T0413639

Undaunted Mind

UNDAUNTED MIND

The Intellectual Life of
Benjamin Franklin

◆

KEVIN J. HAYES

OXFORD
UNIVERSITY PRESS

OXFORD
UNIVERSITY PRESS

Oxford University Press is a department of the University of Oxford.
It furthers the University's objective of excellence in research, scholarship,
and education by publishing worldwide. Oxford is a registered trade mark of
Oxford University Press in the UK and in certain other countries.

Published in the United States of America by Oxford University Press
198 Madison Avenue, New York, NY 10016, United States of America.

CIP data is on file at the Library of Congress

ISBN 9780197554265

DOI: 10.1093/oso/9780197554265.001.0001

Printed by Sheridan Books, Inc., United States of America

In memory of
my father
Richard A. Hayes (1934–2023)

Contents

Prologue: Circles of the Mind

BENJAMIN FRANKLIN'S INTELLECTUAL life was no solo adventure. Picture it as an interconnected chain of circles stretching from the Franklin family in Boston, where he first developed his passion for reading; to the Couranteers, the tradesmen who assembled at his brother James's Boston printshop and wrote entertaining articles for his newspaper, the *New-England Courant*; to the small circle of young literary men whom Franklin befriended shortly after he moved to Philadelphia; to the group of physicians and scientists he met on his first trip to London; to the Junto, the club for mutual improvement that Franklin and some of his ambitious Philadelphia friends created upon his return from London. These are just some of the early links in the chain, which would stretch across nearly the whole eighteenth century and connect Franklin with the best minds in North America, England, and Europe.

Throughout his autobiography, Franklin stresses the importance of friends to his life of the mind. Matthew Adams, the only Couranteer besides his brother that he mentions by name, was "an ingenious tradesman who had a pretty collection of books."[1] Adams invited Franklin to his home to see his library and readily lent him books. In other words, the Couranteer whom Franklin singled out was the one who most encouraged his reading. In Franklin's eyes, the love of books endowed a person with special status.

Describing his earliest circle of Philadelphia friends in his autobiography, Franklin says, "My chief acquaintances at this time were, Charles Osborne, Joseph Watson, and James Ralph, all lovers of reading." John Wigate, Franklin's best friend during his first trip to London, "had been better educated than most printers, was a tolerable Latinist, spoke French, and lov'd reading."[2] Clearly, a pattern was taking shape: Franklin was attracted to people who loved to read, and their passion for reading encouraged his intellectual pursuits and earned them a place in his personal story. Their parallel reading habits and tastes can shed light on his.

The Junto offers more examples. Hugh Meredith, a Philadelphia coworker and quondam business partner, "had a great deal of solid observations" and "was something of a reader." Joseph Breintnall, Franklin's closest friend in the group, was "a great lover of poetry, reading all he could meet with, and writing some that was tolerable." William Parsons was "bred a shoemaker, but loving reading, had acquir'd a considerable share of mathematics." And Nicholas Scull "lov'd books, and sometimes made a few verses."[3]

Recalling all these book-loving friends, Franklin was able to tell a lively story, but readers of his autobiography should see them not only as Franklin's friends in real life, but also as characters in a literary work. They serve as touchstones. To a greater or lesser extent, each friend he mentions is a *Doppelgänger* for him. Emphasizing their shared love of reading, Franklin reinforces their similarities and lets readers contrast their personal and professional decisions with his own.

Comparing Franklin's portrayal of his life in Boston with what he says about Philadelphia, biographer Carl Van Doren observed, "About Boston he speaks chiefly of his studies. About Philadelphia he speaks chiefly of his friends."[4] Nonetheless, there is some continuity between these two segments of Franklin's life. The autobiographical discussion of Philadelphia friends is also a discussion of Franklin's studies because he integrated his intellectual and social life in Philadelphia. Franklin borrowed books from friends, and they borrowed books from him. Together, they discussed their reading, which helped develop their literary tastes, political thought, social conduct, and scientific research. The picture of Franklin's intellectual life is a group portrait, as this book will demonstrate.

Franklin took great pride in his library, which, sadly, was dispersed after his death. During the mid-twentieth century, Edwin Wolf, the director of the Library Company of Philadelphia, embarked on a quest to locate surviving books from Franklin's library and, as much as possible, to reconstruct its contents. Wolf first noticed a distinctive shelf mark in 1947, when he attended an auction of books from Franklin's library that had remained together among his descendants. Other attendees noticed the unusual shelf mark, but none realized it was Franklin's. Not until 1956 would Wolf discover that Franklin made the shelf marks after he returned home to Philadelphia in 1785 and reorganized his library.[5]

The marks indicate the case number and shelf position of each volume. Wolf would spend decades searching for surviving books with Franklin's shelf mark. In addition, he began scouring Franklin's papers in search of references to books he owned that do not survive. Wolf left his catalogue of Franklin's library unfinished at the time of his death in 1991, but John Van Horne, Executive Director of the Library Company of Philadelphia, invited me to complete Wolf's work. I finished *The Library of Benjamin Franklin* in time to celebrate the tricentenary of Franklin's birth in 2006.[6]

Undaunted Mind incorporates additional titles from Franklin's library I have discovered since the publication of *The Library of Benjamin Franklin*. These new finds should be considered additions to the catalogue of Franklin's library. A much greater set of books discussed here are uncatalogued ones. After all, cataloguing a title from Franklin's library requires either a surviving book with evidence of his ownership or documentary proof that he acquired a particular book, but Franklin read other books he knew so well he almost surely owned them, though no documentary evidence survives to prove it. The books Franklin borrowed also enter the discussion, not only the ones he borrowed from friends, but also those he knew from the holdings of the Library Company of Philadelphia. The present work discusses many books Franklin read but did not necessarily own.

Much new information presented here concerns the social contexts of Franklin's reading life. As in Philadelphia, Franklin's social and intellectual activities often overlapped when he was living in London and Paris. Consider an example from the time he lived in London while serving as agent for the Pennsylvania Assembly. He enjoyed weekly suppers at the George and Vulture Tavern with the Monday Club, which included several gentlemen passionate about science and literature, including Captain James Cook.[7]

Since the Monday Club was an informal gathering, it had no officers, no recording secretary, no one to keep the minutes of their meetings. Without surviving records, their suppertime conversations remain a matter of conjecture. Contemporary book subscription lists, a largely untapped resource, reveal some possible topics of conversation, showing that Franklin and his clubmates acquired some of the same books around the same time. In 1758, Franklin and two other Monday Club members, Thomas Collinson and Ingham Foster, subscribed to John Baskerville's new edition of John Milton's poetry. Imagine the discussions that took place around the club table at the George and Vulture when this edition, beautifully printed with a newly designed typeface, appeared.[8]

A chain, on second thought, may not be the best metaphor to illustrate Franklin's various intellectual circles, as it implies a linear progression. His interests branched in many directions, and he often belonged to several interconnected circles simultaneously. A more complex image of overlapping circles may better illustrate Franklin's life of the mind: the Venn diagram.

A combination of practical logic and visual elegance, the Venn diagram offers a way to think about how Franklin's numerous circles intersected.

Take the poet, printer, and ferryman Aquila Rose, for example. Though he and Franklin never met, Rose is a prominent figure in his autobiography. Like Franklin's friends, Rose also serves as a *Doppelgänger*. He continues to function as such in the story of Franklin's life. Both charismatic leaders, Rose and Franklin each became the center of his own Philadelphia circle. Since they shared several of the same friends, their circles overlapped significantly.

Any one of Franklin's circles could include friends, acquaintances, and people he had never met. For example, he was part of an elite group Wolf has characterized retrospectively as the great early American book collectors.[9] Franklin was good friends with three members of this group—Thomas Jefferson, whose personal library would form the basis of the Library of Congress; James Logan, the greatest classicist in colonial America; and Isaac Norris, Jr., Logan's son-in-law and the second greatest classicist in colonial America. Franklin was acquainted with others, including William Burnet, colonial governor of New York and New Jersey, and the Reverend Cotton Mather. Some he had never met: Colonel John Montgomerie, who took over Burnet's gubernatorial position, and William Byrd of Westover.

As a great early American book collector, Franklin shared much with these men, all of whom loved books, not just reading them, but owning them, surrounding themselves with them, making books part of their homes, their lives, their very existence. The reading habits of other early American book collectors create additional parallels that, by analogy, can fill in some of the gaps in the story of Franklin's intellectual life and demonstrate that his experience was by no means unique. The experience of many readers and writers in eighteenth-century America share several similarities.

Franklin personally understood the camaraderie between collectors. After establishing himself as Philadelphia's foremost printer, publisher, and newspaperman, he entered politics, becoming clerk of the Pennsylvania Assembly in 1736. He got along well with all the assemblymen except Norris. Confident that no self-respecting politician would pay "servile respect" to another, Franklin devised a different way to get on Norris's good side.[10]

Hearing that Norris had a rare book in his collection that he wished to read, Franklin asked to borrow it. Happy to learn about Franklin's love of books, Norris sent him the volume. Franklin returned it a week later with a note of thanks. The next time they saw one another in the legislative chamber, Norris talked to Franklin, which he had never done before. Moreover, Norris spoke with great civility, offering to help Franklin whenever he could. From that moment on, they became great friends.

Franklin's interaction with Norris illustrates how a shared love of books could bring people together in colonial America. By asking to borrow the volume, Franklin displayed his passion for books and learning. By loaning him the volume, Norris acknowledged their intellectual kinship. By reading the same book, Franklin and Norris formed an attachment, a mind meld based on its text and ideas. Like so many of his friendships, Franklin's friendship with Norris stemmed from a shared love of books.

The Club of Honest Whigs was one of several intersecting circles Franklin belonged to in London. This supper club met on Thursday nights, first at St. Paul's Coffeehouse and later at the London Coffeehouse. Its members discussed books and reading, scientific experiments, political theory, and many other topics while quaffing drafts of porter, chewing gooey bites of Welsh rabbit, and inhaling fragrant puffs of the coffeehouse's herbal smoking mixture. While seeking to understand Franklin's life of the mind, this book never forgets the life of the body, endeavoring to present what Franklin thought and what he felt. It aims to recapture the sights, sounds, smells, tastes, and textures that surrounded him, from the musty aroma of an old folio from Shakespeare's time to the luxurious feel of a new book freshly bound in tooled calfskin.

Though the details of the contemporary material culture help bring alive the world in which Franklin lived, they directly pertain to his intellectual life in many instances. Take Voltaire, for example. His *Letters Concerning the English Nation* begins with a set of four letters about the Quakers, which gave Franklin a good idea about how the French viewed Pennsylvania Quakers. They celebrated them for their civic virtue, equality, pacifism, probity, religious freedom, and simplicity. In his writings, Franklin adopted different literary personae for different situations; he exerted similar care when it came to shaping his public identity for different circumstances. When he went to France in 1776 as commissioner for the Continental Congress, Franklin used what Voltaire had written about the Quakers to shape his personal appearance, eschewing a wig in favor of his natural hair, wearing a marten fur cap outdoors, and donning a modest suit of clothing. His reading helped Franklin create an unassuming personal appearance, which he sustained even on the most formal occasions, even when he attended the Royal Court at Versailles.[11]

Many of Franklin's intellectual circles can be identified in retrospect. He was one of the Founding Fathers, most notably. Convening in Philadelphia, the Continental Congress brought together the greatest leaders in Revolutionary America, who also happened to be the greatest readers in Revolutionary America: funny how the two so often go together. Few of the delegates had ever had the opportunity to discuss books and ideas on the scale Congress offered.

As one of the century's leading scientists, Franklin joined what is known as the Republic of Letters, an informal, international group of authors, scientists, and various other intellectuals. To advance science and, indeed, all forms of intellectual inquiry, they refused to let political boundaries stop them. The universal quest for knowledge transcended national borders. Franklin's "Passport for Captain Cook," which he wrote during the Revolutionary War, exemplifies his commitment to the Republic of Letters. Addressed to the commanders of U.S. warships, the passport informed them that Cook was returning from a great scientific expedition in the South Pacific. If they encountered him, they should not consider Cook an enemy, nor should they plunder his ship, which would be filled with collections valuable to science. The passport was moot: Cook had been killed by the time Franklin issued it. Nonetheless, it earned Franklin further respect among the European and British intelligentsia. Citizens of the Republic of Letters understood that international strife should not hinder intellectual progress.[12]

Franklin was also part of the circle of great eighteenth-century travelers. Besides crossing the Atlantic eight times and traveling around Great Britain and parts of Western Europe, he journeyed throughout the colonies in his capacity as deputy joint postmaster general of North America. Political and military responsibilities took him to the American frontier. He traveled from Philadelphia to Boston as a member of one congressional committee and from Philadelphia to Quebec as a member of another. Franklin befriended many other great travelers, who often presented him with copies of their work.

In addition, Franklin helped plan some of the greatest expeditions of the era. He sponsored two voyages to search for the Northwest Passage, and, as a member of the Royal Society Council, he helped plan the multiple voyages undertaken in 1761 and 1769 to observe the transit of Venus, the greatest cooperative scientific venture ever undertaken to that time. Franklin's attention to travel literature, perhaps his favorite form of reading, cannot be separated from his travels, his conversations with other travelers, and his efforts to promote travel-based scientific research.

Franklin is one of the finest writers in the history of American literature. The life of every great writer is the culmination of the lives of those who came before and an anticipation of those to come. Studying the authors Franklin read can reveal his life of the mind; so, too, can studying the authors who have read him. Comments from other great writers—Ernest Hemingway, Jack Kerouac, Herman Melville, Edgar Allan Poe, Henry David Thoreau, Mark Twain—cast light back on Franklin's literary life.

Franklin is an American icon. Framed by his natural hair and peering through a pair of wire-framed spectacles, few faces in American history are more recognizable. Given the memorable Poor Richardisms that still circulate in the oral culture, few American humorists are more quotable. As both icon and humorist, Franklin belongs to the popular culture. Much as American literature can help cast light on Franklin, so, too, can popular culture. Movies, television, graphic arts, popular music, stand-up comedy: All can help illuminate his life. In many ways, his innovations to the printed word anticipate modern communication technology. Franklin was doing with broadsides, almanacs, and newspapers what television does today.

When Jean-Luc Godard was asked why he put a reference to Tour de France winner Jacques Anquetil in his 1961 feature film *A Woman Is a Woman*, he replied, "One should put everything into a film."[13] *Undaunted Mind* takes a similarly expansive approach to Franklin's intellectual life. Since so much of what he accomplished continues to affect our lives today, Franklin, perhaps more than any single figure from American history, suits this omnibus approach. In one way or another, Benjamin Franklin overlaps all our circles.

I

Small Chapmen's Books

BORN ON A Sunday and so broke the Sabbath: Though ascribed to Jonathan Swift, these words apply to Benjamin Franklin, who was born on Sunday, January 17, 1706. His parents, Josiah and Abiah Franklin, attended services at Boston's Old South Meeting House that morning. Abiah gave birth to a healthy boy after returning home, and they went back to Old South that afternoon to have him baptized. The day he was born, Franklin joked, he went to church all day.[1]

His parents shared similar religious beliefs, despite their different backgrounds. The daughter of Peter and Mary Folger, Abiah was a native New Englander. In *Moby-Dick*, Herman Melville calls Mary "one of the old settlers of Nantucket and the ancestress to a long line of Folgers and harpooneers— all kith and kin to noble Benjamin."[2] Josiah Franklin came from the East Midlands of England, having learned the silk dyer's trade in Ecton, Northamptonshire, as an apprentice to an older brother.

"Silks and satins put out the kitchen fire": Benjamin Franklin would include this homey English proverb in *Poor Richard's Almanack*. His father did not realize the proverb's ramifications until he emigrated to America, where, to his dismay, he discovered that his trade as a silk dyer was nearly useless. Bostonians preferred hospitality and good housekeeping over sumptuous apparel.[3] To make a living, Josiah Franklin switched to a trade yielding practical products always in demand: He founded a tallow chandlery. Benjamin had eleven living brothers and sisters when he was born, five by Josiah's first wife Ann and six by Abiah, who would give birth to two more children after Benjamin.

The Franklins rented the house where he was born, a small dwelling on Milk Street across from Old South. Josiah's tallow chandlery was located about a block north. In late January 1712, shortly after Benjamin turned 6, Josiah bought a property on the southwest corner of Union and Hanover large enough for both their home and his business. He removed his equipment to their new home, where he hung his sign—the Sign of the Blue Ball—to attract local residents needing soap and candles.[4]

FIGURE 1.1 *The House Where Franklin Was Born.* From Evert A. Duyckinck and George L. Duyckinck, *Cyclopaedia of American Literature* (New York: Charles Scribner, 1856), 1:104. Kevin J. Hayes Collection, Toledo, OH.

The market for everyday necessities grew with the city. The seventeenth-century proverb about Boston being a lost town no longer applied. Boston was now the largest city in British North America. Given its great natural harbor, shipping was the key to the city's economic success. The long wharf extended far into the bay, fostering trade and symbolizing prosperity. Nearby warehouses facilitated commerce. Boston already had several wide streets, well paved and lined with handsome buildings. Its dwellings were mostly brick, and steeples poked into the clouds. In short, Boston was flourishing when Franklin was born.

Daniel Neal's *History of New England*, to use a book from Franklin's library as a source, emphasizes Boston's intellectual and cultural sophistication. The social behavior of local citizens verified their taste and intellect. Their polite conversation could match the conversation in any comparable English city. Boston merchants were well traveled or, at least, well acquainted with British and European fashions. Their homes, furniture, table settings, and clothing were as splendid and showy as those of London's leading tradesmen. The number of booksellers and printing presses indicated that books and learning thrived in Boston more than any other colonial American city during the early years of the eighteenth century.[5]

A precocious lad, Benjamin learned to read when he was quite young. As far back as he could remember, he had always known how to read. In his children's biography of Franklin, Nathaniel Hawthorne calls him "a bright boy at his book." Family tradition says the same. Speaking with Ezra Stiles, the president of Yale College, Benjamin's youngest sister Jane Mecom confirmed her brother's youthful reading ability. Though not born until he turned 6, she told Stiles what was common knowledge in the family: Benjamin read the Bible when he was 5.[6]

In colonial America, learning to read meant learning to read the Bible. Cotton Mather, who shared the pulpit of Old North Church with his father, Increase Mather, stressed the Bible's usefulness as a pedagogical tool, calling it the "sacred grammar." Franklin would minimize the Bible's influence on him in his autobiography, but the numerous biblical references in his writings demonstrate how well he knew its text. He could manipulate scripture so deftly and distinctively that biblical allusions can help identify some of his anonymous writings.[7]

Franklin taught himself many subjects. He related a favorite childhood anecdote to his friend Benjamin Rush, who recorded it for posterity.[8] The anecdote shows young Franklin studying geography. While Josiah prays in their parlor with his little boy nearby, Benjamin examines the maps hanging on the wall. As one bows his head in prayer, the other tilts his upward to study the maps. The father thinks about the next world; his son thinks about this one.

Family tradition and personal anecdotes add much to the story of Franklin's intellectual life, but his autobiography is the most important source to reconstruct his early reading. The genetic text of the autobiography, which is based on Franklin's surviving manuscript, reveals his compositional process. Its editors use arrows, braces, and brackets to mark how and when Franklin deleted unwanted phrases and replaced them with more descriptive and delightful ones. The genetic text's editorial apparatus opens the door to Franklin's study and lets readers peer over his shoulder as he writes.

He drafted part 1 in England in 1771. After a long hiatus, he drafted part 2 in Paris in 1784, part 3 in Philadelphia in 1788 and 1789, and part 4 in 1789 and 1790, also in Philadelphia. In addition, he returned to part 1 in 1789 and revised its text further. "Parts is parts," the saying goes, but the four parts that Franklin's posthumous editors have discerned are not necessarily divisions he made. Differentiating them might imply that Franklin divided the story of his life into distinct periods. He did not. In his fine study of Franklin's autobiography Thomas Haslam argues that it should be considered a set of four unfinished, but related manuscripts, not a single, multipart work.[9]

Pilgrim's Progress is central to Franklin's story of his personal discovery of books. Haslam sees the first part of his autobiography as a secular variation on John Bunyan's Christian classic, "an infidel's progress" so to speak. Franklin's revisions support Haslam's thesis. Franklin says of Bunyan in the draft manuscript, "He was the first that mix'd narration and dialogue, a method of writing very engaging to the reader." Revising this passage, Franklin changed the subject pronoun to the more colorful "Honest John." Instead of drawing religious significance from Bunyan's work, in other words, the autobiography stresses a moral precept transcending religion: honesty.[10]

In his earliest discussion of reading in the autobiography Franklin specifically mentions *Pilgrim's Progress*: "From a child I was fond of reading, and all the little money that came into my hands was ever laid out in books. Pleas'd with the *Pilgrim's Progress*, my first collection was of John Bunyan's works, in separate little volumes. I afterwards sold them to enable me to buy R. Burton's *Historical Collections*; they were small chapmen's books and cheap, 40 or 50 in all."[11] This tale of Franklin's early reading has often been repeated. One anthologist included it as the opening episode in a collection of reminiscences by American authors recalling their childhood love of reading.[12] Despite its familiarity, this passage has never received adequate critical attention. Practically every phrase, nearly every word, deserves further scrutiny. The genetic text can aid the interpretive process.

The passage is a *mise en abyme*. In other words, it is an internal, miniature reduplication of Franklin's autobiography embedded within it. Depicting his youthful discovery of books and reading, the episode mirrors the autobiography, which, in many ways, is a book about reading. The episode reveals the centrality of books to Franklin's life and anticipates the role they would play in his personal story. The conduct of his boyhood self also looks forward to Franklin's behavior as an adult. The child is prelude to the man, as Haslam cleverly observes in his discussion of this episode. Franklin's boyhood self already embodies the opportunism that would be essential to his personal and professional success. Given the chance to buy some histories, he sells Bunyan's books to enable the purchase of Burton's. As he reminisces about his childhood reading, Franklin undercuts his sentimentality by revealing a mercenary attitude toward books. The episode also shows in kernel form a central aspect of Franklin's life: Profit motives are not necessarily incompatible with personal improvement, an idea that reverberates throughout his autobiography.[13]

The sentence about spending all his spare money on books is a classic expression of the true book lover. Literature is filled with similar statements. Upon learning that a New Yorker owned a copy of an obscure annotated edition of Cicero's works, Franklin's friend James Logan offered a sizable sum for its purchase. The owner refused, explaining that he loved books more than money. Logan told another friend that he was more pleased by this explanation that he could have been had the owner complied with his request.[14]

Clarifying that *Pilgrim's Progress* inspired him to obtain more Bunyan books, Franklin revised his text to stress that he was reading a unique set of Bunyan's works that he had collected himself, not some hodge podge assembled in the depths of London's Grub Street by a nameless literary hack. Franklin inserted the prepositional phrase modifying "John Bunyan's works"—"in separate little volumes"—in revision. The insertion reflects his pride as a collector, a habit that began in youth and continued throughout his life.[15]

Franklin does not name the other Bunyan works he owned, but they are easy to discern. The second part of *Pilgrim's Progress* is the likeliest. Whereas the first part relates Christian's allegorical journey, the sequel follows Christian's wife Christiana and their children. She entrusts herself and the children to Mr. Great-heart, who guides them safely past the dangers Christian had encountered. Bunyan's most popular books include his spiritual autobiography, *Grace Abounding to the Chief of Sinners*, and two other fictional works, *The Life and Death of Mr. Badman* and *The Holy War*.

Set in the everyday world of home and shop, *Mr. Badman* has a novelistic realism, though Bunyan made the work a dialogue between Mr. Wiseman and Mr. Attentive, whose graphic conversation chronicles the eponymous reprobate's life. "Some men," Mr. Wiseman says, "have a kind of mystical, but hellish copulation with the devil, who is the father, and their soul the mother, of sin and wickedness; and they, so soon as they have conceived by him, finish, by bringing forth sin, both it and their own damnation."[16]

There is nothing subtle about Bunyan. In *The Holy War*, the Diabolians attack a town called Mansoul. Bunyan wrote around sixty other works, but most are doctrinal and homiletic in nature. His autobiography and his allegorical fiction bring Bunyan's Calvinism alive for readers. In Bunyan's world the individual is a battlefield where mighty forces clash. To prevail, people must surrender themselves to God's grace.[17]

Stressing his youthful attention to *Pilgrim's Progress* and other Bunyan works, Franklin made himself an everyman, letting his readers identify with him. *Pilgrim's Progress* was practically ubiquitous in colonial Boston. Thousands of copies were imported to New England, and demand was sufficient to call for American editions as well. Franklin's Boston friend Thomas Fleet, a printer in Pudding Lane, would issue multiple editions of *Pilgrim's Progress* from the 1730s. Fleet would keep the book in print until his death in 1758. Other eighteenth-century Boston printers subsequently released their own editions.[18]

Franklin used *Pilgrim's Progress* to create a shared point of contact with his readers, enabling them to join him on his literary odyssey. Given the pride Franklin took in his Bunyan collection, the ease with which he disposed of it comes as a modest surprise, but it makes sense in light of his forward-thinking perspective. Contrary to Bunyan, Franklin stressed the power of individuals to control their own lives. Whereas Bunyan's autobiography positions the individual as a passive battleground where good and evil struggle for control, Franklin's autobiography makes the individual a well-equipped combatant. People should have faith in themselves. They need only set personal goals and work toward them with effort and determination: no divinity required.

Besides diminishing Bunyan's Calvinism, Franklin's sale reminds readers that books are commodities that can be turned into cash to buy other goods and services or, in Franklin's case, other books. From childhood, his personal library was a dynamic collection. Once he exhausted a book's usefulness, he sometimes unloaded it, selling a volume when he needed the money, giving it away when he did not. Having matured beyond Bunyan, Franklin no longer wanted him on his bookshelf because Bunyan no longer represented his mind.

Franklin used the proceeds to purchase "R. Burton's *Historical Collections.*" He originally wrote "R. Burton's *Collections,*" adding the adjective in revision. "R. Burton" was the pen name of Nathaniel Crouch, a London bookseller and author. He took the pseudonym "Richard Burton," but usually signed himself "R. B." "Burton's Books" or, even simpler, "Burtons" fully deserve to be called collections. Speaking about Crouch, a contemporary bookseller told a friend, "I think I have given you the very soul of his character, when I have told you that his talent lies at collection. He has melted down the best of our English histories into twelve-penny books." Whether they deserve to be called "historical" is open for debate. This same bookseller admitted that Burtons are "filled with wonders, rarities, and curiosities."[19]

In Puritan New England, one of the most popular books in Crouch's series was *The Kingdom of Darkness: or, The History of Daemons, Specters, Witches, Apparitions, Possessions, Disturbances, and Other Wonderful and Supernatural Delusions, Mischievous Feats and Malicious Impostures of the Devil.* "You must know," our bookseller continued, "his title-pages are a little swelling." If Franklin owned forty or fifty books in the series, then he owned practically every Burton, including *The Kingdom of Darkness*. But the final version of the autobiography stresses their historical nature and downplays the supernatural. In revision, Franklin emphasized that he traded religion for history, superstition for fact.

Miracles of Art and Nature: or, A Brief Description of the Several Varieties of Birds, Beasts, Fishes, Plants, and Fruits of Other Countreys, the first collection Crouch published as "R. B.," appeared in 1678. With this work, Crouch developed the approach he would take in subsequent volumes. He assembled many old, well-respected, but hard-to-come-by works, excerpted their best bits, and gathered the excerpts into small but affordable books all readers could enjoy. Averaging 200 pages each and selling for a shilling apiece, Burtons made learning affordable. Crouch promised similar works if *Miracles of Nature and Art* found favor among contemporary readers.

Once published, Burtons were imported into colonial America. John Usher, a prominent Boston bookseller, ordered several. One 1683 invoice lists *Wonderful Prodigies of Judgment and Mercy*, which presents short biographies revealing the dreadful judgments made on atheists, blasphemers, conjurors, magicians, murderers, tyrants, witches, and other grievous sinners. The book does tell a few positive stories about good people delivered from evil.[20]

Usher tried ordering two other Burtons—*Admirable Curiosities, Rarities and Wonders in England, Scotland, and Ireland* and *The Wars in England, Scotland and Ireland*—but he was initially unsuccessful. Once they were reprinted, Usher received these two works and three more: *Extraordinary Adventures and Discoveries of Several Famous Men*; *Historical Remarques, and Observations of the Ancient and Present State of London and Westminster*; and *The Surprizing Miracles of Nature and Art*, an expanded edition of Crouch's first book.[21]

Edwin Wolf, who considered *The Surprizing Miracles of Nature and Art* Crouch's most fascinating book, cited an episode to illustrate the nature of its contents. As the story goes, a thunderbolt struck a church, broke down its door, and wounded several parishioners before killing a woman while she was praying in the transept. The thunderbolt did not stop there. It kept going, whooshing across town to strike a suburban church, where it singed the hair off the minister's head while he was reading. Wolf recognized the ongoing appeal of such stories: "Franklin and his fellow almanac-makers used similar tidbits of the strange and wonderful to pad their annual ephemerides."[22]

In August 1669, according to another episode Crouch added while expanding his miraculous collection, two whales swam up the Thames. The smaller whale was killed, but the larger one escaped and returned to the sea.

The story is a precedent for Franklin's hilarious newspaper article, "The Grand Leap of the Whale."[23] Speaking as an adventuresome American traveler, Franklin says that he had witnessed whales swimming up the St. Lawrence River as they chased their finny prey. Sometimes they would leap up Niagara Falls!

Though Burtons could be found throughout colonial New England, few book owners recorded reading them. The reason is simple. People saw little need to write about the quotidian. Few living in eighteenth-century America recognized the lasting significance of the popular culture they encountered every day. Paradoxically, readers have left the least information about the most popular books. The dearth of contemporary discussion makes Franklin's reference to Burtons all the more significant.

Calling them "small chapmen's books," Franklin indicated one way Burtons were marketed in colonial America. Though urban booksellers stocked them, chapmen distributed Burtons more widely. Chapmen were traveling salesmen who crisscrossed the countryside. Living on the fringes of colonial American society, they entered the cities just long enough to refill their packs with books before getting back on the road. Country people living far from the nearest bookstore greeted them with excitement. Chapmen carried many informative and entertaining books, including a midwifery handbook known as *Aristotle's Masterpiece*, the most popular book in colonial America after the Bible.[24]

Aristotle's Masterpiece was popular mainly because young men read it as pornography. Even the well-respected and well-educated could not suppress their curiosity when it came to its subject matter. Samuel Johnson, who would become president of King's College (renamed Columbia University), read *Aristotle's Masterpiece* when he was a 24-year-old bachelor.[25] Precisely how this future college president obtained this volume of makeshift pornography is unknown. Chapmen typically met potential buyers at a clandestine location, say, behind Farmer Jones's barn, where they would sell them the book on the sly. The traveling salesman who forms a stock character in countless bawdy jokes in American humor stretches back to the colonial chapman.

Burtons were somewhat different from other chapmen's books. At a shilling apiece, they cost twice the others. During the eighteenth century, chapmen's books or "chapbooks," as they came to be known, would decrease in size and price. The chapbook achieved its most common form as a twenty-four-page duodecimo that sold for a penny.[26] In Franklin's youth, the longer and more expensive chapmen's books could include conduct manuals and how-to books, but most retold centuries-old romances and legends.

Puritan divines cited Burtons as scholarly sources. In *A Modest Enquiry into the Nature of Witchcraft*, the Reverend John Hales, who participated in the Salem witch trials, referenced *The Kingdom of Darkness* and grouped Burton with other "learned writers." In *Remarkable Providences*—another book Franklin read in his youth—Increase Mather cites two Burtons: *Wonderful Prodigies* and *Surprizing Miracles of Nature and Art*. And in *Cases of Conscience Concerning Evil Spirits*, Increase Mather cites *The Kingdom of Darkness*. Cotton Mather read *Delights for the Ingenious*, a work that almost surely was among Franklin's Burtons.[27]

Delights for the Ingenious is an emblem book, and, for the most part, it resembles other emblem books. Each emblem has a visual component and a verbal one: a device and a motto. Franklin explained it best: "An emblematical device, when rightly formed, is said to consist of two parts, a *body* and a *mind*, neither of which is compleat or intelligible, without the aid of the other. The figure is called the *body*, the motto the *mind*."[28]

Emblem books often have other features. At the top of the first page of each emblem in *Delights for the Ingenious*, a roman numeral identifies it. Next comes the device, a woodcut illustrating a fable or an allegory. The device fills most of the page, leaving enough room for a Latin motto beneath it. After a two-line epigram, Crouch ends each emblem by explaining the moral lesson it teaches. Within the emblem book tradition, these explanations are known as commentaries. Emblem books typically present the commentary in prose, but some authors, like Crouch, used verse commentaries.

The unique feature Crouch placed at the back of the book—a feature that sent Cotton Mather into conniptions—differentiates *Delights for the Ingenious* from other emblem books. The volume ends with a wheel of fortune, complete with a spinner to be pinned at its center. The book's users would spin the spinner until it stopped, when it would point to a particular number to indicate their future. The reader would then flip to the numbered emblem; examine the illustration; read the motto, epigram, and commentary; and interpret its personal meaning. Surviving copies of *Delights for the Ingenious* show that early American readers ignored Cotton Mather's warnings and enjoyed playing wheel of fortune.[29]

Emblem 40 in *Delights for the Ingenious* portrays an axe-wielding woodsman chopping down a tree, with the motto *Non uno sternitur ictu*, "Not with a single blow." Though the woodsman has cut partway through the trunk, he has a long way to go. The commentary ends, "Mine *arm*, I know, in time will fell an *oke*, / But, I will ne're attempt it, at a *stroke*." Franklin would use a more succinct version of this idea in *Poor Richard's Almanack*: "Little strokes / Fell great oaks."[30]

The woodcuts in Franklin's newspapers, almanacs, and books reflect the influence of emblem books like *Delights for the Ingenious*. Besides shaping his visual sensibilities, emblem books also affected Franklin's writing style. Some of his best verbal descriptions have an emblematic quality that fixes their imagery in the reader's mind. Franklin thought in emblems. As he perceived the world, he often saw people strike poses resembling emblematic devices.

Though Franklin does not name any particular Burtons in his autobiography, his other writings reveal one volume he read: *Unparallel'd Varieties: or, The Matchless Actions and Passions of Mankind*. A collection of short historical anecdotes, *Unparallel'd Varieties* draws on ancient, medieval, and modern sources to compile historical lessons illustrating the power of love, friendship, courage, magnanimity, and other positive virtues. One chapter provides historical examples demonstrating chastity, temperance, and humility, virtues that Franklin would stress in his autobiography.

Franklin would quote an episode from *Unparallel'd Varieties* in *Poor Richard's Almanack*. His use of the following historical anecdote reflects his open-minded outlook toward women and reinforces their courage, affection, ingenuity, and physical strength when faced with danger:

> *Conradus* the Third, emperour of *Germany*, besieged *Guelphus* duke of *Bavaria*, in the city of *Wensburg* in *Germany*; the women perceiving that the town could not possibly hold out long, petitioned the emperor that they might depart only with so much as each of them could carry on their backs; which the emperor condescended to; expecting they would have loaden themselves with silver and gold; but they all came forth with every one her husband on her back, whereat the emperor was so moved, that he wept, received the duke into his favour, gave all the men their lives, and extolled the women with deserved praises.[31]

Burtons were not the only small chapmen's books Franklin read as a boy. Nearly all literate colonial Americans read chapbooks in their childhood, though few of these little volumes survive. Chapbooks were read and shared until they fell apart and readers used them as toilet paper. Chapbooks worked better than tree leaves, according to Annapolis physician Dr. Alexander Hamilton. Sturdier and more sanitary, chapbook pages minimized the chance of contracting "that most grievous distemper called the piles" and also reduced people's "risque of befowling their fingers."[32]

Doctor Faustus was one of the most popular chapbooks in Boston. A surviving invoice from John Usher's bookshop reflects its relative popularity.

Usher ordered ten copies of Crouch's *Wonderful Prodigies* the same time he ordered thirty copies of *Doctor Faustus*. The chapbook version has disappeared behind the works it inspired—Christopher Marlowe's *Dr. Faustus*, Goethe's *Faust*, Franz Lizst's *Faust Symphony*—but the story of the man whose quest for knowledge prompted him to make a pact with the devil remains compelling. Whereas many chapbooks told stories of exemplary characters their young readers could emulate, *Dr. Faustus* offered a cautionary tale. Franklin learned the lesson, pursuing knowledge without compromising his principles. As one biographer commented, "A life like Franklin's solves the problem stated in the Faust of Goethe; which is how shall a man become satisfied with his life?"[33]

The Mad Conceits of Tom Tram of the West, to take, for example, a chapbook pertinent to Franklin's printer friend Thomas Fleet, chronicles the adventures of a legendary comic rogue. Tom Tram goes through life finding clever ways to avoid working, walking, or going to jail, all while keeping his head buzzing with drink and his belly filled with vittles. Well known for his wit and humor, Fleet felt a kinship for this eponymous ne'er do well and took the character's name as his pseudonym. Signing a facetious article in *The New-England Courant* "Tom Tram," Fleet knew Boston readers would get the reference.[34]

The standard set of children's books remained fairly consistent through the colonial period and across gender lines. The reading of Mary Byles, the elder daughter of the Reverend Mather Byles, another one of Franklin's friends, is representative. In 1762, the year she turned 12, Mary listed all the books she could remember reading. Her adolescent reading parallels Franklin's. Before turning 12, she had read *Pilgrim's Progress* (twice), Bunyan's *Holy War*, and Crouch's *Wonderful Prodigies*.[35]

Franklin read some of the best-known chapbooks during his adolescence. His surviving letters mention two, *Guy of Warwick*, a story of chivalric adventure, and *The Famous History of Friar Bacon*, an episodic account of a legendary conjuror. Traveling through the English Midlands on holiday from his work as London agent for the Pennsylvania Assembly in 1758, Franklin would visit Warwick "to see old Guy's castle." These words reflect his familiarity with Guy of Warwick—the English Hercules—and his ongoing desire to learn more about this legendary hero.[36]

Many versions of *Guy of Warwick* survive, though some of the individual episodes shifted around during the work's centuries-long transmission. In one version Franklin could have read, Guy's reputation for physical strength prompts the earl of Warwick to invite him to his castle, where Guy falls for the earl's daughter Phyllis. She insists he perform martial deeds to prove himself worthy. After slaying a monstrous cow terrorizing the neighborhood, he travels to France and defeats Rumbo, a giant who becomes his sidekick and later gives his life for Guy.

When Guy finally returns, Phyllis agrees to marry him. Her father dies soon after their wedding, so Guy inherits Warwick Castle and the earldom. Sadly realizing how much blood he has shed to attain Phyllis, he turns pilgrim and goes to the Holy Land. Guy comes back to England during the Danish invasion and slays the giant Colbron in single combat. Instead of rejoining Phyllis at Warwick Castle, Guy becomes a cave-dwelling hermit. Not until he is on his deathbed does Guy summon Phyllis, who arrives in time to close his dying eyes.

Measured by the references in his writings, Franklin's favorite chapbook was *The Famous History of Friar Bacon*.[37] As the story begins, young Roger Bacon establishes himself as an excellent student. He surpasses his teacher, who recommends he attend Oxford University. His father quashes that idea, preferring to teach him how to manage the family farm. Roger escapes his family and enters a monastery, where he impresses the other friars, who do send him to Oxford. His necromantic studies progress far enough to attract the attention of King Edward III.

While studying at Oxford, Friar Bacon hires a manservant named Miles. On Good Friday, Miles lies to Bacon, promising that he will keep the fast. Instead, Miles sneaks off to his room to gobble up a "pudding," that is, a sausage. Unbeknownst to Miles, Bacon has enchanted the pudding, and one end gets stuck in Miles's throat. As he gags on the pudding, Bacon initially refuses to help Miles. Not until he repents does Bacon lift the spell, enabling Miles to pull the pudding from his mouth.[38]

The story of the enchanted pudding shares much with traditional stories of trickster heroes. It also anticipates an episode in Franklin's autobiography, the time he convinces his boss Samuel Keimer to become a vegetarian. As Franklin tells the story, Keimer resists eating meat as long as possible, but eventually he can resist no longer and eats an entire roast pig before Franklin and their female dinner guests arrive.

The most iconic episode from *Friar Bacon* was also Franklin's favorite. It concerns Bacon's foolhardy scheme to build a brass wall around England to protect it from invaders. Bacon and his student, Friar Bungay, forge a brass head and strike a deal with the devil. According to their deal, Brass Head will explain how to build the wall, provided they can wait for it to speak. After several uneventful nights, the friars take a break to get a good night's sleep, leaving Miles in charge: a possible error. On Miles's watch, Brass Head finally speaks: "Time is." Miles ignores it. Brass Head speaks again: "Time was." Miles ignores it again. Speaking a third time, Brass Head intones, "Time is past." Upon uttering these three words, Brass Head explodes into a thousand pieces. Terrified, Miles befouls his breeches, and Friar Bacon never gets his wall built.[39]

Franklin would remember the story of Friar Bacon and Brass Head as a story of missed opportunities. Brass Head's famous last words—"Time is past"—would become a catchphrase for Franklin. Repeating it, he would evoke the familiar children's story and underscore the impossibility of recapturing a lost opportunity. The lesson became increasingly relevant as the American Revolution approached. British authorities would ignore the opportunities presented to them until the time for reconciliation with the American colonies was past.

Numerous editions of *Friar Bacon* appeared, some longer than others. One episode relates the death of a wealthy man, who leaves his fortune to one of his three sons, the one who loved him most. Friar Bacon devises a test that proves this to be the youngest son. Many variations of this traditional story exist. Franklin could have read one in Crouch's *Unparallel'd Varieties*. The best-known version, of course, is the one Shakespeare wrote, but *Friar Bacon* and *Unparallel'd Varieties* show that early American readers knew the basic plot before they read *King Lear*.

Another *Friar Bacon* episode illustrates the interaction of folklore and book culture. It incorporates a traditional legend type, "Inexperienced Use of the Black Book," which would remain part of American culture from Franklin to *Fantasia*. In dire need of money, Miles sneaks into Friar Bacon's study and borrows a book of black magic. He heads to the roof to read its magic spells. Miles accidentally summons the devil, who spits fire in his face. To escape the devil, Miles jumps from the roof but lands badly and breaks his leg. Friar Bacon arrives in time to rescue him but refuses to do so until Miles promises never to touch his books again.[40]

Friar Bacon and the other chapbooks Franklin read in his youth significantly influenced his writing style. Despite what he says in the autobiography, Bunyan was not the first author to combine dialogue with narration. He wrote *Pilgrim's Progress* within a popular literary tradition that already blended the two modes of expression. In his youth, Bunyan had read some of the same chapbooks Franklin would read in his. Like Bunyan, Franklin let the chapbook tradition shape his writing, not only in his use of dialogue but also in his use of traditional motifs.

The Famous and Remarkable History of Sir Richard Whittington or, as it was typically called, *Dick Whittington*, is the most obvious precursor to

Franklin's autobiography. *Dick Whittington* tells the story of a poor boy who makes his fortune when he sells his beloved cat to a Moorish king to remedy a rat infestation. Whittington subsequently goes into business and rises to become lord mayor of London. Like *Dick Whittington*, Franklin's autobiography tells a story of a poor boy who goes into business and rises to prominence in his community. Portrayed in the autobiography, Franklin's younger self is as persistent and resourceful as Dick Whittington.[41]

A small chapmen's book is an unassuming thing. Though most were turned into waste paper, a handful still survive. They are yellowed from centuries of age, dingy from frequent bethumbings, pages torn, covers missing, illustrations sliced out. They hardly seem significant at all, but chapbooks introduced Franklin and many other great thinkers and writers of the eighteenth century to the world of books and reading, the world of the imagination. In Franklin's case, the small chapmen's books he encountered during his boyhood provided a foundation for his lifetime love of reading and his approach to writing.

2

Joyful Schooldays

SEVERAL DOZEN VOLUMES strong, Franklin's sizable boyhood library was not his sole source for books. During his adolescence and early teens, he practically read through his father's entire library but named only one book from it when he first drafted his autobiography: "Plutarch's *Lives* there was, in which I read abundantly, and I still think that time spent to great advantage."[1]

Different English translations of Plutarch's *Lives* could be found in colonial Boston. Thomas North's sixteenth-century translation was available in a seventeenth-century edition. More recently, Jacob Tonson had published a new translation in five volumes, and other London publishers released abridgments. Pierre Cabanis confirmed that Franklin read Plutarch as a boy. When the two lived in Paris, Cabanis, a young man who would establish a dual reputation as a physician and a philosopher, had the great fortune to befriend Franklin, who loved sharing tales of his youth with him.

Cabanis's record of their Paris conversations sheds light on Franklin's early reading: "Before he left his father's home he happened on a few volumes by Plutarch: he read them ravenously." Mentioning multiple volumes, Cabanis would seem to mean Tonson's edition, but Franklin also read Plutarch's *Morals* in his youth, so Cabanis could have meant both *Lives* and *Morals*.[2]

The word "ravenously," which applies to many books Franklin read in his youth, captures how he devoured Plutarch's *Lives*. Though lacking the elegance of the finest classical authors, Plutarch nonetheless wrote with energy and precision, rapidly getting to the heart of the people he profiled. His biographical essays pair historical figures from Greece with comparable figures from Rome: Alexander and Julius Caesar, Demosthenes and Cicero, Hannibal and Scipio Africanus, and many more.

Interpreting history in terms of character, Plutarch demonstrated how the ideas and impulses of great individuals can shape their world. Sometimes he used minor episodes to reflect major trends. Plutarch summarizes his approach within his life of Alexander: "My design is not to write histories, but lives.

Besides, the most glorious exploits do not always furnish us with the clearest discoveries of virtue, or vice, in men; sometimes a matter of less moment, a singular expression or a jest, informs us better of their manners, and inclinations, than the most famous sieges, the arrangement of the greatest armies, or the bloodiest battles."[3]

Plutarch gave Franklin an enduring love of history and taught him how to delineate character, a literary skill at which he would excel. His writings often reflect the influence of Plutarch's *Lives*, especially the autobiography. Franklin used jests, memorable expressions, and matters of less moment to enliven his personal story. A dozen years after Franklin drafted part 1, his friend Benjamin Vaughan, who had edited a collection of his political writings, read the manuscript and told Franklin what he thought. Comparing the autobiography with Plutarch's *Lives*, Vaughan urged Franklin to resume the work: "If it encourages more writings of the same kind with your own, and induces more men to spend lives fit to be written it will be worth all Plutarch's lives put together."[4]

Though Plutarch inspired Franklin to read more ancient history, rarely did he take what he read at face value. Intrigued with the speeches that Greek and Roman generals delivered to their armies, Franklin nonetheless questioned their veracity. In Plutarch's *Lives*, Marc Antony, disheveled and straggly haired after fleeing Rome and crossing the Alps, reaches General Lepidus's army, which he harangues, moving the men with his words. It hardly seemed possible to Franklin that a general could address thousands of men at once, but a real-life experience convinced him otherwise. One time when the Reverend George Whitefield was addressing a huge crowd in Philadelphia, Franklin, instead of coming closer, walked away from Whitefield until he reached the limit of his voice. Having paced off the distance, Franklin calculated how many people could fit within the area circumscribed by the distance the preacher's voice carried. He computed that a Roman general very well could have addressed an army of 25,000 troops.[5]

Other Founding Fathers appreciated Plutarch's *Lives*, including Alexander Hamilton and James Madison. Several men whom Plutarch profiled would become role models for the freedom-seeking American Revolutionaries, classical figures who opposed tyranny and warned against the encroachments of corruption and arbitrary power. In addition, by presenting the city-state of Sparta as a free, stable, and civic-minded political entity, Plutarch gave the Founding Fathers a government they could emulate.[6]

Instead of naming additional books from his father's library in the draft of his autobiography, Franklin characterized the collection as a whole: "My

father's little library consisted chiefly of books in polemic and practical divinity, most of which I read, and have since often regretted, that at a time when
I had such a thirst for knowledge, more proper books had not fallen my way."[7]

Franklin's feelings of regret caught Phillips Russell's attention. A North
Carolina journalist turned biographer, Russell may have taken creative liberties in his bestselling life of Franklin, but he had a keen ability to identify
parallels between Franklin's life and subsequent historical, literary, and cultural developments. Russell's biography reveals the continuities between
Franklin's thought and the world to come. Franklin's regret about not reading
"more proper books" in his adolescence, for example, reminded Russell of the
modern man who wishes he had wasted less time reading dime novels during
his inquisitive youth.[8]

For a long time, Franklin remained dissatisfied with the way he had
described his father's library. The conjoined adjectives that define Josiah
Franklin's books of divinity—"polemic and practical"—give the two types
equal status, but they represent opposing attitudes toward religion. Franklin
saw value in practical divinity, not so much in polemic divinity. There was
only one reason to read it, according to a contemporary *bon mot*: "Some men
read polemic divinity, not to confirm them in their own religion, but to out
talk those of another."[9]

The most popular book of practical divinity in colonial New England was
Bishop Lewis Bayly's *Practice of Piety*. The book was well known in the
Franklin family; Benjamin's brother James engraved the frontispiece for a
1718 Boston edition. Despite its Anglican origins, *Practice of Piety* reads like a
Puritan how-to. It contains occasional prayers and advice for practicing devotions, singing psalms, observing the Sabbath, and reading the Bible. One section, for instance, emphasizes why it is important to pray every morning:
"Many a man who rose well and lively in the morning has been seen a dead
man e'er night. So may it befall thee."[10]

Franklin slowly realized how much two particular books had shaped his
life. When he revised part 1 of his autobiography in 1789, he added a sentence
naming two practical books his father had owned. Besides Plutarch's *Lives*,
Benjamin added, "There was also a book of Defoe's call'd *An Essay Upon
Projects* and another of Dr. Mather's call'd *Essays to Do Good*, which perhaps
gave me a turn of thinking that had an influence on some of the principal
future events of my life." Mentioning *An Essay Upon Projects* in his autobiography, Franklin kept Defoe's book alive for new generations of readers. Edgar
Allan Poe, for instance, learned about Defoe's *Essay Upon Projects* by reading
Franklin's autobiography.[11]

Offering many useful ideas for improving society, *An Essay Upon Projects* gave new meaning to the word "projector." A pejorative term during the seventeenth century, a projector was another name for a cheat, a schemer, a promoter of bogus business ventures. Defoe acknowledged that the projector was not far from a swindler but argued that the projector's characteristic inventiveness could generate ideas and produce results. The positive connotations would win out, but the term "projector" retained its negative connotations decades into the eighteenth century.[12]

Given his numerous ideas for community improvement, Franklin personally reinforced the positive connotations of the word "projector." So did H. M. Posnett, an Irishman who established his scholarly reputation while teaching in New Zealand. Calling Franklin the "greatest American projector of his age," he meant it as high praise. Never stingy with his superlatives, Posnett also called Franklin the "greatest statesman of the eighteenth century."[13]

Defoe offered Franklin a clear vision for a better world that was no pie-in-the-sky utopia, but a realm within reach, given good leadership and hard work. One chapter treats friendly societies: organizations that would let people come together for their mutual benefit, helping each other during times of distress, disease, or disaster. The chapter gave Franklin the idea for the first fire insurance company in America.

In a section titled "An Academy for Women," Defoe wonders why girls should be denied an academic education: "If knowledge and understanding had been useless additions to the sex, God Almighty wou'd never have given them capacities." Franklin agreed. After reading Defoe's *Essay Upon Projects*, he enjoyed debating the resolution that women deserve the opportunity for a proper education. Later, Franklin would excerpt a 200-word passage from *An Essay Upon Projects* for one of his Silence Dogood essays. Defoe's emphasis on improving female education crystallizes into an impassioned plea for universal education: "The soul is plac'd in the body like a rough diamond, and must be polish'd, or the lustre of it will never appear."[14]

Essays to Do Good is Franklin's title for Cotton Mather's *Bonifacius*, which means a doer of good. *Bonifacius* deserves recognition as the finest work of practical divinity in colonial American literature. Josiah Franklin's copy was in rough shape. Decades later, Benjamin recalled the book's physical condition: "It had been so little regarded by a former possessor, that several leaves of it were torn out: but the remainder gave me such a turn of thinking as to have an influence on my conduct thro' life; for I have always set a greater value on the character of a *doer of good*, than on any other kind of reputation."[15]

Franklin especially appreciated Mather's emphasis on every individual's responsibility to improve the lives of one another. Mather wrote: "A man must look upon himself as dignifyed and gratifyed by God, when an opportunity to do good is put into his hands. He must embrace it with rapture, as enabling him directly to answer the great end of his being." Mather stressed that religious faith alone is insufficient. It must be accompanied by good works performed with gratitude toward God and compassion for humanity. Indulging his passion for wordplay, Mather observed, "A workless faith is a worthless faith."[16]

Mather's detailed program for charity gave public-minded citizens a way to practice their piety and improve their communities. At one point, he addresses lawyers, quoting a proverb that embodies a derogatory attitude toward them but explaining how to remedy it: "There has been an old complaint, 'That a good lawyer seldom is a good neighbour.' You know how to confute it, gentlemen, by making your skill in the law, a blessing to your neighbourhood." Colonial lawyers were slow to take Mather's advice; the proverb endured. Franklin would repeat it in *Poor Richard's Almanack*.[17] *Bonifacius* helped shape Franklin's philanthropic spirit and anticipated the benevolent American organizations that would emerge over the next two centuries.

Besides encouraging his readers to undertake projects that would benefit the community, Mather's *Essays to Do Good* offered much general advice encouraging people to improve themselves. One suggestion concerns the power of reading. Mather directed his advice to ministers, but it suits every reader: "Good books of all sorts, may employ your leisure, and enrich you with treasures."[18]

Josiah Franklin noticed how much time his youngest son spent reading. His son James was also a reader, but Benjamin surpassed him in his love of books. Instead of having Benjamin serve an apprenticeship and learn a trade like his brothers, Josiah would send him to grammar school. He chose South Grammar School (present-day Boston Latin), "the principal school of the *British colonies*, if not of all *America*," according to the Reverend Thomas Prince. Josiah knew it would prepare Benjamin for Harvard, where he could study for the ministry. He entered South Grammar School when he was 8, meaning he matriculated in 1714.[19]

Benjamin studied incessantly. Jane Mecom said her brother was "addicted to all kinds of reading." His performance in school affirmed his dedication to learning. He advanced quickly, rising from the middle of the class in which he started to its head and then skipping to the next class. Before long he skipped ahead to another class, thus spanning three grades in one school year.[20]

Almost 40 when Franklin matriculated, headmaster Nathaniel Williams was warm and welcoming: "His body was of a middling size, enclining to fatness; his countenance fresh and comely, with a mixture of majesty and smiling sweetness." A Harvard graduate, Williams had been ordained as an Evangelist to Barbados, but its climate disagreed with him. He also trained as a physician with his uncle, Dr. James Oliver, who willed his medical books to him. Though teaching became his passion, Williams abandoned neither medicine nor the ministry. The rest of his life he would mount the pulpit as readily as make a poultice.[21]

In 1703, Williams had become an usher, that is, an assistant teacher at South Grammar under Ezekiel Cheever, colonial New England's most influential schoolmaster. Cotton Mather called Cheever *Corderius Americanus* after the renowned Genevan schoolmaster Maturin Cordier. Cheever had come to Boston in 1637 and opened his first school within two years. A colonial American Mr. Chips, Cheever continued teaching until his death in 1708. His seventy-year career let him teach several generations of New England leaders, profoundly shaping the region's intellectual life.[22]

Herman Melville destroyed the image of all grammar school ushers when he depicted one in *Moby-Dick* as "threadbare in coat, heart, body, and brain," but Williams was an excellent usher. Upon Cheever's death, Williams became headmaster and followed his predecessor's educational philosophy. He found teaching alone difficult, but his own ushers lessened the burden. When Franklin attended South Grammar, Edward Wigglesworth, a recent Harvard graduate, served as usher. Wigglesworth had a reputation as a man of letters. One surviving book from his library suggests his poetic tastes: *Paradise Lost*.[23]

Williams taught students much more than Latin and Greek. In addition to books of divinity, rhetoric, and medicine, his personal library included *Cosmographie*, Peter Heylyn's ambitious attempt to create a geography of the known world. Heylyn painted a glowing portrait of New England, comparing it with ancient Rome: "The growth of *old Rome* and *New-England* had the like foundation: both sanctuaries . . . resorted to by such of the neighbouring nations, as longed for *innovations* in church and state." Williams may have introduced Heylyn's *Cosmographie* to Franklin, who would come to know his brother's copy of the work. Williams's wide-ranging knowledge helped make his students well rounded. Thomas Prince said that Williams gave them a superior education: "With a wise and steady conduct, he happily rul'd them; and was generally both reverenc'd and belov'd among them."[24]

The surviving outline of the Latin curriculum Williams followed at South Grammar reveals what textbooks Franklin studied as he progressed through the three-year program in one year. Williams based his curriculum on his predecessor's. *A Short Introduction to the Latin Tongue* stems from Cheever's handwritten notes, which Williams compiled, edited, and published. It was an accidence, that is, a basic survey of Latin grammar and syntax. Cheever's *Short Introduction* would remain a standard textbook in New England through the eighteenth century.[25]

After mastering Cheever, students read *Nomenclatura*. This title represents one of several possible English–Latin lexicons that helped students build their knowledge by teaching longer units of meaning. It presented many proverbs in English and Latin. With slight variations, some of these textbook proverbs would make their way into *Poor Richard's Almanack*:

> Well begun, is half done.
> No sweat, no sweet; No pains, no gains.
> Many hands make light work.
> Fair winds butter no parsnips.[26]

Whereas Franklin learned English by reading the Bible, he learned Latin by reading traditional saws and sayings that stretched back to ancient Rome.

No author had a greater impact on Williams's curriculum than Charles Hoole, an English schoolmaster who wrote, edited, or translated the most influential Latin textbooks of the era. *Sententiae pueriles*, the work Franklin and his fellow students read after *Nomenclatura*, contains Latin sentences with Hoole's English translations in parallel columns. The text is headed: "Sentences (or Sayings) of Wise Men, Collected for Them that First Enter to the Latin Tongue."[27] Two-word Latin sentences follow, arranged alphabetically by the first word in the sentence. Three- and four-word sentences come next, followed by sentences containing five or more words.

Upon receiving this introductory book, the boys naturally searched for dirty words. The two-word sentences looked promising: *Fuge turpia* ("Avoid filthy things"); *Meretricem fuge* ("Shun a whore"). Though Williams emphasized the importance of rote memorization, it does seem strange to have 8-year-old boys memorizing how to say "shun a whore" in Latin. Not until late in the four-word section would they encounter another naughty sentence: *Nihil turpius sene libidinoso* ("Nothing is more filthy than a lustful old man").[28]

Beyond these few dirty words, the individual items in *Sententiae pueriles* lack the playfulness of the proverbs in *Nomenclatura*. Warning against sloth, selfishness, and dishonesty, Hoole comes across as a metronomic finger-wagger. A few contain memorable imagery: *Rubor virtutis est color* ("Blushing is the colour of virtue"); *Esquilla non nascitur rosa* ("A rose doth not grow upon a sea-onion"); *Saepo sub palliolc sordido sapientia est* ("Wisdom is oft-times under a thread-bare cloak").[29]

From *Sententiae pueriles*, Williams's students progressed to *The Distichs of Cato*. Another one of Hoole's parallel English and Latin textbooks, Cato's *Distichs* gave Franklin additional Latin lessons in the form of moral precepts. It has more literary value than *Sententiae pueriles*, but its built-in morality pleased parents and teachers more than students.

Franklin would later publish James Logan's English translation of Cato's *Distichs*. Unlike Franklin, Logan disagreed with Defoe's argument that women deserved an academic education. Though he was colonial America's greatest classicist, Logan refused to teach his daughters Latin. Unwilling to deny his girls the moral value of *The Distichs of Cato*, he translated the work into English for them. Franklin read the translation in manuscript and liked it so much that he sought Logan's permission to publish it. Logan agreed, provided his own name was left off. In his publisher's preface, Franklin says, "Such excellent precepts of morality, contain'd in such short and easily-remember'd sentences, may to youth particularly be very serviceable in the conduct of life."[30]

Hoole also edited Maturin Cordier's Latin conversation manual. Titled *Colloquia*, the textbook was often called the Cordery after its original author. Hoole adapted it for English speakers. Hoole's Cordery was more attractive to students than either *Senteniae pueriles* or Cato's *Distichs*. Whereas those two works present an adult's admonitory words, the Cordery presents short conversations that let students speak Latin in a voice approximating their own.

Building a reference to Cato's *Distichs* into his Cordery, Hoole provided valuable insight into how Cato's *Distichs* was used in the classroom. The fourth colloquy, which presents a conversation between master and student, illustrates the kind of talk that took place between teacher and student in Williams's Latin class.[31]

"Are you ready to give an account of your study?" the teacher would ask.

"I am ready, as I think," the student would reply.

"Say, then, and have your wits about you."

"This morning we first said a verse out of *Cato*; then we constru'd it in Latin and English: at the last, two and two of us parsed every part of speech, with its things belonging to it, and the signification."

At the end of the third year, Williams's Latin curriculum culminated with the short narratives that comprise *Aesop's Fables*. Related to emblems and proverbs, fables would intrigue Franklin throughout his life. Presumably, he had read *Aesop's Fables* in English before entering school since Nathaniel Crouch had edited an English translation for Burton's Books.[32]

One favorite from Aesop tells the story of a father and son traveling to market to sell a donkey. The father rides the donkey down a muddy road as his son walks. Together, they meet a series of faultfinders. One shames the father for making his son walk, so the boy climbs behind his father, and they proceed. A second shames them for overburdening the donkey, so the father dismounts and lets his son ride. A third wonders why the boy is making his father walk, calling him, in Franklin's words, "a graceless, rascally young jackanapes." Consequently, the two walk and lead the donkey. When a fourth calls them fools for walking through the mud instead of riding, the father tells his son they will toss the donkey over the next bridge and be done with it.[33]

Without further evidence, it is impossible to say which fables Franklin read in school, but Thomas Dilworth's *New Guide to the English Tongue*, a London schoolbook Franklin would later republish, includes a dozen fables, making Franklin's reprint the first American edition of Aesop. Franklin structured his collection of *Aesop's Fables* like an emblem book. Each fits onto a single page. A woodcut illustration appears at the top. A proverb comes next, serving as both caption to the illustration and précis of the ensuing fable. Each page ends with what Franklin called an interpretation that explains the moral lesson the fable teaches. Within the Aesopic tradition, these interpretations are called "applications." They correspond to the commentaries in emblem books.

The first fable in Franklin's edition of Dilworth is "Of the Waggoner and Hercules," which is headed with the proverb, "He that won't help himself, shall have help from no body." While driving his team, the waggoner gets stuck in a hole. He falls to his knees and prays for divine assistance. "Thou fool," Hercules says in reply to the waggoner's prayers and supplications, "whip thy horses, and set thy shoulder to the wheels; and then if thou wilt call upon Hercules, he will help thee."[34]

"Of the Two Thieves and the Butcher" is headed with a proverb Franklin would often repeat: "Honesty is the best policy." "Of the Shepherd's Boy and the Husbandmen" is better known as "The Boy Who Cried Wolf." "Of the Dove and the Bee," a fable about a dove that saves a bee from drowning, concludes with the bee saving the dove from a fowler's snare. It is headed with the proverb "One good turn deserves another."[35]

Franklin left no reminiscences about his fellow grammar school students, and no enrollment records from the period survive. Likely classmates include Jeremiah Gridley, who would emerge as the leading Boston lawyer of his generation, and Mather Byles, who would become a prominent poet. Edmund Quincy was definitely a schoolmate. Quincy was a couple of years older than Franklin, but once Franklin advanced two grades, they would have been reading the same textbooks. Shared interests, a passion for reading, and an omnivorous curiosity reinforced their friendship.[36]

Before Franklin completed his first year at South Grammar, his father started having second thoughts about sending him to Harvard, not just because of its expense, but also because of the poor income college graduates earned. If Benjamin would not be going to college, he hardly needed to attend a Latin school. Pulling him from South Grammar, Josiah thwarted his youngest son's hopes for an academic education. Instead, he sent him to a school for boys and girls conducted by George Brownell, who had come to Boston from South Carolina.

In terms of both organization and curriculum, Brownell's school differed from South Grammar. Williams reported to a committee of municipal overseers and earned a salary set by the city and guaranteed by local taxes. Brownell neither reported to overseers, nor was his salary guaranteed. Instead, his school relied on student fees that parents paid directly. It was a venture school, that is, an entrepreneurial school operated as a household business by an individual teacher and his or her family.[37]

Whereas grammar schools had ushers, venture schools had apprentices. The year before Benjamin Franklin enrolled, Increase Gatchell, a talented 16-year-old, was Brownell's apprentice and helped teach his classes. Brownell taught Gatchell well. He would later open a school of his own. Given his age, Gatchell likely remained Brownell's apprentice when Franklin attended the school.[38]

Since venture schoolteachers depended on tuition for support and did not report to overseers, market demand shaped their curriculum. Brownell did not have total freedom to teach whatever he wished. He had to get special permission to teach dancing, which the city granted in 1713. Some community leaders still disapproved. Cotton Mather, for one, saw dancing as an enterprise fraught with genuine peril. He said, "A dance is a work of Satan, one of his pomps and vanities, which all baptised persons are under vows to renounce."[39] Franklin was one baptized person who would not renounce dancing. The lessons at Brownell's coeducational school gave him a social skill that would prove useful throughout his life.

Brownell also taught music, a subject Josiah Franklin appreciated. Around the Franklin home, Josiah often sang psalms or played psalm tunes on his fiddle. Brownell augmented whatever musical skills Benjamin acquired from his father. He taught treble violin, flute, spinet, and possibly other instruments. Gatchell, also an accomplished musician, could play the fiddle, flute, harpsichord, and mock trumpet, a single-reed instrument that would evolve into the clarinet.[40]

Writing and cyphering (arithmetic) formed the heart of Brownell's curriculum. In his autobiography, Franklin says he did well in writing class but provides no further details about the English curriculum. In a letter to his sister Jane years later, he wrote, "You may remember an ancient poet whose words we have all studied and copy'd at school, [who] said long ago, 'a man of words and not of deeds, / Is like a garden full of weeds.'" Franklin slyly recorded a facetious variation of this proverb in his letter: "'A man of deeds, and not of words / Is like a garden full of. . . .'" Franklin stopped short and inserted a blank instead of the intended rhyme, explaining, "I have forgot the rhime, but remember 'tis something the very reverse of perfume."[41]

The letter to Jane indicates that copying proverbs was a basic assignment in English class. Franklin's skills were already well developed when he came to Brownell's school, but he had apparently copied out proverbs at some point during his education. After mentioning Brownell in the draft, Franklin expanded his reminiscence to describe his teacher's pedagogical approach. Brownell taught students using "mild encouraging methods."[42]

Cyphering was another story. Not even Brownell's pedagogical skill could get young Franklin to learn his arithmetic—or so he says in the autobiography. Franklin initially wrote, "I fail'd in the arithmetic, and made no hand of it."[43] A self-critique on the surface, Franklin's statement implicitly criticizes the classical education he had received at South Grammar. The traditional emphasis on ancient tongues prevented grammar school students from studying more practical subjects like arithmetic. Though Franklin learned the basics of Latin at South Grammar, his education there in no way prepared him for Brownell's rigorous mathematical curriculum.

In light of his future success as a businessman and scientist, Franklin realized that the portrait of his younger self as a mathematical dunce sounded too farfetched. He softened the sentence about flunking mathematics in revision. He changed his wording to "made no progress in it."[44]

Franklin's revision may seem slight. After all, the two phrases are synonymous. The idiom, to make no hand of something, means to make no progress. All Franklin did, really, was to substitute a literal phrase for a figurative one. But this figure of speech has wide-ranging implications. The hand is a prominent motif in Franklin's writings. The memorable Poor Richardism—"Help hands; for I have no lands"—encapsulates Franklin's American Dream.

Though a poor person may inherit neither land nor money, the ability to use the hands, that is, to work hard, can serve as an able substitute. The hand was such an important symbol for him that Franklin did not want to squander it here, especially in a negative expression.[45]

Though the autobiography forms the fullest known appreciation of Brownell, a neglected book supplies vital information about Franklin's teacher. The year before Franklin matriculated, Gatchell prepared an almanac, *The Young American Ephemeris for 1715*, which Brownell agreed to publish. That Brownell had an apprentice capable of performing the complex astronomical calculations necessary to create an almanac is a testament to the scholarly rigor of his mathematical curriculum. By putting his imprimatur on Gatchell's title page, Brownell showed his willingness to support his protégés publicly. In this case, Brownell's support caused some unexpected blowback.

The Loyal American's Almanack for the Year 1715, a weak effort by the otherwise unknown "New Comer into America," inspired Gatchall, whose preface to *The Young American Ephemeris* explains that the mediocrity of New Comer's almanac inspired him to create a better one. New Comer reissued *The Loyal American's Almanack* with a four-page critical appendix. Calling Brownell a "caperer," New Comer demeaned his reputation as a dance teacher. New Comer also called Brownell "an ignorant paper-skull'd fellow, who pretends to have a mighty knack at *writing, cyphering, musick, dancing*, etc. of all which he knows as much as an old horse."[46]

The almanac was one of the colonial printer's most profitable items. The controversy that flared over competing Boston almanacs in Franklin's youth gave him an object lesson that would take on relevance once he started writing and publishing his own almanacs. Hearing that Gatchell hoped to market *The Young American Ephemeris* in Philadelphia, New Comer said he should send his almanacs there quickly. (To understand New Comer's ensuing comment, it is important to know that eighteenth-century housewives rolled their pie crusts on buttered sheets of recycled paper.) New Comer tells Gatchell what to do with his almanacs: "I advise him to make haste, for *Christmas* is now drawing near, and if they don't arrive before they make their *Christmas pyes*, I fear he'll lose his market; for I know not what else they are fit for, unless to wipe their _____."[47]

Less than a year after Benjamin matriculated, his father withdrew him from Brownell's school and thus ended his formal education and put him to work. Brownell remained in Boston until 1721, when he moved to New York before finally relocating to Philadelphia, where he and Franklin would be reunited. By 1723, Gatchell had established his own dancing school with uneven success.

When he denied admittance to some young lads, they retaliated with violence. Before long, a ballet was being fought out in the alley: "After firing several volleys of oaths and curses threatning to kill Mr. Gatchell, and using abundance of obscene discourse not fit to be mention'd, they fell upon the glass windows, shatter'd them all to pieces, and broke one of the iron bars."[48]

Once Josiah put his youngest son to work at the tallow chandlery, the Blue Ball eclipsed Benjamin's light. Since animal fat supplied the raw material for the tallow trade, making soap, ironically, was a dirty job. Benjamin hated it. The smell that emanated from the rendering vat was more than many could stand. The stench of the tallow chandler's cauldron became a measure of smelliness. The body odor of Sir Wilfull, a character in William Congreve's *Way of the World*, is so pungent that another exclaims, "He would poison a tallow-chandler and his family!"[49]

In the autobiography, Franklin recalls his responsibilities: "I was employed in cutting wick for the candles, filling the dipping mold, and the molds for cast candles, attending the shop, going of errands, etc." In one illustration for his edition of Franklin's autobiography, Thomas Hart Benton presents a close-up of two hands with the right holding a pair of scissors as they snip a wick. Presumably, these are young Franklin's hands, but they do not look like a boy's hands. Their gnarly appearance makes them resemble the hands of Atropos, one of the three Fates. Brandishing her abhorred shears, Atropos threatens to cut short Benjamin's life should he continue as a candlemaker.[50]

Beyond the physical discomfort and general tedium, making candles humiliated Benjamin. Having demonstrated his intellectual prowess at school, he knew he could accomplish something greater than candle making, which required no special skill or intellectual ability. Judged by his disregard of Benjamin's intellect, Josiah Franklin seems like an ogre.

Beginning in 1715, the year he turned 9, Benjamin gained another male role model. That year, Uncle Benjamin, for whom he was named, emigrated to Boston. Like his younger brother Josiah, Uncle Benjamin had been raised in Ecton and learned the silk dyer's trade. Uncle Benjamin enjoyed relating his fond memories of Ecton: its church bells, the old fishing stream, childhood games of hide-and-seek, the bakery's fresh bread, and the brewery's nappy ale.[51]

Uncle Benjamin was no ordinary silk dyer. He had many cultural and intellectual interests, which he shared with his namesake. A good listener, Uncle Benjamin enjoyed attending sermons and invented a shorthand to record them. He loved to read and often dabbled in poetry. He wrote several admonitory poems to his nephew, encouraging him to study hard and do his best. Good sentiments do not good poetry make, but Uncle Benjamin's poems show that his nephew's reading life was not limited to the printed word. Colonial American poetry often circulated in manuscript among friends and families. The Franklins were no exception.

Sometimes Uncle Benjamin presented books to his nieces and nephews, but his gifts may not have done Benjamin much good. Years later, Franklin came across one of Uncle Benjamin's presentation copies, Clement Cotton's *None but Christ*, which depicts Christ as both the physician and the medicine to fix a broken soul. Uncle Benjamin also maintained a commonplace book to record memorable passages from his reading. In addition, he drafted a silk dyer's handbook, listing several colors with their symbolic meanings. Red, according to Uncle Benjamin, is the color of defiance.[52]

Uncle Benjamin's library fascinated his nephew. Years later, a London bookseller offered Franklin a multivolume collection of bound pamphlets that had supposedly belonged to his uncle and contained his marginalia. Franklin bought the lot. His acquisition of these volumes was motivated more by personal than practical reasons. A few pamphlets still hold literary value, but most treat minor religious or political controversies. The marginalia was what made them valuable to Franklin. To possess books his uncle had supposedly owned and read and annotated was irresistible.[53]

After working in his father's business for two years, Benjamin realized that if he did not rebel soon, he would be stuck in the tallow chandlery for life. When he threatened to run away to sea, Josiah agreed to introduce him to other trades. He escorted Benjamin on a working man's tour of Boston to let him see how other tradesmen—braziers, bricklayers, cutlers, joiners—performed their work.

The brazier's trade was appealing; better to be the candlestick maker than the chandler. Besides physical strength, a brazier's work required ingenuity and drawing ability. A job as a cutler had a similar appeal. It required a delicate touch that could only come from long experience in the trade. The fee that tradesmen charged parents for accepting an apprentice could prove a barrier. Since Uncle Benjamin's son Samuel had established a cutlery business, Josiah decided to apprentice Benjamin to him but changed his mind when Samuel demanded a fee.[54]

Benjamin had remained a bookish lad even after his father ended his son's formal schooling. Josiah ultimately decided to apprentice Benjamin to his brother James, who had established himself in Boston as a printer after apprenticing in London. At least James would not charge their father an apprenticeship fee for his little brother. Josiah Franklin had matched his son the reader to his ideal trade. A printer he would be.

3

Reading by Candlelight

NINE YEARS HIS senior, James Franklin worked his littlest brother hard. Still, Benjamin managed to carve some personal time from his apprenticeship. He got up early to read before work and stayed up late, often reading through much of the night, or so he says in his autobiography. Mark Twain found his tale of after-hours study a stretcher. Aware that Franklin deliberately shaped himself as a model for posterity, Twain quipped, "With a malevolence which is without parallel in history, he would work all day, and then sit up nights, and let on to be studying algebra by the light of a smouldering fire, so that all other boys might have to do that also."[1]

Franklin must have read by candlelight, not firelight, given the steady supply of candle rejects he and James could have received from the Blue Ball. Despite their defects, Benjamin burned those candles at both ends. Franklin mentions neither candlelight nor firelight as he describes reading after dark. That Twain could envision the pale fire illuminating the printed page as young Franklin read late into the night testifies to his imagination and Franklin's literary skill. Franklin's words bring alive his boyhood love of reading.

Sundays gave him the best chance to read and study. When he lived with his parents, they forced him to attend services at Old South Meeting House every week. Though James was tough on his brother, at least he did not make him go to church. Given the chance to skip services, Benjamin often did. On Sunday mornings, he could dawdle in the printshop by himself and read: a pleasurable diversion that let him dissipate the holy hush of ancient sacrifice.

Franklin's reading material improved once he began his apprenticeship and gained access to a wider range of books. He befriended apprentices from neighboring printshops, who secretly loaned him books, provided he would return them like new the next morning so that neither bosses nor buyers could tell they had been read. Franklin often stayed up to finish one borrowed book or another, so he could return the volume before anyone noticed it was missing.

He enjoyed reading poetry in his youth. The well-stocked library in his brother's printing office held several collections of verse, including John Oldham's *Works*. A seventeenth-century English satirist, Oldham is best known for *Satyrs upon the Jesuits*, though not everyone appreciated the work. John Adams found Oldham's satires "nervous and malignant, or perhaps more properly indignant." Oldham's perceptive vision and ribald wit lent themselves to other topics. John Dryden, who shared his gift for satire, saw the likeness and liked what he saw. Elegizing Oldham, Dryden observed, "One common note on either lyre did strike, / And knaves and fools we both abhorr'd alike."[2]

The most eye-catching title in Oldham's table of contents is "Upon a Lady, Who by Overturning of a Coach, Had Her Coats behind Flung up, and What Was under Shewn to the View of the Company." The action described in this lengthy title has already occurred by the time the speaker of the poem, a young beau, discovers what has happened to Phyllis, the upside-down lady of the title. Unwilling to fall in love, the young man has steeled himself against Phyllis's charms, but he is unprepared for what he sees upon the greeny grass:

> My heart, before averse to love,
> No longer could a rebel prove;
> When on the grass you did display
> Your radiant BUM to my survey,
> And sham'd the lustre of the day.[3]

Franklin would echo Oldham's poem in his mock diatribe *Hoop-Petticoats Arraigned and Condemned by the Light of Nature, and Law of God*: "Instead of covering our nakedness [the hoops in the petticoats] expose it; and upon some emergent accidents, expose those parts that Adam and Eve seem'd to take especial care to cover."[4]

Reading verse gave Franklin the urge to write verse. Not even Oldham's "Satyr Dissuading the Author from the Study of Poetry" could faze him. In this work, the ghost of Edmund Spenser materializes to dissuade the speaker of the poem from becoming a poet. Oldham's humorous version of Spenser clashes with the man John Milton called "our sage and serious poet." Oldham's Spenser finds metaphors in fecal matter. Most so-called poets nowadays, he says, "are troubled with a flux of brains / And each on paper squirts his filthy sense."[5]

Authors of enduring poetry are often neglected in their own time, Oldham's Spenser opines, naming two other English poets. Neither Samuel

Butler, the author of *Hudibras*, nor Abraham Cowley, best known for his Pindaric odes, were recognized by their contemporaries. Franklin knew the verse of Butler and Cowley; his brother had their collected works in his office library. Oldham's Spenser lists alternate methods to make a surer and safer living than writing poetry: "Preach, plead, cure, fight, game, pimp, beg, cheat, or thieve."[6]

Josiah Franklin gave his youngest son much the same advice. He ridiculed Benjamin's verse, telling him that poetry begets poverty. Unlike their father, James saw value in his brother's verse and recognized how he could turn a profit using this skill. James encouraged him to write broadside ballads based on current events.

The Light House Tragedy, a ballad Franklin wrote around the time he turned 13, relates the tragic drowning of local lighthouse keeper George Worthylake, his wife Anne, and their daughter Ruth. Franklin hawked *The Light House Tragedy* through the city streets. Based on an event that had pulled at Boston's heartstrings, the ballad sold well. Franklin was thrilled with its commercial success at the moment but later called it "wretched stuff." It is impossible to test his appraisal because no copies survive, nor do any copies of his second broadside ballad, which told the story of Blackbeard's capture.[7]

After his brief stint as a teenaged balladeer, Franklin shifted his literary ambitions from poetry to prose. A friend helped develop his writing style. Franklin recalled, "There was another bookish lad in the town, John Collins by name, with whom I was intimately acquainted." Franklin's characterization of Collins is also a self-characterization. Franklin was one bookish lad, Collins another. Collins split his reading between literature and science.[8]

Franklin and Collins enjoyed debate. They would take opposite sides of a resolution and continue arguing until they could agree on a winner. Leaving one debate unresolved, Franklin wrote out his arguments and sent them to Collins, who refuted them in a letter of response. Once they had exchanged three or four letters, Josiah Franklin discovered their correspondence and offered his assessment. He critiqued Benjamin's method, judgment, and expression, convincing him to try harder to improve his style. Josiah's sage advice reveals an intellect well above the average Boston tradesman.

Taking his father's words to heart, Franklin sought literary models. He obtained a volume of *The Spectator*, which he read repeatedly. He enjoyed its essays and imitated its writing style. He would list some keywords from an essay, set the volume aside, wait a few days, and then attempt to re-create the essay based on the keywords. Upon completing it, he would check his composition against the original.

No one knows which *Spectator* essays Franklin rewrote, but his autobiography narrows the possibilities. The final text says he obtained an "odd volume" of *The Spectator*; the draft shows it was the third volume, which reprinted eighty-two issues from *Spectator* 170 to *Spectator* 251. Perhaps Franklin cut the reference to the third volume in revision because he soon read the whole eight-volume set, which James also had in the office library. Besides *The Spectator*, James owned other collections of English periodical essays, including *The Lover*, *The Reader*, and *The Guardian*. As their writings demonstrate, both James and Benjamin knew the English essays well.[9]

In "Silence Dogood 14," Franklin quotes a 260-word passage from *Guardian* 80 to support his religious critique. Richard Steele, who wrote that number of *The Guardian*, said the word "church" has often been abused and misused, misappropriated and misapplied: "That important monosyllable drags all the other words in the language after it, and it is made use of to express both praise and blame." Steele's words support Franklin's argument regarding the absurdity of sectarian religious differences and the value of humanitarian ethics.[10]

Spectator 191 helps illustrate how Franklin revised his writing. It contains a proverb he would rewrite for *Poor Richard's Almanack*. Cautioning people against overextending themselves, Mr. Spectator initially uses highfalutin diction: "It is this foolish sanguine temper, this depending upon contingent futurities that occasions romantick generosity, chymerical grandeur, senseless ostentation, and generally ends in beggary and ruin." By the paragraph's end, Mr. Spectator drops the big words and restates the same idea proverbially: "The man who lives by hope will die by hunger." Franklin could see what Joseph Addison, who wrote this number of *The Spectator*, was doing but thought his well-balanced prepositional phrases and careful alliteration made the proverb too neat. Franklin roughed it up, lowering the diction further: "He that lives upon hope, dies farting."[11]

The third volume contains essays on other themes that interested Franklin: the history and power of fable; the stereotype of the hen-pecked husband, which would influence his portrayal of Poor Richard; political arithmetic; a remedy for loud talkers; sculpture as a metaphor for education; and the value of an inquisitive disposition.

Overall, Franklin took much from *The Spectator*: style and structure, subject and purpose. The essays gave him an ideal length for his own writings as he became a "master of the short form," to use Thomas Haslam's felicitous phrase.[12] *The Spectator*'s light-hearted tone also influenced Franklin, who learned how to interject humor in his writings even while addressing the most serious topics.

Spectator 179 has much to say about the relationship between tone and audience. Mr. Spectator identifies two general types of readers: the mercurial and the saturnine. Whereas mercurial readers want to be entertained with wit and humor, saturnine readers want to learn from sensible moral essays. *The Spectator* essays suit both types of readers. The ideal essay is so entertaining that mercurial readers hardly know they are learning as they laugh and saturnine readers learn so much they scarcely mind the accompanying mirth. Franklin found similar advice in Alexander Pope's *Essay on Criticism*, which he could quote from memory: "Men should be taught as if you taught them not."[13] Franklin took such advice to heart, teaching people as he tickled their fancy, both in person and in his writings.

Trying to imitate Mr. Spectator, Franklin realized he lacked a *copia verborum*. This Latin phrase, which means a "copious vocabulary," echoes the title of an Erasmus textbook, *De copia verborum*. Erasmus gave students a set of common Latin sentences with numerous variations enabling them to say the same thing differently. *De copia verborum* helped students build a mental storehouse of words and phrases to vary their spoken and written expression. His textbook was so well known that *copia verborum* had become a common phrase.[14]

Though Franklin used the phrase when he drafted the autobiography, he later replaced it to broaden his appeal. He dipped into the copious vocabulary he had developed since his youth for an English equivalent, telling readers that when he was young, he had lacked a "stock of words or a readiness in recollecting and using them."[15] Abandoning his schoolboy Latin, Franklin substituted the language of commerce. The writer's mind is a vast yet accessible stockroom of words, images, and ideas.

Reading helped Franklin develop his vocabulary. The autobiography mentions several books he read during his apprenticeship, listed more thematically than chronologically. He noted one by Thomas Tryon recommending vegetarianism. Another also influenced his diet. Franklin's mother told a dinner guest that her son learned about eating vegetables by reading "some mad old philosopher." Speaking with Pierre Cabanis, Franklin attributed his vegetarianism to a chapter in Plutarch's *Morals*, "Whether It Be Lawfull to Eat Flesh or No."[16]

Tryon advocated vegetarianism in several works, the fullest and most famous being *The Way to Health, Long Life and Happiness*. Promoting Tryon's vegetable diet, Franklin was in good company. Nineteenth-century whole food enthusiast Sylvester Graham—the inventor of the cracker that bears his name—cited *The Way to Health* to support his argument about whole wheat's "cleansing and opening nature." Graham also praised Franklin for demonstrating how vegetarianism could promote intellectual vigor.[17]

The Way to Health provides more useful recommendations. Tryon emphasized outdoor exercise to stay slim. He also celebrated the working life.
Idleness makes people overweight: "Look amongst ordinary *working people* in
country towns, and you shall very rarely see any of the husband-men or field-
workers very fat." Toward the end of *The Way to Health*, domestic animals
express the cruelty men inflict on them. A sheep, a hog, and even a horse, of
course, speak out. Tryon's talking horse observes, "There are another sort of
things called *idle men*, or *gentlemen*, (but nothing *gentle* do we find from
them,) who finding some of us endued by God with great celerity and swift-
ness of foot, they put us upon running of races one with another, for to grati-
fie their foolish *vanity, pride*, and *covetousness*."[18]

Franklin's vegetarianism contributed to his personal development. He
learned to prepare the dishes Tryon recommended—rice, boiled potatoes,
hasty pudding. Confident in Tryon's vegetarianism and his own culinary skill,
he proposed that if James would pay him half the cost of his board, he would
board himself. James agreed. Franklin discovered he could save half again as
much by purchasing his own food, which gave him more money for books.
Franklin proved himself a true bookman: He skimped on food to buy books!
He also created extra time to read. While James and the other employees went
out for their meals, Benjamin stayed behind in the printshop to read until
they returned.[19]

Dissatisfied with his mathematical performance at Brownell's school,
Franklin found a copy of *Cocker's Arithmetick* and taught himself the subject.
Edward Cocker was best known as an English writing master in his lifetime;
he left his mathematical lessons unpublished. John Hawkins, his successor at
the London school where he had taught, edited them for publication. *Cocker's
Arithmetick* appeared in 1678 and went through dozens of editions by the
mid-eighteenth century. It was the most popular mathematics textbook in
colonial America.

Cocker's pedagogical approach contributed to the book's popularity.
Unlike earlier textbooks, *Cocker's Arithmetick* minimizes explanatory material to let readers learn by practice. It covered such fundamental operations as
addition, subtraction, multiplication, and division. Furthermore, it taught
practical skills: how to calculate exchange rates, compute simple interest, and
convert units of measure.

Next Franklin studied geometry by reading navigation manuals, including
John Seller's *Practical Navigation* and Captain Samuel Sturmy's *Mariner's
Magazine*. Seller's textbook taught readers throuhout colonial America the nec-
essary mathematics to master navigation: arithmetic, geometry, trigonometry,

and the "doctrine of the spheres," that is, nautical astronomy. The work also explains how to use navigational instruments.[20]

In *Mariner's Magazine*, Sturmy instructs readers about geometry before proceeding to navigation, surveying, astronomy, and related subjects. Sturmy was another literary model for Franklin. Like John Bunyan, Sturmy understood how dialogue could function as a rhetorical and literary device. He taught readers navigational commands and responses using dialogue between a captain and his crew. Jonathan Swift enjoyed *Mariner's Magazine* so much he lifted big chunks of Sturmy's dialogue and put them in *Gulliver's Travels*.[21]

Around the time Franklin read Sellers and Sturmy, he also read John Locke's *Essay Concerning Human Understanding*. "The best book of logick in the world," he called it.[22] In it, Locke sets forth his ideas regarding how the mind functions. Beyond its importance to philosophy, the treatise gave Franklin another stylistic model. Few prefaces have as much personal charm as Locke's "Epistle to the Reader." From its opening sentence, Locke evinces the amiability of a good friend. A champion of intellectual endeavor, he is a kindred spirit for his readers, bringing them into his inner circle and his inner sanctum.

In *An Essay Concerning Human Understanding*, Locke presents one of the most famous metaphors in the history of philosophy. A person's mind is originally "white paper, void of all characters, without any ideas." This metaphor occurs in the work's second part. Locke had used a different metaphor to introduce this concept. The mind is an empty cabinet, he said. "The senses at first let in particular *ideas*, and furnish the yet empty cabinet; and the mind by degrees growing familiar with some of them, they are lodged in the memory."[23]

Locke had in mind the cabinet of curiosities, a home fixture for scientifically inclined people who collected objects displaying natural variety and human ingenuity. Beyond their contribution to science, cabinets of curiosities reflected where owners had traveled and what they thought. As a young man, Franklin would become fascinated with cabinets of curiosities, viewing some of the greatest cabinets in London during the mid-1720s. Franklin later created his own cabinet of curiosities and added to it all his life. Furthermore, he would help the Library Company of Philadelphia establish its cabinet of curiosities. Locke's use of the term shows that curiosity-filled cabinets became so influential that they have shaped the knowledge-forming process. The way a collector selects objects and arranges them in a cabinet parallels how the mind accumulates and codifies information.[24]

Franklin read other logic books in his youth. Though he obtained the anonymous *Grammar of the English Tongue* to ameliorate his spotty grammatical education, he enjoyed the appendix, "Logic: or, The Art of Reasoning." Its fourth part discusses the Socratic method of argument, which Franklin made his own. The guise of a humble enquirer and doubter gave him an advantage over disputants without making him seem superior.

Foreseeing the promise of the Socratic method, Franklin sought to learn more. He acquired *Memorable Things of Socrates*, Xenophon's record of what his mentor had taught him. Xenophon presented his Socratic materials with eloquence and integrity. His English translator identified a broad audience for the work, finding it useful for the philosopher, politician, soldier, and tradesman: four roles Franklin would play in his multifaceted career. *Memorable Things of Socrates* affected him perhaps more than any other book he read in his youth. Socrates's common sense, subtlety, and moderation suited Franklin's mind. Cabanis observed, "There was nobody he wanted to resemble more than Socrates: he took him as his model."[25]

Expanding the sentence about Locke's *Essay Concerning Human Understanding* as he revised his autobiography, Franklin named another book: *Logic; or, The Art of Thinking*, which was cowritten by Antoine Arnauld, a French theologian and polemicist, and Pierre Nicole, a French moralist. James had *The Art of Thinking* in his office library. Benjamin liked it so much he obtained his own copy when he was around 16, reinforcing his ownership as he autographed its title page, something he rarely did.[26]

Their English translator called Arnauld and Nicole "eminent sticklers for Jansenism," a school of thought that followed Cornelius Jansen, who defended the theology of Saint Augustine against the Jesuits. Both Arnauld and Nicole were associated with the Port Royal convent, which established several little schools around Paris. Port Royal alumni include the French dramatist Jean Racine. A famous line from Racine's *Britannicus* reflects the quest for truth his *alma mater* symbolized: "No secrets are there time does not reveal." Franklin would make a similar comment: "I believe it is impossible for a man, though he has all the cunning of a devil, to live and die a villain, and yet conceal it so well as to carry the name of an honest fellow to the grave with him, but some one by some accident or other shall discover him."[27]

Though Franklin called it *The Art of Thinking*, the book is generally known as the *Port Royal Logic*. It would develop a lasting reputation as the finest textbook in the field. The Reverend Professor S. S. Nelles, who taught logic at Toronto's Victoria College in the nineteenth century, excerpted it for his classroom text, *Chapters in Logic*. Nelles called the *Port Royal Logic* the best introduction to the subject available.[28]

That Arnauld and Nicole made logic an attractive subject is obvious from their opening sentence: "Nothing is more desirable than good sense and

justness of thought in discerning truth from falsehood." They understood
how lies could mislead the unwary. To help readers, they took a liberal stance
reflecting different, even contradictory, schools of thought. Their openmindedness enhances the book's appeal. They softened the post-Renaissance
hostility toward Aristotelian logic by viewing it with a Cartesian perspective,
which stresses clear and distinct ideas. The Aristotelian syllogism could no
longer reveal truth, they realized, but it could still expose error. They also
introduced a thoroughgoing skepticism that required students to scrutinize
the truth value of historical sources.[29]

Introducing their subject, Arnauld and Nicole explained what was new
about the *Port Royal Logic* and what they had borrowed from previous logic
textbooks. They had wondered about including difficult matters with little
obvious benefit but ultimately retained them; solving knotty questions can
benefit the thinker. Even when a problem-solving exercise does not result in
any particular truth, it can still teach students about the challenges of pursuing truth, a conclusion Arnauld and Nicole punctuated with a Latin phrase
from Martial, the great Latin epigrammatist. The epigrams and aphorisms
Franklin would include in *Poor Richard's Almanack* also demonstrate his
affinity with Martial. Franklin read another version of the same saying as the
motto to *Spectator* 470, which can be translated, "It is disgraceful to engage in
difficult trifles, and the labor spent on frivolities is foolish." Reduced to a two-
word Latin phrase, Martial's epigram became proverbial and entered Franklin's
vocabulary: *difficiles nugae*.[30]

Other echoes of the *Port Royal Logic* occur in Franklin's writings. In one
chapter, Arnauld and Nicole identify the problem that language has as it tries
to express meaning. Any term can mean different things to different people.
Only by understanding the speaker and the context can its meaning be understood. They use the oxymoron "true religion," for example: "If we read in an
historian, that a prince was zealous for the true religion, we cannot tell what
he means by it, unless we know what religion the historian was." Franklin
would say much the same: "Such is the imperfection of our language, and
perhaps of all other languages, that notwithstanding we are furnish'd with
dictionaries innumerable, we cannot precisely know the import of words,
unless we know of what party the man is that uses them."[31]

In his youth, Franklin read another book associated with the Port
Royalists, Blaise Pascal's *Les provinciales*. First translated into English as *The
Mystery of Jesuitism*, it is generally known as *Provincial Letters*. Franklin told
Cabanis he first read Pascal around the same time he read Locke. The work
delighted him so much he reread it several times. According to Cabanis, he

initially read *Provincial Letters* in a bad English translation. How did Franklin know it was a bad translation? Here's how: By the time he spoke with Cabanis, Franklin had reread *Provincial Letters* in French. He knew the English text so well, he remembered it as he read the French and noticed their differences. *Provincial Letters* was one of his favorite works of French literature.[32]

Though it might seem odd for a polemical tract to capture Franklin's attention once he eschewed religious polemics, the book's tone was entrancing. Pascal's rhetoric, more than his religion, gives *Provincial Letters* its appeal. Like the Socratic method, Pascal's method of argumentation shaped Franklin's. Wearing the mask of a humble enquirer and doubter, Pascal inveigles a Jesuit priest into all sorts of logical and doctrinal absurdities. Franklin would often model his literary personae on Pascal's satirical narrator.

Describing how he made the Socratic method his own, Franklin said that it proved handy in religious discussions: "And being then, a real doubter in many points of our religious doctrine, I found this method safest for my self and very embarrassing to those against whom I used it." Revising this sentence, Franklin added a prepositional phrase to explain how he happened to become a "real doubter." The additional phrase reveals two more authors he read but minimizes his personal culpability. Franklin became a doubter, as he says in the final version of his autobiography, "from reading Shaftesbury and Collins."[33]

Anthony Ashley Cooper, third earl of Shaftesbury, is best known as the author of *Characteristics of Men, Manners, Opinions, Times, etc.* One of the eighteenth century's most influential books, Shaftesbury's *Characteristics* showed Franklin the close relationship between individual and social interests, the importance of continual self-examination, and the practical value of a cheerful creed. H. M. Posnett recognized this influence: "Shaftesbury more than any other writer appears to me to have left his marks upon the moral and intellectual character of Franklin." Discussing several authors who influenced Franklin, Stuart P. Sherman argued that Shaftesbury gave him a model of stylistic urbanity.[34]

Shaftesbury's benevolent morality may be his most important contribution to Franklin's thought. He paralleled aesthetic theory and moral philosophy, which, at first glance, hardly seem to belong together. Unlike Thomas Hobbes, Shaftesbury did not think we are entirely selfish in our motivations. Unlike the Christian divines, Shaftesbury did not think we are motivated solely by the expectation of rewards or punishments in the afterlife. He believed we also act on unselfish, benevolent impulses, which constitute our virtue. His ethics coincide with his aesthetics. Both follow the Platonic idea that truth, beauty, and good are the same. Our perception of good functions the same as our perception of beauty. Our abiding moral sense lets us perceive beauty, which functions whether we are perceiving a beautiful work of art or an unselfish act of personal sacrifice.[35]

It would take time for Franklin to absorb Shaftesbury's thought. When he read *Characteristics* in his teens, he was struck mainly by the idea that morality can exist without religion; an innate moral sense makes preachers superfluous. Anthony Collins, the other author whose writings prompted Franklin's religious skepticism, agreed. Collins opposed blind acceptance of religious belief and advocated for the responsibility to use brain power to scrutinize every so-called truth. Franklin told Cabanis that reading Collins shook the fundamental beliefs he had been taught.

Franklin's copy of Collins's *Philosophical Inquiry Concerning Human Liberty*, which survives at the Library Company of Philadelphia, contains his youthful signature. In this work, Collins defends compatibilism, the idea that free will is compatible with determinism. Franklin also knew Collins's *Discourse of Free Thinking*. Its appeal to him is understandable. Collins took the term "freethinking," a pejorative used by his enemies, and gave it positive connotations. For Collins, as for Franklin, freethinking involved the use of reason to dissect any and all accepted beliefs.[36]

The Marquis de Condorcet may have left the most insightful remarks concerning what Franklin learned from Collins and Shaftesbury. Condorcet said that, together, these two authors inspired in Franklin a skepticism that "consists, not in doubting everything, but in weighing all the evidence by submitting it to rigorous analysis; not in proving that man cannot know anything, but in carefully discerning and choosing as the object of his curiosity what it is possible to know."[37]

Locke, who was Collins's mentor, treated him like a son, seeing Collins as his intellectual successor. Years after Locke's death, Collins arranged to publish a volume containing his letters to him and some of Locke's more obscure essays. It appeared in 1720 as *A Collection of Several Pieces of Mr. John Locke*. Franklin obtained a copy of Locke's *Pieces*, as it became known. The title page of his copy bears an autograph like the one in his *Port Royal Logic*.[38]

The letters to Collins appealed to readers like Franklin, that is, bright young men with drive and ambition who used their reason and intellect for the advancement of knowledge and the improvement of society. In one letter, Locke says, "To love truth for truth's sake, is the principal part of human perfection in this world, and the seed plot of all other virtues."[39]

In terms of Franklin's intellectual life, the most important part of Locke's *Pieces* is "Some Thoughts Concerning Reading and Study for a Gentleman."

This essay outlines a program of reading that Franklin could have followed using books he had available in Boston. The office library and Locke's recommendations have enough titles in common to suggest that James Franklin used Locke's essay as a guide to assemble his working collection of books. The essay begins with a bold one-sentence paragraph that defines the purpose of reading: "Reading is for the improvement of the understanding."[40]

The second paragraph identifies a twofold reason to improve the understanding: to increase our knowledge and enable us to share it with others. Before finishing his second page, Locke clarified that he had designed this program of reading for gentlemen, who are "most properly concern'd in moral and political knowledge." Gentlemen should study works that treat the "virtues and vices, of civil society, and the arts of government."[41]

Locke also recommended geography, mentioning two specific works: Peter Heylin's *Cosmography* and Herman Moll's *Geography*. For the countries both cover, Heylin is better than Moll, but the latter contains new discoveries absent from the earlier one. Heylin's *Cosmography* also suffers from its author's inability to break free from traditional religious belief. Happily, Franklin did not have to choose between Heylin and Moll. His brother's office library contained both, letting him decide for himself whose facts were valid.[42]

Closely related to geography, travel literature could give readers a mix of pleasurable and practical reading. Locke specifically recommended the invaluable collections of the two great compilers of English Renaissance travel writing: Richard Hakluyt and Samuel Purchas. Hakluyt may have been hard to find, but Franklin would acquire a copy of *Purchas His Pilgrimage*, and he also read the more extensive collection, *Purchas His Pilgrimes*. George Sandys's *Travels*, another book of travels Locke recommended, chronicles its author's journey from England through Europe to the Levant, which James Franklin also had in the office library. Observant and inquisitive, Sandys showed remarkable moderation and tolerance toward other cultures. Perhaps more than any other book Franklin had encountered so far, Sandys's *Travels* fueled Franklin's wanderlust.[43]

Locke's essay was not the only guide to a gentleman's education Franklin read. In 1758, he would call Obadiah Walker's *Of Education, Especially of Young Gentlemen* "a favourite old book." He had two copies of Walker in his library. Though he gave one away, he kept the other all his life. Learning and study, Walker argued, make a young man attentive, confident, industrious, and wary. Cribbing from Diogenes's life of Aristotle, Walker called learning "an ornament in *prosperity*, a refuge in *adversity*; an entertainment at *home*, [and] a companion *abroad*."[44]

When Walker first published *Of Education* in 1672, it was already a little old-fashioned in terms of both educational theory and literary style, but it still possessed charm and usefulness when Franklin encountered it. In one chapter, Walker emphasizes the importance of cultivating wit, memory, and judgment. Wit, he says, involves fancy and imagination: "It consists (saith *Thesauro*) in 1. *perspicacity*, which is the consideration of all, even the minutest, circumstances; and 2. *versability*, or speedy comparing them together; it conjoyns, divides, deduceth, augmenteth, diminisheth, and in summe puts one thing in stead of another, with like dexterity as a jugler doth his balls."[45] Perhaps the key phrase in this passage is "speedy comparing." To exercise their wit, people must be able to make quick connections between what they see, hear, and read and articulate them in a rapid-fire way.

Locke and Walker formulated their educational advice for gentlemen. What would happen when someone other than a gentleman read their works and followed their recommendations? Or, to be specific, what would happen when a teenaged printer's apprentice in colonial Boston followed the program of study designed for an English gentleman? Can a tradesman who reads a gentleman's books elevate himself to the status of a gentleman? Franklin did not have the answers to these questions, and he may not have reached the point of asking them yet. He did know that the books he read by candlelight during his apprenticeship, those Locke recommended and many others besides, pleased him greatly and taught him much.

4

The Clan of Honest Wags

JAMES FRANKLIN'S PRINTSHOP became a cozy gathering place for some of colonial Boston's brightest young men. Though Benjamin had lost his chance for a formal education, James's friends exposed him to forward-thinking ideas he would not have received at South Grammar or, for that matter, at Harvard. They were neither local church leaders nor politicians, but a band of outsiders. Together, they challenged Boston's religious hegemony and imagined a world based not on religion or class, but one where hard work and stick-to-it-iveness were the only requirements to get ahead.

Like every ambitious eighteenth-century American printer, James hoped to establish a newspaper, but he faced considerable competition. The city already had two papers, *The Boston News-Letter* and the *Boston Gazette*. Founded in 1709, the *News-Letter*, colonial America's first successful newspaper, was edited by John Campbell, who saw it as an "intelligencer," that is, a way to disseminate news from the London papers. Campbell understood how advantageous controlling both the content and distribution of news could be, a lesson Benjamin Franklin would learn.[1]

The Boston News-Letter was not the provincial government's official organ: There was no such thing. Since Campbell opened its pages to the Massachusetts governor and council to publish announcements and government documents, it did resemble an official newspaper. Safe and boring, the *News-Letter* contained almost nothing of literary interest. When Campbell lost his position as postmaster in 1719, he held onto the newspaper. William Brooker, his interim replacement, established the *Boston Gazette* to compete with the *News-Letter* and hired James Franklin to print it. When Philip Musgrave, the new postmaster, arrived from England in 1720, he took over as editor of the *Gazette* and sacked James. Musgrave's newspaper was no better than Brooker's *Gazette* or Campbell's *News-Letter*. Advertisements, extracts from the London papers, and local government announcements filled its pages.[2]

Though these early Boston newspapers were not very good, their existence made it difficult for James to establish another local newspaper, difficult but not impossible. Since both the *Gazette* and *News-Letter* addressed the city's economic and political elite, there was room for a newspaper directed toward the "middling sort," a slice of Boston's population the other papers scorned. With their lively wit and literary talent, James's friends could write articles to fill its columns and make the paper rival London's best weeklies. The newspaper would address controversies that the other Boston papers skirted and bring political discussions from the oral culture into print.[3]

Calling his paper *The New-England Courant*, James echoed the title of London's first daily newspaper, the *Daily Courant*, which was known for its objectivity and its respect for the reader's intelligence. James's title also indicates that he sought a wide audience in terms of geography as well as social class. He covered the waterfront, embracing the whole region and reporting current events from Connecticut, New Hampshire, and Rhode Island. The first issue appeared on August 7, 1721. The timing was propitious. James used a current event to attract subscribers: He launched the *Courant* during a smallpox epidemic.

In late April, a ship had reached Boston from the West Indies carrying at least one person infected with smallpox, a contagious and deadly disease. During the epidemic's early months, Cotton Mather emerged as the leading voice for inoculation. He had learned about it from his body servant Onesimus, a slave from the Gold Coast of Africa whose countrymen practiced smallpox inoculation. Intrigued, Mather had Onesimus explain how they performed it. Mather spoke with other members of Boston's enslaved population, who confirmed the practice. Articles in the Royal Society's *Philosophical Transactions* further informed Mather about inoculation. Convinced of its viability and prudence, Mather devised a scheme to inoculate Boston.[4]

By mid-June, new cases were breaking out across the city. Mather met with Zabdiel Boylston and other local physicians to plan a course of action. Boylston inoculated his family and friends before broadening his inoculations further. His campaign threw Boston into an uproar. Its citizens had several misconceptions about the procedure: that it killed more than it cured; that it would spread, not curtail smallpox; that it meddled with Divine will.

Judging Boylston's behavior to be reckless, Dr. William Douglass could not keep quiet. He was most upset by Boylston's neglect of basic medical precautions, especially his failure to isolate inoculees. Douglass first attacked him in *The Boston News-Letter*. Once James Franklin launched the *Courant*, Douglass started writing for it. Aware that controversy sells papers, James offered the anti-inoculators an open forum. A newspaper and pamphlet war ensued, lasting into the next year, that is, as long as the epidemic.

FIGURE 4.1 Peter Pelham, *Cottonus Matherus S. theologiae doctor regia societatis Londonensis . . . aetatis suae LXV, MDCCXXVII* (Boston, 1728; restrike, 1860). Library of Congress Prints and Photographs Division, Washington, DC, LC-USZ62-108365.

Though the inoculation controversy remained the *Courant*'s predominant theme during its first year, by no means was it the only one. Contributors supplied a steady stream of well-written, sometimes daring articles, the likes of which colonial America had never seen. The "Couranteers," as they became known, influenced James's brother. Benjamin read the articles they wrote, listened to their conversations, and followed Boston's reaction to the *Courant*.

His discussion of *The Spectator* as a literary model in the autobiography has deflected attention from the *Courant*, but the writings of James and his friends shaped Benjamin's growth as a writer.[5] Though he read many books by candlelight during his apprenticeship, in broad daylight Benjamin read the *Courant*. He read its essays in manuscript while setting them in type and reread them while proofreading. Nearly all the Couranteers' articles appeared anonymously or pseudonymously, but Benjamin kept a personal file of the newspaper, recording who wrote what, thus indicating how well he knew each issue.[6]

The articles gave Benjamin stylistic examples to use as he honed his writing skills, but the process of typesetting them also affected his style. In colonial

America, there was perhaps no better way to learn about writing than to apprentice in a printshop. This manual labor reinforced that writing was a physical task as well as a mental one. Handling type with his fingers, Benjamin acquired a delicate touch for words. He could feel the weight of every letter, every word, every line of type. He learned how to avoid unnecessary verbiage. His apprenticeship helped him become a brilliant stylist.[7]

Cotton Mather, the frequent butt of their satirical attacks, had another name for the Couranteers: the Hell-Fire Club. He saw the *Courant* office as a den of iniquity. "A notorious, scandalous paper," Mather called the *Courant*, "full freighted with nonsense, unmannerliness, railery, prophaneness, immorality, arrogance, calumnies, lyes, contradictions, and what not, all tending to quarrels and divisions, and to debauch and corrupt the minds and manners of New-England." Mather refrained from using the phrase "Hell-Fire Club" in print to describe the Couranteers, but he implied as much by referencing them as a New England equivalent of London's Hell-Fire Club, which supposedly consisted of young debauchees of both sexes, who cursed for cursing's sake, ridiculed all religions, played games of chance, abused British liberties, and applauded the wickedest witticisms. King George found the rumors about this elusive club real enough to order the lord chancellor to investigate and prosecute members of any club of blasphemy and debauchery.[8]

James Franklin never shied away from the name Hell-Fire Club, but neither did he do anything that might confirm the heinous charge. He would tease readers with reference to London's Hell-Fire Club. One time he reprinted an article from the British press describing supposed activities that took place within the club. Members erected a black altar and drank toasts to the Prince of Darkness: an ill-omened anti-Eucharist.[9] Mather's accusation that the Couranteers formed a kind of Hell-Fire Club does confirm the clubbish camaraderie of the gatherings at James's printshop. Their playful newspaper contributions, which reflect their close personal interaction, often sound like good-hearted raillery among friends.

Benjamin Franklin's autobiography presents a group portrait of the Couranteers, mentioning one by name, a tanner named Matthew Adams, whose retail goods included buckskin breeches, chamois gloves, and calfskin for shoe leather and book bindings. One of his newspaper advertisements challenges the modern tendency to see the past in sepia tones: Adams sold shoe leather in red and purple. In his spare time, Adams enjoyed reading and writing. His biographer says he possessed a "greater taste for literature than is often discovered by those who labor with their hands for a living. He was inquisitive and fond of reading."[10]

Franklin's reference to Adams occurs in a note to the following passage: "After some time an ingenious tradesman who had a pretty collection of books, and who frequented our printing house, took notice of me, invited me to his library, and very kindly lent me such books as I chose to read."[11] The contents of Adams's library is largely unknown, but he was interested in biography, history, poetry, and theology.[12]

Adams apparently had a good collection of verse. Franklin's interest in poetry began around the time he started borrowing books from him. Adams's own poetry shows his interest in religious controversy. One poem he wrote mentions two books that could have been in his library when Franklin came to know it. In *The Finishing Stroke*, Charles Leslie argues that ecclesiastical, civil, and military government began in the Garden of Eden, hence no independent state of nature ever existed. Franklin became familiar with Leslie's book, later advertising a copy for sale.[13] In *An Epistolary Discourse*—the other book Adams mentioned—Henry Dodwell theorized that baptism can bestow immortality.[14]

An article Adams contributed to the *Courant* indicates a third work that could have been in his library when Franklin was borrowing books from him. The article consists of an introductory headnote followed by a lengthy excerpt from a "great author" who was left anonymous, a common technique among the Couranteers. The unidentified author was John Shower, a Presbyterian minister whose popular treatise *Serious Reflections on Time, and Eternity* compared the tininess of time with the vastness of eternity.[15] Having put polemic divinity behind him, Franklin found little value in such authors as Dodwell or Shower.

Some Couranteers were professional men, but many, like Adams, were tradesmen. Their wide-ranging knowledge demonstrated to Franklin how reading could help surmount class barriers. The tradesmen in the group had gone outside the narrow confines of their trade to cultivate their reading tastes. Through independent study, they had achieved a level of knowledge that let them cross swords with Cotton Mather, Boston's leading Doctor of Divinity.

In November 1721, Mather accosted James Franklin in the street and berated him for publishing anti-ministerial essays in the *Courant*. The encounter became a topic of conversation around the printshop. To make your editorial decisions, Mather advised James, consider what they will mean in the eyes of God when you stand before Him during the Last Judgment. In a signed piece on December 4, James defended himself and his editorial policy. He insisted the *Courant* was not the voice of any religious faction or political party and welcomed articles from everyone. His invitation to possible contributors is inspiring: "I hereby invite all men, who have leisure, inclination and ability to speak their minds with freedom, sense and moderation, and their pieces shall be welcome to a place in my paper." James's tone and word choice echo the seventeenth-century commonwealthmen, who spoke in favor of a free republic, one allowing everyone the liberty of conscience. Thomas Fleet was so impressed with James's words that he would place a similar statement in his own newspaper.[16]

James also welcomed female contributors. Benjamin's annotations show that a woman named "Madam Staples" wrote a twelve-line poem, "The Fool by His Wit." For her pseudonym, Madam Staples used "Renuncles," though no one has ever explained why. Renuncles or, as the word is usually spelled, Ranunculus is a large genus of brightly colored flowers, which includes the buttercup. The pen name is ironic. Combined with her poem's text, it reveals considerable literary sophistication. Madam Staples is Sweet Little Buttercup with an acid tongue.

"The Fool by His Wit" extends a literary battle of the sexes brewing in the *Courant*. Renuncles replies to a male contributor who had treated bachelors with sympathy. She calls him a cuckold and foresees syphilis, a potentially disfiguring disease, in his future. Her poem ends:

> Put up your horns in your pocket,
>   Lest sooner or later,
>   (Without any satyr,)
> Your nose it be sunk in the socket.[17]

The poem suggests its author's knowledge of Restoration drama. Many playwrights applied the same phrase to tell cuckolds to quit lamenting their plight: "Put your horns in your pocket." The following decade Benjamin Franklin would use the cuckold's figurative horns in a Poor Richardism: "You cannot pluck roses without fear of thorns, / Nor enjoy a fair wife without danger of horns."[18]

Besides being the *Courant*'s editor and proprietor, James Franklin was its most prolific contributor. Benjamin avidly read his brother's contributions to the newspaper, which significantly influenced his writing style. At one point, James published an open letter to Musgrave critiquing his slipshod conduct as postmaster. As Benjamin often would, James used a clever pen name. He called himself "Lucilius" after the Roman warrior who supposedly invented satire. James enumerated the various lapses in Musgrave's professional behavior that Bostonians had noticed: reluctance to deliver mail; difficulty staffing the post office; and an inability to stop letters from mysteriously opening and emptying themselves, especially those containing money.

James also made creative use of proverbs. In the open letter to Musgrave, he says: "The old proverb, 'Be not a baker if your head be made of butter,' is very applicable to your self. We all know you have a soft head, which cannot long endure the fire of your own kindling among the people." Benjamin would offer a variation of his brother's proverb in *Poor Richard's Almanack*: "If your head is wax, don't walk in the sun."[19]

Thomas Fleet was another Couranteer whose writing influenced Benjamin's. Though Fleet had his own printing house, he enjoyed the company at James Franklin's printshop, where he could exercise his wit and humor. The week after James's satirical attack on Musgrave, Fleet tackled the same subject and improved upon it. In "A Trip to the World in the Moon," Tom Tram, his fictional alter ego, visits Robinson Cruso's Island. Locating Cruso's Island on the moon, Fleet cleverly combined *Robinson Crusoe* with one of Defoe's earlier works, *The Consolidator: or, Memoirs of Sundry Transactions from the World in the Moon*. In this pioneering work of science fiction, Defoe describes a voyage to the moon, making it resemble the earth to satirize English political conditions and social life.

Fleet's moon resembles Massachusetts. Like Boston, the lunar metropolis has a problem with its post office. Tom Tram interviews several moon men. One calls their postmaster "careless, lazy [and] gump-headed." Another says the postmaster has a "crabbed, surly, snappish temper." Franklin remembered Fleet's article well; years later, he would attempt to write something similar, "A Letter from a Gentleman in Crusoe's Island."[20]

Since its publication three years earlier, *Robinson Crusoe* had captured the popular imagination. Numerous references to it appeared in the colonial Boston press. After reading *Robinson Crusoe*, Franklin always remembered Man Friday's renowned question, "Why God no kill the Devil?" Unable to answer it, Franklin assumed the question was unanswerable. He eventually found the answer, which came in the form of a Scottish proverb: "You would do little for God if the Devil were dead."[21]

Robinson Crusoe influenced Franklin more than the few brief references in his works indicate. He found in Defoe a kindred spirit. Their similarities have often invited comparison. Writing an appreciative essay on Franklin, Desmond MacCarthy identified something they shared: "Defoe, too, preached the gospel of trade and middle-class prosperity, going so far as to assert that statesmen should be drawn from among merchants." Defoe's influence shows in Franklin's writing style as well as his philosophical outlook. Speaking about Franklin's autobiography, D. W. Brogan observed that its admirable style owes as much to Defoe as Addison. And Vernon L. Parrington argued that

Franklin effectively fulfilled Defoe's ideal: "Robinson Crusoe, the practically efficient man making himself master of his environment, was the dream of Daniel Defoe; Franklin was the visible, new-world embodiment of that dream."[22]

After James Franklin, Nathaniel Gardner was the *Courant*'s most active and influential contributor. Besides writing numerous articles for the paper, Gardner sometimes edited the *Courant*. "Agreeable Society and Conversation," Gardner's finest essay, celebrates their talk inside the printshop: "The faculty of interchanging our thoughts with each other, or what we express by the word 'conversation,' is justly accounted one of the noblest priviledges of reason, and that which in a peculiar manner elevates humane nature above the brutal part of the Creation." While we talk with one another, he continued, "there are none superior to others, but all stand on a level, whatever distinctions are to be observ'd at other times. Friends that converse together, do it with a just and equal freedom and dispence their civilities to each other without any difference."[23]

Gardner was good at devising clever pseudonyms. His best one, "Zerubbabel Tindal," is an oxymoron combining the biblical governor of Judah with contemporary freethinker Matthew Tindal. Writing a humorous letter to the editor of the *Courant* as Zerubbabel Tindal, Gardner sought to rebuild the newspaper, arguing that it should abandon the subject of inoculation and publish more entertaining articles. This playful letter addresses the newspaper editor as "Most Hyperbolically Profound, and Superlatively Sagacious and Penetrating Sir." Speaking for a group of potential contributors, he implores, "Give *us* but the hint, and *we* will furnish you with a charmingly various, as well as *copious supply*! For be it known to your *Worship*, that we are all *great, plodding politicians*, and *some* of us (with *Plato*) are owners of a *great genius*."[24]

Reinforcing their respect for the newspaper's editor, Zerubbabel Tindal says they are busy raising a glass to him. Gardner's Latinate diction ironically elevates Tindal's tone to describe the simple act of getting drunk: "We are now exhillerating our spirits over a capacious bowl of inebriating liquor; and *your health* is just going round." Finally, Zerubbabel Tindal supplies a name for his group of would-be *Courant* contributors: the "Clan of the Honest Wags."[25]

Though this club name occurs within Gardner's fanciful letter to the editor, there may be no better name for the Couranteers. They amused themselves by writing articles for the paper, which enhanced its reputation among Boston readers and increased its circulation. The name Clan of Honest Wags suited them far better than the Hell-Fire Club. Benjamin Franklin would echo it with the name he devised for his favorite London club, the Club of Honest Whigs.[26]

Gardner's writings in the *Courant* gave Franklin much to read and ponder. His versatile contributions to the newspapers offered a grab bag of literary styles. A master of many prose genres—essay, letter, dialogue, parody— Gardner showed Franklin what one author could accomplish, how he could use different forms of writing for different purposes. Reading Gardner's prose, Franklin could see that there was a genre for every purpose.

One of Franklin's annotations in his *Courant* file is especially revealing. Identifying Gardner as the author of the facetious "In Favour of Inoculation," Franklin captured his intent: "Mr. Gardner in imitation of Dr. Mather." Two weeks earlier, Gardner had critiqued Mather, implying that his knowledge extended to "a few *ill-pronounced hard words*, but no further." Gardner now aped Mather's overblown rhetoric and his overuse of exclamation and exaggeration: "O! Our brethren in the country, be advis'd! Come into this *safe* and *easy* practice! A practice, which we hope and trust will save millions of lives! And we dare almost *warrant* you, that your lives will be secure against the malignity and danger of this *worst of plagues*."[27]

Gardner recognized the suitability of verse to express feelings of love, but his poetic abilities fell short of his talent as a prose stylist, as "Of Beauty's Sacred, Conquering Power I Sing" clearly demonstrates. Gardner signed this love poem "Corydon." Best known as the name of a rural swain in Virgil's *Eclogues*, "Corydon" was a general term for a rustic, much as the name Phillis symbolized a pretty country girl. In Gardner's poem, Corydon's Phillis is named Eliza. Her appearance is cliché. *Rubor virtutis est color*: Eliza, sure enough, has "rosy cheeks." The poem closes with an awkward couplet, which begs to be read with a lisp: "The fair Eliza's charms inspire the song, / While I but lisp her praises with my tongue." The weakness of this and other poems in the *Courant* would make Benjamin hesitant to publish original poetry once he established his own newspaper. Listing Gardner's poem in his *Calendar of American Poetry*, Leo Lemay offered a one-word critical assessment: "Ugh."[28]

Several Couranteers devised clever pen names and developed fictional personae that gave Franklin additional literary models. In an early instance of investigative reporting, Matthew Adams exposed a landlord who was forcing tenants to vote for the political candidates he favored, either that or face eviction. For his well-meaning persona, Adams created a typename reminiscent of the Restoration stage: "Harry Meanwell." Gardner and James Franklin sometimes used female pen names. Abigail Afterwit, one of James's personae, influenced Benjamin, who appreciated his brother's creative use of a word referring to wisdom acquired after something happened. The word was often used proverbially, as in "Afterwit comes too late," a proverbial equivalent to the more recent variation, "Hindsight is 20/20." Following his brother, Benjamin would create a persona named Anthony Afterwit.[29]

The Couranteers' comic pseudonyms indicate the fictional nature of the newspaper's letters to the editor, distinguishing them from genuine letters to the editor. These strangely named letter writers are not merely mouthpieces for their authors, but fictional characters with distinctive personalities. They became a hallmark of the *Courant* among colonial Boston's readers.[30] These pseudonymous contributions influenced James's brother. In the history of American literature, no one would create more fictional personae or manipulate them with more finesse than Benjamin Franklin.

Listening to James's friends talk, Benjamin longed to join the Clan of Honest Wags, but James restricted his behavior as he would restrict the behavior of any apprentice. Never mind that Benjamin was his brother or that he had a wit to match the cleverest Couranteer. Sometimes, James resorted to corporal punishment to discipline his brother, and every once in a while, Benjamin would have to take a beating. Though he hoped to participate in the witty repartee that went around the printshop when his brother's friends visited, James refused to countenance such uppity behavior from an apprentice who was getting entirely too big for his breeches.

Benjamin found a clever way to circumvent his brother's control. He applied his literary talent to write some pseudonymous articles that would appeal to the Couranteers. He coined a pen name and developed a persona to suit: Silence Dogood, a Boston widow who keeps an eagle eye on her neighbors and critiques their aberrant behavior to reform them. His female pen name echoes the running title of Cotton Mather's *Bonifacius*: "Essays to Do Good." Creating the persona of a middle-aged woman who sticks her nose into everybody's business, Franklin figuratively emasculated Cotton Mather, something the Couranteers often did when they parodied him.

Though doing good would become the central tenet of Franklin's personal philosophy, at 16, he could already see the thin line between a good-doer and a do-gooder. The do-gooder was the type of person who would send Thoreau skedaddling. In *Walden*, he says, "If I knew for a certainty that a man was coming to my house with the conscious design of doing me good, I should run for my life."[31] Silence Dogood's humor stems from her overbearing quality, the way she blithely crosses the line from good-doer to do-gooder.

Franklin disguised his handwriting for "Silence Dogood 1" and secretly submitted it to the *Courant*. Relating the episode for his autobiography, he started in the active voice with the subject pronoun, "He," meaning James. But then Benjamin had second thoughts, crossed out the pronoun and switched to the passive voice, minimizing James's role in the story but leaving the possessive pronoun "his" without a referent: "It was found in the morning and communicated to his intimates when they call'd in as usual." At some point, Franklin substituted a more specific phrase for "intimates": "writing friends." In other words, the men who judged the first Silence Dogood essay were not merely his brother's friends; they were writers themselves.[32]

"Silence Dogood 1" appeared on April 2, 1722. Several more followed, all submitted in a similar fashion. "Silence Dogood 4" castigates Harvard students for their idleness and ignorance. This essay prompted a verse reply by "Crowdero," a poet who took his pseudonym from one of the rabble leaders Sir Hudibras and his faithful sidekick Ralpho encounter in Samuel Butler's *Hudibras*. Crowdero admits that there are some weak Harvard students but asserts that the good ones deserve respect. He agrees with Mrs. Dogood that Harvard's fops should be stopped. Crowdero hopes her satire will compel weak students to reform: "May your sharp satyrs mend the lazy drone, / Who by anothers help ascends the throne. / And not by any merit of his own."[33]

After completing the fourteenth and final number of the series, Franklin revealed his authorship, which elevated him in the eyes of James's friends. Benjamin Franklin's writing initiative was his rite of initiation, letting him become a de facto member of the Clan of Honest Wags.

As the first essay series in American literature, "Silence Dogood" is a landmark in literary history, but it also showcases Franklin's reading life at 17. Silence Dogood's numerous biblical allusions reveal Franklin's deep knowledge of Scripture. The form of his essays reflects the foremost essays in English literature: in *The Spectator* and *The Guardian*. His persona, humor, and satire echo the writings of the Couranteers, especially James Franklin, Nathaniel Gardner, Matthew Adams, and Thomas Fleet. The occasional Latin phrases recall his school days. The essays also indicate the recent direction his reading had taken. Quoting from William Petty's *Political Arithmetick*, Silence reveals Franklin's growing interest in economics and sociology. Before the decade ended, he would read Petty's *Treatise of Taxes and Contributions*, the main source for his first political pamphlet, *A Modest Inquiry into the Nature and Necessity of a Paper-Currency*.[34]

Latin epigraphs preface several Silence Dogood essays. A few are proverbial, such as *Corruptio optimi pessima*, which means, "Bad things when corrupted become the worst." A Latin quote from *Thyestes*, the Senecan revenge tragedy, prefaces "Silence Dogood 6." It can be translated, "Rising day sees a man in pride: / Retreating day sees him brought low." Franklin could have remembered the Latin version from Bayly's *Practice of Piety*. Bayly had used the quote from *Thyestes* to gloss his admonition to pray in the morning to guard against anything that might happen before nightfall.[35]

The other classical authors Franklin quoted for his Silence Dogood epigraphs—Cicero, Plautus, Terence—come from a thus far unidentified source: William Walker's *Dictionary of English and Latin Idioms*. "Silence Dogood 11," for example, uses a Latin epigraph from *Cistellaria*, one of Plautus's comedies, which Franklin found in Walker's *Idioms*: "In all that time I could never get to see my sweetheart."[36]

Walker's *Idioms* was far more useful than Hoole's *Sententiae pueriles*. Hoole had organized his sayings according to the first word in each Latin quote, which rendered it useless as a reference work. Walker organized his excerpts by English keywords, thus allowing readers to find apt Latin quotations by looking them up in English. The Latin epigraph for "Silence Dogood 4," which parodies Harvard College, comes from Cicero's Socratic dialogue *On the Ends of Good and Evil*, but Franklin found it in Walker listed under the keyword "learning": "Am I yet to be learned to speak either Greek, or Latin?"[37] Franklin's use of this epigraph anticipates his subsequent critique of the traditional grammar school education, which stressed ancient tongues to the detriment of more practical subjects.

Reading Walker's *Idioms* as he wrote his Silence Dogood essays, Franklin built on what he had learned at South Grammar School, broadening his Latin vocabulary and mastering Latin syntax. The autobiography says he did not learn Latin until the 1730s, but his use of Walker's *Idioms* as a teenager confirms that Franklin exaggerated his ignorance of Latin. He could read the language of Caesar and Cicero much earlier and much better than he admitted to posterity.[38]

"Silence Dogood 7" begins with an epigraph from "The Adventurous Muse," a lyric poem Isaac Watts published in his collection of verse, *Horae lyricae*. Franklin enjoyed the secular verse of "the celebrated Watts," remembering some of his poems for the rest of his life. "The Adventurous Muse" offers not just an approach to poetry but a philosophy of living. The speaker of the poem longs for a daring muse, one not bound by conventional thinking:

> Give me the muse whose generous force
> Impatient of the reins
> Pursues an unattempted course,

> Breaks all the criticks iron chains,
> And bears to paradise the raptur'd mind.[39]

The approach Watts recommends for poetry Franklin would ultimately apply to his scientific and political thought.

"Silence Dogood 12" celebrates the English language. Mrs. Dogood criticizes drunkards for coining synonyms to avoid admitting they were drunk. Though she looks down on Boston's drunken wastrels, her creator relished their linguistic fecundity. Some synonyms were adjectives: boozey, feverish, foxed, fuddled, mellow, and merry. Others were prepositional phrases: among the Philistines, in a very good humor, or in their altitudes. Yet others combined predicate and object: see the sun, see two moons, or clip the king's English.[40]

"Silence Dogood 6" led *The New-England Courant* for June 11, 1722, but an item James Franklin wrote for that same issue would prove more consequential. After reporting the quick action that Rhode Island had taken against an enemy privateer, the *Courant* facetiously says that Massachusetts might outfit a ship to go after some pirates, perhaps in a month or so, provided the weather would cooperate. Massachusetts authorities disliked James Franklin's snarky tone, reading his critique of their dilatory behavior as an implication that they were colluding with the pirates. Eager to convince the public there was no collusion, the Massachusetts council examined James Franklin the next day, after which it resolved that his report was an affront to its government. It ordered the sheriff to put James Franklin in jail until July 7.

Who would take over the *Courant* in his absence? Though Gardner had edited several issues, he had his own business to run and did not have time to operate a newspaper. There was only one person with the ability to edit, print, and distribute the *Courant*: James's apprentice and brother Benjamin. Keeping the newspaper going, Benjamin did a favor for his brother, but he also took the opportunity to test his editorial skills. Given the chance to edit the paper, Benjamin tried everything he could think of to improve it.

Editing the *Courant*, Benjamin walked a tightrope. Wanting to defend both his brother and the freedom of the press, he knew he could not say too much without getting himself into trouble. For "Silence Dogood 8," he found a solution. Instead of writing an original essay, which could have been actionable, he had Mrs. Dogood quote an essay from the *London Journal* by two prominent British whigs, John Trenchard and Thomas Gordon. The essay was one of several that Trenchard and Gordon wrote under the name "Cato." The quotation begins: "Without freedom of thought, there can be no such thing as wisdom; and no such thing as publick liberty, without freedom of speech." Quoting these words, Franklin made them his own.[41]

Editing the *Courant* while his brother was in jail, Franklin got a taste of running a newspaper. James had taught him how to set type, operate a press, and manage a printing business, but the Couranteers helped teach him to write. Their contributions to the newspaper gave him many different literary approaches in terms of style, tone, and genre. What Benjamin Franklin read as he typeset the *Courant* prepared him to create his own newspaper.

The Courant *Library*

HARD-PRESSED TO find newspaper copy the first week of July 1722, Benjamin Franklin looked around the printshop for ideas. Turning toward the bookcase, he realized he could fill a column by cataloguing the office library. He also wrote a headnote for the catalogue: "We are furnish'd with a large and valuable collection of books; which may be of vast advantage to us, not only in making indexes, but also in writing on subjects, natural, moral, and divine, and in cultivating those which seem the most barren." Calling the published list "a small part of our catalogue," Franklin was feigning modesty. The catalogue is quite substantial.[1]

The catalogue's partial nature makes reconstructing the *Courant* library difficult. Complicating matters further, the listed titles are sketchy. Instead of checking title pages, Franklin listed the books by spine title. Some entries name authors without titles; others supply titles without authors. None list edition, date, or format. Franklin treated multivolume sets inconsistently. Sometimes he provided the number of volumes, other times not. Even with these drawbacks, it is possible to reconstruct a good portion of the *Courant* library.

Franklin wrote a brief closing paragraph to frame the catalogue and indicate the books he would not name. After listing the names of several English divines, he explained, "We have also a great number of Latin authors, and a vast quantity of pamphlets." The catalogue does list one pamphlet title, "The Ladies Pacquet Broke Open," a mistranscription for *The Ladies Cabinet Broke Open*, a twenty-four-page pamphlet containing fanciful letters and poems, most likely the first item in a bound volume of pamphlets.

The Couranteers' articles reveal some pamphlets they read. Supporting his argument that preachers should limit themselves to spiritual matters in "Another Dialogue between the Clergyman and Layman," Nathaniel Gardner quoted Bishop Burnet without naming a specific source. The *Courant* library had Burnet's *History of the Reformation*, but Gardner's extract comes from a Burnet pamphlet, *The Bishop of Salisbury's New Preface to His Pastoral Case, Consider'd*.

Its key sentence states, "The wisest governments have always excluded their clergy from affairs of state." Gardner's quotation forms an early instance of a concept essential to democracy: the separation of church and state.[2]

James Franklin's collection of pamphlets surely contained copies of those he printed. Perhaps no pamphlet he published during Benjamin's apprenticeship is more important than John Wise's *Word of Comfort to a Melancholy Country*. Wise argued for a private land bank that would issue paper money to alleviate the chronic shortage of hard currency in Massachusetts, which had contributed to the colony's economic woes. *A Word of Comfort* foreshadows Franklin's *Modest Enquiry into the Nature and Necessity of a Paper Currency*.[3]

Wise's bold, earthy manner in *A Word of Comfort* also anticipates Franklin's writing style. As Franklin would, Wise used the hand as a synecdoche for the individual: "The means of our relief are in our own hands; and we can save our selves, as easily as say the word." Like Gardner, Wise enjoyed using proverbs. One—"Every spoonful adds to the cistern"—looks forward to Poor Richard's "Every little makes a mickle."[4]

Since Franklin grouped Latin authors together under one general heading, presumably the titles do not represent Latin texts. By their wording, only two catalogue entries could be Latin: "Virgil" and "Josephus Ant." "Virgil" could represent a Latin edition of Virgil's works, and "Josephus Ant" could be Flavius Josephus's *Antiquitatum judaicarum*. More likely these two entries signify English translations. "Virgil" is almost surely Dryden's renowned translation.

By excluding Latin titles from the catalogue, Franklin joined the ongoing ancients-versus-moderns debate. In colonial Boston, the contrast between Latin and English represented a class conflict pitting the Harvard-trained clergy, who saw themselves as the community's spiritual, moral, cultural, and educational leaders, against the tradesmen, who came up through the apprenticeship system and were emerging as leaders of a new and more secular generation. Franklin shared the values of many Couranteers, who found Latin a sign of snobbery and fuddyduddyism.

A few months earlier, Gardner had satirized the Boston clergy for their use of Latin and their scorn for the vernacular in *A Friendly Debate*. Franklin knew the pamphlet well. He may have been the one who set it in type. Gardner's down-home persona reinforces his disdain for the Harvard-trained ministers. The pen name "Rusticus" resembles Gardner's other rustic pen name, "Corydon." Gardner signed his dedicatory epistle, "Rusticus. From the South Side of my Hay-Stack."

As the story goes, Rusticus asks to speak with Academicus, who replies, "What business can you have with me? Do you understand Latin?" In his appendix, Rusticus returns to this theme, criticizing Harvard students, who scatter "scraps of Latin and Greek in their writings (like the weather in an almanack)."[5] Gardner's parenthetical simile challenges the boundaries between elite and popular culture, undermining the differences between the academic writing at Harvard and the practical books Rusticus and his ilk read around the haystack. Similarly, Franklin's *Courant* library catalogue emphasizes the usefulness of English to record and communicate ideas, while marginalizing Latin as a relic of the past.

The catalogue's organization is the most important clue for identifying the books. Books were usually shelved by format: folios, quartos, octavos, duodecimos. The folios—the tallest and heaviest volumes—were shelved at the bottom of a bookcase, the smallest toward the top. Here is what one military-minded collector told his librarian: "Range me the grenadiers [folios] at bottom, battalion [octavos] in the middle, and light-bobs [duodecimos] at top."[6] Cataloguers inventoried the contents of a bookcase from bottom to top. Franklin followed this convention. His catalogue begins with folios. Ending with octavos, his list suggests that he abbreviated the catalogue by leaving off the light-bobs.

Despite the brief spine titles, some books can be identified precisely. The first—"Pliny's Natural Hist."—signifies Philemon Holland's English translation of Pliny's *Natural Historie*. This book gave Franklin a double pleasure, scientific and literary. Pliny synthesized over 500 Greek and Latin works, which he combined with his own thoughts and observations. His *Natural Historie* mixes science and superstition. Skeptical about what he read in Pliny's *Natural Historie*, Cotton Mather coined the term "Plinyism" to mean fables masked as facts. Regardless, the book fired Franklin's imagination, showing him the sheer immensity of what there was to know.[7]

In his eighth book, for example, Pliny discusses land beasts, starting with the elephant. As the largest land beast, the elephant suited Pliny's largest-to-smallest taxonomy, but the elephant also makes a good transition from the seventh book, which concerns humankind. Of all the land beasts, Pliny observed, elephants come closest to humans in terms of intellect and outlook: "They embrace goodnesse, honestie, prudence, and equitie (rare qualities I may tel you to be found in men)."[8]

Holland's text is a celebration of the English language. Instead of adopting an austere manner resembling the original, he exploited the sounds and rhythms of his native language. Holland was a translator who "tricked out his authors with all the resources of Elizabethan English." The *Courant* Pliny may not have been Franklin's first exposure to Holland's exquisite prose, but it was crucial to his reading life. Years later, he would tell William Brownrigg what he remembered most about the book: "I had when a youth, read and smiled at Pliny's account of a practice among the seamen of his time, to still the waves in a storm by pouring oil into the sea: which he mentions, as well as the use of oil by the divers."[9]

Franklin's powers of recall were extraordinary. The passage barely fills three lines in a closely printed, 1,300-page folio, but he remembered it well. Notable for its style as well as its content, the passage highlights the power of Holland's Elizabethan English. His conjoined word pairs contribute to the rhythm of his writing, giving it a cadence reminiscent of the *Book of Common Prayer*. Listen: "And that all seas are made calme and still with oile: and therefore the divers under the water doe spirt and sprinkle it abroad with their mouthes because it dulceth and allaieth the unpleasant nature thereof, and carrieth a light with it."[10]

The teenaged Franklin came to Pliny at a moment when he was so confident in his scientific knowledge that he chuckled over the idea of an author taking superstition seriously. When he learned decades later that oil could indeed calm bodies of water, Franklin would not be chuckling over Plinyisms any more. Holland's Pliny is filled with popular lore as it describes different ways nature can help people. By observing nature and reading its signs, Pliny was saying, we can recognize how to use it to our benefit. Franklin took years to understand what a valuable repository of useful information Pliny's *Natural Historie* was. People should not be so confident in their knowledge, he realized. They should not dismiss folk belief without careful consideration.

Another ancient classic Franklin listed is "Aristotle's Politicks." This spine title can also be narrowed to a specific text, John Dickenson's sixteenth-century English translation, *Aristotles Politiques: or, Discourses of Government*. Aristotle distinguishes three types of political rule: the one, the few, and the many. Each can take two forms: virtuous and corrupt. Tyranny is the corrupt form of monarchy; oligarchy is the corrupt form of aristocracy; and mob rule is the corrupt form of a republic.

Though Aristotle does not say how the virtuous could deteriorate into the corrupt, the possibility remained a concern for everyone involved with creating new forms of government through the eighteenth century, including Franklin. The anxiety about governmental corruption that surfaces in his political writings stretches back to the time he read the office copy of Aristotle's *Politics*.[11]

An experiment in library organization, James Franklin's *Courant* bookcase deserves careful attention. The organization of a personal library has been called a blueprint of the mind, but in the case of Benjamin's catalogue of the *Courant* library, perhaps a different metaphor would be more appropriate. The catalogue is a palimpsest; it retains James's basic organization, but it simultaneously reflects Benjamin's interpretation of the bookcase's contents in terms of both his selection of titles and his deliberate rearrangement of a few of them. Compiling the catalogue, Benjamin imposed his personality on his brother's library. Since no known books survive from the *Courant* collection, James's collection can only be known through his brother's catalogue.

Though principally arranged by format, the library did contain some subject clusters. The seventh item in the list is *The Athenian Oracle*, which assembles individual numbers of *The Athenian Mercury*, a late-seventeenth-century literary newspaper. The *Courant* copy was not the only *Athenian Oracle* in town. In 1705, Judge Samuel Sewall picked up a copy at a Boston bookshop.[12] *The Athenian Oracle* presents queries and answers on a variety of topics. The queries were ostensibly submitted by its readers, the answers supplied by an all-knowing oracle.

The answers are alternately serious or humorous, depending on the question. Sewall was astonished by the strength of the anti-slavery answer to the query: "Whether trading for negroes, i.e. carrying them out of their own country into perpetual slavery, be in it self unlawful, and especially contrary to the great law of Christianity?" Sewall appreciated the lengthy reply so much he had Bartholomew Green reprint the answer to this query as a pamphlet. The impassioned anti-slavery answer is exceptional. Other answers are shorter and lighter in tone.[13]

The British Apollo, which follows *The Athenian Oracle* in Benjamin's catalogue, debuted in 1708. A sequel to *The Athenian Oracle*, it, too, presents queries and answers, some in verse. The first page says the newspaper was edited by a society of gentlemen. Some querists address the gentlemen; others address Apollo. The queries formed such an important part of the work that it was sometimes called "Curious Questions." A fascinating miscellany, *The British Apollo* entertained many inquisitive eighteenth-century readers.

Franklin found several appealing topics in *The British Apollo*. One querist asks how lightning could melt a sword blade but leave its scabbard unharmed. In response, Apollo defines lightning as "nothing else but a very subtle nitro sulphureous matter enflamed, and breaking out of a cloud with very great violence." Apollo's explanation is all wrong, but Franklin did not know that yet. Three decades would pass before he discovered the true nature of lightning.[14]

Some queries concern foodways and human physiology. Another querist asks, "Is pepper eaten with such food we say is windy, because it decreases its inflation, or because it blunts those corroding pungent particles abounding in those aliments?" Apollo replies, "It is doubtless added to windy aliments, to correct their flatuosity, and blunt their acid crudities, and withal to strengthen the digestive faculty of the stomach." Though pepper does not minimize flatuosity, Franklin did wonder if some other food additive might. "To the Royal Academy of Brussels," a bagatelle he would write when he lived in Paris, facetiously offers a prize for the researcher who discovers an additive that would turn farts into perfume.[15]

The editors of *The British Apollo* also used the question-and-answer format to experiment with writing style. Some articles are written in a mock illiterate manner. One forlorn woman asks what she should do about her "brute of a hosband that maks monsters of most of our nabors." Apollo does not answer the forlorn woman's question directly. Instead, he hands it to Joan Woodaveal, his herdsman's wife. The editors of *The British Apollo* thus took the opportunity to write another mock illiterate paragraph. A kindred spirit, Joan gives the querist some practical advice. Speaking about her own brutish husband, Joan says, "The mungie toawd is as dull as a dormouse at hom but a vary town bull abroad."[16]

The term "town bull" literally refers to a bull that was kept at a town's expense to service the local heifers. (During the occupation of Boston in 1775, British troops would cruelly slaughter its town bull, which had been doing its procreative duties for two decades. They sold the meat, and British officers put the profits in their pockets.) The term was also used to designate a town's most notable fornicator and womanizer. Joan Woodaveal controls her bull-brained husband by putting a strong purgative in his vittles.[17]

Franklin would experiment with dialect a few months after he compiled the office library catalogue, contributing to the *Courant* a mock illiterate letter to the editor by "Jethro Standfast." With this persona, Franklin became the first American author to use the biblical name "Jethro" to mock a character's literacy. The name now means any marginally literate country hick. The place and date of Jethro Standfast's letter—New Haven, September 20, 1722—signal a recent religious controversy. The "Great Apostacy" came to a head when Timothy Cutler, rector of Yale College, and some other Connecticut clergymen, including Samuel Johnson, announced their doubts about Congregational ordination. They argued that, in Jethro's words, Congregational ministers "have no more athorriti to administur the ordenanses thun so mani porturs or plow-joggurs."[18]

The following year, Franklin created "Dingo," the first African American persona in American journalism. He took a different approach with Dingo than Jethro. Had he written the article in a mock illiterate manner, it would sound racist. Instead, Dingo dictates his message to an amanuensis. The article reflects the emerging complexity of American newspaper culture. Dingo had heard someone read aloud an article from *The New-England Courant* about the unjust treatment of a poor man. The oral culture transmits the story, but the printed version imbues it with significance and inspires Dingo to communicate his personal story of injustice.[19]

Shelved together, *The Athenian Oracle* and *The British Apollo* indicate that James Franklin recognized their similarities. The presence in the *Courant* library of these two collections—formative works in English periodical history—also reveals James's historical awareness and his desire to situate the *Courant* within its literary heritage.

Beyond their influence on James's newspaper, these two periodicals had a major impact on Benjamin's social and intellectual life. When he and his Philadelphia friends formed the Junto, they generated topics for discussion by submitting queries that members would try to answer. *The Athenian Oracle* and *The British Apollo* are important antecedents for the query-and-answer format that would play a crucial role in the weekly Junto meetings.

Another subject cluster appears among the octavos. *The Ladies Calling* is adjacent to *The Ladies Cabinet Broke Open*. Written by popular devotional author Richard Allestree, *The Ladies Calling* elaborates the virtues a woman should possess—affability, compassion, modesty, piety, timidity—and the successive roles she fulfills: virgin, wife, mother, and widow.

Allestree argued that virginity is not a matter of either/or. There are degrees of defilement. The virgin should stay chaste in mind as well as body: "Every indecent curiosity, or impure fancy, is a deflowering of the mind." He discouraged widows from remarrying: "Marriage is so great an adventure, that once seems enough for the whole life." Women formed a significant part of the *Courant*'s readership. *The Ladies Calling*, which could often be found on the colonial woman's bookshelf, let the Couranteers keep female readers in mind while shaping their newspaper articles.[20]

A subsequent cluster shows that authorship affected the library's organization. Peter Heylyn's *Summe of Christian Theologie*, an extensive commentary on the Apostles' Creed, appears directly after his *Cosmography*. One might expect that Heylyn's *Cosmography* would be better off shelved with Moll's *Geography*, but James put authorship over subject when it came to library organization.

One of the most distinctive but popular works in the *Courant* library was *Letters Writ by a Turkish Spy*, which inaugurated the genre of the satirical, epistolary spy novel. Originally written in Italian by Giovanni Paolo Marana, the English version of the *Turkish Spy* first appeared in a multivolume set in the late seventeenth century. It included many additional letters not in the Italian editions.[21]

The ostensible author of the letters is one Mahmut, an Arab by birth who used to be a slave for some Sicilian Christians but now works for the Ottoman Empire. Mahmut has gone undercover in Paris to report Western culture, manners, and politics. Marana created an aura of verisimilitude. In fact, one querist asked *The Athenian Oracle* if the *Turkish Spy* were true. The oracle replied: "If all a fiction, as we are most inclin'd to believe, 'tis yet so handsomely manag'd, that one may rather suspect than prove it so. Whoever writ it, 'tis plain he was exquisitely acquainted with the Oriental customs and languages; he appears a person of clear sense, wit, and very good humour, and has a valuable collection of history by him." Mahmut's insightful observations about European politics helped promote and popularize political discussion. Franklin left no comments about the work, but he would add a later edition to his own library.[22]

The influence of the *Turkish Spy* on Franklin may have been more literary than political. Mahmut does not write letters solely to his handlers. With more than fifty correspondents, he customizes the tone, persona, and content of his letters for each. Franklin would excel as a letter writer by shaping his epistolary voice to suit each of his recipients. He wrote one way to his sister Jane Mecom, another way to George Washington. *Letters Writ by a Turkish Spy* gave Franklin a model of letter writing.

Toward the catalogue's end, Franklin listed several octavos. Often adjacent volumes can help identify ambiguous titles. The *Courant* Shakespeare appears as "Shakespeare's Works." This spine title could refer to Shakespeare's First Folio—or second or third or fourth—but it might indicate Nicholas Rowe's octavo edition of Shakespeare. Franklin's short title is more appropriate for Rowe's edition. His placement in the catalogue reinforces this identification. It comes between two other octavos, John Oldham's *Works* and Jonathan Swift's *Tale of a Tub*. Since Franklin did not list the number of volumes, the *Courant* Shakespeare could have been the whole six-volume set, or it could have been a broken set.[23]

Two particular catalogue entries stand out: Cotton Mather's history of New England, *Magnalia christi americana*, and John Oldmixon's *The British Empire in America*. Franklin grouped the two titles and italicized them both, the only entries italicized in the whole catalogue. "To get the effect I wanted with them (and it was a strange effect, and they made it,) I had them set in italics. They need those italics."[24] This is Ernest Hemingway talking about italicizing the interchapters of *In Our Time*, but his words suit Franklin's thinking. Throughout his career as both a writer and printer, Franklin would use italics for strategic effect.

Italics gave Franklin one way to link Mather and Oldmixon; the catalogue's organization gave him another. To list them together, Franklin violated the library's shelf organization. Mather's *Magnalia* is a folio, as is the work listed after Oldmixon, George Sandys's *Travels*. But Oldmixon's work is an octavo. Franklin took Oldmixon from where it stood on the shelf and placed it next to Mather in the catalogue. For a moment, he let the infantryman stand with the grenadier. Grouped together, the two titles suggest that Franklin recognized the limitations of arrangement by format and sought a more sensible subject organization.

Another connection between Mather and Oldmixon—a sneakier one—gave Franklin a different reason to list them together. Oldmixon lambastes Mather's *Magnalia* in *The British Empire in America*. A few months before Franklin published the catalogue, Gardner had excerpted Oldmixon's critical remarks in *A Friendly Debate*. Oldmixon called Mather's history poorly organized and badly worded. It is "so cramm'd with punns, anagrams, acrosticks, miracles and prodigies, that it rather resembles school boys exercises forty years ago, and *Romish* legends, than the collections of an historian bred up in a Protestant academy." Gardner was not the only Couranteer to quote Oldmixon. Though William Douglass called him an "erroneous scribler," he quoted with approval Oldmixon's critique of Mather.[25]

Oldmixon gave Mather fits. After reading his critique, Mather defended himself, telling Thomas Prince that there was not one acrostic in the whole book. A dozen years after *The British Empire in America* first appeared, he was still seething. When Daniel Neal presented him with a copy of his *History of New-England* in 1720, Mather replied with a letter of thanks: "Your performance is the reverse of what was done by the malicious and satanic pen of one *Oldnixson* (some such name,) in his account of the *English Empire in America*, whose history of N. E. has far more lies than pages in it."[26] Grouping and italicizing Mather and Oldmixon in the published catalogue, Franklin gave the two books equal status and thus created a parallel guaranteed to upset Mather all over again.

The last title in the catalogue is "St. Augustine's Works," which was not a collection of Augustine's complete works, but Abraham Woodhead's English translation, *S. Augustine's Confessions*, supplemented with biographical information gleaned from Augustine's other writings. The presence of Augustine is consistent with the Jansenist authors in the *Courant* library. Unlike the Jansenists, Augustine did not have much influence on Franklin's thinking. Franklin was, in Vernon L. Parrington's words, "less concerned with the golden pavements of the City of God than that the cobblestones on Chestnut Street in Philadelphia should be well and evenly laid."[27]

Augustine may have influenced Franklin's writing, however. That he knew the *Confessions* during his apprenticeship means Franklin's knowledge of autobiographical literature was greater than formerly assumed. Woodhead's translation makes a good starting point for reconsidering their relationship. In a way, Franklin faced a much more difficult task. Augustine had the advantage of situating his life within God's universality. Franklin's secular autobiography has no such preformed universal. Instead, he had to create his own earthbound world, convincing readers to follow his example and thus join him in a new world unbeholden to a Supreme Being.[28]

Franklin's headnote emphasizes that the office library was helping the Couranteers write about science, religion, and moral philosophy. Furthermore, it would let them cultivate the "most barren subjects." His organic metaphor offers an apt comparison. Books create ideal conditions to germinate stubborn ideas and let them flourish. The articles the Couranteers wrote bear out this figurative comparison. The books in James's office nourished their thought and let it grow. Read against their writings, Franklin's catalogue shows that several Couranteers borrowed words and ideas from the books. Besides James and Benjamin Franklin, Nathaniel Gardner, Matthews Adams, and William Douglass all used the *Courant* library.

James and Benjamin both drew on Mather's *Magnalia* as a source. For the lead article of the January 22, 1722, issue, James took his epigraph from a chapter title in the *Magnalia*: "Bloody Fishing at Oyster River; and Sad Work at Groton." Mather's chapter relates two separate Indian attacks on the back settlements of Massachusetts; James's essay concerns the Mathers' verbal attacks on the Couranteers. James brushed off their criticism with a folksy comparison. "Their heavy curses on the *Courant* and its publisher," he wrote, have been "all to no purpose, for (as a Connecticut trader once said of his onions), 'The more they are curs'd, the more they grow.'"[29]

The critical letter Cotton Mather's son Samuel published in the *Boston Gazette*, James argued, would give readers outside the colonies a pitiful impression of New England. Then a Harvard student, Samuel Mather had addressed his letter to the editor from Cambridge. Imagining what cosmopolitan readers would think, James wrote, "They will certainly conclude, There is bloody fishing for nonsense at Cambridge, and sad work at the colledge." In short, the quotation from Cotton Mather's history is the set-up for James Franklin's punchline. James co-opts Mather's diction and syntax and turns them against him and his son.

Whereas James appropriated language from the *Magnalia*, Benjamin borrowed imagery from it. Mather had an ear for wordplay and an eye for visual imagery, but he often struggled to coordinate them. The *Magnalia* is filled with incongruous combinations of sound and image that sometimes seem insensitive and other times create unplanned hilarity. Few books in the *Courant* library influenced Franklin more than Mather's *Magnalia*, albeit as an object of fun.

In one chapter, "The Death of Mr John Avery," Mather relates what happened when the Reverend Avery left Newberry, Massachusetts, for Marblehead to establish a new ministry. Sailing toward Marblehead, Avery encountered a storm or, as Mather wrote with characteristic hyperbole, "as mighty a storm as perhaps was ever known in these parts of the world." With his ship wrecked, Avery asked God to transport him safely to Heaven. According to the sole eyewitness, once Avery uttered this plea, "he was by a *wave* sweeping him off, immediately washed away to Heaven indeed."[30] Though attempting to relate Avery's last minute on earth, Mather, without intending to, made the tragedy humorous. He depicts Avery deep in prayer at one moment and whooshing off to Heaven the next.

Elsewhere in the *Magnalia*, Mather says how his grandfather John Cotton and his wife Sarah came to New England with two other ministers, Thomas Hooker and Samuel Stone. Mather remarked that the three ministers symbolized three great necessities: Cotton for clothing, Hooker for fishing, and Stone for building. While crossing the Atlantic, Sarah Cotton gave birth to their first child. And what did they name him? Naturally, they named him Seaborn.[31]

Franklin recognized Mather's unintentional humor and borrowed it for "Silence Dogood 1." Like Seaborn Cotton, Silence Dogood was born on a west-bound ship as her parents emigrated from Old England to New. Her father went on deck in exultation. Silence explains: "As he, poor man, stood upon the deck rejoycing at my birth, a merciless wave entred the ship, and in one moment carry'd him beyond reprieve." Franklin understood that Mather's sentimental diction and religious clichés contributed to the unintentionally humorous death of John Avery. He used those same devices intentionally to turn the tragic story of Silence's father into dark comedy.[32]

"Milton," another entry in the *Courant* library catalogue, most likely represents *The Poetical Works of Mr. John Milton*, a collection containing *Paradise Lost, Paradise Regain'd, Samson Agonistes*, and other poems. Franklin had the chance to read Milton the week he published the library catalogue. The same issue containing the catalogue presents a letter to the editor condemning the sin of pride. For support, the contributor quoted a fifteen-line passage from the first book of *Paradise Lost* about how Satan's pride had cast him and his rebel crew from Heaven. The *Courant* copy of Milton let Franklin double-check the quotation before printing the article.[33]

Franklin would often return to Milton. In his personal creed, "Articles of Belief and Acts of Religion," he would incorporate "Hymn to the Creator," a forty-eight-line excerpt from the fifth book of *Paradise Lost*. For his weekly devotions, Franklin would sing these lines from Milton to honor God's Creation.[34]

Gardner also used Milton in the *Courant*. He took his epigraph for "Agreeable Society and Conversation" from a rhetorical question Adam asks God in *Paradise Lost* about the impossibility of finding happiness in solitude. Later in this same essay, Gardner quotes a lengthier piece of verse, which identifies the characteristics of true friends. They are kind, forthright, unselfish, and supportive. They provide comfort and inspire confidence. Gardner did not cite his source, but the ideas came from *The British Apollo*.[35]

Despite their female readership, the Couranteers did not always treat women readers respectfully. For "Female Impudence," Matthew Adams invented a misogynistic persona who describes the bold women who assemble in public to protest *The New-England Courant*. A "certain gentleman" arrives among them. Regular readers could tell that the unnamed man was another caricature of Cotton Mather. Identifying the man's willingness to let the women speak, Adams's narrator calls him a "silent mourner for the loss of his breeches." In response to their anathemas and "tittle-tattle," the man says, "Amen." He also decries the *Courant*: "Oh! the divisions, the quarrelings, the backbitings of the times." After quoting the gentleman's cries, Adams's narrator says, "This puts me in mind of a story I have somewhere read of a mountebank in *Leiscester-Fields*," whereupon he retells a story from Jonathan Swift's preface to *A Tale of a Tub*.[36]

Adams's insouciance may be the most compelling aspect of his use of source material. His quotation is close enough to Swift's original to verify that he had *A Tale of a Tub* open before him as he wrote, but he does not say so. Instead, he feigns ignorance. Exhibiting a Horatian nonchalance toward the story of the mountebank, Adams's narrator says he had read it "somewhere."

Though the Couranteers had an excellent office library for reference as they wrote their articles, they did not necessarily want to admit it. They preferred to strike the pose of a man who has read so widely and so well that he has internalized his readings and cannot always remember where he read what.

In *A Tale of a Tub*, Swift compares people who mention book titles with those who drop names. They use books "as some men do lords, learn their titles exactly, and then brag of their acquaintance."[37] The way Adams and the other Couranteers use books shows that they learned the lesson Swift was teaching. They borrowed from literary sources but typically avoided naming them to avoid showing off their erudition.

Franklin's *Courant* library catalogue exposes the artifice underlying the newspaper's articles. Whereas the Couranteers wore their learning lightly, refusing to boast about their literary knowledge, Franklin's catalogue revealed their trade secret. Literature was not always something they had read in the past and could summon from memory at will. They had a bookcase full of pertinent works to consult as sources and models for their newspaper essays.

Critiques of erudition occur in other works in the *Courant* library. *Spectator* 470 criticizes variorum editions of classical authors that attempt to record every known textual variant. In this number, Addison created a burlesque variorum of an old English ode. His satirical pseudo-erudition ridicules overfastidious editors of ancient authors.

Perhaps no work in English literature mocks the unnecessary display of erudition more than Samuel Butler's *Hudibras*, another work in the *Courant* library. Though *Hudibras* is primarily a send-up of English Presbyterianism, Butler had many satirical targets, including conspicuous erudition. He calls learning a "cobweb of the brain, / Profane, erroneous, and vain." Exemplifying the folly of erudition, Sir Hudibras can "speak Greek / As naturally as pigs squeak." Furthermore, he is an excellent rhetorician: "For rhetorick he could not ope / His mouth, but out there flew a trope."[38]

Dr. Douglass also enjoyed Butler's satire. Butler laughed at the learning of early plastic surgeon Gaspare Tagliacozzi, who, according to legend, would cut flesh from a porter's backside to make noses for patients who had lost theirs to syphilis. Douglass excerpted three lines from *Hudibras* for the title-page motto for *Inoculation of the Small Pox*:

> So learned Taliacotius from
> The brawny parts of porters bum,
> Cut supplemental noses. . .

Douglass does not quote the rest of the third line or the next three lines, which inform readers that when the porter died, the artificial nose would drop off the patient's face. Butler's lines imply that smallpox inoculations would prove as ineffectual as Tagliacozzi's butt noses.[39]

Franklin listed *Hudibras* with Milton, so presumably they were shelved adjacently. In terms of purpose, prosody, and philosophy, *Hudibras* and *Paradise Lost* could hardly be further apart. They did share one major similarity in terms of readership. They were the two best-known English poems in colonial America. Tetrameter couplets with double, triple, or imperfect rhymes became known as hudibrastics, and *Hudibras* inspired two of the greatest poems in colonial American literature: Ebenezer Cook's *Sot-Weed Factor* and Robert Bolling's "Neanthe."

Benjamin Franklin made use of *Hudibras* himself. "Silence Dogood 7" offers a mock literary recipe listing essential ingredients for a funeral elegy. Silence attributes the recipe to her reverend husband. The recipe does not mention *Hudibras*, but it is indebted to Butler's poem. Its sample rhymes are all hudibrastic. The would-be elegist should prepare a "sufficient quantity of double rhimes, such as, 'power, flower; quiver, shiver; grieve us, leave us; tell you, excel you; expeditions, physicians; fatigue him, intrigue him.'"[40]

Franklin returned to *Hudibras* in "Rules for *The New-England Courant*," a facetious article he wrote in the persona of a devout friend of the newspaper. "Rules" proffers guidelines for editing the *Courant*. The fifth rule says: "We advise you to avoid quotations from prophane and scandalous authors which will be but like so many *dead flies* in your *Courant*; and in particular, we think it by no means proper to introduce your speculations with lines out of Butler's *Hudibras*, for he was no *pious author*, but a profane wit, who set himself up to burlesque the *Brethren* and lampoon the *Saints* that liv'd in his time."[41]

The proverbial phrase, "a fly in the ointment," remains common today. In Franklin's time, people would say, "Dead flies corrupt the most precious ointments."[42] "Rules" forms an early example illustrating how Franklin incorporated proverbs in his writing. In this instance, he combined folklore and book culture. His proverbial dead flies complement his use of *Hudibras*. The proverb and the poem heighten the article's humor even as they suggest that the stern rule-writing persona lacks a sense of humor.

"Rules for *The New-England Courant*" resulted from an odd set of circumstances. On January 14, 1723, Gardner published "Satire on New England 'Saints'" in the *Courant*, exposing Boston's leaders as religious hypocrites. The following day, the Massachusetts Council censured James Franklin as the newspaper's publisher and subjected it to review prior to publication.

Philadelphia printer and publisher Andrew Bradford, who read the story, was shocked by the Massachusetts authorities' ruling to limit the freedom of the press. He reported it in his newspaper, *The American Weekly Mercury*, and added some satire, a rarity for him: "By private letters from Boston we are informed, that the bakers there are under great apprehensions of being forbid making any more bread, unless they will submit to the Secretary, as Supervisor General and Weigher of the Dough, before it is baked into bread and offer'd to sale."[43]

At first, James Franklin did not let the Massachusetts Council faze him. He kept publishing the *Courant* as usual. But when the court issued a warrant for his arrest, James went into hiding. Benjamin took charge of the *Courant* again. "Rules" is his satirical reply to the sanctimonious Boston officials who sought to censor the press.

Since the Massachusetts government prevented James from publishing the *Courant*, he and the Couranteers pondered their options. They considered changing the paper's name. Instead, they kept the name of the newspaper but changed the name of its publisher. "Benjamin Franklin" would appear on the masthead. James canceled Benjamin's old indenture so that it would not appear he was publishing the paper through his apprentice. He also wrote a new indenture for the rest of Benjamin's apprenticeship, which he would keep secret from the authorities.

The case against James Franklin was dismissed, a major victory in the development of the freedom of the press. Once the controversy died down, James and Benjamin settled back into a routine, meaning that James returned to abusing his little brother, who was not so little any more. Taking advantage of the canceled indenture, Benjamin decided to leave, knowing full well James could not produce the new secret indenture without opening himself up to court action. Benjamin felt badly about taking advantage of his brother's situation, but, given the chance to escape, he escaped.

Benjamin Franklin's apprenticeship had lasted long enough for him to learn how to manage a printing house. His brother had taught him the trade that would help make his reputation and his fortune. James Franklin's excellent office library played no small part in his brother's education. It gave Benjamin information about geography and travel, natural history, political science, poetry, and the art of the essay. The *Courant* library supplied the literature that shaped Franklin's intellectual life.

6

Reader on the Road

ONE LATE SEPTEMBER day in 1723, John Collins delivered an urgent message to Captain Arnout Schermerhorne, skipper of the New York sloop *Speedwell*. My friend, Collins said, meaning Benjamin Franklin, got a girl pregnant. A "naughty girl," Franklin would say when he spiced up the story in his autobiography, placing the onus for such behavior on the female, not the male. Collins told the captain that his friend had to leave town before her friends forced them to marry. The story was not true. Collins, a regular Tom Sawyer at scheming, helped Franklin devise the ruse to provide a reason for sneaking aboard the *Speedwell* before anyone got wind of his departure.[1]

Having left his brother's printshop days earlier, Franklin hoped to find work with another local printing house. Determined to get Benjamin back under his thumb, James warned the other Boston printers not to hire him. James also informed their father what had happened. Josiah Franklin said he would try to force his wayward son back to James's printshop, hence the ruse.

Then in his thirties, Schermerhorne was young enough to sympathize with the teenaged runaway and willing to help him escape trouble—provided he could pay his way. Franklin sold some books to afford the trip, but he held onto his favorite volumes, including the *Port Royal Logic*. The Burtons seem the most likely ones he sold since their high demand and low cost made them easy to unload. He did not sell them all. Remember he kept one—*Unparallel'd Varieties*—long enough to quote from it in *Poor Richard's Almanack*. The sale reveals Franklin's desperation. Already he took pride in his personal library and considered it part of himself. The sale was akin to self-sacrifice. But it was a necessary sacrifice, enabling him to get a fresh start somewhere else.

On Wednesday, September 25th, he was aboard the *Speedwell* when it left Boston harbor. Pierre Cabanis found the story of Franklin's departure from Boston akin to the end of *Paradise Lost* or the start of Tom Jones's adventures. His reminiscence gives Franklin's journey the aura of a mythical quest: "Here he was, like Adam and Tom Jones, with the world before him, with no other guide than his good fortune, or rather his common sense, which had not yet been honed by experience."[2]

Reaching New York on Friday, the 27th, Franklin asked William Bradford for a job. The city's sole printer, Bradford had introduced printing to New York three decades earlier. Franklin would later characterize him as a "crafty old sophister"—a phrase typically applied to Satan—but Bradford gave this young journeyman a helping hand. Bradford was not hiring, but he pointed Franklin toward Philadelphia, where his son operated a printing house. Andrew Bradford, who had lost his principal employee, needed a capable replacement. The lost employee was Aquila Rose, a charismatic young man best known as a poet. Rose had caught a chill while retrieving a boat from the Schuylkill River during a storm. The chill developed into a fever that took his life.[3]

Franklin's autobiography does not say how he felt about filling a dead man's shoes, but he needed the work. Instead of dawdling in New York, he hastily sought passage to Philadelphia, a little too hastily as things turned out. On Tuesday, October 1st, he and some others left for Perth Amboy, New Jersey, in an open boat. The passage normally took a few hours, but as they crossed New York Harbor, an unexpected squall shredded the boat's decrepit sails. The squall stopped them from reaching Kill van Kull, the sheltered channel separating Staten Island from New Jersey.

The storm drove them east across the harbor toward Long Island, where they washed about in the heavy surf, rocking like a broken cradle and almost crashing onto the stony beach. Unable to land on Long Island or return to Manhattan, they spent the night bobbing on the chop. The storm did not abate until the next morning, when they turned toward Perth Amboy, which they did not reach until Wednesday afternoon, thirty hours after their journey had started. Franklin came ashore burning with fever. In his hurry to take Aquila Rose's place, he seemed to be following his fate. Franklin found a friendly tavern in Perth Amboy: a safe haven for the night.

Relating the adventure, Franklin wrote, "Having read somewhere that cold water drank plentifully was good for a fever, I follow'd the prescription, sweat plentifully most of the night, [and] my fever left me."[4] With the word "somewhere," which he added in revision, Franklin took a cue from Matthew Adams, who had used the word in "Female Impudence" to mask his literary source. Franklin assumed a similar nonchalance toward his medical reading. Before the revision, the sentence makes him sound too careful, too knowledgeable, as if he had prepared for illness beforehand. Putting "somewhere" in the sentence, Franklin showed the value of desultory reading. By pure chance, he had read a cure for fever, but he remembered it well enough to use the information to save himself. Though forced to sell some books to finance his trip, Franklin had internalized his reading. Neither poverty nor distress could take away his knowledge.

Franklin was recalling an anti-fever article from *The Boston News-Letter*, which summarized John Hancocke's *Febrifugum magnum: or, Common Water the Best Cure for Fevers*. A short book written in a nonmedical language, *Febrifugum magnum* appealed to general readers. Franklin enjoyed the newspaper's summary so much he would add the book to his library.[5] Hancocke recommended drinking a pint or two of cold water and then sweating out the fever. His hydrotherapy offered a common-sense alternative to other procedures—bleeding, blistering, purging, vomiting—that supposedly cured illness by rebalancing the humors. In the Perth Amboy tavern, Franklin drank plenty of water before retiring to stew himself in sweat. He had the fever all through the night but awoke the next morning relaxed, refreshed, and ready for a new challenge: a walk across New Jersey. He took to the road like a Shetland pony in fine fettle.

On Friday, the 4th, he reached a Bordentown inn run by local surgeon John Browne. His autobiography captures the moment: "He entered into conversation with me while I took some refreshment, and finding I had read a little, became very sociable and friendly."[6] This, the second time in three days, Franklin's reading came in handy, taught him something different from the fever prescription. Whereas Hancocke had provided some specific medical advice, his general reading now benefited Franklin socially.

Speaking with Browne, Franklin realized something nonreaders never realize, that people's conversation reflects their reading. The Couranteers were men who read much and talked well. Now, the tables had turned. His encounter with Browne showed Franklin that reading, a solo activity, could have social benefits. His literary knowledge endeared him to Browne, and they formed a lifelong friendship.

Browne was a poet as well as a man of science, a dual impulse many of Franklin's friends shared. "He had some letters," Franklin wrote, using a curious phrase that means Browne had a good knowledge of literature. "He had some letters, and was ingenious, but much of an unbeliever, and wickedly undertook some years after to travesty the bible in doggerel verse as Cotton had done Virgil. By this means he set many of the facts in a very ridiculous light, and might have hurt weak minds if his work had been publish'd: but it never was."[7]

Franklin was referring to Charles Cotton's *Scarronnides: or, Virgile Travestie*, a burlesque of *The Aeneid*. Though Cotton established the tetrameter couplet as an apt medium for satirical English verse, he would be overshadowed by *Hudibras*, which lent its name to this style of poetry. *Scarronnides* begins:

> I *sing the man*, (read it who list,
> A *Trojan* true as ever pist)
> Who from *Troy Town*, by wind and weather
> To *Italy*, (and God knows whither)
> Was packt, and wrackt, and lost and tost,
> And bounc'd from pillar unto post.[8]

Scarronnides was well known throughout colonial America. Take, for example, *The Association*, Jacob Bailey's verse travesty. A Loyalist poet who transposed his initials to create the pseudonym "Bob Jingle," Bailey aligned his verse travesty of Congress's non-importation and non-exportation agreement with *Scarronnides*. He adapted Cotton's first two lines for his title-page motto, pluralizing the object of the verse sentence to refer to all congressional delegates: "I sing the *men*, read it who list, / *Bold* Trojans true, as ever pist."[9]

The reference to Cotton let Franklin's readers imagine Browne's biblical travesty. Mentioning that Browne wrote this work several years later, Franklin confirmed that they kept in contact. In other words, Browne shared his satirical poem with him after Franklin had founded his printing house. Browne may have asked him to publish the poem. Presumably, Franklin talked him out of making it public.

Franklin did not necessarily disagree with his friend's biblical interpretation. Browne's poem apparently revealed how ridiculous parts of the Bible could be. But Franklin recognized the danger. Having read both scripture and *Scarronnides*, Franklin could appreciate Browne's satire because he knew its literary and cultural contexts. Reading helps people develop critical thinking skills enabling them to understand and interpret information. Franklin knew that people who lacked sufficient background reading would have had trouble recognizing Browne's satirical tone and interpreting his lampoon.

When he reached Philadelphia, Franklin left the Delaware River at Market Street Wharf. The autobiography famously gives a block-by-block report of his entry into the city. He walked up High Street or, as it is better known, Market Street. He purchased three puffy rolls at Second Street, passed the home of John and Sarah Read, and continued as far as Fourth, where he turned left toward Chesnut Street.

He does not say why he turned off Market at Fourth Street, but it is not hard to fathom. Market Street continued all the way to the Manayunk or Schuylkill River. The Dutch name for the river stuck, but the Lenape name "Manayunk," which means "the place to drink," survives to describe a neighborhood in northwest Philadelphia. But in 1723, there were almost no buildings on Market Street beyond Fourth. Market Street was heavily wooded between Fourth Street and the Schuylkill.

Franklin had a reason for being so specific about his entry into Philadelphia. He created a memorable image of himself at this moment in his life as a contrast to the familiar image of his older and more successful self. His narrative strategy worked. Franklin's first walk through Philadelphia is one of the most iconic scenes in American literature, repeated, parodied, and paralleled by countless authors.

Jack Kerouac recalls the scene in *Lonesome Traveler*. Writing in the mid-twentieth century, Kerouac saw the American hobo as a vanishing breed. His admiration for the hobo is exceptional. Contemporaries saw the hobo not as a person to be admired, but one to be shunned. Kerouac looked to American history to support his perspective. Melville had linked Franklin with the whaleman to establish the nobility of whaling; Kerouac linked him with the hobo to establish the American hobo's essential dignity: "Benjamin Franklin was like a hobo in Pennsylvania; he walked through Philly with three big rolls under his arms and a Massachusetts halfpenny on his hat."[10]

The halfpenny—Kerouac's embellishment—is an anachronism, but it enhances the story's literary sophistication. Reinforcing Franklin's Massachusetts roots, Kerouac stressed a personal connection the two shared. Kerouac was also a man from Massachusetts. But there is more. Best known for the three conjoined heads on its obverse, the Massachusetts halfpenny creates a parallel with Franklin's three puffy rolls and thus integrates sustenance for the body with the powers of the mind. Three heads looking in three different directions convey Franklin's ability to appreciate the past, perceive the present, and foresee the future.

After spending the night at the Crooked Billet Tavern on Water Street or, as it is better known, Front Street, Franklin walked to the Sign of the Bible on Second, which designated Andrew Bradford's shop. He introduced himself and stated his business. Bradford said he had no full-time work available, but he offered Franklin some "smouting," printers' slang for intermittent part-time work, as well as a temporary place to stay.[11]

Franklin went to Samuel Keimer's shop, located on the south side of Market Street between Third and Fourth. Having arrived from London the previous year, Keimer had purchased a ramshackle press but had yet to start printing. Franklin found him composing an elegy to Aquila Rose. Instead of using pen and paper, Keimer was literally composing the elegy, that is, setting it in type from his head.[12]

Keimer lacked the skill to operate his press since printers' apprentices in London either learned how to set type or how to operate a press, not both. Franklin, like other American printers' apprentices, had learned both typesetting and presswork. Keimer offered him a position as pressman. Franklin accepted the offer, tightened up the rickety old press, and printed *An Elegy on the Much Lamented Death of the Ingenious and Well-Belov'd Aquila Rose*, the first issue of Keimer's Philadelphia press. One modern commentator has called Keimer's tribute to Rose "perhaps the worst elegy ever written."[13]

Though severe, this critical judgment is not unique. Literary history has treated Keimer shabbily, and Franklin is the one to blame. Franklin could be merciless when it came to business matters, as his portrayal of Keimer shows. The autobiography depicts Keimer as a buffoon, and history has followed suit. Keimer deserves more credit. He was a better man and a better printer than Franklin says.[14]

In 1724, Keimer published one of his most notable imprints, *The Independent Whig*, a new edition of the radical weekly that John Trenchard and Thomas Gordon had written and edited, which would influence the thought of many Founding Fathers besides Franklin. Since Keimer published the first twenty numbers in weekly installments, his edition could be considered the first magazine published in America, but its status as a reprint, not an original, typically disqualifies it from the history of American periodicals. After the twentieth number, Keimer collected the remaining issues of *The Independent Whig* and released them as a book.[15]

In his preface to the first issue, Keimer explains that *The Independent Whig* had been printed numerous times and widely circulated with positive results. He was reprinting it "for the benefit, and delight of those who have any relish for useful knowledge, and are not contented to be led blindfold into the boggy mazes of ignorance and superstition."[16] Keimer's preface testifies to his commitment to the Whiggish principles Trenchard and Gordon espoused. As a whole, *The Independent Whig* places individual conscience above religious authority and celebrates the freedom to determine our fate. Keimer's edition of *The Independent Whig* makes him a leader in disseminating the ideas of religious and political freedom in America.

Regardless of his contribution to early American book culture, there is no denying that Keimer was an oddball. Seeking to humanize Franklin and depict his personal interactions with sympathy and understanding in his 1965 biography, Owen Aldridge used two modern character types to contrast him with his employer. Franklin is a varsity letterman; Keimer is a beatnik.[17]

Keimer's beatnik proclivities went beyond his scruffy beard and questionable hygiene. A fringe dweller, he enjoyed experimenting with alternate modes of thought and new religions. In London, Keimer had joined the French Prophets or the Camisards, a Protestant sect whose members preached doomsday, spoke in tongues, and swooned into fits. Sometimes the French Prophets would be taken by the Holy Spirit, which triggered wild gesticulations. Franklin remembered Keimer reenacting the enthusiastic agitations of the French Prophets to entertain his employees. Keimer stimulated his curiosity. Franklin would later obtain a volume of pamphlets about the French Prophets.[18]

After falling out with the French Prophets, Keimer wrote *Brand Pluck'd from the Burning*. Part autobiography and part exposé, this tell-all reveals the secrets of the French Prophets. Describing their elaborate physical movements during a prophesy, Keimer called them "violent and strange agitations or shakings of body, loud and terrifying hiccups, and throbs, with many odd and very surprizing postures." Sometimes, Keimer continued, the prophets would turn the world upside down, assuming odd positions "such as boys in their play commonly call 'bending the sea-crab,' walking on his hands, with his legs erect, etc."[19]

Soon after Franklin began working for Keimer, William Keith, the colonial governor of Pennsylvania, visited his printing house. Having heard he had a bright new journeyman, the governor asked if he could speak with him. Shocked by Keith's request, Keimer could do little but introduce him to Franklin, whereupon the governor invited the youngster to a nearby tavern, where they enjoyed the double pleasure of conversation and madeira.

Despite Franklin's youth, Keith saw in him a powerful ally. Their meeting was the first of many. Keith cultivated a friendship with the ambitious journeyman, encouraging Franklin to start his own printing house. With a printer on his side, Keith would have a forum and a platform for his administrative policies. Sometimes he invited Franklin to his home to discuss plans for the future.

Though Keith never recorded his friendship with Franklin, he did leave some general comments that shed light on their interaction. *Observator's Trip to America*, a pamphlet Keith would write two years later, shows what visiting his Philadelphia home was like. Franklin may have read this pamphlet; he compliments Keith's writing abilities in his autobiography. Keith structured it as a set of dialogues between Observator and Roger, two figures who represent Whig political philosophy. Observator is witty and urbane; Roger is a plain-speaking man and thus forms a good comic foil.

One dialogue presents a fictional episode that parallels Franklin's real-life visits to the Pennsylvania governor's mansion. Observator goes to see Governor Keith around seven o'clock one morning to deliver a package. A jolly man with a rubicund visage welcomes Observator, sits him down, and says the governor will appear soon. Less than three minutes later, Keith breezes into the room like Caesar in his nightgown. He shakes Observator by the hand, takes a seat, and begins speaking with him. Governor Keith offers his guest an eye-opener in the form of a fine cordial. Before Observator leaves, Keith says he will do what he can for him.[20]

Keith told Franklin that if he could secure his father's support, then he would also contribute to the venture. In late April 1724, Franklin returned to Boston to ask his father for the capital to establish his own printing business. Suspicious of Keith's motives and uncertain whether Benjamin was ready for such responsibility, Josiah Franklin refused to loan him the necessary sum.

Franklin visited others during this brief return to his birthplace. Colonial travelers conventionally called on Boston's leading citizens. Franklin went to see Cotton Mather. The cordiality of his visit suggests that Mather did not associate him with the Couranteers who had attacked him in the press. Though Franklin had lampooned Mather with the character of Silence Dogood, his satire was subtle, and, besides, his authorship was unknown outside the small circle of Couranteers. Furthermore, Franklin sided with Mather against the Couranteers regarding the central issue for which they attacked him: smallpox inoculation. A few years later, Franklin would emerge as a vocal advocate for inoculation.

Once he reached Mather's home, his host welcomed him inside and escorted Franklin to his library, which held the greatest private collection of books in colonial New England. Now 61, Mather had spent a lifetime amassing his library. By the time he turned 18—Franklin's age—Mather already had assembled an extensive collection. When Franklin visited in 1724, Mather's library had swelled to nearly 4,000 volumes. His collection rivaled that of William Byrd of Westover, who had the greatest library in the colonial South.[21]

His extensive collection of divinity, ecclesiastical history, and biblical scholarship held little interest for Franklin, but Mather was more widely read than his religious books suggest. While believing a minister should know Latin, Greek, Hebrew, and Syriac, he thought a well-rounded education

should include modern languages as well. A minister should avoid being an
"odd, starv'd, lank sort of a thing, who had lived only on Hebrew roots all his
days."[22]

Mather recommended reading poetry. Placing Homer and Virgil atop
his pantheon, he reflected a conventional taste in verse. He did recommend
some English poets, including Richard Blackmore, a recommendation that
reveals Mather's verse aesthetic. Blackmore belonged to a group of English
poets known as the "physico-theological poets," a name derived from
Physico-Theology, William Derham's hugely popular contribution to natural
theology, a scientific approach that saw the study of nature as an act of
devotion. Studying the natural world could reveal the power and wisdom
of God.[23]

The Creation, a seven-book epic poem that is a veritable encyclopedia of
physico-theology, is Blackmore's greatest work. Though his verse often falls
flat, few poems excel Blackmore's *Creation* in terms of scientific comprehen-
siveness. Examining numerous topics from the construction of the universe to
the anatomy of the human body, Blackmore shows how nature illustrates the
shaping hand of the Supreme Being. A physician by trade, Blackmore is at his
best as he delineates human anatomy, devoting 150 lines to the circulatory
system and 125 to the digestive. The poem culminates in a lyrical hymn to
the Creator.[24]

Like Mather, Franklin enjoyed Blackmore's *Creation*. A few years later
when he wrote his private liturgy, "Articles of Belief and Acts of Religion,"
Franklin made reading devotional literature part of his idiosyncratic religious
practice. He specifically mentioned Blackmore's *Creation* and another fundamental work of natural theology, John Ray's *Wisdom of God Manifested in the
Works of Creation*. First published in 1691, Ray's *Wisdom of God* connected
science and religion to form the foundation on which the physico-theological
poets built their work.[25]

When Franklin rose to leave Mather's library, his host showed him out the
back way. They walked through a narrow passage crossed by a low overhead
beam. With Franklin ahead and Mather behind, the two continued their conversation. When Franklin turned to look back toward his host, Mather yelled,
"Stoop, stoop!" Franklin did not understand what Mather meant, that is, not
until he knocked his head on the beam. Never one to miss a teaching moment,
Mather told Franklin, "Let this be a caution to you not always to hold your
head so high; stoop, young man, stoop—as you go through the world—and
you'll miss many hard thumps." Relating this episode to Mather's son Samuel
years later, Franklin concluded, "This was a way of hammering instruction

into one's head: And it was so far effectual, that I have ever since remember'd it, tho' I have not always been able to practise it."[26]

In addition to seeking funds, Franklin had come to Boston to retrieve the valuable belongings he had left behind: his books. The precise contents of the library he brought from Boston is unknown, but his collection was substantial enough to impress the captain of the sloop that took him back to Philadelphia. How did this printer's apprentice assemble such an impressive library? Here is one theory: During his apprenticeship, Franklin often came across books Bostonians sold for scrap. Instead of passing them to the pulper, he kept many for himself. This theory helps explain the sixteenth-century black-letter volumes in his library.

When they reached New York, the captain informed Governor William Burnet about the bookish lad aboard. The scholarly governor asked to meet him. Franklin's autobiography chronicles their encounter: "The governor treated me with great civility, show'd me his library, which was a very large one, and we had a good deal of conversation about books and authors."[27]

Franklin came away with an appreciation for the governor's intellect. Burnet had done much to advance scientific inquiry in New York. For example, he had made numerous astronomical observations attempting to ascertain latitude and longitude. Burnet was the son of Gilbert Burnet, bishop of Salisbury. Among the volumes in his collection were finely bound editions of his father's works, such as his *History of the Reformation* bound in red morocco with gilt edges. Franklin knew the work from the copy in the *Courant* office.[28]

Governor Burnet also had an excellent collection of *belles lettres*, scientific works, and travel books. Containing 1,600 titles totaling around 3,000 volumes, Burnet's library approached the collections of Byrd and Mather. Franklin was impressed. He would acquire for himself several works that Burnet owned. The most important aspect of their encounter is the deference the governor paid to this young tradesman. Franklin's library let him surmount substantial class barriers, giving this son of a tallow chandler the opportunity to talk books with a colonial governor and son of a bishop. Knowledge of books, Franklin realized, offered an entry to society.

Franklin's account of meeting Burnet in his autobiography echoes the chapbooks he had read as a child. When the earl of Warwick learns about Guy's reputation for physical strength, he invites him to his castle. When King Edward III learns how well Friar Bacon excels at his necromantic studies at Oxford University, he invites him to his castle. When Governor Burnet learns about a young man with an excellent library, he invites him to the governor's mansion. Whereas Guy's physical strength attracts the earl and

Friar Bacon's supernatural ability attracts the king, Franklin's extensive reading attracts the governor. In the modern, secular world, reading is what empowers the hero.

Back in Philadelphia, Franklin returned to Keimer's, settling into a regular work routine. Franklin integrated his reading life with his social life in Philadelphia. His best friends were avid readers, and they often discussed what they read. Speaking about his friendships outside Keimer's printing office, Franklin recalled that his three closest friends, Charles Osborne, Joseph Watson, and James Ralph, were all "lovers of reading."[29] As the four young men spent their Sundays walking through the woods along the Schuylkill, the forest would echo with laughter. Often they would read to one another and discuss what they read. Osborne was a little too critical, Ralph too full of himself, but their literary interests kept the friends together.

After Franklin gave Keith the disappointing news that his father would not finance their printing venture, Keith said he would still support him. He told Franklin to start arranging a business trip to London, where he could obtain the necessary equipment and supplies, including a printing press, type, paper, everything. Not only did Keith promise a letter of credit sufficient for Franklin to purchase whatever printing supplies he needed, he also promised letters of introduction to London friends.

The chance to go overseas thrilled Franklin, and the possibility of visiting London sweetened the opportunity. The center of the British world, London occupied a special place in the colonial mind. It was where Parliament met to make laws and where the Lords of Trade and Plantations convened to decide colonial policy. Yet, London was much more than the seat of empire, it was also a capital of culture. From the first century, when Caesar entered Londinium, it had been one of the leading cities of the world. And one of the leading cities of the world it remained.

Franklin foresaw London as a land of literature and philosophy, a place where intellectuals gathered at coffee houses to discuss new books, contemporary plays, current politics, and recent scientific discoveries. London was where literary tastes and critical standards were set, where any author who failed to live up to those standards was subject to harsh, yet always witty ridicule. The city was the home of the virtuoso, the cultured gentleman who excelled at many different pursuits. The virtuoso could read a musical score and play the violin or maybe the flute or oboe. He kept up with developments in science and technology and knew how to use a telescope. Heroic couplets fell trippingly off his tongue, and he could write letters clever enough to impress the most educated men or flatter the most fashionable women. For a young man with intellectual ambitions, London promised to be an exciting place.

Since James Franklin and Samuel Keimer had both lived in London, they could have related their impressions of the metropolis. But much of what Franklin learned about London came from his reading. *The Spectator* offered considerable information. *Spectator* 28, for example, presents a letter from a public-minded projector wanting to regularize London's streets. While criticizing the city's countless signboards, the author creates a vivid picture of life in London. He disparages the signs that go against nature, such as the Flying Pig or the Lamb and Dolphin. Since pigs can't fly, images of them should not have wings. And since lambs and dolphins never consort in nature, they should not consort on a London signboard.

Mr. Spectator's projector may protest too much, but he does so with charm and vivacity. He also critiques signs with no correlation to the products being sold, like the perfumer located at the Sign of the Goat. The projector seeks to impose order on the disorderly streets, but the impression that lingers from *Spectator* 28 is one of alluring disorder: The vivid, colorful, humorous, iconic signs compete for the attention of passersby, beckoning them to cross their thresholds, purchase their wares, or drink their ale.

If Franklin had any qualms about leaving Philadelphia to visit London, they concerned Deborah Read. A talkative but feisty young woman, Deborah lived with her parents on Market Street next door to Keimer's printshop. Deborah's father John Read was Keimer's landlord. Since Franklin came to Philadelphia, he and Deborah had grown close. They talked about marrying but had settled nothing definite before he left for London.

Franklin purchased his passage aboard the *London Hope*, a renowned ship that had been making the Philadelphia-to-London run for years. The ship's name augured well—unlike the governor's inexplicable behavior. Every time Franklin visited Keith's home to obtain the promised letters of introduction and credit, the governor had yet to finish them.

The *London Hope* had already been delayed several times this year. By November 1724, its departure was imminent. Franklin tried to see Keith again to take his leave and get his letters. Franklin eagerly approached the governor's mansion one final night, the night before the ship left Philadelphia. No jolly man with a rubicund visage greeted him. Instead, Dr. Patrick Baird, a shadowy character who acted as the governor's confidential secretary, met Franklin at the door, opening it no wider than necessary. Baird said Keith was so busy he could not see him but assured Franklin that the governor would give him the letters when the *London Hope* stopped at New Castle, a Delaware town about 30 miles south.

Perhaps Franklin should have been suspicious, but he left Philadelphia believing Governor Keith would keep his word. Surely, no one would send a friend across the Atlantic empty-handed. Ralph, who would accompany Franklin to London, was less naïve and more familiar with humankind's capacity for deceit, but Franklin stayed mum about the governor's role in his business plans. Ralph's own motivations for making the trip puzzled Franklin. Since his young wife had recently given birth to their daughter Mary, Franklin found it strange that Ralph would leave them for a lengthy overseas trip. He understood that Ralph was going to London to establish an importing business.

Captain John Annis, longtime skipper of the *London Hope*, had established a reputation for transporting goods, people, and letters of personal, political, and economic importance safely across the ocean. He was naturally kind and nautically savvy. But while in Philadelphia, he had come down with a violent fever and died. Thomas Annis and his younger brother William, who had been sailing with their father to learn the trade, also contracted the fever, but they recuperated. As Thomas buried his father and recovered his health, he realized that he was now the captain of the *London Hope*. Added to these troubles, three crew members, all indentured servants, took advantage of his father's death and ran away.[30]

When Benjamin Franklin and James Ralph boarded the *London Hope*, they found their initial accommodations disappointing. By the time they had booked passage, all five berths in the great cabin had been taken, so they got stuck in steerage. Not long after they boarded, Colonel John French, another one of the governor's henchmen, came aboard. French paid his respects to Franklin and handed the governor's dispatches to the new captain, who placed them in the mailbag. Once the letters had been stowed away, Franklin asked to see what Keith had written for him.[31]

Who did this young steerage passenger think he was to make such a special request? In light of the costly runaways, the new captain asserted his authority and denied the request. He told Franklin all the letters had been put into the mailbag together, so he could not access them until they neared England. His statement was not exactly true: A last-minute letter James Logan had written found its way into the mailbag. While denying Franklin's request, Captain Thomas Annis was not brusque or rude. He responded with kindly firmness, telling Franklin he could rummage through the mailbag before they docked in London to remove whatever letters Keith had written on his behalf. The captain's words satisfied Franklin, who was content to wait until the end of the voyage to retrieve the letters.[32]

The prominent Philadelphia lawyer Andrew Hamilton and his teenaged son James were among the five passengers who had reserved berths in the great cabin. Seeing off the *London Hope* had become a local tradition; Hamilton traveled from Philadelphia to New Castle with a large entourage—seventy horse altogether—to wish him well. The entourage indicates Hamilton's level of respect among Philadelphians. The city's most formidable lawyer, he would earn a lasting reputation as a defender of free speech. James Hamilton would become deputy governor of Pennsylvania, one of the colony's few governors who tried to reconcile the opposing views of the assembly and the Pennsylvania proprietors.[33]

Before the *London Hope* departed, Hamilton was called back to Philadelphia to defend a high-profile case. Taking James with him, he left two berths available in the great cabin. Having witnessed Colonel French pay his respects to Franklin, the cabin's three remaining passengers were impressed and invited him and Ralph to leave steerage and join them in the great cabin. The upgrade to first class gave them the chance to enjoy comfortable quarters and unexpected luxury. Hamilton was unable to remove the copious provisions he had brought aboard to ease the lengthy ocean voyage: a boon for hungry travelers like Franklin and Ralph.

The pleasant company enhanced Franklin's first ocean crossing. He could see in the others parallels of himself. Two were ironmongers: Stephen Onion and Thomas Russell. Both deserve credit for establishing Maryland's iron industry. Together, they constituted the driving force behind the Principio Company. So far they had prospected for iron ore, leased tracts of land, built a furnace and two forges, and arranged the sale of bar- and pig-iron. Having put their business on a solid footing, they left their ironmaster in charge and now headed to London to promote the venture and raise some capital.[34]

Little is known about Thomas Russell, but Stephen Onion possessed both style and character. To oversee his iron works, he built a genteel home close to his forges. At 30, Onion presented a personal example of a successful young businessman.[35] His profession as an ironmonger reinforced the current relationship between the colonies and the metropolis. America had the natural resources; London had the investment capital. And an ocean separated the twain, a distance that took three weeks to cover at the very best but could take seven or eight weeks with contrary winds.

Of more importance to Franklin was the third passenger in the great cabin, Thomas Denham, whose background had until now remained a mystery. Born on December 5, 1687, in Bristol, England, Denham was the son of Thomas and Rebeccah Denham, a working-class Quaker couple. His father, a shoemaker, died in 1696. Rebeccah remarried the following year but died herself the year after that, leaving Thomas an orphan. The Quaker church in Bristol tried to find the boy an apprenticeship. A local weaver offered to apprentice him, but nothing came of the offer. Denham's whereabouts for several years thereafter still remain a mystery.[36]

Denham next surfaces as a young Bristol merchant. Franklin's autobiography provides the fullest information about his professional activities. Denham had borrowed from British creditors to establish his mercantile business. Financial setbacks and unscrupulous business partners rendered him unable to pay his outstanding debts, so he left the Old World for the New, where his luck changed for the better. The successful business he established in Philadelphia enabled him to pay his old debts with honor—and with interest.[37]

Neither Franklin nor the other passengers in the great cabin left records of their conversations aboard the *London Hope*. There were two subjects they did not discuss: Franklin kept quiet about Keith's role in his business plans, and Ralph did not divulge his real reason for leaving America. Perhaps Onion had the most to discuss. The two tracts where he established his iron forges he had leased from Ebenezer Cook, the agent for Lord Baltimore who is best known as the author of *The Sot-Weed Factor*. The terms for one tract required Onion to pay an annual rent of fifteen shillings, sixpence and two fat capons.[38]

Onion had literary inclinations himself. He named one of the tracts *Vulcan's Rest*, the other *Vulcan's Trial*. These names associate Onion's foundries with the god of fire who invented iron, according to Roman mythology. Vulcan is lame, a physical deformity he got after defying Jupiter, who shoved him down Mount Olympus. Vulcan thus embodies rebellion and represents the superiority of the intellectual over the spiritual world. Perhaps most importantly, Vulcan has a reputation for industry. He inspires others to learn practical skills that can contribute to the good of society. Symbolizing useful arts and community improvement, Vulcan was a mythological figure after Franklin's heart.

The Lair of the Green Dragon

THE STORMY WEATHER throughout the voyage was a trial for the young skipper of the *London Hope*, but Captain Thomas Annis safely navigated the vessel into the English Channel seven weeks after leaving Delaware. True to his word, he let Franklin search the mailbag once they entered the chops of the Channel. The mailing addresses gave Franklin a glimpse of the personal and professional correspondence between Philadelphia and London. From a literary standpoint, the most interesting letter may have been the one inside the envelope James Logan had addressed to his old friend Josiah Martin. Eager to learn more about the customs, history, and literature of the Near East, Logan, whose linguistic expertise included a reading knowledge of Arabic, asked Martin to purchase several Arabic texts for him.[1]

Franklin and Logan had yet to become friends. He turned over his letter to Martin as he rummaged through the rest. Pawing through the mailbag, Franklin grew more and more anxious. He emptied the sack without finding any letters for him, so he selected six or seven that, by their handwriting style and London addresses, could have been from the governor to members of the printing trade. One was addressed to John Baskett, who had held the office of king's printer for many years and who also had a monopoly on printing for Oxford University Press. Another was addressed to a London stationer, whose name time has forgotten.

After passing the cliffs of Dover, Captain Annis brought the *London Hope* to Deal, where, according to one version of history, Julius Caesar had landed when he came to conquer Britain. Deal had remained a small, poor village for centuries, but in recent decades the burgeoning mercantile trade helped it thrive. Ocean-going ships took on provisions at Deal; returning vessels found pilots there to guide them up the Thames.

The *London Hope* reached the Custom House in London on Christmas Eve, when Franklin and Ralph disembarked. The previous Custom House, designed and built by Christopher Wren, had been ravaged by fire and since rebuilt. The Long Room was its most distinctive feature. Two hundred feet long with a ceiling five stories high, the Long Room caused first-time visitors to gasp in awe. Stepping inside this cavernous room, Franklin and Ralph entered another world.[2]

Daniel Defoe captured the look and feel of the Long Room. In *Tour through Great Britain*, a work Franklin enjoyed for its detailed descriptions of Britain's public buildings, Defoe observes, "The Long Room is like an exchange every morning, and the croud of people who appear there, and the business they do, is not to be explained by words, nothing of that kind in Europe is like it." The sight of so much business occurring in one place fired Defoe's imagination. He used the Long Room as a setting for his picaresque crime novel *Colonel Jack*. The Long Room is where Jack enters the pickpocket trade.[3]

Once they cleared customs, Franklin and Ralph entered London. The quay at the Custom House welcomed visitors, giving them a broad and pleasant walk along the Thames. "Here at mid-day," said one, "the rays of the winter's sun seem less feeble than elsewhere."[4] Franklin's growing uneasiness about the letters turned him from the river toward the first addressee: the stationer with no name.

London was intimidating. Having left Philadelphia, with a population of 10,000, Franklin found himself in a city of 700,000. Ralph, who was familiar with London, showed Franklin around and helped him find the shop. Upon reaching the stationer's, Franklin delivered the letter from the mailbag. He said it was from Governor Keith. The stationer was unimpressed.

"I don't know such a person," he replied as he opened the letter. "O, this is from Riddlesden; I have lately found him to be a complete rascal, and I will have nothing to do with him, nor receive any letters from him."[5]

Franklin left astonished and humiliated. The letter was not from Keith but from William Vanhaesdonck Riddlesden, a criminal mastermind who had been swindling people on both sides of the Atlantic for years. After committing various felonies in England, Riddlesden was convicted and transported to Maryland, where he committed so many land swindles the Maryland Assembly passed a special act deeming him a "person of matchless character in infamy."[6] Riddlesden returned to England but was transported back to America, this time to Philadelphia, where the victims of his fraudulent schemes included Deborah's father, John Read. Franklin found himself an unwitting messenger for an international swindler.

Leaving the stationer's, Franklin was in a tough spot. Keith had undermined his trip to London, not by writing a bellerophonic letter, but by writing no letters, neither the promised letter of credit nor the letters of introduction.

What did Franklin do next? Did he open the other five or six letters to see that none concerned him? Doing so would have been an uncharacteristic breach of privacy and propriety. The only other option was to deliver the rest and thus suffer a series of similar humiliations. Having taken responsibility for the letters, this future postmaster apparently delivered them. If any good came from the experience, it did help Franklin learn his way around London. Familiar with Abraham Cowley's poetry, perhaps he heard an echo from "Of Solitude": "Methinks, I see / The monster London laugh at me."[7]

Since the stationer had opened the Riddlesden letter, Franklin read that one. Though not from Keith, it revealed that the governor was in league with Riddlesden. Together, they were plotting some kind of secret scheme against Andrew Hamilton. Franklin knew what he had to do next: He would give the letter to Hamilton, who had successfully defended the case that had called him back to Philadelphia, collected his fee, gone to New York, and caught a ship from there to England. Hamilton was happy to see Franklin, especially since the thoughtful young man brought him Riddlesden's sneaky letter. Going forward, Franklin and Hamilton became good friends and political allies.[8]

Without the promised letters, Franklin had no idea what to do. He was stranded in London, his ambitious business plans in shambles. The Atlantic separated him from home, and he lacked the wherewithal to return. Ralph was no Ralpho: Far from being a faithful sidekick, he took advantage of his friend. Having spent all his money for the passage, Ralph relied on Franklin to support him in London. With nowhere left to turn, Franklin approached Thomas Denham, revealed Keith's role in his predicament, and asked for advice.

Denham offered some insight into Keith's character, confirming the unlikelihood that he had written the letters and telling Franklin that anyone who knew Keith also knew how flaky he was. Denham scoffed at the idea of Keith giving Franklin a letter of credit. A King Midas in reverse, Keith could not give anyone letters of credit because he had no credit to give.

Aware that skilled printers were hard to come by, Denham urged Franklin to seek a position with a London printing house, which would provide invaluable experience he could apply on returning to Philadelphia. Without a letter of credit, Franklin could not raise sufficient capital to buy the equipment he needed. Denham gave him a new way to view his predicament: Knowledge could become a kind of capital. What Franklin learned while working as a printer in London would provide further know-how to help him establish a successful printshop. Perhaps, Denham intimated, Franklin could rise in the world without the help of Governor Keith.

Following Denham's advice, Franklin headed for Bartholomew Close, a part of London just north of St. Paul's, where several printers worked. Keimer had served as a journeyman for Thomas Ilive on Aldersgate Street, so perhaps he told Franklin about this neighborhood. Ilive died soon after he reached London, but Franklin did befriend his widow Jane Ilive, who continued the family printing business and whose bold freethinking he admired.[9]

Besides looking for work, Franklin and Ralph had to find somewhere to live. In their search for lodgings, they turned onto Little Britain, a narrow lane just off Aldersgate hard by St. Botolph's Church. Little Britain had a reputation as a good place where young literary men could afford to live. The experience of Thomas Gordon resembles Franklin's situation. Though best known for his collaborative work with John Trenchard, Gordon was also a classical scholar, essayist, and pamphleteer. Early in his career, he took a room above a printshop in Little Britain. Having to climb three flights up a back staircase to reach his room, Gordon longed for the day he could afford to leave the neighborhood.[10]

Known in the previous century as the best place to buy secondhand books in London—the "ancient mart of bibliopolists," one bookman called it—Little Britain was going downhill. When Washington Irving visited the following century, all the bookshops were gone, but Franklin discovered several booksellers, many specializing in used and rare books. Traveling through London, John Macky found other shopping districts better for histories, law books, and French books, but Little Britain was the best place to get old books in ancient languages. Jonathan Swift quipped, "Pox on the modern phrase Great Britain, which is only to distinguish it from Little Britain, where old cloaths and old books are to be bought and sold." Swift's words sound condescending, but he, too, shopped for books in Little Britain.[11]

Logan, who had visited London the previous year, also came to Little Britain. Newton's, one of its most renowned shops, had a reputation for scarce and uncommon books. Here, Logan found a seventeenth-century history of the Arabian peninsula in Arabic. The book appealed to him, but it was too pricey. Logan found better bargains down the street at Francis Jackson's shop, where he got some good deals on several erudite works, including Ambrogio Calepino's polyglot dictionary: eleven languages for only 4 shillings! Two decades later, Logan was still boasting about the good deals he got at Jackson's.[12]

Little Britain presented a charming sight to Franklin's eyes. As he walked down the narrow street, signboards stretched above his head from either side, almost meeting in the middle. (A danger to pedestrians, overhead signage would soon be outlawed.) The Rose and Crown usually indicated a tavern, but in Little Britain, Jackson used the Rose and Crown for his bookshop. John and Benjamin Sprint, having inherited their father's bookshop, kept it going at the sign of the Blue Bell. The Rising Sun identified the shop of Thomas Ballard, the first of an eminent line of London booksellers. His kinsman Samuel Ballard's shop could have reminded Franklin of home; it was located at the sign of the Blue Ball. Samuel's son Edward would keep the Blue Ball rolling long after the other booksellers abandoned Little Britain for Paternoster Row. Three Golden Fleurs-de-Lis, the Golden Ring, the Green Dragon, the King's Arms: All marked other Little Britain bookshops.

The Sign of the Green Dragon typically indicated a public house, but John Wilcox's use of the Green Dragon perfectly suited his bookshop. It presented an image of the dragon the Red Cross Knight battles in Edmund Spenser's *Faerie Queene*. Who can forget the dragon's deep, devouring jaws that resemble the grizzly mouth of hell or its iron teeth thick with raw gobbets of human flesh? Wilcox's sign invites customers to enter his shop and, in so doing, to enter the dragon's maw, that is, the world of imagination his books represented. No wonder the Green Dragon became Franklin's favorite bookshop in Little Britain.

For the time being, the Golden Fan, the retail establishment next door to the Green Dragon, meant more to Franklin and Ralph. Happily, this fan shop had affordable rooms to let. Though grateful to its proprietor for putting a roof over their heads, Franklin hesitated to mention the Golden Fan in his autobiography. Describing their early days in London, he wrote a simple declarative sentence about where they lived before adding two prepositional phrases to pinpoint the spot: "at a fan shop in Little Britain."[13]

Franklin's textual revisions confirm his literary craftsmanship. After inserting these two phrases, he reconsidered their symbolic resonance. As a mecca for book lovers, Little Britain added much to his story, reinforcing the personal significance of books and reading. Franklin questioned the symbolism of the phrase "fan shop." Nathaniel Gardner had shown how frivolous fans could be when he ridiculed young Boston women who brought them to church. They would smile and play with their fans, which Gardner called "an indication of criminal carelessness, and unthoughtfulness of the awful presence they are in."[14] Franklin decided the phrase "fan shop" sounded too feminine or too frivolous. He deleted it.

Once Franklin and Ralph put a roof over their heads, they could go next door and browse the old books inside the Green Dragon. This bookshop appealed to Franklin more than the neighboring ones because of its huge inventory and amiable proprietor. Franklin was one of several young men

with literary ambitions who sought John Wilcox's friendship and advice.
Wilcox's interaction with other young literary men approximates his contact
with Franklin.

That same decade, Wilcox befriended Anthony Purver, an unemployed
Quaker schoolmaster who had come to London from Hampshire. Wilcox
agreed to publish Purver's verse broadside, *Youth's Delight*. Wilcox's confidence
in him was not misplaced. Purver would establish his literary reputation with a
new translation of the Holy Scriptures, which became known as the *Quaker's
Bible*. Franklin would add a copy of Purver's translation to his personal library.[15]

Purver simplified the language of the English Bible. Take Psalm 22, for
example. In the King James Version, the 14th verse laments: "I am poured out
like water, and all my bones are out of joint: my heart is like wax; it is melted
in the midst of my bowels." Purver translated this verse differently: "I am
poured out like water, and all my bones come apart, my heart is like wax,
being melted in my inside." The phrase "out of joint" makes sense, but Hamlet's
figurative usage—"The time is out of joint"—had made its literal meaning
obsolete. Purver found a more natural expression instead. Franklin's acquisition of the *Quaker's Bible* reflects his interest in the history of English usage.[16]

Samuel Johnson also met Wilcox when he was starting out and, with the
brashness of youth, declared he would make a living as a writer. Wilcox sardonically suggested an alternate line of work: "You had better buy a porter's
knot." For a stout young man like Johnson, he implied, working as a market
porter offered surer success than writing books.[17] Like Purver and Johnson,
Franklin became good friends with Wilcox, who did what he could to aid the
young American.

Since Wilcox specialized in auctioning large private libraries, his shop was
filled with secondhand books. Wilcox occasionally published sale catalogues,
only one of which survives from before Franklin first visited the Green
Dragon, an auction catalogue Wilcox had co-published before relocating his
business to Little Britain. Issued in 1709, the catalogue is much too early to
illuminate Franklin's reading. The books Wilcox published do suggest some
general interests: field sports, such as hunting and falconry; medicine, both
diagnosis and treatment; moral philosophy; natural religion; and poetry.[18]

Seeing so many books in one place, Franklin proposed an innovative
scheme: He asked to borrow individual volumes for a small fee. To encourage
the young man's literary pursuits, Wilcox agreed. With minimal expense,
Franklin indulged his love of reading and continued the rigorous self-
education he had begun in Boston. Living in London, he borrowed numerous
books from the Green Dragon. Beyond the books, Wilcox also gave Franklin

a personal model of behavior. Later in his life, Franklin would similarly encourage the bright young men who entered his orbit.

Less than a week after reaching London, Franklin found work as a compositor for Samuel Palmer, a master printer located in the converted Lady Chapel of the Church of Saint Bartholomew-the-Great in East Smithfield, a few blocks from the Golden Fan. His printing room was impressive: 65 feet long by 27 feet wide. As a former chapel, it had a high ceiling with large windows that admitted great shafts of light.[19]

The warmth of Palmer's fireplace often allured Franklin, but he did not dawdle there unnecessarily. He had a work-related reason that brought him mothlike to the flame. After being used, the compositor's type would be washed and replaced in the case. The case of wet type would then be carried to the fireplace, set down nearby, and tilted toward the fire to dry. Franklin had not encountered this practice in Boston or Philadelphia, but he quite liked it. He especially enjoyed handling the warm type while composing. Sometimes Franklin would warm his dry type beside the fire, but he quit doing so after an old timer warned him he was in danger of the "dangles," a palsy symptomatic of lead poisoning. Tilted toward the fire, Franklin's case of type, in short, formed the angle before the dangles.[20]

When Franklin arrived, Palmer was at the peak of his career, publishing a series of bold and groundbreaking books that exemplified his high aesthetic standards and serving as an elected official of the Stationers' Company. Some books Palmer printed were beyond the abilities of most London printers. He was unafraid to tackle projects in other languages and, indeed, other orthographies: Greek, Hebrew, Arabic. In 1721, Palmer had begun printing an Arabic translation of the Psalter for the Society for Promoting Christian Knowledge (SPCK). Founded by the Reverend Doctor Thomas Bray, the SPCK propagated Christianity by establishing libraries and charity schools in England and abroad. Palmer's psalter was intended for distribution to Arabic-speaking Christians in Lebanon. He had finished it before Franklin arrived but printed 500 extra copies to sell. Consequently, Franklin had the chance to take a long look at this beautiful language.[21]

Palmer knew printing from the perspective of a historian as well as a practitioner. While Franklin worked for him, Palmer was writing a history of printing, which George Psalmanazar would complete after Palmer's death. It appeared as *A General History of Printing*. Weighted toward the early days of printing, Palmer's history is an introduction to incunables. After Franklin and his friends established the Library Company of Philadelphia the following decade, they would add a copy to its collection.[22]

Whereas Franklin quickly found a job, Ralph had trouble obtaining employment. He stuck close to his friend, confident Franklin would not let him starve. Ralph had no marketable skills. His plan to establish an importing business was a ruse. Once in London, Ralph disclosed his real reason for leaving Philadelphia: he had abandoned his young American wife and their newborn daughter Mary. Franklin and Ralph became friends because both loved to read. For Franklin, the love of literature could mask a multitude of sins. Though shocked at Ralph's selfish and inconsiderate decision, he remained his friend.

Ralph's job search was hopelessly unrealistic. Fancying himself an actor, he sought work on the stage. He did have a natural eloquence: Franklin had never known a "prettier talker."[23] Ralph spoke with Robert Wilks, the manager of Drury Lane Theatre and one of its busiest actors. All his pretty talking could not help him become an actor. Wilks was blunt. He told Ralph it would be impossible for him to succeed on the London stage.

Ralph next went to see James Roberts, a printer and bookseller near the Oxford Arms, a tavern in Warwick Lane. He offered to write an essayistic weekly paper like *The Spectator*. Since Ralph had no more experience as a journalist than he had as an actor, Roberts said no. Next, Ralph headed toward Grub Street, unsuccessfully seeking work as a hack writer. He remained unemployed and continued sponging off his kind-hearted friend. With plenty of free time, Ralph explored the city, leaving valuable descriptions of London, which help reconstruct the look and feel of the city when Franklin lived there.

What little pocket change Franklin had after paying for shelter and sustenance, Ralph helped him spend at the theater. For the 1724–1725 season, Drury Lane and Lincoln's Inn Fields monopolized the performance of English plays. The Royal Academy of Music presented Italian opera at King's Theatre, and Haymarket Theatre staged some French plays, including Moliere's *Tartuffe*.[24]

Franklin attended enough plays starring Robert Wilks and Colley Cibber to get a good sense of their contrasting styles of performance.[25] Whereas Wilks had a more natural acting style, Cibber's was more affected. They complemented one another on the stage and performed together to great acclaim. Franklin's attention to Wilks and Cibber provides a vital clue to identify the possible performances he saw.

The plays produced that season ranged from the standards of Renaissance drama to current comedies. Franklin had the opportunity to see a variety of Shakespeare plays: comedies, histories, and tragedies. Shakespeare would remain a presence in Franklin's life and writings. Shakespearean quotations would pepper his periodicals, and references to the plays, especially *Othello*, would surface in his correspondence. Franklin would stock multivolume editions of Shakespeare's works in his bookshop and obtain a new edition for his personal library, which he would share with his first grandson. Franklin's surviving copy of Shakespeare, which has just recently come to light, reflects his enduring appreciation.[26]

John Dryden may have been Franklin's favorite playwright after Shakespeare. Lincoln's Inn Fields staged *The Prophetess*, a new production with an original score and fresh scenery and costumes, and Drury Lane staged *The Spanish Friar*, a tragicomedy with Wilks in the role of the duplicitous Lorenzo. Once William Congreve published his six-volume edition of *The Dramatick Works of John Dryden* the following decade, Ralph acquired a set for his personal library. When Ralph's books were sold after his death, Franklin attended the auction and purchased his old friend's copy of Dryden. Reading Dryden's plays from the comfort of home in the coming years, Franklin could relive the times he and Ralph spent together attending the London stage.[27]

William Congreve wrote the greatest comedies of the Restoration stage. Four of his plays were performed in London during the 1724–25 season. At Lincoln's Inn Fields, Franklin could have seen *The Old Batchelor* and *The Double Dealer*. *The Old Batchelor* displays Congreve's talent for what Samuel Johnson called "quick and sparkling" dialogue. *The Double Dealer* is a dark comedy whose action unfolds in real time. At Drury Lane, Franklin could have seen *The Mourning Bride*. Congreve's only tragedy, *The Mourning Bride* is best known for its opening line: "Music has charms to soothe a savage breast" or "savage beast," as it is often misquoted. Drury Lane also produced *The Way of the World*, a comic masterpiece despite its convoluted plot. Phillips Russell has argued that Franklin thoroughly enjoyed Congreve's comedies while in London. Once he opened his Philadelphia bookstore, Franklin would stock the three-volume edition of Congreve's *Works*.[28]

Ben Jonson's seventeenth-century comedies delighted eighteenth-century audiences. During the 1724–25 season, *Volpone* played at Drury Lane, *Everyman in His Humour* at Lincoln's Inn Fields.[29] Franklin reveals his knowledge and appreciation of Jonson's writings in the conduct book he would write two decades later, *Reflections on Courtship and Marriage*: "We should make it our mutual study to render ourselves agreeable and amiable by all the *innocent arts* of invention, and every laudable stratagem of conduct: remembering old *Ben. Johnson*'s, '*That love comes by chance, but is kept by art*.' Which should be wrote with indelible characters on the memory of every married person."[30]

Franklin's quotation is slightly paraphrased from Jonson's love elegy, "To Make the Doubt Clear, That No Woman's True," which compares falling in love with catching a disease before concluding:

> But, being got, it is a treasure, sweet,
> Which to defend, is harder than to get;
> And ought not be prophan'd, on either part;
> For though 'tis got by chance, 'tis kept by art.

Franklin may have encountered this poem in a collection of Jonson's work or in one of several anthologies that reprinted it.[31]

Both a comedy and tragedy by Joseph Addison ran concurrently during the 1724–25 season: *The Drummer: or, The Haunted House* at Lincoln's Inn Fields and *Cato* at Drury Lane. For his comedy, Addison made use of a local legend, a ghost story known as "The Drummer of Tedworth." Franklin would reuse Addison's *Drummer* a half-dozen years later in "Letter of the Drum," a newspaper essay satirizing superstition and slyly attacking religious belief. The slapstick nature of "The Letter of the Drum" shows that Franklin had learned to use aspects of London stage comedy in his writings.[32]

One of Franklin's favorite plays, *Cato* was a favorite of many other Founding Fathers as well. Cato's resistance to Julius Caesar's tyranny became an object lesson for the American Revolutionaries in their stand against British tyranny. Franklin's references to *Cato* suggest that he drew a somewhat different lesson from the other Founding Fathers. Three years later, he would use a four-line excerpt from the tragedy as the epigraph for "Articles of Belief and Acts of Religion":

> Here will I hold—If there is a pow'r above us
> (And that there is, all Nature cries aloud,
> Thro' all her works), He must delight in virtue
> And that which he delights in must be happy.[33]

These lines come from the soliloquy that opens act 5. Cato utters them as he debates what he must do in the face of Julius Caesar's seemingly unstoppable power. Unable to uphold his principles of liberty, Cato knows he must follow the Roman code of honor and throw himself upon his sword, but he nonetheless hesitates. He conveys these lines as he contemplates what his virtuous life means in the eyes of God. Cato's words helped Franklin understand the true meaning of religious devotion and reinforced what he read about practical divinity. Devotion to God must involve benevolence toward fellow human beings.

The name "Cato" shows up elsewhere in Franklin's writings, which he continued to associate with admirable behavior. In "Busy-Body 3," Franklin presents a character sketch of a virtuous man named "Cato." His whiskers unshaven and his coat "old and thread-bare," Cato is nonetheless the most respected man in town due to his virtue: "Integrity renders him calm and undaunted in the presence of the most great and powerful, and upon the most extraordinary occasions." Franklin punctuated his piece with an excerpt from Nicholas Rowe's *Fair Penitent*, another play he could have seen performed on the London stage in 1725. His quotation, which offers a definition of bravery, implies that virtue, like bravery, shines brightly, even in the light of day.[34]

Though Franklin and Ralph enjoyed the stage, they spent many evenings at the Golden Fan, which had charms of its own. Two single women also let rooms there. Mrs. T was a milliner, and her roommate was a mantua-maker. Streamlining their story for the autobiography, Franklin would combine the two women into one character and thus confuse readers for centuries.[35]

Besides mantuas—loose gowns worn by eighteenth-century women— mantua-makers also made nightgowns, petticoats, and *robes de chambres*. Milliners made aprons, caps, handkerchiefs, neckties, ruffles, smocks, and "as many etceteras as would reach from Charing Cross to the Royal Exchange." Though the articles of clothing that mantua-makers produced were more luxurious, milliners formed the pinnacle of the clothing pyramid. Often mantua-makers did not have their own shops but did piecemeal work for milliners. Most likely, her roommate worked for Mrs. T, who did have her own shop in the Cloisters. The prefix "Mrs." does not refer to her marital status; it signals her status as a shop owner. She was not a widow, as many have assumed.[36]

For some people, the Cloisters was a dangerous place. Defoe has Colonel Jack steal a big bag of money from a feeble country gentleman standing by Cloister Gate. Mrs. T faced a different kind of danger. At the Golden Fan, Ralph, no doubt taking advantage of Franklin's book-borrowing agreement with Wilcox, read plays to Mrs. T in the evenings. Ralph's pretty talk had been unable to secure him any acting roles, but it was effective in another way. As Ralph chatted up Mrs. T, the two grew close. The results were predictable. Before long Mrs. T found out that she was pregnant with Ralph's child: another fact Franklin obscured as he revised his autobiography. When he initially mentioned the baby, Franklin wrote, "his child," but he later revised the text to read "her child."[37]

Ralph led to Mrs. T's ruin. The couple left Little Britain for other lodgings. Since Mrs. T was an enterprising businesswoman, Ralph thought they could live on the proceeds of her shop while he wrote poetry. As a young, unwed mother trying to run her own business, she had a tough go. Because of Ralph, Mrs. T, in Franklin's words, "lost her friends and business." This is one phrase Franklin did not temper in revision. Losing her shop, Mrs. T consequently lost whatever investment her family had made in it. She lowered her ambitions and sought piecemeal work as a mantua-maker.[38]

When Ralph moved away, he left owing Franklin a sizable amount of money. On the bright side, Ralph's departure from the Golden Fan did save Franklin from supporting him any further. For all Ralph's personal failings—his selfishness, his irresponsibility, the ease with which he took advantage of others—Franklin maintained a soft spot in his heart for him. Ralph was an intellectual, a lover of literature, and life often treats such types hard, especially those who, unlike Franklin, lack a practical side. Ralph had the dreamer's disease, so he was inevitably surprised whenever his dreams failed to come true. When he and Mrs. T left the Golden Fan, Franklin had no idea what would happen to them.

Franklin could not be rid of Ralph so easily. In a half-hearted attempt to support Mrs. T and their child, Ralph left London for Berkshire, a village where he found employment as a schoolmaster. While there, Ralph turned epic poet. Perhaps no one has described Ralph's situation better than John Dos Passos, who, having put his best novels behind him, turned his attention to history. Chronicling Franklin's first time in London, Dos Passos said Ralph wanted to climb into "preferment and place on an endless ladder of heroic couplets."[39] Seeking Franklin's advice, Ralph started sending him installments of a long manuscript poem he was writing. Since Franklin enjoyed reading poetry, he was not necessarily against Ralph sending him installments of the poem—except that he sent them postage due. Franklin responded reluctantly; he thought the idea of becoming an epic poet foolhardy.

In 1725, Franklin was reading *The Universal Passion*, Edward Young's series of numbered satires about ambition and the quest for fame. Once complete, Young would gather the individual satires and republish them under the title, *Love of Fame*. Ambitious men often read *Love of Fame*. Ezra Stiles, whose ambition would carry him to the Yale presidency, obtained a copy when he was single and 26. At the same time he bought *Love of Fame*, this future college president acquired another book reflecting his youthful desire: *Onania: or, The Heinous Sin of Self-Pollution, and All Its Frightful Consequences (in Both Sexes) Considered*.[40]

Franklin excerpted a passage from *Love of Fame* and sent it to Ralph to try and dissuade him from a poetical career. Franklin does not say which satire he excerpted. Years later, he would quote *Satire I* in response to a friend who said something about the love of praise. Franklin replied, "What you mention concerning the love of praise is indeed very true; it 'reigns more or less in every heart.'"[41] The way Franklin described what he sent Ralph makes it sound like a passage toward the end of *Satire II*. Using the second person, the poet speaks to himself, questioning his desire for fame and his use of poetry to achieve it:

> Thou too art wounded with the common dart,
> And love of fame lyes throbbing at thy heart;
> And what wise means to gain it hast thou chose?
> Know, fame, and fortune both are made of prose.

Ralph ignored Franklin's implicit admonition and kept writing poetry until Alexander Pope demolished him in *The Dunciad*, after which Ralph did indeed switch to prose.[42]

Ralph had promised to send part of his teacher's salary back to Mrs. T. He could not afford to support her, so she remained in dire financial distress. Feeling sorry for her, Franklin visited Mrs. T several times and grew quite fond of her. Aroused in her presence, Franklin "attempt'd familiarities": big mistake. After repulsing Franklin's advances, she informed Ralph what had happened. Franklin's behavior allowed Ralph a convenient indignation, providing a perfect excuse to avoid repaying the money he owed him.[43]

The story of Franklin's first time in London resembles a Congreve comedy. The cast of characters includes a scheming governor who cannot keep his promises; an international swindler, who is in league with the governor in an effort to overthrow a powerful attorney; and a best friend whose intellectual abilities and lofty ambitions have no correlation to his low moral conduct, who abandons a wife and child only to seduce another woman and father another child, both of whom he fails to support. In this drama of moral ambiguity, Franklin himself plays a part. Even as he helps the lover of his friend from financial hardship, he attempts to take advantage of her. Like so many Americans after him, Benjamin Franklin lost his innocence abroad. In London, he learned much about printing and much about literature, but he also learned, morally speaking, that the world was a much more complicated place than it had seemed on the other side of the Atlantic.

8

What Franklin Read in London

NO ONE KNOWS what books Franklin borrowed from the Green Dragon, but we do know what books Palmer printed during Franklin's time at his shop. The title pages of eighteenth-century books do not always name their printers. Palmer printed many books or parts of books in which his name does not appear. Hazel Wilkinson, a British researcher, has examined almost every London imprint from 1725, seeking distinctive typographical ornaments that can be traced to Palmer's printing house during Franklin's employment, and compiled a checklist of titles issued by Palmer that Franklin could have set in type, proofread, or read soon after they were printed. Her research expands the list of possible books Franklin read and gives a sense of his robust intellectual life during his first London sojourn.[1]

Palmer printed a variety of books Franklin could have found useful, entertaining, or both—ideally both. The third edition of Anthony Blackwall's *Introduction to the Classics*, for example, could have filled some gaps in his classical education. Blackwall designed the book for current students as well as gentlemen who had finished school but now wished to read more on their own. "Gentlemen" is the operative word identifying Blackwall's intended audience. But there is no reason why a tradesman could not read Blackwall's *Classics*. When Scottish educator William Mavor reissued it, he recommended Blackwell's *Classics* to readers without the advantages of a learned education.[2]

Blackwall's *Classics* let Franklin brush up his knowledge of ancient literature. It includes many thumbnail appreciations of prominent Greek and Roman authors. His treatment of Horace is representative. Blackwall enjoyed Horace's characteristic nonchalance, the unforced ease that runs through his work. Horace's style presented an ideal for Augustan satirists to follow. In terms of satirical tone, no Latin author was more important to Franklin. To read Horace during spare moments, he obtained a slim, small-format edition of his verse. Less than 5 inches tall, the edition let Franklin put his Horace in his pocket.[3]

In many cases, Blackwall confirmed what Franklin had already discovered. His positive comments about *Memorable Things of Socrates*, for example, reinforced Franklin's respect for Xenophon. Blackwall praised his cleverness, simplicity, and use of language. He also paid tribute to Xenophon's teacher. Socrates argued with the reason of a philosopher, spoke with the authority of a leader, and counseled with the kindness of a friend.[4]

The second part of Blackwall's *Classics* provides specific directions to help writers improve their style. Blackwall reformed some inadequacies of English education. To demonstrate how to write well, he presented figures of speech that could lend strength and grace to the English language. Textbook publisher Robert Dodsley recognized the usefulness of Blackwall's *Classics*. He retitled its second part "Rhetoric and Poetry" and reprinted it in *The Preceptor*, an English textbook that could be found throughout British North America. In 1774, Franklin would obtain a copy of Dodsley's *Preceptor* for his first grandson.[5]

Christopher Pitt's English translation of Marco Girolamo Vida's *Art of Poetry* is another book Palmer printed while Franklin worked for him. A sixteenth-century neo-Latin poet and theorist, Vida furthered the aesthetic paradigm Horace had formulated, which would hold throughout Europe over the next two centuries: to delight and instruct. Vida's *Art of Poetry* is essential reading for everyone interested in the critical history of literature. Alexander Pope celebrated him in *An Essay on Criticism*: "Immortal Vida! on whose honour'd brow / The poet's bays and critick's ivy grow." Samuel Johnson found that in terms of elegance, imagery, and prosody, Pitt's verse translation was faithful to Vida's original.[6]

Like Blackwall's *Classics*, Vida's *Art of Poetry* could have advanced Franklin's literary knowledge and reinforced his critical judgment. Vida also understood the importance of a *copia verborum*:

> But e'er with sails unfurl'd you fly away,
> And cleave the bosom of the boundless sea;
> A fund of words and images prepare,
> And lay the bright materials up with care,
> Which at due time, occasion may produce,
> All rang'd in order for the poet's use.[7]

Inspired by the success of his Vida translation, Pitt would translate Virgil's *Aeneid*. Johnson was less enthusiastic about Pitt's Virgil, preferring Dryden's translation, even with its drawbacks. "Dryden's faults are forgotten in the hurry of delight," Johnson observed. "Pitt's beauties are neglected in the langour of a cold and listless perusal." He concluded, "Pitt pleases the critics, and Dryden the people." Franklin disagreed. Seeing popular appeal in Pitt's *Aeneid*, he would excerpt it for *Poor Richard's Almanack*.[8]

Franklin's time in London coincided with rising interest in Spanish America. Not only were English readers curious about the conquistadors, they also yearned to know about the anthropology and natural history of the people and lands the Spanish conquered. Palmer started printing Antonio de Herrera's *General History of the Vast Continent and Islands of America* in an English translation prepared by Captain John Stevens, the leading Spanish translator of the day. Palmer printed the first volume of Stevens's translation in individual parts, some of which Franklin may have set in type. Once finished, the volume stood in need of company: The translation would swell to six volumes.[9]

Herrera's *History of America*, as Franklin called it, introduced readers to early Spanish colonization. King Philip II of Spain had appointed Herrera the first historiographer of the West Indies and thus given him unprecedented access to state papers and other authentic sources. Scottish historian William Robertson applauded the fullness and accuracy of Herrera's history as well as his impartiality and candor. Robertson did find fault with Herrera's perplexing organization, which forced readers to make sense of its disconnected episodes. Franklin may not have read all six volumes in London, but the Library Company of Philadelphia would acquire the whole set.[10]

No work Palmer printed in 1725 was more important to the development of Franklin's moral philosophy than Pierre Daniel Huet's *Philosophical Treatise Concerning the Weakness of Human Understanding*. Born in 1630 and trained as a classical scholar, Huet achieved an extraordinary level of classical, historical, scientific, and philosophical erudition and became bishop of Avranches. His friend Leibniz considered Huet the most learned man of their era. Bishop Huet had a reputation for devoting his spare time to study. According to one traditional story, a member of his diocese, who had unsuccessfully tried to see Huet several times, hoped the next bishop would finish his studies before being ordained.[11]

The bishop's literary output was prolific. As assistant tutor to the Dauphin, Huet coedited the renowned Delphin Classics. He wrote much else as well. Franklin would add to his library the French edition of Huet's *History of the Commerce and Navigation of the Ancients*. Huet spent his final days at the Jesuits' House in the Rue Saint Antoine in Paris, dying in 1721. *Philosophical Treatise Concerning the Weakness of Human Understanding*—his most famous book—appeared posthumously. The work was a sensation: It revealed that a leading French bishop advocated Pyrrhonism, a form of ancient Greek skepticism that encouraged the suspension of judgment in all theoretical matters. William Douglass summarized the Pyrrhonists best: "They doubted of every thing."[12]

Huet reinforced and extended the skepticism Franklin had learned reading Collins and Shaftesbury. He denied he was a skeptic, but even Huet's denial is skeptical: "If any man ask me what I am, since I will be neither *academick* nor *sceptick*, nor *eclectick*, nor of any other sect; I answer, that I am of my own opinion, that is to say, free, neither submitting my mind to any authority, nor approving of any thing but what seems to me to come nearest the truth."[13]

Franklin's skepticism often surfaces in his writing. In "The Prodigious Growth of Infidels," a facetious essay he wrote the following decade under the pen name "Marcus," he criticizes contemporary skeptics, but Marcus is so obtuse and his argument so absurd that the article affirms the value of skepticism and reveals how foolish the writers who critiqued it could be. Through the voice of Marcus, Franklin mocked those who lacked the reasoning power of the people they attacked.[14]

Palmer also printed a small, but important section of *The Rule of Conscience*, an abridgement of Jeremy Taylor's *Ductor dubitantium*. In this weighty tome of moral theology, Taylor argues that conscience can reconcile natural law with Christ's teaching. Palmer printed the seventh chapter of the second volume, "Of the Interpretation, Diminution and Abrogation of Human Laws." The chapter's first rule says: "When the letter of a law is burthernsome and unjust, the intent and charity of the law does only bind the conscience." Taylor's rule anticipates the political discourse of the Revolutionary era. Facing burdensome and unjust laws, Franklin and his fellow patriots would question their obligation to obey them. Taylor's chapter on conscience and injustice is a neglected source in the intellectual background of the American Revolution—though perhaps it should not be. John Adams had a copy of the folio edition of *Ductor dubitantium* in his library.[15]

The printing house's output during Franklin's time with Palmer included several religious books. Franklin had put polemic divinity behind him; his Huet-inspired skepticism did nothing to encourage him to resume it. Still, the religious books Palmer published in 1725 did give Franklin some perspective on their demand. One of Palmer's imprints sounded familiar, John Shower's *Serious Reflections on Time and Eternity*, the work Matthew Adams had excerpted for *The New-England Courant*. This, the sixth edition of Shower's treatise, reinforced the popular fascination with life after death. Franklin never gave Shower's religious beliefs much thought, but he did recognize the book's appeal. Once he began retailing books in Philadelphia, Franklin would keep Shower in stock.[16]

Two works Palmer printed confirm that attacks on the freethinking Anthony Collins had become something of a cottage industry. Anglican and dissenting ministers alike sought to refute Collins's dangerous ideas, seeing him as a formidable threat to Christianity. Franklin could have helped print two different books that attacked Collins's freethinking.[17]

William Wollaston's *Religion of Nature Delineated*, the most renowned religious book Palmer printed during Franklin's tenure, is one of many treatises of moral philosophy the eighteenth century embraced but the nineteenth abjured. Franklin recognized its faults while setting the book in type. Of Wollaston, he says, "Some of his reasoning not appearing to me well-founded, I wrote a little metaphysical piece, in which I made remarks on them."[18]

The little metaphysical piece is *A Dissertation on Liberty and Necessity, Pleasure and Pain*. Franklin's discussion of liberty and necessity—free will and determinism—is quite sophisticated. On the surface, it is a dryasdust treatise of moral philosophy. Lurking beneath is a vicious satire. Franklin's *Dissertation* also reflects his skepticism. He uses logic to show the ultimate absurdity of the principles underlying the belief in God. Only by denying our common sense can we accept God's existence.[19]

Setting forth his doctrine of philosophical necessity, Franklin presented a series of propositions that mock all systems of morality. Whereas eighteenth-century intellectuals who questioned some tenets of Christianity took refuge in Deism, Franklin exposed its flaws as well. In the history of American literature, no one would approach the skepticism of Franklin's *Dissertation* until Mark Twain penned a set of bleak statements about religion during the 1880s.[20]

Another book printed at Palmer's during Franklin's time there touches on many of the same issues as Franklin's *Dissertation*: John Reynolds's *View of Death; or, The Soul's Departure from the World: A Philosophical Poem*. Like Richard Blackmore, Reynolds is a physico-theological poet. A Presbyterian minister, he had originally published this book-length poem under the title *Death's Vision*. Upon its appearance in 1709, *Death's Vision* became the first consciously scientific long poem in the English language. In his preface, Reynolds identifies science as a proper subject for "eminent and lofty poems." In addition, Reynolds included numerous notes citing the day's most prominent scientific literature.[21]

The View of Death, as Reynolds retitled his poem for the 1725 edition, contains many additional notes, which cite scientific books published since 1709.

As an author of a physico-theological poem, Reynolds belongs to the eighteenth century, but the verse form he chose was a throwback to the seventeenth. Eschewing heroic couplets, Reynolds wrote *The View of Death* using the irregular lines lengths and elaborate figures of speech characteristic of the metaphysical poets. His footnotes reveal his knowledge of and fascination with the latest scientific developments, incorporating recent work in astronomy, microscopy, and natural theology.

Assuming that departed spirits have a fuller perspective on the world, the speaker of *The View of Death* summons a ghost to tell him what happens after death and let him know what realms of knowledge will be available to him then. The ghost agrees, and, together, they set off on a cosmic voyage. Besides showing the speaker of the poem how the wisdom of God manifests itself in the celestial harmony, their conversation touches on prevailing theories about the soul's properties, which Franklin also considers in his *Dissertation*.

Both Reynolds and Franklin ponder the implications of the soul's immortality. Franklin contends that after death the soul, though immaterial, is still capable of thought, echoing an observation Reynolds makes in a note: " 'Tis evident, the soul has its rational operations, in discourse, reflexion, abstraction, as well as strange flights of fancy, when it is not assisted by the sensory instruments."[22] Franklin's *Dissertation* also has a similar tone as Reynold's *View of Death*. Though serious treatments of their subject, both works occasionally shade into sarcasm.

The second half of Franklin's *Dissertation*, which defines the relationship between pleasure and pain, continues his attack on any and all belief systems. Suggesting that pain is humankind's sole motivating factor, Franklin portrayed God as a sadist who enjoys watching us writhe in agony. During every person's life, pain and pleasure equal out, not necessarily in terms of duration, but in absolute terms. To aid his explanation, Franklin used a scientific analogy. Ten thousand cubic feet of gas could be compressed to 1 cubic inch; a single moment of pleasure could outweigh an age of pain.[23]

This analogy echoes Boyle's law, which holds that the volume and pressure of a gas are inversely related. Franklin had great respect for the Reverend Robert Boyle's scientific research but found his devotional practice suspect. In *Occasional Reflections on Several Subjects*, Boyle says that man could appreciate Creation by meditating on natural and sometimes even on manmade objects. In other words, the physical world provided analogies that could reinforce religious belief. Franklin would parody Boyle's devotional practice in "Meditation on a Quart Mugg."[24] *A Dissertation on Liberty and Necessity* foreshadows that parody. Franklin suggests the impossibility of using scientific analogies to understand moral conduct. If such analogies are valid, then man is nothing more than machine, something totally subject to the physical laws of the universe.

Franklin's time with Palmer gave him the opportunity to read Boyle. Palmer printed the first volume of Boyle's *Philosophical Works*. Editor Peter Shaw called the edition an abridgement, but this collection of Boyle's scientific work fills three thick quartos. Only the first was printed at Palmer's, but that volume contained much to interest Franklin. After a general discussion about the usefulness of experimental philosophy, it presents the method and results of numerous scientific experiments. Besides Boyle's work on air pressure, it offers a brief discussion of electricity, which could have introduced Franklin to the subject. Boyle used his air pump to experiment with electricity, discovering that electrical attraction can operate in a vacuum. Franklin did not acquire Shaw's abridgement in London, but after a second edition came out the following decade, he would add it to his library and use it in his research.[25]

Besides its scientific analogy, Franklin's *Dissertation* contains another feature that reflects his London reading: a title-page epigraph from Dryden:

> Whatever is, is in its causes just
> Since all things are by fate; but purblind man
> Sees but a part o' th' chain, the nearest link,
> His eyes not carrying to the equal beam
> That poises all above.

These words reflect an optimistic view of the world, one suggesting that, as Pope would put it more succinctly in *An Essay on Man*, "Whatever is, is right." Quoting the Dryden passage from memory years later, Franklin would accidentally substitute Pope's line for the first line of the Dryden excerpt.[26]

Essentially, Dryden was saying that even though we cannot perceive all the links in the chain, we can accept the premise that they extend to God. The quotation does not exactly pertain to the ideas Franklin expresses in the pamphlet. Instead, his title-page epigraph adds irony: Franklin's text satirizes the jejune optimism these lines articulate. Franklin's editors have identified his source as *Oedipus*, the adaptation of the Sophocles tragedy by John Dryden and Nathaniel Lee. Franklin would not add *Oedipus* to his library until after he wrote *A Dissertation on Liberty and Necessity*. Most likely, he took the Dryden quotation from a secondary source.[27]

He could have found his title-page epigraph in one of two possible anthologies, Edward Bysshe's *Art of English Poetry* or the anonymous *Thesaurus dramaticus*. Published two decades earlier, Bysshe's work had gone through several editions since. *Thesaurus dramaticus* first appeared the year before Franklin wrote his *Dissertation*. Both works present selected quotations arranged topically. The quotation from *Oedipus* appears under the same subject in each: "Fate."[28]

Though reading Wollaston's *Religion of Nature Delineated* gave him the idea to write and publish a pamphlet against it, Franklin also had personal and social reasons for writing his *Dissertation* and printing it at his own expense. Deprived of Keith's letters of introduction, Franklin lost the side benefit he had been expecting from them. He had come to Britain hoping to meet some of its leading men of science. Without the letters of introduction, he would find it difficult to enter London's intellectual scene.

Franklin's decision to write *A Dissertation on Liberty and Necessity* was an ingenious solution to compensate for the absent letters. The pamphlet functioned as a letter of introduction, a document helping Franklin display himself as a man of ideas. It was a calling card that demonstrated his creativity and intellect, his ambition and audacity. As the erudite title suggests, he intended the pamphlet for learned readers, that is, those who enjoyed moral philosophy. The first paragraph reinforces his intended audience, asserting that the author had not designed the work for those who would not understand it.[29]

In terms of physical appearance, the pamphlet's title page reveals much. It has a spare quality, partly because Franklin left off his name as well as the names of any printers, publishers, or booksellers. These omissions identify the work as a contribution to the radical press. Aware how dangerous its ideas were, Franklin did not want to put himself or his employer at risk by naming names on the title page. Yet, there is another reason for the elegance of Franklin's title page, a purely aesthetic one. Palmer had a reputation for his title pages, which were models of clarity and balance. The title page of Franklin's *Dissertation on Liberty and Necessity* indicates what he learned from his employer in terms of design and layout. After Franklin established his own printing house in Philadelphia, he would develop a reputation for clean, well-balanced title pages that utilize much white space.

Concluding his treatise, Franklin shifted from the persona of moral philosopher to interject a nugget of traditional wisdom. Admitting that some readers might find his ideas unpalatable, he softened them with an appropriate proverb. Typically, the proverb says, "Every man thinks his own geese, swans." Franklin wrote: "But, (to use a piece of *common* sense) our *geese* are but *geese* tho' we may think 'em swans; and truth will be truth tho' it sometimes prove mortifying and distasteful."[30]

Franklin's conclusion to *Dissertation on Liberty and Necessity* marks a new development in his use of traditional wisdom. Resorting to a proverb, his moral-philosopher persona appears exhausted with his readers. In case you still do not get it, he implies, let me rephrase my argument in simple, down-home terms. On the other hand, Franklin may be abandoning the persona he has sustained throughout the treatise. Bringing his theoretical argument to a close, he seems to outgrow the work even before finishing it. In the coming years, Franklin would continue substituting proverbs for theoretical arguments to convey his moral philosophy.[31]

With his social and intellectual life looking up, Franklin decided to improve his professional position. Though he had learned much from Palmer, he left his shop to take a position with John Watts, whose printing house was located in Wild Court near Lincoln's Inn Fields, about a mile west of Little Britain. James Ralph found Lincoln's Inn Fields one of the neatest squares in town. Some thought it had an unsavory reputation, but Ralph corrected that misconception. He admitted the square was imperfect on one side but thought the defect created beauty, showing off its gardens. No area in London, Ralph said, was cleaner and more beautiful by day or safer and more decorous by night.[32]

Franklin continued living at the Golden Fan after he started working for Watts but eventually moved closer to his new employer. He found lodgings in an Italian neighborhood on Duke Street a few blocks south of Watts's. Coming from Little Britain, he would enter Duke Street through a shadowy archway on the western edge of Lincoln's Inn Fields. A few doors further, on the north side of the street, he found rooms to let at an Italian warehouse. His flat was located two flights up a back staircase.[33]

Like many people who lived in the neighborhood, Franklin's landlady was a Roman Catholic. Though raised a Protestant, she had converted to Catholicism upon her marriage to an Italian. Now a widow, she retained fond memories of her husband, who had known several distinguished Londoners stretching back to the reign of Charles II. She peppered her conversation with numerous anecdotes about these famous people. Her stories reinforced the social and historical value of personal anecdotes. Franklin enjoyed her company, and they often ate together. His autobiography brings the experience alive, even describing their thrifty suppers: half an anchovy each on a slice of bread with butter, washed down with half a pint of ale.[34]

Watts, whose printing house was twice the size of Palmer's, had a reputation for producing some of the era's handsomest books. His partnership with publisher Jacob Tonson, an intimate of the Kit Kat Club, put him in touch with the day's most distinguished authors and editors. Whereas Franklin had worked as a compositor for Palmer, he worked in the press room when he started at Watts's printing house. The choice was his. While working for Palmer, Franklin missed the rigorous physical exercise that came with press-work. Working the press, he would not have read his early Watts imprints as closely as the Palmer ones. But Franklin remained in the press room for just a few weeks. Watts needed him more as a compositor, so Franklin switched to the composing room.[35]

Several of Watts's imprints were new editions of works that Franklin already knew, including *The Guardian* and *The Spectator*. Watts also printed Thomas Tickell's three-volume collection of Addison's *Miscellaneous Works*. Before coming to London, Franklin mainly knew Addison as an essayist. Tickell let him read Addison's poetry, translations, criticism, drama, and anti-quarian studies. Tickell's edition is a testament to the lofty stature Addison held in the eighteenth century.

The edition gave Franklin the chance to read *The Campaign*, Addison's enthusiastic tribute to John Churchill, 1st duke of Marlborough, upon his decisive victory at the Battle of Blenheim during the War of the Spanish Succession. *The Campaign* teems with memorable phrases. As the poet considers the battle in the opening stanza, he sees an "*Iliad* rising out of one campaign." Sending troops to aid the Grand Alliance against the French and Spanish forces, England proves itself to be the "guardian of the continent," Marlborough the army's "god-like leader."[36]

Franklin remembered one particular couplet: "Great souls by instinct to each other turn, / Demand alliance, and in friendship burn." These lines refer to the first meeting between Marlborough and the renowned Austrian commander, Prince Eugene of Savoy. Franklin excerpted this couplet from its context and used it in *Reflections on Courtship and Marriage* to describe the meeting of two lovers destined to wed and spend their lives together. The difference between Franklin's excerpt and Addison's original suggests that Franklin was quoting the lines from memory. Instead of "Great souls," he says, "Great minds."[37]

Addison's *Miscellaneous Works* also contains his most inspired poetic passage, his apostrophe to Liberty in the verse epistle "A Letter from Italy." Appearing with a parallel Italian translation, "A Letter from Italy" let Franklin start learning Italian. After praising its literary heritage and geographical wonders, the speaker of the poem says that Italy is nothing without liberty, whereupon he launches the eight-line apostrophe, which begins: "Oh Liberty, thou goddess heavenly bright, / Profuse of bliss, and pregnant with delight!"

During the Revolutionary War, these lines would be quoted countless times to celebrate American liberty.[38]

The travel writing that Watts printed includes *The Voyage and Adventures of Captain Robert Boyle*. An imaginary journey by Anglo-Irish novelist William Chetwood, Boyle's *Voyage* was just the kind of book Franklin enjoyed. It shares much with the better-known contemporary works, *Robinson Crusoe* and *Gulliver's Travels*. Franklin called *Gulliver's Travels* "a severe satyr and ridicule upon the follies, infirmities, and vices of particular nations, and the human race."[39] Not that there is anything wrong with that: Follies, infirmities, and vices should be satirized and ridiculed.

For *Miscellaneous Poems by Several Hands*, an anthology Watts printed during Franklin's employment, the poet David Lewis assembled 300 pages of verse. An usher at Westminster School, Lewis recruited several alumni to contribute. Despite the background his contributors shared, Lewis selected poems that varied in tone and style, mixing ballads, occasional verse, songs, and translations. To create an "agreeable variety," Lewis used a random organization and separated poems by the same author.[40]

Nearly all the poems in Lewis's miscellany were original contributions, but the best ones have been reprinted since. "Winifreda," its most frequently reprinted poem, celebrates conjugal love. Winifreda's husband—the speaker of the poem—projects their future life together: "Through youth and age, in love excelling, / We'll hand in hand together tread." The poet also praises the humble life. The husband and wife do not need pompous inherited titles: "We'll shine in more substantial honours, / And, to be noble, we'll be good."[41]

Lewis preserved the anonymity of his authors, but external evidence permits some identifications. "The Monument," for example, was written by Samuel Wesley. This eight-line poem tells the story of a vicious monster of a man, who has bequeathed his ill-gotten fortune to a grateful heir. The heir erects a marble bust in his memory, carving in stone the man's pure virtue. The last four lines go:

> If on his specious marble we rely,
> Pity a worth like his shou'd ever die!
> If credit to his real life we give,
> Pity a wretch like him should ever live![42]

The most renowned poem in Lewis's miscellany is the final version of John Dyer's "Grongar Hill," a landscape prospect poem written in the tradition of John Denham's *Cooper's Hill*, which combines topographical description with historical, moral, philosophical, and political reflection. It is almost impossible to overestimate the significance of *Cooper's Hill* to literary history. It culminates the Renaissance and anticipates the Restoration.[43] Like the speaker of *Cooper's Hill*, the speaker of "Grongar Hill" stays nearly fixed in space as his eyes wander across the landscape and the view elicits moral reflections.[44]

Dyer first wrote "Grongar Hill" as a Pindaric ode, an irregular verse form reflecting Abraham Cowley's influence. He restructured it for David Lewis's *Miscellaneous Poems*, rewriting "Grongar Hill" in tetrameter couplets: a daring choice since Charles Cotton and Samuel Butler had already established the tetrameter couplet as the verse form for raucous satire, not quiet contemplation. But Dyer's decision to restructure the poem was a good one. The couplets give the final version of "Grongar Hill" a directness and simplicity the Pindaric version lacks. Dyer omitted the abstractions of the earlier version in favor of concrete, straightforward imagery.[45]

Combining landscape description with meditative reverie, "Grongar Hill" creates a contemplative vision that evokes its time and place. Once the speaker of the poem climbs Grongar Hill, he looks around at the ruins of old castles on the surrounding cliffs, a scene that prompts the poem's most famous lines:

> A little rule, a little sway,
> A sun beam in a winter's day,
> Is all the proud and mighty have,
> Between the cradle and the grave.[46]

Wilfred P. Mustard traced two poems in *Poor Richard's Almanack* to Lewis's miscellany. Besides "The Monument," Franklin also borrowed "The Thracian," an epigrammatic poem that says how Thracian parents used to grieve upon an infant's birth but rejoice on the child's death.

Professor Mustard in the library with steely determination: Lewis's *Miscellaneous Poems* was one of several sources for the poetry in *Poor Richard's Almanack* that Mustard identified. Additional evidence confirms Franklin's appreciation of David Lewis. The success of *Miscellaneous Poems* encouraged Lewis to compile a new sequel with the same title four years later. Franklin would add the 1730 *Miscellaneous Poems* to his library.[47]

The belletristic literature Franklin could have seen through the press at Watts's printing house also included drama. In March 1726, Watts printed Thomas Southerne's *Money the Mistress*. This comedy, which had premiered at Lincoln's Inn Fields the month before, was Southerne's last play: a sad and sorry ending to an otherwise brilliant career as a dramatist. Franklin may have seen one of the February performances of *Money the Mistress*—or not. His London theater-going had waned after he and Ralph parted.

Money the Mistress is a comedy of morals, a dramatic genre that tends toward preachiness. As its title suggests, the play shows money's power to allure and destroy. Mariana, the heroine, is betrayed by both her friend and her lover. All three characters are flat, their dialogue stilted and overly obvious. The only aspect of *Money the Mistress* that saves it from oblivion is the anecdote that survives from opening night. During the last act, the audience hissed dreadfully. Theater manager John Rich was standing in the wings with Southerne and asked him if he heard the audience. Southerne replied, "No, sir, I am very deaf."[48]

Franklin had the chance to read the seventh and final installment of *The Universal Passion*, Edward Young's series of satires on ambition and the quest for fame, which Watts also printed. Already *The Universal Passion* was one of Franklin's favorite works. Imagine the joy he felt given the chance to help print the book. He would read Young's satire over and over in the years to come. For *Poor Richard's Almanack*, he would quote or adapt lines from all seven numbers of *The Universal Passion*.[49]

Swift, who recognized Young's hypocrisy, was less enthusiastic about *The Universal Passion*. While satirizing the impulse for fame, Young used his verse as a path to preferment. Young cannot castigate those searching for fame without condemning himself. Before *Satire VII* ends, the speaker of the poem finds something positive to say. He concludes that the love of fame is justifiable if combined with virtue, benevolence, and genuine ability. Young used Isaac Newton to illustrate his case. Newton's pursuit of fame let him share and propagate his scientific ideas.[50]

Franklin did not share Swift's view of Young's satire. He had used *The Universal Passion* to warn Ralph against seeking fame as a poet but admitted that he, too, felt the passion for fame. Franklin had come to London hoping to meet its leading scientists. Without Keith's promised letters of introduction, he had trouble fulfilling that hope. Franklin took the initiative and found a way around the nonexistent letters. The book he wrote helped initiate his entry to British society, and the books he read gave him the knowledge and sophistication to mix with gentlemen.

9

Sailing Home with Memories
of London

AT WATTS'S PRINTING house, Franklin befriended his coworker John Wigate, whose background differed from that of most tradesmen. A well-educated member of an affluent family, he knew Latin and French. Best of all, he loved to read. Sometimes they met outside the shop. Franklin taught him to swim, and they spent one memorable day with Wigate's country cousins sightseeing in Chelsea. When Franklin grew restless after eighteen months in London, Wigate, who shared his wanderlust, proposed a poor man's Grand Tour. Since good printers were everywhere in demand, the two could travel around Europe together, pausing to work whenever they needed cash.

Wigate's adventuresome proposal tempted the wayfarer in Franklin, but responsibility tugged from a different direction. Thomas Denham, who thought Franklin should return to Philadelphia, offered him a job and agreed to loan him passage money. A mercantile career, Denham argued, would not preclude travel. The merchant trade could take him to the Caribbean occasionally. Franklin accepted Denham's offer. On July 21, 1726, the two set sail aboard the *Berkshire*, skippered by Captain Henry Clarke.[1]

"Journal of a Voyage," Franklin's detailed account of the trip, contributes to both literary history and the history of science. It marks an advance over *A Dissertation on Liberty and Necessity*. Stylistically, Franklin's travel narrative is reminiscent of Joseph Addison's *Remarks on Several Parts of Italy*, another work he may have read in London. John Dos Passos called Franklin's journal the first instance of his new literary manner: "clear, cool, selfless, faintly amused." With its compelling oceanographic detail, Franklin's journal also deserves a place in the history of sea voyages. It conveys an Enlightenment attitude toward the sea, depicting the perceptive gaze of a modern observer who understands the importance of recording natural phenomena.[2]

Though Franklin would cross the Atlantic Ocean six more times, never again would he record his travels in such detail. "Journal of a Voyage" is worth an extended look, which can serve as an example of Franklin's subsequent voyages across the Atlantic, illustrating the personal, social, and intellectual activities that occupied him during a trip that lasted several weeks.

Despite its wealth of information about everything from sharks to sargasso, "Journal of a Voyage" omits many facets of the voyage. It says almost nothing about books. Several days into the trip, Franklin recorded a typical shipboard behavior: "I rise in the morning and read for an hour or two perhaps, and then reading grows tiresome." The journal does not say what he read on those Atlantic mornings. Nowhere does his travelogue record authors or book titles. In the autobiography, Franklin says he spent little money on himself while in London "except in seeing plays, and in books," but he never mentions what books he bought.[3]

Franklin's later ocean crossings indicate how he packed his books for a transatlantic voyage. He would keep several volumes handy to read during a passage. The rest he stowed. His reluctance to name specific books in the journal was a holdover from the admonitions of Samuel Butler and the Couranteers against ostentatious erudition. Given such reticence, the books Franklin had aboard the *Berkshire* are difficult to identify. Many items in his library date before 1726, but when he obtained them is unknown. Still, the books he brought home from his first visit to London are not beyond all conjecture.

Three pieces of evidence supplement Franklin's library catalogue to indicate what books he had with him on the *Berkshire*. His autobiography contains several clues regarding books he acquired in London. A letter he wrote decades later names one book and reveals how and why he read it. Even without specific titles, his travelogue is detailed enough to identify a few additional books Franklin read during the voyage.

What he brought from London helped Franklin reflect on the year and a half he had spent there. His new books elicited recent memories: authors he met, printers he encountered, bookshops he patronized, and coffeehouses he enjoyed. Franklin's comment that reading grew tiresome after an hour or two each morning conveys the difficulty he had concentrating aboard the *Berkshire*. Sailing home to Philadelphia, his mind returned to London.

Flashback to Franklin's *Dissertation on Liberty and Necessity*. This little pamphlet had worked like magic. It ingratiated him to London's intellectual elite, showing he was a thinker, someone to be taken seriously, someone worth getting to know. The pamphlet's readers encouraged his intellectual and literary pursuits, none more than John Lyons, another thinker whom John Wilcox had taken under his wing. Wilcox published the first edition of Lyons's *Infallibility of Human Judgment*, a treatise celebrating the power of reason.

Wilcox saw similarities between Franklin's pamphlet and Lyons's work and apparently introduced the two men, who shared a dedication to common sense for solving problems. He gave Franklin a copy of the latest edition of his work. Lyons believed that by relying on reason, solely on reason, humankind could rise to immeasurable heights. Franklin caught his excitement and shared *The Infallibility of Human Judgment* with others. Philadelphia friend Joseph Breintnall would add the work to his personal library. Summarizing Lyons's outlook, the *Philobiblion* said that he "depicts with bright colors the great benefits which would accrue to the world from the general diffusion of his principles."[4]

Much confusion surrounds John Lyons. Since Franklin identifies him as a surgeon in the autobiography, many commentators call him "Dr. Lyons," but there is no evidence he had a medical degree. Practicing surgery in the early eighteenth century did not require one. Dr. John Jones, Revolutionary America's leading surgeon and Franklin's last physician, was a staunch advocate for rigorous medical training. Jones scorned the traditional belief that surgery was a "low mechanical art, which may be taught a butchers boy in a fortnight." His advocacy helped professionalize surgery in late-eighteenth-century America, but it remained an amateur pursuit in Franklin's London.[5]

Regardless of his surgical ability, Lyons was, to quote the *Philobiblion* again, "a man of candor, and a sincere inquirer after truth."[6] In addition, he was a friendly, helpful soul happy to assist another ambitious young man. He enjoyed Franklin's *Dissertation* and recognized his intellect. Lyons obtained a second copy, marked it up, and returned it to Franklin should he wish to publish a revised edition. Franklin thought better of republishing his radical treatise but treasured Lyons's annotations and retained the marked-up copy.

Though Franklin appreciated the intellectual content of Lyons's notes, perhaps this annotated copy meant more to him as a memento from a friend. Well connected with the city's intellectual elite, Lyons escorted Franklin to the coffeehouses and taverns where physicians and virtuosi congregated and introduced him to some of London's greatest thinkers.

The Horns, a pale-ale house, was one place Lyons brought Franklin. The Horns was situated in a little pocket of London between St. Paul's and the Pennsylvania Coffee House. Here, Franklin met Bernard Mandeville, a Dutch physician living in London. With a joke, a *bon mot*, or an anecdote always at the ready, Mandeville was an entertaining companion. He formed the soul and center of the club that gathered at The Horns. Despite his convivial nature, Mandeville could do little to change Franklin's viewpoint when their talk turned to moral philosophy.[7]

The humor of Mandeville's verse is consistent with the tenor of his ale-house talk. *The Fable of the Bees*, the work that made his literary reputation, started as *The Grumbling Hive*, a hudibrastic poem. Taking Thomas Hobbes's theory about the fundamental selfishness of human nature one step beyond, *The Grumbling Hive* articulates Mandeville's basic thesis: Society must tolerate its private vices, which create public benefits. In closing, the poem tells people to stop complaining about vice and accept it.

According to Mandeville, society thrives as a whole because individuals indulge their greed for money, power, and possessions. These private vices produce beneficial results by employing people and contributing to social prosperity. Vice and self-interest, Mandeville argued, produce the same results as virtue and public spirit. But vice and self-interest have an advantage over virtue and public spirit, according to Mandeville's cynical view of human nature. Public spirit must be learned and cultivated; selfishness just comes naturally.

Though *The Fable of the Bees* is quite funny, optimistic readers found it madness. So many objected to Mandeville's disheartening thesis that he republished the poem with an extended commentary. *The Grumbling Hive* and Mandeville's commentary together form *The Fable of the Bees*, which appeared in 1714. Mandeville republished *The Fable of the Bees* with additional commentary nine years later. For the 1723 edition, he softened his argument, clarifying that public benefits did not automatically arise from private vices but required the management of a skilled politician.[8]

With an eye for bestsellers, Jacob Tonson saw the money-making potential of *The Fable of the Bees*, secured the rights, and reissued the work in 1724 and again in 1725. Given the personal charisma of its author, the pertinence of its thesis to Franklin's moral philosophy, and the close professional association between Tonson and Franklin's employer John Watts, *The Fable of the Bees* is another likely work he had with him on the way home. Though Franklin disagreed with Mandeville's thesis, *The Fable of the Bees* challenged his thinking and encouraged him to devise alternatives for achieving public benefits without the necessity of private vice.

Before he and Franklin met, Mandeville had published *A Modest Defence of Publick Stews*. The obsolete term in the title may require some explanation. When he said "public stews," Mandeville was not talking about some kind of Hungarian goulash. The word "stew" meant a sauna or steam bath. From the frequent use of steam baths for immoral purposes, it had become a synonym for a brothel. Assuming the persona of "Phil Porney," a civic-minded projector, Mandeville identified prostitution as a necessary vice and proposed a system of public stews or state-run brothels. With his satirical tone and humorous pseudonym, which means both friend to and lover of prostitutes, Mandeville burlesqued the public-minded schemes of eighteenth-century projectors.[9]

Almost as soon as Defoe turned the community-minded projector into a respectable figure who sought to change the world for the better, the projector was ripe for parody. Despite Mandeville's satire, his pamphlet identifies a serious social issue: the proliferation of prostitutes on London streets. *A Modest Defence of Publick Stews* uses a rhetorical pattern Franklin would repeat in his own satirical writings, which often propose outrageous solutions for social problems. Their sheer outrageousness emphasizes the need to devise serious solutions. Mandeville's influence on Franklin has yet to be measured fully. One recent scholar argues that Franklin's inclusion of chastity in his renowned list of virtues refutes Mandeville's claim in *A Modest Defence of Publick Stews* that prostitution is a necessary vice.[10]

Lyons also brought Franklin to Batson's, perhaps the most important coffeehouse he visited during his first trip to London. Batson's was located on the north side of Cornhill adjacent to the Royal Exchange. Its regular customers lent distinction to the place. Many were intellectuals who patronized Batson's to enjoy its lively conversation. Once physicians started using Batson's as a house of call, quacks gathered there to legitimize their medical practice by association. *The Connoisseur* had no high opinion of either real or pretended physicians, calling them "the dispensers of life and death, who flock together, like birds of prey, watching for carcasses at Batson's. I never enter this place but it serves as a *memento mori* to me."[11]

Though *The Connoisseur* lumped together physician and quack, the two groups segregated themselves inside Batson's. The reputable physicians sat apart from the disreputable ones, who gathered toward the room's upper end. Like the leading physicians, Franklin cracked wise about quacks. Whereas some people could not understand how quacks could successfully practice medicine, Franklin blamed their patients. Quacks succeeded because patients refused to expose them. Doing so, patients would have to confess their own ignorance and credulity. Instead, they extolled the virtues of quack remedies. Explaining the situation, Franklin called quacks the "greatest lyers in the world, except their patients."[12]

Among those who gathered at the lower end of Batson's, one physician was better known than the rest: Dr. Richard Mead. Though Franklin does not mention Mead in his autobiography, he almost surely met him at Batson's.

Sometimes Mead settled himself at the coffeehouse in the morning and lingered there all day. When an apothecary visited to tell him how his patients were doing, Mead would write prescriptions for the apothecary to fill for them. Though not unique to him, this practice did subject Mead to contemporary criticism. No amount of criticism could diminish his reputation as a diagnostician and medical experimenter.[13]

Lyons first became acquainted with Mead in a roundabout way. In 1723, the year after the third edition of *The Infallibility of Human Judgment* appeared, Lyons was arraigned on a charge concerning the book and imprisoned in Newgate. The charge was blasphemy, but the personal narrative Lyons appended to the fourth edition—the one Franklin read—is deliberately vague: "The most that ever I, or any of my friends, cou'd learn of it, was, that it was a piece of ironical drollery (of a certain young noble lord) which being ill timed, created some heat, and was either improv'd into, or mistaken for, a serious complaint."[14]

When Lyons came up for trial at the Old Bailey, the prosecution dropped the case. *The Daily Journal* reported, "We hear it was at the intercession of some persons of distinguishable learning." The newspaper did not elaborate, but one person of distinguishable learning was Dr. Mead, whom Lyons thanked in the fourth edition of *The Infallibility of Human Judgment*.[15]

Mead's friendship was the silver lining to Lyons's legal trouble; Lyons was the conduit connecting Mead to Franklin, two kindred spirits. What Lyons said about Mead equally suits Franklin: "There is continually some new thing discover'd, either for publick or private benefit, which demonstrates him to be a general friend to mankind."[16] Given his efforts to encourage the improvement of useful arts and sciences, Mead served as a model for Franklin.

In 1720, Mead had established his literary reputation with *A Short Discourse Concerning Pestilential Contagion*, a prolegomena to the plague. Copies circulated around Boston during the smallpox epidemic in the early 1720s, when Franklin would have first encountered the work. He enjoyed Mead's writing and later acquired his handbook of practical cures for common diseases, *Medical Precepts and Cautions*.[17]

While in London, Franklin had seen Europe's greatest medical library, which formed part of Sir Hans Sloane's 30,000-volume collection of books. He had approached Sloane and offered to sell him an American curiosity: an asbestos purse. Sloane accepted his offer and invited Franklin to tour the vast cabinet of curiosities at his home in Bloomsbury Square. Sloane's collection of curiosities would form the core of the British Museum, and his library would form the core of the British Library. His medical books apparently impressed Franklin, who would assemble the finest private medical library in Revolutionary America.[18]

Franklin also met Martin Folkes, another leading figure in the Royal Society, the prestigious scientific organization established in London the previous century. Since Franklin's autobiography does not mention him, Folkes has escaped the story of Franklin's life, but eighteenth-century accounts attest to their meeting. An antiquarian as well as a scientist, Folkes collected and studied Roman coins. He, too, could have encouraged Franklin's interest in collecting. Folkes also had an in-depth knowledge of literature. A well-rounded virtuoso, he was friendly, affable, and willing to help others who shared his interests. For someone who had reached London without any letters of introduction, Franklin came to know several distinguished men of science.[19]

Henry Pemberton, a Leyden-trained physician, was another regular at Batson's. Lyons introduced Franklin to him as well. Pemberton, in turn, offered to introduce Franklin to Isaac Newton. Pemberton was well positioned to bring the young American into the orbit of the venerable Newton. After Pemberton impressed Newton with his work on physics, he collaborated with him on a scientific paper. Newton chose Pemberton to edit the third edition of the *Principia*. Franklin accepted Pemberton's magnanimous offer and looked forward to meeting Newton.[20]

The books Franklin added to his personal collection suggest that he studied Newton's writings as he prepared to meet him. Franklin owned the 1721 edition of Newton's *Opticks*, which he most likely read soon after Pemberton promised to introduce him to its author.[21] Newton's *Opticks* was a revelation for Franklin. Whereas the *Principia* appeared in Latin, Newton published *Opticks* in English, a shift toward the vernacular Franklin appreciated.

Opticks was much different in its scientific approach as well. Whereas the *Principia* is a challenging mathematical and theoretical work, *Opticks* chronicles Newton's experiments in the field. Its opening sentence belongs among the great opening sentences in the literary history of science: "My design in this book is not to explain the properties of light by hypotheses, but to propose and prove them by reason and experiments." Owen Aldridge observed that after Franklin's *Dissertation on Liberty and Necessity*, his thinking shifted from the theoretical to the empirical. More than any other book, Newton's *Opticks* was responsible for this shift.[22]

Many curious people read Newton's *Opticks* in the eighteenth century. The other Newton book Franklin acquired is more unusual: *Commercium epistolicum*. Based on the Newton correspondence collected by seventeenth-century

English mathematician John Collins, the *Commercium* assembles the letters in which Newton discusses his theoretical work in the field of infinitesimal calculus. A controversy flared regarding who invented calculus: Newton or Leibniz. First published under the auspices of the Royal Society, the *Commercium* was designed to prove Newton's priority, but it only fueled the controversy.[23]

Watts's printing business provides the evidence to approximate when Franklin acquired the *Commercium*. Again working with Tonson, Watts published a second edition in 1722. In this instance, Tonson's market sense failed him. The *Commercium* sold poorly. The year Franklin started working for him, Watts had so many copies left over, he decided to print a new title page and reissue the book.[24] Most likely Watts gave Franklin one of the extra copies lying around. The presence of the *Commercium* in Franklin's library indicates how much effort he put into his planned meeting with Newton. Why, he was trying to read a book about calculus in Latin!

Franklin's strenuous effort to read about Newton's calculus research shows how much he looked forward to meeting the famous scientist and mathematician, though there is some question whether Newton was healthy enough to make new friends. When James Logan saw him at the Royal Society in 1724, Newton looked quite feeble. Watching him walk toward Crane Court, the stately house off Fleet Street where the Society had met for the past decade and a half, Logan saw Newton "bending so much under the load of years as that with some difficulty he mounted the stairs of the Society's room."[25]

Perhaps Newton's frailty prevented him from making Franklin's acquaintance. For whatever reason, their meeting never occurred. Newton died less than a year after Franklin left London. In *Poor Richard's Almanack*, he would call Newton the "prince of astronomers and philosophers" and repeat Pope's memorable epitaph: "Nature and nature's laws lay hid in night; / God said, '*Let* Newton *be*,' and all was light." After returning home, Franklin had little further use for the *Commercium* and donated his copy to the Library Company of Philadelphia.[26]

One book Franklin definitely had with him on the *Berkshire* was Professor Marcus Zuerius Boxhorn's *Arcana imperii detecta: or, Divers Select Cases on Government*. An English translation of *Disquisitiones politicae*, a set of lectures the professor had delivered to his students at Leyden University, *Arcana imperii* digested his theory of good governance. Franklin could have learned about the book from Mandeville, Boxhorn's countryman. *The Fable of the Bees* draws on Boxhorn's political theories about the relationship between private interests and the maintenance of the commonwealth.[27]

Franklin mentions Boxhorn's *Arcana imperii* directly in his correspondence, indirectly in his travel journal. Writing to the mysterious "Charles de Weissenstein" in 1778, Franklin reveals how he read Boxhorn. In this letter, Franklin recalls hearing that a great personage—presumably George, Prince of Wales—had studied Boxhorn's *Arcana imperii*. The prince's interest in the book was what prompted Franklin to obtain a copy and read it. To become a great man, one should read the same books great men read.[28]

Boxhorn synthesized the learning, judicial theory, and state policy of many nations across Europe and throughout history to demonstrate how government should work. The London edition of *Arcana imperii* reflects the growing desire for political knowledge. One English reviewer questioned the propriety of Boxhorn's approach. The review begins: "We are got into an age, wherein every man sets up for a sage politician, and talks as confidently of the affairs of state, as if he was seated at the helm, and had been for several reigns past bred up in the *secretary's office*, or born a *privy counsellor*." The reviewer appears quite uncomfortable with this development, with the idea of making the secrets of how to run a government available to anyone who could read. It threatened to undermine the basic order of society. Instead, the reviewer contended, every man should stay "within his own sphere and province."[29]

Franklin's attention to a leadership handbook read by a prince shows he was far more ambitious as a young man than formerly acknowledged. Twenty years old when he sailed home on the *Berkshire*, Franklin was already studying how to be a successful leader. The fact that he remembered Boxhorn's treatise a half-century after first reading it indicates how the books he read as a young man would contribute to the development of his thought during the Revolutionary era.

Boxhorn's *Arcana imperii* was a rare work in colonial America, but it was not totally unknown. The Reverend Jonathan Boucher, a Maryland schoolmaster, had a copy in his library. Boxhorn was a prolific scholar, and two of Franklin's Philadelphia friends owned some of his other works. Logan had two of Boxhorn's Latin works, a world history and a study of the Gaulish language. Contributing to Logan's in-depth linguistic studies, Boxhorn argued that old Gaulish was the same language the ancient Britons spoke and that survivals of it could be found in modern Welsh. Rural Pennsylvania had an extensive Welsh population, and Franklin grew curious about their language. *Poor Richard's Almanack* would include several proverbs in Welsh.[30]

Isaac Norris, Jr. owned another Latin work, Boxhorn's *Institutiones politicae*. Norris would emerge as a leading figure in Pennsylvania politics, serving as speaker of the assembly for a decade and a half. One wonders how much Boxhorn's political theory affected Norris's work in the Pennsylvania

Assembly. The story of Boxhorn's influence on American politics has yet to be written.[31]

In the letter to Weissenstein, Franklin says of Boxhorn's *Arcana imperii*, "There are sensible and good things in it; but some bad ones." Boxhorn organized the book as a set of case studies. Each poses a question and then proceeds to answer it. Regarding one particular case study, Franklin recalled the question it asks, "Whether a prince who, to appease a revolt, makes promises of indemnity to the revolters, is obliged to fulfil those promises?"[32] Writing from Paris in 1778, Franklin did not have access to his copy of Boxhorn, so he could not double-check the reference. Citing it from memory, his question varies from the original in its wording, but not in its basic gist. The fact that Franklin started his discussion with a question reinforces the importance of Boxhorn's question-and-answer format.

Franklin was referring to a case discussing the Milanese rebellion against Louis XII of France, who then ruled Milan. Wishing to end their rebellion, the Milanese sought terms with the French king, who offered a general amnesty to the rebels. Once they accepted his terms, he ignored the amnesty and executed several leading citizens.[33] Paraphrasing the case study and applying it to the American rebellion against Britain, Franklin wrote an answer to the question about whether a prince must fulfill the promises he made:

> Honest and good men would say, Ay. But this politician says, as you say, *No*. And he gives this pretty reason, that tho' it was right to make the promises, because otherwise the revolt could not be suppress'd; yet it would be wrong to keep them, because revolters ought to be punish'd to deter future revolts. If these are the principles of your nation, no confidence can be plac'd in you, it is in vain to treat with you, and wars can only end in being reduc'd to an utter inability of continuing them.[34]

Franklin understood that Boxhorn's view of the Milanese rebellion was pertinent to the Americans as they rebelled against the British Crown.

After its London passengers boarded but before it went to sea, the *Berkshire* stopped at Portsmouth. Touring the city, Franklin heard scary stories about its former lieutenant governor, Sir John Gibson. He also visited a miserable dungeon near the town gate that was known as Johnny Gibson's Hole. According to legend, Gibson struck fear into his men. He would confine soldiers for trifling misdemeanors until they almost starved to death. Generalizing from Gibson's behavior, Franklin found that it manifested the severe discipline required to control rabble-rousing soldiers.[35]

If a commander cannot make his men love him, then he must make them fear him, Franklin said. But, he continued, the best leaders can and do make their men love them. For proof, Franklin mentioned Alexander and Caesar, two renowned generals who "received more faithful service, and performed greater actions by means of the love their soldiers bore them, than they could possibly have done, if instead of being beloved and respected they had been hated and feared by those they commanded."[36]

Franklin's journal does not mention Boxhorn, but his comments about Alexander and Caesar come from another case study in *Arcana imperii*: "Whether a prince ought to leave his own dominions and head his army in a foreign country in person, and upon whose grounds the same is advisable to be done?" To answer this query, Boxhorn used the same two examples that Franklin would use.[37]

Two months after leaving London, the *Berkshire* remained at sea, but Franklin felt they were getting close to home. He ended his journal entry for September 24 with a heroic couplet: "On either side the parted billows flow, / While the black ocean foams and roars below." Derived from Pope's recent translation of Homer's *Odyssey*, these lines occur shortly before Ulysses spots Ithaca. Not everyone can bend the bow of Ulysses, but with this couplet Franklin compared himself to Homer's great hero. Franklin, too, was returning home from a long and life-shaping adventure.[38]

Reading Boxhorn the same time he was reading Homer, Franklin received two contrasting lessons in leadership. Ulysses rules his men through force of personality. He is brave when bravery is required, crafty when craftiness demands it, and honest and straightforward when it does not. A risk taker, Ulysses does not hesitate to improvise, coming up with original but expedient solutions to achieve his goals. Despite his sometimes ruthless conduct and acrimonious behavior, he never loses the sense of responsibility for his men or the dedication to his mission.

Whereas Homer depicts Ulysses as a leader in battle and at sea, Boxhorn situates his ideal leader within the context of running a state and showing how to use the machinery of government to maintain control. Boxhorn's ideal leader makes agreements with other nations when they benefit his own but breaks them when they do not; treats citizens fairly to avoid civil war but crushes them to end civil strife; treats other nations differently according to their circumstances; and actively shapes the citizenry to benefit the nation. That Franklin found both good things and bad in *Arcana imperii* suggests that he read it carefully, scrutinizing what he read and weighing the quality of Boxhorn's advice. Instead of trusting what Boxhorn wrote, Franklin decided for himself what was good and bad.

There is one more type of book Franklin had during the voyage home: an almanac. He apparently brought one from London; he knew there would be a lunar eclipse on Thursday night, September 29th. No almanacs from 1726 survive among his books, but Franklin's extant collection of English almanacs shows that Salem Pearse's *Coelestial Diary* was a personal favorite. Pearse said the lunar eclipse would begin in London at 3:52 A.M. and last for two hours and twenty-one minutes. Franklin was unsure when the eclipse would take place at sea. There was still no way to determine longitude beyond fumbling along by guess and by gosh. The lunar eclipse offered a rare opportunity to pinpoint their position by comparing the time it occurred with the time the eclipse occurred in London. Franklin resolved to stay up late to take observations.

Seeing the night sky as a harbinger of earthly events, Pearse interpreted what the lunar eclipse foretold. Often considered a bad omen, an eclipse could mean disaster. Pearse predicted: "The moon eclipsed in the 7th house, which denotes detriment to noblemen, scarcity of the fruits of the Earth; and *Mars*, being lord of this eclipse stirs up much mischief, wars, quarrels, duels, massacres, etc: hot air, thunder and lightning, and shipwrecks, and loss by pyrates at sea."[39]

Franklin brushed aside the traditional superstitions and put his mathematical instruments and brain power to work. His observations and calculations let him determine the position of the *Berkshire* and compute the remaining distance. Once finished, he gave fellow passengers welcome news. They were only a hundred leagues from Philadelphia.[40]

"Land! Land!" cried a member of Franklin's mess on Sunday afternoon, October 9th. Hearing these words, his messmates gazed westward. Franklin did not see the land at first; tears of joy blurred his vision. As they approached Cape Henlopen around noon on Monday, the pilot boat met their vessel. The pilot boarded the *Berkshire* with a peck of apples. Hercules had to slay a hundred-headed dragon to obtain the golden apples of the Hesperides; Franklin took the apples from the pilot with a smile of delight. Crunching into one after another, he found them the most delicious apples he had ever eaten. With a fair wind, they made excellent time. By 10 Monday night, they had entered the Delaware River and almost reached New Castle when the *Berkshire* cast anchor to await the morning tide.

Tuesday was bright and sunny, and the people along the shore hailed the men aboard ship to welcome them home. Franklin filled his journal with evocative details. Covered with woods and dotted here and there with farmhouses, Delaware was a bucolic painting come to life. Ranging from elm yellow to sassafras red, the fall color was nearing its peak. Puffy clouds floated across bright blue skies. A breeze from shore wafted toward the ship, promising passengers they would soon have land beneath their feet.

Some disembarked at Chester to take the road to Philadelphia, but Franklin and others stayed aboard, hoping the water would be faster. To Franklin's chagrin, the wind slackened about 8 that evening. The *Berkshire* weighed anchor at Redbank, 6 miles from Philadelphia. They faced another night aboard ship. Some young Philadelphians out sailing for pleasure in a light craft passed by and offered them a ride into town. Franklin and three other passengers accepted the kind offer. About 10 o'clock that evening, they landed at Philadelphia, happy to set foot on American soil once more.

The Junto

ON OCTOBER 12TH, the day after Franklin reached Philadelphia, he and Thomas Denham got to work. They unloaded the retail goods Denham had shipped aboard the *Berkshire* and located a suitable house on Front Street just a few doors from the Crooked Billet. They could sleep upstairs and operate their general store downstairs. A natural salesman, Franklin manned the store and kept the books. That fall, Franklin bought some appealing items from Denham's store, including a new cap. No matter how warm the cap was, it could not safeguard him against pleurisy, a life-threatening pulmonary disease that struck late that winter. Denham also fell ill. Franklin recovered. Denham did not. His illness lingered for months, taking his life the following year.[1]

Once Franklin recovered, he unsuccessfully sought retail work elsewhere in Philadelphia. Keimer, who had moved to a better location, now operated both a stationer's shop and a printing house. Wanting to concentrate on his retail business, Keimer invited his former journeyman to manage the printshop. With no other prospects, he accepted his old boss's lucrative offer.

Franklin oversaw a staff of five, whom he would profile in the autobiography. Initially, he emphasized Hugh Meredith's farming background, calling him a "Welsh-Pensilvanian, thirty years of age, bred to country work." This description did not quite capture Meredith's essence; Franklin added that he was "honest, sensible, but given to drink." All true, but the concluding remark sounded too harsh. Franklin expanded his description further. Between "sensible" and "given to drink," he added that Meredith "had a great deal of solid observation" and "was something of a reader."[2] Calling him a reader before mentioning his predilection to drink, Franklin minimized his central flaw. In the final version, Meredith's bibliomania mitigates his dipsomania.

Stephen Potts was also raised on a farm. Since Franklin had given Meredith's age, he added a similar comment about Potts to make their character sketches parallel. Potts, he wrote, was "of full age," meaning he was an adult. Franklin added that Potts was "of uncommon natural parts, and great wit and humour, but a little idle."[3] This description reinforces the structural parallel with Franklin's description of Meredith; it lists positive qualities before ending with a single flaw. But Potts's sense of humor was his defining trait.

Finishing his description of the employees, Franklin mentioned David Harry—Keimer's apprentice—and two indentured servants. Calling Harry a "country boy," Franklin made him seem younger than he was. Harry was only two years younger than him. When Franklin returned to Keimer's shop, Harry had almost finished his apprenticeship. He came from the Welsh Barony, a settlement west of Philadelphia where many Welsh-speaking Quakers lived.

One indentured servant was a "wild Irishman" named John, the other an "Oxford scholar" named George Webb. Franklin's ethnic stereotype characterizes John's personality. As William Byrd says in *The History of the Dividing Line*, "The wild Irish find more pleasure in laziness than luxury." Webb, who had attended Oxford, called himself "Oxford Scholar." The phrase may have stuck as a facetious nickname around the shop, as in "Hey, Oxford Scholar, sweep the floor and take out the trash."[4]

Aware that an Oxford student serving an indenture in a Philadelphia printing house would surprise his readers, Franklin developed Webb's story further. Webb starred in some school plays, joined a literary club, and wrote essays and poetry for the local newspaper in Gloucester. On July 18, 1724, he matriculated at Oxford, entering Balliol College when he was 16.[5]

"Balliol made me," sings the poet. Webb would not stay at Balliol long enough for it to make or break him. Dissatisfied with college life after a year, he longed to tread the boards of the London stage. When his father sent the next quarterly allowance of 15 guineas, Webb quit school. He was still wearing his academic robes when he ran away. Upon escaping Oxford city limits, he stopped at the first convenient furze bush, stripped off his cap and gown and hid them in its foliage: the Oxonian equivalent of the proverbial bustle in the hedgerow. Divested of his academic regalia, he walked the rest of the way to London.[6]

Webb knew no one in the metropolis and fell into bad company. Before he had met any thespians or theater buffs who could get him on stage, his guineas were gone. Hungry and penniless, he pawned his clothes next. The proceeds did not last long. Webb soon found himself hungry and penniless again.

Alone, he roamed around London, unsure of what to do, easy pickings for a crimp's evil clutches. A "crimp" was someone who procured seamen, soldiers, or indentured servants through underhanded means. Crimps would ply their nefarious trade well into the nineteenth century. In *White-Jacket*, Melville castigates the crimps who lured innocent young men into the navy. Sure enough, a crimp approached Webb and offered him food and shelter, if he would bind himself to serve in America. With his options exhausted, Webb signed the indenture and boarded the next ship for Philadelphia, his destiny the setting sun.[7]

Except for Harry, Keimer's employees lacked the skills to do their job. Meredith had no idea how to operate a press; Potts knew nothing about bookbinding, except possibly the joke about a local customer who wanted to have a valuable book finely bound. When the bookbinder told him he could have it done in russia or morocco, the customer said he wanted it done in Philadelphia. Keimer had rehired Franklin to train his new employees. Once they acquired the necessary skills, Franklin would be superfluous, so Keimer could fire him. Aware Keimer was taking advantage, Franklin nonetheless enjoyed the work and the camaraderie.

Hearing a loud noise outside one early October day, Franklin poked his head out the window to see what was the matter. "Mind your own business," Keimer yelled. Their neighbors witnessed Keimer's abusive treatment of his shop foreman. Upon reentering the shop, he gave Franklin three months to clear out. Franklin did not need three minutes. He left instantly.

That evening, Franklin and Meredith discussed what to do. With his own printing house, Meredith argued, Franklin could drive Keimer out of business. He liked the idea, but lacked the capital. Meredith proposed a partnership. His father would supply the capital; Franklin would supply the expertise. Franklin accepted Meredith's proposal, and they ordered the necessary equipment from London. Months would pass before everything arrived, so Franklin returned to Keimer, who had undergone a change of heart.

Meredith, Potts, Webb, and Franklin socialized outside the shop. Around the time Keimer dismissed him, Franklin and the others formed a club for personal and social improvement. Limiting membership to twelve, they had no trouble filling the remaining slots. Young and ambitious, its members would eventually become, in Benjamin Vaughan's words, "men considerable for their influence and discretion." They called their mutual improvement society the Junto.[8]

John Locke's *Pieces* came in handy as Franklin and his friends planned the Junto. One piece presented the rules of a society that met weekly to foster the search for truth and the pursuit of knowledge. The Junto would meet every Friday night. Franklin borrowed from Locke a set of questions potential members would have to answer, such as "Whether he loves and seeks truth for truth's sake; and will endeavour impartially to find and receive it himself, and to communicate it to others?"[9]

Three years younger than Franklin, Robert Grace was quite wealthy. Since his parents died when he was an infant, his grandparents raised him. Grace inherited the family's luxurious estate while in his teens. His inheritance included his grandfather's home and property, which extended from Market Street to Jones Alley or Pewter Platter Alley, a name it gained due to the large pewter platter that formed the sign of a fashionable tavern at the corner of Jones Alley and Front Street. Grace's presence invigorated the Junto meetings. Franklin called him a "young gentleman of some fortune, generous, lively and witty, a lover of punning and of his friends."[10]

Nicholas Scull, a part-time surveyor who would later serve as surveyor-general of Pennsylvania, joined the Junto and became its first host. The group initially gathered at the Indian Head Tavern, which Scull owned and operated. Later, it would assemble at Scull's new establishment, the Bear Tavern, at Second Street and Vine. Within its first year, the Junto began meeting at Grace's home. Members entered his property from Pewter Platter Alley through an arched carriageway. His well-appointed home added class and comfort, and Grace set aside a room for their meetings.

Though a poor speller, Scull was an expert linguist. While training for his career, he had surveyed much of Pennsylvania's backcountry, acquiring an extensive knowledge of Native American dialects, several of which he could speak fluently. Scull even used a Native American phrase for the title of a pamphlet he wrote supporting the military defense of Pennsylvania against Quaker pacifism, *Kawanio che keeteru*. In a prefatory note, Scull explains his title: "Imagine a man, with his wife, and children about him, and with an air of resolution, calling out to his enemy, 'All these God has given me, and I will defend them.'"[11]

Scull generally got along well with the Native American population. He did not always need his knowledge of native dialects to understand them. One time, after Scull had unpacked his chains and started surveying some land near the Delaware Gap, a large group surrounded him. An elder placed his hand on Scull's shoulder and said, in English, "Put up iron string, go home." Scull went.[12]

His adventures in the Pennsylvania wilderness did nothing to detract from Scull's refined behavior at home in Philadelphia. Scull loved to read and enjoyed writing poetry. His literary activity reflects his extensive reading. He was the only member who left an account of a Junto meeting. But there is a problem with using Scull's account as documentary evidence: He wrote it in verse. Still, there are enough similarities between the Junto's rules and Scull's poem to verify many details.

Scull left two versions of the poem: "The Junto" and "The Junto Room." In both, the speaker of the poem, a traveler and Junto member, grows weary after a long horseback ride. He dismounts to rest and soon falls asleep, whereupon he dreams about a meeting: "Three queerys in philosophy were first / Gravely considerd and at length discurst." According to the Junto's rules, each member had to prepare for discussion at least one query about morality, politics, or natural philosophy, as science was called then.[13]

After the group had been active for a few years, Franklin compiled a numbered list of standing queries. Some were lighthearted. The second one shows his passion for personal anecdotes: "What new story have you lately heard agreeable for telling in conversation?" Medicine forms another topic: "Have you or any of your acquaintance[s] been lately sick or wounded? If so, what remedies were used, and what were their effects?" The eleventh query asks, "Do you think of any thing at present, in which the Junto may be serviceable to *mankind*? to their country, to their friends, or to themselves?" This query looks forward to Franklin's ambitious community improvement projects—firefighting companies, fire insurance, police reform—most of which started in the Junto. The queries also reflect its members' Whiggish political philosophy. The fifteenth one asks, "Have you lately observed any encroachment on the just liberties of the people?"[14]

Franklin's list of standing queries forms a good outline for any mutual improvement society. Appending the list to his edition of Franklin's political writings, Vaughan titled it, "Rules for a Club Formerly Established in Philadelphia." Once Vaughan published these rules, they caught the attention of many readers. Contemporary magazines reprinted them, and an edition of *The Spectator* published in Franklin's lifetime glossed Joseph Addison's discussion of proper clubs with a footnote referencing Franklin's rules. The footnote is a fitting tribute. *The Spectator* had helped Franklin develop his writing style; now his writings were being used to gloss *The Spectator*.[15]

The queries also show that reading was an important activity for Junto members. The first asks: "Have you met with any thing in the author you last read, remarkable, or suitable to be communicated to the Junto? Particularly in history, morality, poetry, physic, travels, mechanic arts, or other parts of knowledge?"[16] This standing query encouraged members to follow current literature. Each would share the most memorable parts of their reading. When several members read the same book, the Junto resembled a modern-day book club. Franklin's subject list indicates their diverse interests. Mechanics and physics provided useful information. Poetry offered pleasure reading. Other subjects—history, moral philosophy, travels—combined pleasure with instruction.

In his essay "Of Studies," Francis Bacon famously says, "Some books are to be tasted, others to be swallowed, and some few to be chewed and digested." A later and less famous sentence in the same essay goes, "Some books also may be read by deputy, and extracts made of them by others." Franklin proposed to the Junto an activity following Bacon's later sentence. Any member who mentioned a noteworthy text at one meeting should transcribe an extract or write an abstract for the next. Extracts would let Junto members disseminate information and make their reading more efficient. If one member read a book and shared its best bits, the rest would not have to read the whole thing. Collectively, they could process reading material easier than they could individually.[17]

After the queries, the speaker of "The Junto Room" continues:

> A declamation next was read in course
> Wherein keen wit did virtues laws enforce
> Where strength of thought in lofty language shone
> Such as famd Swift or Addison might own.[18]

Comparing their essays with those of two leading British authors, Scull showed that Franklin was not the only Junto member who patterned his writings on those of Joseph Addison and Jonathan Swift.

Each member had to read aloud an original essay once every three months. The queries and essays together formed the Junto's main business. Members then turned to music, poetry, and drink. The music varied from one week to another, depending on who played what instrument. In Scull's poem, one member plays the flute. Others get something to drink, and they begin reading poems. The book club transforms into a poetry reading. Scull's poem does not say what they drank, but his accounts provide a clue. One night, Franklin and Meredith each spent 5 pence at the Bear Tavern: the price of a quart of "best beer."[19]

"Waller" recites the first poem in "The Junto":

> Turned Waller next a Pennsylvania bard
> Whose muse sometimes on Delware banks is heard
> Renownd of old for soft harmonious lays
> Pastorals sometimes write and sometimes plays.[20]

The name is a reference to seventeenth-century poet Edmund Waller, who found many appreciative readers in colonial America, including Franklin, who often quoted Waller's verse. In *Poor Richard's Almanack*, he excerpts

Waller's poem on the death of Oliver Cromwell and supplies an accompanying anecdote. According to the anecdote, Waller wrote a congratulatory poem to King Charles II upon the Restoration. The king asked Waller why his Cromwell poem was so much better than the poem about him. "We poets," Waller replied, "always succeed better in fiction than in truth."[21]

Waller helped introduce the heroic couplet to English literature, thus initiating the form that would define Augustan poetry. John Denham also pioneered the heroic couplet in *Cooper's Hill*. Dryden observed that the "sweetness of Mr. Waller's lyric poesy was afterwards followed in the epic by Sir John Denham, in his *Cooper's Hill*, a poem which . . . for the majesty of the style, is, and ever will be, the exact standard of good writing."[22]

In his anthology of colonial American verse, Kenneth Silverman identifies Joseph Breintnall as "Waller." Breintnall hailed from Derby, England. About ten years older than Franklin, he had started in the mercantile trade but now worked as a scrivener. Breintnall had read some of the same books as Franklin in his youth, including Plutarch's *Lives*, Plutarch's *Morals*, and Xenophon's *Memorable Things of Socrates*. Overall, Breintnall's reading embraced many subjects: antiquities, biography, botany, commerce, geography, history, moral philosophy, poetry, and political science. Furthermore, he was the Junto's most accomplished poet.[23]

Breintnall—the "phantom of colonial literary history," David S. Shields called him—is slowly coming into view. Four years after Shields coined this evocative sobriquet, an unrecorded Breintnall poem surfaced, *The Death of King George Lamented in Pennsylvania*. Breintnall wrote this elegy once news of the king's death reached Philadelphia in August 1727. He had Keimer publish it, meaning that Keimer set it in type and Franklin physically printed it.[24]

Though Breintnall wrote *The Death of King George* in the heroic couplets characteristic of the neoclassical era, he structured his elegy as a fragment from a greater work, thus anticipating a technique more common to the Romantic era. Breintnall's use of persona shows considerable sophistication. He assumed the identity of a non-Quaker addressing a Quaker friend: "And tho' two different creeds our sects divide, / One is our faith in friendship often try'd." King George merited the Quakers' regard: He had settled the differences between them and the Anglicans and freed the Quakers from swearing oaths.[25]

"Waller" and the names of other members mentioned in "The Junto" convinced Silverman that they borrowed their club names from English poets. Scull's revisions challenge Silverman's interpretation. Revising "The Junto" into "The Junto Room," Scull changed Breintnall's poetic name from "Waller" to "Withers" and thus changed the reference from Edmund Waller to George Wither, an English pastoral poet.[26]

The case of Joseph Breintnall reflects the danger of drawing conclusions based on incomplete evidence. Changing his poetic name from Waller to Withers, Scull created a misleading picture of Breintnall's poetry. The partial evidence of Breintnall's library provides another misleading clue. A copy of Richard Crashaw's *Steps to the Temple* survives with Breintnall's ownership inscription.[27] Breintnall's verse has neither the stylized diction and imagery that characterizes pastoral verse, nor the ornate syntax and baroque tropes of Crashaw's religious verse. Breintnall's poetry shows that he preferred concrete, realistic detail.

Even when Breintnall wrote about religion, which was rare, he concentrated on what he could perceive with his senses. In an appreciation of the speaking style of Quaker preacher John Salkeld, Breintnall focuses on the appearance of his face and the volume of his voice:

> His first words would be soft, but might be heard;
> He look'd resolv'd,—yet spoke as if he fear'd.
> Then gain'd attention, in a gradual way,
> As morning twilight ushers in the day.[28]

For "The Junto," Scull named Franklin after the author of *Cooper's Hill*, but he did not stop his compliment there. Scull's poem contains the earliest known recognition of Franklin's genius: "Denham whos birth is by fair Boston claimd / And justly is for a great genius famd." Scull's poem provides enough detail about the poem Franklin read that evening to suggest it was "The Rats and the Cheese, A Fable."[29]

The Junto members generally read their own poems, but in this instance, Franklin read one he encountered in his reading. "The Rats and the Cheese" appeared anonymously in the London *Weekly-Journal*. Not until the twentieth century would it be attributed to Bernard Mandeville.[30] With other items from the same newspaper, "The Rats and the Cheese" would be anthologized in *A Collection of Miscellany Letters, Selected out of Mist's Weekly Journal*. Franklin would not add this miscellany to his personal library until 1762, but he could have seen it earlier, reading a copy he had for sale or borrowing one from another Junto member.[31]

When Franklin published "The Rats and the Cheese" in *The Pennsylvania Gazette*, he applied it to a current Massachusetts gubernatorial controversy. Once John Montgomerie became colonial governor of New York and New

Jersey, William Burnet left New York to take over as governor of Massachusetts. Burnet requested a fixed salary of £2000. The Massachusetts Assembly balked at his steep request and appointed Jonathan Belcher to visit London and lodge a formal protest. Appointed to replace Burnet while in London, Belcher returned to Boston and demanded the same salary he had been sent to protest!

The whole situation sickened Franklin, making him see how patriotism and principles went by the wayside once a person achieved power. As it concludes, "The Rats and the Cheese" gives voice to a solo rat. Though no magic rat, this one does possess insightful powers of perception. It is "not quite so blind / In state intrigues as humankind." Reading the poem to fellow Junto members, Franklin made the rat's sentiments his own:

> Your politicks are all a farce;
> And your fine virtues but mine arse:
> All your contentions are but these,
> Whose rat shall best secure the cheese.[32]

Revising "The Junto" into "The Junto Room," Scull added one more poetry-reading member, whom he named "Young Oldham," a reference to the seventeenth-century satirist whose works Franklin had known since his apprenticeship. "Young Oldham" stands for George Webb. "The Junto Room" provides enough detail to identify the poem Webb read: "No More a Willing Muse Her Aid Bestows." Webb's direct reference to Waller's "Battell of the Summer Islands" in this poem provides another reason why Scull changed Breintnall's poetic name to Withers: He did not want to confuse Breintnall and Webb.[33]

Scull's placement of poets from English literary history into his account of the Junto lends his poem considerable sophistication. The dream vision conflates the meeting with his reading. The idea of *translatio*—the westward movement of arts and civilization—would become a prominent theme in Webb's poetry.[34] "The Junto Room" also reflects this theme. Naming Junto members after the English poets who established the literary characteristics that would define neoclassical verse, Scull had the Junto recreate the history of English poetry in the New World.

In their surviving accounts of the Junto, both Franklin and Scull emphasize the structure of their meetings, but members also had time for casual conversation. Franklin's friend Hugh Roberts, a Quaker merchant, joined the Junto once a space opened. His personal experience shows the impact of

Franklin's playful conversation. Grace was not the club's only lover of punning. After receiving a pun-filled letter from Roberts, Franklin took credit for
making him a punster.[35]

The Junto would affect Franklin's social, intellectual, and professional life.
In mid-May 1728, he and Meredith quit Keimer's printing house to establish
their own. They left amicably; Keimer had no idea the two would become his
competitors. Their new equipment had arrived from London, and they found
an ideal house on the south side of Market a few doors below Second Street.
They called it the New Printing Office. Using part of the first floor for their
printshop, they rented the rest to Thomas Godfrey, another Junto member, to
use as his glaziery. Godfrey rented the building's upper floor for his wife and
family. With their arrangement, the Godfreys would provide room and board
for Franklin and Meredith.[36]

Once they set up their press and opened the New Printing Office, another
Junto member helped Franklin and Meredith secure their first big project.
Breintnall arranged to have them print part of *The History of the Quakers*,
William Sewel's authoritative chronicle of the Society of Friends. The
Philadelphia Monthly Meeting of Friends sponsored the edition. Keimer had
started printing it years earlier but it proved far too laborious and time-
consuming. He never finished it.[37]

FIGURE 10.1 Carol M. Highsmith, *Benjamin Franklin's Printing Press* (2013). Library of
Congress Prints and Photographs Division, Washington, DC, LC-DIG-highsm-56717.

The New Printing Office issued a variety of forms and other business documents: apprenticeship bonds, arbitration bonds, bills of lading, book labels,
lottery tickets, marriage surety bonds, mortgage bonds, powers of attorney,
quit-rent notices, real estate advertisements, receipts, and warrants. For
Philadelphia's churches, Franklin printed catechisms, psalm books, religious
tracts, and sermons. Books he printed at his own risk included conduct
manuals, medical handbooks, poems, songbooks, and spelling books.
Franklin's friendship with Andrew Hamilton proved invaluable. In 1730, the
Pennsylvania Assembly voted to name Franklin its official printer. Hamilton,
who was speaker of the assembly, had used his influence to help Franklin
secure this lucrative government contract.[38]

Once he established his business, Franklin began considering his marriage
prospects. While he was in London, Deborah Read had married John Rogers, a
union she now regretted. Rogers turned out to be a lout and a cad and a dead-
beat. He deserted her, fleeing Philadelphia for the West Indies in December
1727. One rumor said he had a wife abroad. Another said he perished at sea.
A third possibility: Rogers could make a Chillingworthian return at any
moment. Benjamin remained fond of Deborah, but, given her situation, he
hesitated to reignite their romance and looked elsewhere for affection.

A sexual indiscretion on Franklin's part resulted in an unplanned pregnancy. Around 1728, one of his lovers gave birth to a baby boy whom he
named William and agreed to raise. The identity of William's mother has
escaped history. Though Franklin did not always take the advice of his Latin
textbook—*Meretricem fuge*—William's mother was probably not a prostitute, as some have conjectured. If she were, Franklin could not have been certain he was the father. She must have been a woman of higher status, one
unwilling to raise or even acknowledge the boy.[39]

An illegitimate child limited Franklin's marital prospects. After William's
birth, he and Deborah rekindled their romance. She hesitated to assume responsibility for a stepson, but, given her uncertain situation, she had few marriage
prospects. To her credit, Deborah agreed to raise William as hers. Because
Rogers's fate remained unknown, Benjamin and Deborah could not legally
wed. They formed a common-law marriage, announcing to friends on September
1, 1730, they would from that point forward live together as man and wife.

When Franklin and Meredith quit Keimer's printing house, Webb
remained there. They still saw him on Friday nights at the Junto. Somehow
Webb managed to charm a wealthy woman into buying out his indenture.
Freed by the fall of 1728, he approached Franklin and Meredith for work.
They had nothing for him, but since they were planning a newspaper, they

might need him soon. Having written newspaper articles back in England, Webb looked forward to editing a paper but knew Franklin would serve as editor, leaving him little but manual labor. Webb revealed Franklin's secret plans to Keimer. His behavior violated both his friendship with Franklin and Meredith and the Junto's rules against revealing club members' secrets.

Learning Franklin's plans for a newspaper to compete with Bradford's *American Weekly Mercury*, Keimer drafted a proposal for his own newspaper. He attacked the *Mercury*, then Pennsylvania's sole newspaper, calling it "not only a reproach to the province, but such a scandal to the very name of printing, that it may, for its unparallel'd blunders and incorrectness, be truly stiled *Nonsence in Folio*." Keimer's proposal stopped Franklin and Meredith from starting their newspaper.[40]

Keimer quashed whatever hopes Webb had for editing the paper. He would edit it himself, so Webb's duplicitous behavior gained him nothing. Keimer titled his newspaper *The Universal Instructor in All Arts and Sciences: and The Pennsylvania Gazette*. Its first issue appeared on December 24, 1728. His long-winded title reflects Keimer's long-range plan for the paper, which would take advantage of the current interest in general knowledge that English encyclopedist Ephraim Chambers represented. Chambers's *Cyclopaedia* appeared in 1728, and copies reached Philadelphia that September. When Keimer started serializing it, he was reprinting a brand-new work. He never calculated how long the serialization would take. Franklin did. Without exaggerating, he figured it would take fifty years for the *Universal Instructor* to serialize Chambers.[41]

Franklin, a shrewd and ruthless businessman, went after Keimer's *Gazette*. He proposed to Bradford an essay series for the *Mercury*, hoping to enhance the popularity of Bradford's newspaper and thus expedite Keimer's failure. Aware the essays would increase his newspaper's circulation, Bradford accepted the proposal, perhaps without realizing that once Franklin had run Keimer out of business, he might turn against him. Sure enough, Franklin and Bradford would develop a heated rivalry in the coming years.

"The Busy-Body," as Franklin titled the essay series, began in February 1729. Mr. Busy-Body observes in his first installment that few people have access to high-quality literature. Instead of reprinting outdated European articles, Bradford could entertain readers with literary extracts. Though Bradford was gracious enough to run this essay series, Franklin used his first number to criticize the contents of the *Mercury*. But Franklin's point was valid. Not only would a good extract entertain and instruct newspaper readers, it would also improve their conversation. Good books make good talk.

With "Busy-Body 4," Franklin followed his own advice, presenting a well-chosen extract from a book of travels and making it relevant to Philadelphia society. When paying a social visit, how long should a person stay? A guest who left too soon risked offending the host, but one who stayed too long became an annoyance. How could both host and guest agree on the ideal time to end a social call? Having found a solution to this thorny matter of etiquette in his reading, Mr. Busy-Body shares it with his readers, extracting a passage about the Turkish manner of entertaining visitors.

Mr. Busy-Body does not name his source, which has just recently come to light. Franklin took the extract from Henry Maundrell's *Journey from Aleppo to Jerusalem*, a work consistent with his earlier reading. At the *Courant* office, Franklin had familiarized himself with George Sandys's travels in the Near East. The publisher's preface to *A Journey from Aleppo to Jerusalem* says that Maundrell intended his book as a sequel to Sandys. But Maundrell deserves credit in his own right as an important figure in the history of English travel writing.[42]

Maundrell recounted a typical social call in Turkey, explaining how it would end. "Busy-Body 4" repeats his account of the perfuming of the beards. Prior to this ceremony, the Turkish host would put some hot coals in a small silver chafing dish with a perforated lid. Onto the coals, he would place a piece of aromatic agarwood before shutting the lid. The dish would then be held beneath the chin of each male guest as smoke escaped through the holes. The pleasant odor would permeate each beard, turning it into a wearable nosegay.[43]

Maundrell admitted that the perfuming-of-the-beards ceremony may sound silly, but it served an important social function, telling houseguests it was time to go. Once their beards have been perfumed, guests could leave without fearing they would offend their host. After relating the Turkish ceremony, Mr. Busy-Body informs readers that he has adapted it for himself. He now provides French brandy for men and citron-water for women. Having treated them, he expects his guests will leave, so he can resume his studies.

Franklin's use of Maundrell's *Journey* in "Busy-Body 4" parallels the use of books in the Junto. Given its rules and proposals about reading, it is not hard to imagine how Maundrell's *Journey* would have been discussed in the Junto. Having just finished reading and enjoying the book, one member would discuss its contents with the others. They would take what Maundrell says about Turkish culture and apply it to their own. One member might enjoy what he heard about the book so much he would ask the person who introduced it to copy the memorable passage for him.

When Keimer learned that Breintnall was helping Franklin with the essay series, he wrote a fanciful essay, "Hue and Cry after the Busy-Body," depicting them as conjoined twins, a colonial American Luigi and Angelo. Writing in the second person, Keimer described Mr. Busy-Body's appearance: "You saw two heads, belong to one trunk, and when so united, form the *Busy-Body*."[44] After writing the sixth and seventh numbers, Breintnall completely took over the series starting with number 9.

"The Busy-Body" stopped being part of Franklin's writing life once Breintnall took control, but it became part of his reading life. Breintnall's "Busy-Body" essays fall short of Franklin's, but not too short. Number 9 incisively contrasts how good men and bad react to accusations of wrongdoing. Whereas good men react in a calm and temperate manner, bad men "have the *truth* to fear; falsehood and darkness are their refuge; hence they appear so uneasy when their conduct is like to come under the least examination."[45]

Number 16 incorporates a mock-illiterate letter from a country hick signed "G. L." This badly spelled letter ironically addresses the issue of proper spelling. G. L. explains that his cousin bet the local schoolmaster about the spelling of certain words. G. L. asks Mr. Busy-Body to settle the bet because the method the schoolmaster has chosen is laughable. With its mock-illiterate dialect, "Busy-Body" rivals another American literary classic: G. W. Harris's *Sut Lovingood*. G. L. explains: "Now the skool-mastur haz lade a wagur that hee spells ritest, and will be dissyded by the *Uneversal Instrukter*; and therefore my cuzzin laffs at him for he sez that hee haz casted it up, and he fynds that theze wards woant wun off um be printed in the *Struckter*, in less tyme then sevvinti fyve yeers, and twelv wekes."[46] Franklin's fifty-year estimate lowballed the time it would take Keimer to serialize Chamber's *Cyclopaedia*. G. L.'s cousin says it will take over seventy-five years.

Keimer continued publishing the *Struckter* and serializing Chambers's *Cyclopaedia* into September without leaving the "A's." Before the month's end, he had had enough. With the September 25th issue, his last, Keimer announced that Franklin and Meredith had purchased the newspaper. With the sale, Keimer threw in his copy of Chambers's *Cyclopaedia*, expecting Franklin would want to continue reprinting articles from it. He would not. David Harry, whose apprenticeship had ended, purchased Keimer's press and types and set up his own printing business. Seeing Harry as a rival, Franklin proposed a partnership, but Harry scorned the offer. Keimer moved to Barbados.[47]

Breintnall had continued the essay series in the *Mercury* through the summer, but after "Busy-Body 32," which appeared in the September 25th issue, he abruptly ended it. In other words, as soon as Franklin took over Keimer's newspaper, Breintnall stopped helping Bradford. In its eight-month history, "The Busy-Body" had transformed *The American Weekly Mercury* from a fact-based newspaper into a weekly that presented entertaining essays in the manner of *The Spectator*. Bradford lost the best part of his paper at the exact moment he started competing with a formidable newspaper editor: Benjamin Franklin.[48]

Franklin and Meredith published the first issue of their newspaper without missing a beat—or a week. Retitled *The Pennsylvania Gazette*, the first issue appeared on October 2nd. It reveals the work and thought Franklin put into it. Pennsylvania's annual election took place on October 1st of that year. Franklin reported the results the very next day! His report gives the election returns from Chester County as well as Philadelphia County. He must have stationed a man with a fast horse at the Chester County Courthouse that night to await the results. Franklin ended the article apologizing for the absence of returns from two other counties, Bucks and Lancaster. Though characteristic, this self-effacing apology detracts from Franklin's extraordinary achievement. His planning and expedience put him a week ahead of Bradford, who would not report the election returns until the 9th.[49]

The New Printing Office and *The Pennsylvania Gazette* prospered until April 1730, when Franklin and Meredith faced a financial crisis of existential proportions. The merchant who had imported the press and types had only received half his fee, so he sued for the rest. Franklin feared they would lose their entire printing plant. The Junto to the rescue: Two members—Robert Grace and William Coleman—approached Franklin separately and offered to advance the necessary funds. A clerk in a mercantile firm when he joined the Junto, Coleman had since become a successful merchant in his own right. Franklin said he had the "coolest dearest head, the best heart, and the exactest morals, of almost any man I ever met." The two men had one caveat. Neither Grace nor Coleman wanted Franklin to continue with Meredith, who, they said, "was often seen drunk in the streets, and playing at low games in alehouses."[50]

Meredith's father had hoped that business responsibilities and Franklin's influence would cure his son's debauchery. They had not. Franklin dissolved their partnership and became sole proprietor of the New Printing Office. Meredith left for North Carolina and turned farmer. Within a decade, he was back in Philadelphia. Franklin advanced him hundreds of chapbooks, so Meredith could enter the chapman's trade. With a pack full of books, Meredith left Philadelphia and faded into the countryside. Franklin never saw him again.

Richard Lewis and the News

FRANKLIN'S PRINTING BUSINESS limited his reading time. Whereas the books he had worked on while a London journeyman often made good reading, those he published at the New Printing Office seldom did. Since Philadelphia was a much smaller book market than London, Franklin had to select titles carefully. He could ill afford to publish books with little chance of turning a profit. Instead, he published mainly practical books, rarely belletristic writings.

One facet of Franklin's printing business did bring together his working life with his reading life. As editor and publisher of *The Pennsylvania Gazette*, he exchanged copies of it for other colonial newspapers from Boston to Barbados, which allowed him to read much recent poetry. Since Franklin seldom wrote literary criticism, his thoughts about American verse have gone unrecorded, but he chose several poems to reprint in the *Gazette*. These selections reflect his tacit critical approval.

In January 1730, Franklin reprinted a 219-line poem that had appeared in *The Maryland Gazette* the previous month, "To Mr. Samuel Hastings (Shipwright of Philadelphia) on His Launching the *Maryland-Merchant*, a Large Ship Built by Him at Annapolis." The poem appeared anonymously, but it was written by Richard Lewis, the greatest Augustan poet in American literature.[1]

"To Mr. Samuel Hastings" uses several literary techniques characteristic of contemporary English verse but also incorporates unique American imagery. Three short-verse paragraphs form its introduction. Save for some occasional triplets for emphasis, the whole poem is written in heroic couplets. Ending the introduction, the speaker of the poem beckons Hastings to listen while he relates the history of shipbuilding. He presents it as a "progress" piece, a common technique of long Augustan poems.

The history begins the moment Adam's descendants build a vessel to cross the Euphrates. To characterize this early boat, Lewis used a Native American term—a canoe—and thus applied his knowledge of indigenous culture to interpret biblical times. Since all human life stretches back to Adam and Eve, according to the Bible, culture has developed more slowly in the New World than the Old. America thus offered a unique opportunity to gaze into the past and understand how other parts of the world have developed.

Lewis's progress piece mentions some famous ships and their captains, including Jason, who "In the fam'd *Argo* did the seas explore, / (A golden ram, upon her stern she bore)." Melding biblical history and classical mythology, Lewis demonstrated his forward-thinking ability to combine different literary and cultural traditions. His wide-ranging references enhance the complexity of his verse and challenge the belief systems on which they are based. Lewis would not be the last American poet to take such an eclectic approach. His literary and cultural references anticipate T. S. Eliot's in *The Waste Land*.[2]

The poem stresses that the American shipbuilding industry has helped the colonies thrive. Maryland ships have brought products from around the globe to North America. Besides putting colonists in touch with the world at large, international trade has let them obtain whatever goods they need: "What Nature has to Maryland deny'd / She might by ships from all the world provide."[3] Having finished the progress piece, the speaker of the poem starts the next major section, which personifies the rivers that empty into the Chesapeake Bay, their father-king. Summoned by the Chesapeake, the rivers arrive one by one, culminating with the Susquehanna. Once they have arrived, the Chesapeake delivers an address paying homage to the ship Hastings has built.

The day after Franklin reprinted "To Mr. Samuel Hastings" in his newspaper, Andrew Bradford reprinted it in his. Franklin had scooped Bradford again. When it comes to poetry, "To Mr. Samuel Hastings" is an exception in the rivalry between Franklin and Bradford. During the late 1720s and early 1730s, Bradford was quicker to print American poetry than Franklin. Their treatment of newspaper verse indicates their contrasting editorial policy.

As a Junto member, Franklin enjoyed poetry on a weekly basis. Every Friday night, he listened to fellow members read their poems. Sometimes he wrote poetry himself and read it at their meetings. Other times he revised or adapted poems he had read. From the time Franklin founded the Junto until he started editing *The Pennsylvania Gazette*, he believed most poetry should remain in manuscript form. Poems should be shared among family, friends, and club members but not necessarily published.

The uneven quality of the verse James Franklin had printed in *The New-England Courant* made his brother wary about publishing poems in the

Gazette. Thomas Fleet came away from his experience with the Couranteers feeling much the same. Almost two years passed between the time Fleet began editing the *Weekly Rehearsal* and the time he published the first poem under his editorship. Even then, Fleet still had some misgivings. His introduction to the poem says, "Poetry does not look overgraceful in a newspaper."[4] Bradford was more open to local poets. As Franklin matured as a newspaper editor, he would adopt Bradford's open-minded stance toward publishing verse.

After Franklin started publishing poetry in *The Pennsylvania Gazette*, he sometimes took Bradford to task when his newspaper verse fell short of acceptable poetic standards. One week, Bradford published an eight-line poem attacking the character of a mutual friend. The poem is signed with the initials, "B. L." The following week Franklin assumed the poet's identity and wrote a letter to *The Pennsylvania Gazette*. Wanting to appear open and above board, he had asked Bradford to publish his name. The "B. L." with which the poem is signed are not his initials, he says, but the first two letters of his name, which Bradford had accidentally truncated. He now supplies the remaining letters to complete his name: BLOCKHEAD.[5]

As a publisher of newspaper verse, Bradford had already gone through a metamorphosis similar to what Fleet and Franklin would undergo. Though he started *The American Weekly Mercury* in 1719, Bradford did not publish any local poetry in his newspaper for several years. This is not to say that Philadelphia did not have an active poetry scene. It did. But poetry writing belonged to the city's manuscript culture. Henry Brooke, who lived in Lewes Town, Delaware, often came to Philadelphia and shared his manuscript verse with a coterie of coffeehouse friends.[6] Another poetic circle formed around Aquila Rose, the charismatic young man who had died before Franklin reached Philadelphia and whom Franklin had sought to replace in Bradford's printing house.

From his christening, Aquila Rose was destined to live a romantic life. Since *aquila* is Latin for "eagle," his name embodies the image of an eagle rising high above the land. Having left England the victim of unrequited love, Rose traveled the world as a sailor, reaching Philadelphia around 1719. Though a rose cannot grow on a sea-onion, Aquila Rose blossomed in Philadelphia. His work as a journeyman printer gave him a livelihood, but his literary activities established Rose's enduring reputation. He befriended the city's leading writers: Joseph Breintnall, Samuel Keimer, William Keith, and Jacob Taylor.

Rose's romantic background drew others to him, but he also had a gift for conversation and a talent for reconciling people with different viewpoints. Breintnall honored his people skills in "An Encomium to Aquila Rose, on His

Art in Praising." The poem remained in manuscript until Franklin published it in *Poems on Several Occasions*, a collected edition of Rose's poetry that would appear several years after his death. The volume is the first posthumously published collection of verse in American literature.[7]

Breintnall's elegy, "To the Memory of Aquila Rose, Deceas'd," also appears in *Poems on Several Occasions*. This verse biography is a literary breakthrough. David S. Shields observed that Breintnall gave the poem an archetypal quality, creating a pattern that American literature would often repeat. He framed Rose's life as the story of a man who suffered before winning renown. Breintnall is the first writer in American literature to transform a poet into a romantic figure. Rose's poetry, which follows Breintnall's verse biography in the collection, verifies and illustrates the romantic life he led.[8]

"To the Memory of Aquila Rose" also reflects the transatlantic nature of much colonial American poetry. Its final verse paragraph addresses British readers: "Ye *Rose's* friends, that in *Britannia* dwell / Who knew his worth, and best the loss can tell."[9] Besides contributing to literary history, this elegy helps reconstruct Rose's life. The poem contains much realistic detail, chronicling what Breintnall learned as their friendship developed.

Rose shared his poems with Philadelphia friends and encouraged them to write verse. His personal life also flourished in the New World. He wed a local woman named Mary, who bore him a son, Joseph. To support his young family, Rose sought more permanent employment. In 1723, his friendship with Governor Keith helped him secure an appointment to operate the ferry across the Schuylkill River at the end of Market Street, a position that also involved running an inn. Rose signed a twenty-one-year contract, started operating the ferry, and began making improvements on both sides of the Schuylkill. But tragedy struck one day that summer when a violent gust broke the ferry loose from its moorings.

An expert seaman, Rose retrieved the ferry but caught a chill, which developed into a fever, or, as Breintnall says in his elegy, "Freezing juices into boiling turn'd / Scalded the veins, and sore the vitals burn'd." Sometimes Breintnall is more clinician than poet: "Then soon defluxions thro' bowels rush, / Nor stay for Nature's kind digesting push." Four lines later, Aquila Rose is dead. He was 28.[10]

In death, Rose continued to affect local poetry. By no means were Keimer and Breintnall the only ones who elegized Rose. Bradford published two other elegies for him in *The American Weekly Mercury*. Not counting a brief poem Keimer had written as an advertisement, the Rose elegies are the earliest American poems to appear in Bradford's newspaper. These elegies changed the local poetry scene, expanding the audience for poetry from a few small, overlapping circles to Philadelphia's entire newspaper-reading public.[11]

Though Bradford began publishing newspaper verse in 1723, he had published poetry in other formats. In 1720, Rose proposed writing and publishing a broadside poem that Bradford's apprentices could distribute to *Mercury* subscribers on New Year's Day, January 1, 1721. The poem would help them coax a tip from the subscribers on their newspaper route. This, the first North American newspaper carriers' address, was a resounding success. Rose would write additional poems for New Year's Day in 1722 and 1723. His broadsides do not survive, but Franklin reprinted Rose's New Year's Day verse in *Poems on Several Occasions*. Rose's last, "To Bring New Years, Revolving Time Makes Haste," is his best. It celebrates the power of the printed word to gather news and disseminate it throughout the world.[12]

After Rose's death, Bradford would keep issuing annual newspaper carriers' addresses. So would Franklin, once he began publishing *The Pennsylvania Gazette*. In late 1741, Franklin put an apprentice in charge of recruiting a poet to write the annual poem. That apprentice was none other than Joseph Rose. Franklin never took Aquila Rose's place in Bradford's shop, but he did become a father figure to his son. That year, Joseph Rose wrote a letter to Jacob Taylor, asking him to compose the annual poem.

Taylor's reply does not survive, nor do any copies of the January 1, 1742, poem, but Joseph Rose's letter reveals much about the genre. It explains that he was writing to Taylor because Breintnall, who usually wrote the New Year's Day poem, was too busy. Explaining that the apprentices who delivered the paper sorely needed a poet, Rose told Taylor, "Their former bard, is now so fatigued with business, that he can't perform his usual kindnesses that way."[13] Rose's plural—"kindnesses"—reveals that Breintnall had written the annual poem for at least two years. Rose's letter to Taylor tells him to structure the poem around that year's leading news stories. Rose even listed some possible headlines to cover. The headlines poem had originated while Breintnall was writing the annual verses.

Though published anonymously, the poem for January 1, 1739, has the concrete detail characteristic of Breintnall's best poetry. It mentions how news spreads throughout Philadelphia. The personification of "News" running around perplexed is charming:

> *To taverns, inns, and coffee-houses*, next
> The rambling News runs crowding in, perplext,
> But scrutiniz'd, discuss'd and modell'd, thence
> It sometimes goes with more of truth and sense.[14]

The poem ends as *The Pennsylvania Gazette* synthesizes all the various news stories and presents the truth to its readers.

The poem for January 1, 1740, suggests that Franklin's apprentices had given Breintnall a list of headlines to use in his poem. Initially, he bristled at such a formulaic approach. His poem shows considerable personality: "I'm out of sorts, and know not what to write; / The war's begun with *Spain*—but who will fight?" Breintnall was talking about the War of Jenkins's Ear, which started after Captain Robert Jenkins, the skipper of a British merchant vessel, was maimed by Spanish sailors who had boarded his ship. The War of Jenkin's Ear would continue until 1742, when it would be subsumed within a wider conflict, the War of the Austrian Succession. After this attempt at relating the news in verse, the speaker of the poem gives up and selects a different approach: "Unfitted for this task, a tale I'll tell, / In hopes the substitute may do as well."[15]

By January 1, 1741, Breintnall had mastered the news-headlines poem, developing the basic structure Rose would outline in his letter to Taylor. It takes readers on an international journey from Russia to Corsica to Pennsylvania. News carriers' addresses would remain an annual tradition through the nineteenth century. Often new poems would be written for the occasion, but sometimes old poems would be recirculated. In the 1870s, newsboys would distribute copies of Edgar Allan Poe's mellifluous poem *The Bells*. Though the New Year's poem disappeared in the early twentieth century, the approach Breintnall used for the January 1, 1741, poem has had a longer life. Visual imagery and verbal commentary have replaced the heroic couplet as its medium, but the year-in-review remains a vital journalistic tradition.[16]

The almanacs Bradford published also contain poetry, sometimes very good poetry in the case of Jacob Taylor's almanacs. Born in England around 1670, Taylor emigrated to America before the seventeenth century ended. He published his first American almanac in 1699. Within a few years, they earned a good reputation. After he issued his almanac for 1702, James Logan informed William Penn that Taylor "wrote a pretty almanac for this year."[17]

Before writing almanacs, Taylor had written *Tenebrae*, a twenty-year guide to solar and lunar eclipses calculated from 1697, the year of its publication. Within this work—the first mathematical book published in British North America—Taylor included an essay about the science of measurement. After *Tenebrae*, Taylor would apply his mathematical precision, classical learning, and poetic ability in his almanacs. His talents would draw him to Franklin, and the two became friends.[18]

An accomplished poet, Taylor has largely escaped literary history because he published most of his verse in his almanacs. Franklin enjoyed reading

Taylor's poetry, which influenced *Poor Richard's Almanack*, but modern readers have been denied a similar experience. Taylor wrote almanacs every year for decades, but few survive. Taylor's almanac for 1737, one that does, contains a poem that pays tribute to Francis Quarles's *Enchiridion*, a collection of maxims.[19]

Most people threw away their almanacs at year's end, but Breintnall kept his copies of Taylor's almanacs. Rereading Taylor's 1737 almanac a couple of years later, Breintnall came across the reference to Quarles. Taylor noted how almanac-makers excerpted Quarles's *Enchiridion* to fill the blank spaces in their almanacs. Breintnall imagined reversing the process for Taylor, that is, gathering the miscellaneous tidbits of poetry and erudition scattered throughout his almanacs and assembling them into a collection. Breintnall proposed that Bradford publish an "*Enchiridion* that shall contain a collection from his almanacks for some number of years past; of poetry, pieces of history and useful observations of divers kinds with some of his prefaces and chronologies."[20] Breintnall's proposed collection could have preserved many of Taylor's poems, but nothing came of it.

Though Aquila Rose had promoted camaraderie within his poetic circle, its members did not get along as well after his death. Keimer took advantage of Taylor's reputation as an almanac maker. In late 1725, he published *A Compleat Ephemeris for 1726* under Taylor's name. After Franklin had returned to Philadelphia in 1726, this is the almanac he would have used for the rest of the year. Deborah's mother Sarah Read sold it at the little shop she ran from their home. So did Mary Rose, who ran a shop from her home after her husband's death. In his preface, Keimer argues that girls should receive an education equal to boys: "I know not why the former should not be as capable to receive and improve useful knowledge as the latter, since God himself has made use of women for the most honourable, most noble and most heavenly employments."[21]

Following his preface, Keimer included a typical feature of contemporary almanacs, a woodcut illustration depicting the Man of Signs with the parts of his body keyed to the constellations of the Zodiac that controlled them. The Man of Signs perpetuated the Renaissance concept of the human body as a microcosm of the universe, a scientifically untenable idea that nonetheless continued to shape the popular imagination.[22]

Seated atop the world, Keimer's naked Man of Signs resembles those in earlier American almanacs. He has short, curly hair, narrow shoulders, and flabby hips. He even has a little paunch. Keimer distinguished his Man of Signs by giving him a voice. He speaks a hudibrastic poem that appears beneath the illustration, "A Prologue Suppos'd to be Spoken by the Anatomy Above." It begins: "Behold kind readers, here, I'm come, / Without a rag to hide my bum."[23]

This prologue introduces "An Arch Young Wag, in Time of Night," a verse fable dramatizing how ignorant and gullible stargazers could be. As poetry, "An Arch Young Wag" excels Keimer's elegy on Aquila Rose. Manifesting his playful humor, this poem may be the best one Keimer ever wrote. Using a lit candle to dupe the public, Keimer's young wag anticipates "The Burning Shame" in *Huckleberry Finn*. He places the candle in a lantern and attaches it to a kite, which he launches into the night sky to see how Philadelphia stargazers will react. Fear is their first reaction, as the behavior of a stargazer named Will shows:

> As soon as Will espies the light, sir,
> He runs away, in piteous fright sir,
> (Like an old miser losing riches,
> Or boy with looseness, in his breeches,)
> And roars aloud, with lips wide open,
> As Cape May parts from Cape Henlopen.

Keimer's scatological humor creates an earthy contrast to the stargazers' skyward glances. His local geography lends the poem additional significance. To illustrate how wide Will opens his lips in fear, Keimer uses a hyperbolic simile comparing them to the two capes where the Delaware Bay opens into the Atlantic. Keimer's simile thus parallels the male body with the North American continent in a manner not dissimilar to Sylvia Plath's "Daddy," whose eponymous subject has "one gray toe / Big as a Frisco seal / And a head in the freakish Atlantic."[24]

"An Arch Young Wag" catalogues the various interpretations of local stargazers, who mistake the kite for a star, a comet, or some other heavenly body. A lengthy moral ends the poem. The poet lambastes the stargazers, again using scatological humor for emphasis: "[They] scarce know how to split an *atom*; / Nor can they (mighty sons of art) / Take the dimensions of a fart." Keimer's scatological humor does not end here. To gloss these lines, he added the following footnote, a brilliant example of mock erudition: "Its said a famous mathematician, among the many wonderful and useful discoveries he has made for the use of the learned, has found out that a *fart* does not weigh in the *hydrostatical balance*, the thousandth part of a grain, yet it shall expand it self so far as to occupy the whole atmosphere of a large drawing-room."

Taylor was not amused. Not only did Keimer publish this almanac under his name, he also used it to ridicule the science of measurement that Taylor held dear. Taylor placed a notice in Bradford's *Mercury* to disavow the "filthy foolish pamphlet . . . flying about in my name. Know all men that I am not the author of that fulsom garbage, nor any part thereof." With this protest, Taylor included an eighty-eight-line poem, "To S. K." Without stooping to hudibrastics, Taylor showed that he could give as well as he got. He critiqued the educational schemes that Keimer discusses elsewhere in the almanac: "All students in the mathematic arts / Imploy'd by thee, shall measure turds and farts."[25]

Junto members appreciated Bradford's willingness to publish their verse. Before placing poems with the *Mercury*, no doubt they read them aloud at their regular Friday night gatherings. In June 1729, Bradford published Breintnall's "Plain Description of One Single Street in This City." Breintnall's title reflects his method. Describing Market Street, he abandoned poetic diction to capture its look. Breintnall's urban street scene departs from the topographical poetry of John Denham and John Dyer. Whereas Dyer looked at castle ruins and saw the evanescence of human life, Breintnall looked at the flourishing city street and saw promise for the future.[26]

"A Plain Description" starts on the banks of the Delaware River, looking westward:

> At *Delaware's* broad stream, the view begins,
> Where jutting wharfs, food-freighted boats take in.
> Then, with th' advancing sun, direct your eye;
> Wide opes the street, with firm brick buildings high:
> Step gently rising, o'er the pebbly way,
> And see the shops their tempting wares display.

Like his elegy for Aquila Rose, Breintnall's "Plain Description" has much documentary value. No contemporary description of Philadelphia is more detailed. Breintnall's poem is the single best street view of Philadelphia in American literature before Franklin's autobiography. But Breintnall had an advantage over Franklin, who described Philadelphia of the 1720s using fifty-year-old memories. Breintnall recorded how the city looked at the time.

While avoiding poetic language, "A Plain Description" is not without literary sophistication. It is no coincidence that the speaker of the poem directs the reader's gaze to follow the sun. Much as Scull uses the names of English poets in his Junto poems to suggest that English poetry is being recreated in

America, Breintnall's poem reflects the idea of *translatio*. From the Delaware River to the Schuylkill, Philadelphia developed from east to west.

George Webb also wrote some poems about Philadelphia. The month after Breintnall's "Plain Description" Webb published "Let Philadelphia's Generous Sons Excuse" in the *Mercury*. His poem is technically superior to Breintnall's "Plain Description." In other words, it shows a greater mastery of the tropes and language of poetry writing, but Breintnall's documentary poem has more lasting power. Its realistic detail has helped his poem transcend fleeting literary trends.[27]

A poem about Philadelphia that Webb published in Titan Leeds's *American Almanack* is stronger than "Let Philadelphia's Generous Sons Excuse." "Goddess of Numbers, Who Art Wont to Rove" consists of twelve six-line verse paragraphs, each appearing near the top of every monthly page in the calendar. The one for March is the best:

> Stretch'd on the bank of *Delaware's* rapid stream
> Stands *Philadelphia*, not unknown to fame;
> Here the tall vessels safe at anchor ride,
> And *Europe's* wealth flows in with every tide
> Through each wide ope the distant prospect's clear;
> The well-built streets are regular and fair.

Webb's verse still lacks Breintnall's specific details, but the grandeur of the ocean-going vessels crowded in the Delaware River is impressive. The couplet that closes May's verse paragraph shows Webb also using the *translatio* theme. He depicts a decrepit Europe as civilization has traveled westward to America: "*Europe* shall mourn her ancient fame declin'd, / And *Philadelphia* be the *Athens* of mankind."[28]

Webb also wrote a poem about the Philadelphia Bachelors' Club, *Batchelors-Hall: A Poem*, which Franklin published in a handsome twelve-page pamphlet as a keepsake for Webb's friends. When Franklin advertised it, he announced, "There is but a small number printed, so that few will be left for sale after the designed presents are made by the author." James Hamilton was one reader who obtained a copy of *Batchelors-Hall*.[29]

Two commendatory poems preface the pamphlet. Breintnall wrote the first, Taylor the second. "The Generous Muse Concern'd to See" lacks the documentary quality of Breintnall's best verse, but the poem is notable as an experiment in style. Eschewing heroic couplets, Breintnall wrote the poem in tetrameter lines rhyming a-b-a-b, a step toward the ballad stanza that would not return to favor until the Romantic era. Taylor used heroic couplets for "In Ancient Greece the Muses Flourish'd Long," which also treats the theme of *translatio*.

Webb stressed the conviviality that prevailed at the Bachelors' Club. To characterize the clubical humor of its members, he applied two terms Joseph Addison had defined in *Spectator* 62: "false wit" and "true wit." False wit is more superficial; it depends on a resemblance of words. True wit involves a resemblance of ideas. The term "true wit" does more than characterize the humor that Webb's bachelors enjoy; it embodies their social code: decorum, good nature, refinement, and urbanity.[30]

Philadelphia's colonial poets gave the city a literary atmosphere and established poetry as a vital mode of expression. The city would remain the center for American poetry throughout the eighteenth century.[31] Franklin was vital to the colonial poetry-writing tradition. Besides encouraging Junto members to write poetry, he eventually encouraged poetry writing as the editor of *The Pennsylvania Gazette*. In addition to reprinting the best poetry he read in other colonial papers, he began publishing original poems. His newspaper's growing popularity further expanded the readership for poetry.

In 1731, Franklin read another poem by Richard Lewis, "A Journey from Patapsco to Annapolis," which he reprinted in *The Pennsylvania Gazette*. This poem—Lewis's masterpiece—initially appeared in a now-lost issue of *The Maryland Gazette*, but Franklin was the first to republish it. British magazines reprinted "A Journey from Patapsco to Annapolis." Edward Kimber, who read the poem in *The London Magazine*, enjoyed it so much he clipped it out and carried the clipping with him throughout his American travels. Lewis's poetic journey was both guide and inspiration for Kimber's American odyssey.[32]

"A Journey from Patapsco to Annapolis," the greatest neoclassical poem to emerge from the colonial American experience, also anticipates Romantic verse. A poem of self-exploration, it is a precursor to Walt Whitman's "Song of Myself." In addition, Lewis's poem celebrates the natural world of North America and includes set pieces on two indigenous birds: the mockingbird, a prominent motif of Southern colonial literature, and the hummingbird, another distinctive American motif. Lewis's paean to the hummingbird anticipates Emily Dickinson's hummingbird in "A Route of Evanescence."[33]

Lewis's trip functions at both the literal and metaphysical level. His trek from Patapsco—the site of present-day Baltimore—to Annapolis is also an excursion to the center of the soul. Trying to understand where he belongs in the universe as he confronts recent scientific discoveries, the speaker of the poem asks earth-shattering questions in a more frank and forthright manner than any previous poet in American literature.

Franklin would encounter at least one more poem by Richard Lewis. Published as a pamphlet in 1732, *Carmen seculare* is an occasional poem commemorating Maryland's centennial and celebrating Lord Baltimore's visit. Franklin read *Carmen seculare* in one form or another. If he did not see the pamphlet, then he saw the poem when it was reprinted in *The Gentleman's Magazine*, which he had in his personal library.[34]

Even while praising Maryland's beautiful waters, abundant natural resources, and extraordinary progress, *Carmen seculare* is not without criticism. Lewis directed his ire toward the colony's overreliance on the single-crop system. Tobacco cultivation exhausted the land, impoverished farmers, and limited their opportunities: "Despondent, they impending ruin view, / Yet starving, must their old employ persue."[35]

Kenneth Silverman compared Lewis's sympathy with the Southern planters, who are starving amidst lush virgin land, to Allen Ginsberg's portrayal of burned-out American hipsters starving in the quintessential land of opportunity. Though he did not develop his comparison, Silverman was thinking about the first line from *Howl*: "I saw the best minds of my generation destroyed by madness, starving hysterical naked."[36] Franklin would address similar concerns in his promotional writings.

Lewis's *Carmen seculare* was one of many American poems Franklin could have encountered in *The Gentleman's Magazine*, which gave him another way to read the latest verse. He would eventually accumulate thirty-two volumes of *The Gentleman's Magazine*. Its regular poetry column featured such American poets as Thomas Dale, Adam Thomson, and Charles Woodmason. Its poetry also inspired Franklin. When he founded *The General Magazine* in 1741, he would make a poetry column one of its regular features.[37]

The story of Franklin's magazine illustrates another way that poetry from *The Gentleman's Magazine* inspired him. As Franklin planned his magazine, he spoke with John Webbe, a local attorney with an Irish heritage and literary hopes. Franklin offered him the position of editor. Much as George Webb (no relation) reported Franklin's plan to publish a newspaper to Samuel Keimer, who then scooped him, John Webbe reported Franklin's plan to publish a magazine to Andrew Bradford, who hired him to edit *The American Magazine*, which appeared just a few days before Franklin could publish his *General Magazine*.[38]

Franklin took his revenge in verse. Having read "Teague's Orashion," a satirical poem written in a mock Irish brogue that had appeared in *The*

Gentleman's Magazine, Franklin used the poem as a model for his satire of Webbe, which he titled "Teague's Advertisement." The name "Teague," a derogatory term, embodies the ethnic stereotype of the stupid, blundering, lazy Irishman. In *Magnalia christi americana*, Cotton Mather tells a typical Teague story. Mather's Teague makes the dubious decision to pull a canoe with butt of his musket, which forces him to hold its muzzle in his hand: a formula for disaster. Teague accidentally shoots himself in the arm.[39]

In terms of genre, "Teague's Advertisement" is a versification, a type of parody that involves transposing a serious work of prose into satirical verse. During the Revolutionary era, the versification became a prominent form of political poetry as American authors versified the political speeches and proclamations of British governors and generals. Published in 1741, "Teague's Advertisement" shows Franklin pioneering the genre.[40]

A half dozen years later, Franklin would make another memorable contribution to the genre, "The Speech Versyfied." Using the pseudonym "Ned Type," he versified Governor William Gooch's speech about the Virginia Capitol fire. Written in unryhmed verse with irregular line lengths, "The Speech Versyfied" adumbrates modern free verse. Franklin's daring experiment in form has earned appreciation from both contemporary and modern readers. Dr. Alexander Hamilton said that Ned Type converted Gooch's "lame prose into hobbling verse." Reading Leo Lemay's edition of Franklin's writings, John Updike enjoyed "The Speech Versyfied," which he found a hilarious parody of Governor Gooch's speech.[41]

"Teague's Advertisement" concerns *The American Magazine*. Whereas Franklin had designed his *General Magazine* as an anthology of the best newspaper writing of the day, Webbe tried to make the contents of his *American Magazine* original, which accounted for its expense, as he says in his own advertisement. Paraphrasing Webbe, Franklin has Teague say, "'Tis true, my book is dear; but de reashon is plain. / The best parts of it ish de work of my own brain."[42]

Readers remembered "Teague's Advertisement." After Webbe moved to Maryland and began contributing to *The Maryland Gazette*, the local wits burlesqued him and, in so doing, recalled Franklin's satirical poem. Dr. Adam Thomson, Hamilton's friend and former classmate at Edinburgh, had emigrated from Scotland and settled in Prince George's County. Ridiculing an article Webbe contributed to the *Gazette* about the tobacco inspection law, Thomson wrote "Teague Turn'd Planter." In a footnote, Thomson says that Teague's advertisement "was extremely well burlesqu'd in the *Pennsylvania Gazette*."[43]

"Teague Turn'd Planter" illustrates how the poetry Franklin published in his newspaper inspired other colonial American poets. Having read "Teague's Advertisement," Thomson took inspiration from Franklin's poem to write his own verse satire of Webbe. Other newspaper poems Franklin published similarly influenced colonial American poets. Jacob Taylor read "A Journey from Patapsco to Annapolis" in *The Pennsylvania Gazette* and liked it so much he paid homage to Lewis by writing an imitation of his poem. Taylor's imitation, which appeared in Bradford's *Mercury*, demonstrates the power of the original by contrast. Taylor borrowed much from Lewis: imagery, diction, and figures of speech. Having begun writing poetry in the seventeenth century, Taylor had difficulty adjusting to Lewis's neoclassicism or broaching his religious skepticism, but Lewis's progressive outlook did not stop Taylor's appreciation of his poetry-writing ability or reduce his desire to write more like him.[44]

Despite its uneven quality, Taylor's poem illustrates how the work of one poet, disseminated through the pages of a newspaper, could influence and encourage others. Though hesitant to bring poetry from the privacy of the Junto to the pages of a public newspaper, Franklin ultimately realized that by publishing high-quality poems, he could contribute to the development of American verse. To write good poetry, after all, one must read good poetry.

The Library Company of Philadelphia

AT ONE JUNTO meeting, Franklin proposed that members should combine their personal book collections to form a communal library far surpassing what any could assemble individually. They accepted his proposal, brought their books to Pewter Platter Alley, shelved them in Grace's home, and began borrowing. The books trickled back in rough enough shape to anger their owners. Clearly, the communal library was not working.

In this instance, Franklin had neglected the personal importance of books. Not just repositories of ideas, books are icons of their owners, who hate seeing cherished volumes mistreated. Having failed in its first attempt, the Junto would not abandon their newfound dream of a great library. Members imagined other ways to create a collection they could all enjoy. The result was the Library Company of Philadelphia, the first subscription library in North America.

Franklin led this new organization from its planning stages. Each subscriber would pay 40 shillings to join and 10 for annual dues, which would create an initial fund to establish the collection and a perpetual fund to maintain and expand it. Their subscriptions would let them borrow items from the library and suggest others to acquire. Subscribers would elect a ten-member board of directors and a treasurer annually. The board would choose the secretary. To formulate the rules, Franklin hired local conveyancer Charles Brockden, who filed the Articles of Association on July 1, 1731. Initially, Franklin would appoint a treasurer, secretary, and board of directors. All would serve until proper elections could be held at the first annual subscribers' meeting the following May.

By early November, fifty men were willing to join. Breintnall—Franklin's choice for secretary—called the first directors' meeting, held on November 8th at Nicholas Scull's Bear Tavern. The names of other officers may sound familiar. Franklin chose William Coleman as treasurer. Thomas Godfrey and William Parsons, two more original Junto members, also became directors. So did Dr. Thomas Cadwalader. Thomas Hopkinson, another Junto member, brought his conviviality to the library's board of directors. After Hopkinson's death, Franklin would say that his "virtue and integrity, in every station of life, public and private, will ever make his memory dear to those who knew him." Philip Syng, another Junto member, also joined the library's board of directors.[1]

A silversmith by trade, Syng would engrave the Library Company's official seal from Franklin's design. For its device, Franklin depicted two open books surrounded by beams of light. Between the books, water pours into a big urn. Vents channel the water into smaller urns. Franklin's Latin motto circumscribes the device: *Communiter bona profundere deum est*, "To pour forth benefits for the common good is divine."[2]

The books on the seal represent the library's holdings, but they also function as general symbols of knowledge. Surrounded by light, they recall the iconic volumes that emblem books depict. In his emblem book *Delights for the Ingenious*, Nathaniel Crouch portrays a man reading, even though he is at death's door. Well, he is not actually at death's door, but he does have one foot in the grave, literally in the grave. Creating visual equivalents for traditional metaphors, devices reinforce the close relationship between proverbs and emblems. Though the sun has set, moonlight illuminates the pages of the open book the man holds.[3]

Another man in *Delights for the Ingenious* similarly seeks wisdom. He holds an open book in one hand, and starlight brightens its pages.[4] Light often symbolizes divinity. In Franklin's view, as in these examples from Crouch, light represents the power of books to provide intellectual enlightenment. Water, a symbol of fecundity, gives knowledge a dynamic quality, showing that it flows in a never-ending stream. The one urn pouring into many demonstrates how the Library Company will improve its members, who, in turn, will share their knowledge with others. The urns represent the outpouring of knowledge for the community and the ages.

The directors would receive subscriptions from interested parties at Bear Tavern a few days after the directors' meeting. Franklin printed receipts for all subscribers. They would each receive an individual share, numbered in the order they subscribed. Grace, who volunteered his home to house the library, received share no. 1. Hopkinson subscribed next, receiving share no. 2, and Franklin got share no. 3. John Jones, a cordwainer and another original Junto member, subscribed fourth with Breintnall fifth.[5]

When James Logan learned about the planned library, he offered to help. Logan did not join. He did not need to: He already had the greatest library in colonial Pennsylvania at Stenton, his large estate near Germantown. Logan had come to Philadelphia in 1699 as William Penn's secretary. He rose quickly in colonial government, joining the governor's council and serving on it for decades. He also established a lucrative fur-trading business. Neither political responsibilities nor business opportunities stopped his diverse intellectual pursuits. His surviving books contain substantial marginalia, showing how closely he read them. Logan shared his knowledge with others. Besides loaning books to friends, he wrote papers on astronomy, botany, geometry, mathematics, and navigation. He also encouraged others to develop their intellectual abilities.[6]

When the directors met on Wednesday, March 29, 1732, Godfrey reported that Logan would be happy to recommend books for the Library Company. The directors agreed that Logan was, in Franklin's words, a "gentleman distinguish'd for his universal knowledge, no less than for his judgment in books." They accepted his offer and appointed Godfrey to meet with him and prepare a list of possible titles to order. The following night, Godfrey went to Stenton to see Logan. Franklin accompanied him. Speaking of Logan's library, Franklin said, "It contains many hundred volumes of the best authors in the best editions."[7] The other directors, who assumed the meeting would not take too long, waited at Bear Tavern that night for their return.

No record of their conference survives. What does survive is the initial list of titles the directors ordered from London. Several reflect the discussion that took place at Stenton. No entry on the list shows Logan's input more than Jan Jonston's big book of animals, *Theatrum universale omnium animalium*, a Latin work he owned.[8]

Their passion for mathematics had drawn Logan and Godfrey together. The directors ordered several mathematical works, the most substantial being Jacques Ozanam's *Cursus mathematicus*, a five-volume course of study J. T. Desaguliers had translated into English from the original French. Logan respected Ozanam, but when he read *Cursus mathematicus*, he was disappointed to find an error in the chapter about how to take square roots of fractions.[9]

The list also reflects Franklin's tastes. Having read Cato's letters in *The London Journal*, Franklin was eager to share them. Authors John Trenchard and Thomas Gordon had since published a collected edition. Besides *Cato's Letters*, the list names some of Franklin's other boyhood favorites, including Plutarch's *Lives* and Xenophon's *Memorable Things of Socrates*. It stipulates "Plutarch's Lives in small vols," meaning the directors did not want Thomas North's Renaissance translation, but the newer English translation Tonson published. A few entries represent books Franklin could have helped print in London, including Joseph Addison's *Miscellaneous Works*.[10]

Another item indicates Franklin's recent reading: Jean Barbeyrac's edition of Samuel Pufendorf's *Of the Law and Nature and Nations*. Franklin had used Barbeyrac's preface, "An Historical and Critical Account of the Science of Morality," to write "A Glorious Passage in Perseus," an essay he published in *The Pennsylvania Gazette* that spring. Barbeyrac supplied the Latin quotation from Perseus for his epigraph. That Franklin was reading moral philosophy while writing an appreciation of classical satire is no coincidence. Satire is a mirror of morality, a funhouse mirror.[11]

There is one aspect of the Stenton conference known for sure: It lasted far longer than anyone had imagined. The directors waited hours for Franklin and Godfrey to return to Bear Tavern that night, but they never did. Eventually, Scull had to call out, "Hurry up please, it's time," or something to that effect.

The directors, including Godfrey and Franklin, returned to Bear Tavern Friday night to finalize the list. Once finished, it went to Hopkinson, who was leaving for London soon. The directors also provided instructions. To minimize costs, they had Hopkinson obtain as many books as possible unbound. They also told him to buy additional books with any leftover funds, selected at his discretion. Hopkinson would bring a note from Robert Grace for £45 drawn on Peter Collinson.[12]

Upon reaching London, Hopkinson contacted Collinson, whose home and business were located at the Red Lion in Gracechurch Street near London Bridge. Collinson was an importer/exporter specializing in silk and other fine fabrics, but his passion was botany. He famously said the pleasure of cultivating a garden either attracted temperate and virtuous men or made men temperate and virtuous. A great supporter of public improvement projects, Collinson happily aided the fledgling library.[13]

With Thomas Cadwalader, who had come to London earlier to resume his medical studies, they started shopping for books. The forty-five titles on the list covered a variety of subjects: agriculture; architecture, including Andrea Palladio's *Architecture*, a work that shaped colonial American homebuilding; essays; histories; law, including Thomas Wood's *Institute of the Laws of England*, a standard work that could be found in law libraries throughout colonial America; medical handbooks; poetry, including Pope's *Iliad* and *Odyssey*; and science, including Herman Boerhaave's *New Method of Chemistry*.[14]

One history title, "Vertot's Revolutions," represents a set of works about political uprisings from ancient Rome to modern Europe by the Abbé René Aubert de Vertot, who used the term "revolution" to mean any major event producing significant political change. His works, which would appeal to American readers as the Revolutionary War approached, had already found a receptive American readership. Governor John Montgomerie owned three of Vertot's *Revolutions*, those about Rome, Portugal, and Sweden. James Hamilton acquired a copy of Vertot's *Revolutions of Portugal* when he was in his teens, and, in 1726, Isaac Norris, Jr. obtained Vertot's *History of the Revolutions in Sweden*, which he annotated as he read.[15]

Even with Collinson's love of literature and his in-depth knowledge of London's bookshops and back streets, they could not locate some works, which were out of print, too expensive, or otherwise unavailable. *Cato's Letters* was popular enough that a new edition of it was printed almost every year. Their inability to locate a copy testifies to the allure of its Whiggish politics. It sold so fast the publisher could not keep it in print. The Library Company would acquire *Cato's Letters* when Charles Read, Jr., a kinsman of Deborah Franklin, donated a copy.[16]

Thomas Salmon's *Modern History*, another work Hopkinson could not locate, combined travel writing with world history. Salmon knew little about North America. Instead of doing any original research among primary documents, he copied from secondary sources. William Douglass grouped Salmon with the hack writers, whose accounts of North America were obsolete, erroneous, or just plain silly. Douglass demanded that historians treat their task with seriousness and professionalism and insisted that North America was a historical subject deserving accurate and up-to-date information. Franklin would reach a similar conclusion in the coming years.[17]

John Parkinson's *Theatrum botanicum*, a vast compilation of botanical writings, fell into the too expensive category, but a generous benefactor would donate a copy to the Library Company. The four-volume folio edition of Pierre Bayle's *Historical and Critical Dictionary* was unavailable, but when London publishers announced the serial publication of a new edition in 1733, Breintnall wrote Collinson and asked him to obtain Bayle's *Dictionary* as the individual parts appeared. Together, the parts would form a five-volume set. Jonston's *Theatrum animalium* was also unavailable. The directors wanted to make the Library Company mainly a collection of English books; Jonston's *Theatrum* had never been translated into English.[18]

Hopkinson could not locate *A Collection of Voyages*, either. This title refers to a four-volume anthology Knapton published three years earlier. Though considered the best edition of William Dampier's *Voyages around the World*, this anthology has the unmistakable whiff of Grub Street. Since its original publication in 1697, Dampier's *Voyages* had gone through several editions, proving itself a masterpiece of English travel writing. For *A Collection of Voyages*, Knapton padded out Dampier with some slow-selling travel narratives. The strategy worked. By the time Hopkinson started looking for *A Collection of Voyages*, it was out of print.[19]

The Library Company would eventually acquire *A Collection of Voyages*, which became a Franklin favorite. Dampier put new emphasis on accurate observation and detailed description. His work marks the start of scientific exploration, paving the way for the likes of Captain Cook. Despite his scientific accuracy, Dampier had a sense for popular literature. He gave *Voyages* a wide-ranging appeal, combining elements of spiritual autobiography, pirate stories, and shipwreck narratives.[20]

Dampier's powers of discrimination helped him select compelling details to drive his narrative. His story also shows much personality. While visiting Mexico, Dampier was struck with a fever that turned into dropsy. The local remedy for dropsy was a concoction made from dried and pulverized alligator testicles. "I would have tried it," he began. "I would have tried it, but we found no alligators here."[21]

Franklin would read and reread Dampier's *Voyages*. Assembling evidence for "Notes on Colds" to prove that catching a cold did not come from getting cold, he remembered something he had read in Dampier's account of Mindanao. Franklin excerpted the following passage from Dampier: "You see abundance of people in the river from morning till night washing their bodies or clothes. If they come into the river purposely to wash their clothes, they strip and stand naked till they have done; then put them on and march out again."[22]

Dampier's account is not about catching cold. Rather, it describes people who sometimes spend all day in the water naked but remain healthy. Though Franklin is known for his Rabelaisian humor, in this instance his excerpt is inexact. Franklin cleaned up Dampier's text, which has one more gender and lots more fluid: "You shall always see abundance of people, of both sexes, in the river, from morning till night; some easing themselves, others washing their bodies or cloaths."[23]

Many of Dampier's details became common knowledge. In "Maritime Observations," a work Franklin would write half a century later, he mentions Chinese junks that are divided into several tightly caulked chambers. Franklin called this ship-building technique the "well-known practice of the Chinese." Chinese shipbuilding practices were well known among eighteenth-century English readers because Dampier made them so.[24]

Hopkinson chose eleven substitute books. One, John Quincy's *Lexicon physico-medicum*, reflects Cadwalader's influence. Dr. Quincy introduced his readers to a fascinating sphere of medicine, its terminology. The substitutes also include a work that no good library should be without: *Paradise Lost*. Hopkinson obtained the edition prefaced with Elijah Fenton's "Life of Mr. John Milton," which Franklin came to know. The substitutes also included Andrew Ramsay's *Travels of Cyrus*, a didactic fictional voyage designed to teach leadership skills.[25]

As part of the first shipment, Collinson donated two books to the Library Company: Henry Pemberton's *View of Sir Isaac Newton's Philosophy* and the first volume of Philip Miller's *Gardener's Dictionary*. Having befriended Pemberton in London, Franklin understood his passion for Newtonian science. While the scientific community appreciated Newton's ideas, Pemberton sought to disseminate them among general readers. His goal of mass scientific literacy was both impressive and unprecedented. In Collinson's view, Miller's *Gardener's Dictionary* contained the "whole system of gardening and botany." It was a must-have among colonial planters. After Miller published his second volume, Collinson would present the Library Company with a copy of that, too.[26]

Collinson encouraged his London friends to donate books to the Library Company, and he continued his donations, sometimes giving the Library Company prized volumes from his own collection. He presented his personal copy of Captain John Smith's *Generall Historie of Virginia*, which contains Collinson's extensive manuscript notes. Though Smith had established the first permanent English settlement in America in 1607, he would not gain the status of a romantic American hero until the early nineteenth century. Collinson's notes provide a rare glimpse into mid-eighteenth-century attitudes toward Smith.[27]

By the second week of August, Hopkinson had packed the Library Company shipment aboard the *Molly*, skippered by Samuel Cornock. With the original order, Hopkinson's substitutes, and Collinson's donations, the shipment amounted to fifty-six titles in 141 volumes. After a lengthy crossing, Captain Cornock brought the *Molly* to Philadelphia the last week of October. The directors had the boxes sent to Stephen Potts.[28]

Since Franklin taught him bookbinding, Potts had established himself in the trade. When Godfrey left Franklin's house after a domestic squabble, Potts's bindery took over the commercial space Godfrey's glaziery had occupied. Surviving examples of Potts's work show that Franklin taught him well. His bindings are solid, yet conservative. Occasionally, Potts outdid himself. His two-toned, paneled calf binding for Bayle's *Dictionary* is quite handsome.[29]

Potts's business was never very profitable. The Library Company and Benjamin Franklin were his two best clients. He often repaired volumes for the Library Company or rebound volumes beyond repair. He remained a bookbinder for several years but eventually left the trade. At the end of his life, Potts was operating a small public house in Philadelphia. The lack of success did not bother him. Franklin remembered Potts "in the midst of his poverty, ever laughing!"[30]

Though the directors had stipulated that Hopkinson obtain the books unbound, he discovered that the kind of books the Library Company ordered were available in unbound sheets only to the wholesale trade. The Library Company's new books arrived in their London trade bindings. Upon receiving them, Potts used sheathing paper to make dust jackets to help protect the leather-bound volumes. The books were then brought to Pewter Platter Alley. The room Grace provided to shelve the books became known as—what else?—the Library Room.[31]

A week after the books arrived, Breintnall wrote Collinson to thank him for his donations and for his help procuring the books. Collinson would continue to assist the Library Company. He kept donating books and also donated some scientific instruments. For over twenty years, he would serve as the Library Company's London agent, purchasing books and shipping them to Philadelphia, but always refusing any remuneration for his efforts.[32]

On Tuesday, November 14, 1732, the directors met in the Library Room for the first time. Their responsibilities included appointing a librarian. Louis Timothée was the logical choice. After he learned the printing trade in Holland, Timothée emigrated to Philadelphia in 1731 with his wife Elizabeth and their children. Fluent in several languages, Timothée first advertised himself as a French teacher but later took a job as a journeyman at Franklin's New Printing Office: a position with more career potential.

Timothée's linguistic expertise made it possible for Franklin to publish the first German-language newspaper in colonial America. Edited by Timothée, the *Philadelphische Zeitung* folded after two issues, but it remains a milestone in German American history. Since Timothée was renting Grace's home, it would be easy for him to attend the library. Already a shareholder in the Library Company, Timothée accepted the appointment, becoming the first professional librarian in North America.

His responsibilities involved attending the Library Room on Wednesday afternoons from 2 to 3 o'clock and on Saturdays from 10 until 4 o'clock. Members could borrow only one book or one multivolume set at a time, and they had to sign a promissory note for its return undamaged. If the book were not returned in good condition, the borrower would have to pay double its value.[33]

The minutes for the November 14th meeting also stipulate that the library would be catalogued to facilitate the lending process. The catalogue would list a borrowing period for each book. Different-sized books could be borrowed for different lengths of time. In other words, subscribers could borrow folios for a longer time than octavos, and multivolume sets could be borrowed longer than single volumes. One column would indicate the length of time an item could be loaned out. The next would list each item's value, which would be used for the promissory notes. This manuscript catalogue does not survive. Presumably, it formed the basis for the catalogue Franklin would print.[34]

At the December 11th meeting, the other directors asked Franklin what he would charge to print enough copies of the catalogue for all the shareholders. Nothing, Franklin said. He would print copies gratis as presents for them. Franklin printed the catalogue as a broadside, but no copies of his first printed catalogue for the Library Company survive, either. When Franklin printed the catalogue is unknown. Breintnall had a copy in his possession on May 30, 1733, when he added to it the titles of books received since Franklin issued the catalogue. Several members had donated additional books to the library.[35]

Breintnall himself donated books from many different subject areas. In the field of political science, he donated his copy of *Leviathan Drawn Out with a Hook*, Alexander Ross's challenge to Thomas Hobbes's *Leviathan*. Hobbes's masterpiece was not well known in colonial America, but it could be found in the best libraries. When Franklin obtained a copy to resell in the 1740s, he noted that the work was "very scarce."[36]

There is a reason why *Hudibras* has an ancient sage philosopher read Alexander Ross over. A Scot and a schoolmaster, Ross lived and died by Aristotle's works. He measured new philosophical ideas by how closely they hewed to Aristotlean thought. Ross tried to expose the dangerous consequences of Hobbes's theories. He was more interested in religious views than political ideas, but Ross did attack Hobbes for equating kings with tyrants, offering a necessary corrective: "A king governs, and is governed by lawes; a tyrant hath no law but his will."[37]

Franklin donated several volumes, including personal favorites that had been with him since boyhood: Locke's *Pieces* and the *Port Royal Logic*. Why would Franklin donate books that meant so much to him? To understand his donations, recall the book discussions that took place in the Junto. Franklin had members copy favorite passages from books they discussed, so others could read them. Franklin apparently talked up these old favorites so much he decided that giving them to the Library Company would be the most efficient way to share their contents. Most Junto members were also Library Company shareholders, so they could borrow whatever books Franklin recommended.

The donations would not prevent him from rereading these books. He, too, could borrow them whenever he wished.

The Library Company made its first purchase beyond the original order in March when a mysterious stranger offered to sell Amédée François Frézier's *Voyage to the South-Sea*, which chronicles the exploration of the west coast of South America. Franklin could see the book's charm from its opening sentence. Frézier's youthful attention to geography parallels Franklin's: "The structure of the universe, which is naturally the object of our admiration, has ever also been the subject of my curiosity: From my very infancy I took the greatest pleasure in all such things as could advance me in the knowledge of it: globes, charts, and books of travels." The Library Company accepted the stranger's offer and added Frézier's *Voyage* to its holdings.[38]

In October 1733, Franklin learned that his business partner Thomas Whitmarsh had died in Charleston, South Carolina, the previous month. He now invited Louis Timothée to take over the Charleston operation. Eager to be his own boss, Timothée accepted the offer and sailed for South Carolina, where he would anglicize his name to Lewis Timothy. Before leaving, Timothy donated to the Library Company two Russian manuscript rolls written in Cyrllic, though at the time no library members could tell what language it was.[39]

Timothy gave his wife Elizabeth power of attorney, so she could settle their affairs before joining him in South Carolina. A smart businesswoman, Elizabeth Timothy arranged a partnership agreement with Franklin. Since this new partnership deprived the Library Company of its librarian, Franklin would fill the position until the directors could appoint a permanent replacement.

They selected William Parsons as librarian in March 1734. Born in England, Parsons came to Philadelphia with his family as an infant. He shared many similarities with other members of the Junto. Like Jones, he apprenticed as a cordwainer. Like Hopkinson, he broadened his business interests to include the mercantile trade. Like Scull, he taught himself mathematics and began working as a surveyor. Like Breintnall, he also worked as a scrivener. And, like Potts, he was an odd character, at least in Franklin's view. Potts was a wit who seldom acted wisely; Parsons was a wise man who often acted foolishly.[40]

The books remained at Pewter Platter Alley, but after serving as librarian for two years, Parsons found the arrangement cumbersome, In April 1736, he had the collection moved to his home. Four years later, that arrangement became awkward, so the directors found a location for the library outside anyone's home. Franklin successfully petitioned the Pennsylvania Assembly to have it moved to the State House. Parsons would serve as librarian until 1746.[41]

The books would remain at the State House until 1773, when the collection, having grown too large for the room that held it, was moved to the second floor of Carpenters Hall, a new building on Chestnut near Fourth Street. The First Continental Congress would convene at Carpenters Hall the following year, when the library directors granted the congressional delegates borrowing privileges. Thus, the Library Company of Philadelphia was the first Library of Congress.[42]

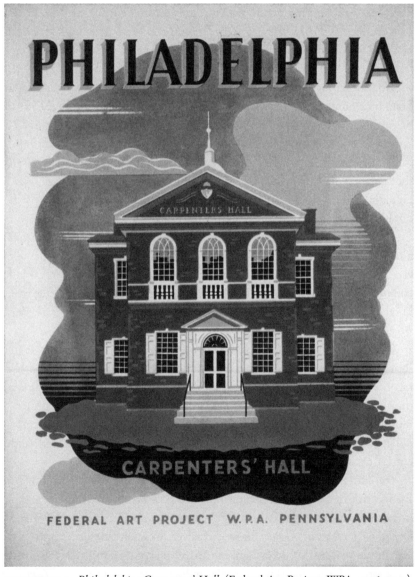

FIGURE 12.1 *Philadelphia: Carpenters' Hall.* (Federal Art Project, WPA, 1936–1941). Library of Congress Prints and Photographs Division, Washington, DC, LC-USZC2-1888.

Though the Library Company thrived during the 1730s, it was not the only way Franklin's friends borrowed books. He ran an impromptu lending library from his printing house, which is known by a 1734 advertisement in *The Pennsylvania Gazette*. Franklin did not keep close tabs on who borrowed what. His advertisement names five books he had loaned but had forgotten to whom and asks the borrowers to return them.[43]

Whoever borrowed Richard Steele's *Dramatick Works* apparently returned it. Two years later, Franklin would cite one of Steele's comedies in his essay, "On Amplification," which recalls a comment by Mr. Puzzle, the conveyancer in *The Funeral: or, Grief a la Mode*. Mr. Puzzle looks forward to the day "when it will require as much parchment to convey a piece of land as will cover it."[44]

No one knows whether the remaining books were returned. Years later, Franklin would tell Benjamin Rush "that a man lost ten percent on the *value*, by lending his books, [and] that he once knew a man who never returned a borrowed book, because no one ever returned books borrowed from him." Franklin admitted that sometimes he was slow to return borrowed books. In the same advertisement asking for the return of Steele's *Dramatick Works*, Franklin said he possessed the second volume of Abraham Cowley's *Works*, but had forgotten who loaned it to him.[45]

By 1735, the Library Company collection had expanded enough to warrant a new printed catalogue. Franklin printed the catalogue, but no copies survive.[46] The earliest Library Company catalogue to survive is the one Franklin compiled and printed in 1741. In fact, the 1741 catalogue is the first surviving library catalogue of any kind Franklin compiled since that of the 1723 *New-England Courant* library.

Contrasted with the *Courant* catalogue, the Library Company catalogue shows how Franklin's bibliographical skills had matured. Whereas he had recorded spine titles for the *Courant* catalogue, he consulted the title pages of the library books. In addition, he recorded places and dates of publication for most books. He also recorded the donors' names, an acknowledgment designed to thank the donors and encourage further donations. For some entries, he supplied critical or anecdotal comments.

Franklin paraphrased some titles to make the catalogue more useful. The English title of Christian Helwig's *Theatrum historiarum et chronologicum* is a literal translation of the Latin: *The Historical and Chronological Theatre of Christopher Helvicus*. Used almost exclusively in book titles, the term "theater" in this context means a comprehensive view of its subject, but the word was approaching obsolescence. For the catalogue, Franklin retitled it *Helvicus's*

Chronology, in which the Time of the Most Remarkable Events in the World Is Assigned, and When the Most Famous Men Lived, etc. Franklin's paraphrase gave library users a better idea of the book's contents, helping them decide whether to read it.[47]

Paraphrasing the title of Pierre Bayle's *General Dictionary, Historical and Critical*, Franklin listed it as *Mr. Bayle's Historical and Critical Dictionary, Newly and Accurately Printed; Containing the Lives, Actions and Works of All the Most Famous Men, with a Vast Variety of Other Knowledge.* Onto this title, Franklin added that Bayle was "for his prodigious learning and industry, esteemed the wonder of this latter age."[48]

Bayle found other early American readers. Charles Carroll of Carrollton, to take another signer of the Declaration of Independence, for example, owned what is considered the best edition of Bayle's dictionary, the four-volume folio printed at Rotterdam in 1720. James Monroe owned the five-volume French edition, which appeared in 1734. Bayle's stature would diminish after the eighteenth century, but his dictionary still found some American enthusiasts. Upon adding a copy of the four-volume folio edition to his library, Herman Melville told a friend, "I bought a set of Bayle's *Dictionary* the other day, and on my return to New York intend to lay the great old folios side by side and go to sleep on them thro' the summer." Though knowledge of his *Dictionary* has continued to wane, Bayle—"the forgotten hero of the Enlightenment"— deserves to be better known.[49]

Bayle's *Dictionary* has an odd shape. It contains informative articles combined with lengthy footnotes, which dwarf the articles they gloss. In his footnotes, Bayle reveals his erudition and expresses his controversial opinions. The article about the Roman god Jupiter, for instance, mentions the ridiculous stories that form the foundation of pagan religion. Even more absurd are the scholars who have attempted to explicate these stories in terms of logic and science.

Though ostensibly about pagan religion, the article implicitly critiques the same phenomenon that occurs among exegetes who interpret the Bible's most outrageous details. In one footnote, Bayle applies the Latin quotation from Martial about the uselessness of pursuing difficult trifles. Trying to solve the mysterious follies of religion, Bayle argued, is hardly worth the effort. Bayle's translator Pierre des Maizeaux rendered Martial's Latin into a charming English distich: "'Tis labour misapply'd, and ill-judg'd toil, / When trifles only waste our time and oil."[50]

Throughout his dictionary, Bayle emphasizes the ongoing value of Pyrrhonism. His footnotes reinforce ideas that Franklin had encountered in

Shaftesbury, Collins, and Huet. Bayle believed people should have the liberty to worship whichever religion they wished or no religion, if they wished. Bayle's contentious footnotes reinforce an anecdote about him. When the Abbé de Polignac quizzed him about his religious views, Bayle disclosed his Pyrrhonism: "I am most truly a protestant; for I protest indifferently against all systems and all sects."[51]

Franklin's annotations to the 1741 library catalogue begin with Thomas Gordon's two-volume English translation, *The Works of Tacitus*. The coauthor of *Cato's Letters* and the *Independent Whig*, Gordon aligned Tacitus with Whig political philosophy. Through Gordon's translation, Tacitus became a prominent source of political ideas in Enlightenment America. Franklin said this edition contained "some fine political discourses prefixed by the translator."[52]

Annotating the entry for Paul de Rapin de Thoyras's fifteen-volume *History of England*, Franklin commended his historical authority and critical reputation: "The author employed seventeen years in composing it, and as he had (by consulting the ancient records of the Tower) much better helps than any historian that went before him, it is esteemed the best history of *England* yet published." Readers throughout British North America shared Franklin's high opinion of Rapin. When Loquacious Scribble and Philo Dogmaticus quarrel over a fine point of medieval English chronology in Dr. Alexander Hamilton's *History of the Tuesday Club*, they dispatch a messenger to fetch the relevant volume of Rapin to settle the dispute, a bottle of arrack hanging in the balance.[53]

A French Huguenot, Rapin served in the army that came to England in 1688 with William of Orange. Rapin's participation in the revolutionary battles that year did much to shape his understanding of the English Constitution. He saw the history of England as a struggle between the prerogatives of the Crown and the privileges of the people. Liberty results when the two achieve balance. Demonstrating that the ideal government was parliamentary and constitutional, Rapin traced it back to Anglo-Saxon times. Subsequent upheavals, like the Revolution of 1688, represent the struggle to maintain the Anglo-Saxon system of government.[54]

Onto the entry for Algernon Sidney's *Discourses on Government*—another seminal work in the development of Whig political philosophy—Franklin added an anecdotal remark, observing that Sidney's manuscript had been "found in his closet, [and] cost him his life, in the reign of King Charles II." Franklin would elaborate on the December page of *Poor Richard, 1750*: "On the 7th of this month, 1683, was the honourable Algernon Sidney, Esq; beheaded, charg'd with a pretended plot, but whose chief crime was the writing an excellent book, intituled, *Discourses on Government*. A man of admirable parts and great integrity."[55]

The catalogue entry for John Wilkins's *Essay towards a Real Character and a Philosophical Language* is another one Franklin annotated. Published in 1668, Wilkins's *Real Character* set forth an artificial language based on the classification of all human knowledge, organized hierarchically according to nature. Franklin observed that this work contains a "distribution of all things in nature into their proper genuses, differences, species, etc. with a natural grammar, and a most excellent English dictionary."[56]

Franklin's observation encapsulates Wilkins's Schema. Wilkins divided the universe into forty genuses, which are subdivided into differences and further subdivided into species. Each genus is denoted by a two-letter consonant-and-vowel combination, each difference by one of nine consonants, and each species by one of nine vowels. (Wilkins had to raid the Greek alphabet to get enough vowels for his scheme.) When the number of species exceeded nine, Wilkins added an extra consonant after the first letter. For example, *za* means fish; *zan* means the ninth difference of fish, that is, squamous (scaly) river fish; *zana* means salmon, the second species of squamous river fish. *Zlana* signifies gudgeon, the eleventh species (second in the second nine) of squamous river fish.[57] With the gudgeon—his own example—Wilkins plays straight man for his readers. To accept his arbitrary and speculative universal language, we must swallow the proverbial gudgeon.

Though Wilkins's universal language never caught on, his ambitious organization of knowledge set a precedent for later classification schemes that would take hold. Umberto Eco has identified the fundamental problem with Wilkins's philosophical language: It taxonimizes but does not define.[58] To compensate for this drawback, Wilkins appended the dictionary, which functions separately from the work. Franklin thought the dictionary gave Wilkins's *Real Character* its lasting usefulness.

Shareholders continued to donate books to the Library Company, as Franklin's annotations verify. Having inherited his grandfather's library, Grace donated several items from it, including a three-volume elephant folio edition of John Foxe's *Actes and Monuments* or, as it is better known, *The Book of Martyrs*. This luxurious edition is illustrated with many copperplate engravings. It became one of the Library Company's bibliographical treasures.[59]

William Rawle, another director of the Library Company, donated John Hughes's six-volume illustrated edition of Edmund Spenser's *Works*. The edition stands out for Hughes's willingness to preserve Spenser's language, which many Augustan readers saw as hopelessly archaic. At a time when Shakespeare's blank verse was being rendered into heroic couplets, Hughes would neither modernize nor regularize Spenser's verse.[60]

Spenser was not widely read in colonial America, though there were a handful of exceptions. Governor Montgomerie had a copy of Hughes's edition in New York, and Dr. Alexander Hamilton read the *Faerie Queene* in Annapolis. Hamilton dismissed it as "intirely allegory and fiction," but one time he and other members of the Tuesday Club wrote a group poem in imitation of the *Faerie Queene*, proving that the ability to write Spenserian stanzas was a shared talent among men of letters in colonial Maryland.[61]

Perhaps no one in colonial America was a better Spenserian that Samuel Henley, a William and Mary professor whose library included a critical study of Spenser's masterpiece, Thomas Warton's *Observations on the Faerie Queene*. Before Warton, Spenser's commentators typically traced his work to classical and Italian sources, but Warton emphasized his debt to Romance literature and the English literary tradition. Rawle's generous donation let fellow Library Company members enter the fantastic world Spenser imagined. The edition obviously generated interest in Spenser; the Library Company would acquire a copy of Warton's *Observations*.[62]

Several nonmembers donated books. The directors granted Logan borrowing privileges, and he continued his support. His donations include Garcilaso de la Vega's *Royal Commentaries of Peru*, which forms part of the library's outstanding collection of European Americana. Franklin's mother-in-law Sarah Read donated *Philosophia*, a three-volume Latin introduction to the subject by Father Guillaume Chabron. How she ended up with this mid-seventeenth-century Paris publication is a mystery; perhaps she took it in trade at her shop.[63]

Isaac Greenwood donated a Latin edition of Thomas Stanley's *History of Philosophy*. The Library Company already had the English translation, which Hopkinson had obtained in London. Professor Greenwood's gift was an expression of thanks. Greenwood, whose bibulosity overpowered his bibliography, had been dismissed from Harvard for excessive drinking. He now supported himself as an itinerant scientific lecturer. Acting as his impresario, Franklin had arranged for Greenwood to lecture at the Library Company. Greenwood's lecture shows that the library was becoming much more than a place for members to borrow books. It was emerging as a prominent intellectual and cultural institution.[64]

Though Franklin noted most donations by providing the donors' full names, he marked his own donations with his initials. Like the *Port Royal Logic* and Locke's *Pieces*, when Franklin donated Montaigne's *Essays*, he was parting with a work that he enjoyed very much and had put to good use. He often used Montaigne's *Essays* as a source in his writings. Perhaps he obtained a new edition and donated his old one to the Library Company, or perhaps he donated it, like the others, to share a favorite with friends.[65]

Before Franklin donated Montaigne's *Essays*, he used the work while writing *The Nature and Necessity of a Paper Currency*. A Latin quotation from Persius's *Satires* forms Franklin's title-page motto. Like most of his Latin quotations, Franklin took this one from a secondary source. He found it in Montaigne's essay, "Of the Education of Children." Charles Cotton, Montaigne's translator, not only supplied Montaigne's Latin, he also provided a translation: "What's money's natural use, / What to be liberal is, and what profuse."[66]

After donating the book to the Library Company, Franklin continued using Montaigne's *Essays*. Some Poor Richardisms come from Montaigne. In "Of Experience," Montaigne asks, "Have you known how to compose your manners? You have done a great deal more than he who has compos'd books." Franklin simplified Montaigne to craft a well-balanced sentence: "He that can compose himself, is wiser than he that composes books." Montaigne's prose also affected Franklin. Continuing his survey of Franklin's literary influences, Stuart P. Sherman noted similarities with the great French essayist: "Like Montaigne, he loves frank and masculine speech, and he likes to enrich the language of the well bred by discreet drafts upon the burry, homely, sententious, proverbial language of the people."[67]

Besides demonstrating Franklin's bibliographical skill, the 1741 catalogue showcases the library's success. What started as an order for forty-five titles in 1732 had swelled to 375 titles. The catalogue ends with Franklin's "Short Account of the Library." This one-page history reinforces the Library Company's success: "It is now ten years since the company was first established; and we have the pleasure of observing, that tho' 'tis compos'd of so many persons of different sects, parties and ways of thinking, yet no differences relating to the affairs of the library, have arisen among us; but every thing has been conducted with great harmony, and to general satisfaction, which happy circumstance will, we hope, always continue."[68]

Franklin's epithet for the Library Company of Philadelphia—"the mother of all North American subscription libraries"—captures its significance to American library history.[69] Between its establishment in 1731 and American independence in 1776, major cities from Boston to Charleston founded libraries, and each followed the pattern Franklin had established. Library historian Dorothy F. Grimm found appropriate the phrase Diodorus Siculus had used to describe Ozymandias's famous library. The Library Company of Philadelphia is a "dispensary of the mind."

13

How to Make an Almanac

AWARE AN ALMANAC would provide a steady income for the New Printing Office, Franklin and Meredith looked for an able mathematician to compile one. They did not have to look far, since they shared a house with Thomas Godfrey, the colony's best mathematician. Godfrey welcomed the chance to undertake the work. Like today's calendars, almanacs for the next year usually appeared around November. Franklin and Meredith followed suit. Once Godfrey had finished his astronomical calculations, they issued *Godfrey's Almanack for 1730*.

Instead of the familiar pamphlet format, *Godfrey's* appeared as a single-sheet almanac designed to hang in the home, the equivalent of a modern wall calendar. Franklin took pains to make their first published almanac accurate and appealing. No copies survive, but he advertised that *Godfrey's Almanack* was "beautifully printed in red and black, on one side of a large demi sheet of paper, after the London manner."[1]

A printing house did not have to restrict itself to one almanac. The more it published the more its potential profit. The year Franklin and Meredith issued their first almanac, Andrew Bradford released three. Besides Jacob Taylor's, he published almanacs by Titan Leeds and William Birkett. Almanac makers did not limit themselves either. Leeds wrote one almanac for Bradford and another for David Harry, who claimed that readers preferred Leeds over other American almanac-makers. Still, Harry hedged his bets, issuing a second almanac by another local philomath, John Jerman.[2]

Neither was enough to save Harry. Within a year, he was out of business. Like other competitors whom Franklin profiles in the autobiography, Harry's plight shows how not to succeed in business. He was "very proud, dress'd like a gentleman, liv'd expensively, took much diversion and pleasure abroad, ran in debt, and neglected his business, upon which all business left him."[3]

Harry packed up his press and moved to Barbados, becoming that colony's first printer. Since Keimer was still roving around Bridgetown idle and unemployed, Harry hired his former master as his journeyman. Harry fared no better in Bridgetown than Philadelphia. Once his printing house failed, he sold his equipment to Keimer, returned to the mainland, and became a farmer.

Keimer flourished given the chance to be his own boss again. After starting *The Barbados Gazette*, Bridgetown's first newspaper, he kept it going for years. He edited selections from the paper as *Caribbeana*, a major anthology in the literary history of the West Indies. Franklin's portrayal of Keimer as a buffoon masks his respect for his work in Barbados. He kept an eye on Keimer's career and added a copy of *Caribbeana* to his library.[4]

In late 1730, Franklin published another single-sheet *Godfrey's*. He also took over Jerman's almanac. Franklin was not considering making an almanac himself, at least not yet, but Jerman's work may have inspired him. While Jerman's *American Almanack* is competent enough in its astronomical calculations, it shows little personality. It includes one folk rhyme—"Good sowing I do foresee / But if it miss then blame not me"—but otherwise lacks literary value.

Almanacs became another battleground in the Franklin–Bradford rivalry. Franklin again published the Godfrey and Jerman almanacs for 1732, but Bradford still had three almanac-makers in his pocket. The following year Bradford offered Godfrey and Jerman better terms than Franklin and secured their almanacs, bringing his output to five.[5]

Bradford's success did not mean he had won Philadelphia's almanac wars: Franklin had a secret weapon. Deprived of the others, he wrote his own almanac for 1733. He did not do so until quite late in 1732, that is, not until Bradford had published his. Appearing in December, *Poor Richard, 1733* shows signs of haste: Franklin transposed the September and October pages. But it did well enough to require a second printing before the end of 1732, and a third in January.[6]

The third impression was overambitious. Two months into the year, Franklin had a thousand copies left. In August, he sent 300 to his brother James, who had moved to Newport, where he established Rhode Island's first press. Having developed a business relationship with Thomas Fleet, Benjamin Franklin sent him 200 "Poor Dicks" that same month, but he still had heaps of leftover copies. Suffice it to say that Deborah's Christmas pies did not want for waste paper that year.[7]

Poor Richard, 1733 begins with a two-paragraph epistle to the reader by its ostensible author, Richard Saunders. The hoaxy second paragraph, which predicts Leeds's death, is more renowned, but the first paragraph is more entertaining. The paragraph is a skit, that is, a lighthearted personal satire. With

Richard's opening epistles in this and subsequent almanacs, Franklin proved himself a master of the skit. The first one initiates a domestic drama he would sustain into the next decade. Introducing himself and his wife, Richard Saunders tells readers that he is excessively poor and she is excessively proud.

Bridget, unnamed in 1733, has little respect for her lazy husband, given her vast amount of household work. There are no Rumpelstiltskins in real life. Bridget is stuck home all day endlessly spinning her spinning wheel, but she never gets any new clothes herself. As she works, Richard gazes at the stars. To motivate him, Bridget threatens to burn all his books and mathematical instruments—"rattling traps," she calls them—if he does not turn them to profit.

Franklin recognized marital conflict as an entertaining theme for an almanac, which uses recurring characters year after year. *Poor Richard's* roots extend back to the Restoration stage. Franklin's attention to stage comedy as a reader and a theater-goer helped him develop both Richard and Bridget Saunders. English periodicals also provided inspiration. Richard Saunders is reminiscent of Sir Roger de Coverley, the lovable country squire in *The Spectator*. He is the "Sir Roger of the masses."[8]

A more recent form of entertainment also makes a good comparison. Though popular culture has taken many different forms throughout history, traditional themes and motifs have carried over to new genres and new media. Almanacs share much with television shows. Franklin's humorous take on marital conflict adumbrates its portrayal in sitcoms. Over 200 years before television, Franklin imagined comedic situations to dramatize and satirize marriage. Richard and Bridget are the Ricky and Lucy of colonial America.

The final page of *Poor Richard, 1733* reinforces the couple's humorous, yet antagonistic relationship. Richard lists the birth dates of kings and princes of Europe, ending with: "Poor Richard, an American prince, without subjects, his wife being viceroy over him, 23 Oct 1684, 49." Franklin, who turned 27 in 1733, created a persona two decades older than himself. Richard's birth date enhances the complexity of Franklin's humor. It is the date the Crown revoked the original charter of colonial Massachusetts and thus made it a royal colony. Franklin's joke creates a parallel between the macrocosm—the British Empire—and the microcosm—the Saunders family. Much as the British Crown rules colonial Massachusetts, Bridget Saunders rules her husband.[9]

At 49, Richard has finished 70 percent of his biblically allotted three score and ten doing as little work as possible. The Poor Richard persona clashes with another public identity its author was creating: "B. Franklin, Printer." While establishing his business, Franklin made a point not only to be industrious but also to look industrious. He got up early and worked late but made sure people saw him getting up early and working late. Franklin depended upon a wheelbarrow to enhance his public image. He would haul reams of paper through Philadelphia, striking the pose of a hard-working tradesman.[10]

The story of Franklin's painstaking effort to look industrious and the image of him wheeling his wheelbarrow through Philadelphia both come from the autobiography. The picture of his hard-working younger self is central to the American Dream. The nation's cultural history is filled with young go-getters following Franklin's example. One modern reader found his iconic wheelbarrow-pushing self-portrait as American as Norman Rockwell's paintings for the *Saturday Evening Post*. An avant-garde example from the history of art also works for comparison. Early in his career as a commercial artist, Andy Warhol bicycled around Manhattan delivering drawings to clients. He appeared so wan and hungry that editors and art directors feared he was starving and gave him extra work, though Warhol was already living comfortably by that point in his career.[11]

A remark Keimer made confirms how carefully Franklin shaped his public image as he started his printing business. Once he and Meredith established the New Printing Office, Keimer attacked Franklin in the *Universal Instructor*, finding his "merits as threadbare as his great coat."[12] Wisdom is oft-times under a thread-bare cloak, as the saying goes. Franklin hid his under a Gogolian overcoat.

Poor Richard forms an alter ego for "B. Franklin, Printer." Richard Saunders cares nothing about working hard or getting ahead. He is happy to take life as it comes, messing about with his mathematical instruments or reading for pleasure. Poor Richard is a precursor to Rip Van Winkle, who sleeps for twenty years and outlives his wife to become the town sage. Even as Franklin used his public image to define the American Dream, he created an anti-hero who undermines what the American Dream symbolizes.

With the epistle to the reader at the beginning of *Poor Richard, 1733* and the joke about Richard's wife at the end, Franklin sustains the Richard Saunders persona throughout his first almanac. Readers must guard against attributing what Richard Saunders says to Benjamin Franklin. In other words, Poor Richard's personal advice is not always Franklin's. Their behavior does coincide in terms of source material. Bridget urges Richard to capitalize on his books; Franklin used his to compile the almanacs.

Richard has a dual audience in mind as he assembles his almanac. Several epigrams are directed toward Bridget. He resents that she makes him work to compile the almanac. Its practical material—astronomical data, weather predictions, folksy sayings—are designed for general readers, though a few also reflect Richard's animosity toward his wife. Having documented her complaints about sitting at her spinning wheel, Richard says on the July page of *Poor Richard, 1733*, "Many estates are spent in the getting, / Since women for tea forsook spinning and knitting."[13] Given Bridget's portrayal of Richard's laziness, his wise saws and sayings appear ironic. A lazy, good-for-nothing husband should not be dispensing commonsense folk wisdom about hard work.

The first epistle to the reader spills onto the second page. Next comes the Man of Signs, for which Franklin prepared an original woodcut. Like many of his visual creations, this woodcut has both symbolic and rhetorical value. In Franklin's hands, the Man of Signs resembles an image from an emblem book.

Like those in previous American almanacs, Franklin's Man of Signs sits atop a globe naked. Though striking the same pose, Franklin's Man of Signs otherwise differs considerably.[14] Gone are the narrow shoulders, flabby hips, and pot belly. Franklin's has an athletic build. His muscular arms resemble link sausages, and he has washboard abs, a natural mane of long wavy hair, and a clear and impressive manhood. Franklin made the traditional figure into something it had never been before: a sex symbol.

An inch, perhaps two, under 6 feet, Franklin himself was powerfully built. At Watts's printing house, he had shown off his strength by carrying two heavy printing forms while his fellow printers carried one each. He had also demonstrated his athletic ability in London by stripping off his clothes and swimming the 4 miles from Chelsea to Blackfriars. In the history of endurance swimming, his effort rivals Lord Byron's swim across the Hellespont. Years later, Franklin would regularly use dumbbells, making him an early American advocate for strength training.[15] With the Man of Signs, Franklin upholds physical fitness as an aspect of his masculine ideal.

Whereas Keimer's Man of Signs recites a poem, Franklin's is silent—at least in *Poor Richard, 1733*. For *Poor Richard, 1734*, Franklin took a cue from Keimer. He reused the same illustration from the previous year, but this time his Man of Signs recites a poem, which functions like a commentary in an emblem book:

> Here I sit naked, like some fairy elf,
> My seat a pumpkin; I grudge no man's pelf;
> Though I've no bread, nor cheese upon my shelf;
> > I'll tell thee *gratis*, when it safe is,
> To purge, to bleed, or *cut*, thy cattle, or—*thy self.*

Franklin's Man of Signs speaks humbly. Seated atop the world, he depicts himself sitting on a pumpkin, which was not an unusual place to sit in rural America around harvest time. The poem foreshadows something Thoreau says in *Walden*: "I would rather sit on a pumpkin and have it all to myself, than be crowded on a velvet cushion."[16]

After shrugging off his poverty, Franklin's Man of Signs starts sounding like Poor Richard, that is, like an almanac-maker who studies the stars to determine when Venus and Mars are alright to let people administer medical or veterinary treatment. Adding to the psychology of Franklin's almanac-making persona, the Man of Signs is Richard's self-projection. Richard Saunders sees himself as a strong, virile, muscular man, a self-image that diverges from Bridget's derogatory view.

Despite its entertainment value, *Poor Richard's Almanack* was first and foremost a practical book to be read daily. In addition to the regular almanac, Franklin also sold an interleaved version, that is, an almanac bound with blank leaves between its pages to let people keep notes throughout the year. Isaac Norris, Sr., for example, obtained a copy of *Poor Richard, 1733* and used its blank leaves as a diary.[17]

In *Poor Richard, 1733* the monthly pages are structured similarly. The top line names the month, and an epigram follows. Beneath the epigram several columns supply information about weather conditions and phases of the moon. Richard tucks his aphorisms into the spare white spaces, usually in the rightmost column. Sometimes astronomical information interrupts the longer Poor Richardisms. The fact that the moon would set at 2 o'clock in the morning one day in January interrupts the following distich: "Visits should be short, like a winters day, / Lest you're too troublesom hasten away." Using a short winter's day as a simile, this maxim suits January.

Professor Mustard identified *Witts Recreations*, a seventeenth-century poetical miscellany, as a precursor to *Poor Richard's Almanack*. Many poems in *Witts Recreation* come from authors associated with Oxford University, then a center for the production of brief, lighthearted verse. This miscellany was rare in colonial America, but Franklin was not the only one who read it. Seaborn Cotton read *Witts Recreations* and excerpted several passages for his commonplace book.[18]

Franklin stayed in the mindset of his persona to select epigrams from *Witts Recreation* that form Richard's running commentary about Bridget. The January epigram provides a bachelor's recipe for a good wife. She should be wise, fair, rich, and young. She should be neither proud, nor churlish. She should have a country housewife's domestic skills and a city woman's sophistication. The epigram concludes by telling the optimistic bachelor he would have to bespeak his ideal wife. Otherwise, he was trying to find a woman who had never been born.[19]

Interpreted from Richard's perspective, the March epigram, which also comes from *Witts Recreations*, reads like a fantasy piece. It portrays a scene of marital bliss, as man and woman exchange playful kisses. Seaborn Cotton enjoyed this epigram so much he transcribed the whole thing in his commonplace book. Reproduced in *Poor Richard, 1733*, it tells Bridget to drop her ornery ways and become the affectionate woman in the poem. Franklin developed Bridget's character so well that he enabled readers to imagine her reaction. Reading Richard's implication that she should behave more like the kiss-dispensing woman in the poem, we can hear what Bridget is thinking: "Fat chance."[20]

The October epigram more accurately represents the relationship between Richard and Bridget. Franklin revised the version from *Witts Recreations* but retained its gist. A husband and wife argue about what it means for marriage to make a couple into one whole. The wife says they must both become one woman; the husband says they must both become one man. The argument persists until the wife gets her way. The husband, who is the speaker of the poem, concludes, "Thus we contended daily, but the strife / Could not be ended, till both were one wife."[21]

The epigram for December, which is titled "On a Proud Maid" in *Witts Recreations*, also sends a message to Bridget. Richard drops the original title but otherwise sticks to his source:

> She that will eat her breakfast in her bed,
> And spend the morn in dressing of her head,
> And sit at dinner like a maiden bride,
> And talk of nothing all day but of pride;
> God in his mercy may do much to save her,
> But what a case is he in that shall have her.[22]

Franklin published *Poor Richard, 1734* around the time people were reading the December page of *Poor Richard, 1733*. Advertisements in *The Pennsylvania Gazette* connect the new almanac with the previous one. According to Franklin's advertising copy, *Poor Richard, 1734* will conclude with "Verses by Mrs. Bridget Saunders, in Answer to the December Verses of Last Year." This advertisement represents the first time Bridget's name appears in print.[23]

In his second epistle to the reader, Richard thanks the book-buying public for purchasing his first almanac. The proceeds have improved their situation: "My wife has been enabled to get a pot of her own, and is no longer oblig'd to borrow one from a neighbour; nor have we ever since been without something of our own to put in it. She has also got a pair of shoes, two new shifts, and a new warm petticoat." As a result, he continues, her temper is "so much more pacifick than it us'd to be, that I may say, I have slept more, and more quietly within this last year, than in the three foregoing years put together."[24]

This opening epistle reinforces Franklin's mastery of his persona. Richard boasts about his success, never mind that he now displays the pride he had critiqued in his wife. Richard also shows how oblivious he is to Bridget's feelings. He reveals way too much personal detail. Why, he even talks about her underwear! Once more Franklin prompts readers to imagine how Richard's wife will react.

Bridget would respond to what her husband says in *Poor Richard, 1734*, but first she must refute the December epigram from the previous year. For the December page of *Poor Richard, 1734*, Bridget insists he use a poem she has written. Richard provides the heading: "By Mrs. Bridget Saunders, My Dutchess, in Answer to the December Verses of Last Year." Without directly saying that Richard behaves like the man in her poem, she implies as much:

> He that for sake of drink neglects his trade,
> And spends each night in taverns till 'tis late,
> And rises when the sun is four hours high,
> And ne'er regards his starving family;
> God in his mercy may do much to save him,
> But, woe to the poor wife, whose lot it is to have him.[25]

If Bridget's epigram truly characterizes her husband, then Richard is an arch-hypocrite. In his almanac's first two years, he has supplied the following aphorisms: "Nothing more like a fool, than a drunken fool"; "Be temperate in wine, in eating, girls, and sloth; / Or the gout will seize you and plague you both"; and "No man e'er was glorious, who was not laborious."[26]

Recognizing that Professor Mustard had left many of Franklin's sources unidentified, Owen Aldridge encouraged Robert Newcomb, a student from his graduate seminar in eighteenth-century American literature at the University of Maryland, to undertake a more extensive study for his doctoral dissertation. Keen to undertake the task—keen as mustard, one could say—Newcomb threw himself into the project. After meat comes mustard, the proverb goes. Newcomb reversed this traditional saying. Following Professor Mustard, he wrote a beefy tome that remains the single finest study of Franklin's sources for *Poor Richard's Almanack*. Newcomb never published his dissertation, but for years it was a cult classic on the interlibrary loan circuit.

Newcomb proved that Franklin's use of *Witts Recreations* was more extensive than Professor Mustard had realized. It was the main source of the epigrams for the first four years of *Poor Richard's Almanack*. Newcomb also identified additional sources, including *A Collection of Epigrams*, which Franklin added to his library before compiling *Poor Richard, 1737. A Collection of Epigrams* would become the principle source for *Poor Richard's* verse over the next several years.[27]

Like those from *Witts Recreations*, the epigrams from this new anthology sometimes form comments about Bridget. For the December page of *Poor Richard, 1737*, Franklin revised "On Women," a poem comparing women with books. In *A Collection of Epigrams*, the closing couplet is in the first person: "If they are books, I wish that my wife were / An almanack, to change her every year." Richard knows Bridget would never let him get away with the first-person point of view, so he changes it to the third person, substituting the name "Hodge" for the first-person pronoun. A familiar abbreviation for Roger, "Hodge" was a generic name for a rustic: "Are women books? says Hodge, then would mine were / An *almanack*, to change her every year."[28]

Bridget takes her revenge the next year. After compiling *Poor Richard, 1738* but before sending it to the printer, Richard must leave Philadelphia for business. He seals his manuscript and asks Bridget to send it to the printer. Suspicious, she breaks the seal "to see if he had not been flinging some of his old skitts at me." Sure enough, his epistle to the reader confirms her suspicions. She scratches out his epistle and writes one herself, in which she asks a rhetorical question and continues from there: "Cannot I have a little fault or two, but all the country must see it in print! They have already been told, at one time that I am proud, another time that I am loud, and that I have got a new petticoat, and abundance of such kind of stuff; and now, forsooth! all the world must know, that Poor Dick's wife has lately taken a fancy to drink a little tea now and then."[29]

Bridget tells readers she had planned additional corrections, but, having broken her spectacles, she cannot make any further changes and must publish the rest as it stands. It is easy to see what she disliked. The January epigram is the most misogynistic poem to appear in *Poor Richard's Almanack*. Two doctors attend "Dick's wife," who questions their medical skill. Both rely on the traditional humoral theory of medicine, but each prescribes a different cure. The first recommends purging; the second recommends bleeding. After the first says that bleeding would mean certain death, they let her husband decide. Richard's reply sounds like a Henny Youngman punch line: "'Ise no great skill,' quo' Richard, 'by the rood; / But I think bleeding's like to do most good.'"[30]

From the standpoint of Franklin's reading life, *Poor Richard, 1738* contains one of his finest aphorisms: "Reading makes a full man, meditation a profound man, discourse a clear man." Newcomb traced this saying to Bacon's *Essays.* In "Of Studies," Bacon observes, "Reading maketh a full man; conference a ready man; and writing an exact man."[31]

Franklin's changes to Bacon are revealing. For the second clause, he altered both action and result. Bacon gives the reader a social activity: conferring with others to make reading useful. Franklin gives the reader a solo activity: meditation, which can enhance understanding. Franklin's second clause reiterates a traditional Christian practice that crossed denominational boundaries: closet devotions. After reading some scripture, devout Christians would meditate on the text to understand its meaning. Though Franklin makes meditation secular, he nonetheless reinforces its importance to the reading process.

His third clause also modifies Bacon. Whereas Bacon had used the word "writing," Franklin used the broader term "discourse," which could involve both writing and speech. Franklin also changed Bacon's "exact man" to a "clear man." Both terms suggest precision, but Franklin's clear man also embodies the process of communication. Having omitted the communication process when he revised Bacon's second clause, Franklin restored it in the third. Clarity is essential to communication.

Poor Richard, 1739 does not mention Bridget's substitute preface from the previous almanac, but Franklin had developed their personalities so well by this point that he enabled long-time readers to imagine what had happened in the Saunders home. When Richard returned from his business trip and discovered what his wife had done to the almanac, no doubt Bridget had some explaining to do.

Richard does include a disparaging reference to Bridget in the June page of *Poor Richard, 1739.* Borrowing Jonathan Swift's "On His Late Deafness" from *A Collection of Epigrams,* Richard modifies the second half of this eight-line poem to suit his personal situation. In the anthology Swift's poem goes:

> At thunder now no more I start,
> Than at the rumbling of a cart:

> Nay, what's incredible, alack!
> I hardly hear a woman's clack.[32]

Richard makes some key revisions. He keeps the term "clack"—"cackle" might be a modern equivalent—but adds some scatological humor and a specific reference to his wife:

> At thunder now no more I start,
> Than at the whisp'ring of a fart.
> Nay, what's incredible, alack!
> I hardly hear my Bridget's clack.[33]

Skip ahead seven years. Franklin's advertisement for *Poor Richard, 1746* says it will contain Richard's "Account of Himself and His Way of Life with His Dame Bridget." Richard wrote the account in verse. "Who Is Poor Richard?" is consistent with contemporary poems in the colonial press offering prescriptions for true happiness. Williamsburg printer William Parks published similar poems in *The Virginia Gazette*. They emphasize reason, virtue, equanimity, and a good wife.[34]

As Richard Saunders paints his picture of wedded bliss, a state in which husband and wife share their responsibilities, he again seems oblivious to his wife's feelings. Her domestic duties are way out of proportion to his literary efforts. While he writes his almanac, she plants trees, plows the field, harvests grain, presses cider, churns butter, and makes cheese. Her household work may have been more strenuous than his literary tasks, but their marriage has reached an equilibrium of sorts. They are not exactly Darby and Joan, but neither are they Punch and Judy. Elsewhere in that year's almanac Richard says, "A good wife and health / Is man's best wealth."[35]

Like other Augustan poets who describe how to achieve true happiness, Richard makes reading essential. He follows a commonplace critical standard, emphasizing that books worth reading are those that please even as they teach. According to Richard, there are not many that accomplish this dual goal, but, then again, there need not be. Good books can be read over and over again. As Richard says in an almanac from an earlier year, "Read much, but not many books."[36]

This aphorism comes from *Directions, Counsels and Cautions*, a collection of admonitory sayings Dr. Thomas Fuller compiled as a conduct book for his son. Many other Poor Richardisms come from Fuller, but Franklin typically revised what he borrowed. In this instance, he changed only one word. Fuller had written, "Read much; but not many things." Franklin changed Fuller's "things" to "books."[37]

Though the revision eliminates Fuller's vague noun, it does alter the meaning. Franklin's version reinforces the process of reading intensively, not extensively. Whereas extensive reading involves reading many books, intensive reading involves reading the same books over and over again. Besides making Poor Richard support intensive reading, Franklin's revision does something more. By substituting "books" for "things," he contradicts Fuller's advice. Telling people to read much, Richard gives them license to read many things and thus advocates a figurative reading process: to read the fine print, to read someone's mind, to read a person's face, to read the terrain, to read between the lines, to read the writing on the wall.

Fuller's *Directions* was Franklin's most frequent source for his almanac's saws and sayings. Franklin treated collections of aphorisms as he treated collections of epigrams. He would use one until he exhausted it and then switch to another. He also took proverbs from James Howell's *Lexicon tetraglotton*, a multilingual dictionary containing a substantial collection of English, Italian, French, and Spanish proverbs. After Fuller, Howell was Franklin's most frequent source for Poor Richardisms.[38]

Howell's *Lexicon* gave Franklin his most famous maxim: "Early to bed, and early to rise / Makes a man healthy, wealthy and wise." This was one saying that needed no revision. Franklin repeated it word for word. Though Franklin took several other proverbs from Howell, he left many behind. The unused ones help reveal his selection process. Here's one Howell recorded, which Franklin did not use: "All work and no play makes *Jack* a dull boy."[39]

Franklin selected proverbs to empower his readers. The early-to-bed proverb challenges the established social order, providing a formula for success anyone could follow. It gave readers self-improvement advice. The dull-boy proverb, on the other hand, denigrates hard work and implies that play, not work, leads to self-improvement. Were he to propagate the dull-boy proverb, Franklin would have been giving readers a convenient excuse to quit work early and turn their attention to fun. Franklin had nothing against fun, but he did not want to elevate it above hard work. The descent to Avernus is rapid: A proverb encouraging people to quit work and have fun is far too easy to repeat.

Poor Richardisms have their roots in the proverbial maxims and moral reflections that fill Hesiod's *Works and Days*, but the oldest printed source Franklin used is *Houres of Recreation*, James Sandford's English translation of Lodovico Guicciardini's Italian collection of jokes, anecdotes, and proverbs published in 1576 in black letter. Largely obsolete in English printing by Franklin's time, black letter survives today under the misnomer "Old English" in such specialty uses as sports logos, college campus signage, and front-page newspaper titles. Franklin's great grandson William J. Duane, who later owned the book, enjoyed showing it to friends and boasting about how his great-grandfather mined it to create his famous sayings.[40]

Franklin often pulled down *Houres of Recreation* from the shelf as he compiled his almanac. Translating one Italian proverb, Sandford wrote, "He that goeth to bedde with dogges, aryseth with fleas." For *Poor Richard's Almanack*, Franklin modernized this proverb and improved its diction and syntax. He juxtaposed two rhyming verbs and paired them with opposing prepositions: "He that lies down with dogs, shall rise up with fleas."[41] Franklin's memorable version would endure. In *A Dog's Life*, Charlie Chaplin makes a joke by literalizing the proverb, having the Little Tramp use his pet dog as a pillow one night and wake up with fleas the next morning.

The most recent source for *Poor Richard's* aphorisms is Samuel Richardson's *Clarissa*. Richardson scattered memorable sayings throughout this lengthy novel. Though Franklin published the first American edition of Richardson's *Pamela*, he was never much of a novel reader. He did not have to read all eight volumes of Richardson's *Clarissa* to find some sayings that would work well. Richardson compiled the sayings in an appendix, organizing them by keyword, volume, and page. Franklin borrowed over twenty aphorisms from *Clarissa*, though he typically improved them. Here is one he found in the novel: "The greatest punishment that can be inflicted on us, would often be the grant of our own wishes." Franklin restructured and reworded Richardson's cumbersome sentence, making the comma a fulcrum to balance its two clauses: "If a man could have half his wishes, he would double his troubles."[42]

Poor Richard's Almanack is an outstanding contribution to science as well as literature. When Jacob Taylor read Franklin's account of the solar eclipse for April 1744, he wrote a poetic tribute, which he published in his own almanac the next year. As a poet and a mathematician, Taylor could appreciate *Poor Richard's Almanack* on multiple levels. He said that anyone who enjoyed the beauty of numbers would appreciate Richard's precise description of the solar eclipse.[43]

Taylor's tribute suggests that something strange and wonderful had happened to *Poor Richard's Almanack* since Franklin had started it a dozen years earlier: His fictional persona had matured. No longer was Richard Saunders the lazy, spiteful husband who used his almanac to avenge his wife. Richard had developed a greater sense of purpose and spoke with a new level of seriousness. Taylor's death in 1746 would further enhance Richard's maturity.

Poor Richard, 1747 includes an obituary for Taylor, whose almanac, Richard observes, had contained "the most compleat ephemeris and most accurate calculations that have hitherto appear'd in America." Richard continues, "He was an ingenious mathematician, as well as an expert and skilful astronomer; and moreover, no mean philosopher, but what is more than all, he was a pious and an honest man. *Requiescat in pace*."[44]

The epistle to the reader for the following year includes a poetic tribute to Taylor. Franklin adapted the poem from "The Ecstasy," John Hughes's Newtonian poem, substituting Taylor's name for Newton's.[45] Franklin's new format also reflects Taylor's influence. *Poor Richard Improved*, as Franklin retitled the almanac starting with the 1748 issue, is improved partly because it is one and a half times longer. Unlike other contemporary almanacs, Taylor had devoted two pages to each month, which made his almanac easier to read and gave him more space for poetry. With Taylor's death, Franklin adopted his format and started using two pages for each month. Franklin thus enabled Richard to write lengthier epistles to the reader and include more jokes, anecdotes, and poems.

The December 1748 pages reprint the story from Nathaniel Crouch's *Unparallel'd Varieties* about the Bavarian women who protected their city by carrying their husbands to safety. After presenting it, Richard adds a query: "Is this story more to the honour of the wives or of the husbands? My dame Bridget *says* the first, I *think* the latter: But we submit our dispute to the decision of the candid reader."[46]

Though Franklin would continue his almanac for another decade, Bridget's approval of these strong, smart, loving, and courageous Bavarian women marks her final appearance in *Poor Richard's*. Television again provides an apt comparison. The Richard-and-Bridget saga resembles a story arc in a television series. Much as a story arc spans several episodes, the story of Richard and Bridget Saunders spans several almanacs. Like a good television producer, Franklin could tell when his story arc was exhausted. *All in the Family* would give way to *Archie Bunker's Place*: Franklin quietly canceled the Richard and Bridget show and let Richard carry the almanac himself.

With *Poor Richard Improved*, Richard Saunders undergoes a metamorphosis. Since his *General Magazine* folded, Franklin channeled his magazine-making impulses to *Poor Richard's Almanack*. The lengthier epistles to the reader and the supplemental texts often resemble magazine articles. The Poor Richardisms continue, but they lose their ironic quality. No longer are they admonitions to work hard from someone who does not. Richard now seems to follow the folk wisdom he dispenses.

Poor Richard, 1753 filled some of its extra space to present information about a forthcoming astronomical event, the transit of Mercury. Franklin provided a long list of statistics allowing stargazers throughout colonial America to observe the path of Mercury across the sun's face and take accurate readings. He also provided a diagram illustrating the approximate path Mercury would take, making it memorable with a homey simile. Mercury would appear "like a small black patch in a lady's face."[47]

Joseph-Nicolas Delisle, a prominent French astronomer, wrote to encourage colonial astronomers to record the transit of Mercury. Having recorded previous transits, Delisle knew Mercury was too close to the sun to measure its distance accurately, but he encouraged observations of Mercury because it would let stargazers practice for a more rare and useful astronomical event the following decade: the transit of Venus. Franklin's New York friend James Alexander translated Delisle's instructions into English, sent it to Franklin, and urged him to encourage others to observe the transit of Mercury.[48]

Franklin printed fifty copies of Delisle's instructions as a pamphlet and inserted a hand-drawn illustration into each. To one correspondent he included a copy of *Poor Richard, 1753* with the pamphlet, which let him boast a little: "You will see by our almanack, we have had this transit under consideration before the arrival of these French letters."[49] Franklin's astronomical discussion in *Poor Richard, 1753* put him in the vanguard of astronomers planning to observe the transit of Mercury and the transit of Venus.

Distributing the pamphlet across colonial America, Franklin sent half a dozen copies to Antigua, where he had established a partnership with Benjamin Mecom. Franklin's nephew and namesake, Mecom was the son of Edward and Jane Mecom. Upon completing his apprenticeship with New York printer James Parker, Mecom moved to Antigua with Franklin's support. On May 6, 1753, cloudy skies hid the transit of Mercury from mainland observers, but the skies were clear in Antigua. Since Mecom had shared the pamphlet with a local astronomer, they were able to take excellent readings, which circulated in manuscript and appeared in the scientific press.[50]

The extra space in *Poor Richard Improved* also gave Franklin room for longer poems. As he scanned his books for material, sometimes he could not find poems long enough for the space he had to fill, so he would create composite poems that combined lines from multiple works. Franklin felt no compunction to cite his sources. Perhaps he could be accused of plagiarism, but Franklin did not see his anonymous borrowings that way. His method of composing poetry for his almanac anticipates Jorge Luis Borges's belief that literature is a collective endeavor.

In "The Flower of Coleridge," Borges sanctions the practice of borrowing from other authors. The whole idea of plagiarism, he observes, is based on a false premise, that literature is proprietary. Literature does not belong to the individual creator. Borrowing from a predecessor, an author lifts literature above the level of individual creation. Ideally, all poets—past, present, future—must combine their efforts to advance their art.[51]

To write "Learn of the Bees," a poem that appears on the July pages of *Poor Richard, 1756*, Franklin searched Henry Baker's *Medulla poetarum romanorum*, a collection of excerpts from Roman poets in parallel Latin and English texts. Baker's *Medulla* contains selections from three different poems that Franklin used to compose "Learn of the Bees." Baker arranged the excerpts topically. Franklin took his first six lines from Christopher Pitt's translation of Virgil's *Aeneid*, which was excerpted under the topic "Labour" in the second volume of Baker's *Medulla*. Franklin's selection describes how bees work hard to make honey.[52]

Franklin found his next four lines in the first volume of Baker's *Medulla* under the topic "Industry." The passage, which takes the ant, for instance, comes from Francis Creech's translation of Horace's satires. The passage begins: "The little ant (example she to man / Of care and labour,) gathers all she can." Franklin canceled the first "she" and substituted "too," thus linking the ant with the bee and creating a smooth transition between excerpts from different sources.[53]

The last six lines of "Learn of the Bees" Franklin found in the second volume of Baker's *Medulla* under the topic "Sloth." The lines come from Ovid's *Tristia*. Like the other two selections, Franklin indented the excerpt from Ovid, making the whole sixteen-line composition into a poem with three verse paragraphs. Coming after the ants and the bees, the third verse paragraph begins, "Man's understanding, dull'd by idleness / Contracts a rust, that makes it daily less."[54] These lines have the quality of a turn in a sonnet, applying the examples from the animal kingdom to humans. "Learn of the Bees" shows that Franklin saw poems from the past as building blocks he could assemble to create original combinations expressing his personal philosophy.

Franklin kept his almanac going into 1757, when he wrote *Poor Richard, 1758*, his twenty-sixth and final one. This work contains his longest epistle to the reader, which he structured as a frame tale. Richard relates a time when he was riding through the city and encountered a large crowd of people waiting for a public auction. Father Abraham, a voluble greybeard, gives the people sage advice, recommending prudence and emphasizing thrift. Father Abraham enhances his aphorisms with the tag clause, "as Poor Richard says." At one point, for example, he tells the crowd, " 'The cat in gloves catches no mice!' as Poor Richard says."⁵⁵

One of Franklin's finest literary achievements, the epistle to the reader of *Poor Richard, 1758* has been reprinted countless times. Mecom, who dissolved his partnership with Franklin, left Antigua, and established a printshop in Boston, was the first to reprint Franklin's preface separately, which he titled *Father Abraham's Speech*. Other printers followed Mecom, issuing their own pamphlet versions of Franklin's preface under the title, *The Way to Wealth*, which remained in print through the nineteenth century. In his children's biography of Franklin, Nathaniel Hawthorne said *The Way to Wealth* made him the "counsellor and household friend of almost every family in America."⁵⁶

The Way to Wealth solidified many traditional sayings and made them more memorable. Father Abraham's mantra-like tag clause itself became proverbial. People often tacked it onto proverbs they repeated. Benjamin F. Palmer, an American POW during the War of 1812 who had been named after Franklin, kept a diary during his imprisonment, in which he says: "Fortune is a slippery jade, and as poor Richard says there is many a slip between the cup and the lip."⁵⁷ Though Franklin knew this proverb, Richard never uses it in the almanac. Palmer gave the traditional saying extra oomph by introducing it with the familiar tag clause.

The phrase "as Poor Richard says" has fallen from usage, but Franklin's catchy sayings endure, which is not necessarily a good thing. They stick in the memory and trip off the tongue so well that they have given people convenient ways to summarize a problem and save themselves the burden of analyzing it and devising their own solution. A memorable aphorism lets people quote instead of think. Yvor Winters called this process the "method of the New England farmer who meets every situation in life with a saw from *Poor Richard*." Winters was talking about T. S. Eliot's quotations in *The Waste Land*, but his observation applies more broadly. The ease of quotation "betokens the death of the mind and of the sensibility alike."⁵⁸

The Way to Wealth proves that Franklin was too good a writer for his own good. It became so well known that it blotted from the cultural memory any Poor Richardisms omitted from Father Abraham's speech. *The Way to Wealth* gave posterity the impression that Franklin's maxims were exclusively concerned with the world of getting and spending. Reducing Richard Saunders and his creator to penny-pinching maxim mongers, *The Way to Wealth* established a materialistic philosophy that became so deeply engrained in American culture that, according to Phillips Russell, it practically went unchallenged until Walt Whitman sang, "I loafe and invite my soul."⁵⁹

So influential was *The Way to Wealth* that it effaced Franklin's early concept of Richard Saunders, a loafer long before Whitman. It also minimized the character's psychological complexity by ignoring Richard's gradual maturation over his almanac-making career. Though Russell says that "Song of Myself" challenged the philosophical materialism of *The Way to Wealth*, what he does not say is that the challenge was unsuccessful. In Gilded Age America, Whitman's barbaric yawp could hardly be heard above the ringing cash registers of Poor Richard's progeny.

14

Science

THE SCIENCE BOOKS Franklin read during the mid-eighteenth century indicate that different scientific fields had reached different stages of development. Long-standing fields—medicine, most significantly—progressed slowly, whereas new ones, such as optics and electricity, made rapid strides. Even within specific areas, separate aspects progressed at different rates. In medicine, groundbreaking discoveries in diagnostics took place while centuries-old remedies stymied advances in treatment.

In 1734, Franklin acquired a copy of John Tennent's *Every Man His Own Doctor: or, The Poor Planter's Physician*, which William Parks had published in Virginia. Tennent's work parallels other contemporary self-help books that gave general readers knowledge formerly restricted to professionals. These works include *Every Man His Own Lawyer* and *Every Man His Own Broker*. When London bookseller Edmund Curll reissued *Medicinia gymnastica*, Francis Fuller's treatise about the therapeutic value of physical exercise, he retitled it *Medicina gymnastica: or, Every Man His Own Physician*. Franklin joked that soon a publisher would issue *Every Man His Own Priest*.[1]

Recognizing its potential, Franklin reprinted *Every Man His Own Doctor*. The work's appeal is obvious from its opening sentence, which sounds like something Franklin would say: "The most acceptable service we can render God, is beneficence to man." A new appendix clarifies one aspect of this Virginia medical handbook for readers in Pennsylvania, Delaware, and New Jersey. Engaging in a bit of intercolonial one-upmanship, Franklin warned that Pennsylvania ipecac or "Indian physick" was stronger than Virginia ipecac, so he adjusted the dosages to be taken for a vomit or a purge.[2]

That ipecac was one of Tennent's principal remedies shows his reliance on the humoral theory that stretched back to Galen. Many people in Franklin's day still believed illness came from disturbances among the four humors: blood, phlegm, black bile, and yellow bile. To restore health, one must rebalance the humors using such cures as bleeding and vomiting, which were often repeated to the patient's detriment. When Dr. William Douglass first reached

Boston, he found local medical practice appalling: "bleeding, vomiting, blistering, purging . . . if the illness continued, there was *repetendi*, and finally *murderandi*."[3] Tennent's recommended medical equipment reinforced this traditional approach. Every home should have a lancet, a syringe, and a clyster pipe, which looks even scarier than its modern equivalent, the enema bulb. The modern implement the clyster pipe most resembles is the caulking gun.

Every Man His Own Doctor is organized by illness. After describing the relevant symptoms, each section provides a cure. Tennent started with pleurisy. Upon showing symptoms, the patient "must, without loss of time, take away 10 ounces of *blood*, and repeat the same three or four days successively, if the pain go not away before. On the third day, he may vomit with 80 grains of Indian physick." Tennent ended the pleurisy section with recipes for herbal concoctions the patient should drink and plasters to apply.[4]

Tennent's first section was pertinent to Franklin, who had caught pleurisy at 21. In 1735, the year after he published *Every Man His Own Doctor*, pleurisy struck again. Tennent had designed his medical handbook for people who lived far from the nearest doctor. Since Franklin was friends with several good physicians, including Dr. Thomas Bond and Dr. Samuel Chew, he did not have to treat himself using lancet and ipecac.

In 1736, Franklin obtained a copy of Tennent's new book, *An Essay on Pleurisy*. Weighed down with dubious medical theories, *An Essay on Pleurisy* contains less practical information than *Every Man His Own Doctor*, but its treatment for pleurisy is more detailed. When he issued the next edition of *Every Man His Own Doctor*, Franklin added a postscript summarizing Tennent's new cure. It still involved bleeding and vomiting, but Tennent introduced a new ingredient: rattlesnake root, *Polygala senega*.[5]

Rattlesnake root manifests the doctrine of signatures, a theory stretching back to Paracelsus. Some contemporary physicians had put such ancient practices and practitioners behind them. Dr. Alexander Hamilton, for one, condemned "the puerilities of *Paracelsus*." But many still followed the doctrine of signatures, which held that plants are marked by signs indicating their medicinal use. Furthermore, the doctrine of signatures stipulated that wherever a particular disease arises, nature provides its cure nearby. Rattlesnake root was plentiful where rattlesnakes were plentiful. "To the Author of the *Poor Planter's Physician*," a blank-verse tribute Franklin reprinted in *The General Magazine*, begins with an apostrophe to Virginia, which reiterates this concept, "Oh happy virgin land! still self-producing / A remedy, for every noxious ill."[6]

A parallel doctrine of signatures developed among Native Americans, who used rattlesnake root to cure snakebite because the plant's root resembled the snake's rattle. Tennent went beyond the doctrine of signatures, seeing rattlesnake root as a wonder drug that could cure many illnesses. Though Franklin accepted rattlesnake root as a cure for pleurisy, Tennent had trouble convincing the medical profession of its therapeutic value.[7]

Franklin read all he could about another medical topic: smallpox. Philadelphia started inoculating for smallpox in 1730 when rumors from Boston foretold the arrival of a new epidemic. Franklin emerged as a strenuous advocate for inoculation. He published an article about the practice of inoculation in *The Pennsylvania Gazette* and recorded statistics verifying that inoculation was safe and effective.[8]

Franklin's medical library shows him keeping up with the latest literature about inoculation. Joseph Rogers's *Essay on Epidemic Diseases*—the earliest book on the subject in his library—appeared in 1734. Based on his extensive medical practice in Cork, Ireland, Dr. Rogers's treatise covers both typhus and smallpox. His smallpox section discusses the practice of inoculation and emphasizes its advantages.[9]

Inoculation lets the surgeon minimize people's exposure to contagious disease, Rogers explained. Those who contract smallpox through infection cannot control the amount of disease that enters their bodies, nor can they control the strength of the strain: "Every column of *air* we breath in [carries] its own *harbinger* of destruction." Rogers used an epic simile to punctuate his argument. Contracted through infection, smallpox rushes "naked and unguarded into every *pore* like so many sharp pointed daggers; cut, tear and destroy every thing they meet with and commit ravage without controul."[10]

Another smallpox epidemic struck Philadelphia in 1736. Thomas Cadwalader, along with Bond, Chew, and other local physicians, administered some inoculations, but far fewer than they wished. Francis Franklin, the first child Benjamin and Deborah had together, was now 4 years old. They planned to have Franky inoculated once he recovered from another illness. Sadly, he contracted smallpox before his parents could have him inoculated. Franky died on November 21, 1736. The January epigram for *Poor Richard, 1737*, which Franklin composed around this time, is poignant. He found its last four lines in *A Collection of Epigrams* but wrote the first four himself. They express his disappointment with thoughtless people who ignore the underlying science: "Tho' 'tis life's great preservation / Many oppose *inoculation*."[11]

The Franklins would not have another child until Sarah or Sally, as they nicknamed her, was born in 1743. They would have her inoculated when she was 2.

Besides promoting smallpox inoculation in *The Pennsylvania Gazette* and *Poor Richard's Almanack*, Franklin printed separate works on the subject. In late 1750, he published Dr. Adam Thomson's *Discourse on the Preparation of the Body for the Small-Pox*. Though Thomson had first settled in Maryland, he moved to Philadelphia in 1748. Known to posterity as a poet, Thomson had a thriving medical practice in Philadelphia, partly because of his success as an inoculator. His pamphlet explains how to administer mercury and antimony as preparatives for smallpox inoculation. Other physicians attacked Thomson's method. Dr. John Kearsley, his most vocal opponent, critiqued Thomson in *A Letter to a Friend*.[12]

A third pamphlet in the controversy defended Thomson. Written by Dr. Alexander Hamilton, *A Defence of Dr. Thomson's Discourse* was published by Andrew Bradford's nephew William Bradford, who had established his own printing house in Philadelphia. Like his uncle, William Bradford was a business rival to Franklin; he founded *The Pennsylvania Journal* to compete with Franklin's *Pennsylvania Gazette*.

In the smallpox pamphlet war, William Bradford came out the winner, at least in terms of literary worth. Hamilton applied his consummate writing skills to defend Thomson's method. His defense is based on logic, reason, and sound medical theory, but, try as he might, Hamilton could not silence his saucy wit. Refuting Kearsley's argument that Thomson's method went against nature, Hamilton repeated a story he had heard Kearsley tell about a new method of curing dysentery, which hardly followed nature.

Afflicted with the bloody flux, one of Kearsley's patients was having trouble breathing. The patient ordered a servant to perform mouth-to-mouth, a first-aid procedure in its infancy. The servant applied his lips and blew forcefully to inflate his master's lungs. After the servant repeated this procedure several times, his master recovered. Hamilton quipped: "Whether such a whimsical cure as this be natural, I leave you to judge: for I shall make no remark upon it; only, I think, the gentleman might easily make an improvement on this discovery by applying his mouth to a certain part, through which he might convey his air or *flatus* more immediately into the place, where that distemper has its seat."[13]

Hamilton's flight of fancy notwithstanding, scientific literature appealed to a small segment of the colonial book-buying public. Other subjects had a wider appeal. After befriending the itinerant evangelist George Whitefield, Franklin became his publisher. He also published religious works opposing Whitefield, including the Reverend George Gillespy's *Remarks upon Mr George*

Whitefield, Proving Him a Man under Delusion. A shrewd businessman, Franklin could see how well religion sold. Though putting words in his mouth, Ezra Pound best summarized the situation: "For as Ben Franklin said, with such urbanity: / 'Nothing will pay thee, friend, like Christianity.'"[14]

Five years before Thomson's *Discourse*, Franklin had published his first original scientific work, Thomas Cadwalader's *Essay on the West-India Dry-Gripes*. Though not published until 1745, Cadwalader had been working on this book since 1738, when he lost his manuscript. Cadwalader advertised for its return, saying he had dropped it somewhere in the streets of Philadelphia. Rewriting the lost work, he correctly hypothesized that the lead condensers used in distilling Jamaica rum caused the colic or the dry gripes, a condition marked by severe abdominal cramps that could develop into a debilitating disease that adversely affected the personality and hindered motor skills. Though Cadwalader hesitated to attribute the West-India dry gripes directly to the use of lead equipment in distilling, his pamphlet is a seminal contribution to the study of lead poisoning.[15]

Publishing Cadwalader's treatise was just one of Franklin's efforts to inform people about the dangers of lead poisoning, which he had known about since his Boston boyhood. While in London serving as agent for the Pennsylvania Assembly, Franklin would befriend Dr. George Baker, the leading British expert in the field, who presented him with a copy of his treatise, *An Essay, Concerning the Cause of the Endemical Colic of Devonshire*. Franklin informed Baker about the use of "leaden worms," that is, the coiled tubing used as condensers in the distillation of New England rum. Baker would incorporate what he learned from Franklin in a paper he presented before the Royal College of Physicians.[16]

Franklin's interest in medicine extended beyond the walls of his library. When Bond approached him in 1751 with the idea of establishing a hospital in Philadelphia, Franklin was happy to lend a hand. To help Bond raise money, he wrote "Appeal for the Hospital." This essay shows how Franklin could use his learning to create a powerful argument for contributing to the public good.[17] Their fund-raising campaign succeeded. The Pennsylvania Hospital opened a temporary facility in 1752. Designed by Franklin's architect friend Samuel Rhoads, the new building opened four years later. The first hospital in North America, the Pennsylvania Hospital thrives today.

In 1763, Cadwalader Evans, a physician at the Pennsylvania Hospital, proposed that a portion of medical student fees be allocated toward the purchase of books to create a hospital library. Evans argued that a library would "tend greatly to the advantage of the pupils, and the honor of the institution." With

FIGURE 14.1   Robert Scot, *1755, The Pennsylvania Hospital* (1782–1793), engraving. Library of Congress Prints and Photographs Division, Washington, DC, LC-DIG-pga-14303.

his proposal's approval, the Pennsylvania Hospital Library was born. Evans wrote Franklin, then in London, to tell him the news. Franklin endorsed the idea and sent the hospital Baker's *Essay Concerning the Cause of the Endemical Colic of Devonshire*. Furthermore, Franklin asked Evans for a catalogue of the hospital library, so he could solicit additional volumes from his philanthropic doctor friends in London.[18]

Mathematical books helped Franklin in an odd way. When he was appointed clerk of the Pennsylvania Assembly in 1736, he obtained a position that gave him considerable social, political, and commercial benefits, but it had one major drawback. Long legislative sessions could be tedious. Franklin looked to the mathematical literature for surcease of boredom. Bernard Frénicle de Bessy's "Tables magiques," which appeared in a collection of mathematical essays published in Paris by the Royal Academy of Sciences, helped him cope. Frénicle taught Franklin how to make magic squares, that is, large squares containing many little ones. An eight-by-eight square, for instance, contained sixty-four squares. The challenge was to place a different number in each little square so that every column and every row would total the same. Making magic squares, Franklin filled hours of legislative debate. Sometimes, after a long day in the assembly, he would be left without a square to spare.

While entertaining Franklin one day, Logan brought up the subject. In a letter to Peter Collinson, another magic-square devotee, Franklin reported their encounter, complete with dialogue. Though Logan knew about

European mathematicians who had distinguished themselves with mathematical games and puzzles, he could recall no Englishmen who had created anything like magic squares, which demonstrated great ingenuity in the manipulation of numbers.[19]

"Perhaps," Franklin responded, it is "a mark of the good sense of our English mathematicians, that they would not spend their time in things that were merely *difficiles nugae*, incapable of any useful application."

"Many of the arithmetical or mathematical questions, publickly proposed and answered in England, [are] equally trifling and useless," Logan replied.

Franklin's follow-up comment echoes the *Port Royal Logic*. "Perhaps the considering and answering such questions," he said, "may not be altogether useless, if it produces by practice an habitual readiness and exactness in mathematical disquisitions, which readiness may, on many occasions, be of real use."

"In the same way," Logan said, "may the making of these squares be of use."

Franklin then boasted to Logan about the magic squares he had created. Though Logan showed him several more of Frénicle's magic squares, Franklin was unimpressed. Logan asked to see his. The next time Franklin visited Stenton, he brought an eight-by-eight square he had made. Logan appreciated Franklin's magic square but wished to challenge him further. He pulled down another volume, Michael Stifel's sixteenth-century algebra handbook *Arithmetica integra*, which contained a sixteen-by-sixteen square.

Unwilling to be outdone by a crusty German professor, Franklin went home and started a sixteen-by-sixteen square. Not only did each row and column add up to the same total, so did the diagonals. Furthermore, Franklin created sixteen-square patterns within the larger square that also reached the same total. Logan found Franklin's square astonishing, stupendous even. Logan told Collinson that Franklin had out-Frénicled Frénicle. Besides praising Franklin's mathematical skill, Logan called him "an extraordinary man in most respects . . . one of a singular good judgment, but of equal modesty."[20] In his letter to Collinson, Franklin cuts short Logan's effusive praise, but before the letter ends, he throws modesty to the wind and says his sixteen-by-sixteen square is the "most magically magical of any magic square ever made by any magician."

When neither his printing house nor his responsibilities as assembly clerk occupied him, the indefatigable Franklin started new projects. During the winter of 1737–38, he purchased some steel plates and built a home-heating stove. His design improved on the traditional fireplace, directing heat into the room, not up the chimney. It also conserved firewood and thus reduced fuel costs, the colonial homeowner's single biggest expense. Preventing sparks from flying up the chimney, the new stove minimized potential house fires. Franklin designed the front to open, giving people the greatest asset of the traditional fireplace: the hypnotic pleasure of staring into the flames.

After Franklin began manufacturing his stoves, he gained a partner in the business. Robert Grace was overseas when Franklin built his first stove, but he had since returned to Philadelphia. Little evidence survives to document Grace's activities in England and Europe. He did befriend Collinson, whose correspondence reveals that Grace took "pains to make himself master of fluxing metals." He studied metallurgy with an eye toward entering the iron mining and manufacturing business. Grace had the great fortune to meet Mrs. Rebecca Nutt, a young but wealthy widow, whom he would soon marry. Her dowry included the forges and furnaces of Coventry and Warwick, Pennsylvania. Grace threw his energy into improving them.[21]

Franklin was pleased to be reunited with his friend. He would compliment Grace's playful wit in his autobiography. Family tradition has preserved one of his pranks. The Graces had a stone chapel on their estate. Riding past the chapel one day, Grace saw his wife's saddle horse tied to a tree. He dismounted and chalked a distich on the chapel door: "Your walls are thick and your people are thin, / The Devil's without, and Grace is within."[22]

Since Grace was spending most of his time in Warwick, he leased his property on Pewter Platter Alley to the Franklins, which was just four doors down toward the Delaware River from their former home and printing house. Having become Philadelphia postmaster, Franklin had been operating the post office from his printing house. The new location would provide more room for both the printshop and the post office, and also let Benjamin and Deborah live in a dwelling detached from the printing house. Pewter Platter Alley would remain the Franklins' home and place of business for years to come.[23]

Grace invested in Franklin's new stove and became his primary steel supplier. He also encouraged Franklin to write a pamphlet promoting the stove and financed its publication. *An Account of the New Invented Pennsylvania Fire-Places* marks a new phase in Franklin's literary development. Though a promotional pamphlet, the work is also a scientific treatise, his first. Theodore Hornberger observed, "Science brought into play all of Franklin's best qualities as a writer. It demanded clarity and conciseness. The persona of the humble inquirer fitted perfectly, for in science there is little respect for dogmatism. Yet there was room for imagination, since from the phenomena observed hypotheses had to be constructed, and for persuasion, because these hypotheses had to be supported."[24]

Franklin abandoned the nonchalance he had learned from the Couranteers. Gone are such phrases as "I read somewhere" or "a learned writer says." In his scientific writings, Franklin cites his sources with precision. Some citations in the fireplace pamphlet do seem uncomfortable. Describing a French stove, Franklin cited the French title of his source, Nicholas Gauger's *La mechanique de feu*. Franklin had a fair reading knowledge of French by the 1740s, but he almost surely read Gauger's work in J. T. Desagulier's English translation, *Fires Improved; or, A New Method of Building Chimnies*, which Grace had donated to the Library Company.[25]

Since Franklin often celebrated the expressive power of the English language, his use of the French title seems pretentious. Alternately, he appears insecure, as if citing an English translation of a French work would be amateurish and unscientific. His use of a Latin source later in the pamphlet conveys a similar insecurity, again making him seem uneasy with erudite material.

Fireplaces, Franklin argued, draw air through the cracks in the house and thus create disease-producing jets of cold air. (Later, Franklin would challenge the traditional belief that cold air could produce disease.) To support the pamphlet's argument, he switched from erudite French and Latin sources to more familiar material: proverbs. The switch seems to put him at ease. Franklin first made literary use of proverbs while writing for *The New-England Courant*, which he had since elevated to an art form with *Poor Richard's Almanack*. Incorporating a proverb in his fireplace pamphlet, Franklin gave folk wisdom an authority commensurate with scientific research. He observed, "The Spaniards have a proverbial saying, 'If the wind blow on you thro' a hole, make your will, and take care of your soul.'"[26]

To bolster his folk wisdom, Franklin bowed to Martin Clare's expertise. Assuming a humble pose, he spoke in the third person: "As the writer is neither physician nor philosopher, the reader may expect he should justify these his opinions by the authority of some that are so." Consequently, he quoted from *The Motion of Fluids*, Clare's pioneering treatise in the field of fluid mechanics. When Franklin catalogued the Library Company's books, Clare's work was shelved next to Gauger's *Fires Improved*.[27]

Histories and travels from around the world broadened Franklin's medical knowledge. A few years earlier, he had read Jean-Baptiste Du Halde's *General History of China*. He now reread it to strengthen his argument about the dangers of a cold, sharp wind. Du Halde incorporated a Chinese medical handbook as part of his history, *Tchang-Seng: or, The Art of Procuring Health and Long Life*. *Tchang-Seng* combines folk wisdom with medical advice. Wind that enters a home through a narrow passage can cause gout, palsy, and similar diseases. From this work, Franklin repeated an ancient Chinese proverb: "Avoid a blast of wind as carefully as the point of an arrow."[28]

Franklin also introduced empirical evidence from closer to home. During the smallpox epidemics of 1730 and 1736, Pennsylvania's German settlers suffered fewer fatalities because, he argued, they kept their homes at a high, but even temperature, which discouraged smallpox. To support his argument, Franklin cited other people he had read about—Danes, Swedes, Russians—who kept their homes quite hot. He did not draw any definitive conclusions but instead submitted his theory to the judgment of physicians.

Besides designing the stove, Franklin also designed a device to be cast into a front panel, which reflects his ongoing fascination with emblems. The front of his stove portrays a smiling sun with the Latin motto, *Alter idem*, meaning a second self. The pamphlet closes with a poem, "On the Device of the New Fire-Place," that explicates the stove's emblem. The poem reinforces the interaction between science and poetry in Franklin's world. The author is identified as "a friend," Breintnall presumably. Differing from the sun in the sky, this new sun will neither scorch in the summer nor abscond in the winter: "But, faithful still to us, this new sun's fire, / Warms when we please, and just as we desire."[29]

The fireplace pamphlet circulated throughout colonial America and made its way to Europe. One day, John Bartram showed Franklin a translation that leading Dutch naturalist J. F. Gronovius had sent. Bartram had begun corresponding with British and European botanists after Chew and Breintnall recommended him to Peter Collinson as someone who could send them American seeds, plants, and other specimens of natural history. In his cover letter to the Dutch translation of Franklin's fireplace pamphlet, Gronovius told Bartram that it had elicited "great applause in this part of the world." *An Account of the New Invented Pennsylvania Fire-Places*, Franklin's first overseas publication, marks the beginning of his international scientific reputation. The pamphlet's history also illustrates how the transatlantic exchange of botanic information and specimens fostered an exchange of information in other scientific fields.[30]

Bartram's European correspondents encouraged him to commit his vast knowledge of botany to paper. In the summer of 1743, he took a six-week wilderness trip through Pennsylvania and New York to Fort Oswego on Lake Ontario. He kept a journal during the trip, which he sent to England. His journal circulated in manuscript form until Collinson arranged for its publication. It appeared in 1751 as *Observations on the Inhabitants, Climate, Soil, Rivers,*

Productions, Animals, and Other Matters Worthy of Notice. Franklin added a copy to his personal library, one of many works of natural history he owned.[31]

The European scientists were disappointed with Bartram's *Observations*. They knew from their correspondence with him and the seeds and plants he sent that his knowledge of the natural history of North America was far more extensive than *Observations* indicates. Franklin reacted differently. He quite enjoyed books that combined narratives of travel with natural history. Other travel books in his library contain extensive information about everything from botany to zoology.

Louis Feuillée's *Journal des observations, physiques, et botaniques*, for example, describes the flora and fauna he encountered during his exploration of South America in the first decade of the eighteenth century, the same decade John Reynolds published his physico-theological poem *Death's Vision*. The timing is not coincidental. Feuillée, a friar of the Minim order, was motivated by the same basic impulse as the physico-theological poets, that is, to study nature to appreciate the wisdom and power of God.[32]

Father Feuillée exemplified the scientific heroism of the eighteenth century; he was willing to risk his life and endure countless hardships to make discoveries that contributed to scientific knowledge and, in so doing, reinforced his belief in the Supreme Being. His strenuous research suited the belief system of the Minim order, showing the spiritual value of scientific exploration and contrasting the humility of the observer with the grandeur of the observed.[33]

Trained in astronomy, botany, and cartography, Feuillée explored and mapped much of the South American coast, describing many plant specimens for the first time. His *Journal*, part ship's log, part monastic diary, and part scientific treatise, offered Franklin a hybrid form written with an elegant simplicity that similarly exemplified Father Feuillé's religious and philosophical outlook. His *Journal* contains dozens of illustrations depicting the species he discovered drawn with a minimalism consistent with its prose style and his belief system.[34]

The time Franklin spent in Europe over the ensuing decades gave him more opportunities to expand his library of natural history. Living in London, he met many of Britain's leading scientists and bookmen. Initially, he had been unable to subscribe to George Edwards's *Gleanings of Natural History, Containing Birds, Insects, Plants, etc.*, but Franklin did subscribe to the work before Edwards released his third volume.[35]

Illustrated with Edwards's hand-colored engravings, *Gleanings* was both a beautiful book and a contribution to scientific knowledge. Reviewing Edwards's *Gleanings* for *The Monthly Review*, William Bewley observed that many of his subjects had never before been delineated or described so that they "are real acquisitions to natural history, and increase our knowledge of the numberless species of objects with which the Almighty Creator has decorated our terrestrial abode."[36]

Compared with such lavishly illustrated works as Feuillée's *Journal* and Edwards's *Gleanings*, Bartram's *Observations* is quite modest. One can see why the European botanists were disappointed, but Franklin enjoyed Bartram's book, not only because he was a good friend, but also because he had done much to encourage Bartram's botanical research. He raised funds to support his American travels and gave him free access to the Library Company. As Philadelphia postmaster, he franked specimens Bartram sent through the mail: an early American example of government-subsidized scientific research.

A book Franklin published in 1751 presents Bartram's botanical knowledge in greater detail. Five years earlier, Scottish physician Thomas Short had published *Medicina britannica*, an encyclopedia of medicinal plants. For the first American edition, Franklin recruited Bartram to annotate Short's entries, supplying information pertinent to the plants in North America. Bartram's notes indicate that he grew in his garden many European species of plants, which reflect his strenuous transatlantic efforts to exchange seeds and cuttings. For example, Bear's breeches, *Acanthus spinosus*, was "a great softener, often used in emollients and pain-easing clysters." It once flourished in his garden, Bartram explained, but "the late hard winters have destroyed the root and branch." Bartram got several other European species to grow, but many others similarly had trouble surviving the Pennsylvania winters. In one instance, however, a non-native species flourished all too well. Toadflax or *Linaria vulgaris*, "a troublesome, stinking weed, is no native," Bartram explained, "but we can never I believe eradicate it." The local name for this species reflects the contempt Americans had for it: "dog piss weed."[37]

Bartram identified some species that were native to both Europe and America. In other cases, he did not find the exact species but did find similar ones. In his travels, Bartram never saw the species of devil's bit that Short describes, *Succisia pratensis*, but he did see *Liatris scariosa*, a species known as devil's bit and blazing star. Several entries show what a meticulous observer Bartram was during his travels. He found *Potentilla anserina*, a species of silverweed used to treat fluxes and loosenesses, in the backwoods of New York: "This plant I saw growing on the salt-plain four miles beyond Onondango, and no where else."[38]

Franklin also read the latest science news. As publisher of *The Pennsylvania Gazette*, he received numerous exchange papers, which let him keep up with

FIGURE 14.2 *John Bartram House and Garden, House, 54th Street and Lindbergh Boulevard, Philadelphia, PA*. Library of Congress Prints and Photographs Division, Washington, DC, HALS PA-1-A.

the latest developments throughout British North America. The Boston papers contained the best science news, mainly due to the efforts of Dr. William Douglass, who brought together several Boston physicians to found the Medical Society of Boston, which reported new medical practices and procedures. When they were not attending their patients, its members enjoyed botanical excursions into the surroundings woods. In one issue of *The Boston Gazette*, the Medical Society filed a report on poisonous jimsonweed, *Datura stranomium*. The article called for a detailed botanical catalogue of indigenous plants, partly to save people from accidentally poisoning themselves. After reading the article, Franklin passed it along to Bartram to apprise him of the botanical research being done in Boston.[39]

In 1743, Bartram and Franklin planned a colonial scientific society, partly inspired by Douglass's Medical Society of Boston. With *Proposal for Promoting Useful Knowledge among the British Plantations in America*, Franklin coined the group's name—the American Philosophical Society—and established its founding principles. Since the long stretch of land that formed colonial America extended through different geographical regions, it provided a natural laboratory for scientific research and offered diverse resources that could contribute to the improvement of the colonies. American virtuosi needed an organization to coordinate their individual studies. Franklin understood that their scientific research had the potential to benefit the world. His wistful tone enhances his rhetoric: "Many useful particulars remain uncommunicated, die with the discoverers, and are lost to mankind."[40]

Franklin also traveled to New England in 1743. In Boston, he caught Archibald Spencer's scientific lectures. Though Franklin thanked Spencer for introducing him to electrical research, his influence was slight. Spencer's basic electrical demonstrations formed a small part of his general scientific lectures, which also discussed Isaac Newton's theories of light and color and William Harvey's research into the circulatory system. Spencer demonstrated the circulation of blood through the human body with an elaborate model. Dr. Alexander Hamilton acknowledged the popularity of his lectures but personally found Spencer a sour and self-centered pedant. "Dr. Rhubarb," Hamilton called him. He may have sounded ingenious to unsophisticated lecture audiences, but the Edinburgh-trained Hamilton saw that Spencer could not tell chalk from cheese.[41]

Passing through New York during his trip to New England, Franklin met New York botanist, historian, physicist, and statesman Cadwallader Colden for the first time. Their chance meeting sparked a warm friendship. Besides botany, medicine, and Native American culture, Colden took an interest in physics. A few years later, he sent Franklin several copies of his theoretical treatise, *An Explication of the First Causes of Action in Matter*, asking him to keep one and distribute others to his scientist friends.[42]

Having interleaved his copy to give himself room for notes, Franklin told Colden he was "reading it and making remarks as time permits." Franklin distributed copies to Bartram, Logan, and others. Colden hoped to solicit their opinions and then publish an authoritative version of his treatise. Audaciously, he sought to discuss something Newton had not: the cause of gravity.[43]

Colden published the enlarged edition in 1751 as *The Principles of Action in Matter*. He divided matter into three basic substances: resisting matter, that is, bodies having mass, occupying space, and capable of action; moving matter, which he equated with light; and ether, a reacting medium, contiguous everywhere with resisting and moving matter, that transmits action and movement between material bodies distant from each other. According to Colden, gravity is the force exerted by the ether on all the planets and stars.

Though it seemed to some that Colden was trying to outdo Newton, he really was not. Rather, he was attempting to explain queries Newton had appended to *Opticks*. The physical processes Colden identified were also

FIGURE 14.3 *Cadwallader Colden*. From Evert A. Duyckinck and George L. Duyckinck, *Cyclopaedia of American Literature* (New York: Charles Scribner, 1856), 1:80. Kevin J. Hayes Collection, Toledo, OH.

responsible for thought, according to his theory. Perception occurs as external objects make impressions on the brain. Ideas arise from the impact objects have on our senses.[44]

Colden joined the American Philosophical Society once it was organized. All the early officers were friends Franklin knew from the Junto, the Library Company, or the St. John's Lodge of Freemasons, another organization in which he was active. In 1744, the American Philosophical Society elected Thomas Hopkinson president, William Coleman treasurer, and Franklin secretary. Others members would oversee individual scientific departments. Bartram became the society's botanist, and Bond oversaw medicine. Rhoads directed mechanical studies. The American Philosophical Society also attracted men from other colonies, including James Alexander, the attorney general of New Jersey.[45]

Despite their enthusiasm, the founding members could not sustain the society. Franklin had so many community improvement projects going he scarcely had time for them all. Bartram's farm slowed his scientific research. In

April 1744, he wrote Colden, "I am full as much hurried in business as our friend Benjamin for I can hardly get any time to write but by candle light after a very hard days labour about my plantation for the subsistence of my family." Bartram's figurative comparison—busy as Benjamin—incidentally reveals Franklin's untiring activity on behalf of his various professional and community-improvement projects. Other members lacked such good excuses. Bartram said they could have made the philosophical society work if more members had been willing to trade their time at the coffeehouse or the chess-board for the "curious amusements of natural observations." Two decades would pass before Bond and Rhoads revived the American Philosophical Society and reestablished it on a permanent basis, electing Franklin president in absentia.[46]

When Bartram initially considered forming the American Philosophical Society, he had sought Peter Collinson's opinion. Collinson was not hopeful. He wondered whether there would be sufficient public interest and govern-mental support to make the organization viable. Instead, Collinson said the Library Company could perform the same function as a scientific society. Collinson's gifts confirm his view of the Library Company as a scientific society. In 1745, he presented it with a long glass tube and a pamphlet describing the electrical research of Swiss scientist Albrecht von Haller. Experimenters could rub the tube to generate the static electricity needed to replicate Haller's experi-ments. The pamphlet is a "ghost," a technical term meaning that no copies sur-vive. One lasted long enough to inspire Franklin's earliest electrical research.[47]

The Library Company did have other books about electricity before Haller's, including Francis Hauksbee's *Physico-Mechanical Experiments on Various Subjects* and Desaguliers's *Course of Experimental Philosophy*, which Franklin had cited in the fireplace pamphlet. Franklin also broadened his per-sonal scientific library. He started acquiring the *Philosophical Transactions of the Royal Society*, beginning with the transactions for 1743.[48]

As Franklin continued his electrical experiments, he obtained the latest treatises in the field. William Watson was doing important work in England. In 1747, Franklin acquired Watson's *Experiments and Observations Tending to Illustrate the Nature and Properties of Electricity* and his follow-up work, *A Sequel to the Experiments and Observations*, which Franklin bound with Benjamin Martin's *Essay on Electricity*. By the time he received these books, Franklin's own research had progressed far enough to let him identify the flaws in theirs.[49]

Though his personal collection of electrical books would continue to grow, Franklin's knowledge reached a point where books alone could not

FIGURE 14.4 *Franklin's Experiment, June 1752: Demonstrating the Identity of Lightning and Electricity, from which He Invented the Lightning* Rod (New York: Currier and Ives, c. 1876). Library of Congress, Prints and Photographs Division, Washington, DC, LC-DIG-pga-08719.

supply what he needed to know. His electrical experiments helped him make several new discoveries. He discerned how Leyden jars collected electricity. He discovered that electricity separated itself into positive and negative charges. He invented the electrical battery. He theorized that lightning was electricity. And he invented the lightning rod. Franklin's electrical research established his international scientific renown.

His reputation helped further expand his library, as he received presentation copies from other scientists. In 1754, for example, Giambatista Beccaria presented Franklin with a copy of the Italian edition of his *Treatise upon Artificial Electricity*.[50] Franklin's correspondence shows that he read the book: the first indication that he was now fluent in Italian. Franklin would acquire several of his other works. Beccaria's excellent electrical research notwithstanding, by the time Franklin finished assembling his collection of electricity books, the most important one was *Experiments and Observations on Electricity*, that is, the one he wrote himself.

A landmark work, Franklin's *Experiments* defined the various problems and methods of research in the field of electricity. Thomas S. Kuhn observed that Franklin's *Experiments*, like other landmark works in the history of science, was sufficiently unprecedented to attract a group of dedicated adherents away from other competing scientific theories in the field. Furthermore, his book was open-ended enough to leave numerous problems for subsequent electrical researchers to solve. Franklin's *Experiments* was a seedbed of electrical research for generations to come.[51]

As Franklin's electrical research progressed, Philadelphia friends crowded into his home to witness the experiments. To encourage them to pursue their own research, he had a local glassblower manufacture several green glass tubes like the one Collinson had sent, which would let others generate the static electricity necessary for experiments. Hopkinson discovered that pointed metal rods not only drew off, but also threw off electricity. Syng invented a slick machine operated by a crank arm that could generate static electricity more efficiently than the tiresome rubbing the glass tube required.[52]

No one did more to spread the news of Franklin's electrical research than his friend Ebenezer Kinnersley. Franklin encouraged Kinnersley to tour colonial America presenting lectures on electricity. Franklin outlined two lectures for him, arranging the material so that the successive electrical demonstrations built on one another to give audiences a clear understanding of how electricity worked.[53]

Franklin's encouragement broadened the scientific horizons of his friends and readers. He urged some to master the microscope. One article in *Poor Richard's Almanack* surveys the potential research the microscope made possible. Upon reading Henry Baker's *Microscope Made Easy*, Nicholas Scull grew curious about the wonders of the unseen world.[54] Baker's work extended the research initiated by Dutch microscopist Anton van Leeuwenhoek, who had discovered protozoa and observed bacteria.[55] If Scull wished to develop his microscopic studies further, the Library Company made a microscope available to its members.

Franklin continued reading scientific poems, the most important being James Thomson's *Seasons*. In 1745, Franklin mentioned *The Seasons* to a friend, revealing how Thomson had affected him: "That charming poet has brought more tears of pleasure into my eyes than all I ever read before. I wish it were in my power to return him any part of the joy he has given me."[56] Classifying Thomson's *Seasons* as a scientific poem does not do justice to its wide-ranging eclecticism, but it may offer a way to explain why it moved Franklin so profoundly.

The Seasons is the greatest of all the physico-theological poems. Describing nature over the course of a year, Thomson illustrates how it manifests the shaping hand of a benevolent deity. He discusses such Newtonian topics as the gravitational pull of the planets and the refraction of light and touches on such scientific fields as astronomy, botany, geology, mineralogy, and physics. Throughout this 240-page poem, Thomson celebrates the plenitude and variety of nature, which overwhelms the human intellect.[57]

In the "Spring" section, Thomson imagines a botanist seeking to catalogue and classify what he encounters: "Then spring the living herbs, profusely wild, / O'er all the deep-green Earth, beyond the power / Of botanist to number up their tribes." Though Thomson creates an attractive image of the botanist going about his work, stealing "along the lonely dale / In silent search," he emphasizes that the natural world is so plentiful that the human intellect cannot grasp it.[58]

Some of the latest scientific verse Franklin read was physico without being theological. After Scull discovered a new species of wild raspberry near Reading, Pennsylvania, Breintnall chronicled his discovery in a poem titled "On the Lately Discovered Wild Raspberries," which begins by comparing Scull's discovery with Bartram's explorations:

> Had Bartram's eye been there, it had descry'd
> This curious plant, which Nature seem'd to hide;
> But, as to chance great benefits we owe,
> Scull was the first, this rarity to know.

Whereas Thomson's botanist cannot hope to classify nature in its entirety, Breintnall celebrates the botanist's ability to discover a species no one had discovered before him. Paraphrasing Scull's notes, Breintnall describes the plant in the middle of the poem. Though written in verse, Breintnall's description is as precise as an entry in Miller's *Gardener's Dictionary*. The poem ends with a paean to the wild raspberry:

> The lovely berries in rich purple vye,
> And tempt the fingers as they charm the eye;
> But more excel, in taste and size, all those,
> That gard'ners in their choicest walks dispose.[59]

Celebrating the wild raspberry over cultivated ones, Breintnall looks forward to the Romantic poets. The ability of art to improve on nature was a central tenet of Augustan aesthetics, but Breintnall, like the Romantics, emphasizes the superiority of nature.

Breintnall's personal story, though tragic, suits the literary history of scientific verse. On Sunday, March 16, 1746, he mysteriously disappeared. The next morning, someone found Joe's clothes on the Pennsylvania side of the Delaware River, but there was still no sign of him. On Tuesday, Breintnall's body turned up on the Jersey side.

Some said his drowning was accidental; others thought it was suicide. John Smith, a prominent Philadelphia Quaker, recorded both possibilities in his diary but leaned toward the latter: "He was remarkable for deistical principles, and much distrest in his circumstances. When once religion is banished from the mind, I know not what can relieve a man in deep distress, but death, and the mean, low hope of annihilation therein."[60] Smith read too much into Breintnall's deism. No one can say what trials Joseph B. underwent before his tragic death. Suffice it to say that no more on Delaware's banks would his muse be heard.

Breintnall's death signals the end of the scientist-poet and symbolizes the beginning of a new era in scientific literature. With the increasing professionalization of science in the coming decades, fewer and fewer scientists would have the inclination to write poetry. There are exceptions, of course. Erasmus Darwin, to cite one of Franklin's English friends, for example, was a leading botanist who wrote a book-length poem called *The Botanic Garden*. But the underlying purpose of *The Botanic Garden* was more scientific than literary. Erasmus Darwin—Charles Darwin's grandfather—used poetry to attract readers to scientific inquiry, "to inlist imagination under the banner of science."[61]

By the Romantic era, scientists found poetry an inappropriate medium for scientific inquiry and poets, conversely, thought that science unnecessarily restricted the imagination. In "Sonnet to Science," Edgar Allan Poe asks his subject: "Why preyest thou thus upon the poet's heart, / Vulture, whose wings are dull realities?"[62] Writing poems about a city street, deathbed illness, a home-heating stove, and wild raspberries, Joseph Breintnall had no trouble turning dull realities into verse. His life ended when he stopped seeing the poetry in reality.

The Philadelphia Academy

TWO DECADES AFTER its founding, the Junto was still going strong. Though Franklin had previously pitched several community improvement projects to the group, in the mid- to late 1740s he introduced his most ambitious project yet: a school. It would start as an academy, but Franklin foresaw an institution of higher learning: a college next and then a university. Despite his youthful antagonism toward Harvard, he regretted that Philadelphia lacked a comparable school. After gaining the support of the Junto and other civic-minded Philadelphians, Franklin drafted *Proposals Relating to the Education of Youth in Pensilvania*, a milestone in the history of learning.

Given the chance to start the Philadelphia Academy from scratch, Franklin imagined a school that would differ from other colonial American academies, which were based on the Greek and Latin curriculum inherited from Europe. Franklin dared to suggest a new kind of academic education. His concept was radical: Modern students need not learn ancient tongues to get a good education.

Aware that community leaders would resist his innovative curriculum, Franklin carefully set forth his argument. Though *Account of the New Invented Pennsylvania Fire-Places* seems hesitant in its use of scholarly sources, Franklin's footnotes in *Proposals* show more confidence. The main text of *Proposals* is quite short, less than 2,500 words. The text of its footnotes are three times longer. On most pages, the notes occupy more space than the main text. The text-to-notes ratio follows Bayle's *Dictionary*.

A list of authorities prefaces the main text. Besides providing bibliographical citations, Franklin introduced his authorities individually, making them resemble participants in an educational symposium. Arranged for maximum impact, the list starts with John Milton. "The famous Milton," Franklin called him, "whose learning and abilities are well known, and who had practised some time the education of youth, so could speak from experience." Instead of mentioning Milton's role as poet and polemicist, Franklin stressed a minor aspect of his career. Having served as schoolmaster for two nephews and some other boys, Milton articulated the theoretical basis of his pedagogical approach in a pamphlet, *Of Education*. Franklin would cite this work throughout *Proposals*, but his list of authorities does not mention it. Milton's teaching, not his writing, is what earns him the top spot on Franklin's list.[1]

John Locke comes second, followed by the author of *Dialogues Concerning Education*. Franklin misattributed the work to Francis Hutcheson. David Fordyce, a different Scottish philosopher, wrote *Dialogues Concerning Education*. Franklin's misattribution anticipates Fordyce's unfair historical reputation as a lesser Hutcheson. The two thinkers shared a similar moral philosophy.[2]

Obadiah Walker, who wrote *Of Education, Especially of Young Gentleman*, comes next. Having enjoyed Walker's educational treatise in his youth, Franklin returned to it as he planned the academy. Walker's pedagogical approach coincided with Franklin's. Having benefited from the "mild encouraging methods" of his teacher George Brownell, Franklin found in Walker a parallel approach to teaching. Walker observed, "Many times also we see a word cast in by chance, or in merriment, to have greater force than a formal admonition."[3]

Charles Rollin, the author of the four-volume work *The Method of Studying and Teaching the Belles Lettres*, follows Walker in Franklin's list. John Adams, who read Rollin's *Method* in college, found all four volumes "worth their weight in gold." George Turnbull, who ends the list, was the author of *Observations upon Liberal Education*. Franklin shared Turnbull's belief in the dual purpose of education. It should improve the individual and help the individual improve the community.[4]

Simple on the surface, Franklin's list of authorities is actually quite sophisticated. Basing his proposal for a new curriculum on the thought of leading figures from the history of education, Franklin made it difficult for contemporaries to critique his pedagogical scheme. Upon closer scrutiny, Franklin's list of authorities resembles a rhetorical sleight-of-hand trick. While revealing his historical sources, it masks the source of its most innovative educational ideas, which Franklin derived from his own thought and experience.[5]

The main text of *Proposals* begins boldly: "The good education of youth has been esteemed by wise men in all ages, as the surest foundation of the happiness both of private families and of common-wealths." Franklin's first note stresses the unique opportunity Pennsylvanians have as they plan the school. Several educational theorists agreed that the traditional academic education does not work, but, being so embedded in the culture, it was difficult to change. Franklin wished to avoid the mistakes of the past. Educators should let reason, not custom, be their guide.[6]

Easing into his controversial approach to education, Franklin discussed physical fitness before academic studies. He considered both diet and exercise. Student meal plans should be plain and simple, frugal and temperate. In addition, students should engage in rigorous physical exercise: running, jumping, swimming, and wrestling. To support his argument, Franklin cited several historical examples. In his boyhood, King Henry IV of France ran, jumped, and went rock climbing. Furthermore, he limited his diet to coarse bread, beef, cheese, and garlic. His clothing was unadorned, and he often went barefoot and bareheaded. Franklin's ideal student sounds like Huck Finn.

Turning to the academic curriculum, Franklin expressed the basic problem with any educational scheme: Students do not have time to learn everything. To help readers grasp this idea, he applied a proverb: "As to their studies, it would be well if they could be taught *every thing* that is useful, and *every thing* that is ornamental: But art is long, and their time is short. It is therefore propos'd that they learn those things that are likely to be *most useful* and *most ornamental*, regard being had to the several professions for which they are intended."[7]

Repeating the proverb elsewhere, Franklin named Hippocrates's *Aphorisms* as his source, but this proverb had been circulating in colonial America for decades. John Wise had used it. Arguing that men should begin serving as ministers when they are young in *The Churches Quarrel Espoused*, Wise observed, "That considering theology, as well as art, is a long study, and life is very short, why may they not begin young?"[8]

Franklin used the proverb in *Proposals* for the same reason Wise had used it in *The Churches Quarrel Espoused*. This nugget of traditional wisdom strengthened his argument. A familiar saying helps make an unfamiliar idea acceptable. Though Franklin's educational scheme makes sense now, it represents another radical innovation: The curriculum should be shaped to suit each student's intended profession.

Before he reaches any academic subjects in *Proposals*, Franklin emphasizes good handwriting skills. In addition, students should learn drawing, which is a kind of universal language. Aware that gentlemen may look askance at drawing—a skill associated with tradesmen—Franklin preempted that argument, quoting Locke's observation that drawing would be useful for leisure travel, a gentlemanly pursuit. Drawing gave travelers an accurate way to record what they saw: buildings, machines, public works projects.

Franklin quoted Locke again to support his first set of academic subjects: arithmetic, bookkeeping, geometry, and astronomy. From his boyhood, Franklin knew that the traditional emphasis on ancient tongues deprived students of a proper mathematical education. Arithmetic also offered considerable potential for social studies. Lately, he had been rereading William Petty's *Political Arithmetick*, which showed how demographic statistics could be used to predict trends and shape the future. A couple of years later, Franklin would write "Observations Concerning the Increase of Mankind," the greatest work of political arithmetic in American literature. Franklin argued that North America would surpass England to become the most populous and important part of the British Empire.

Considering how ingrained the classical education was in Western culture, Franklin knew the study of languages presented his toughest argument. Before addressing other languages, he stressed the importance of English: "The English language might be taught by grammar; in which some of our best writers, as Tillotson, Addison, Pope, Algernon Sidney, *Cato's Letters*, etc. should be classicks: The *stiles* principally to be cultivated, being the *clear* and the *concise*."[9]

What stands out most in this sentence is Franklin's use of the word "classics" to characterize eighteenth-century English writings. The term usually meant ancient Greek and Roman literature, as in Blackwall's *Introduction to the Classics*. Franklin proposed a new concept of the classic. Recent English works deserve consideration as classic literature, which can supply models for students learning to write. Like the Library Company's holdings, the authors Franklin recommends in *Proposals* demonstrate the power of the English language.

Joseph Addison, Alexander Pope, Algernon Sidney, John Trenchard, and Thomas Gordon: Franklin had already expressed his respect for these authors. To his canon of classic English writers, he added Archbishop John Tillotson, who offered writers a model of clarity. Abram Taylor, a member of the Pennsylvania Council and a shareholder in the Library Company, owned a three-volume folio edition of Tillotson's *Works*. The presence of this work in Taylor's library confirms his reputation as a "gentleman of genteel taste" possessing a "great many publications of the first character."[10]

Franklin had known Tillotson's *Works* since his youth; his brother James had had a copy in the office library. Like his brother, Franklin used Tillotson as a literary model. Stuart P. Sherman recognized in Benjamin Franklin's writings Tillotson's lean, vigorous style. Adding Tillotson to the recommended list of authors for students at the Philadelphia Academy, he provided another example students could follow to improve their writing.[11]

After explaining how English authors could help students become better writers, Franklin reached the central subject of his curriculum: history, under which he subsumed other subjects: ancient customs, chronology, geography, moral philosophy, oratory, and political science. Making moral philosophy part of history, Franklin hoped to teach it by example. Studying the rise and fall of historical figures can reveal their personal impulses—frugality, industry, order, perseverance, temperance. Reading well-written history would impress on students the usefulness of virtue, fortitude, and public spirit. Besides indicating his educational theory, Franklin's *Proposals* can help gloss his autobiography, which, after all, tells the story of a man who shares exemplary characteristics with leading figures from history.[12]

History can also teach moral philosophy by letting students debate the causes underlying historical events. Debate would let them apply logic and reason. To prepare themselves for debate, students would want to study natural law. Franklin named two key texts: Pufendorf's *Of the Law of Nature and Nations* and Grotius's *Rights of War and Peace*. Both would help students debate questions of right and wrong.[13]

Franklin discussed ancient and modern languages under history. Not all students needed to learn Latin and Greek. He saw nothing wrong with letting them read Latin and Greek histories in English translation. Language courses should be tailored to suit each student's program of study. Divinity students should learn Latin as well as Greek, the language of the oldest surviving version of the New Testament. Medical students should learn Latin, Greek, and French. Law students should learn Latin and French, since some fundamental English legal texts were written in a hybrid language known as Law French. Students planning a career in the mercantile trade should learn the modern languages: French, German, and Spanish. Franklin made courses in ancient and modern languages electives, not requirements. Students who wanted to study Greek and Latin could still study Greek and Latin—provided their attention to ancient tongues did not detract from English, arithmetic, or other essential subjects.

Natural history would provide students with subject matter for literary compositions during school and useful knowledge after graduation. Merchants would trade natural commodities; preachers could apply figures of speech from the natural world to strengthen their sermons. No matter what profession they chose, students would benefit from natural history. It would improve their conversation, giving them a widespread knowledge that would let them make natural observations to amuse and instruct their friends.[14]

Health fell under the general heading of natural history. Though *Proposals* recommends few specific books overall, Franklin names three in his discussion of health education: John Arbuthnot's *Essay Concerning the Effects of Air*, a study of pulmonary disease Franklin had in his own library; Louis Lémery's *Treatise of All Sorts of Foods*, which analyzes how food and drink affect the human body; and Sanctorius's *Medicina statica*. Franklin's title for the third work reflects its theme: "Sanctorius on Perspiration." Sanctorius emphasized how perspiration affects health. His theory confirms the wisdom of Franklin's self-administered water cure in Perth Amboy all those years ago.

The study of agriculture also stems from natural history in Franklin's educational scheme. To reinforce his argument about expanding the curriculum to include practical agriculture, he borrowed a metaphor from Rollin, whose figurative language compares the study of a farm with reading: "A garden, a country, a plantation, are all so many books which lie open to them; but they must have been taught and accustomed to read in them."[15] All students should develop agricultural skills. They need to go outdoors and get their hands dirty. While reading natural history, they could learn how to plant, graft, nurture, and harvest. Franklin said that students should visit nearby farms, meet the best farmers, and learn their methods. Students today owe him a debt of gratitude: Benjamin Franklin invented the field trip.

Franklin distributed *Proposals Relating to the Education of Youth in Pensilvania* gratis with the October 23, 1749, issue of *The Pennsylvania Gazette*. The pamphlet answered "On the Need for an Academy," an article he had published in the *Gazette* two months earlier. The combination of an anticipatory newspaper article and an ensuing pamphlet illustrates Franklin's characteristic one-two rhetorical punch. He would often lay the groundwork for a social or political cause in a newspaper article and then answer it with a lengthier work. Time and again, Franklin would apply this literary strategy to great effect.[16]

"On the Need for an Academy" reveals another book he had been reading: *The Letters of Pliny*. It reprints a letter by Pliny the Younger—not to be confused with his uncle and guardian, Pliny the Elder, who wrote the *Natural Historie*. Pliny the Younger advocates a new academy to benefit local students: "Where can they be placed more agreeably, than in their own country, or instructed with more safety, and less expence, than at home, and under the eye of their parent?"[17]

Though not named in his list of authorities, Pliny's *Letters* was another source Franklin consulted for *Proposals*. Emphasizing the importance of teaching English, Franklin cited Pliny's letter to Hispulla, recommending a Latin tutor for her son. Franklin observed that Pliny did not recommend a Greek master of rhetoric, a subject at which the Greeks excelled, but a Latin master because Latin was her son's native tongue.[18] Aware of the opposition *Proposals* would face, Franklin turned the tables on the advocates of a classical curriculum, using a Latin author to support his argument for teaching English grammar.

Once *Proposals* sunk in, Franklin established a subscription fund to finance the Philadelphia Academy. Many found the plan for an English school attractive. The subscription proved so successful that Franklin made the Philadelphia Academy a reality. Working with Tench Francis, Pennsylvania's attorney general, he drafted the "Constitution of the Academy of Philadelphia."

The first trustee meeting for the Philadelphia Academy occurred on November 13, 1749. The trustees included several men who have already entered the story of Franklin's intellectual life: Thomas Bond, William Coleman, Thomas Hopkinson, James Logan, Philip Syng, and Abram Taylor. They elected Franklin president and Coleman treasurer. They also approved the constitution he set before them. In addition, they named a committee to meet with the trustees of the New Building to negotiate its purchase and solicit estimates for remodeling it into a suitable classroom space.[19]

The New Building, a product of the evangelical religious movement known ironically as the Great Awakening, had been erected ten years earlier for George Whitefield. Banned from established churches, Whitefield would preach outdoors to thousands at a time, but he needed an indoor venue during inclement weather. His supporters found a suitable lot at Fourth and Arch Streets. A huge building—100 × 70 feet—was soon erected. Upon its completion toward the end of 1740, it became the single largest building in Philadelphia.

The building was designed so that it would not violate any particular religion. Franklin's autobiography says the New Building let ministers of all faiths preach to the people of Philadelphia: "If the Mufti of Constantinople were to send a missionary to preach Mahometanism to us, he would find a pulpit at his service." Franklin's account sounds enlightened, and it would be if it were true. But the building was not quite so accessible. According to its deed, the New Building was open to ministers of different faiths—as long as they were Protestant.[20]

The New Building was a white elephant. It stopped being used, fell victim to vandals, and slid into debt. Franklin, who had been elected a trustee of the New Building in 1746, arranged its sale to the Philadelphia Academy. Some might accuse him of a conflict of interest, but his role as a trustee for both the New Building and the Philadelphia Academy helped him save the structure. Franklin turned a house of worship into a place of enlightenment.

The huge assembly hall had to be split into two floors and subdivided into classrooms. Franklin oversaw its remodeling. He negotiated with the workmen and settled disputes among them. He purchased building materials and supervised the day-to-day work. Furthermore, he raised additional funds to cover unanticipated expenses.[21]

The trustees had approved Franklin's constitution for the Philadelphia Academy, but a majority questioned his plans for the English school. Making their preference clear, they voted to give the Latin master double the salary of the English master for half the work. The Latin master would receive a salary of £200 to teach twenty students; the English master would receive a salary of £100 to teach forty students. The trustees also displayed their favoritism toward the Latin school by allocating £100 toward purchasing Latin and Greek books for the school library, but nothing for English books.[22]

Though Franklin had trouble convincing the other trustees of the English school's value, there can be little doubt that the Philadelphia Academy was his baby. No one worked harder to make it a reality. The Reverend Richard Peters, another trustee and a member of the Pennsylvania Council, informed Thomas Penn about the school, telling him that Franklin was "the soul of the whole."[23]

Franklin also recruited its faculty. For headmaster, he wanted to hire Samuel Johnson, a Connecticut minister and educator he had known about since the Great Apostasy, but circumstances prevented him. Johnson would become president of King's College (now, Columbia University). For the dual position of rector and Latin master, Franklin recruited David Martin. He hired David James Dove as English master, Theophilus Grew as mathematics master, and Charles Thomson as tutor in Latin and Greek.[24]

Though a classicist, Thomson shared Franklin's educational philosophy. He believed practical skills were no less valid than linguistic ones. Sketching out some thoughts on education in his memorandum book, Thomson observed, "Learning should be connected with life and qualify its possessor for action."[25] Stone masons, metalworkers, sailors, farmers: All possessed useful knowledge that could contribute to the common good. Given these thoughts, it is unsurprising that Thomson and Franklin became lifelong friends. Thomson, too, would contribute much to the founding of the United States. Once the Continental Congress was formed in 1774, he would serve as congressional secretary throughout its duration.

Still uncomfortable with the English school, the other trustees asked Franklin to write down his plans in detail. The result was "Idea of the English School," which outlines the curriculum more fully than *Proposals*. Its opening sentence leaves blank the starting age for its students, but Franklin told

Johnson that he expected the boys would range in age from 8 to 16. Franklin defined six different classes for the English school. The boys who started the first year at 8 would end the sixth at 14. Those who started when they were 10 would not end until 16.[26]

Discussing the books that students in the first or lowest class would read, Franklin named one in particular and others by a general type: "Croxall's *Fables*, and little stories." By "little stories," he meant the same kinds of chapbook tales he had read as a child. These storybooks could accomplish similar educational objectives as collections of fables. They would help students develop their reading proficiency and build their vocabulary. In addition, fables and stories could teach morals, displaying virtues to emulate and vices to avoid.[27]

English editions of *Aesop's Fables* came in all shapes and sizes. Roger L'Estrange's edition—the version Abram Taylor had in his library—appeared as a 500-page folio. Samuel Croxall first published his *Aesop* as a 400-page octavo, but he issued subsequent editions in a handier duodecimo format, though they were each nearly 400 pages long. The Library Company of Philadelphia had a duodecimo edition of Croxall's *Aesop*.[28] Nathaniel Crouch published his, the English edition Franklin most likely read as a child, as a 200-page duodecimo. Samuel Richardson, who also published his edition as a duodecimo, made it fifty pages longer than Crouch's. All these editions had appeared before Franklin wrote "Idea of the English School," but he stipulated Croxall's *Aesop*.

Though more manageable than L'Estrange's, Croxall's *Aesop* was still a substantial book for first-year academy students to handle, especially compared with the storybooks Franklin recommended, which were typically a few dozen pages long. Crouch's *Aesop* may have been out of print by 1750, but Richardson's was not. Published as a challenge to Croxall, Richardson's *Aesop* first appeared in 1740 and was reprinted in 1749. Franklin had great respect for Richardson, but he did not assign his *Aesop* to the students of the Philadelphia Academy.

Aesop's English editors defended their editions against their competitors'. Croxall complained that L'Estrange's applications made his *Aesop* inappropriate for children. Richardson leveled the same complaint against Croxall, whose text seemed more suitable for adults. According to Richardson, Croxall scattered "pedantick quotations and Latin scraps . . . thro' his own applications, in a piece design'd for the earliest part of childrens education."[29]

Croxall's political orientation distinguishes his *Aesop* from the others. Whereas L'Estrange's translations and applications embody a reactionary political outlook, Croxall made his edition of *Aesop's Fables* Whiggish. In Croxall's view, Aesop took "all occasions to recommend a love for liberty, and an abhorrence of tyranny." British children, Croxall continued, "are born with free blood in their veins; and suck in liberty with their very milk." He designed his edition of *Aesop's Fables* to perpetuate the natural liberty of British children: "Let the minds of our *British* youth be for ever educated and improv'd in that spirit of truth and liberty, for the support of which their ancestors have often bravely exhausted so much blood and treasure."[30]

Franklin recommended Croxall's *Fables* because he shared Croxall's politics. Though it appeared too late for him to read in his boyhood, Franklin had read Croxall's *Aesop* by 1734 and began sharing it with others. He chose this edition for the Philadelphia Academy to give students a distinctive political perspective. Like the British children Croxall described, Franklin wanted to educate American children in the "spirit of truth and liberty."[31]

"The Dog and the Sheep," one of Aesop's shortest fables, exemplifies Croxall's method. Here's the whole fable: "The dog sued the sheep for a debt; of which the kite and the wolf were to be judges. They, without debating long upon the matter, or making any scruple for want of evidence, gave sentence for the plaintiff; who immediately tore the poor sheep in pieces, and divided the spoil with the unjust judges."[32]

Croxall's application begins with the following statement: "Deplorable are the times when open barefac'd villainy is protected and encouraged, when innocence is obnoxious, honesty contemptible, and it is reckon'd criminal to espouse the cause of virtue." Croxall's application is timeless: "It is amazing how mankind could ever sink down to such a low degree of base cowardice, as to suffer some of the worst of their species to usurp a power over them, to supersede the righteous laws of good government, and to exercise all kinds of injustice and hardship, in gratifying their own vicious lusts."[33]

For students in the second class at Philadelphia Academy, Franklin listed several literary genres to read: a preacher's sermon, a general's harangue to his men, a tragic soliloquy, an excerpt from a comedy, a fictional story, a letter, and three different types of poetry: blank verse, heroic couplets, and hudibrastics. But he emphasized the periodical essay most.

Students in the second class could read essays around the same length as *The Spectator* essays. Indeed, they could read *The Spectator* essays themselves, at least the easier ones. Beyond its contents, the periodical essay was valuable to students as a unit of length. It was the ideal size to capture their attention and hold it until they had finished reading. The essay could train students to focus.[34] In addition, students could read periodical essays to learn English composition. They could analyze individual sentences, learning by example how syntax could enhance meaning and increase a sentence's impact.

Third-year students would read history. They should start with Rollin's histories: no mean feat. Recommending Rollin to students, Franklin prescribed an ambitious program of reading. Rollin's *Ancient History of the Egyptians, Carthaginians, Assyrians, Babylonians, Medes and Persians, Macedonians and Greeks* fills thirteen octavo volumes in the English translation, his *Roman History* sixteen. By reading history, students would learn the causes of the rise and fall of states and understand the character of nations and great men in history. They would learn to search for truth.[35]

Though ambitious, Franklin's recommendation of Rollin's *Ancient History* and *Roman History* is not unusual. From the appearance of the English translations in the 1730s into the nineteenth century, Rollin's histories taught American readers about history. Tench Francis had a set of Rollins's *Ancient History* in his library. Schoolmasters at classical schools often assigned Rollin to add historical context to their linguistic studies. When Thomas Jefferson assembled the library for the University of Virginia, he obtained Rollin's histories in their original French, which would let students learn ancient history while enhancing their knowledge of French. The strategy worked, at least in the case of one renowned student. Edgar Allan Poe borrowed from the university library three volumes of Rollin's *Histoire ancienne* and two volumes of *Histoire romaine*.[36]

As Franklin saw it, reading Rollin in their third year, Philadelphia students would establish a pattern of study they could continue throughout their education. After mastering ancient history, they could then read the history of Great Britain and its colonies. Franklin does not name any more history books, but he wanted students to keep reading history. The term "crossover skill" had yet to enter the pedagogical vocabulary, but Franklin's program of study encouraged habits students could sustain. People who learn to love history in school will keep reading history all their lives.

Natural history could take a similar trajectory. Franklin had recommended Noël Pluche's *Spectacle de la nature: or, Nature Displayed* as a good possible textbook in *Proposals*. "Idea of the English School" reinforces the earlier recommendation. Franklin appreciated Pluche in terms of both style and substance. He enjoyed his easy-going manner and his scientific yet practical information. Unlike many scientific authors, Pluche did not bog down his writing with too much mathematics.[37] Students could read Pluche's *Spectacle* in their third year and read additional books about natural history in the following years.

When Francis Bacon classified knowledge, he subsumed arts, crafts, and technology within the larger category of natural history. Pluche followed Bacon's approach. So did Franklin. Pluche's encyclopedic work stresses the importance of artisanal skills, celebrating tradesmen, who have contributed so much to society. At every opportunity, Pluche's text reinforces the idea of a universal work ethic as the basis of society.[38]

Many American readers shared his perspective. Patrick Henry had a copy of Pluche's *Spectacle* in his Virginia library. Like Henry, Franklin found in Pluche a kindred spirit. He designed the curriculum of his English school to prepare students for many possible careers. Pluche's *Spectacle* would help them develop a multifaceted perspective toward the working life. Merchants would better understand the commodities they traded; craftsmen would better understand their raw materials; and farmers and developers would better understand the land they improved.[39]

English composition should dominate the fourth-year curriculum. For literary models, Franklin recommended some collections of letters. An excellent letter writer himself, Franklin understood the importance for students to develop good letter-writing skills. Few would ever write for publication, but all would have to express themselves in their personal and business correspondence.

William Temple's *Letters* is one collection Franklin recommended to help students polish their prose. Temple's understated tone appealed to eighteenth-century readers. His ingratiating letters reveal an engaging personality. Even as he described his most impressive diplomatic accomplishment—the Triple Alliance of 1668—Temple remained modest. Negotiating the treaty, he said, was simply a matter of taking things that had been drawn out of their center and recentering them.[40]

In one letter, Temple wishes that Abraham Cowley had lived long enough to commemorate in verse the heroic death of Captain Archibald Douglas, who went down with the *Royal Oak* after the Dutch fleet had set it aflame. Temple lamented that present-day Englishmen "neither act things worth relating, nor relate things worth the reading." Temple was not the first to make this observation. Another model letter writer—Pliny the Younger—had said much the same: "Happy I esteem those to be, whom providence has distinguished with the abilities either of doing such actions as are worthy of being related, or of relating them in a manner worthy of being read."[41]

Temple would not be the last to make this observation, either. Franklin, whose writings reflect the influence of both Temple and Pliny the Younger, adapted their words for *Poor Richard's Almanack*. Whereas Temple had put his observation in negative terms, Franklin phrased his as a piece of positive advice:

> If you wou'd not be forgotten
> As soon as you are dead and rotten,
> Either write things worth reading;
> Or do things worth the writing.[42]

The Reverend Samuel Johnson's textbooks formed an important part of Franklin's curriculum. Fourth-year students would read Johnson's *Ethices elementa: or, The First Principles of Moral Philosophy*, the earliest colonial American textbook on the subject. Fifth-year students would read Johnson's *Noetica*, an introduction to the sciences. Franklin would combine the two works and publish them together in 1752 as *Elementa philosophica*.[43]

A follower of Bishop George Berkeley, Johnson based his course of moral philosophy on Berkeleyan epistemology. Nothing exists outside the mind, Berkeley theorized. What we perceive as external reality is merely our mental concept of ideas produced by the divine mind. God shows us what He wants us to know in the order He wants us to know it. By cultivating our intellect, we can develop a greater understanding of the order of the universe. Studying nature, we are not studying physical objects; we are studying the language that articulates divine thought. William Douglass had trouble taking the bishop's epistemology seriously. He said that Berkeley "seems to affirm, in a whimsical manner, that every thing we see is an illusion, that the whole series of life is a continued dream."[44]

Like Berkeley, Johnson believed in a knowable divine truth. He sought to give students the intellectual tools necessary to perceive truth without distortion. Johnson divided all knowledge into philosophy and philology. Philosophy concerns what people knew absolutely—logic, moral philosophy, the sciences; philology concerns how people transmit knowledge. It involves such subjects as grammar and rhetoric. Understanding how people transmit knowledge, students could see how information could be expressed and how it could be distorted.[45]

Though Franklin appreciated Johnson's moral philosophy, like Douglass, he had little patience for Berkeleyan metaphysics. He did enjoy the bishop's more practical writings, such as *The Querist*. Consisting of a series of numbered queries, this book mainly concerns political economy. Franklin's copy of Berkeley's *Miscellany*, which includes *The Querist*, survives at the Library Company of Philadelphia. It shows that Franklin answered Berkeley's queries as he read: He wrote his answers into the book. When the querist asks what makes a wealthy people, Franklin replied, "Industry and frugality."[46]

Franklin's reading list for students in the sixth and final class also reflects Johnson's influence. Before presenting "Idea of the English School" to the board of trustees, Franklin sent a draft to Johnson for his input. Johnson named some additional English books and authors that students should read but found little to change. Johnson told him, "You might do well to mention Milton and Telemachus and the *Travells of Cyrus* with the works of Shakespear, Addison and Pope and Swift."[47] Franklin added all the authors Johnson recommended except Shakespeare, whom he had already assigned earlier. He had not mentioned Shakespeare by name, but when he assigned second-year students some tragic soliloquies, Franklin had *Hamlet* in mind.

The Philadelphia Academy opened on January 7, 1751, when the Pennsylvania governor led a procession of trustees from his home to the New Building, where Richard Peters presented his *Sermon on Education*. Though Peters had been a staunch advocate of the classical school, he did say good things about the English school in his sermon. The New Building was not quite ready; the first day's classes convened in a warehouse two blocks away.

Franklin published Peters's *Sermon on Education*, appending to it "Idea of the English School." New York educator William Smith recognized the pamphlet's value. Born in Scotland and educated at Aberdeen, Smith emigrated to New York, where he took a position as a domestic tutor, though his vaulting ambition directed his sights much higher. Smith articulated his thoughts on education in *A General Idea of the College of Mirania*, which he published in 1753. A contribution to American utopian literature, Smith's *College of Mirania* conveys his educational theory as an idealistic vision. Smith's utopian educational system facilitates Mirania's commercial prosperity and cultural refinement.

A "mechanics' school" forms a branch of Smith's utopian college. He patterned it on Franklin's English school. Mirania's mechanics' school does not teach ancient tongues, instructing students in more practical subjects instead. Smith also said that the mechanics' school would teach moral conduct, reinforcing his link to Franklin's educational scheme. A shameless sycophant, Smith flattered Franklin within the work, praising the English school "sketch'd out by the very ingenious and worthy *Mr. Franklin*."[48]

Smith aped Franklin's emphasis on history and his Whiggish political philosophy. The study of history at Mirania lets students perceive the dreadful effects of tyranny and, conversely, the health and prosperity that liberty makes possible. "The very Sun himself [seems] to dart his choicest beams on the favor'd land," Smith wrote. To support his point, he quoted Addison's apostrophe to Liberty, though the prudish Smith omitted the part about Liberty being "pregnant with delight." To curry Franklin's favor, Smith sent him a copy of *The College of Mirania*.[49]

His strategy worked. Franklin enjoyed *The College of Mirania* very much. He wrote Smith, "I know not when I have read a piece that has more affected me, so noble and just are the sentiments, so warm and animated the language." Seeking a rector for the Philadelphia Academy, Franklin saw Smith as a possible candidate. Smith came to Philadelphia in late May, met Franklin, and toured the academy. Sensing opportunity, he wrote a poem commemorating his visit, dedicated it to the trustees, and convinced Franklin to publish it. *A Poem on Visiting the Academy of Philadelphia* praises the students whom Smith observed. By this time, Franklin was seeking to turn the academy into a college. He mentioned the possibility to Smith, and together they discussed what role he might play.[50]

Franklin had a blind spot when it came to Smith, which seems surprising in retrospect. In his business dealings, Franklin was quite shrewd; his own climb to the top of his profession was marked by opportunism. After becoming active with the freemasons, for example, Franklin sought to lead the St. John's Lodge. The month before one annual meeting, he reprinted James Anderson's *Constitutions of the Free Masons*, the standard masonic handbook. The timing was perfect. When St. John's Day rolled around, sure enough, his lodge brothers elected Franklin grand master.[51]

In 1753, Smith would go to England to take holy orders, a move that would help advance his career, whichever direction it took. Smith introduced himself to Peter Collinson, who could see him without the blinders that narrowed Franklin's vision. Collinson called Smith ingenious but wished he were "more solid and less flighty." Smith also met Thomas Penn. It did not take long for either man to see how they could benefit one another. By convincing Penn to support the academy, Smith practically assured himself of a position in the school. Penn's support came at a price. He wanted Smith to spy on Franklin and secretly offered him a £50 salary. Untroubled by qualms or conscience, Smith accepted the position and became Penn's spy. When he returned to Philadelphia in May 1754, the trustees offered Smith a £200 salary to teach logic, rhetoric, natural philosophy, and, ironically, ethics.[52]

Once he obtained a foothold in the Philadelphia Academy, Smith began to muscle Franklin out. In December, when Franklin was in New England on a postal inspection tour, Smith proposed to the board of trustees that the academy grant college degrees. The trustees agreed and had a new charter drafted. In Franklin's absence, they approved the new charter. In March 1755, the trustees appointed Smith provost of the college. Franklin, who had always hoped the academy would become a college but who had yet to perceive Smith's duplicity, was pleased with the developments. Present at the March meeting, he made no objections to Smith's appointment.[53]

Unlike Franklin, Charles Thomson saw through Smith. After he became provost, Thomson resigned his position as Greek and Latin tutor, taking a position as head of Latin at the Friends' School in Philadelphia instead.[54] As provost, Smith would shore up his power base and help oust Franklin as president of the trustees. All of Smith's self-serving machinations could not deny one essential fact: Benjamin Franklin was the true founder of the Philadelphia Academy, the school that would become the University of Pennsylvania.

16

The Northwest Passage

FRANKLIN UNDERTOOK SO many projects in the middle third of the century that following them requires some occasional backtracking. By the summer of 1743, he had three printing houses under his control. In addition to his Philadelphia operation, he was a partner in the Charleston, South Carolina, printing house operated by Elizabeth Timothy, who had taken over the business in 1738 after her husband perished in a mysterious accident. Franklin had also established a partnership with James Parker to run a printing house in New York. He would establish several more partnerships to assist a new generation of printers and extend his influence throughout colonial America.

A few years earlier Deborah Franklin's kinsman James Read had met William Strahan, a prominent London publisher and bookseller, and the two had begun corresponding. Read showed Franklin a letter from Strahan about an ambitious journeyman printer seeking a greater opportunity in the trade than he could find in London. Franklin wrote Strahan and invited the man to America with an enticing offer. If Franklin liked him well enough, they could establish a partnership. If he wished to return to England, Franklin promised him enough smouting to afford the return passage.[1]

Within a year, David Hall, the journeyman in question, left London for Philadelphia. Hall went to work at the New Printing Office, but Franklin's reticence puzzled him. He could not tell what business plans Franklin had in mind. Hall wrote Strahan wondering what to do. Trust the kind-hearted Franklin, Strahan said: good advice, as things turned out. Hall's technical skill and business savvy impressed Franklin. Instead of establishing him as a partner in a distant colony, Franklin kept Hall close, making him partner in his Philadelphia operation.

When Hall arrived in June 1744, he brought a present from Strahan, a copy of Arthur Dobbs's *Remarks upon Capt. Middleton's Defence*, the latest salvo in the controversy over the Northwest Passage. Strahan sensed what Franklin liked to read; his thoughtful gift sparked their friendship. Franklin replied, "I have long wanted a friend in London whose judgment I could depend on, to send me from time to time such new pamphlets as are worth reading on any subject (religious controversy excepted) for there is no depending on titles and advertisements."[2]

Franklin enjoyed Dobbs's *Remarks* but wished to learn more about his conflict with Christopher Middleton before passing judgment. He wondered what had been published in Middleton's defense. Strahan sent two works: *A Vindication of the Conduct of Captain Christopher Middleton*—the book that had provoked Dobbs's *Remarks*—and Middleton's follow-up work, *Reply to the Remarks of Arthur Dobbs*. Franklin received them in February 1745. Dobbs and Middleton would issue additional pamphlets in their acrimonious war of words, but these three volumes gave Franklin the gist of the controversy.

By 1731, Arthur Dobbs, an Irish Member of Parliament (MP), had become convinced the Northwest Passage existed. He drafted a memorial arguing that Britain should send explorers to find the passage before France did. Dobbs circulated his manuscript among British leaders to elicit governmental support for an expedition, basing his argument on previous tidal observations for Hudson Bay. Dobbs had no personal experience there and never understood how the ice-choked channels on the bay's west side rendered such observations unreliable.[3]

No one knew more about the bay than the ship captains of Hudson's Bay Company. ("Hudson Bay" is the standard geographical name now; earlier commentators called it Hudson's Bay, and the trading company was named Hudson's Bay Company.) Dobbs approached Middleton—the company's leading captain—to pick his brain. With a long-standing interest in its discovery, Middleton hoped to find the passage himself. So far, the more information Middleton gathered, the more confident he became that the Northwest Passage existed.[4]

Dobbs was unable to organize an expedition during the 1730s. Middleton, who made annual trips to Hudson Bay for the company through the decade, stayed in touch. The day after Middleton returned from his annual voyage in October 1739, England declared war against Spain, marking the start of the War of Jenkins's Ear. Middleton told Dobbs the war would prevent any possible voyage of discovery. Dobbs drew the opposite conclusion. War with Spain lent urgency to the discovery of the Northwest Passage, which would let the Royal Navy sail through it to pillage the Pacific coast of Spanish America from California to Panama.[5]

Unbeknownst to Dobbs, the Admiralty was planning a voyage with a similar purpose, which would follow a more conventional route. Commanding a squadron of warships, Commodore George Anson would round Cape Horn into the Pacific, disrupt Spanish trade, and intercept the great Manila galleon. The successful expedition was not without sacrifice. Anson lost hundreds of men before the voyage was half over. The expedition would be chronicled in *Anson's Voyage Round the World*, another masterpiece of English travel writing.[6]

Though called *Anson's Voyage*, the book was not written by Commodore Anson but by the Reverend Richard Walter, chaplain to the expedition. *Anson's Voyage* is not listed in Franklin's library catalogue, but he knew the work, the most popular travel book in colonial America. Thomas Godfrey had *Anson's Voyage* in his personal library. In March 1749, Franklin advertised *Anson's Voyage* for sale. With a lot of other books he acquired for resale, he obtained another copy from William Bradford.[7]

The men Anson lost mostly perished from scurvy. Once the expedition reached Juan Fernandes, Walter took stock of the situation. In three of Anson's ships, over 600 men had died, two-thirds of the entire crew. Franklin found stories of death from scurvy heartbreaking, mainly because they were so unnecessary. Scurvy was a preventable disease, as some had known since the Renaissance. Franklin had read about an anti-scorbutic in one of the voyages that Samuel Purchas had collected for *Purchas His Pilgrimes*: James Lancaster's "First Voyage Made to East-India."[8]

Commanding four ships on the inaugural expedition of the East India Company, Lancaster was becalmed for months. The expedition lost over a hundred men to scurvy, but those aboard the *Red Dragon*, Lancaster's flagship, suffered much less. They remained healthy because, on Lancaster's order, each drank three spoonfuls of lemon juice every morning. Writing in the mid-1760s, Franklin observed, "This was printed 150 years ago, and yet it is not become a practice."[9]

Franklin's attention to Lancaster's voyage reveals much about the general importance of books and the usefulness of travel writing. Travel books are repositories of practical ideas people can use for their own health, benefit, and, indeed, survival. Franklin's comments also reveal a key problem: Books are useful only when people read them, remember what they read, and put the information to use. Though Purchas had published a way to prevent scurvy a century and a half earlier, it was not being practiced by English sailors, who continued dying from scurvy. No one at the Admiralty knew Lancaster's account, at least no one who could influence policy. *Purchas His Pilgrimes* was out of print, and Lancaster's advice went unheeded. The story Franklin told illustrates the tragedy that can result from the failure to read.

Purchas His Pilgrimes also let Franklin read the story of the explorer for whom the bay is named, Henry Hudson. After considerable experience in search of an Artic passage for the Dutch East India Company, Hudson was recruited by an English syndicate to find the Northwest Passage. He left England on April 17, 1610, in command of the *Discovery*. In early July, he entered what would become known as the Hudson Strait, emerging from it into the bay a month later. Ice crowded the bay throughout the summer, as Hudson tried crossing it to find a westward passage. Abacuk Pricket, a fine writer who had joined his crew, borrowed an image from Greek mythology to characterize their search for the Northwest Passage. He said they "spent three moneths in a labyrinth without end."[10]

Despite his ambitions as an explorer, Hudson was a poor leader. After wintering at the southernmost part of the bay and nearly exhausting their supplies, the men mutinied. Facing starvation, Pricket reluctantly joined the mutineers. They put Hudson, the few who stuck with him, and the sick men into a shallop, which they set loose in Hudson Bay before taking off in the *Discovery*. Hudson and the others aboard the shallop were never heard from again. Natives killed several of the mutineers; the survivors returned to England, where they were tried for murder but acquitted.

Purchas printed a brief document Hudson had written at the start of the voyage, after which Pricket's narrative provides nearly all the details of the voyage and mutiny. Purchas's title for Pricket's narrative, "A Large Discourse of the Same Voyage, and the Successe Thereof," does not do it justice. Modern retellings of Pricket's story call it "Mutiny on the *Discovery*." Regardless, Pricket's nail-biting personal narrative is the most exciting story in the literary history of the Northwest Passage.

In 1741, Dobbs convinced the Admiralty to make the new voyage to discover the Northwest Passage an official expedition of the Royal Navy. He arranged a naval commission for Middleton and had him appointed commander. Middleton oversaw the refitting of the *Furnace*, a bomb vessel converted to a sloop and strengthened to endure the rugged Arctic conditions. The vessel that accompanied the *Furnace* was named the *Discovery*, a name that did not bode well given the fate of Hudson's *Discovery*. On June 8, 1741, the *Furnace* and the *Discovery* weighed anchor, marking the first naval expedition to seek the Northwest Passage. Aboard the *Furnace* and serving as Middleton's clerk was none other than John Wigate, Franklin's old friend from Watts's printing house. After several disappointing years in the London printing trade, he had found a way to satisfy his wanderlust, though winter at Hudson Bay was not exactly what Wigate had in mind when he proposed to Franklin that they travel the world.[11]

Middleton did not reach Prince of Wales Fort at Churchill—the northernmost fort of the Hudson's Bay Company—until August. To search for the Northwest Passage, he would have to winter at Hudson Bay and conduct his exploration once the ice melted the following summer. The fort lacked sufficient room for Middleton's men, who would have to stay at Old Factory, a semi-derelict fort 5 miles up Churchill River. Given its state of disrepair, Old Factory was scarcely an ideal place to endure the lethal cold.

Besides keeping the official journal, Middleton made supplemental scientific observations that winter, which he sent home with the first Hudson's Bay Company ship that returned to London after the thaw. His observations appeared in the Royal Society's *Philosophical Transactions* as "Captain Middleton's Account of the Extraordinary Degrees and Surprizing Effects of Cold in Hudson's Bay, North America." The article earned Middleton the Copley Medal, the Royal Society's highest honor. It also gained the attention of Benjamin Franklin, who developed more respect for Middleton after reading his article in the *Philosophical Transactions*.

Franklin adapted Middleton's article for *Poor Richard, 1748*, having Richard Saunders excerpt it in his epistle to the reader. Richard mentions Pennsylvania winters as a segue to Middleton's article: "We complain sometimes of hard winters in this country; but our winters will appear as summers, when compar'd with those that some of our countrymen undergo in the most northern British colony on this continent."[12]

Whereas the saga of Richard and Bridget Saunders gives *Poor Richard's Almanack* the quality of a television sitcom, Franklin's version of a Hudson Bay winter looks forward to another television genre: the reality show. His use of Middleton's text anticipates television shows that depict survivors in extreme conditions to astonish stay-at-home audiences with the hardships that humans can endure. Choosing the most dramatic examples from Middleton's article for illustration, Franklin portrayed nature's awesome power.

Thermometers at the time could not record extremely low temperatures; Middleton illustrated the cold with a series of graphic descriptions. Lakes less than 12 feet deep, for example, would freeze straight through, chilling and killing all the fish. In deeper lakes, fish could be caught throughout the winter by cutting a hole in the ice and dropping lines into it. As soon as the fish were brought into the open air, they would freeze stiff and could be preserved that way until spring. Slaughtered in the late fall, beef, pork, mutton, and venison could be preserved similarly until spring.

Indoors was no refuge. The relentless cold penetrated their living quarters. The ice wreaked havoc with the fort's wooden structure. Joists, rafters, trusses—pretty much all building materials that held moisture—sounded like enemy gunfire as they refroze and cracked in the middle of the night. Copper pots accidentally left overnight with beer or water in them would split to pieces by morning.[13]

The Reverend James Sterling also enjoyed Middleton's vivid detail. Better known as a poet than a preacher, Sterling used a technique common to eighteenth-century verse in his epic poem *An Epistle to the Hon. Arthur Dobbs*: He glossed his own references. Having coined the poetic phrase, "the fury of the lawless north," Sterling cited Middleton's article to explain that he was referring to the rugged wintertime conditions at Hudson Bay.[14]

A glance at Middleton's article can show what Franklin, Sterling, and so many other contemporary readers found fascinating. Middleton's details, which Franklin reported in *Poor Richard's Almanack*, continue to intrigue:

> The walls of the houses are of stone, two feet thick; the windows very small, with thick wooden shutters, which are close shut 18 hours every day in winter. In the cellars they put their wines, brandies, etc. Four large fires are made every day, in great stoves to warm the rooms: As soon as the wood is burnt down to a coal, the tops of the chimneys are close stopped, with an iron cover; this keeps the heat in, but almost stifles the people. And notwithstanding this, in 4 or 5 hours after the fire is out, the inside of the walls and bed-places will be 2 or 3 inches thick with ice, which is every morning cut away with a hatchet. Three or four times a day, iron shot, of 24 pounds weight, are made red hot, and hung up in the windows of their apartments, to moderate the air that comes in at crevices; yet this, with a fire kept burning the greatest part of 24 hours, will not prevent beer, wine, ink, etc. from freezing.[15]

The winter cold, especially when the wind was blowing from the north, was merciless. It blistered exposed skin on the face and hands. Many lost toes to frostbite. Despite the perilous winter, outdoor exercise could forestall the onset of scurvy. Men who remained indoors to stay warm succumbed to scurvy more quickly than those who ventured outdoors to collect firewood or hunt for game. Indoors or out, nearly all the men were afflicted with scurvy to some degree. Several died from it: more unnecessary loss of life.

After supplying further examples from Middleton's account of the debilitating cold, Richard Saunders adds an upbeat conclusion that echoes the Book of Psalms: "Thus far Captain Middleton. And now, my tender reader, thou that shudderest when the wind blows a little at n-west, and criest,

'Tis extrrrrrream cohohold! 'Tis terrrrrrrible cohold! what dost thou think of removing to that delightful country? Or dost thou not rather chuse to stay in Pennsylvania, thanking God that *He has caused thy lines to fall in pleasant places.*"[16]

Having survived the winter, Middleton finally started exploring. In July, he and his men traveled further north than any previous explorers, discovering a large inlet that Middleton shrewdly named after Sir Charles Wager, First Lord of the Admiralty. Weeks of additional exploration let Middleton know the inlet was not the entrance to a west-bound strait, but a closed bay. Farther north, they discovered Roe's Welcome, which gave them new hope, but that, too, was a closed inlet. Disappointed, but now convinced there was no Northwest Passage, Middleton decided to abandon the search and go home. Like condemned men learning of a last-minute reprieve, his crew—"poor scorbutic creatures"—cheered Middleton's decision.[17]

Frustrated with his conclusions, Dobbs thought Middleton was dissembling to protect the interests of the Hudson's Bay Company. Some took Dobbs's side; others, like William Douglass, could see through him. Relating the controversy in his history of North America, Douglass took Middleton's side. He saw that Dobbs's disappointment with the unsuccessful voyage is what prompted him to accuse Middleton of neglect, misconduct, and corruption. In his zeal, Dobbs coaxed a few of Middleton's men to turn against him. Peter Collinson informed Cadwallader Colden, "Some malicious people have opposed Capt. Middleton and rendred his journals suspicious att the Admiralty."[18]

The "malicious people," sad to say, included Wigate, who joined Dobbs's campaign to smear Middleton. Given the friction between Wigate and Middleton aboard the *Furnace*, Dobbs easily turned him against his captain. According to Wigate's deposition, which Dobbs appended to *Remarks*, Middleton said that "no man but himself should be able to know whether there was a passage or not." That the deponent was an old friend may have prevented Franklin from seeing through Dobbs as Douglass did. Wigate continued to support Dobbs, issuing a map, which shows the "Wager Strait" leading from Hudson Bay westward.[19]

Intrigued with the prospect of finding the Northwest Passage and convinced that its discovery remained possible, Franklin obtained additional books on the subject, including Henry Ellis's *Voyage to Hudson's Bay*. A family friend of Arthur Dobbs, Ellis served as hydrographer, that is, science officer for the new expedition Dobbs had organized. The *Dobbs Galley* and an accompanying vessel, the optimistically named *California*, left England on

May 20, 1746. They entered Hudson Strait that summer and wintered near the mouth of the Hayes River. The following summer, they tried to locate a passage through Wager Strait, which, as Middleton had concluded, was not a strait at all.

Ellis's *Voyage to Hudson's Bay* is the finest book to emerge from the search for the Northwest Passage. A dedicated and patient observer, Ellis created vivid pen pictures of what he saw, including beaver lodges, seal habitats, periwinkles, and partridge berries. Ellis also recorded much about the language and culture of the region's native people. He introduced many terms to the English language, including "snow-blindness." His description of "snow-eyes," that is, goggles to prevent snow-blindness, shows what readers could learn from the native culture. Snow-eyes are made from bits of bone or ivory that cover the eyes and are tied behind the head. Into each piece are cut narrow, horizontal slits, one for each eye, through which users can see. The snow-eyes are just one of Ellis's many examples demonstrating the native "spirit of invention."[20]

Despite the expedition's failure to find the Northwest Passage, Ellis's ending is upbeat. Reusing Abacuk Pricket's mythological imagery, he explained: "We may consider *Hudson's-Bay*, as a kind of labyrinth, into which we enter on one side through *Hudson's-Straights*, and what we aim at, is to get out on the other side." Attempting to find the passage by trial and error would be tedious and time-consuming, but the explorer could find vital clues to navigate the labyrinth. Ellis continued, "The tide is a kind of clue, which seems to lead us by the hand through all the windings and turnings of this labyrinth, and if studiously and steadily followed must certainly lead us out."[21]

Perhaps no book about the Northwest Passage affected Franklin more than Ellis's *Voyage to Hudson's-Bay*. The quest for the unknown thrilled him. Throughout his life, he took great pride in identifying and solving problems. Whenever Franklin was faced with a mystery, he worked hard to solve it. Finding a route through Ellis's labyrinth would be difficult, he reckoned, but not impossible. Franklin was Theseus in spectacles, a string of printed words his thread of Ariadne.

Franklin obtained another book about the *Dobbs Galley*: *An Account of a Voyage for the Discovery of a North-West Passage*. According to its title page, this work was written by the "Clerk of the *California*." Franklin's editors call the clerk Charles Swaine, but he had other aliases. Whatever his name, he was a man of many talents, including considerable literary skill. Like Ellis, he created memorable comparisons to bring their voyage alive. Describing the icebergs they sighted while approaching Hudson Strait, Swaine wrote, "The afternoon continuing clear and pleasant, [we] saw more islands of ice, one equal in size and much resembling a large *Gothick* church."[22]

In the second volume of *An Account of a Voyage*, Swaine included a letter from one Admiral Bartholomew de Fonte, who supposedly sailed from Lima, Peru, in 1640 up the west coast of North America and found a water route to Hudson Bay. First published in 1708 in *The Monthly Miscellany*, a short-lived periodical edited by James Petiver, Fonte's letter is now considered a hoax. But the Fonte letter fooled Swaine, as it had fooled Dobbs and as it would fool Franklin. It did not fool Douglass, who laughed at Dobbs's gullibility, calling him a "wild projector, and notoriously credulous."[23]

Fonte's letter fell into neglect after its initial appearance in Petiver's *Monthly Miscellany*, but once Dobbs reprinted it in *An Account of the Countries Adjoining to Hudson's Bay*, it got some traction. John Campbell included it in his revised and expanded edition of John Harris's *Complete Collection of Voyages and Travels*. Besides reprinting it in *An Account of a Voyage*, Swaine added interpretive commentary and published the first map of Fonte's supposed discovery.[24]

Peter Collinson sent Franklin the first volume of Swaine's *Account of the Voyage* in 1748. The second volume appeared the following year. Franklin acquired it by April 1753, when he mentioned both volumes to his friend Jared Eliot. Franklin could have reread Fonte's letter in Dobbs's *Account of the Countries Adjacent to Hudson's Bay*, which Swaine, who was living in Chestertown, Maryland, in 1750, had given him. Wanting to believe Fonte's letter, Franklin sought independent corroboration.[25]

After entering Hudson Bay, the story goes, Fonte encountered a ship from Boston navigated by a Captain Shapley, who sold him his detailed charts and journals. Given Shapley's skill as a navigator and mapmaker, Franklin thought there must be some trace of him in Boston. Douglass had never heard of Shapley, but Franklin hoped that Thomas Prince, colonial New England's greatest antiquarian, might know about him.

Eager to help, Prince consulted the written records—to no avail. Prince considered the oral tradition next. He asked Deacon Marshal, a local nonagenarian, if he had ever heard of Captain Shapley. As a boy, Marshal had heard others mention Shapley, who was a native of Charlestown, Massachusetts. His learning was so great, the other boys said, that Shapley must have dabbled in the black arts. The association between learning and black magic echoes centuries-old legends and superstitions. The way Marshal's friends talked, Captain Shapley was more Friar Bacon than Francis Drake.

Prince put little stock in the stories about Shapley and the black arts, but he did see the significance of Charlestown, where he had yet to search. There, Prince located some Shapley descendants, who testified to their kinsman's nautical skill. The information from the descendants added weight to Fonte's letter, Prince concluded. Franklin concurred.[26]

When Swaine emigrated to America, it was not by coincidence that he settled at Chestertown, Maryland, where James Sterling lived. A close associate of Arthur Dobbs, Sterling had begun writing his lengthy verse epistle to him after the *Dobbs Galley* and the *California* returned to London. Learning of Dobbs's plan to lead an expedition himself, Sterling found the projected voyage a suitably epic subject.

In the second part of *Epistle to Dobbs*, Sterling traces the prospective route from Britain to Hudson Bay. Though drawing on fact, he loved to embellish. When he visited the Tuesday Club in Annapolis one evening, Dr. Alexander Hamilton dubbed him the Reverend Mr. Rodomantus after the vainglorious boaster in Ariosto's *Orlando furioso*. That night, Sterling mentioned two-headed bulls, talking monkeys, drunken salamanders, cockatrices that could kill with a look, and a squirrel that could skipper a little boat using nothing but its tail for a sail. Sterling's wonders of nature reflect a literary interest he shared with Franklin. Skipper Squirrel comes from one of Franklin's favorite emblem books, Joachim Camerarius's *Centuries*.[27]

Sterling's poem recommends that Dobbs visit Orkney, where he would find further proof of the Northwest Passage: "There by communicating oceans borne / See fruited trees from coasts of *Corea* torn." Much as he cites Middleton's article elsewhere in the poem, here Sterling glosses his reference to Korean fruit trees in Orkney: "These products of the *East-Indies*, said to be sometimes found on the shores of the *Scotch* islands, are urged as proof of the North-West Passage."[28]

The reference to Korea adds an exotic quality to Sterling's colonial American epic and reinforces the poem's importance to literary history. Owen Aldridge asserts that the Korean pirates in Franklin's 1786 magazine article "Letter Relative to the Present State of China" represent the earliest reference to Korea in American literature. But Sterling's reference to Korean fruit trees antedates Franklin by decades, making *Epistle to Dobbs* the first work in American literature to mention Korea.[29]

Swaine, who planned his own voyage of discovery, persuaded several Maryland men to finance it. Governor Samuel Ogle found Swaine so convincing he granted him a passport permitting his search for the Northwest Passage. Swaine also approached Franklin, the greatest fundraiser in colonial

America. The reason why he gave Franklin a copy of Dobbs's *Account of the Countries Adjacent to Hudson's Bay* was to curry his favor and convince him of the Northwest Passage's existence: another example of the social power of books.

Franklin did not need much convincing, nor did other prominent Philadelphians. The Northwest Passage fascinated them. Abram Taylor, who made his living as a merchant, could see its commercial possibilities. Taylor had both Ellis's *Voyage* and Swaine's *Account of a Voyage* in his library.[30] With several other prominent Philadelphians, including William Allen—chief justice of Pennsylvania—Franklin established a subscription fund and organized the North-West Company. Additional subscribers came from Maryland, Massachusetts, and New York. Sterling was one of the Maryland subscribers. Together, they raised £1500 to purchase and outfit a schooner for Swaine to sail to Hudson Bay.

Around November 1751, Sterling left Maryland for a trip to England. He planned to see *Epistle to Dobbs* through the press and hoped to obtain a lucrative civil post, collector of customs for the head of Chesapeake Bay. While in London, Sterling revealed the secret plans for Franklin's North-West Company. He and several London investors founded a competing company to organize a search for the Northwest Passage. They applied for a 99-year trading monopoly along the Labrador coast as both an incentive and reward for their proposed exploration.

When the Philadelphians heard about Sterling's shenanigans, his duplicity astonished them. "A scoundrell of a parson," Allen called him. Sterling never received his monopoly, but he did finagle the lucrative post as collector of customs and also got *Epistle to Dobbs* published in Dublin and London. Though Collinson recognized his underhanded double-dealing, Sterling's behavior did not stop him from enjoying *Epistle to Dobbs*. He called Sterling a "volatile blade and great poet."[31]

Franklin's North-West Company found a suitable schooner in Massachusetts. They renamed it the *Argo* after the ship Jason sailed in search of the Golden Fleece. The name suits Pricket's earlier use of Greek mythology: What better vessel to navigate the labyrinth of Hudson Bay than the *Argo*? The voyage of the *Argo* had a threefold purpose: scientific, commercial, and diplomatic. In addition to searching for the Northwest Passage, it sought to explore Labrador. These geographic endeavors represent the *Argo*'s scientific purpose. The North-West Company also gave Swaine the commercial tasks of opening trade and promoting fisheries. In terms of diplomacy, Swaine sought to befriend the native inhabitants.[32]

Sailing from Philadelphia, Swaine had several advantages over the explorers who began in London. The British expeditions had to winter in Hudson
Bay and perform their explorations the following summer. Ideally, Swaine
could have an equal amount of time to explore without wintering at Hudson
Bay, saving time, money, and, almost surely, lives. On March 4, 1753, the *Argo*
set sail with Swaine at the helm. John Patten, an Indian trader, came along as
mapmaker and mineralogist.[33]

The winter of 1752–53 proved to be the coldest in decades. "It was a great
year for ice," Swaine quipped. Ice blocked the entrance to Hudson Strait.
After repeated attempts, Swaine found it impossible to enter. Unable to reach
Hudson Bay, he explored Labrador instead. The approach to the upper falls
was breathtaking. A lush green woods surmounted by barren rocks pointing
into the sky made the scenery resemble a painting. The beauty amazed them:
"The freedom of nature, the gloom of the evening, the slow steady course of
the water, and the echoes of the rumbling fall, afforded such a scene as affected
even those that rowed; and they said, it was the pleasantest place they had
ever seen."[34]

Swaine would not publish his account of Labrador until the following
decade. Temporarily, he left his journals and charts with Franklin for safe-
keeping. Franklin read the manuscript journals and recognized the commercial and scientific potential of Swaine's voyage. The discoveries he had made
along the Labrador coast would help others exploit its natural resources.[35]

After Swaine returned, his Philadelphia sponsors hosted a gala dinner for
him at a local tavern. They unanimously voted him a handsome present.
Though his search for the Northwest Passage had failed, some investors were
willing to outfit him for a second attempt. Others were not. The *Argo*, its
tackle, and its stores went up for sale to let disappointed investors recoup part
of their costs. Franklin, Allen, and the other investors willing to finance a second voyage bought the *Argo* and refitted it for a new expedition.[36]

On May 2, 1754, Franklin announced the departure of the *Argo*'s second
voyage. Swaine returned on October 20, less than six months later. Surprised
by his early return, people wondered what had happened. Franklin knew, but
he was not saying. *The Pennsylvania Gazette* reported that Swaine's search for
the Northwest Passage had been unsuccessful but provided no further
details.[37]

William Bradford offered more information in *The Pennsylvania Journal*,
reporting that three of Swaine's men had been killed in Labrador. Bradford
did not name the victims, but John Patten was one of them. William Parsons
had heard from a friend that natives had killed Patten and two of the sailors

while they were fishing a considerable distance from the *Argo*. There was more to the story than Parsons's friend revealed.[38]

Not until the following decade would Swaine publicly reveal what had happened. Satisfied with Patten's service the previous year, Swaine rehired him as mapmaker and mineralogist for the 1754 voyage. What Swaine did not know at the time was that Patten had brought back some ore samples from Labrador, which he had shared with an otherwise unidentified investor, who secretly hired Patten to search for gold.[39]

When they returned to Labrador, Swaine ordered Patten and two sailors to explore the immediate area. Searching for gold, Patten led them well beyond where Swaine had directed. Natives ambushed them, killing all three and stealing their boat. Though now short-handed, Swaine still planned to continue to Hudson Bay, but, given the deadly attack, some men were afraid to proceed. Dreading a mutiny, Swaine returned to Philadelphia. In classical mythology, the quest of Jason's Argonauts symbolizes the search for spiritual strength through purity of soul. Motivated by greed, fear, and self-interest, Franklin's Argonauts were all too human.

Swaine did not return empty-handed. He acquired some parkas as well as some utensils and other curiosities the native people used in everyday life. In the name of the North-West Company, Swaine donated these items to the Library Company of Philadelphia for its cabinet of curiosities. By 1828, Swaine's artifacts had disappeared. Some may have disappeared sooner. The 1757 library catalogue lists "Cloathing, instruments and utensils of the *Eskimeaux*, given by the *North West* Company," but the next catalogue, which appeared in 1764, lists only the instruments and utensils. The parkas were gone.[40]

Though the failure of the 1754 voyage of the *Argo* ended Franklin's active involvement in the exploration for the Northwest Passage, he remained convinced of its existence. In 1768, Swaine published *The Great Probability of a Northwest Passage*, presenting further speculations about Fonte's letter and printing his "Account of Labrador." Then living in London and serving as agent for the Pennsylvania Assembly, Franklin acquired a copy for his personal library and also helped Swaine market the book.[41]

When Jonathan Carver came to London the following year, he befriended Franklin and helped sustain his interest in the Northwest Passage. Three years earlier, Carver had explored much of what is now Minnesota. Unable to raise enough subscriptions to publish his journals in Boston, he had come to London to publish them there but still had trouble getting them into print. They would not appear until 1778 under the title *Travels through the Interior*

Parts of North America, in the Years 1766, 1767, and 1768. Franklin added a copy of Carver's *Travels* to his library and shared it with others.[42]

Carver impressed Franklin. After first meeting him, Franklin appreciated the "opportunity of being acquainted with so great a traveller." Surviving documents do not say what they talked about, but Carver's discussion of the Northwest Passage in *Travels* offers a good indication. Carver ended his book with some hints for successfully discovering the passage. Instead of entering Hudson Bay, as previous explorers had done, they should start from a promising place on the Pacific coast and try to find the bay by traveling east. Explorers trying to find the Northwest Passage from the Hudson Bay always had to cut their explorations short because they were understandably terrified of being trapped there until the following summer. Traveling east, alternatively, would allow explorers more time to explore and assure them of a safe retreat to the open sea.[43]

FIGURE 16.1 Robert Rogers, American Commander (Nürnberg: G. N. Raspe, 1778). Library of Congress Rare Book and Special Collections Division, Washington, DC, LC-USZ62-45269.

From London, Franklin also followed Robert Rogers's efforts to raise funds for his proposed journey to discover the Northwest Passage. Rogers had established his reputation during the French and Indian War, when he commanded a group of irregular soldiers who became known as Rogers's Rangers. A master of the *petite guerre*, Rogers had extraordinary success during the war. He chronicled his wartime exploits in *Journals*, another work that Franklin added to his library. After the war, Rogers fell on hard times. He, too, came to London in 1769 and peppered the government with petitions for several ambitious projects. To help his cause, Rogers contacted Franklin.[44]

In 1771, Rogers drafted a petition to search for the Northwest Passage. His premise was simple. Earlier attempts to find the passage were flawed because they went by water. The best way to find it would be an overland journey and the best person to find it would be the leader of Rogers's Rangers. Rogers hoped for government sponsorship, but he also sought the Royal Society's scientific heft. He had his petition printed and gave a copy to Franklin, hoping he would present it to the Society. There is no evidence that Franklin put Rogers's petition before the Royal Society. It survives with other books from his library at the American Philosophical Society.[45]

Franklin's reluctance to support Rogers's ambitious overland journey reflects his doubts about Rogers's ability as an explorer. It does not reflect any doubt about the existence of the Northwest Passage. In 1783, Franklin still upheld the validity of Fonte's letter, informing John Adams that the English version had been translated from the now-lost original Spanish letter. Reinforcing his belief in the letter's validity, Franklin also told Adams what he had learned from Thomas Prince about Captain Shapley. The following year, Franklin ordered Daines Barrington's *Miscellanies*, a collection of scientific papers about new approaches to polar exploration.[46] Franklin never found the way out of Ellis's labyrinth, but never did he stop believing in its possibility.

The Art of War

BENJAMIN FRANKLIN LEARNED military tactics mainly by reading history and biography, but he did own some specific books on the subject. His modest military collection ranged from ancient classics to seventeenth-century instructional manuals to personal narratives by French and English officers. Little did Franklin realize on acquiring these books that he would ultimately face war. His military miscellany gave him valuable background information to use as the leader of the Pennsylvania militia, first during the War of the Austrian Succession, next during the Seven Years' War.

The oldest and most important military title listed in Franklin's library catalogue is consistent with the leadership handbooks he read in his youth: a Greek manual published in English as *Onosandro Platonico: Of the General Captain and of His Office*. The Greek philosopher Onasander wrote it in the first century, and Peter Whitehorne translated it in the sixteenth. *Onosandro Platonico* is a conduct book for generals, serving as both a guide for personal behavior and a treatise on strategy and tactics. Whitehorne did not translate the work from Onasander's Greek, but from an Italian translation: a common practice. His cumbersome English title is a literal rendering of the Italian.[1]

The succinct title of the modern English version clarifies Onasander's purpose: *The General*. Written in Rome during the reign of Claudius and Nero, *The General* begins by defining what makes a good leader. A general should not be selected for his wealth or noble birth, but for his personal traits. He should be temperate, self-restrained, vigilant, hard-working, and free from avarice. He must also perfect his organizational skills. After all, the commander's responsibility is not to lead troops, but to command commanders. *Onosandro Platonico* is vital for understanding the historical development of the chain-of-command concept.[2]

Instead of supplying examples from Greek and Roman military history, Onasander painted his portrait of the ideal general in broad strokes. The approach has helped his manual transcend its times. His advice was as applicable in Franklin's era as it had been in Claudius's. The aphoristic quality of Onasander's prose also appealed to Franklin. So did his common sense. Discussing the proper age for a military commander, Onasander recommended a middle-aged general, one young enough to retain both force and strength, but old enough to have developed prudence. The general must proceed with patience and cool deliberation. Franklin possessed many of the same personal qualities as Onasander's ideal leader. The similarities may be coincidental, or they may reflect what Franklin learned reading *The General*.[3]

A sixteenth-century black-letter volume, Franklin's copy of *The General* could have been part of his library since his apprenticeship, but when he acquired it is unknown. He had at least four other military manuals in his library by 1746: *The Art of War*, a four-part French work translated into English; and three shorter works bound together in one volume: Louis de Gaya's *Art of War*, Robert Harford's *English Military Discipline*, and Sieur de La Fontaine's *Military Duties of the Officers of Cavalry*. Together, these works gave Franklin knowledge of military tactics, techniques, and weaponry.

Four French officers, each with their own expertise, collaborated to write *The Art of War*. Little else is known about them beyond three of their four names. Sieur de Birac discusses the cavalry in the first part, and Monsieur de Lamont discusses the infantry in the second. The anonymous third part treats the soldier in general, and the Chevalier de la Valière discusses the rules and practice of war in the final part.

Addressing soldiers who believed that service and experience are better teachers than books, the preface explains how *The Art of War* could enhance their military knowledge, letting them know what experience has yet to teach and facilitating whatever new knowledge they will gain on the battlefield: "War is one of those arts in which a man can never be perfect, but must still be learning."[4] Books have a crucial advantage over personal instruction. Soldiers who are loath to show their ignorance can learn in private what they are unwilling to learn in public. In addition, military books can provide expertise in the absence of experts. As a further advantage, the knowledge soldiers gain from reading can help them rise in the ranks.[5]

Louis de Gaya's *Art of War*, the first item in Franklin's bound volume of military manuals, presents a brief introduction explaining how war is waged. Gaya establishes his authority early in the book, telling readers his expertise stems from combat experience. Though Gaya designed the work for French nobility and gentry, his translator tailored it for English readers, telling them how to interpret this French military manual. The translator said he was merely introducing them to the French method of making war, not elevating the French above the English method or telling readers how to wage war.

Gaya's *Art of War* appealed to Franklin's linguistic curiosity. The work introduced several military terms to the English language, including "contravallation," meaning a chain of interconnected redoubts and breastworks constructed between the besiegers' camp and the besieged town. Contravallation is related to circumvallation, a rampart or entrenchment encircling a town. Both terms soon started being used figuratively. Franklin could have encountered them elsewhere. When a querist in *The Athenian Oracle* asks how to approach a lover who refuses his letters, Oracle looks on the bright side. Consider the savings in pen and paper, time and trouble: "All this is clear gains to you, (for, a penny sav'd, you know, etc.) and you may e'en besiege the town without all these lines of circum-and-contravallation."[6]

Harford's *English Military Discipline*, the second item in the bound volume, is largely a translation of Gaya's *Traité des armes*. An encyclopedist of weaponry, Gaya was among the first to describe military arms without going into tactics. Published in 1678, *Traité des armes* captures a major turning point in military history, a time when defensive armor was being discarded due to the increased efficiency of firearms.

Gaya did not limit his discussion to firearms. The opening chapter, "Of Sharp-Weapons," has sections devoted to swords, scimitars, and bayonets. Subsequent chapters treat staff arms, such as pikes, halberds, axes, and maces; arms of the ancients; defensive arms; and many more. Gaya provided much practical information, sometimes with a touch of humor. Vinegar was being used to cool down cannons after firing, but Gaya said water would work equally well. Save the vinegar to season salads.[7]

Sieur de la Fontaine's *Military Duties of the Officers of Cavalry*, the third item in Franklin's bound volume, provides further information about the French military. Like Gaya's *Art of War*, this work required a delicate touch on the translator's part. While informing English readers of French tactics, the translator never tells them to follow the French method. Instead, he says that the best way to defeat the enemy is to understand how they fight.[8]

William Franklin tried running away to sea around 1742, but his father stopped him. Franklin could not stop his son's urge for adventure. As the War of the Austrian Succession escalated, William became anxious to join the fight. The most remarkable incident of King George's War, as the conflict was known in North America, was the 1745 capture of the French Canadian fortress of Louisbourg by a British expeditionary force manned by colonial militiamen.

Contemporary observers chalked up this unexpected victory to Providence. William Douglass observed, "If any one circumstance had taken a wrong turn on our side, and if any one circumstance had not taken a wrong turn on the French side, the expedition must have miscarried, and our forces would have returned with shame." No matter the reason, the success encouraged many young colonial men, William Franklin included, to join the next military expedition planned against the French in Canada. The victory also contributed to the history of journalism. On June 6, 1745, Benjamin Franklin published a woodcut depicting Louisburg and its harbor in *The Pennsylvania Gazette*, making it the paper's first illustrated news story.[9]

In 1746, when William was around 18, his father let him enlist as an ensign in one of four companies raised in Philadelphia for a campaign against Canada. To help prepare him for the army, his father presented William with two volumes from his library, the four-part *Art of War* and the bound volume featuring the work of Louis de Gaya. William could follow the advice given in *The Art of War*, learning much about military service before entering combat.[10]

Commissioned under Captain John Diemer, William joined a company of a hundred men who left Philadelphia in September 1746 for Albany, where they would spend the winter. The expedition to Canada never materialized, and the Albany winter proved dreadful. But William thrived in the army. After attaining the rank of captain, he briefly returned to Philadelphia in May 1747. This was no idle visit. He came home to retrieve some deserters and escort them back to Albany. Franklin could see that William was enamored of military life. To reward him, Franklin ordered from Strahan a lavish present, a six-volume annotated edition of the standard French translation of Polybius.[11]

Franklin's order reveals much about how he sought to educate William. He took advantage of his son's newfound interest in the military to broaden William's education. Polybius was an accomplished warrior and man of learning: a rare combination. He accompanied Scipio on his military campaigns and distinguished himself in battle. Polybius's history is well respected for its accuracy and authenticity. He was the only ancient Greek historian who wrote about the battles he fought.

Ordering the French edition of Polybius, Franklin planned to double up William's education, letting him polish his French as he read ancient Greek and Roman military history. A knowledge of French would help advance his military career. Though English writers hesitated to say so, the French wrote the best military treatises in the world. (There is a reason why French would be a required subject at West Point.) Furthermore, since France was England's perennial enemy, a knowledge of French would have practical value when it came to reading confiscated enemy communiqués or negotiating a peace.

Strahan was unable to obtain the edition of Polybius that Franklin ordered, which turned out just as well. William soon left the army, not from dislike but from the lack of opportunity. The prospect of peace between Britain and France quashed William's dreams of glory on the battlefield. There were few opportunities for military advancement in peacetime, and colonial officers were always at a disadvantage against British regulars, as George Washington would discover to his chagrin the following decade. Seldom were colonial officers promoted above the rank of captain. The military manuals that Benjamin Franklin had given his son returned to his library.[12]

War always sparks an interest in books about war. King George's War encouraged Franklin to expand his military reading beyond manuals to military history. In 1747, he ordered two pertinent works from Strahan, Captain Robert Parker's *Memoirs of the Most Remarkable Military Transactions for the Years 1693, to 1718* and the Marquis de Feuquières's *Memoirs Historical and Military*.[13]

Robert Parker, an officer in the British army, kept a journal during his various campaigns. Upon retirement, he started shaping it for publication. He died around 1718 without finishing the book. His son put the final touches on the manuscript and issued his father's memoirs in 1746. Parker had been present for most of Marlborough's campaigns during the War of the Spanish Succession, so his memoirs form a valuable account of a marching officer's life and responsibilities in Marlborough's army.[14]

Since Parker's military adventures concerned the War of the Spanish Succession, they gained new relevance during the War of the Austrian Succession. Its publisher told readers that Parker's *Memoirs* would elevate the "martial spirit of the nation, by representing how gloriously *Britons* have behaved in defence of the liberty and independency of *Europe*."[15]

Though a personal narrative, the Marquis de Feuquières's *Memoirs* also functioned as a military manual. His English translator faced the same problem as the earlier translators. While recognizing the importance of French military literature, they did not want to glorify England's traditional enemy by stressing the value of its writings. To soften De Feuquières's French outlook, the translator supplemented his text with passages from an Englishman who had written about some of the same battles, the distinguished diplomat William Temple.[16]

The most substantial set of military works to survive from Franklin's library is a two-volume folio collection of manuscripts made by John Lindsay, the twentieth earl of Crawford. After attending the University of Glasgow, he went to the military academy of Vaudeuil in Paris. Lindsay entered the army in 1726 and became a captain of the Third Foot Guards in 1734. He did not establish his military prowess until he joined the Austrian army as a volunteer under Prince Eugène in 1735. In 1739, Lindsay became colonel in a Highland regiment, the Black Watch.[17]

Lindsay's manuscripts combine military history with practical know-how. Some items record English campaigns of the late-seventeenth and early-eighteenth centuries. Others discuss more recent Russian campaigns. One is a manual for infantry soldiers; another describes fortification and geometry. Together, these manuscript works form a unique chapter illustrating how military information was digested and disseminated in Franklin's time.[18]

The Library Company of Philadelphia contains another military manual Franklin read, Joseph Moxon's *Epitome of the Whole Art of War*. Moxon's *Epitome* presents a series of illustrations accompanied by explanatory text. A derivative work, it reuses plates and text from Captain John Stevens's *Military Discipline*. Franklin appreciated the book's fine copper engravings, not only for how they illustrated the text, but also for their aesthetic appeal.[19]

His military reading acquired a more realistic edge when French privateers attacked ships and settlements on the Delaware River in late 1747. In addition, French troops and their Native American allies attacked Pennsylvania's back settlements: the latest salvos in King George's War. Committed to pacifism, the Quakers who controlled the Pennsylvania Assembly refused to authorize a militia to defend the colony.

In response to the pacifist Quakers' refusal to defend themselves, Franklin wrote *Plain Truth*, a call to arms highlighting the danger Pennsylvania faced. Since their colony would not defend itself, Franklin urged Pennsylvanians to arm themselves. The title page of *Plain Truth* underscored his wide appeal. A lengthy Latin quotation from Sallust's *Conspiracy of Catiline* comes after the author's pseudonym: "A Tradesman of Philadelphia." Making his persona a tradesman who could quote Latin, Franklin challenged traditional class barriers. The title page of *Plain Truth* appeals to both tradesmen and gentlemen. The current danger threatened all Pennsylvanians, not just one segment of the population.

The Latin text is italicized, save for one clause in small caps. A contributor to *The Pennsylvania Gazette* known only as Mr. X translated the entire passage for those unable to read Latin. When Franklin published the translation in the *Gazette*, he again used small caps for its key passage: "Divine assistance and protection are not to be obtain'd by timorous prayers and womanish supplications."[20] On the verso of the title page of *Plain Truth*, Franklin repeated the Latin phrase in abbreviated form as the caption to an illustration from Dilworth's *New Guide to the English Tongue*. The illustration forms the device, and Sallust's key phrase is the motto. In combination, they create an emblem showing what *Plain Truth* means.

In Dilworth's *New Guide*, the illustration accompanies "Of the Waggoner and Hercules," the fable emphasizing the importance for people to help themselves before resorting to prayer. Transferred to Franklin's *Plain Truth*, the illustration retained its message of self-reliance but now formed a comment on current events. Reprinted in *Plain Truth*, the illustration became a political cartoon, the first in American history. Turning an emblem into a political cartoon, Franklin updated a traditional form for modern times. Using his extensive knowledge of the emblem tradition, he invented a visual form of political discourse that thrives today.

Franklin printed a thousand copies of *Plain Truth* for the first edition, which appeared on November 14, 1747. Less than three weeks later, he published a second edition, also a thousand copies. In addition, he had *Plain Truth* translated into German, loaning the woodcut to the German printer and thus reinforcing the political cartoon's power to transcend language. When Franklin advertised the second edition of *Plain Truth* in December, he also advertised the forthcoming publication of General William Blakeney's *New Manual Exercise*, a brief handbook of infantry drill and tactics.[21]

Another veteran of the War of the Spanish Succession, Blakeney had revitalized his military career during the War of Jenkins's Ear. A specialist in officer training, he was appointed adjutant-general to an expedition to attack Spanish colonies in the West Indies. Blakeney traveled through the mainland colonies raising a force of 3,000 troops to form the American regiment. He wrote *New Manual Exercise* as a set of instructions for his regiment. Franklin had previously published the text of Blakeney's drill manual in his *General Magazine*.[22]

Plain Truth and Franklin's 1747 edition of *New Manual Exercise* were companion volumes. *Plain Truth* called for the formation of a militia; Blakeney's work showed how to train one. After publishing *Plain Truth* but before issuing *New Manual Exercise*, Franklin founded the Association, as the colonial Pennsylvania militia became known. Democratic principles guided the Associators. They elected company officers, who, in turn, elected the higher officers. On January 1, 1748, the company officers elected Franklin their colonel. Aware that Thomas and Richard Penn, the proprietors of Pennsylvania, would resent his leadership, Franklin declined the position and nominated Abram Taylor instead.[23]

Franklin's choice of Taylor was less a military maneuver than a political move. As a member of the Pennsylvania Council, Taylor created an alliance between the Associators and the government. Like Franklin, Taylor had gained his military knowledge from reading. Taylor owned the bible of the British army: Humphrey Bland's *Treatise of Military Discipline*. Franklin also knew "Old Humphrey," which he sold at his printing house and which he excerpted in an appendix to Blakeney's *New Manual Exercise*.[24]

Colonel Taylor used Bland's military treatise to get the Associators into fighting shape. In May, he arranged for the Pennsylvania Council to review his regiment of Associators in the field. Many others witnessed the demonstration. The *Gazette* reported, "Strangers who were present agree, that the progress the regiment has made in military discipline in so short a time, was truly extraordinary."[25]

Adam Thomson paid homage to the Association in "An Ode, Humbly Inscribed to the Associators of Pennsylvania," which reflects what many Pennsylvanians felt:

> Drums beat, and trumpets sound alarms,
> And thronging crowds appear in arms;
> Inflam'd by noble patriot rage,
> For lives and fortunes to engage.[26]

Though Colonel Taylor commanded the Associators, Franklin involved himself in every aspect of the Association, down to designing company flags. Harford's *English Military Discipline* let him know that company flags could promote camaraderie and expedite rallying in battle. Franklin's emblem books taught him the power of visual iconography. Though none of the Associators' flags survive, Franklin published a two-part list describing their emblems. The devices Franklin created for the Associators' flags are quite diverse. Some show soldiers ready for battle. Others feature weaponry. Some present traditional symbols to illustrate abstract concepts: hope, glory, liberty. Five feature animals, though three of the five are leonine. The best one portrays a sleeping lion with the motto, "Rouze me if you dare."[27]

Many of the mottoes are Latin, but some are English: a departure from the highfalutin emblematic tradition. The greatest motto Franklin coined is an English one: "In God we trust." The Associators' flags mark the earliest usage of this phrase in American history. Not until 1956 would Franklin's words be adopted as the official motto of the United States. For another flag, Franklin used an eagle descending from the skies. A symbol of victory, Franklin's eagle exemplifies the motto *A Deo victoria*, "Victory from God." Franklin used Pliny's greatest land beast, the elephant, to symbolize a warrior who is always ready, *Semper paratus*.[28]

The first part of the list of flags appeared the second week of January 1748, with the second part coming in April. One contemporary reader transcribed the first part into his own copy of *Plain Truth*, creating a personal record of Franklin's emblems. It is prefaced with the following headnote: "In consequence of the above proposal an Association was entered into by the people of all ranks, but the Quakers, and the following is an account of the devices and mottos on some of their colours."[29] Emphasizing that people of all ranks joined, this reader confirmed the effectiveness of Franklin's egalitarian scheme.

Pacificist Quakers spoke out against the Association. The pamphlets on the subject in Franklin's library track the controversy. After the Reverend Gilbert Tennent, a Presbyterian minister, published a sermon conveying his support, *The Late Association for Defence, Encourag'd: or, The Lawfulness of a Defensive War*, the Quaker John Smith responded with *The Doctrine of Christianity, as Held by the People Called Quakers, Vindicated*. Smith issued his pamphlet with the approval of the Philadelphia Meeting. Refusing to let their politics interfere with their business, Franklin and Hall printed Smith's attack on the Association. Smith arranged for Hall to print a thousand copies, taking 500 to his home to give away and leaving 500 with Hall to distribute. Once the pamphlet appeared the last week of January, the printing house was, to use Smith's simile, like a fair because so many people crowded around it. Hall had never seen such demand for a pamphlet, not even when he worked in London.[30]

Smith's *Doctrine of Christianity* would continue to influence Philadelphia Quakers. Parodying a pacifist Quaker at the start of the Seven Years' War in *Kawanio che keeteru*, Nicholas Scull has him read the pamphlet:

> Smith *on Defence*, he had read o'er,
> With many a pious author more,
> Who with enthusiastick din,
> Make *self-defence* a deadly sin.[31]

Though they never had to battle the French, the Associators struck fear into Thomas Penn. William Penn, the colony's founder, had overseen

Pennsylvania with benevolent compassion. Thomas, his son and heir, who held a three-quarter stake in the proprietary colony, let greed be his guide. Richard Penn, who held the remainder, supported his older brother's administrative decisions. Both had abandoned their father's Quaker faith and joined the Anglican church to smooth their way through English society. Anyone who endangered his income Thomas Penn saw as a threat. He feared Franklin's leadership. Calling him "a dangerous man," Penn said, "I should be very glad he inhabited any other country, as I believe him of a very uneasy spirit."[32]

The Associators drifted apart once the Treaty of Aix-la-Chapelle ended the War of the Austrian Succession, but Franklin remained a local hero. The Association is an important precursor to the American Revolution. Working outside the structure of the British colonial government, the Associators defended the lives and rights of colonial Americans, whose safety was being ignored by those in power.

A report from the Board of Trade Franklin read in 1751 in his capacity as assembly clerk showed him that those in power ignored, nay deliberately undermined, the safety of colonial America. Shockingly, the Lords of Trade had concluded that transporting felons to America contributed to the "improvement and well-peopling of the colonies." Franklin was incensed by their callousness. British administrators neither understood nor sympathized with the American men and women they governed. Subsequent events reinforced Franklin's indignation. A few months after reading this report, he learned about a gory double homicide committed by a transported felon in Maryland, a barbarous act that formed part of a huge wave of violent crime perpetrated by transported felons—robbery, rape, murder—sweeping across Maryland and Pennsylvania.[33]

The Board of Trade report and the ensuing crime wave led to "Rattlesnakes for Felons," a satire Franklin published that May. Signing the article "Americanus," Franklin used a persona identifying with the land where he lived. Since the British were transporting felons to America, colonists should transport rattlesnakes to Great Britain. Franklin quoted the memorable phrase from the Board of Trade, sardonically observing, "Our *mother* knows what is best for us. What is a little *housebreaking, shoplifting,* or *highway robbing;* what is a son now and then *corrupted* and *hang'd,* a daughter *debauch'd* and pox'd, a wife *stabb'd,* a husband's *throat cut,* or a child's *brains beat out* with an axe, compar'd with this 'improvement and well peopling of the colonies!'"[34] In the coming years, Franklin would repeat this phrase in some of his most memorable political satires. It was a continual reminder of the callous insensitivity of the British administrators.

To take a more active role in shaping Pennsylvania's future, Franklin successfully stood for election to the assembly in 1751. Becoming an assemblyman, he vacated the clerk's seat but arranged for William to fill the vacancy.
Franklin's nepotism may be the least attractive aspect of his personality—and
the most inconsistent. His public writings stress the importance of hard work
and self-reliance, but he spoiled his son and, later, his first grandson, doing
whatever he could to help their careers and place them in prestigious
positions.

After the Treaty of Aix-la-Chapelle had ended the War of the Austrian
Succession, Franklin continued to keep abreast of the latest military literature.
No way would he be caught off guard when next the colony was threatened. In
1752, he ordered from Strahan a sizable number of books for the Library
Company, including three military works. Having acquired De Feuquières's
Memoirs for himself, Franklin now ordered a copy for the Library Company.
He also ordered two new works, John Pringle's *Observations on the Diseases of
the Army* and Charles Sackville's *Treatise Concerning the Militia*.[35]

Pringle, the British physician-general during the war, used his experience
as the basis for *Observations on the Diseases of the Army*. Pringle recognized
that hospitals, ironically, were a primary cause of sickness and death in the
army. Pringle's *Observations*, the first scientific account of epidemiology in the
field, explains how to prevent cross-infection. Leeuwenhoek's research contributed to Pringle's thought, helping him see that microscopic bacteria—
"animacula," to use Pringle's term—caused the bloody flux and facilitated its
transmission between soldiers.[36]

Sackville's *Treatise Concerning the Militia* provides a general history of militias going back to ancient Rome and proposes a new plan for a national militia.
Echoing Lord Bolingbroke's concept of a patriot king, Sackville advocated a
monarch who would strengthen Great Britain without regard to party. Though
well intended, his scheme seems like a frightful abuse of power in retrospect.
Sackville narrowed the distinction between the Crown army and the militia,
placing the militia solely under the king's command. He wanted to turn the
militia into a standing army to strengthen the monarchy.[37]

Franklin's burgeoning knowledge of military matters worked well with
other responsibilities, including his work for the post office. Having served as
Philadelphia postmaster since 1737, he now set his sights on the top colonial
job, postmaster general of North America. He solicited Collinson's help and
began campaigning for the position. In 1753, Franklin was named joint postmaster general with Williamsburg printer, newspaper editor, and postmaster
William Hunter.[38]

The following year, soon after Franklin had returned home from his first postal inspection tour with Hunter, a letter from George Washington reached Philadelphia reporting that the French had captured the uncompleted British fort near present-day Pittsburgh and begun erecting Fort Duquesne, which would give them control of the Ohio River and make it easier to attack Pennsylvania's frontier settlements. The French and Indian War, as the American theater of the Seven Years' War would become known, had yet to be declared, but the skirmishes on the Pennsylvania frontier anticipated the conflict.

Franklin knew intercolonial cooperation would provide the best defense. In the May 9, 1754, issue of *The Pennsylvania Gazette*, he published the first newspaper cartoon in the history of American journalism and the earliest symbol of colonial American unity. Another brilliant example of Franklin's mastery of emblems, this cartoon famously depicts a snake cut into parts, each representing a different colonial American region. Its stark motto dramatizes the serpentine device and stresses the urgency of taking action: "Join or die."

The cut-snake cartoon was not the only sign pointing toward colonial American unification. The Albany Conference, held the month after the cartoon appeared, brought Franklin together with delegates from several other colonies. Its purpose was to arrange a common defense of the frontier against

FIGURE 17.1 Benjamin Franklin, *Join or Die* (1754). Library of Congress, Prints and Photographs Division, Washington, DC, LC-USZ62-9701.

French forces and their Indian allies. On the way to the conference, Franklin drafted "The Albany Plan of Union."

Persuading delegates from other American colonies to accept his plan for federation, Franklin was at his best. Imagining Franklin at Albany, H. M. Posnett found his political performance awe-inspiring: "When I picture to myself the greatest statesman of the 18th century at his greatest moment, it is Franklin at Albany in June, 1754, projecting his plan for the defensive union of the American colonies, that takes my fancy as the supreme example of this man's amazing political ability."[39]

After much debate and some revisions, the conference delegates approved Franklin's plan, but the colonial legislatures rejected it, worrying that an American federation would minimize their powers. The Board of Trade also rejected it, fearing a colonial union would spark American independence.

Despite its failure, "The Albany Plan of Union" deserves recognition as the most important design for a colonial federation before "Proposed Articles of Confederation," which Franklin would draft in 1775 while serving in the Second Continental Congress. During the Constitutional Convention in 1787, Franklin, along with many other delegates, recalled the Albany Conference. They recognized that the new federal government was the culmination of a political design that began in June 1754.[40]

The impact of Franklin's Albany Plan extends beyond the boundaries of the United States. Within the British Empire, Posnett was not alone in his appreciation of Franklin's efforts to form a federation. While teaching at the University of Aukland, Posnett befriended Sir George Grey, former colonial governor and premier of New Zealand. Both outdoorsmen, they enjoyed summer mornings together rambling through the wooded headlands of Waiwera just north of Aukland. As they hiked, their talk turned to Benjamin Franklin. Grey agreed with Posnett that Franklin's work at Albany was the "finest example of political foresight known to modern days."[41]

Grey had served as governor of Cape Colony and high commissioner for South Africa in the 1850s, when he sought to create a union reminiscent of Franklin's Albany Plan. Grey wanted to create a South African federation that included the Afrikaner republics of Orange Free State and the Transvaal. The British government, which most certainly did not want a South African federation, recalled Grey upon learning of his plans. After his second term as New Zealand's colonial governor, he returned to London in the late 1860s. Grey sought to implement a new federal plan, this time for the entire British Empire. Inspired by Franklin, Grey became one of the leading voices in the nascent imperial federation movement.[42]

After Franklin became joint postmaster general, he arranged for William to take his position as Philadelphia postmaster. Post office business brought them to Maryland and Virginia in April 1755. They established a new post office in Winchester, Virginia, before proceeding to Frederick, Maryland, the third week of April to meet General Edward Braddock, the new commander of British forces in North America.

Franklin's wilderness journey has gained considerable significance in American cultural history. Having read about Franklin's wartime mission as postmaster, Jack Kerouac recalled it as he followed Franklin's footsteps in *On the Road*: "I thought all the wilderness of America was in the West till the Ghost of the Susquehanna showed me different. No, there is a wilderness in the East. It's the same wilderness Ben Franklin plodded in the oxcart days when he was postmaster. . . . There were not great Arizona spaces for the little man, just the bushy wilderness of eastern Pennsylvania, Maryland, and Virginia, the backroads, the black-tar roads that curve among the mournful rivers like Susquehanna, Monongahela, old Potomac and Monocacy."[43]

Franklin's purpose for meeting Braddock was to discuss the establishment of a military postal service. Braddock had been disappointed with the paltry colonial support he had received so far. Franklin introduced him to Pennsylvania politics, describing the conflict arising from the pacifist Quaker legislators and a governor who could neither think nor act for himself. Franklin promised to supply Braddock with what he needed. In a Herculean effort, he persuaded numerous Pennsylvania farmers to provide wagons and horses for Braddock's march. He also convinced them to drive the wagons but said they would not have to fight. In addition, Franklin personally guaranteed the farmers against loss: a guarantee that would almost ruin him.

As Braddock and his troops neared Fort Duquesne in early July, George Washington, then serving as his aide, warned him that the French fought differently in America than in Europe and recommended they attack Indian-style. Braddock ignored his advice. Washington offered to lead the provincial troops separately. Braddock scorned the offer. On July 9, 1755, General Braddock led the British and colonial troops to slaughter. During the Battle of the Monongahela, as it became known, French troops and their Indian allies ambushed the much larger British force, killing hundreds, including many officers. Braddock was mortally wounded. Washington, who had two horses shot from under him, escaped unwounded and led the survivors to safety.

During Franklin's tenure as an assemblyman, Pennsylvania went through several governors. Their individual names hardly matter. All puppets of the proprietors, the colonial Pennsylvania governors acted under secret instructions forbidding them to approve any bills levying taxes on proprietary lands. The Penns also refused to contribute to other colonial expenses, not even those that materially benefited them, such as Indian treaties.

In November 1755, after the latest governor vetoed the assembly's latest military spending bill, Norris appointed Franklin to a committee to answer the veto. Franklin's report emphasizes that the legislators had done all they could in the face of the Penns' intransigence, which prevented the governor from approving any military spending bills. The legislature had taken every possible step short of violating the rights of Pennsylvania citizens. Concluding the report, Franklin wrote a lofty sentence Americans would quote time and again when faced with balancing national security and civil liberty: "Those who would give up essential liberty, to purchase a little temporary safety, deserve neither liberty nor safety."[44]

After the Battle of the Monongahela, the British troops fled to Philadelphia, leaving the Pennsylvania frontier undefended. Local men established a patchwork of volunteer companies in a haphazard attempt to defend the colony. Franklin knew the colony needed a more thorough and systematic wartime effort. For the time being, he provided military advice to those in the field. Once again, his reading came in handy.

When Franklin shipped fifty muskets to James Read, who was serving as a major of two volunteer companies in Reading, Pennsylvania, he also provided some military advice, recommending large, strong, fierce dogs for patrolling enemy territory. To stop them from running after squirrels and tiring themselves out, their handlers should lead each dog in a slip string. Only when the patrol approached thick woods or other suspicious places should the soldiers let slip the dogs of war: "In case of meeting a party of the enemy, the dogs are then to be all turn'd loose and set on. They will be fresher and fiercer for having been previously confin'd, and will confound the enemy a good deal, and be very serviceable. This was the Spanish method."[45]

Franklin found this tactic in a popular book of pirate adventures, Alexandre Olivier Exquemelin's *History of the Bucaniers*. Exquemelin related the difficulties the Spanish colonists on Tortuga had against the native islanders. Upon fleeing into the wilderness, the natives were safe from enemy pursuit. The colonists wrote to Spain and requested dogs, which arrived in vast numbers. The dogs, mainly mastiffs, let them locate the natives "in the most solitary and intricate thickets, whereby they forc'd them to leave their old sanctuaries, and to submit to a most cruel sword." The slip string is Franklin's improvement on the Spanish method, which did not provide an effective way to control the dogs.[46]

Franklin drafted a bill to establish a voluntary militia. The assembly passed the bill, and the governor approved it, thus giving this new militia legal standing, unlike the earlier Association. But like the Association, the new militia was based on democratic principles, letting the militiamen elect their leaders.

Before the new militia was organized, the latest Indian attack demanded swift action. A Shawnee war party had attacked Gnadenhütten, a Moravian mission village 75 miles northwest of Philadelphia whose name means "huts of grace." The Shawnee killed everyone who could not escape into the woods and torched the village. On January 5, 1756, the governor appointed Franklin military and civilian commander of the Pennsylvania frontier. Franklin arranged for William to serve as his aide. Together, they led 500 troops into the wilderness.

Despite Gnadenhütten's proximity to Philadelphia, its story deserves recognition as a classic tale of the American West. Situated on the opposite side of Lehigh Gap, Gnadenhütten's strategic location gave the French and Indian forces a stronghold from which to launch attacks. Lehigh Gap—a narrow passage through the Blue Mountains—provided a dramatic setting that established a standard motif in stories of the West. Rocks overhung the road on either side, letting a small party inflict massive casualties onto any who dared ascend the pass. On January 10, 1756, William Franklin led the Pennsylvania troops through the gap unscathed.

Entering Gnadenhütten, they encountered a gruesome scene of unimaginable horror. The once bustling village was now silent. The houses lining its streets were in ruins, set aflame and reduced to ashes and rubble. The inhabitants who had been unable to escape into the surrounding woods—men, women, and children—had been butchered in a shocking manner, their mangled bodies left in the streets, carrion to be devoured by the beasts of prey that emerged from the Pennsylvania wilderness and sniffed their way into town.[47]

Overcoming the feelings of revulsion at the sight of such carnage, Benjamin Franklin and his men solemnly buried the dead. They also built a stockade, thus giving hope to the survivors, who trickled back from their hiding places in the woods. Perhaps the instructions and illustrations in Moxon's *Epitome* helped Franklin design this fort. One of Lindsay's manuscript works also taught him about the subject, *A Short Treatise of Fortification and Geometry*.[48] After Franklin secured the village, the governor unexpectedly recalled the Pennsylvania Assembly. Leaving an experienced officer in charge, Benjamin and William Franklin returned to Philadelphia.

Franklin's work for the Pennsylvania Assembly required much time, but he also devoted considerable effort organizing the new militia. When the company officers had elected him colonel in February, he accepted the command. Colonel Franklin did not serve for long. The Privy Council soon disallowed the militia bill, considering it too democratic.

Before the Privy Council quashed the Pennsylvania militia, Franklin had to travel to Virginia on post office business. The officers of his regiment decided to escort him out of town. Just as he was mounting his horse, thirty or forty mounted men in uniform surprised Franklin. As they accompanied him, they drew their swords and rode with naked swords all the way out of town. When Thomas Penn heard about the episode, he had a fit. No one had ever given him a parade.

In 1756, a new governor arrived. Same as the old one, the new governor refused to approve any taxes on proprietary lands. No matter that all the other Pennsylvania landowners paid their fair share of taxes. No matter that a war was under way and the colony's back settlements were being attacked. In January 1757, the governor vetoed the assembly's latest bill to finance the war because it taxed the proprietors' estates. The assembly prepared a remonstrance, and the assemblymen marched en masse through the streets of Philadelphia on Thursday, January 27th, to deliver it to the governor.[49]

To no one's surprise, the governor rejected the remonstrance. The Pennsylvania Assembly had had enough. That Friday, it resolved that two members go to London on its behalf. On Saturday, the assembly decided which two: Isaac Norris and Benjamin Franklin. Norris's poor health stopped him from making the trip, but Franklin agreed to do whatever his fellow lawmakers resolved. He was ready to go anytime, anywhere. In anticipation, he wrote Strahan, "Our assembly talk of sending me to England speedily. Then look out sharp, and if a fat old fellow should come to your printing house and request a little smouting, depend upon it 'tis your affectionate friend and humble servant B Franklin."[50]

The military books Franklin read during the period between the War of Jenkins' Ear and the Seven Years' War gave him vital knowledge to use in his role as a leader of the Pennsylvania militia, but Franklin would fight his greatest battles in the political arena. Thomas Penn had resented Franklin's leadership in Pennsylvania. The two would now go head to head. But Franklin had to reach London first. While the Seven Years' War raged, crossing the Atlantic remained a dangerous endeavor. The speedy packet boats had reduced the time between New York and Falmouth, a port on the Cornish coast, to less than thirty days, but solo vessels were moving targets for French warships and privateers. Before Franklin could challenge Thomas Penn, he had to run the gauntlet of the North Atlantic.

18

An American Intellectual in London

AFTER COUNTLESS DELAYS, Franklin finally sailed from Sandy Hook on June 20, 1757. Aware that his diplomatic mission would take several months at least, he had hoped to bring the whole family, but Deborah was deathly afraid of crossing the ocean. She would stay home with Sally, now 13, manage their business affairs, and oversee the post office, updating her husband by correspondence. Historians have treated Deborah harshly, misinterpreting her poor spelling as a lack of intelligence. John Bartram and Nicholas Scull were both bad spellers, but history has not treated them with the venom and vitriol dished out to Deborah. She deserves more credit. The responsibilities she undertook in Franklin's absence testify to her strong character and powerful decision-making abilities.

William Franklin, now in his mid-twenties, would accompany his father. Going to London to defend the rights of the Pennsylvanians, Franklin, paradoxically, brought two slaves with him. Peter would serve as a personal servant for him; King would serve William in a similar capacity. Only 11 or 12 years old, King was young for a manservant. Peter's age is unknown; presumably, he was around the same age. Benjamin Franklin did write a new will before leaving Philadelphia, which would free Peter's parents, Peter and Jemima, upon his death. Franklin's broad-minded contacts in London would help enlighten his perspective on the problem of slavery.[1]

Reaching Falmouth on July 17th, they faced a 300-mile overland trek that almost seems like a journey through time. Their stop at Stonehenge took them back to the prehistoric era, and Wilton House let them experience the glory that was Greece and the grandeur that was Rome. A preeminent example of English Palladianism, this quadrangular mansion housed an impressive collection of ancient statuary and paintings.[2]

A symbol of heroic determination, Hercules appeared more often than any other figure inside Wilton House. A colossal statue in the Great Hall gave Hercules an air of satisfaction after taking the apples from the Hesperides.

FIGURE 18.1 Joseph Andrews, *Mrs. Franklin* (Boston: Tappan and Dennet, 1840–1845). Library of Congress Prints and Photographs Division, Washington, DC, LC-DIG-ds-09831.

A nearby sarcophagus showed him turning the river Achelous, represented as an old man with snake-like legs. In the billiard room, one statue depicted Hercules killing the serpents sent to destroy him in his cradle. Another showed him wrestling with Antaeus, whom he raises from the ground to sap his strength.

The Franklin party reached London the last week of July. They found permanent lodgings at a boarding house on Craven Street with plenty of room for Franklin, his son, Peter, and King. The house even had a spacious backyard. Stretching between the Thames and the Strand just east of Charing Cross, Craven Street was within easy walking distance of Whitehall and the Houses of Parliament. Margaret Stevenson, the widow who ran the boarding house, was about the same age as Franklin, and they got along well. He also befriended her daughter Mary, nicknamed Polly. Tall and slender, Polly Stevenson looked as if she had stepped from a painting by Jan van Eyck. She loved discussing literature and science with her mother's distinguished American boarder.

While living in the country to nurse a wealthy aunt, Polly corresponded with Franklin. Her insatiable curiosity encouraged him to teach her the sciences. Franklin's letters to her are among the finest he ever wrote. He occasionally sent books to aid her scientific studies. One time, he sent the early volumes of Noël Pluche's *Spectacle de la nature*. He recommended reading with pen in hand to transcribe attention-grabbing details, which would help her remember what she read.[3]

Their correspondence resembles a scientific primer. Some contemporary textbooks for female readers are structured as dialogues. Consider John Harris's *Astronomical Dialogues between a Gentleman and a Lady*, a work the Library Company had on its shelves.[4] Within their correspondence, Benjamin Franklin and Polly Stevenson resemble Harris's gentleman and lady. Their correspondence could be published as an introductory scientific text. In fact, Franklin would include eight letters to her with other miscellaneous scientific correspondence in the fourth edition of *Experiments and Observations on Electricity*.[5]

In one letter, Franklin discusses a wintertime experiment he performed to test how color absorbed light. He took little squares of broadcloth from a tailor's sample—black, purple, dark blue, light blue, green, yellow, red, and white—and placed them on the snow one sunny morning. After a few hours, the white square still rested atop the snow, but the others had sunk to different depths, the black square sinking deepest. Drawing some conclusions from this experiment, Franklin suggested several uses for different-colored clothing from the Arctic to the tropics. Beyond its practical applications, this experiment forms a striking visual composition. Robert Rauschenberg found Franklin's multicolored experiment one of the most beautiful exercises he had ever encountered. Rauschenberg's postmodern collages often echo Franklin's inventive experiment.[6]

Franklin liked Polly so much he hoped she and his son would marry. But William Franklin ignored her intellectual accomplishments and sought a match to help him rise in colonial British society. Before he found a suitable woman to marry, a casual dalliance resulted in an unplanned pregnancy. Born in 1760, William Temple Franklin was named after the letter-writing English diplomat. Aware an illegitimate son would hinder his marriage prospects, William Franklin refused to raise the boy and placed Temple with a foster mother.

The detailed accounts Franklin kept during their early months in London show where they went and what they spent. He immersed himself in London's world of books. One of the earliest establishments he patronized was also one of the closest. At the corner of Craven and the Strand, Josiah Graham's book-shop welcomed Franklin inside on August 1st. He often returned, buying sta-tionery and newspapers and making use of Graham's bookbinding skill.[7]

Franklin planned to complain to the British government about the Penns. Dr. John Fothergill said he should appeal directly to the proprietors, who might be willing to settle their differences with the Pennsylvania Assembly without fuss or publicity. Unsure of Fothergill's advice, Franklin consulted Peter Collinson, who recommended first contacting Lord Granville, presi-dent of the Privy Council. Franklin took Collinson's advice and went to Whitehall to meet Granville, who told him that the king's instructions to colonial governors are "the *law of the land*; for the king is the legislator of the colonies."

"I told his lordship," Franklin wrote as he recalled the episode, "this was new doctrine to me."[8]

FIGURE 18.2 James McArdell, after a painting by Benjamin Wilson, *B. Franklin of Philadelphia - L.L.D. F.R.S.* (1761). Library of Congress, Prints and Photographs Division, Washington, DC, LC-DIG-pga-11573.

The meeting with Granville represents a moment of growth for Franklin. He came to London convinced the Penns were responsible for the colony's problems, but Granville showed him that leaders in the British government did not understand who the Americans were, what the colonies represented, or how they contributed to the British Empire. Franklin realized that his work as London agent for the Pennsylvania Assembly would require him to assume a much larger role. He became a propagandist for the colonies, taking responsibility to educate the British public about America.

After seeing Granville, Franklin reverted to Fothergill's advice. Later that month, he went to Thomas Penn's Spring Garden mansion to meet him and his younger brother Richard. Thomas Penn looked much older than he had when Franklin first met him in Philadelphia two decades earlier. As they began their discussion, Franklin said something about himself and his mission on behalf of the Pennsylvania Assembly, but Penn already knew who he was and why he had come.

"You're an errand boy sent by Quaker merchants to collect a bill." Well, perhaps Penn did not use these exact words, but he said something to their effect. He obviously could not mask his contempt for the assembly or its messenger. Afterward, Franklin wrote that both sides declared themselves open to reasonable accommodation but, upon reflection, added, "I suppose each party had its own ideas of what should be meant by *reasonable*."[9]

Though the conniving proprietors refused to change their position, relinquish their power, or pay their taxes, the Penns devised a strategy for handling the shrewd man the assembly had sent across the Atlantic. As they spoke with Franklin, Thomas and Richard Penn gave him the impression that he might sway them. They said that if he submitted his complaints in writing, they would consider the document.

Using the legislative committee's report to the Pennsylvania Assembly, Franklin drafted what is now known as "Heads of Complaint." Upon receiving it, the Penns forwarded the document to their attorney, Ferdinando John Paris. Having corresponded with him while assembly clerk, Franklin understood Paris well. Pride and anger were his defining traits. Paris would never agree to anything Franklin said on the assembly's behalf.[10]

Refusing to deal with Paris, Franklin insisted on direct talks with the Penns. They, too, were aware of Paris's unscrupulous legal strategy; they counted on it. Paris recommended forwarding "Heads of Complaint" to the attorney general: a sure way to slow negotiations even further. While pretending to consider "Heads of Complaint," the proprietors let Franklin stew in his own juices. He could tell their answer would take a long, long time.[11]

Awaiting their decision, Franklin began enjoying London's intellectual and cultural life and started befriending its leading scientists and poets. While he was feeling chipper as you please, serious illness brought him to his knees. "Heads of Complaint" gave way to complaints of the head, and Dr. Fothergill went from political advisor to personal physician. Tension, pressure, pain: Franklin's headaches would persist for two months. Some were so severe they made him dizzy.[12]

Fothergill cautioned Franklin against overexertion, forbidding him from strenuous activity and denying him the use of pen and paper: torture for any writer. To relieve his pain, Fothergill arranged for him to be cupped on the back of his head. Considering Franklin's diagnostic ability and extensive knowledge of medical literature, Fothergill let him decide the procedure's frequency.

Cupping involved placing small heated cups onto the patient's skin. As the cups cooled, each would create a vacuum that would supposedly alleviate the pain. Though practitioners championed its curative powers, some people joked about cupping. William Congreve described a beau in a bagnio, who cupped for his complexion and sweated for his shape. In Franklin's London, the Royal Bagnio had itinerant practitioners who cupped people in their homes.[13]

Cupping is related to the humoral theory of medical treatment, which Franklin never fully abandoned. He even acknowledged the therapeutic power of some of the bizarre cures designed to rebalance the humors. He told Polly Stevenson that thousands of people owed their lives to "Spanish fly," but he did acknowledge that, like any medicine, Spanish fly could be harmful if applied indiscriminately.[14]

Not to be confused with Spanish flea, Spanish fly was a medicinal powder made from an emerald green beetle, *Lytta vesicatoria*. Containing a strong irritant, this beetle would be dried and crushed into a powder also known as cantharides. Spanish fly would be mixed with lard to form a paste. In the proverb the fly spoils the ointment, but in medical practice the fly is the ointment. Applying Spanish fly to the patient's skin, the physician would leave the ointment there until it raised blisters, which would be popped to release the pus and, in theory, rebalance the humors. More likely it would create infection, which was not well understood in Franklin's day.

Visiting his friend Lord Cardross one day, Franklin found him suffering from a fever and about to undergo a blister over his entire back at the hands of his physician. A blister, especially one so extensive, hardly seemed like an appropriate cure for fever. A couple of glasses of cold water and a good night's sleep would be better therapy. Franklin could not see why his friend used

Spanish fly; perhaps he would die. Stopping the treatment, he may have saved his lordship's life.[15]

Feeling better in October, Franklin went out one day to take care of some business on the assembly's behalf and do a little shopping. He stopped at a bookshop, where he caught up with the news. Though he read the London papers regularly, Franklin received more detailed news through the latest pamphlets. His library catalogue lists hundreds of pamphlets, but his account books record few by title. When he acquired most is unknown. Given their topical nature, he presumably obtained the pamphlets as they were published.

Franklin continued to follow the war. During the second week of October, he bought *A Genuine Account of the Late Grand Expedition to the Coast of France*, which relates the British navy's secret attempt to capture the French port of Rochefort. Its author identified himself as a "Volunteer in the Said Expedition." *The Monthly Review* concluded that a gentleman had written the pamphlet, "the language flowing in an easy and lively strain, with nothing of the *fumet* of authorism about it."[16]

The previous month the British captured Île d'Aix, intending to use this offshore island to attack Rochefort, but the water between the island and the French coast was too shallow; ships could not get close enough to bombard the coastal fort. The British abandoned the poorly conceived operation. Volunteer exclaimed, "Henceforth, adieu to all secret expeditions! I will put off my military garb, and retire to the Sabine farm of my forefathers, fully determined neither to converse with a politician, nor to read another newspaper so long as I live."[17]

Volunteer was not the only critic of the Rochefort expedition. Franklin would continue to follow the controversy as it unfolded. Admiral Charles Knowles, second in command of the expedition, spoke up to defend himself. Franklin obtained a copy of his defense, *The Conduct of Admiral Knowles on the Late Expedition Set in a True Light*. Knowles comes off well in his personal narrative: dignified, responsible, conscientious.[18]

Franklin's health recovered by late November, letting him explore London with renewed gusto. He could visit several bookshops within a mile of Mrs. Stevenson's. East of Craven Street, Paul Vaillant's shop stood on the Strand opposite Southampton Street. Vaillant's had long been the best shop in London for imported French books, but other London booksellers were venturing into the field. Further east on the Strand, John Nourse's shop at the Sign of the Lamb was more appealing. Franklin went elsewhere to have some books bound in vellum; he went to the Sign of the Lamb for scientific books. A prominent man of science, Nourse stocked an excellent collection of mathematical treatises and also imported French books.

Before leaving Philadelphia, Franklin had encouraged Sally to study French. One of her first written efforts in the language—a letter to her father—was disappointing, not because it was filled with mistakes, but because it was not. Franklin could tell that her French master was helping Sally too much. He preferred she do her own work and learn from her mistakes. One day, Franklin stopped by the shops of both Vaillant and Nourse, picked up some books and pamphlets for himself, and bought one book for her, a French edition of *Pamela*. Sally knew Richardson's novel in English from the edition her father had published. By rereading a familiar work in an unfamiliar tongue, she might have an easier time learning the language.[19]

Franklin's library catalogue indicates what other subjects caught his eye in 1757. Though he bought *Pamela* for Sally, he seldom bought novels for himself. Current events meant more to him than recent fiction. He obtained pamphlets on numerous political and economic issues: coinage, the leather trade, military financing, monetary policy, mortality, population, taxation, and the war.

His son's literary tastes did run toward current fiction. During their first year in London, William Franklin subscribed to *The Brothers*, Susan Smythies's sentimental novel of social intrigue about a man trying to seduce a young woman who continues his devious seduction even after learning she is his half-brother's daughter. Few books better illustrate the clash between what William Franklin wanted to read and what his father wanted him to read. Smythies's seduction novel is a far cry from the scholarly French edition of Polybius.[20]

In 1757, Edmund Burke published the second edition of his first book, *A Vindication of Natural Society*, which Franklin added to his growing London library. Burke's *Vindication* satirized Lord Bolingbroke. Some readers did not get Burke's satire. Franklin did. His own satirical writings have much in common with Burke's. *A Vindication of Natural Society* anticipates Franklin's parody of the British government before the Revolutionary War, "Rules by Which a Great Empire May Be Reduced to a Small One." Burke's *Vindication* and Franklin's "Rules" both indicate authors who had mastered logical irony. H. M. Posnett returned to superlatives to characterize Franklin's satire, calling it "perhaps the most condensed and truthtelling piece of irony ever written."[21]

Before the year ended, Franklin had made several friends among the fellows of the Royal Society, including Dr. John Pringle. One dark December night, he took a coach to Pringle's home, where chess was usually on the evening's agenda. The two proved to be worthy opponents. Toward the end of one match, Pringle started taking Franklin's pulse and his own. He discovered that their pulses rapidly increased as a match neared completion. Franklin's passion for chess reflects his fiercely competitive nature. Seeking an edge over Pringle, he soon bought a chess handbook by Philidor, a legendary French champion.[22]

Franklin acquired his new chess manual at Thomas Osborne's shop in Gray's Inn. He preferred buying books from his friend William Strahan, but Franklin went to Osborne's because Isaac Norris had seen some books on husbandry and gardening listed in one of Osborne's sale catalogues and asked Franklin to obtain them. Franklin loved shopping for books so much he was happy to help Philadelphia friends improve their libraries. Writing from London, he told Junto member Hugh Roberts, "Send your orders for buying books as soon as you please."[23]

Osborne had a shifty reputation among colonial American bookmen. He considered the colonies a good place to dump inferior books and sent to New York or Philadelphia otherwise unsaleable merchandise.[24] Osborne's London reputation was no better. Pope made him the loser of a pissing contest in *The Dunciad*. After a futile first attempt, Osborne tries again and accidentally sprays himself in the face:

> A second effort brought but new disgrace,
> The wild Meander wash'd the artist's face:
> Thus the small jett, which hasty hands unlock,
> Spirts in the gard'ner's eyes who turns the cock.[25]

Despite Osborne's unsavory reputation, Franklin got along well with him. One time, Osborne told Franklin about William Smith's latest plot to destroy him. Not content to muscle Franklin out of the Philadelphia Academy and undermine his personal and political reputation, Smith now sought to ruin his business. He asked Osborne to ship a large cargo of books to Philadelphia. Smith planned to sell them at reduced rates, thus undercutting David Hall's retail trade and driving Franklin and Hall out of business. Once Franklin told him about Smith's history of underhanded double-dealing, Osborne refused to have anything more to do with the conniving Smith.[26]

The Franklins had reached London during a propitious moment in the history of printing, around the time John Baskerville was implementing the new typeface he had designed. Baskerville's subscription proposal for a new edition of Virgil had reached Philadelphia before Franklin left. Subscribing for six copies, he revealed his confidence in Baskerville's publishing venture. Franklin knew they would make excellent gifts. Not only did Baskerville design a typeface that was a treat for the eyes, he also developed better-quality ink, manufactured high-quality wove paper, and invented a process to glaze the paper, using all these new techniques for his Virgil. Soon after reaching London, Franklin received his copies and had Graham cover them in luxurious but sturdy bindings.[27]

Several people whom Franklin befriended in London shared his love of books. He would join two supper clubs. The Monday Club, which gathered at the George and Vulture, included some scientifically inclined gentlemen. Besides Thomas Collinson, the members of Franklin's Monday Club included John Ellicott, a professional watchmaker and amateur astronomer; and Ingham Foster, an ironmonger with a fine personal library and a fossil-filled cabinet of curiosities.[28]

Since Thomas Collinson also subscribed to Baskerville's Virgil, this handsome edition made an ideal topic for Monday night suppertime conversation. Collinson would assemble a huge personal library reflecting his scientific interests and critical judgment. He spoke in an animated and energetic manner, and his knowledge of books contributed to his conversational skill. Collinson's prodigious memory let him recall anecdotes appropriate to practically any topic, an ability he and Franklin shared.[29]

The Club of Honest Whigs, Franklin's retrospective name for the Thursday Club, first met at St. Paul's Coffeehouse but later switched to the London Coffeehouse, Ludgate Hill. Its members included political thinkers, scientists, and dissenting ministers: James Burgh, John Canton, John Densham, Philip Furneaux, Andrew Kippis, Richard Price, Joseph Priestley, Abraham Rees, William Rose, and others. Since Furneaux subscribed to Baskerville's Virgil, the book could have entered the Thursday night table talk. Furneaux was a booklover without a bookish manner. When it came to his favorite topics, he spoke with passion and excitement.[30]

James Boswell, who also joined the Thursday Club, found its conversation formal, yet furious. A great gourmand, Boswell recorded what they ate and drank: Welsh rabbit, apple-puffs, porter, and beer. Josiah Quincy, Jr. clarified what Boswell meant by formal conversation. A young Bostonian who attended the club while visiting London, Quincy recorded one evening's topic of conversation in his diary: "A question was debated by assignment whether capital punishments are in every case warrantable." Quincy did not record their debate, but Franklin's correspondence offers an approximation.

After reading Martin Madan's *Thoughts on Executive Justice*, Franklin wondered, "To put a man to death for an offense which does not deserve death, is it not murder?" Quincy's diary entry does show that the Thursday Club, like the Junto, planned its conversation topics in advance. The preplanning did not prevent heated conversation, as Boswell suggested, but it did give their discussions some structure.[31]

Not all their conversation was formal. Rees, who called Franklin "the life of the club," remembered discussing the Royal Society's latest research, and Densham mentioned the "good sense [Franklin] genteelly treats us with at the club." Franklin's air-bath was another topic of conversation. He boasted that every morning he would rise and pass half an hour in the nude reading or writing. Sometimes he would return to bed afterward for another hour or two of sweet and restful sleep.[32]

Kippis contributed much to the Thursday night conversations at St. Paul's Coffeehouse. Well read and quick-witted, he could discuss any subject in an instant. Religious toleration was one interest Franklin and the dissenting ministers shared. One night the conversation turned to John Abernathy, the Irish Presbyterian divine who tirelessly defended the civil rights of dissenters. Franklin, it turned out, owned a manuscript about Abernathy's efforts to emancipate Irish dissenters from the Test Act, which banned dissenters from holding public office. Kippis later recalled, "I remember to have read some years ago, a curious manuscript narration of the proceedings in this whole affair, which was then in the hands of Dr. Benjamin Franklin. I know not from whence the Doctor had it, nor whether he carried it with him to America, or left it behind him in England."[33]

The Thursday Club brought Franklin in contact with many other figures in London's literary world. Club membership and Ralph Griffiths's circle—men who wrote for *The Monthly Review*—overlapped significantly. Griffiths had founded his magazine in 1749, and it became known for its critical acumen and Whiggish principles. Club members who contributed to *The Monthly Review* include Furneaux, Kippis, Price, Rees, and Rose.[34]

Reading *The Monthly Review* regularly, Franklin became familiar with William Bewley's contributions to it. A surgeon apothecary, Bewley spent most of his life in Great Massingham, a village in Norfolk. His articles in *The Monthly Review* attracted Priestley's attention, and the two developed an extensive correspondence. Bewley also contributed to his scientific research. He called himself Priestley's "satellite," but Bewley need not have been so modest. He excelled at so many scientific fields—anatomy, chemistry, electricity, pharmacology—that he became known as the "Philosopher of

Massingham."[35] His areas of expertise also included literary criticism. Bewley wrote over 400 essays for *The Monthly Review*. He was a careful reader with the capacity for discerning a book's finest features and summarizing them with wit and precision.

Legal writer Owen Ruffhead, another contributor who befriended Franklin, gave him a copy of his book about public welfare, *A Digest of the Poor Laws*. Ruffhead's presentation copy came with a caveat. He wanted Franklin's advice on the subject. Suspicious of welfare fraud, Franklin told Ruffhead that every parish in Britain should print an annual report of each disbursement and each receipt of its officers to hold both the poor and the officers accountable.[36]

Franklin's correspondence reveals what happened to his extra copies of Baskerville's Virgil. He donated one to Harvard. His cover letter calls Baskerville's Virgil the "most curiously printed of any book hitherto done in the world." Franklin sent others home for Deborah to disperse. A close friend of the family by now, Charles Thomson visited her to get one. Thomson enjoyed Baskerville's elegant font: the perfect excuse to reread Virgil.[37]

Having intended to subscribe to Baskerville's Virgil, Isaac Norris had forgotten to send his subscription fee, an understandable oversight given his weighty legislative responsibilities. Norris was happy to receive Franklin's gift. He liked it so much he wanted more examples of Baskerville's work. Norris asked Franklin if Baskerville published other classical authors in the same font, so he could purchase them and thus encourage Baskerville's work.[38]

Baskerville was planning a two-volume edition of John Milton's poetry. He circulated his proposal throughout Britain and the colonies. Franklin subscribed to it. So did Abram Taylor. After receiving Norris's thank-you letter, Franklin added his name to the list of subscribers for Baskerville's Milton, which also includes three of Franklin's London clubmates: Collinson, Foster, and Furneaux.[39]

Another familiar name appears among Baskerville's subscribers: Thomas Penn. Franklin had known about Penn's bookish interests for years. When Penn was living in Philadelphia during the 1730s, Franklin printed a thousand copies of his armorial bookplate.[40] An interest in fine printing was about all Franklin and Penn shared. Having resumed their talks after recovering from his illness, Franklin visited Penn's Spring Garden mansion several times. His meetings with Thomas and Richard Penn came to a head on Saturday, January 14, 1758.

Franklin told them that their father's charter gave the Pennsylvania Assembly "all the power and privileges of an assembly according to the rights of the freeborn subjects of England." Thomas Penn said that whatever his father said did not matter. The only rights the Pennsylvanians had were those the royal charter stipulated. If people who emigrated to Pennsylvania misunderstood his father, then it was their own fault. Recording what Thomas Penn said, Franklin captured his tone, saying he spoke it with "a kind of triumphing laughing insolence, such as a low jockey might do when a purchaser complained that he had cheated him in a horse." Franklin was shocked to see how readily Thomas Penn sacrificed his father's reputation. At that moment, Franklin told Norris he felt more contempt toward Thomas Penn than any man living. But he held his tongue, a personal strategy Franklin would apply whenever he felt himself "getting warm."[41]

British intellectual life continued to compensate Franklin for political disappointment. In May, he and William visited Cambridge. Franklin joined Professor John Hadley's experiments on the phenomenon of evaporation. He and his son stayed a week, met many leading academics, and took advantage of what Cambridge had to offer. Their hosts enjoyed the Franklins so much they invited them back to attend commencement in July.

Benjamin Franklin's first trip to Cambridge did him a world of good, improving his health and his spirits. He agreed to return for commencement, after which he would embark on a longer journey. The road trip would not detract from his official business because nearly everyone who could help his cause left town for the summer. The Franklins attended the Cambridge commencement exercises; ate in the dining halls; and met the chancellor, the vice chancellor, and the college deans. Though his electrical research had made him one of the world's leading scientists, this Philadelphia tradesman was nonetheless astonished to find himself rubbing elbows with berobed dons.

Once the commencement exercises ended, Benjamin, William, and Peter traveled through Northamptonshire, visiting many Franklin relatives. Peter's easygoing nature and capacity for hard work had convinced the Franklins to bring him along on the trip. King had become so mischievous, they left him with Margaret Stevenson. He took advantage of their absence and ran away. At Ecton, the Franklins' trip became a tombstone tour. They met the local rector and his wife, who escorted them to the churchyard. Covered with moss, the Franklin gravestones were illegible. Obtaining a basin of water and a hard-bristled brush, Peter scrubbed them clean, enabling William to copy their inscriptions.[42]

This trip is the one that took Franklin to Warwick. He told Deborah they went there to see the castle of Guy of Warwick. Many contemporary travelers took the same trip. The townspeople were proud of their local hero and showed off relics associated with him: staff, helmet, two-handled sword. The tour sometimes included the cave where Guy of Warwick supposedly spent his last years and the nearby chapel where he was buried.[43]

Warwick, though the only destination on this trip without family associations, did let Franklin indulge his nostalgia by visiting the home of a boyhood hero. Other destinations helped him reconstruct his family heritage. Being the most prominent member of his extended family, Franklin took responsibility for compiling its history and gathering pertinent relics. Thomas Haslam labeled him the "de facto *pater familias*."[44]

Nostalgia and the search for family motivated Franklin's behavior in the Midlands. His travel correspondence does not mention shopping for books, but one surviving volume from his library shows that he did. His copy of Daniel Neal's *History of New-England* is adorned with the armorial bookplate of the Reverend Stephen Langham, the rector of Cottesbrooke in Northamptonshire, who had died a couple of years earlier and whose library had since gone up for sale. Franklin bought his copy, the first edition of Neal's *History*, and thus acquired a book describing the Boston of his boyhood.[45]

Another book Franklin added to his personal library around this time he had known since his apprenticeship: Cotton Mather's *Magnalia christi americana*. Inside its back cover, Franklin scribbled some notes from the text. One concerns his grandfather Peter Folger, who had taught the native islanders of Martha's Vineyard how to read. Franklin's attention to Mather's *Magnalia* is consistent with his other activities during this tombstone tour. He reread Mather as part of his genealogical research.[46]

William Douglass's *Summary, Historical and Political, of the First Planting, Progressive Improvements, and Present State of the British Settlements in North-America* was another volume of American history Franklin added to his London library. Having published the work in parts, upon his death in 1752, Douglass left unfinished *British Settlements in North-America*, as its title is best abbreviated. London publishers recognized the book's potential and reissued it in 1755. The London edition sold well enough to require another one in 1760. Franklin had the 1755 edition in his London library and also acquired a copy of the 1760 edition.[47]

The defining stylistic feature of Douglass's history is the digression. Some may interpret his digressions as a failure to focus, but he consciously shaped *British Settlements in North-America* as a literary work. Douglass savored his digressions, which are purposeful as well as intentional. His attitude adumbrates Laurence Sterne's famous exclamation in *Tristram Shandy*: "Digressions, incontestably, are the sunshine: they are the life, the soul of reading!"[48]

Given Douglass's digressions, Franklin's friend William Rose observed that reading *British Settlements in North-America* "requires a very considerable share of patience." Rose found Douglass's critical outlook quite refreshing: "The author appears to be a man of sound judgment, and extensive knowledge; he delivers his sentiments of persons and things with a blunt freedom, which is not always disagreeable; an air of integrity appears through the whole of his work."[49]

Franklin shared Rose's opinion. He, too, liked Douglass's bluntness and recognized his ingenuity. Franklin also enjoyed Douglass's memorable figures of speech. In his own writings, he recalls what Douglass said about British military officers stationed in New York. French officers successfully recruited Native Americans to fight on their side partly by instructing them in the European art of war. The British officers of all four independent companies of fusiliers in New York made no such effort. Instead, Douglass observed, they "lived like military monks in idleness and luxury." Appreciating Douglass's observation, Franklin repeated his simile and extended his argument.[50]

British Settlements in North-America, in Franklin's words, was the "most complete work on the British colonies in North America." Though Franklin knew its author personally, his acquisition of Douglass's history, unlike his acquisition of Neal's, was motivated less by nostalgia and more by practical considerations. Living in London and serving as a colonial agent, Franklin needed as much information about America as he could get.

From his first conference with Lord Granville in 1757 through his meetings with many other British officials over the next two years, Franklin reached the same conclusion from personal experience that Douglass had reached by reading: The British knew little about America. Franklin embarked on a publicity campaign, contributing numerous articles to the London press, starting with "A Defense of the Americans," a rousing celebration of the American character he wrote for *The London Chronicle* in 1759. This essay refutes two articles in the *Chronicle* impugning the courage and intellect of the colonists. Franklin informed readers that America enjoyed widespread literacy and refuted the cliché about the cultural lag between the Old World and the New. There was no cultural lag. The latest London publications reached the colonies in a matter of weeks, not years.

One of the earlier *Chronicle* contributors was an army officer who championed the bravery and professionalism of British soldiers over provincial troops. Franklin cited examples of colonial soldiers who had acquitted themselves with skill and bravery and, conversely, of craven British soldiers. During the Battle of the Monongahela, the Indians had thrown Braddock's redcoats into a panic. In their confusion, the British regulars had shot one another and fled a much smaller force, abandoning their guns and ammunition.[51]

Other books in Franklin's London library show him following events in Philadelphia. He acquired William Smith's 1759 collection of occasional sermons, *Discourses on Several Public Occasions during the War in America*. When serving as college provost, Smith's animosity toward Franklin and support of the proprietors had become more blatant. Deborah wrote her husband about further disturbances at the college. Privately, Franklin blamed himself for recruiting Smith and admitted that he had not seen through the power-hungry provost until it was too late.[52]

Franklin kept thinking about Smith. Three years after *Discourses on Several Public Occasions*, William Whitehead published *A Charge to Poets*. Using his authority as Great Britain's poet laureate, Whitehead gave would-be poets some words of wisdom. Do not confuse what an author says with who an author is: "Avoid all authors, 'Till you've read the man." After this line comes a ten-line elaboration. The passage reminded Franklin of Smith so much that he took down his copy of Smith's *Discourses* and transcribed all ten lines from *A Charge to Poets* onto its flyleaf. Franklin's transcription begins:

> Full many a peevish, envious, slanderous elf
> Is, in his works, Benevolence itself
> For all mankind, unknown, his bosom heaves,
> He only injures those with whom he lives.[53]

When Smith was back in London in 1763 and Franklin was in Philadelphia, Polly Stevenson wrote to inform her friend that Smith was badmouthing him. Franklin was unsurprised. In response, Franklin sent Polly the same ten lines from Whitehead, emphasizing the adjectives "peevish," "envious," and "slanderous."[54]

Read against what Franklin says in his correspondence, his excerpt from *A Charge to Poets* becomes an admonition to himself. Having first encountered Smith as the author of *The College of Mirania*, he judged him by his writing and missed the schemer behind the screed. Franklin's lapse in judgment threatened the very existence of the college he had founded.

The second week of August 1759, Benjamin and William left London on holiday, bringing Peter with them again. Around September 1st, they reached Edinburgh, staying for two weeks before taking a loop through Scotland. They visited the University of St. Andrews, which earlier that year had awarded Franklin an honorary doctorate of law in absentia. The degree prompted "B. Franklin, Printer" to start calling himself "Dr. Franklin."

When Franklin returned to London from Scotland, the Seven Years' War was waning. News of both the British victory on the Plains of Abraham on September 13th and the subsequent capitulation of Quebec reached London the following month. People began debating possible peace terms. Should Britain keep Canada, or should it keep Guadeloupe, a rich, sugar-producing island in the West Indies, which it had seized during the war? The answer seems obvious now, but at the time it involved the fundamental purpose of the British colonies. Were the colonies primarily a source of raw materials for Great Britain, or did they represent new opportunities for marketing British manufactured goods?

John Douglas, later Bishop of Salisbury, started a pamphlet war when he published *A Letter Addressed to Two Great Men*. Ostensibly written to the Duke of Newcastle and William Pitt, first earl of Chatham, this pamphlet stresses the importance of retaining Canada to remove the French threat from North America and thus prevent further bloodshed. After its appearance in late 1759, dozens more pamphlets ensued. Franklin followed the controversy and added several pertinent pamphlets to his London library, including Ruffhead's *Reasons Why the Approaching Treaty of Peace Should Be Debated in Parliament*.[55]

The pamphlet that irked Franklin most was *Remarks on the Letter Address'd to Two Great Men*. Though it appeared anonymously, this pamphlet has been attributed to William Burke, Edmund Burke's cousin. Franklin heavily annotated his copy. A careless binder cropped Franklin's marginalia, but enough survives to reveal his anger. A manuscript note in another hand identifies the pamphlet's author and also says, "Dr. Franklin was alarmed by this and wrote a pamphlet entitled *The Interest of Great Britain Considered*."[56]

Few works better illustrate how Franklin's reading affected his writing than *The Interest of Great Britain Considered*. He found the preference for Guadeloupe short-sighted. Canada was far more significant, not only for its natural resources, but also as a place for British emigrants to settle. Canada would be both a source of raw material and a new market for British manufactured goods.

Onto *The Interest of Great Britain Considered* Franklin appended "Observations Concerning the Increase of Mankind" to form a sixty-page octavo pamphlet, which has become known as the *Canada Pamphlet*, a title Benjamin Vaughan coined. It could be called "How to Build an Empire." The same year the *Canada Pamphlet* appeared in London, publishers in

Dublin, Boston, and Philadelphia reissued it. The Boston edition is the only one identifying Franklin as its author. Published by Benjamin Mecom, the Boston edition says on its title page: "As the very ingenious, useful, and worthy author of this pamphlet (B———n F———n, LL.D.) is well-known and much esteemed by the principal gentlemen in *England* and *America*; and seeing that his other works have been received with universal applause; the present production needs no further recommendation to a generous, a free, an intelligent and publick-spirited people." Mecom's praise is so effusive that it no doubt embarrassed Franklin, who understood his nephew's personal motives. Mecom's bookselling business depended on a steady stream of London imports from Strahan, so Mecom hoped his uncle could help keep the books flowing, despite the younger man's chronic inability to pay his debts.[57]

The Boston edition of the *Canada Pamphlet* sold well enough that Mecom published a second edition. He repeated the title page note and added excerpts from two London reviews. The first comes from *The Gentleman's Magazine*: "The pamphlet seems to be written with great force of argument, and compleat knowledge of the subject." The second comes from *The Monthly Review*: "The author of the pamphlet before us, which is penned with great good sense and moderation, is a very masterly writer." The second review appeared anonymously, but Ruffhead wrote it.

As Haslam first recognized, David Hume spoke about the *Canada Pamphlet* in the same breath as one of England's best-loved books, Laurence Sterne's *Tristram Shandy*. Moral philosopher William Paley observed, "The true *summum bonum* of human life consists in reading *Tristram Shandy*, in blowing with a pair of bellows into your shoes in hot weather, and in roasting potatoes in the ashes under the grate in cold." Hume thought of something even better: reading Franklin's *Canada Pamphlet*, which he ranked above *Tristram Shandy*.[58]

British politicians worried that Canada would strengthen British North America so much that it would threaten to become independent. Franklin allayed their concerns in the *Canada Pamphlet*. Recalling the reluctance of colonial legislatures to approve his Albany Plan, he said that it was unlikely the colonies could unite against Great Britain. Franklin did add an example. A union of the American colonies would be possible should they face "grievous tyranny and oppression." He continued, "While the government is mild and just, while important civil and religious rights are secure, such subjects will be dutiful and obedient. The waves do not rise, but when the winds blow."[59]

Like his finest Poor Richardisms and his mottoes for the Association flags, this metaphorical sentence demonstrates Franklin's ability to write short, pithy phrases destined to be remembered and repeated. As British encroachments on American freedoms escalated in the coming years, Franklin would repeat the sentence. He used a slightly revised version for the epigraph to his essay, "Causes of the American Discontents before 1768": "The waves never rise but when the winds blow."[60]

In the past, Franklin had used traditional wisdom to bolster his arguments. Lacking a convenient saying from the oral tradition in this instance, he invented one and palmed it off as a proverb. Having done so, he could now use it to strengthen his argument. Publishing "Causes of the American Discontents" in the London press, Franklin made sure his readers knew that British winds were raising white caps off the American strand.

19

The Call for Racial Tolerance

FRANKLIN ATTENDED MANY meetings of different organizations during his time in London. On Thursdays when he was not at St. Paul's Coffeehouse with the Club of Honest Whigs, he would go to the Mitre Tavern on Fleet Street to attend the Royal Society Club, a select group of Fellows of the Royal Society who gathered for dinner before their meetings. Franklin never officially joined the Royal Society Club, but he was always welcome. As a Fellow of the Royal Society himself, he continued to attend its meetings regularly. Already a corresponding member of the Society for the Encouragement of Arts, Manufactures, and Commerce, he attended its meetings as well. Also known as the Premium Society, this organization paid premiums to stimulate the industrial arts. Having established himself as a leader of the Freemasons in America, Franklin became active with London's Grand Lodge. In terms of American cultural history, perhaps no London organization Franklin joined is more important than the Associates of Dr. Bray, a group that sought to educate and Christianize African American slaves.

A central figure in colonial American library history, the Reverend Dr. Thomas Bray established parochial and provincial libraries throughout the English colonies in the late seventeenth and early eighteenth centuries. These collections were assembled for the clergy's benefit, but Bray believed that understanding God's works required a broad range of knowledge. Besides theological books, the Bray libraries included European and English history, books on gardening, and Latin classics in the well-respected Delphin editions. Recognizing the book needs of isolated communities that clergymen did not serve, Bray also established laymen's libraries composed mainly of devotional works.[1]

Holding over a thousand volumes, Maryland's Annapolitan Library— Bray's greatest colonial library—was a model for smaller ones in Boston, New York, Philadelphia, and Charleston. These collections encompassed twelve subject categories, eleven theological and one "historical and geographical," that included subcategories: trade, medicine, poetry, and rhetoric. With the advent of the Library Company of Philadelphia and similar subscription libraries, Bray's efforts to establish public collections had faded by the mid-eighteenth century.[2]

Industrious and indefatigable, Bray sought additional ways to extend his dual goal of promoting literacy and Christianity. He discussed the spiritual condition of the enslaved population in America with Abel Tassin, sieur d'Allone, King William's secretary at The Hague. Bray's passion and devotion inspired D'Allone, who bequeathed a fund at his death in 1723 that would make Bray's project a reality. With D'Allone's bequest, Bray planned to establish "Negro schools" in America. After his death in 1730, the Associates of Dr. Bray would slowly carry out his work. But the organization accomplished little until Franklin joined the effort.[3]

In January 1757, the Reverend John Waring, secretary of the Associates, wrote Franklin for advice. Familiar with the circulating schools in Wales, Waring wondered if they could be a model for Negro schools in America. His letter shows that the Associates were considering itinerant schoolmasters, not permanent facilities. Before it reached Philadelphia, Franklin had left for London. Deborah shared Waring's letter with the Reverend William Sturgeon, assistant minister at Christ Church and catechist to the Negroes for the Society for the Propagation of the Gospel in Foreign Parts (SPG). Sturgeon wrote Franklin recommending the establishment of a Negro school in Philadelphia.

Franklin agreed with Sturgeon, as he told Waring in January 1758. He explained that few slaveholders in Philadelphia educated Negro children because they believed a literate slave was a dangerous slave. Furthermore, schoolmasters hesitated to accept Black students, fearing that White parents would not want their children integrated with Black children in the classroom or on the playground. Franklin shared Sturgeon's proposal with Waring and said it could be implemented in other colonial American cities as well.[4]

The Philadelphia Negro school opened on November 29, 1758, with a mistress and thirty pupils. Sturgeon, who served as superintendent, reported the school's success the following year. His report was not the only positive one to reach London. Deborah Franklin also had good things to say about the school. The impressive performance of its students convinced her to enroll the other slave child in their household. The following year, she informed her husband: "I went to hear the Negro children catechized at church. There were 17 that answered very prettily indeed, and 5 or 6 that were too little, but all behaved very decently. Mr. Sturgeon exhorted them before and after the catechizing. It gave me a great deal of pleasure, and I shall send Othello to the school."[5]

After Franklin brought Peter to London, Deborah had obtained Othello, an adolescent slave to take Peter's place in the Franklin home. Since purchasing him two years earlier, she had become quite fond of Othello. Her willingness to enroll him in school shows that Deborah did not share her neighbors' prejudice against educating slaves. Sadly, Othello would receive little schooling; he soon contracted a grave illness. Deborah tried her best to nurse him back to health without success. Othello perished the next year.[6]

With the Philadelphia school's success, the Associates of Dr. Bray planned additional schools and again sought Franklin's advice. On January 17, 1760, two weeks after the Bray Associates elected him a member, he visited Thomas Bird's bookshop at the Sign of the Angel and Bible, where the Associates held their regular meetings. At this, his first meeting, Franklin actively participated, recommending they establish Negro schools in New York, Newport, and Williamsburg. The organization took his advice, founding schools in each of those cities.[7]

The Associates also sent textbooks to the Negro schools. The box of books they sent to the Williamsburg school in Virginia is representative. It included fifty copies of *The Child's First Book*, a printed alphabet designed to be pasted on wood to make a hornbook; forty copies of Henry Dixon's *English Instructor*, a spelling book; twenty-five copies of *The Church Catechism Broke into Short Questions*; ten copies of another catechism, *An Easy Method of Instructing Youth in the Principles and Practice of the Christian Religion*; and many other basic devotional manuals.[8]

Dixon's *English Instructor* may be the most interesting textbook among those sent to the Negro schools. A schoolmaster in Bath, Dixon used his personal experience to compile this spelling book. Instead of bogging students down with consonants and vowels, the work begins with some common English syllables, after which it supplies a list of one-syllable words, grouped in rhyming sets of four—"got rot shot spot"; "dip chip ship clip." Divided into subjects, additional one-syllable words follow. Next comes a series of lessons containing complete sentences constructed from one-syllable words. Some are proverbial. For students born into slavery, one proverb seems downright cruel: "All work and no play makes *Jack* a dull boy."[9]

The books for the Negro schools reflect the purpose of the Bray Associates. Though the organization sought to ameliorate the condition of the enslaved population in America, it was not an abolitionist society. Its members were less concerned with the slaves' lives than their afterlives. The Negro schools taught their pupils how to read, so they could read the devotional literature that would help save their souls.

In his professional career as a printer, Franklin had already befriended some early American abolitionists. Ralph Sandiford, who had become a Quaker as a young man, emigrated from Liverpool to Philadelphia, where he established himself in the mercantile trade. When the Pennsylvania Assembly reduced the duty on importing slaves, Sandiford protested with *A Brief Examination of the Practice of the Times*. Franklin printed this work in 1729, but Sandiford financed its publication himself and distributed copies of the book for free.[10]

Sandiford's was not the first anti-slavery tract published in America, nor was the anti-slavery essay from *The Athenian Oracle* that Samuel Sewall had reprinted in Boston in 1705. A handful of anti-slavery tracts had appeared in the late seventeenth century. Toward the end of his life, Franklin would discover one of them and add it to his personal library: *An Exhortation and Caution to Friends Concerning Buying or Keeping of Negroes*, a six-page pamphlet New York Quaker George Keith wrote in 1693.[11]

Keith emphasizes that slavery goes against the fundamental principles of Christianity. Furthermore, he stresses the essential humanity of everyone regardless of race: "*Negroes, Blacks* and *Taunies* are a real part of mankind, for whom Christ hath shed his precious blood, and are capable of salvation, as well as *White Men*." Quakers should only buy slaves to set them free. During their enslavement, their masters should teach them to read and give them a Christian education.[12]

Though Keith had set a precedent for anti-slavery activity within the American Quaker community, Sandiford's *Brief Examination* stirred up considerable resentment, and he was expelled from the Philadelphia Meeting. He returned to the New Printing Office the following year and had Franklin print an expanded edition of his anti-slavery tract, which he retitled *The Mystery of Iniquity*. Business took Sandiford to England in late 1730, but he left copies of the new edition for his lawyer to distribute. Franklin kept some copies of *The Mystery of Iniquity*, but they sold poorly. A year later, he still had plenty on hand, so he sent three dozen copies to his brother James in Newport. Two years later, Franklin sold fifty copies to Sandiford's friend and fellow abolitionist Benjamin Lay, who would give them away.[13]

Distributing copies of Sandiford's *Mystery of Iniquity* was one of Benjamin Lay's numerous anti-slavery activities. Hunchbacked and barely four and a half feet tall, Lay nonetheless casts a long shadow across history. Folklore tells of a heroic dwarf with superhuman powers; Lay's superpower was his moral strength, his profound conviction that it was wrong for one human being to own another. Lay's equally diminutive wife Sarah was impressive in her own right. She was a preacher for the Society of Friends.

In 1718, Benjamin and Sarah Lay emigrated from England to Barbados, where they first encountered slavery and, therefore, where he first became a virulent anti-slavery advocate. One modern biographer characterizes his public anti-slavery demonstrations as guerrilla theater.[14] Not coined until the 1960s to describe the histrionic counterculture protests, the term "guerrilla theater" is an anachronism, but it suits Lay's public activities.

Before attending one Philadelphia Yearly Meeting, Lay made some elaborate preparations. He hollowed out a large folio volume, filled a bladder with red pokeberry juice until it was taut, placed it in the hollow, and closed the book. He then donned a military coat, tucked a small sword into his belt, and put on his great coat, fastening it with a single button. After entering the Quaker meeting house, he took a seat in a conspicuous place and awaited the right moment.[15]

Partway into the proceedings, Lay interrupted to proclaim the evils of slavery, which, he said, was in "direct opposition to every principle of reason, humanity, and religion." As he spoke, Lay undid the button that held the lapels of his great coat together and shrugged it off to exhibit his warlike appearance to the peace-loving audience. God Almighty, he continued, "beholds and respects all nations and colours of men with an equal regard." Owning slaves is tantamount to murdering them, he said. You might just as well thrust a sword through their hearts, "as I do through this book," whereupon Lay removed the sword from his belt and stabbed the book, piercing the bladder and spraying its bloodlike contents over those seated nearby. Guerrilla theater indeed.

Like Sandiford, Lay wrote his own anti-slavery treatise, *All Slavekeepers that Keep the Innocent in Bondage, Apostates*, which Franklin would print in 1737. Before printing it, Franklin read the work carefully but found it quite confusing. He told Lay that his manuscript seemed to have no order or arrangement whatsoever. "It is no matter," Lay replied. "Print any part thou pleasest first." A recent biographer called Lay's writing style a "stream-of-consciousness flow of words and ideas," associating his compositional approach with modernist literary technique.[16]

Given his reply to Franklin, Lay's technique sounds more like William Burroughs's cut-up method, whereby a work is disassembled and then reassembled at random. Lay said the parts of his manuscript could be printed in any order; they would still be effective. Both "stream of consciousness" and the cut-up method are also anachronisms when applied to Lay's book. Perhaps it is appropriate that the terms that best suit his anti-slavery activities are anachronisms. Benjamin Lay was a man ahead of his time.

The text of Lay's anti-slavery treatise is forward-thinking as well. Toward the end of the eighteenth century, anti-slavery literature would make use of the latest developments in moral philosophy advanced by Francis Hutcheson and Adam Smith, who both identified indignation as a moral sentiment related to but distinct from sympathy. Anti-slavery advocates would get their readers riled up by compelling them to sympathize with slaves and thus inspire a righteous indignation against slavery.[17]

Before either Hutcheson or Smith identified the psychological process underlying indignation, Benjamin Lay was already compelling his readers' indignation against slavery. Lay lumped slave traders with thieves and murderers, all close cousins to the "Devil's own children" who take "hellish delight" in the evil they perpetuate. But Lay went further. Anyone who condones slavery, even if they are not slaveholders themselves, is still complicit in its evil. They "shall drink the wine of the wrath of God, which is poured out without mixture, into the cup of his indignation."[18]

Lay continued to speak out against slavery for the next two decades. Deborah Franklin was one Philadelphian he inspired. His advocacy, combined with her affection for Othello, prompted Deborah to question the morality of slaveholding. Less than a year after purchasing Othello, she acquired a portrait of Benjamin Lay and hung it in their home. After Othello's death, Deborah never bought another slave.[19]

Three years after printing Lay's tract, Franklin published an anti-slavery article in *The Pennsylvania Gazette*, "A Letter from the Rev. Mr. George Whitefield to the Inhabitants of Maryland, Virginia, North and South Carolina." The first anti-slavery article to appear in the *Gazette*, Whitefield's letter is the second anti-slavery article to appear in any American newspaper. Later that year, Franklin would reprint it as part of *Three Letters from the Reverend Mr. G. Whitefield*.[20]

Whitefield's stance is less extreme than Lay's. Whereas Lay advocated abolition, Whitefield stopped short. He urged slaveowners to educate and Christianize their slaves, arguing that Christianity would make them better and more behaved workers. Whitefield's travels through the South had shown him that the slaves on Southern plantations had not been converted to Christianity. He witnessed many profaning the Lord's Day "by their dancing, piping and such like."[21] Whitefield would prefer to take away the one day of fun in the slaves' otherwise miserable lives and force them to attend religious services instead. He thought Sundays should be all church and no play.

Franklin's willingness to print and distribute the anti-slavery writings of Sandiford, Lay, and Whitefield suggest that he was sympathetic to the anti-slavery cause, but he was not too sympathetic, at least not yet. Franklin may have owned a slave in 1737 when Lay asked him to print his book, but the story of his slave ownership is rife with uncertainty. His 1735 accounts record the purchase of a pair of shoes and some breeches for someone named Joseph. In 1742, he bought Joseph a beaver hat from local hatter Charles Moore. These references to "Joseph" could refer to a slave named Joseph but may refer to Joseph Rose. The documentary evidence indicates other slaves in Franklin's household. In 1745, Moore charged Franklin 15 shillings for a "raccoon hat for your negro." By 1750, Benjamin and Deborah owned a slave couple, Peter and Jemima, whose son they had inoculated for smallpox.[22]

The first version of "Observations Concerning the Increase of Mankind," which Franklin drafted in 1751, touches on the issue of slavery, explaining how it adversely affected slaveholding families. Slavery shredded their moral fiber, imbuing them with a sense of entitlement and depriving them of the personal characteristics necessary to succeed and thrive: "The white children become proud, disgusted with labour, and being educated in idleness, are rendered unfit to get a living by industry."[23]

The changes Franklin made to "Observations" when he republished it as the appendix to his *Canada Pamphlet* reflect another moment of growth on Franklin's part. They show him becoming more sensitive to the issue of race. As he reread his earlier version of "Observations," he found passages that could be interpreted as racist, so he revised or deleted them. In his first version, Franklin had refuted the commonplace notion that slavery makes labor less expensive, arguing that slaveholders incur expenses that wage-paying employers do not. The slaveholder's expenses include: "Loss by [the slave's] neglect of business (neglect is natural to the man who is not to be benefited by his own care or diligence), expence of a driver to keep him at work, and his pilfering from time to time, almost every slave being *by nature* a thief."[24]

The way he had worded it, Franklin now realized, made the sentence sound like a racial slur. He seemed to have said that thievery and dishonesty were innate to Blacks. He revised the passage to eliminate the ambiguity, changing the phrase "almost every slave being *by nature* a thief" to "almost every slave being from the nature of slavery a thief." The revision clarifies that slavery itself was corrupting Blacks and shows its adverse impact on them. Eliminating the ambiguity, the revision indicates Franklin's newfound sensitivity to the issue of race.[25]

Franklin abbreviated the second-to-last section of "Observations," reducing its two paragraphs to one. He kept the paragraph comparing a nation's population growth to the procreation of a polyp, which can be subdivided *ad infinitum* to create copies of itself. Given a nation's ability to increase its population organically, Franklin questioned the need to encourage immigration to increase population.

The second paragraph of the section, as Franklin originally wrote it, launches an angry critique against German people, language, and customs: "Why should Pennsylvania, founded by the English, become a colony of *aliens*, who will shortly be so numerous as to Germanize us instead of our Anglifying them, and will never adopt our language or customs, any more than they can acquire our complexion?"[26] A decade after writing this rhetorical question, Franklin recognized it as jingoistic, ethnocentric, and, in retrospect, unfounded. Franklin now saw the danger his paragraph could incite among narrow-minded readers. He cut the whole paragraph as he revised "Observations."

Franklin remained active with the Bray Associates into 1762. As with other organizations, he naturally took a leadership role. Two months after attending his first meeting, he was elected chairman of the Bray Associates for the 1760–61 year. In March 1761, he was reelected for a second term. He presided over the Bray Associates until March 1762, when he stepped down as chair, mainly because he would return to Philadelphia later that year.[27]

Preparing to go home, the Franklins had to do something about King. After he had run away in 1758, they learned that King had found a place in Suffolk with a woman who wanted to educate and Christianize him. She had him baptized "John King," sent him to school, taught him music, and dressed him in livery. Since King was pretty much useless to the Franklins, they had left him in Suffolk for the time being. In 1762, William apparently offered to sell King to her, but she refused to purchase him. William thus reclaimed him as his property and brought King back to Craven Street. He did not stay for long. King soon ran away again.[28]

Franklin left London for Philadelphia in August 1762. Presumably, Peter, whose parents lived in Philadelphia, returned with him, but he disappears from history around this time. Franklin returned without his son, who had become something of a dandy during their time in London. Poet and Harvard alumnus Jacob Bailey, who visited London in the early 1760s, came to Craven Street to meet Benjamin Franklin. He recorded his impressions of William Franklin in his diary: "He is a gentleman of good education, but has passed away the flower of his youth in too many extravagancies."[29]

William Franklin stayed behind to marry Elizabeth Downes, the daughter of a wealthy Barbados planter. Benjamin Franklin's connections in the British government, especially his friendship with newly elected prime minister Lord Bute, helped William secure a commission as royal governor of New Jersey. William would return to America with his new bride and settle in New Jersey to assume his new position.[30]

Back in Philadelphia on November 1st, Benjamin Franklin caught up with his post office business. He would spend nearly half a year traveling through the colonies inspecting post offices. He also visited one of the Negro schools the Bray Associates had established and observed their students. So far, Peter had shaped Franklin's understanding of the African intellect. Franklin's current observations showed him that Peter's willingness to learn was by no means unique. The students he observed impressed him. Franklin's statement of racial equality in his report of the school that he wrote for the Bray Associates is inspiring: "I was on the whole much pleas'd, and from what I then saw, have conceiv'd a higher opinion of the natural capacities of the black race, than I had ever before entertained. Their apprehension seems as quick, their memory as strong, and their docility in every respect equal to that of white children."[31]

Franklin continued to follow the pamphlets that appeared with the end of the Seven Years' War; sometimes their subject matter overlapped with books about the slave trade. *A Plan for Improving the Trade at Senegal* was one 1763 pamphlet he added to his library. Before getting to the plan, the pamphlet's anonymous author offered some general comments on slavery. Refuting the racial stereotype "Blacks are naturally lazy and wicked," the author presents the same argument Franklin uses in the *Canada Pamphlet*, that such characteristics are not indigenous to any race. Rather, the institution of slavery is what makes slaves lazy and wicked.[32]

Though anonymous, the author had ties to Pennsylvania. The colony appears throughout the pamphlet as a positive example. Whereas the mistreatment of slaves in the West Indies has corrupted them, the benevolent treatment of them in Pennsylvania has made slaves "chearfully industrious, and their manners equal to those of the natives of that province."[33] The author admits that slavery is firmly entrenched in the West Indies but argues that new colonies should avoid the practice. Most of the pamphlet concerns colonizing Senegal, formerly a French colony, which the British had seized during the war. By keeping its native population free and introducing good government, the pamphleteer argues, Britain could create a society more productive than a slave-holding one.

Though the French and Indian War officially ended with the Treaty of Paris in 1763, violence continued to flare up on the Pennsylvania frontier. Some feared the Indians would soon attack Philadelphia. Such fears provide the backdrop for a little-known Franklin anecdote, which T. J. Hogg recorded in his *Life of Shelley*. In a digression on nudity, Hogg used Franklin—"the father of air-bathing"—for example.[34]

A Philadelphia neighbor, who was traveling to a nearby town, agreed to retrieve a message from one of its townspeople for Franklin. The neighbor returned to Philadelphia much too late to give him the message. The next morning, he sent his maidservant to deliver it. She arrived when Franklin was indoors taking his air-bath. Looking out the window, he saw her approach. Eager to obtain the message, he walked outside to receive it, accidentally neglecting to put on his clothes. Upon seeing the naked man, she fled in fright and ran home screaming.

"What is the matter?" the neighbor asked her. "Did you see the Doctor?"

"Oh! No! Poor old gentleman; we shall never see him again; he has been barbarously murdered, no doubt! The Indians got possession of the farther end of the village in the night; the chief is in the poor Doctor's house, and as soon as he saw me he ran out, tomahawk in hand, to scalp me!"

Almost surely apocryphal, this humorous anecdote nonetheless reveals much about racial prejudice in colonial America. Seeing a naked man traipsing around the Franklin property, the maidservant could not imagine it was Franklin. A naked man in public must be an Indian, she assumed. Her assumption also reflects a racial stereotype equating naked Indians with violent murderers. The maidservant's behavior demonstrates the ease with which people accept stereotypes and react accordingly. To her, the presence of a naked man in public could only symbolize an incipient Indian attack.

Its humor keeps the anecdote light, but the racial stereotypes the maidservant holds were shared by many Pennsylvania settlers. The story of their activities has a much darker tone. On December 14, 1763, men from Paxton, a frontier village, massacred six Susquehanna Indians as a reprisal for a recent attack. The Indians whom the so-called Paxton Boys murdered were not those who had perpetrated the attack; they were peace-loving Christian Indians. Fourteen Susquehanna Indians were placed in the workhouse in Lancaster for their protection, but the ruthless Paxton Boys stormed the workhouse and slaughtered them all.

Mobs do not respond to logic. "A mob's a monster: heads enough, but no brains," as Poor Richard says. The first week of February, the Paxton Boys marched on Philadelphia, determined to kill the Indians there. The governor did little to stop them, so Franklin organized the city's defense. Franklin confronted the rioters, met their leaders, asked them to present a list of grievances, and persuaded them to disperse. Personally confronting the mob, Franklin demonstrated his leadership and, indeed, his bravery.[35]

Franklin denounced the Paxton Boys in *A Narrative of the Late Massacres*, a work John Updike called Franklin's "fiercest and most eloquent pamphlet."[36] It begins by mentioning the treaty of friendship William Penn negotiated with the Indians, which was supposed to endure "as long as the sun should shine, or the waters run in the rivers." According to Native American oratory, the renewal of a treaty was known as brightening the chain. In *Narrative of the Late Massacres*, Franklin observed, "This treaty has been since frequently renewed, and the *chain brightened*, as they express it, from time to time. It has never been violated, on their part or ours, till now." This expression was one of Franklin's favorite figures of speech. He used it so often he became identified with it. John Fothergill gave him a silver cream pot engraved with the words "Keep bright the chain."[37]

Condemning the Paxton Boys, Franklin emphasized that the slaughtered Indians were Christians, and he supplied some Christian names and brief personal descriptions. Stressing the victims' Christianity and individuality, Franklin made the murders more heinous. *A Narrative of the Late Massacres* combines early American discourse with anti-racist rhetoric. The work resembles a case of conscience, a popular genre of devotional literature among New England Puritans, as it asks, "If an Indian injures me, does it follow that I may revenge that injury on all Indians?" Franklin's answer to this question presents an impassioned plea for racial tolerance: "The only crime of these poor wretches seems to have been, that they had a reddish brown skin, and black hair; and some people of that sort, it seems, had murdered some of our relations. If it be right to kill men for such a reason, then, should any man, with a freckled face and red hair, kill a wife or child of mine, it would be right for me to revenge it, by killing all the freckled red-haired men, women and children, I could afterwards any where meet with."[38]

Franklin shamed the murderous actions of the Paxton Boys, whose violent behavior exhibited an almost unprecedented level of savagery. Instead of behaving savagely ourselves, we Christians, he argued, should set an example when it comes to the knowledge and practice of what is right. For comparison, he used several examples to show how people in different times and different cultures extended their hospitality, even to their enemies. Taking his first example from Homer, Franklin would seem to be structuring his work as a progress piece. Though his examples move in a forward and westward path, they do not illustrate progress. Rather, they illustrate continuity. Throughout history, people have consistently behaved in a hospitable manner until, that is, the Paxton Boys committed their foul murders.

Some of Franklin's examples in *A Narrative of the Late Massacres* come from his reading, but others—the most memorable ones—are his own invention.[39] One anecdote tells the story of a Spanish cavalier who escapes after murdering a young Moorish gentleman and accidentally enters the garden of a neighboring Moor, who extends his hospitality to the Spaniard. Upon learning that the murder victim was his son, the Moor does not avenge the Spaniard because he has already extended his hospitality to him.

Another anecdote tells the story of a Black named Cudjoe, who worked for William Murray, a White man. When some Blacks were seized and forced into slavery, others sought revenge by trying to kill Murray. Answering the door, Cudjoe meets a mob of fellow Blacks but refuses them entry. Franklin dramatized the clash between the mob of Blacks and Cudjoe, who tells them, "You must not kill a man, that had done no harm, only for being white. This man is my friend, my house is his fort, and I am his soldier. I must fight for him. You must kill me, before you can kill him."[40]

A Narrative of the Late Massacres ends with an eloquent observation: "*Cowards* can handle arms, can strike where they are sure to meet with no return, can wound, mangle and murder; but it belongs to brave men to spare, and to protect; for, as the poet says, 'Mercy still sways the brave.'" Franklin's source for this closing line of verse is Pope's translation of Homer's *Odyssey*. The beggar Irus insults Ulysses, then disguised as an itinerant old man. One of Penelope's suitors—an Ithacan Ransy Sniffle—tries to goad the two into fighting. Ulysses knows he could smite Irus dead with one vengeful blow, but he resolves to save his life, for "mercy sways the brave."[41] Inserting the adverb "still," Franklin identified a continuity between ancient Greece and colonial America. Certain human values transcend time and place.

Though one of the finest defenses of racial tolerance in American literature, Franklin's *Narrative of the Late Massacres* alone was insufficient to open people's minds in an enduring way, as its author understood. The battle against racial prejudice must be fought incessantly. In *The Querist*, George Berkeley asks "whether a single hint be sufficient to overcome a prejudice." Franklin answered this query in his copy of Berkeley's work: "Seldom." In a follow-up query, Berkeley asked "whether even obvious truths will not sometimes bear repeating." "Yes," Franklin replied.[42]

Franklin's leadership also manifested itself in the Pennsylvania Assembly. Despite his work in London, the political animosity between the assembly and the proprietors continued to fester. To strengthen the argument for a royal charter, Franklin wrote *Cool Thoughts on the Present Situation of Our Public Affairs*, which explains a royal charter's advantages and reassures Pennsylvanians that they would not lose the rights that William Penn's original charter guaranteed. Franklin circulated gratis copies of *Cool Thoughts* for maximum impact.

When Norris resigned as speaker of the assembly in late May, Franklin replaced him. The assembly adopted his petition to King George III to change the government from a proprietary to a royal government. *Cool Thoughts* had not persuaded Franklin's increasingly vocal and increasingly numerous political enemies, who believed he wanted a royal colony to make himself governor. They circulated ugly rumors—that Franklin had bilked public funds while in England, that he was an Indian lover, that William's mother was a maidservant. The anger culminated in a bitter election that October. Franklin lost his seat in the assembly.

On the plus side, the anti-proprietary party retained its majority and appointed Franklin to serve as joint agent in London. Deborah, again refusing to cross the ocean, would stay home and oversee construction of the new home Samuel Rhoads was designing and building for them on a court off Market Street between Third and Fourth. Like Penelope saying farewell to Ulysses, Deborah said goodbye to Benjamin, unsure when or if she would ever see him again. He left Philadelphia on November 7, 1764.

By the second week of December, Franklin was back at Craven Street. Margaret and Polly Stevenson were doing well. Temple, his 4-year-old grandson, had suffered a series of foster mothers, but his grandfather now arranged for him to attend a boarding school operated by educational reformer James Elphinston, where his classmates included William Caslon III, of the famous type-founding family. During vacations, Temple would return to Craven Street, where he became Margaret Stevenson's little darling.

As he had during his first mission, Franklin contributed numerous articles to the London press that championed America. In one instance, he found that his advocacy of colonial rights and his growing attention to slavery coincided. Some British observers noticed an inconsistency among the colonists. How could they clamor for their rights while continuing to hold slaves? Franklin addressed the issue in "A Conversation on Slavery." This article reveals that Franklin read Granville Sharp's anti-slavery tract, *A Representation of the Injustice and Dangerous Tendency of Tolerating Slavery*.

"Englishman" and "American" are the two main speakers in the conversation. Englishman tells American to read Sharp's book. When American says he has already read it, Englishman solicits his opinion. While American likes Sharp's basic premise, he disagrees with his impulse to draw general conclusions about all Americans based on the behavior of a few. Thousands of colonial Americans abhorred slavery. Furthermore, Englishman's critique of American slavery ignores his own countrymen, who are complicit in the slave trade. The colonial legislatures had passed numerous bills preventing the importation of slaves, but the king disallowed them.

As their conversation continues, American identifies British labor practices that are tantamount to slavery. Colliers, he argues, "are bought and sold with the colliery, and have no more liberty to leave it than our negroes have to leave their master's plantation." The impressment of sailors is another British practice akin to slavery: "The sailor is often *forced* into service, torn from all his natural connections." And British soldiers can be forced to serve a foreign prince: "Soldiers must, on pain of death, obey the orders they receive; though, like Herod's troops, they should be commanded to slay all your children under two years old, cut the throats of your children in the colonies, or shoot your women and children in St. George's Fields." With this statement, American gets the last word.[43]

Franklin continued to acquire a variety of books pertinent to the slave trade. In 1769, he purchased Michel Adanson's *Voyage to Senegal, the Isle of Goree, and the River Gambia*, an abridged translation of *Histoire natural du Sénégal*. Previously, the only Westerners who had visited the parts of Africa that Adanson explored were slave traders or ivory poachers. Adanson went there solely for scientific purposes and stayed for five years.[44]

The Paris edition of Adanson's natural history of Senegal appeared in 1757. By the time the English translation appeared two years later, Senegal was a British colony, and this new geopolitical reality shaped the translation. Prefacing Adanson's narrative, the translator observes, "He informs us of whatever relates to the manners and customs of the Negroes, to their dress, habitations, repasts, dances, superstitions, and poverty: neither does he forget to mention their sociability, good-nature, docility, and respect for the French nation, which we make no doubt, but they will be equally ready to shew to the new conquerors of Senegal."[45]

Though Adanson accepts and repeats many of the stereotypes about Africans, he does make several positive comments. Describing Sor, a region adjacent to Saint-Louis, Adanson compared the situation of the local inhabitants to that of Adam and Eve in paradise: "Which way soever I turned my eyes on this pleasant spot, I beheld a perfect image of pure nature: an agreeable solitude, bounded on every side by a charming landskip; the rural situation of cottages in the midst of trees; the ease and indolence of the Negroes, reclined under the shade of their spreading foliage; the simplicity of their dress and manners; the whole revived in my mind, the idea of our first parents, and I seemed to contemplate the world in its primeval state."[46]

Adanson also enjoyed the fables, dialogues, and witty stories that formed part of traditional Senegalese entertainment. In addition, he was impressed with their knowledge of the constellations: "It is amazing, that such a rude and illiterate people, should reason so pertinently, in regard to those heavenly bodies: for there is no manner of doubt but that, with proper instruments and a good-will, they would become excellent astronomers."[47]

William Bollan's anonymous pamphlet *Britannia libera: or, A Defence of the Free State of Man in England* was another anti-slavery tract that Franklin added to his library. After being dismissed from his lengthy service as London agent for Massachusetts, Bollan remade himself as a political pamphleteer, writing at least thirteen pamphlets. *Britannia libera*, which mainly concerns keeping slavery out of Great Britain, offers an erudite history of the subject, tracing it from antiquity to the present. Bollan touches on the European introduction of slavery to America, which, he explains, has proliferated due to the union of pride and power, "the lust of domination, avarice, injustice, and cruelty."[48]

Britannia libera reflects Bollan's extensive reading, but it lacks the outrage and indignation characteristic of the best examples of anti-slavery literature. Andrew Kippis, Franklin's friend and a fellow member of the Club of Honest Whigs, noticed *Britannia libera* for *The Monthly Review* and captured the work's central problem: "The spirit of liberty which this publication displays, deserves the highest commendation; but its author appears to have more learning than judgment. He has well stored his memory with facts and observations; but we are mistaken if he is not yet to learn how to employ them with the greatest advantage."[49]

In 1772, the year Bollan published *Britannia libera*, Franklin received a package containing several different works from Anthony Benezet, the foremost anti-slavery propagandist in Revolutionary America. In a follow-up letter, Benezet mentions that he had sent some "tracts on the slave-trade" and a "treatise" on the subject. Benezet's terminology draws a distinction between two print genres, tract and treatise. The reference to the treatise is specific enough to identify it as Benezet's *Some Historical Account of Guinea*, a 144-page work. Benezet's other anti-slavery publications can be classified as tracts; nearly all were pamphlets ranging from sixteen to forty-eight pages in length. In short, Benezet sent Franklin a copy of *Some Historical Account of Guinea* and several of his anti-slavery pamphlets.[50]

In his introduction to *Some Historical Account of Guinea*, Benezet explains that he will describe the regions in Africa where the slaves come from to give readers a view of the lives that the Africans lead and, therefore, to refute the baseless assertion on the part of slave traders and slaveholders that they were supposedly removing Africans from the life-threatening cruelties they faced in Africa and giving them better lives as slaves in America.

The treatise is largely assembled from other works. Adanson's *Voyage to Senegal* was one of Benezet's key sources. Early in *Some Historical Account of Guinea*, Benezet quotes his Adam-and-Eve comparison. He also mentions Adanson's enjoyment of the Africans' fables, dialogues, and witty stories and their impressive knowledge of astronomy. Benezet's use of Adanson and other sources proves his point, that Africans lived a harmonious life in their native land, which the slave traders destroyed.[51]

The escalating problem between Great Britain and the American colonies would occupy Franklin's time and mind over the next decade, so the issue of slavery would temporarily take a backseat in his thinking. Not until American freedom was secure, and the United States was established would Franklin return to the issue, when he would emerge as one of the staunchest abolitionists in America.

20

Travels in a Time of Strife

TO PROMOTE AMERICA and defend American rights, Franklin contributed numerous articles to the London papers. Despite their shared purpose, they reflect different moods for changing moments. Some are angry and impassioned, others cool and humorous. The personae Franklin used for his newspaper articles are equally diverse. "The Grand Leap of the Whale," which appeared in *The Public Advertiser* in May 1765, is one of his most entertaining pieces. Making fun of British misinformation about America, Franklin used two examples of what would become a defining feature of American humor: tall talk. Besides asserting that whales swam inland and even jumped up Niagara Falls, he said that American sheep were so laden with wool that they must pull little trailers to hold their tails and keep them from dragging on the ground. Franklin signed the article, "A Traveller," a pseudonym appropriate to the subject matter, but one that also reflects his personal love of traveling and travel writing.

Franklin hoped to keep taking annual summer vacations, as he had during his previous mission to England, but political responsibilities kept him in smoky London all summer his first year back. Though he had returned to petition the king to change Pennsylvania's status from a proprietary colony to a royal colony, the Stamp Act took precedence upon his arrival.

Having passed the House of Commons in February, the Stamp Act received royal assent the following month. Scheduled to take effect on November 1st, it would require Americans to pay taxes on all sorts of printed material. Initially accepting the Stamp Act, Franklin advocated forbearance, naïvely believing that Britain would not oppress the colonies for long. Other Americans were neither as patient nor complacent. Led by Patrick Henry, Virginia's House of Burgesses passed a set of resolves protesting the Stamp Act and denying the British government the right to tax the colony.

Franklin's complacency was taken as tacit approval, and, on September 16th, a wild-eyed Philadelphia mob threatened his home. Deborah got Sally to safety but stayed behind herself, angry and armed and ready to fight.

Samuel Rhoads and other friends arrived to help Deborah thwart the mob. Additional protests took place throughout the colonies. The royal governors, William Franklin included, were helpless to stop the protesters or enforce the stamp duties.

Parliament had underestimated colonial opposition. Inspired by the American resistance, Franklin spoke out against the Stamp Act. In February 1766, the House of Commons debated the issue. Informed, serious, and dedicated to the cause of American rights, Franklin testified on the 13th. He answered the legislators' questions with reason and precision, force and spirit.

His testimony was published as *The Examination of Doctor Benjamin Franklin*, a pamphlet that circulated widely in Britain and America. Printers in Boston, New York, Philadelphia, and Williamsburg republished it. A German translation also appeared in Philadelphia. American readers back home and American sympathizers in England found Franklin's testimony awe-inspiring. It still is. Stuart P. Sherman called *The Examination of Doctor Franklin* "one of the most interesting and impressive pieces of dramatic dialogue produced in the eighteenth century."[1]

Partly swayed by Franklin's words, Parliament repealed the Stamp Act. The repeal was a victory for all Americans, but their celebrations ignored an act passed directly afterward. The Declaratory Act let Parliament implement whatever laws they deemed necessary to control the colonies. Parliament now had "full power and authority to make laws and statutes of sufficient force and validity to bind the colonies and people of America . . . in all cases whatsoever." The Declaratory Act unequivocally asserted the Crown's sovereignty over the colonies.[2]

The Stamp Act symbolizes an issue central to the American Revolution: no taxation without representation. In a democratic society, people should be taxed solely by their elected representatives. Colonial legislatures like the Pennsylvania Assembly could levy taxes, but Parliament could not since the colonies did not elect any members to represent them. The solution seemed obvious to many American colonists: Give the colonies seats in Parliament. But Franklin knew Parliament would never allow them representation commensurate with their population.

Cadwalader Evans broached the issue in a letter to Franklin. Replying the first week of May, Franklin told Evans it would be ideal if the different regions of Great Britain and its colonies each had their own legislatures for local issues and representation in Parliament for national issues. But such a government should have been formed early in colonial history: "In the infancy of our foreign establishments, it was neglected, or was not thought of. And now, the affair is nearly in the situation of Friar Bacon's project of making a brazen wall round England for its eternal security. . . . *Time is past.*"[3]

The second week of June 1766, Franklin wrote Deborah to tell her about his forthcoming trip to Germany with John Pringle. Having been sickly through the winter into the spring, he blamed his poor health on the lack of a vacation the previous summer. The trip to Germany, he hoped, would revitalize him. Franklin's letter evinces an unprecedented attitude toward summer vacations. Owen Aldridge called Franklin the "first man in modern society to recognize the benefit of an annual vacation."[4]

By late June, Franklin and Pringle were in Bad Pyrmont. This renowned spa was best known for its natural sparkling water, which supposedly had healing powers. Pringle was anxious to test them out. Franklin doubted the healing powers of sparkling water. What would improve his health, he sensibly thought, would be the fresh air and vigorous exercise he got during the trip.[5]

They went to Hanover in July. Franklin left a detailed account of a side trip to the saltpeter works 2 miles outside of town. He was astonished by how much and how cheaply the Germans could manufacture saltpeter. All the gunpowder for 12,000 troops and their forts were munitioned from the saltpeter the Hanover works produced. Little did Franklin realize at the moment that what he learned at Hanover would prove useful when he was appointed to a congressional committee in charge of locating sources for saltpeter to manufacture sufficient gunpowder for the Continental Army.[6]

Franklin and Pringle left Hanover for Göttingen, where they were both inducted into its Royal Academy. They proceeded through Cassel and Frankfort to Mainz. From Mainz, they sailed down the Rhine to Holland, where both became fascinated with canals and canal boats, making observations about drag, buoyancy, and water depth. The canals fired Franklin's scientific curiosity so much that after they returned to London, he quizzed the London watermen on the Thames and performed some experiments himself.

Franklin and Pringle had such an enjoyable time traveling together that they planned a trip to France the following summer. They would leave the last week of August. Gathering with others at Dover to board the boat to Calais, Franklin could tell which passengers were crossing the English Channel for the first time: those eating breakfast. Concerned that if the wind failed they would not reach Calais until suppertime, they were eating a hearty breakfast to tide them over, so to speak. Franklin knew better. Once they reached Paris, he reported the crossing to Polly Stevenson. The letter demonstrates his skill as a travel writer. He told Polly what the greenhorn passengers did wrong: "Doubtless they thought that when they had paid for their breakfast they had a right to it, and that when they had swallowed it they were sure of it. But they had scarce been out half an hour before the sea laid claim to it, and they were oblig'd to deliver it up. So it seems there are uncertainties even beyond those between the cup and the lip."[7]

Once he and Pringle reached Paris, Franklin went to a perruquier to be fitted for a new wig. The full-bottomed grizzle he had worn to Whitehall looked dowdy in the Paris salons. Continuing his letter to Polly, Franklin offered an amusing self-portrait upon leaving the perruquier: "Only think what a figure I make in a little bag wig and naked ears! They told me I was become 20 years younger, and look'd very galante."[8]

A fashionable French wig that gathered the hair at its back in an ornamental bag, the bag-wig was an object of humorous derision in England. When Master Elphinston showed up at school wearing one, his students had no end of fun. Revealing Franklin's ability to laugh at himself, his self-portrait calls to mind Christopher Smart's verse fable, "The Bag-Wig and the Tobacco-Pipe." Tobacco-Pipe says England was better off before French fashions crossed the channel, "When none sought hair in realms unknown, / But every blockhead bore his own." Powdered and perfumed, Bag-Wig takes offense at Tobacco-Pipe's obnoxious smell: "Hideous! sure some one smoak'd thee, Friend, / Reversely, at his t'other end."[9]

One day when they were in Paris, Pringle went to visit Hôpital de la Charité, a hospital renowned for treating the colic of Poitou, which was the French version of the Devonshire colic or the West-India dry gripes. Returning from the hospital, Pringle brought Franklin a pamphlet listing the names of patients treated there, along with their professions. Franklin read the list carefully and discovered that the patients belonged to trades with a traditionally high instance of exposure to lead—glaziers, painters, and plumbers. Two professions listed did not seem to fit the pattern, stonecutters and soldiers. Curious as always, Franklin went to the hospital and spoke with a physician there, who informed him that stonecutters often used melted lead in their work and that painters often hired soldiers to mix their paints. Wherever Franklin went, he found more evidence of the pervasive danger of lead poisoning.[10]

While in France, Franklin and Pringle went to Versailles and dined with the king and queen. Though Franklin was flattered by the attention he received at the royal court, another French dinner party during the trip meant more to him. One night he dined at the villa of François-César Le Tellier, Marquis de Courtnavaux. A French nobleman who had established a reputation for his military prowess fighting in Bohemia and Bavaria, Courtnavaux now devoted himself to scientific research, becoming acutely interested in finding a quick and easy way to determine longitude.

The Royal Academy of Sciences offered a prize to the person who built a marine chronometer that could be used for calculating longitude. Courtnavaux had a ship built, *Aurore*, that he would sail on a months-long cruise in all sorts of weather conditions to put his chronometer through its paces. The next year, Courtnavaux would write up his account of the cruise of the *Aurore* as *Journal du voyage*, a copy of which Franklin added to his library. Besides contributing to his collection of travel writing, the volume was a reminder of the memorable night he spent with its author.[11]

No record of his conversation with Courtnavaux survives, but Franklin had been fascinated with the problem of determining longitude at least since he had observed a lunar eclipse aboard the *Berkshire* four decades earlier. Franklin was reminded of the inability to determine longitude more recently. Sailing to England on his first mission for the Pennsylvania Assembly, his ship was much closer to land than its captain realized. They almost wrecked on the Scilly Isles.

There were two ways to determine longitude: the celestial method and the mechanical method. The celestial method involved taking several measurements of the moon and the stars and performing numerous calculations. Each measurement and every calculation offered an opportunity for error. The mechanical method was much simpler: just compare local time with the time at a standard fixed location, say, Greenwich, England. It sounds simple enough, but there was a major obstacle to the mechanical method: Given all the movement of a ship on the waves and all the changes in latitude, humidity, and temperature, current timepieces, no matter how sturdy, could not accurately keep time at sea.

Courtnavaux was not the only scientist working on the problem. John Harrison, a British watchmaker, had invented an ingenious clock that could keep time at sea with extraordinary accuracy. Harrison's clock met resistance from members of the British scientific establishment. Their resistance stemmed from class prejudice. Since the celestial method involved numerous complex calculations, it required practitioners to have a superior mathematical education. Harrison's approach was that of a craftsman, not a gentleman scientist. Franklin had visited his workshop and saw Harrison's clock during his first mission to England. Later, while serving on the Council of the Royal Society in 1761, Franklin helped plan an expedition to Jamaica to test Harrison's clock.[12]

Jean-Baptiste Chappe d'Auteroche, a French astronomer, came to Courtnavaux's for dinner the same night Franklin did. Chappe was busy putting the final touches on a book of travels about his recent adventures, *Voyage en Siberie*. Witty and perceptive, Chappe was a charming dinner guest. Abraham Rees, who left a brief character sketch of him, may have learned about Chappe from Franklin. Rees observed, "Chappe was of a lively, cheerful, social disposition, upright in his views, and candid in his conduct: devoted to the pursuit of science, and in a great degree regardless of all considerations of private interest."[13]

Chappe had gone to Siberia in 1761 for a specific purpose: to observe the transit of Venus across the face of the sun. Transits of Venus always occur in pairs eight years apart. The last transit had occurred in 1639, but another would occur eight years later in 1769. After that, over a hundred more years would pass before the next one. No matter how successful, a single observation of the transit of Venus was insufficient. Multiple observations taken as far apart as possible would enable astronomers to merge the data to determine the solar parallax, the angle formed between two lines of sight. After determining the parallax, they could calculate the distance between Earth and the sun, which would let them calculate the distance between the other planets as well. Observing the transit of Venus would make it possible to map the heavens.

European scientific societies sent astronomers around the globe to observe the transit. Having taken his seat on the Council of the Royal Society on December 8, 1760, Franklin participated in the last-minute planning for the expeditions that the Royal Society was sponsoring to observe the 1761 transit. The Reverend Nevil Maskelyne had gone to St. Helena, and Charles Mason and Jeremiah Dixon, who would later earn their lasting reputation for surveying the line that bears their names, left for Bencoolen, Sumatra. Franklin's reading reinforced his responsibilities for the Royal Society: He obtained James Ferguson's *Plain Method of Determining the Parallax of Venus, by Her Transit over the Sun*, a book every lover of astronomy would enjoy, according to William Bewley.[14]

Since Britain and France remained at war, astronomers from both sides risked attack from enemy naval vessels and privateers. Soon after Mason and Dixon left Portsmouth aboard the *H.M.S. Seahorse*, it came under attack from a French warship. The *Seahorse* hobbled back to Portsmouth badly damaged. Fearing for their lives, Mason and Dixon refused to return to sea. Under threat from the Council of the Royal Society, they begrudgingly left Portsmouth again. They never did make it to Sumatra, but they did reach Sable Bay, Cape of Good Hope, to witness the transit there.[15]

Chappe traveled overland, so he did not face the perils of wartime ocean travel, but his overland journey to Tobolsk, Siberia, presented dangers of a different sort. All astronomers who left their homes for far-flung parts of the globe were risking their lives for the sake of science. Beyond life-threatening danger, these intrepid astronomers faced a disheartening possibility even when they reached their destinations: A cloudy day would render their months of strenuous travel useless.

Traveling by sledge across the melting snow of a Russian spring, Chappe reached Tobolsk on April 10th, setting up his observatory in time to witness the lunar eclipse on May 18th, which would allow him to ascertain the city's longitude: an essential measurement for observing the transit. Superstitious Russian peasants complicated Chappe's efforts, blaming his strange behavior and mysterious scientific apparatus for the floods that were devastating local farms. When the transit occurred on June 6th, ideal weather conditions at Tobolsk let Chappe observe the event in its entirety. Bringing his results home proved more difficult. His route took him through swamps infested with the double threat of thirsty mosquitoes and angry Russian rebels. He did not return to France until 1762.[16]

Chappe also studied the natural history of Siberia during his travels. The mastodon fossils discovered there intrigued him. The subject came up in conversation the evening Franklin dined with him and Courtnavaux. Franklin had much to say on the subject. George Croghan, a renowned wilderness guide, had sent him some fossilized tusks and teeth from the American mastodon, *Mamut americana*, discovered at Big Bone Lick, a salt marsh south of present-day Cincinnati. Chappe asked to borrow them. Once Franklin returned to London, he sent a mammoth tooth to Chappe, who thanked him in *Voyage en Siberie* and summarized their conversation at Courtnavaux's villa. Though *Voyage en Siberie* was not translated into English, Bewley translated the part about Franklin and published it in *The Monthly Review*.[17]

Franklin had more opportunities to speak with other world travelers once he returned to London. In November 1766, the month after he arrived back from France, Captain Cook returned from Newfoundland, where he had spent four years surveying its coast and the surrounding islands. Since Cook belonged to Franklin's Monday Club, geography no doubt formed a prominent topic of conversation at St. Paul's Coffeehouse that winter. Reelected to the Council of the Royal Society in 1766, Franklin took his seat on December 8th. Elected to another term the following year, Franklin continued to serve on the Council until December 1768, meaning that he helped plan the expeditions the Royal Society sponsored to observe the 1769 transit of Venus.

Their plans heated up in December 1767. The Royal Society wanted to send one expedition to Hudson Bay and another to the South Pacific. Franklin's in-depth reading about the exploration of Hudson Bay had not helped him find the Northwest Passage, but it did qualify him to plan the expedition there to observe the transit of Venus. He interviewed potential observers for both the Hudson Bay and South Pacific expeditions. Furthermore, he oversaw lists of technical equipment the observers would need. Though Franklin could have seen Cook at their Monday Club, he formally interviewed him once the Admiralty appointed Cook to command the *H.M.S. Endeavour*, the ship that would carry the Royal Society's expedition to the South Seas.[18]

Before embarking, Cook gathered as much useful information as he could. A couple of weeks after Cook met with Franklin and the Council of the Royal Society, Samuel Wallis returned from the South Pacific. As commander of the *Dolphin*, Captain Wallis led a search for the great continent, *Terra australis incognita*. Wallis did not find it, but he did discover and chart fifteen islands in the South Pacific, by his own count. Wallis stayed in Tahiti for five weeks. His narrative of the voyage portrays Tahiti as a lush and fertile land, where the women traded sexual favors with the sailors. His portrayal did much to establish Tahiti's erotic reputation.

Wallis's time in Tahiti paved the way for Cook, who would use it as his base for observing the transit of Venus. An excellent commander, Wallis also treated his men well and saved them from scurvy. They appreciated his humane and sensitive treatment and worried about their captain when he fell ill toward the end of the voyage. Wallis remained quite ill as the *Dolphin* reached England. The illness limited his contact with others once he came home. It is unknown whether he and Cook met, but Cook did learn much about Wallis's journey from others—including Benjamin Franklin.

As British ships traveled further and further from the North Atlantic, they were afflicted by the shipworm, genus *teredo*, a bivalve mollusk known as the termite of the sea because it voraciously chewed through unprotected wood. William Douglass aptly observed that the tip of its head resembled the double-bit of an auger. The *Dolphin*, one of the first British warships protected by copper sheathing, safely avoided the ravages of the shipworm. Captain John Byron—grandfather of the poet—had circumnavigated the globe at the helm of the *Dolphin* before Wallis. Having demonstrated the value of copper sheathing, Captain Byron, with characteristic hyperbole, called it the "finest invention in the world." Though Byron did not discover the great southern continent, he did find signs of its existence. His discoveries had encouraged Wallis's expedition.[19]

While in Tahiti, Wallis inspected the *Dolphin* the first week of July 1767: "On the 3rd, we heeled the ship, and looked at her bottom, which we found as clean as when she came out of dock, and to our great satisfaction, as sound." Franklin also examined the *Dolphin*. Reading this sentence in Wallis's account of the voyage, he placed an asterisk after it, which corresponds to a note he inscribed and initialed on the lower margin of the page. To this time unpublished, the note adds a new episode to the story of Franklin's life, placing him at the shipyards inspecting the *Dolphin*: "She was sheathed with copper, and was as clean when she came home. I saw and examined her bottom at Woolwich."[20]

Cook did not have time to get the hull of the *Endeavour* refitted after Wallis's return. He left on August 28, 1768, without the copper sheathing that had protected the *Dolphin*. Sure enough, the shipworm wreaked havoc with the underside of the *Endeavour*. Cook would have to careen the ship twice during the voyage. The numerous challenges he faced throughout the journey remained a mystery to everyone back home. Cook would not return to England until July 1771, nearly three years after he had left.

The books Franklin added to his London library during the late 1760s also reflect his passion for travel. In May 1769, he attended an auction held by Wilson and Nicol, booksellers in the Strand. During the auction, Franklin successfully bid on many travel books. His purchases include older works such as John Ray's *Travels through the Low Countries, Germany, Italy and France*—a botanist's progress through Western Europe—and George Shelvolcke's *Voyage Round the World*, an early account of the South Pacific that was an important source of information for Byron, Wallis, and Cook. The more recent travel books that Franklin acquired at the Wilson and Nicol sale include Frederick Hasselquist's *Voyages and Travels in the Levant* and Niels Horrebow's *Natural History of Iceland*.[21]

Reviewing Hasselquist's *Voyage* for *The Monthly Review*, Griffiths addressed an issue applicable to travel writing in general. Should travel writers polish their prose to a high sheen, or should travel books present bare facts? Griffiths wondered:

> With respect to Dr. Hasselquist himself, he appears to be a very honest man, and a sensible observer, both of men and things. He is not, however, an elaborate writer; at least, there are in this work, no extraordinary proofs of his talent for literary compositions. His remarks are cursorily set down, without any great regard to order or system; and have the appearance of a mere journal, published in the same negligent

undress in which it was originally written, in the very course of the travels to which they relate.—But a naked beauty is not perhaps the less engaging for the want of ornaments, which sometimes only serve to obscure those charms they were intended to embellish.[22]

Franklin's bookish activities in 1769 also involved preparing the fourth edition of *Experiments and Observations on Electricity*, which included letters about other scientific topics. Some contribute to the travel-writing tradition. In one letter, Franklin relates the passage to Madeira on his voyage home in 1762. The weather was so balmy he kept his cabin window open at night, but the breeze kept blowing out the candle. Experimenting with whale oil, he designed a lamp that would burn steadily.[23] Many travelers can relate to Franklin's shipboard behavior. Encountering situations unprecedented in their personal experience, they must invent ways to adjust and innovate. The best travel writers, to Franklin's mind, were those who not only described their travels but also related what they learned from them.

Regardless what *Experiments* contributes to travel literature and other fields of scientific inquiry, it remains first and foremost an essential text in the field of electricity. Bewley, who reviewed the fourth edition at length, coined a memorable epithet for Franklin's *Experiments*. He called it the "*principia* of electricity."[24]

Franklin's responsibilities as colonial agent limited his summer travels for the next three years. Perhaps more than his work as agent for the Pennsylvania Assembly, his work as an American propagandist encouraged other colonial legislatures to recruit him to represent them. Three other colonial legislatures appointed Franklin their London agent in the coming years: the Georgia Assembly in 1768, the New Jersey House of Representatives in 1769, and the Massachusetts House of Representatives in 1770.

In the summer of 1771, Franklin had the chance to escape London on vacation. In mid-June, he went to Twyford, where he spent a week with Bishop Jonathan Shipley and his family. Before leaving for Twyford, Franklin may have spoken with Captain Cook, who had just returned from the South Pacific. He had successfully observed the transit of Venus in Tahiti. In addition, he had secret instructions to search for the great southern continent. He surveyed New Zealand, discovered Botany Bay, confirmed that Australia was not connected to New Guinea, claimed the whole east coast of Australia in the name of George III, and named it New South Wales. Cook stopped in Batavia on the way home, where dozens of crew members died from a disease contracted there. Cook's voyage was nonetheless deemed a brilliant success.

Chappe, who had gone to San José del Cabo at the southern tip of Baja California to observe the transit, was less fortunate. Aware of a typhus epidemic as he arrived, Chappe insisted that the Spanish vessel on which he was sailing land him and his men. He observed the transit from start to finish. Not until after the transit did things go awry. Struck with typhus on June 11th, Chappe was determined to survive for at least another week; the lunar eclipse on June 18th would let him determine the longitude of San José del Cabo, a measurement essential for ascertaining his transit observations. Chappe observed the eclipse, but perished two weeks later. The engineer and the painter, the sole survivors from Chappe's expedition, buried their leader, collected his notes, and returned to Paris. The only one to observe the 1761 and 1769 transits from start to finish, Chappe gave his life in the service of science.

After the survivors of Chappe's expedition reached Paris and Cook returned to London, all the data from the 1769 transit could be collated to determine the solar parallax and thus the distance between the earth and the sun. On behalf of the Royal Society, Thomas Hornsby calculated that the earth was 93,726,900 miles from the sun. Hornsby's calculation differs only eight-tenths of 1 percent from today's high-tech calculation of the distance. Several men perished to get that number, but got it they did. Their efforts exemplify the scientific heroism that helped define the Enlightenment.

In July 1771, Franklin returned to Twyford, where he spent another two weeks with Bishop Shipley and his family. Shipley had five daughters ranging in age from 11 to 23. Georgiana, at 15, was the most precocious. Franklin became her mentor, and they began corresponding. Shipley had a study in his garden, which Franklin found an ideal place to write. Here is where he started his autobiography. Averaging 2,000 words a day, Franklin wrote 87 manuscript pages to form part 1. His writing complemented his attention to Shipley's daughters. Dwelling on his boyhood in the autobiography, he created a self-portrait that would have amused the Shipley girls. And when he reached the story of running away from Boston, he turned himself into a romantic hero.[25]

Part 1 also deserves a place in Franklin's travel writings. As he escapes Boston, the pace of his narrative quickens, and the tension increases. He sustains the excitement throughout his journey to Philadelphia. At times, his autobiography takes on the quality of a picaresque novel. D. W. Brogan wondered if Franklin did not outdo the contemporary fiction: "What picaresque novel ever began with a better scene than that of Franklin's arriving in Philadelphia for the first time, soaked, scrubby, unknown, taking refuge in a

Quaker meeting house and falling asleep?"[26] Additional segments in part 1 relate Franklin's return trip to Boston, his journey to London, and his return from London to Philadelphia. The travel literature Franklin read before 1771 helped him write the travel sections of part 1, the most thrilling part of his autobiography.

The tour of England that Franklin and Pringle took in the summer of 1772 turned out to be an odyssey of intellectual discovery and rugged adventure. After leaving London in mid-June, they went to Ormathwaite, the country estate of Dr. William Brownrigg, whose home could boast a scientific laboratory, mineral museum, art collection, and library. He was best known for his research into salt production. During Franklin's stay, Brownrigg presented him with a copy of his treatise *The Art of Making Common Salt.*[27]

While sailing from New York to England in 1757, Franklin had learned that sailors already knew that oil could calm the waves. While living in London, he had begun experimenting on Clapham Common. Franklin was astonished that a tiny amount of oil would spread itself across a large body of water. He had a walking cane custom-made with a built-in vial to hold a small measure of oil, which he could use any time he wished to experiment or demonstrate the properties of oil on water. His demonstrations took on the quality of a parlor trick. Ever the merry prankster, Franklin would astonish friends with his seemingly magical power to calm the waves. Ormathwaite overlooked Derwent Water, an ideal location for Franklin to demonstrate oil's capacity to calm the waves. One day, Franklin went out on Derwent Water with Pringle and Brownrigg to demonstrate oil's wave-stilling properties.[28]

This vacation also took Franklin to the top of Wild Boar Fell. One of the finest peaks in the Pennines, it was the legendary home of England's last wild boar, which had been hunted down in the sixteenth century. Franklin took in the breathtaking view from the top and enjoyed the surrounding hills, farms, fields, and villages.

From Wild Boar Fell, Franklin headed to Whitehaven, where he began his descent to the underworld. In other words, he toured the large coal mine there. His correspondence chronicles the experience. In one letter, he tells Jacques Barbeu-Dubourg about it. Busy preparing a French edition of Franklin's writings, Barbeu-Dubourg liked the letter so much he printed it as part of his edition. Franklin wrote, "Descending by degrees toward the sea, I penetrated below the ocean, where the level of its surface was more than eight hundred fathoms above my head, and the miners assured me, that their works extended some miles beyond the place where I then was, continually and gradually descending under the sea." Franklin told Deborah about mountain climbing and exploring the undersea coal mine all in the same breath: "I have been nearer both the upper and lower regions than ever in my life before."[29]

While Franklin was on vacation, his dwelling place on Craven Street was being remodeled. During the late 1760s, Polly Stevenson had become acquainted with William Hewson, a young physician, lecturer on anatomy, and medical researcher. His research into the lymphatic system earned him the Copley Medal, but his personal qualities won Polly's heart. She paid tribute to him in verse:

> Fond to record the graces of his mind:
> Prudence with liberality combined:
> Sweet gentleness, integrity unswayed;
> And wisdom, by no vanity allayed.[30]

When the couple married on July 10, 1770, Franklin gave the bride away, and when Polly gave birth to their son William, Franklin became his godfather.

The Hewsons moved to Craven Street after their wedding, and, in 1772, William decided to remodel the house, filling the backyard with a lecture hall, where he could deliver his anatomical lectures. The new construction began while Franklin was on vacation. Polly wrote to reassure him that his door remained locked and his apartment undisturbed. With 27 Craven Street becoming the Hewsons' home and William Hewson's anatomical school, Margaret Stevenson found another house on the street for her boarding house. She relocated to 1 Craven Street.[31]

Franklin wrote his son to inform him of the move. His letter provides the fullest description of his London library: "I am almost settled in my new apartment; but removing, and sorting my papers and placing my books and things has been a troublesome jobb. I am amaz'd to see how books have grown upon me since my return to England. I brought none with me, and have now a roomfull; many collected in Germany, Holland and France; and consisting chiefly of such as contain knowledge that may hereafter be useful to America."[32]

He continued adding to his collection of travel writings. The following year, Franklin acquired *An Account of the Voyages*, a three-volume work edited by his friend John Hawkesworth compiling the explorations of Byron, Wallis, and Cook. This compilation of recent South-Sea voyages gave readers much new information about an unexplored region of the world. In Bewley's words, Hawkesworth's *Voyages* enabled the geographer "to fill up that wide-extended and opprobrious *blank*, so conspicuous in our maps of the southern hemisphere, without the assistance of mermaids, dolphins, and flying fishes."[33]

Franklin's copy of Hawkesworth's *Voyages* survives at the American Philosophical Society. Wormholes have partially ruined the first volume. The damage is ironic. Copper sheathing had stopped the shipworm, but bookworms damaged the stories of Wallis's copper-sheathed vessel. Considered in retrospect, the wormholes seem oddly appropriate. In science fiction, wormholes in outerspace let astronauts explore distant parts of the galaxy. Hawkesworth's *Voyages* let readers learn about distant parts of the world.

His copy of Hawkesworth also contains previously unpublished marginalia in his hand. The margins of Hawkesworth is where he recorded inspecting the hull of the *Dolphin*. A manuscript annotation to Byron's voyage reveals Franklin's ongoing curiosity about copper sheathing. In one paragraph, Byron observes that early in the voyage no fish followed their ship, attributing the phenomenon to its copper sheathing. Franklin partly underlined Byron's paragraph and wrote the word "Query" in the margin. He was obviously curious about how copper affected marine life.[34]

At the end of the same paragraph, Byron mentions that the drinking water on the *Dolphin* had become putrid: "We purified it with a machine, which had been put on board for that purpose: it was a kind of ventilator, by which air was forced through the water in a continued stream, as long as it was necessary." Franklin wrote in the margin: "An Invention of Dr. Hales." This note supplies information Byron omitted, but Franklin acknowledged Stephen Hales's role in inventing a device to make long-distance ocean travel safer and more convenient. Franklin owned a copy of Hales's *Account of a Useful Discovery to Distill Double the Usual Quantity of Sea-Water*, which he shared with Polly Stevenson.[35]

After mentioning the distillation of seawater, Byron observed that fresh meat would rot quite rapidly aboard his ship: "I procured three bullocks for the people, but they were little better than carrion, and the weather was so hot, that the flesh stunk in a few hours after they were killed." Franklin underlined the phrase "so hot" and wrote a query in the margin: "How hot?—had they not a thermometer?"[36] Franklin found such imprecise statements frustrating. If one captain has trouble with meat spoiling in hot weather, he should supply enough information to help the next captain avoid the problem.

Hawkesworth's *Voyages* is somewhat unusual among surviving books from Franklin's library. Normally, he did not annotate his books, but there is a major exception to this rule. As the London press issued more and more anti-American pamphlets after the Stamp Act, Franklin became increasingly upset with callous British attitudes toward colonial America. He expressed his scorn in the margins of the pamphlets. Published in 1773, Hawkesworth's *Voyages* appeared during a time when Franklin developed the habit of annotating political pamphlets. His marginalia in Hawkesworth is a carryover from his concurrent marginalia in contemporary political pamphlets.

With the tensions between Great Britain and colonial America escalating, Franklin soon had little time for traveling or reading travel literature. As the agent for Massachusetts, he learned that Governor Thomas Hutchinson and Lieutenant Governor Andrew Oliver had spearheaded the repressive measures the Crown was taking against the colony. Somehow Franklin obtained their correspondence with Thomas Whately, undersecretary of state, which he sent to Thomas Cushing, speaker of the Massachusetts Assembly. Franklin assumed the correspondence would pacify Massachusetts radicals and allay their ire toward the British authorities. He was wrong. It had the opposite effect, increasing tension between the governor and legislature, which petitioned to remove both Hutchinson and Oliver from office.

Hutchinson obtained a copy of the letter Franklin had written Cushing, which urged colonial assemblies to resolve never to aid Britain in any general war unless and until both Parliament and the Crown acknowledged American rights. Hutchinson sent a copy to the colonial secretary, who judged it treasonable and asked General Thomas Gage to obtain Franklin's original letter, so he could be prosecuted. Gage could not locate the original, which a quick-thinking Boston patriot had apparently destroyed to protect Franklin.

After Franklin forwarded to the British government the Massachusetts petition to remove Hutchinson and Oliver, a preliminary hearing took place on January 11, 1774. Soon, the explosive news about the Boston Tea Party reached London. Furious with Massachusetts, the British sought a scapegoat. The hearing on the petition took place before the Privy Council on January 29th at Whitehall in the Cockpit. Originally built for cockfighting, the Cockpit retained the aura of conflict.

Once Solicitor General Alexander Wedderburn began speaking, it was obvious he came not to prosecute Franklin but to humiliate him. For over an hour, he spewed a torrent of lies, rancour, innuendo, and mean-spirited misinformation. Priestley, who had obtained special admission to the Cockpit, saw and heard members of the Privy Council laugh at the solicitor general's sarcastic attacks. Spectators watched Wedderburn excoriate Franklin as if they were witnessing an *auto-da-fé*. He demanded that Franklin be branded a criminal. Wedderburn was not speaking figuratively. He wanted a red-hot iron to sear Franklin's flesh with the brand of a criminal.

Lond Mag Aug

Lord Loughborough

FIGURE 20.1 *Alexander Wedderburn, Lord Loughborough* (1780). Library of Congress, Prints and Photographs Division, Washington, DC, LC-USZ62-45275.

Jeremy Bentham, another guest in attendance, left the best description of Franklin that day. Franklin remained "the whole time like a rock in the same posture, his head resting on his left hand; and in that attitude abiding the pelting of the pitiless storm." Bentham's metaphor alludes to a prayer King Lear makes after taking shelter during the tragedy's famous storm scene. Lear's prayer emphasizes the power that comes from enduring adversity.[37]

Franklin would remain in London until March 1775, attempting some last-ditch efforts to achieve a peaceful and equitable coexistence between Britain and its American colonies. The story of his negotiations with British go-betweens culminates on February 1, 1775, the day William Pitt, 1st earl of

Chatham, presented a speech to the House of Lords. Considering Chatham's prestige, Franklin was shocked by how the legislators received his bill. John Montagu, 4th earl of Sandwich, who assumed Franklin had written Chatham's proposal, encouraged the House of Lords to reject it. Speaking to his face, he called Franklin "one of the bitterest and most mischievous enemies this country had ever known."[38]

Franklin was fuming when he left the House of Lords. He found it absurd that these narrow-minded legislators claimed sovereignty over 3 million virtuous, sensible Americans. "They appear'd to have scarce discretion enough to govern a herd of swine. Hereditary legislators!" Frankling thought. "There would be more propriety, because less hazard of mischief, in having [(as] in some university of Germany,) hereditary professors of mathematicks!"[39]

Seeing little hope of reconciling Britain and America, Franklin longed for home. Some sad news he received in late February made him all the more anxious to return. Deborah Franklin had suffered a stroke in mid-December. After lingering for a few days, she succumbed to her illness on Monday, December 19, 1774. The funeral took place on Wednesday. As a heavy snow fell, Hugh Roberts and some of Franklin's other old friends bore Deborah's casket to Christ Church Burial Ground, where she was laid to rest near Little Franky. Benjamin Franklin had not seen his wife in ten years. Now, he would never see her again.[40]

Sunday, March 19th, was Franklin's last day in London. He spent it with Priestley reading the latest American newspapers. Franklin let his friend know what to extract for the London press: a draining experience. Priestley recalled, "In reading them, he was frequently not able to proceed for the tears literally running down his cheeks."[41]

The next day, Franklin and his grandson Temple left London for Portsmouth, where they embarked for America. The six-week passage was quite pleasant. Instead of keeping a journal of the trip, Franklin wrote the story of his final negotiations on behalf of the colonies. He also pursued his oceanographic studies. Fascinated with the Gulf Stream and its capacity for making transatlantic travel more efficient, he hoped to study it further and began taking daily water temperature readings. They varied so little he abandoned the effort. But when the ship entered a meadow of sargasso on April 26th, this grandson of a Nantucket whaleman, sighted a whale and resolved to continue his temperature readings. Franklin's innovative study of the Gulf Stream would make the Atlantic crossing speedier for future travelers.

The Emblems That Made America

WEDDERBURN'S BEHAVIOR IN the Cockpit emboldened Franklin's London enemies to step up their attacks on him. Discussing Franklin's role as colonial agent, one newspaper paragraphist observed, "This living emblem of Iniquity in Grey Hairs thinks, because he is agent for four colonies, that he leads the whole continent by the nose, but he is greatly mistaken."[1] This clever British observer draws on the emblem book tradition to give readers a striking visual image. Though their politics differed, Franklin shared with this observer an ability to harness the power of emblems. Few contemporaries were more familiar with emblem books or more adept at manipulating their conventions than Franklin. With the start of the Revolutionary War, he would draw on the emblem books in his library for purposes of propaganda and, in so doing, create symbols that would define the new nation.

Upon reaching Philadelphia on Friday, May 5, 1775, Franklin heard some shocking news from New England. While he had been at sea, 800 British troops had marched on Concord, Massachusetts. The Minutemen, that is, the local militia, had assembled at Lexington ready to fight. When the British commander ordered the Americans to disperse, they refused. The redcoats fired on them, killing eight and forcing the rest to retreat toward Concord. The Minutemen established a new position on the farther side of Old North Bridge over the Concord River. This time they resisted the redcoats, forcing their retreat to Boston and harassing them as they went.

The news outraged the American colonists. The letters Franklin wrote to English correspondents after his arrival capture the prevailing animosity toward the British. He explained that the Battle of Lexington and Concord effectively united the colonies against Great Britain. To Joseph Priestley, he mentioned the conciliatory proposal Lord North had sent to the colonies and Governor Thomas Gage's plan to introduce it to the Massachusetts legislature, using the proverbial sword and olive branch for illustration: "The governor had called the assembly to propose Lord North's pacific plan; but before the time of their meeting, began cutting of throats; You know it was said he carried the sword in one hand, and the olive branch in the other; and it seems he chose to give them a taste of the sword first."[2]

The day after Franklin came home, the Pennsylvania Assembly elected him as a delegate to the Second Continental Congress, which would convene in Philadelphia the following week. Always willing to volunteer, Franklin served on numerous congressional committees. He chaired a committee for establishing a postal system, while serving on other committees to regulate commerce, locate supplies of saltpeter, negotiate with Native Americans, and protect American trade.

Franklin also served with Thomas Jefferson on a committee to consider North's conciliatory proposal. As prime minister, North tried to pacify the colonies with a tax exemption, only to burden them with a perpetual tax. Beyond the issue of taxes, North's proposal did nothing to reconcile the Americans' other grievances. His lordship was trying to use the sneaky proposal to divide the colonies but failed to understand how united they had become. Congress refused his conciliatory proposal.

Jefferson and Franklin also served together on a committee to draft the *Declaration of the Causes and Necessity for Taking up Arms*, a document General George Washington would present to the Continental Army, which he had started forming in Massachusetts once Congress elected him commander-in-chief. The activities of one particular committee belong to Franklin's intellectual life. The committee to arrange for printing paper currency gave him the chance to use his library and consult some of his most treasured volumes.

On June 22nd, the day that news of the Battle of Bunker Hill reached Philadelphia, the Continental Congress approved an emission of 2 million dollars to be issued in bills of credit for the defense of America. The next day, a committee was appointed to arrange for printing paper currency. The committee was responsible for getting plates engraved in ten denominations, locating supplies of paper, and arranging with printers to produce the bills. Franklin went beyond the basic responsibilities Congress stipulated. He took it upon himself to design the currency, choosing separate devices and mottoes for each bill.

Familiar with emblem books since boyhood, Franklin had been thinking more about them recently. Two years earlier, Peter P. Burdett, an English engraver, had sent him some specimens of transferware, that is, ceramics adorned with images transferred from paper printed with copperplate engravings. Franklin told Burdett that he had had the same idea over two decades earlier. In the late 1740s, Franklin had asked his friend Dr. John Mitchell, then living in London, to locate the plates that had been used for *Moral Virtue Delineated*, an emblem book by Marin Le Roy, sieur de Gomberville.[3]

Since each copperplate engraving in the volume illustrates an individual moral virtue, Franklin thought they would be ideal for transferring to ceramic tiles, which could be mounted in the home around the chimney and thus provide an alternative to the biblical illustrations that adorned Dutch delft-ware tiles. The chimney tiles would let children see the illustrated moral virtues every day and thus give parents the chance to explain the pictures to their children and impress on them their moral sentiments.

Though ideally suited for the home, the emblems from *Moral Virtue Delineated* would not work for the Continental currency. They were too complex and too heavy-handed. Besides, they primarily contained human or humanlike figures—angels, nymphs, satyrs. Franklin decided against human figures for the bills. He wanted more symbols than scenes.

Once he had finished designing the currency and it had been issued, Franklin wrote "An Account of the Devices in the Continental Bills of Credit." In this essay, he explains what each device symbolizes. A brilliant piece of political propaganda, the essay reads like a linked series of commentaries from an emblem book. Nowhere does it say where he found the emblems. Though he did not take any from *Moral Virtue Delineated*, he took most of them from two other emblem books.

The first emblem that Franklin discusses in "Account of the Devices" comes from Diego Saavedra's *Royal Politician*. Saavedra, a Spanish diplomat, had written this emblem book as a conduct manual for princes. It consists of 100 emblems, each with a commentary. Saavedra's commentaries are much longer than those typically found in emblem books. Each amounts to an essay on an individual aspect of leadership.

There is no evidence that Franklin owned a copy of the *Royal Politician*, but he might have read it in his youth with other leadership manuals or found it elsewhere in Philadelphia. James Logan had had a copy in his personal library at Stenton. Upon his death in 1750, Logan bequeathed his library to Pennsylvania. A building was erected for the Loganian Library on Sixth Street in Philadelphia, and it opened its doors every Saturday afternoon to welcome the general public. Few people were interested in scholarly editions of the books in Greek, Latin, Hebrew, and Arabic that dominated the collection, but those familiar with Logan's library knew about his other bibliographic treasures. One Saturday in the summer of 1775, Franklin could have gone to the Loganian Library and examined his old friend's copy of the *Royal Politician*.[4]

In Saavedra's second volume, Franklin found the emblem of a harp with the motto *Majora minoribus consonant*, which he would use for the 8 dollar bill. He kept the Latin for the currency but translated it for "Account of the Devices": "The greater and smaller ones sound together." Containing strings of different length within a strong frame, all in tune, the harp symbolized the Continental Congress. The strings represented the different-sized colonies and different ranks of American people working together in harmony.[5]

While adapting Saavedra's emblematic harp, Franklin ignored his commentary. Saavedra warned against altering the established form of government: "A prudent prince tunes the strings in the same order they stand in." Thinking the harp's strings symbolized a nation's people, Saavedra nonetheless took a dim view of the public. People are flighty and fickle. Rarely do they think through decisions. Seldom can they distinguish truth from falsehood. It takes a strong leader to harmonize them.[6]

The harp was the only emblem Franklin took from the *Royal Politician*. He had a different emblem book in his personal library that worked much better, Joachim Camerarius's *Centuries*. A German botanist and physician, Camerarius used his knowledge of botany and zoology to create his emblem book. *Centuries* depicts emblems with matter derived from four general areas: herbs and plants, four-legged animals, creatures of the air, and creatures of the sea. For Camerarius, the purpose of studying nature was not merely to describe and identify species. It was also to understand their figurative meanings. He sought to know what the flora and fauna symbolized. Camerarius's *Centuries* established the emblematic approach as a valid way to study natural history.

Though he conceived his natural history as a four-part work, Joachim Camerarius did not live to see his fourth volume to completion. He issued the first three in his lifetime, letting his son finish the fourth. Ludwig Camerarius issued his father's final volume in 1605. The complete work went through several editions, including the 1702 Mainz edition, the one Franklin owned.

Camerarius's work is highly structured. Each emblem fills two pages, and all contain the same components: emblem number, motto, device, epigrammatic distich, and commentary. Camerarius's commentaries include botanical or zoographical information but also provide moral wisdom in the form of proverbs and aphorisms. In addition, he supplied advice for future leaders. All the devices appear in a circular frame, thus reflecting their affinity with medallions and making them suitable to adorn currency.[7]

Camerarius encouraged his illustrator to make the engravings as accurate and realistic as possible, but his commentaries show less concern for realism. His most important source was Pliny's *Natural Historie*. Organized from largest to smallest, the volume about land animals follows Pliny's section on land beasts, starting with the elephant. Redoing Pliny in emblem form, Camerarius considered himself *Plinius emblematicus*.[8]

For what Franklin wanted, Camerarius was more useful than Saavedra. The number of emblems Franklin took from each volume suggests that he went through the work page by page searching for ideal devices and mottoes. With his selections, Franklin preserved the integrity of his source. In other words, he did not take a motto from one emblem and a device from another. Though he simplified the imagery of some devices, he kept both motto and device together, seeing them as integral components of the same emblem.

As he paged through *Centuries*, Franklin sought mottoes that would give Americans messages of strength, freedom, unity, and righteousness. Franklin's currency inspired Revolutionary America. Carefully selecting his emblems, he created pocket propaganda, notes of currency that people would carry with them and look at often. Every time they earned wages or bought goods, Americans would see the emblems Franklin had chosen to represent their cause and receive inspiration and encouragement.

Devoted to herbs and plants, Camerarius's first volume presented one major problem. Many of the botanical devices look similar. Each depicts a different plant, but it is hard to tell the flowers from the leaves. With the plant centered in the middle of the circular device, the imagery around its edges is more appealing. A puffy-cheeked face in the clouds blows wind through the tree branches in emblem 11. Emblem 17 shows another personified cloud in the act of blowing wind. The imagery looked familiar to Franklin. Emblem 8 in *Moral Virtue Delineated* uses the same motif to show how nature wafts the hero toward temptation.[9]

Paging through Camerarius's first volume, Franklin finally reached one he could use, emblem 41. He translated its Latin motto—*Sistine vel abstine*—in two possible ways: "Bear with me, or let me alone," or "Either support or leave me." The device portrays a disembodied hand attempting to uproot a thorny bush. The sharp thorns cause the hand to bleed. Franklin would use this emblem for the 5 dollar bill, though the reduced size of the device makes it hard to tell that the hand is bleeding. In his commentary, Franklin says the thorny bush represents America, the hand Britain. He wishes the bleeding would stop, the hand would heal, and wisdom and equality would guide its future operations. He also hopes the thorny bush will flourish, forming a hedge around it to guard against invading enemies. Franklin's language echoes the Old Testament: "I will hedge up thy way with thorns, and make a wall." It also calls to mind a saying from *Poor Richard's Almanack*: "Love your neighbour; yet don't pull down your hedge."[10]

Emblem 41 helped Franklin select others from Camerarius's first volume. It taught him that devices combining plant life with human elements would work well as propaganda. As he scanned the rest of the volume for useful emblems, Franklin looked for ones displaying an interaction between man and nature. Emblem 50 depicts a laurel wreath atop a marble plinth with the motto *Si recte facies*, "If you act rightly." Franklin found this emblem appropriate for the 30 dollar bill, the largest denomination Congress had approved. He explained that it promised to reward Americans for acting righteously in the face of British injustice. It also encouraged Americans to be brave and steady in their defense of liberty. Those who persevere would be rewarded with laurel wreathes and marble monuments.[11]

Emblem 58 portrays an acanthus plant onto which has been placed a heavy weight. The plant flourishes regardless, sprouting from beneath the weight. This device illustrates the motto, *Depressa resurgit*, "Tho' oppressed it rises." Camerarius had cited Vitruvius's *De architectura* as a source. Though Franklin does not mention *De architectura* in "Account of the Devices," he does repeat Vitruvius's architectural imagery, asserting that the accidental placement of a weight atop an acanthus plant inspired the capital of the Corinthian column. Placing this emblem on the 1 dollar bill, Franklin reassured Americans that British oppression would not destroy them. Instead, it would encourage them to work harder, find new ways to fulfill their political goals, and establish American prosperity on a foundation of liberty.[12]

Emblem 84, the last one Franklin took from Camerarius's first volume, presents another combination of man and nature. A disembodied hand holds a flail over several sheaves of wheat, illustrating the motto *Tribulatio ditat*, "Affliction enriches." Franklin used this emblem for the 2 dollar bill. For his commentary, he translated the Latin to suit the device: "Threshing improves it." The thresher's flail represents the British; the sheaves of wheat symbolize the Americans. No matter how hard the British strike them, the Americans will only improve. The beatings will bring forth chaffy grains of genius in the arts and manufactures that are hidden inside the husk. Franklin's commentary reflects the democratic belief that all people have the potential for genius. The hardships Americans faced would soon bring out their finest qualities.[13]

The land animals in Camerarius's second volume gave Franklin mottoes and emblems for three more bills. Emblem 22 depicts two bears engaged in a

Graeco-Roman wrestling match. Behind them, rain appears on one side of the device, clear skies on the other. The motto is *Serenabit*, "It will clear up." Franklin used this emblem for the 7 dollar bill, but it was difficult to render the ursine combatants with sufficient detail, so he cut the bears and displayed a storm with clear skies approaching. The image reassured Americans. They may not have serenity now, but they will achieve it later. Their present strife will end, and they can look forward to a calm and bright future.[14]

Franklin used emblem 58 from the second volume for the 4 dollar bill. Its motto is *Aut mors aut vita decora*, "Either death or an honorable life." Franklin translated the Latin less precisely, but more dramatically: "Death or liberty."[15] A few months earlier, Patrick Henry had delivered his famous line at St. John's Church in Richmond during the Virginia Convention: "Give me liberty or give me death!" Franklin may have learned about Henry's speech from the Virginia delegates to the Continental Congress. Franklin's similar phrasing shows that, like Henry, he recognized the rhetorical power underlying the dramatic contrast between liberty and death.

The accompanying device portrays a wild boar rushing toward the point of a spear. Printed on the 4 dollar bill, this image let Americans know that they could take inspiration from the wild boar, a strong and courageous animal. The boar is peaceful and inoffensive when allowed to enjoy its freedom, but when a hunter rouses it, the boar often turns and makes the hunter pay for his injustice.

Emblem 96, the last one Franklin took from Camerarius's second volume, depicts a beaver gnawing down a large tree with the motto, *Perseverando*, "By perseverance." He selected it for the 6 dollar bill. In his commentary, Franklin emphasizes the enormous power Britain has over the Americans, which it is enforcing with deadly arms, arbitrary taxes, and capricious legislation, "binding us in all cases whatsoever." Franklin's phrase repeats the language of the Declaratory Act, but the emblem reverses the current power structure, showing the beaver, an indigenous American animal, taking control. In American culture, the beaver's capacity for hard work had already become proverbial. Franklin's emblem for the 6 dollar bill incorporates this traditional association. Through hard work and perseverance, the beaver will take down the rigid and inflexible tree that is Britain.[16]

Franklin used emblem 32 in Camerarius's third volume for the 3 dollar bill. An eagle has swooped down to snatch a crane. Camerarius's crane was an inspired choice: Cranes traditionally symbolize justice, goodness, and longevity. As they struggle in the air, the crane jabs its beak into the eagle's throat. The crane's act of violence is Franklin's innovation. Camerarius had not depicted the crane's beak penetrating the eagle's throat. Franklin captured their struggle at a moment of uncertainty. The eagle must release its grip on the crane to survive but hesitates to do so. The motto is *Exitus in dubio est*, "The event is uncertain."[17]

Of all the emblems Franklin selected for the Continental currency, none more closely coincided with his writings than the crane and the eagle. During an evening with some London friends, Franklin demurred when one suggested that the era of fables was over. He said the subject was inexhaustible. Many new fables were just waiting for the right pen to come along. When one friend asked who would be the person to write these new fables, Franklin said he would. Taking pen and paper in hand, he wrote a new fable in a few minutes, "The Eagle and the Cat."[18]

Flying over a barnyard one day, an eagle sees a furry creature basking in the sun. Thinking it was a rabbit, the eagle swoops down, seizes the creature, and carries it high into the air. Not until the eagle is aloft does he realize that he has a cat in his clutches. The cat sets her claws into the eagle's breast. Realizing the mistake, the eagle opens his talons to drop the cat, but she refuses to relax her grip until the eagle puts her back where he had snatched her.

Substitute the word "cat" for "crane," and Franklin's commentary on the emblem could be an application for the fable. The eagle represents Great Britain; the crane symbolizes America. The device has a message for both the crane and the eagle. It warns the crane against depending on diplomatic means for success; it must be prepared to use its natural means of defense. In addition, it cautions the eagle against relying on its superior strength since a weaker bird could destroy it.[19]

With the works of Saavedra and Camerarius, Franklin had found emblems for all the bills Congress requested except the 20 dollar bill, but he did not need any more sources. Ever since he wrote the *Canada Pamphlet*, Franklin had an idea for an emblem he wanted to use somehow. He had repeated a slightly revised version in "Causes of the American Discontents before 1768": "The waves never rise but when the winds blow." The Continental currency gave Franklin the chance to reuse this memorable saying again, this time in visual form.

Camerarius could have supplied some visual iconography to help Franklin convert his aphorism into imagery: the personified and puffy-cheeked clouds from two emblems in the first volume of *Centuries*. They blow violently on the waters and raise its waves. For the motto Franklin used *Vi concitatae*, "Raised by force." He explained: "From the remotest antiquity, in figurative language, great waters have signified *the people*, and waves an insurrection.

The people of themselves are supposed as naturally inclined to be still, as the waters to remain level and quiet. Their rising here appears not to be from an internal cause, but from an external power, expressed by the head of *Aeolus*, God of the winds (or *Boreas*, the *North* wind, as usually the most violent) acting furiously upon them." Identifying the wind as the "North wind," Franklin slyly attacked Lord North, whose ill-conceived conciliatory proposal had reflected his ignorance of and insensitivity to the plight of the Americans.[20]

The emblems Franklin chose for the currency worked well. People enjoyed interpreting the images for themselves. Franklin's motivation underlying "Account of Devices" was mainly propagandistic, but he also wanted to clarify the symbolism for the devices. Franklin's essay proved quite popular. After he published it in *The Pennsylvania Gazette* that September, it was reprinted in newspapers and almanacs from Delaware to New Hampshire.[21]

The Reverend Wheeler Case, a Revolutionary Connecticut poet, enjoyed the device on the 3 dollar bill so much he wrote a poem about it, "A Contest between the Eagle and the Crane." Case structured his poem like an emblem, describing the device and adding some narrative drama in the first part and then offering a verse commentary in the second.[22] Case's "Contest" is not very good poetry, but it does verify that Franklin's designs for the Continental currency captured the imagination of the American people.

Even Loyalists had to admit the currency was effective. Nicholas Cresswell, for one, criticized the Continental Congress's right to release its own currency, but he complimented the care with which the emblems had been selected. While in Boston during its occupation by British troops, William Browne wrote a letter describing the Continental currency. He informed his British correspondent that Franklin had invented the emblems.[23] Though Franklin's authorship of "Account of the Devices" was not discovered until the late twentieth century, Browne's statement shows that Franklin's responsibility for designing the currency was general knowledge in Revolutionary America.

Browne interpreted some of the devices for his correspondent. He described the storm scene on the 7 dollar bill as a "heavy shower of rain falling on a new settled country." Since Franklin had taken the device from an emblem created before British North America was first settled, the original emblem had nothing to do with a new country. Browne shows that people interpreted the emblem to suit their circumstances. Since the blood of the British hand that had attempted to pluck the American thorn bush on the 5 dollar bill is unclear, Browne reversed the symbolism Franklin had intended. With the Boston Tea Party a recent memory, Browne saw the device as an image of an American hand attempting to pluck a British tea plant.[24]

Though Franklin took the harp on the 8 dollar bill from a Spanish emblem book, Browne gave it a different nationality. He called it an "Irish harp." Browne may have been onto something. Franklin had great sympathy for Ireland, whose situation was not dissimilar to British North America. The Irish followed current events and reprinted pro-American political pamphlets. In the bold articles of confederation Franklin would write the following year, he not only made a provision to include Canada as part of the United Colonies of America, he also offered to include Ireland. Perhaps Franklin did have this iconographic Irish symbol in mind while thumbing through Saavedra's *Royal Politician* in search of useful emblems.

The clearest evidence concerning the symbolic impact of Franklin's currency comes from the emblems that individual regiments in the Continental Army chose. Many borrowed their regimental emblems from the Continental currency. The Third Pennsylvania Regiment used the harp and its accompanying Latin motto for its flag. The Sixth Pennsylvania Regiment used Franklin's wild boar and its accompanying death-or-liberty motto, and the Seventh Pennsylvania Regiment used the tree-gnawing beaver and the motto *Perseverando*.[25]

The same week Franklin wrote "Account of Devices," he also wrote a letter to Bishop Shipley. He stressed that the strength of America comes from its soil. Its agricultural potential will provide the power to resist all invaders. To make his point, Franklin applied a classical reference. His simile demonstrates that Franklin's use of emblems went beyond selecting devices and mottoes for the Continental currency. The letter gives Shipley an emblematic simile that creates a vivid image illustrating Franklin's point: "Agriculture is the great source of wealth and plenty. By cutting off our trade you have thrown us *to the Earth*, whence like *Antaeus* we shall rise yearly with fresh strength and vigour."[26]

The most famous emblem to emerge during the Revolutionary War is the device of a coiled rattlesnake with the motto, "Don't tread on me." This emblem was first used on a drum for the Continental Marines. Franklin did not create the emblem, but it does echo one he did create, the Join-or-Die cut-snake emblem he had invented earlier. Why did it have to be snakes? Franklin would attempt to say why in "The Rattle-Snake as a Symbol of America," the fullest contemporary explication of the coiled snake emblem.

"The Rattle-Snake as a Symbol of America" also reads like a commentary in an emblem book. Franklin published it under the pseudonym "An American Guesser." In the opening paragraph, his pseudonymous commentator lets readers know a little about himself. Having seen this emblem on a drum, he says, "As I have nothing to do with public affairs, and as my time is perfectly my own, in order to divert an idle hour, I sat down to guess what could have been intended by this uncommon device."[27] This self-characterization seems like a fantasy piece. Few men in America were more involved with public affairs than Benjamin Franklin. Congress had reconvened in September, and Franklin had been appointed to a committee to travel to George Washington's headquarters at Cambridge, Massachusetts. Having since returned, Franklin was serving on several other congressional committees when this article appeared in *The Pennsylvania Gazette*. Traditionally, the rattlesnake was a measure of valor. Dr. Alexander Hamilton recorded the proverb, "No one can be called a colonel who has not killed a rattlesnake."[28] American Guesser says that an emblematic animal should exemplify the animal's worthy characteristics, but initially he cannot think of any worthy characteristics a rattlesnake possesses. As an indigenous creature, the rattlesnake could represent America, something that Franklin had recognized decades earlier when he suggested that since Britain was transporting convicted felons to the American colonies that colonial America should send rattlesnakes to Britain.

The more he thinks about it, the more worthy qualities American Guesser can see in the rattlesnake. Since it has no eyelids, the snake symbolizes vigilance. Since the snake never begins an attack, but, once engaged, never surrenders, it symbolizes both magnanimity and courage. In addition, the snake never wounds until it has given notice by shaking its rattle, which seems to be a "strong picture of the temper and conduct of America."[29]

After counting thirteen rattles on the snake's tail, American Guesser observes, " 'Tis curious and amazing to observe how distinct and independent of each other the rattles of this animal are, and yet how firmly they are united together." The sound of the snake's rattle reinforces the idea of unity. One rattle alone is incapable of producing sound, but when the thirteen ring together, the sound produced is "sufficient to alarm the boldest man living." Counting the rattles, American Guesser reiterates Franklin's belief that Canada should join the American Revolution: "Perhaps it might be only fancy, but, I conceited the painter had shewn a half formed additional rattle, which, I suppose, may have been intended to represent the province of Canada."[30]

Congress was still not ready to declare independence. Canada remained one unsettled issue. Would it join the American cause? Congress appointed Franklin as a commissioner to Canada. The late winter journey from Philadelphia to Montreal would be arduous, but he accepted the appointment.

He and his fellow commissioners left Philadelphia on March 26th. Now 70, Franklin suffered from swollen legs and suppurated boils during the trip but returned from Canada with little gains for his pains. Needless to say, the commissioners failed to convince Canada to join the American cause.

In June, Congress selected a committee to draft the Declaration of Independence: Thomas Jefferson, John Adams, Benjamin Franklin, Robert Livingston, and Roger Sherman. As the first name listed, Jefferson chaired the Committee of Five and therefore determined how it would proceed. He chose to write the Declaration of Independence himself and then submit his draft to the committee for its input.

On Friday, June 28th, the Committee of Five presented the Declaration of Independence to Congress, which delayed its debate until Monday. Despite the grueling July heat, debate continued all day Monday and into Tuesday. On Thursday, the Fourth of July, Congress approved the Declaration of Independence with its final changes and ordered it printed. Copies were sent to General Washington, who had relocated the Continental Army to New York after retaking Boston. Washington arranged for the Declaration to be read aloud to all his troops.

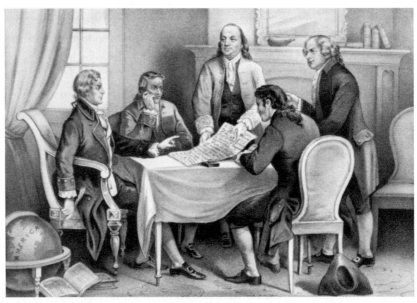

FIGURE 21.1 *The Declaration Committee* (left to right: Thomas Jefferson, Roger Sherman, Benjamin Franklin, Robert R. Livingston, and John Adams). Lithograph by Currier and Ives, 1876. Library of Congress, Prints and Photographs Division, Washington, DC, LC-USZ62-820.

As busy as Franklin was in the Continental Congress, he had other legislative responsibilities. On July 8th, he was elected to the Pennsylvania state convention and, on the 16th, chosen its president. The convention had the responsibility to draft the state constitution. Similar conventions took place in other states. Most state constitutions created a governor and a bicameral legislature, but Franklin suggested something more democratic. He argued against a bicameral legislature. The picturesque simile he used to support his argument reinforces the relationship between emblems and figurative language. "It appears to me," Franklin argued, "like putting one horse before a cart and the other behind it, and whipping them both. If the horses are of equal strength, the wheels of the cart, like the wheels of government, will stand still; and if the horses are strong enough, the cart will be torn to pieces."[31] Pennsylvania followed Franklin's preference for a unicameral legislature and an executive council in lieu of a governor, thus creating a more purely democratic form of government.

Also that July, Congress appointed Franklin, Adams, and Jefferson to a committee to design a seal for the United States of America. The assignment let Franklin use his extensive knowledge of emblem literature again. Jefferson and Adams had plenty of ideas, too. Jefferson took inspiration from *Aesop's Fables*, suggesting that a good device to symbolize the United States would be the father who presents a bundle of rods to his sons. Aesop tells the story of three quarrelsome sons. Their father initially gives each a rod, and they easily break them. When the father gives them a set of rods bundled together, the rods are unbreakable, proving the old adage that there is strength in unity. This fable became so well known in America, it gave rise to a proverbial simile: "like a bundle of rods."[32]

Adams recalled an engraving from Shaftesbury's works. As Hercules rests on his club, Virtue personified gestures toward a rugged mountain in the distance, encouraging him to ascend. Sloth, on the other hand, tries to persuade Hercules toward vice. Neither Franklin nor Jefferson thought the Hercules imagery would work for the seal. They kept brainstorming.[33]

Jefferson now suggested that one side of the seal could portray the children of Israel tramping through the wilderness led by a cloud during the day and a pillar of fire at night. The other side could depict Hengist and Horsa, the Anglo-Saxon chiefs who, according to Jefferson's interpretation of political history, established the basic principles on which the American government was formed.[34]

All these suggestions lacked the elegant simplicity of the emblems Franklin had used for the Continental currency. Unlike Camerarius's emblems, they do not come from natural history, but from fables, mythology, or ancient history. All contain human figures, in fact, several human figures in each group. Regardless of how well his emblems for the Continental currency had worked, Franklin was hesitant to reuse Camerarius. He, too, wanted human figures for the Great Seal of the United States.

Franklin had another emblem book in his library, Christoph Weigel's *Ethica naturalis*.[35] Unlike Camerarius, Weigel included numerous human figures. Except for a small group of animals toward the end, Weigel's devices typically portray two human figures in the foreground, with the subject of each depicted in the background. One figure gestures toward the background to identify the emblem's subject. Nearly all take place outdoors, usually in a natural or rural setting. A handful of devices occur in urban settings. The clothing of the figures indicates ancient Roman times, but a few are more recent. They portray a wide variety of subjects: natural phenomena, natural disasters, illnesses, stages of life, and many more. The last one, *Mundi negocia*—business of the world—portrays a busy marketplace that serves as a microcosm.

Franklin did not use any of Weigel's individual emblems, but the composition of his proposed devices reflects Weigel's influence. Inspired by Jefferson, Franklin suggested an image of Moses standing on the shore, extending his arm over the sea and causing it to overwhelm the pharaoh, who sits in his chariot oblivious of the danger. Rays streaming from a pillar of fire in the clouds reach Moses, giving his conduct divine sanction. The motto for this device is "Rebellion to tyrants is obedience to God."[36]

This motto comes from "Bradshaw's Epitaph," a hoax Franklin had written some months earlier, which ostensibly honors the regicide John Bradshaw. The fake epitaph ends with the admonition: "Never forget that rebellion to tyrants is obedience to God." These words would not become the motto for the United States, but Jefferson liked them so well that he did make Franklin's phrase his personal motto.[37]

Deadlocked, the committee decided to consult the French artist Pierre du Simitière to get his thoughts. He came up with a much different concept. A six-part shield would have different symbols for each of the nations whose people formed a significant part of the American population, including, for example, an Irish harp. Du Simitière also placed Lady Liberty in the device and an American soldier, adorned in a hunting shirt and holding a tomahawk and a rifle. The appearance of Du Simitière's soldier verifies the frontiersman as a defining symbol of America. Du Simitière also coined a motto for the seal, one that would stick: *E pluribus unum*. The committee submitted its report on August 20th, using Du Simitière's idea for one side and a simplified version of the Moses-and-pharaoh image for the other. Congress tabled the matter without reaching a decision.[38]

The same day the committee submitted its report to Congress, Franklin began drafting a letter to Lord Howe, who had reached America, prepared for one last attempt to negotiate a peace. In his draft, Franklin recalls his negotiations with Howe in London but concludes that it is now impossible for Americans to submit to British control. Echoing the words of Friar Bacon's Brass Head, Franklin says, "To propose now to the colonies a submission to the crown of Great Britain, would be fruitless. The time is past." Franklin never finished the letter, but, with Congress's approval, he went to New York with John Adams and Edward Rutledge to meet Howe in person. The meeting came to naught.[39]

Later that year, Congress appointed Franklin to a three-man commission to visit Paris and negotiate a treaty with France, the first delegation appointed to represent the United States abroad. The two other commissioners, Silas Deane and Arthur Lee, were already in Europe. Deane was in France, seeking to purchase munitions and other goods for America; Lee was in London, acting as confidential agent for Congress's Committee of Secret Correspondence. On October 27th, the day before the British attacked White Plains, Franklin, accompanied by two grandsons, Temple Franklin, now 16, and Benny Bache, who was 7, boarded the *Reprisal* bound for France.

Not until 1780 would Congress return to the issue of a great seal. A new committee was appointed that March, and it produced a report on the seal, which was recommitted two months later. Two more years would pass with no further action, but in 1782 Congress asked its secretary Charles Thomson to come up with a final design. A close friend of the Franklin family, Thomson returned to Franklin's principle source for the emblems on the Continental currency: Camerarius's *Centuries*. Though Thomson had an excellent library himself, he did not own a copy of Camerarius; apparently, he visited Sarah Bache and borrowed her father's copy. Thomson started thumbing through the work for an appropriate emblem. It did not take him long to find an ideal device, the first one in the third volume. This device reinforces the close relationship between proverbs and emblems. It presents a heraldic eagle depicted with an olive branch and a variation on the proverbial sword: a cluster of lightning bolts, which represents the weapon Zeus used to mete out punishment.[40]

While adopting this device, Thomson made several changes. He substituted the bald eagle for the heraldic eagle, thus using an indigenous American animal. He kept the olive branch and also retained the bundle of weapons, substituting arrows for lightning bolts. The arrow had precedents in both the classical European and Native American traditions. Furthermore, the bundle of arrows recalls the bundle of sticks the father presents to his sons in *Aesop's Fables*, a symbol of unity.

Thomson stipulated thirteen arrows, symbolizing the thirteen original states. The bundle of arrows is just one of many uses of the number thirteen in the Great Seal. On its chest, Thomson's eagle wears a shield adorned with thirteen alternating stripes, seven red and six white. Thirteen stars appear above the eagle's head. The eagle holds in its beak a scroll bearing the motto, which has thirteen letters: *E pluribus unum*. Though Thomson deserves most of the credit for creating it, the Great Seal of the United States—the greatest emblem in American history—has its roots in a book from Benjamin Franklin's library.

22

Solon and Sophocles

WHEN ERNEST HEMINGWAY entered Paris in 1922 to make his name as a writer, he compared himself with Benjamin Franklin entering Philadelphia two centuries earlier to make his name as a printer. Describing his arrival in Paris, Hemingway reminded Ezra Pound of the "fine thrill enjoyed by Benj. Franklin when entering Philadelphia with a roll under each arm." When Franklin entered Paris in December 1776, he cut a much different figure from his younger self entering Philadelphia. He never reached his Paris years in the autobiography, but he described his appearance to some English correspondents. Telling them he was alive and well and living in Paris, he mentioned his plain attire and thin, grey, straight hair, which poked out from under a marten fur cap that came down his forehead, almost touching the top of his ever-present spectacles.[1]

Hemingway was a nobody when he came to Paris; Franklin was the most famous American in the world when he arrived. France adored him. His distinctive look, combined with his renowned scientific accomplishments and winning personality, made him the darling of Paris. Parisians hung his portrait in their homes, and Franklin medallions made from Sèvres porcelain became chic accessories. His face appeared on clocks and rings, snuffboxes and handkerchiefs. Franklin dolls became favorite toys for French schoolgirls, and Franklin himself became a favorite toy for their grandmothers, at least those *salonnières* lucky enough to lure Franklin into their orbit.

He made such an appealing subject for Parisian artists that Jean-Antoine Houdon, France's greatest sculptor, joined the fun. The two would become friends later, but Houdon made a terra-cotta bust of Franklin after first seeing him in public. Franklin carefully shaped his personal image for the French public; Houdon's bust re-creates the impression Franklin conveyed. Houdon portrayed him as worldly and wise, yet friendly and approachable. Nineteenth-century American sculptor Richard Saltonstall Greenough, who would base his sculpture of Franklin on Houdon's bust, said that Franklin's face had two sides, the left philosophic and reflective, the right funny and smiling.[2]

FIGURE 22.1 *Benjamin Franklin and His Hat* (1855). From Evert A. Duyckinck and George L. Duyckinck, *Cyclopaedia of American Literature* (New York: Charles Scribner, 1856), vol. 1, frontispiece. Kevin J. Hayes Collection, Toledo, OH.

Houdon and the staff of his workshop created several copies of the bust in marble and plaster, but they could scarcely meet the demand. Besides capturing Franklin's personality, Houdon's bust documents the emergence of modern celebrity culture, a phenomenon that, needless to say, extends to the present. It is no coincidence that Andy Warhol, whose work reflects the ongoing proliferation of celebrity culture, would obtain one of Houdon's busts of Franklin, which he kept in the front hall of his Upper East Side townhouse.[3]

Within months of Franklin's arrival, Paris publisher Nicolas Ruault released the French edition of *The Way to Wealth*. *La science du bonhomme Richard*, as it was titled, reinforced Franklin's popularity, letting French readers see another side of him. The book was a bestseller, and the French took to calling Franklin "Bonhomme Richard." His formula for success caught on, and his penny-saving maxims were repeated throughout France. Ruault would offer an additional homage to Franklin, dedicating his collected edition of Bernard Palissy's scientific writings to him.[4]

The lightning rod had done more than any other single object to establish Franklin's worldwide reputation as both a scientist and a humanitarian. His scientific and philanthropic accomplishments reinforced his political reputation. Europeans considered him the leader of the American Revolution. The view of contemporary French playwright Jean-François de La Harpe is typical. He called Franklin the "patriarch of America, and the founder of her liberty."[5]

After the Revolutionary War began, the British sought ways to cut Franklin down to size. In May 1777, they found one possible way. When Franklin was living in London, the British Board of Ordnance approached him and asked how to protect its powder magazine against lightning. He recommended pointed lightning rods. His recommendation came before the Royal Society, which established a committee to analyze his advice. All the committee members approved Franklin's idea except Benjamin Wilson.[6]

Arguing that pointed rods would attract lightning, Wilson recommended lightning rods topped with spherical knobs instead. Franklin's pointed rods were erected at Purfleet, where the royal gunpowder magazine was located, and atop other public buildings, including the Queen's House (later, Buckingham Palace). Lightning struck the powder magazine at Purfleet in May 1777. It did no damage, but Wilson took the opportunity to reassert his argument for spherical knobs to safeguard buildings against lightning. The politicization of science is not a modern phenomenon: King George III agreed with Wilson this time. His Majesty was not about to let a rebel tell him what to do. He changed Franklin's pointed rods on the powder magazine for Wilson's knob-topped lightning rods. He also began changing rods at Buckingham Palace.

Franklin still had plenty of British supporters, both wits and scientists. In "Poet's Corner," *St. James's Chronicle* published the following occasional poem:

> Whilst you, great George, for knowledge hunt,
> And *sharp conductors change for blunt*,
>> The empire's out of joint;
> Franklin a wiser plan pursues,
> And all your thunder useless views,
>> By keeping to the *point*.[7]

Franklin read this newspaper poem and enjoyed it enough to keep a clipping, which survives among his papers at the American Philosophical Society. John

Almon reprinted the poem in *An Asylum for Fugitive Pieces*. Franklin would obtain a copy of this anthology as well.[8]

Since Franklin had already made a convincing argument for pointed rods, he was content to leave the matter to science. Refusing to speak out against Wilson, Franklin informed a correspondent: "I have never entered into any controversy in defence of my philosophical opinions; I leave them to take their chance in the world. If they are right, Truth and Experience will support them."[9] Itching for a fight, Wilson framed their clash as a contest of masculinity, but Franklin declined to compare his rod with Wilson's knob.

Though Franklin instantly became the most famous man in Paris upon his arrival, there was another who matched him as the most famous man in France: Voltaire. But Voltaire lived at Ferney, which was practically Switzerland. He wanted to return to Paris, but every time Voltaire came back to the capital, it seemed, he would do something or say something or write something that offended the Catholic Church or the French government or both, usually both, and the city would ban him again. Toward the end of his life, Voltaire's reputation as a champion of freedom of speech and religious toleration grew so great that almost nothing could keep him from Paris.

The humanitarian interests and celebrity status they shared were bound to bring Voltaire and Franklin together. They also shared a frankness that was refreshing. Desmond MacCarthy observed, "Franklin was one of those men who, like Voltaire (with whom he has affinities) could not speak without expressing themselves characteristically."[10] Though tangential to the saga of Franklin's diplomatic mission to France, his contact with Voltaire forms a major episode in Franklin's intellectual life, one that has never been told fully. The diplomatic situation between France and the United States provides the backdrop for the story of Franklin and Voltaire.

A few weeks after he and his grandsons reached Paris, Franklin secretly met Charles Gravier, comte de Vergennes, the French foreign minister. Together, Vergennes and Franklin laid the groundwork for diplomatic relations between France and the United States. Vergennes was a heady amalgam of shrewdness and sympathy. His profound dislike of Britain made him amenable to the American cause, but he would not commit France fully unless and until victory seemed certain.

The other two American commissioners—Silas Deane and Arthur Lee— did some preparatory work before Franklin arrived. For one thing, they enlisted the help of Franklin's grandnephew Jonathan Williams. Having traveled to London on family business in 1770, Williams had stayed with Franklin on Craven Street. Franklin recognized the young man's intellect and ambition,

FIGURE 22.2 *Voltaire*, after a painting by Louis Carrogis, called Carmontelle (1900). Library of Congress, Prints and Photographs Division, Washington, DC, LC-USZ62-72043.

made Williams his private secretary, and welcomed him into his ever-widening circle of scientific friends. When Franklin returned to Philadelphia in 1775, Williams went to France, where Deane and Lee appointed him their agent for inspecting arms and supplies being shipped to America.[11]

The three commissioners had the responsibility to negotiate military and commercial treaties between France and the United States. They also sought France's financial assistance. On January 5, 1777, they formally requested French aid and, within two weeks, received a verbal promise of 2 million livres. Throughout the Revolutionary War, Franklin would coax further loans from the French government, which could ill afford what the Americans asked. That Franklin continued to secure loans from France is a testament to his ability to parlay his personal charm into diplomatic currency. The treaties proved more elusive.

In late February 1777, Franklin moved to Passy, settling into the Hôtel de Valentinois, a villa located on the crest of a bluff overlooking the Seine. Valentinois became the headquarters of the American legation. From

February through November, Franklin and his fellow commissioners had little success reaching an agreement with the French. The situation would not change until after the Continental Army trounced the British at Saratoga in October. When news of this exciting victory reached Paris the first week of December, it reignited negotiations with the French. On Friday, February 6, 1778, the United States and France signed two treaties, a treaty of alliance for mutual defense and a treaty of amity and commerce.

Franklin's efforts to ingratiate himself to the French took many different forms. His friendship with Voltaire suits his wider diplomatic efforts. The day before the treaty-signing ceremony, Voltaire had left Ferney for Paris with great fanfare. Practically everything Voltaire said and did in Paris was newsworthy. Franklin could tell that if he were to befriend Voltaire, everyone in Paris would know about it almost instantly. Their friendship would have great propaganda value, confirming the amity between France and the United States.

The friendship would not be just for show. In terms of personal and political philosophy, Franklin was drawn toward Voltaire, whom he had been reading for decades. Franklin first encountered his work when he read *The History of Charles XII*, Voltaire's biography of the great Swedish warrior-king, which came in the initial shipment of books for the Library Company that had reached Philadelphia in 1732. The work was not part of the library directors' original order, but Thomas Hopkinson selected it as an attractive substitute. Later, Franklin would stock the work at the New Printing House.[12]

With *The History of Charles XII*, Voltaire created a biography that Franklin—or anyone who grew up reading Plutarch's *Lives*—could appreciate. Voltaire followed Plutarch's approach toward biography. He agreed that sometimes a gesture, a joke, or an anecdote could say more about history than stories of great battles. Voltaire made his inspiration apparent by comparing the Swedish king with Alexander the Great. He ended the biography with a sobering moral, concluding that the life of Sweden's renowned warrior-king illustrates the folly of conquest.[13]

By the time the Library Company released its 1757 catalogue, it had added several more Voltaire volumes to its shelves, including *The Age of Lewis XIV*, a history of seventeenth-century France with the drama, suspense, and grandeur of stage tragedy. When he was 9 years old, Franklin had heard Increase Mather preach about King Louis XIV. Mather called him "that wicked old persecutor of God's people." Portraying the king as a bogeyman, Mather's words stayed with Franklin. Voltaire offered a new perspective on old King Louis, showing that the reign of Louis XIV was a period during which arts and literature flourished.[14] When Peter Collinson sent *The Age of Lewis XIV* to the Library Company, he wrote Franklin separately, predicting that the book would please him.[15]

Other Voltaire works the Library Company acquired before 1757 include *The Elements of Sir Isaac Newton's Philosophy*, a popularization of Newton's scientific research that dared to say that Newtonianism superseded Cartestianism, which was tantamount to heresy among the French; *The General History and State of Europe*, a translation of Voltaire's great philosophical survey of the history of mankind, which reflects the paradox of history, that is, the coexistence of destruction and progress; and *Letters Concerning the English Nation*, a by-product of Voltaire's time in England.[16]

Voltaire related the eccentricities of English life in *Letters Concerning the English Nation*, but his underlying purpose was to contrast French religious and intellectual prejudice with British liberty and toleration. *Letters Concerning the English Nation* is the work in which Voltaire famously said, "If one religion only were allowed in England the government would very possibly become arbitrary; if there were but two, the people wou'd cut one another's throats; but as there are such a multitude, they all live happy and in peace."[17]

Most likely Franklin read *Zadig*, a philosophical novel that Voltaire set in ancient Babylonia. *Zadig* is best known for its eponymous hero's powers of ratiocination, which would influence the development of detective fiction. Though Franklin does not mention *Zadig* in his writings, he does echo it. After being appointed a judge, Zadig fills the position with wisdom and fairness, believing "that 'tis much more prudence to acquit two persons, tho' actually guilty, than to pass sentence of condemnation on one that is virtuous and innocent." Franklin would say much the same: "That it is better 100 guilty persons should escape, than that one innocent person should suffer." Franklin could have encountered other versions of this proverb elsewhere, but *Zadig* is one possible source.[18]

A classic in the history of world literature, *Candide* contributes to the literary history of the Seven Years' War and thus suits the numerous other books and pamphlets on the subject in Franklin's library. In this, his most renowned work, Voltaire offers an unflinching view of the war. As Cunégonde and Martin approach England, she asks him about the English, wondering if they are as crazy as the French. "They have a different kind of folly, said Martin; you know that these two nations are at war, for a few acres of barren land in the neighbourhood of Canada, and that they have spent a great deal more in the prosecution of this war than all Canada is worth."[19]

Pomponne Vincent, a French lawyer, assumed that Franklin knew *Candide*. Vincent told Franklin about his desire to write a book to express his sympathy with the American cause, comparing himself with Voltaire's hero. Much as Candide must cultivate his garden at the end of the novel, Vincent must write his book. Vincent wrote it in the form of an epistolary political novel, which he called *Lettres d'un membre du congres ameriquain*. Franklin added the book to his Paris library, presumably a presentation copy from its author.[20]

Franklin's philosophical attitude toward humanity often seems contradictory. André Maurois titled his children's biography *Franklin: The Life of an Optimist*, but Franklin was never as optimistic as Maurois makes him out to be. Occasionally, he sounds like Candide's teacher Pangloss, who calls this world "the best of all possible worlds." In one letter to his sister Jane, Franklin says, "Take one thing with another, and the world is a pretty good sort of world, and 'tis our duty to make the best of it and be thankful." Other times, Franklin sounds more like Pangloss's creator. Franklin's satires and other writings on human nature are often pessimistic. Satirizing the same Leibnizian optimism as Voltaire, Franklin questioned whether this world really is the best of all possible worlds.[21]

One episode from his autobiography sounds like something pilfered from the pages of *Candide*. At the end of a treaty conference, the Pennsylvania commissioners' Native American hosts drank all the rum and raised a horrible ruckus throughout the night. The next morning, a native orator spoke with Franklin to apologize and blamed the rum for their behavior: "The great spirit who made all things made everything for some use, and whatever use he design'd anything for, that use it should always be put to; now, when he made rum, he said, 'Let this be for Indians to get drunk with.' And it must be so." In terms of its sardonic tone and specious use of reason to justify the ways of the world, this episode shares much with *Candide*.[22]

Franklin mentions Voltaire several times in his correspondence. His fullest remarks come in a letter to Henry Bouquet, in which he discusses Voltaire's *Treatise on Religious Toleration*. Voltaire published the work anonymously, but Franklin recognized his style when he read it. He told Bouquet: "There is in it abundance of good sense and sound reasoning, mix'd with some of those pleasantries that mark the author as strongly as if he had affix'd his name."[23]

That Franklin recognized Voltaire's authorship is astonishing. Voltaire had written the work, not as one extended argument, but as a series of short, independent essays using a variety of styles and perspectives, though irony and satire predominate. Franklin's ability to recognize Voltaire's authorship attests to his familiarity with his work.

In his letter to Bouquet, Franklin quotes Voltaire's paragraph about the harmony that reigns among the Pennsylvania Quakers. The following passage from the English translation corresponds to the French passage Franklin quoted:

> And what shall we say of those pacific primitive Christians, who have, by way of derision, been called Quakers; and who, though some of their customs may perhaps be ridiculous, are yet remarkable for the virtue and sobriety of their lives, and for having in vain endeavoured to preach peace and good-will to the rest of mankind? There are at least a hundred thousand of them in Pennsylvania; discord and controversy are unknown in that happy spot where they have settled: the very name of their principal city, Philadelphia, is a continual memento to them, that all men are brethren, and is at once an example and reproach to those nations who have not yet adopted toleration.[24]

Before quoting Voltaire's *Treatise of Religious Toleration*, Franklin told Bouquet, "I will give you a passage of it, which being read here at a time when we are torn to pieces by factions religious and civil, shows us that while we sit for our picture to that able painter, tis no small advantage to us, that he views us at a favourable distance."[25]

Franklin continued to follow Voltaire's career while living in London. After Pierre Henri Larcher attacked Voltaire's *Philosophy of History*, which he had published under the name of Ambrose Bazin, Voltaire assumed the persona of Bazin's nephew to defend his approach to history, *La défense de mon oncle*. Reviews were mixed. Franklin's friend William Rose panned Voltaire's defense in *The Monthly Review*. While admitting the book contained strokes of humor and pleasantry, he thought it would disgust liberal men of learning. In conclusion, Rose exclaimed, "Strange, that men of superior genius, of the greatest eminence in the republic of letters, should thus disgrace both themselves and their profession!" Imagine the conversation that went round the club table at St. Paul's Coffeehouse the month Rose's review came out. Franklin did not let Rose's negative opinion stop him from making up his own mind about Voltaire's new book. He added a copy of *La défense de mon oncle* to his personal library.[26]

Time has rehabilitated the reputation of Voltaire's impassioned defense of his historical method. Owen Aldridge, whose scholarly work includes a biography of Voltaire as well as a biography of Franklin, found *La défense de mon oncle* the most amusing of its author's polemics, but recognized its serious intent. The work makes a significant statement about the nature of scholarship: "It is not the incessant compiling or the repetition of statements which others have made but which nobody believes; rather it is the presentation of truth, based upon judging and weighing, and upon appropriateness as well as accuracy."[27]

Franklin's correspondence with Polly Hewson reveals their mutual interest in Voltaire. Having translated some of his poems, she shared them with Franklin, who read both her translations and Voltaire's French. Franklin returned them to her, declaring, "The translations I think full as good as the original." He asked her to send the translations back, so he could keep them.[28]

Another Voltaire work surfaces in their correspondence. In one letter, Franklin tells Polly, "Voltaire in his *Questions sur l'encyclopedie*, which I have been reading this morning, gives translations of several Greek epigrams into French, to show that the latter language was as capable of correctness as the former." Franklin asked her to render the epigrams into English, hoping her translations would prove his theory that the "English language is denser than the French."[29]

Franklin was reading the article about epigrams in the fifth volume of Voltaire's *Questions*. Having selected a dozen epigrams a year for *Poor Richard's Almanack* during its twenty-six-year history, Franklin understood the art of the epigram well, but he knew there was always more to learn. Reading Voltaire's *Questions*, he indulged his curiosity about this literary form.

Since Voltaire returned to the city in February 1778, the *Journal de Paris*, the newspaper that Franklin's friend Antoine-Alexis Cadet de Vaux had founded the previous year, published his latest utterances on a daily basis. Franklin knew if he visited Voltaire that Cadet de Vaux and other Paris newspaper editors would report the event. Coming soon after France and the United States had signed treaties of amity and commerce, the personal meeting between these two great sages would amount to an emblem of France and America coming together.

On Sunday, February 15, Franklin did indeed visit Voltaire. They spoke in English. Madame Denis, Voltaire's niece, interrupted their conversation and asked her uncle to speak in French, so those present—about twenty people altogether—could understand what the two great men were saying.

"My dear," Voltaire told his niece, "I for a moment indulged my vanity to speak in the language which is the mother tongue of a Franklin."[30]

Continuing their discussion, Franklin asked what he thought about the United States. Voltaire had great respect for the new nation. Why, if America had achieved independence forty years earlier, he would have emigrated there himself to enjoy its freedom. Ultimately, Franklin asked Voltaire to say a benediction for his grandson.

"My child, God and Liberty; remember those two words."

Sure enough, the Paris newspapers reported the momentous event, complete with Voltaire's benediction. Exhibiting the Rashomon effect, contrasting stories about their encounter circulated privately. Less than a week later, Voltaire himself retold the story to a correspondent, partly to correct all the different versions: "I shall say to you exactly what I said when I gave my blessing to the grandson of the wise and famous Franklin, the most honored of American citizens. I spoke only these words, 'God and liberty.' All present were greatly moved."[31]

Voltaire's words show that he understood what Franklin was doing. By no means was Franklin's interest in emblems limited to flags, political cartoons, or currency. He could see how to create *tableaux vivant* that could endure in the cultural memory. By introducing his grandson to Voltaire, Franklin created a living composition with the quality of a device in an emblem book: Age passing the Torch to Youth. Voltaire recognized what was missing: a motto to accompany the device. The phrase "God and liberty" forms an ideal motto for the moment.

None of the contemporary accounts say which grandson met Voltaire. Young Benny makes for a better story than the teenaged Temple. La Harpe combined the published reports and unpublished rumors to write one of the fullest contemporary accounts of the meeting. His version does not say which grandson, but it does say the boy was about 15, a description that better suits Temple. Here's the most convincing evidence that Temple was the grandson who received Voltaire's benediction: He would have a wax seal made for himself with the motto "God and liberty."

Franklin's library catalogue adds further evidence in Temple's favor. Recently, Temple had acquired a copy of Voltaire's memoirs, inscribing its title page, "W. T. Franklin 1777."[32] Given the interest in Voltaire that this acquisition reflects, it would seem a terrible snub were his grandfather to ignore Temple and take his little cousin to meet Voltaire instead. In short, it was Temple, not Benny, who received Voltaire's benediction.

During their time in Europe, Benny and Temple would take separate paths. Franklin initially placed Benny at a school in Passy, where he would remain for three years before his grandfather sent him to Geneva to study. Franklin had different plans for Temple. He wanted him to become fluent in French before he began reading law. Since Congress continually ignored his requests for a secretary, Franklin hired Temple as his unofficial secretary. Temple would continue in that capacity throughout their time in France. Franklin groomed his oldest grandson for the world of international diplomacy. He hoped that Temple's hands-on experience would lead to a full-time position in the U.S. diplomatic corps.[33]

Newspapers throughout Europe and the United States also reported the meeting between Franklin and Voltaire. The British newspapers omitted the God-and-liberty line, but otherwise they repeated the French reports. One anecdote about Franklin's meeting with Voltaire differs wildly from the rest, however, the one Arthur Lee told his family. Richard Henry Lee, his nephew and biographer, recorded it for posterity in his *Life of Arthur Lee*: "Mr. Lee often related an anecdote which occurred soon after the American commissioners arrived. Voltaire was then dangerously ill in Paris, where he shortly after died. He had warmly espoused the cause of the Americans. The commissioners requested to be permitted to wait on him, which Voltaire cheerfully granted. As they entered the room he raised himself feebly up in his bed, and in a momentary glow of enthusiasm, repeated some beautiful lines from Thompson's *Ode to Liberty*, commencing, 'Oh Liberty, thou goddess ever bright.'"[34] This version indicates the errors that crept into the story through repeated retellings. Voltaire's "God and liberty" became Addison's "Oh Liberty, thou goddess," and Addison's famous line got misattributed to James Thomson.

The Lee version of the story has the three commissioners calling on Voltaire together, but the other versions mention neither Lee nor Deane. With a fiery temper and a sense of self-importance characteristic of the Virginia aristocracy, Arthur Lee made such a nuisance of himself by February 1778 that Deane and Franklin dealt with him as little as possible. Lee slandered them every chance he got. His vocal disagreements undermined their diplomatic mission, giving France the impression that the so-called United States was not united at all.

Lee's cantankerous nature disappointed Franklin, who made some general remarks about personal quarrels in conversation with Pierre Cabanis. He alluded to Homer's *Odyssey*, another example showing that the books Franklin read a half-century earlier remained pertinent to his life. "The most fraught quarrels, the most violent hatred are often caused," he said, "by small stings, such as those which unleashed the storms trapped in Ulysses's bag of wind. Much grief, many misfortunes can easily be avoided by a little self-control, and thoughtfulness toward others."[35]

Self-control became an ongoing theme in his conversations with Cabanis, who learned about Franklin's personal scheme for achieving moral perfection. Using an ivory table book—a pocket notebook with erasable ivory leaves—Franklin famously listed thirteen virtues he hoped to attain. He worked on them individually, marking with a black spot each day he found fault with himself regarding whichever virtue he was working on. At week's end, he would erase the marks and start afresh. Franklin had long since abandoned his scheme for achieving moral perfection, but he kept the ivory notebook and used it to record dinner invitations and other appointments.[36]

Though dedicated to the American cause, Lee continued stirring up trouble. He accused Deane of embezzling congressional funds, which resulted in Deane's recall. Lee decried Franklin's method of carrying out their commission and grumbled about the lackadaisical support from the European nations. Lee grew frustrated with Franklin's prudent and more patient diplomatic approach. Franklin understood that diplomacy takes time, that the nations of Europe had to be courted, persuaded, and convinced of the American cause before they would recognize or aid the United States in its war against Great Britain.

Lee's Voltaire anecdote should be read in light of his animus toward Franklin. Instead of repeating the standard version of the anecdote featuring Franklin and his grandson, Lee retold it by placing himself in the story, thus doing with the anecdote what he was unable to do in France, that is, to put himself in Franklin's place.

Franklin and Voltaire would come together twice more. A few months after their first meeting, Franklin helped induct Voltaire into the Lodge of the Nine Sisters. This Masonic lodge was the brainchild of renowned philosopher Claude-Adrien Helvétius, who had longed to create a lodge resembling a learned society that celebrated and encouraged the arts and sciences. Helvétius died before he could see his dream become a reality, but his widow, Anne-Catherine de Ligniville, Madame Helvétius, with the help of Joseph-Jérôme de La Lande, a learned astronomer, created the Lodge of the Nine Sisters, which they named for the nine muses.[37]

Voltaire was inducted on April 7, 1778. Then in his eighties, he went through an abbreviated induction ceremony. He was blindfolded prior to the ceremony. Franklin, who was in his seventies, took Voltaire by the arm and led him into the lodge chamber. His examiners asked Voltaire several questions, informed him about the secret signs and symbols of Freemasonry, and proclaimed him a member of both the order and the Lodge of the Nine Sisters.[38]

John Adams's arrival in Paris marks a new phase in Franco-American relations, but not necessarily a better one. Perhaps André Maurois put it best when he said, "John Adams did not like the French and the French did not like John Adams."[39] Since Adams kept a detailed diary, his arrival does mark a considerable rise in the amount and quality of information about Franklin's life in Paris. Adams recorded several memorable anecdotes, some of which reflect Franklin's reading.

One night, Franklin related a story he derived from Quevedo's *Visions*, one of the greatest works of satire in the history of Spanish literature. In Franklin's version, a civil and well-bred demon leads the Spanish writer through Hell, showing him all the apartments in the place. After visiting the hall of deceased kings, the Spaniard asks to see the rest of the kings. "The rest?" the demon asks. "Here are all the kings who ever reigned upon earth from the creation of it to this day, what the Devil would the man have?"[40]

Franklin's words reveal how he used his reading to generate anecdotes. The version in Adams's diary varies from the parallel episode in Quevedo's *Visions*. In Quevedo's sixth vision, the demon guides the Spanish narrator to the hall of kings. Before long, the Spaniard needs some fresh air and asks the demon to guide him out.

To appreciate the following excerpt from the English translation of Quevedo, a quick scatological vocabulary lesson may help. A house-of-office, saith Thesauro, is a privy. Tail-timber is toilet paper. "Saving your reverence" is a traditional apology for any expression considered indelicate, much the same as saying, "Pardon my French." In its contracted form—"sir-reverence"—the expression acquired a filthier, more specific meaning. "Sir-reverence" is a synonym for human excrement. Here endeth the vocabulary lesson: on to the excerpt. The Spaniard says: "He carry'd me away by a *back-passage*, into *Lucifer's house-of-office*; where there was I know not how many tun of *sir-reverence*, and bales of *flattering panegyricks*, not to be number'd; all of them licens'd, and *enter'd according to order*. I could not but smile at this provision of *tail-timber*."[41]

Franklin cleaned up his source for Adams. He could have told a version closer to Quevedo—"sir-reverence" was in his vocabulary—but he omitted the dirty bits. He also added a humorous punchline condemning the whole concept of royalty as something inherently evil. In terms of political theory, Franklin's anecdote goes farther than Quevedo, whose living depended on the favor of the Spanish court. Franklin also went further than Adams was willing to go. After recording the anecdote in his diary, Adams commented that some kings would reach Heaven.[42]

Adams saw Voltaire in person on April 29th when he attended a meeting of the Paris Academy of Sciences. As other attendees realized that both Franklin and Voltaire were present, they clamored for them to be introduced. The two came on stage, bowed, and spoke to one other. The audience wanted more. Franklin and Voltaire shook hands, but the crowd remained dissatisfied. The two must kiss one another on the cheek, the French insisted. So they did. The Marquis de Condorcet, who was also in attendance, compared Franklin with Solon, the renowned Greek legislator, and Voltaire with Sophocles, the renowned Greek tragedian. He was not the only one to make the comparison. Adams recorded the French reaction, but his sardonic tone reflects his disdain: "How charming it was! Oh! it was enchanting to see Solon and Sophocles embracing!"[43]

After Voltaire's death on May 30, 1778, Franklin grew anxious for a summer vacation, but his responsibilities as American minister to France prevented him from the kind of annual travels he had enjoyed during his time as London agent. The best he could manage was an occasional day trip. In the summer of 1778, he accompanied Madame Brillon to Moulin-Joli, a luxurious estate on an island in the Seine.

Anne-Louis d'Hardancourt Brillon de Jouy was Franklin's neighbor in Passy, where she lived with her husband and their two daughters, Cunégonde and Aldegonde. Twenty-four years older than his wife, Brillon spent little time with her, so she enjoyed the attention of her charming American neighbor. Their flirtatious relationship has contributed to Franklin's legendary but unwarranted reputation as an old lecher during his Paris years. *Nihil turpius sene libidinoso.*[44]

Franklin and Madame Brillon enjoyed an intimate friendship, and he habitually spent two evenings a week at her home. Besides being a good conversationalist, she was also a talented musician and composer. Cunégonde and Aldegonde both sang well, and the three, sometimes accompanied by other musical friends, often entertained Franklin. In addition, Madame Brillon was a good chess player, so she and Franklin played chess on quieter evenings.

The excursion to Moulin Joli inspired "The Ephemera," a bagatelle Franklin wrote after returning to Passy. His title refers to French mayflies, which live and die in less than a day. This bagatelle consists of two parts: a general introduction in Franklin's voice and a soliloquy by an "old greyheaded" mayfly. The introduction shades into fantasy as Franklin claims he can understand the insects' language. As he listens, he hears them arguing over two arthropodal musicians. Franklin is astonished that they were spending their time "seemingly as regardless of the shortness of life, as if they had been sure of living a month."[45] He thus established the world of the ephemera as an analogue for Parisian society, which was currently debating the relative merits of Christoph Willibad Gluck and the German school of music and Nicolò Piccinni and the Italian school. Franklin's comparison stresses the triviality of the debate, making the music in question little more than the sound of buzzing mosquitoes.

The old grey-headed mayfly, Franklin's six-legged alter ego, laments the brevity of life and wonders if all his political and scientific accomplishments will be forgotten once he is dead and rotten. He also wonders what is left for him in the hours or minutes he has remaining. He concludes, "To me, after all my eager pursuits, no solid pleasures now remain, but the reflection of a long life spent in meaning well, the sensible conversation of a few good lady-ephemeres, and now and then a kind smile, and a tune from the ever-amiable *Brillante*."[46]

"The Ephemera," which barely fills two pages in Franklin's papers, is one of his finest pieces of writing. It has elicited effusive praise from some of Franklin's finest readers. Upon quoting his conclusion, Theodore Hornberger observed, "In that gallant commentary on fame and old age Franklin comes alive more fully than he ever does in the *Autobiography*." Leo Lemay called it a "brief but glorious work of art," and Stuart P. Sherman compared it with one particular artwork, Jean-Antoine Watteau's *Embarkation for Cythera*.[47] Much as Watteau depicted an amorous celebration on the Greek island where Venus, the goddess of love, was born, Franklin's "Ephemera" resulted from his trip to an island in the Seine with a woman he adored.

FIGURE 22.3 *Le tombeau de Voltaire.* A print showing the continents of Europe, Asia, Africa, and America personified, respectively, as d'Alembert, Catherine II, Prince Oronoco, and Benjamin Franklin; they are almost to honor the tomb of Voltaire, when the personification of the Prejudice of Ignorance rushes in from the right to disrupt the proceedings, 1778? Library of Congress, Prints and Photographs Division, Washington, DC, LC-USZ62-45436.

On November 28th, the Lodge of the Nine Sisters held a memorial service for Voltaire. That evening, the auditorium was draped in black and dramatically lit. Eulogies of Voltaire alternated with original music composed by Gluck and French composer Jean-Philippe Rameau. Voltaire's niece—a rare female attendee—presented the lodge with Houdon's bust of Voltaire. In addition, the lodge unveiled a huge painting of Voltaire's apotheosis. On stage for its unveiling, Franklin removed the laurel crown from his head and placed it beneath the painting.[48]

Despite his diplomatic responsibilities, Franklin still enjoyed reading for pleasure throughout his Paris years. In or around 1780, he obtained *La pucelle d'Orléans*, Voltaire's mock epic of Joan of Arc. When this poem appeared in English as *The Maid of Orléans*, *The Monthly Review* refused to believe Voltaire had written it, calling the work a "gross assemblage of buffoonery, profaneness, obscurity, and nonsense."[49] *The Maid of Orléans* has much in common with other Voltaire works Franklin admired. It satirizes French historical tradition, hero worship, religious superstition, and the literary genres of epic and romance.[50] The presence of a new edition of *The Maid of Orléans* published after its author's death in Franklin's Paris library reveals his enduring interest in Voltaire's work and thought.

The Mystery of the Book Lists

IN NOVEMBER 1781, Franklin received stupendous news. Lord Cornwallis had capitulated at Yorktown, ending Britain's chances of winning the land portion of the Revolutionary War. Before the month was out, Franklin wrote fellow peace commissioner John Adams, who had gone to the Netherlands to negotiate both a loan and a treaty. Connecting Cornwallis's defeat at Yorktown with Burgoyne's defeat at Saratoga, Franklin found a classical metaphor appropriate: "The infant Hercules in his cradle has now strangled his second serpent." Franklin would incorporate this mythological image as part of the device for the peace medal he would design. It was another opportunity to put his passion for emblems and his knowledge of emblem literature to work.[1]

Though Franklin was under no illusions that a peace treaty with Britain would come any time soon, a flurry of activity at Valentinois toward the end of the year suggests that he and his staff were anticipating their eventual departure. Two book lists from late 1781 survive among his papers. One is dated, the other is not. The undated one is titled "List of Books." To use its short French title, the dated one can be called "Liste des livres." Its long title identifies it as a catalogue of books shelved in Franklin's private quarters that were being shifted to the office library. The dated list was begun on December 31, 1781, and finished on January 8, 1782, when the listed items were moved.[2]

Many books Franklin acquired in Paris before 1781 are not named on either list. From Passy, he continued his subscription to *Monde primitif*, Court de Gébelin's nine-volume treatise of comparative mythology and linguistics, but it does not appear in either list. Neither are the books Franklin loaned to French friends in 1778, nor the several known works Franklin acquired in 1780, nor are hundreds of other books and pamphlets Franklin obtained during his Paris years.[3] Together, "List of Books" and "Liste des livres" represent a small fraction of Franklin's Passy library.

Handwriting analysis reveals that Temple began "List of Books." The rest of the list is in the handwriting of Gurdon Saltonstall Mumford, a teenaged American who was working for Franklin at Valentinois. Cataloguing a library was a two-person task. One would read the spine titles aloud; the other would record them. Having spent hours and days in his grandfather's London library, Temple knew how to create a catalogue. Perhaps he started the list to show Mumford how to compile one, and then they switched roles, Temple reading the titles aloud and Mumford recording what he heard. Once they finished, Temple went through the list to correct the errors. Though most entries are in Mumford's hand, Temple was the driving force behind "List of Books."

Several autographed volumes from the "List of Books" collection survive, which can help identify its contents, illuminate its nature, and distinguish it from the "Liste des livres" collection. Other surviving books provide further clues. So do the Franklins' letters about books and some scattered bills from Paris booksellers. Taken together, the evidence can help reconcile the ambiguities and uncertainties of both lists.

Temple and Mumford recorded the books as they were shelved. Though the collection did not have an overarching organizational scheme, some subject clusters are discernible. Three titles early in the list form one subject cluster. The first item in the cluster is Abel Boyer's two-volume French and English dictionary. Franklin's correspondence shows him using this dictionary in 1772, when he was living in London and corresponding with Jacques Barbeu-Dubourg.[4]

Two smaller dictionaries follow. One is Thomas Nugent's *New Pocket Dictionary of the French and English Language*. Nugent made his dictionary manageable by defining individual words but omitting multiword phrases. To understand idiomatic expressions, according to his introduction, people must read the finest French authors often and deeply. Nugent did add some words the Académie Française had excluded from its standard dictionary of French, conveying his frustration with the academy's stuffy attitude toward the language. (William Byrd shared the feeling: He filled the back flyleaf of his copy of the academy dictionary with a lengthy list of French words it had excluded: the dirty words!) The Passy copy of Nugent's pocket dictionary survives with Temple's autograph.[5] The third French dictionary is Pierre Restaut's edition of Charles Le Roy's treatise of French orthography, which contains a fifty-page appendix presenting rules of versification. Temple's dated title-page autograph shows he acquired the book in 1777.[6]

Listed directly after Le Roy is a French novel, Louis de Cahusac's *Grigri*. Identifying this work as a romance, Abraham Rees dismissed it without another word. Baron von Grimm was more critical, calling it "the insipid *Grigri*" and attributing to it the same faults as other bad novels: raillery, frivolity, licentiousness. Unlike his grandfather, Temple enjoyed novels. Pierre Cabanis gave

Franklin a copy of *Julie*, Rousseau's epistolary novel inspired by his love for Sophie d'Houdetot. Franklin's friendship with her made Rousseau's novel interesting from a personal standpoint. Otherwise, his library catalogue shows little interest in prose fiction beyond standard works like *Pilgrim's Progress* and *Don Quixote*. But Temple said *oui, oui* to *Grigri*. He would continue to show an interest in French fiction. When Pierre Choderlos de Laclos published *Les liasons dangereuses* in 1782, Temple would obtain a copy for himself.[7]

This cluster—three dictionaries and a novel—tells a story. Around the time he and Mumford compiled the list, Temple was apparently reading *Grigri*, which he shelved with the French dictionaries. The shelf placement let him easily consult the dictionaries while reading the novel. When in doubt, he could take down a dictionary and look up an unfamiliar word. Temple acquired two of the French dictionaries on his own; his grandfather had either loaned or given Temple his copy of Boyer's dictionary. He did not give his grandson the dictionary just so he could read insipid French novels, however. Franklin had a higher purpose in mind. Hoping his first grandson would join the diplomatic corps, Franklin wanted Temple to deepen his knowledge of French, the international language of diplomacy.

Later in the list, six consecutive titles form another cluster of French reference books. Two items from this cluster survive at the Free Library of Philadelphia: Pierre Olivet's *Remarques sur la langue françoise* and Pierre Hurtaut's *Dictionnaire des mots homonymes*. Hurtaut's *Homonymes* suited Temple's linguistic study. The work was ideal for readers studying French as a foreign language. Temple autographed and dated the title pages of both: "W. T. Franklin 1777."[8]

Two other entries in this cluster represent companion works for the French dictionaries: Abel Boyer's *Compleat French-Master* and Pierre Restaut's *Principes généraux et raisonnés de la grammaire françoise*.[9] Though association copies of these two grammars do not survive, most likely they belonged to Temple. The work of educational reformer Charles Rollin inspired Restaut's French grammar, which used French, not Latin, as the foundation for learning other Romance languages.

Another cluster of five related Italian books comes directly after the cluster of French reference works and verifies Restaut's pedagogical approach. Though no association copies from this Italian cluster survive, it belongs with Temple's library. Since his grandfather could already read Italian, he did not need basic textbooks in the language.

The first item in the Italian cluster is Francesco d'Alberti's *Nouveau dictionnaire françois-italien*. Ferdinando Altieri designed his *Grammatica inglese* to help native Italian speakers learn English, but it could work in the opposite direction. The cluster also included another Italian grammar. The last two entries represent works of fiction: *Telemaco*, an Italian edition of Fénelon's *Adventures of Telemachus*, and a three-volume Italian edition of Boccaccio's *Decameron*, a work Benjamin Franklin had known for decades.[10]

The Italian cluster follows the same pattern established by *Grigri* and the three French dictionaries. Coming after a dictionary and two grammars, *Telemaco* gave Temple a fictional work he could use to master Italian. Since *Telemachus* was the most popular French book in eighteenth-century America, the Italian edition provided a familiar work in an unfamiliar language. Once Temple had read *Telemaco*, he could turn to a more challenging Italian author and read Boccaccio.

Another cluster of related works can be called the Latin cluster. It included a Latin edition of Caesar's works; a parallel French and Latin edition of Cicero; a collection of Horace's verse; Juvenal's *Satires*; Livy's *Historiarum*; Sallust's works; and a French and Latin edition of Virgil. The copy of Caesar's works, which survives at the American Philosophical Society, is inscribed "W. T. Franklin," suggesting that the other books in the Latin cluster were Temple's as well. The last volume in the cluster is Jean-Louis Le Bel's *L'art d'apprendre sans maitre*, a work that let French readers learn Latin independently. Temple, it seems, was using his knowledge of French to brush up his Latin. Though unnecessary for a diplomatic career, Latin would help Temple rub elbows with members of French society, who were generally well educated in the ancient tongues.[11]

In short, the Passy books that survive with ownership inscriptions help identify the precise nature of "List of Books." It is not a catalogue of Benjamin Franklin's Passy library at all; it is a catalogue of William Temple Franklin's Passy library. One entry refers to John Byrom's *Universal English Short-Hand*. The Passy copy survives at the Huntington Library. Benjamin Franklin autographed its flyleaf and added an inscription recording that John Pringle had presented the book to him.[12] Since Franklin considered his library a dynamic collection, he had no qualms about sharing useful works with his grandson. Having given military manuals to his son when he was planning an army career, Franklin now gave or loaned this shorthand manual to his grandson while he was serving as a diplomatic secretary. For someone responsible for taking minutes of meetings, shorthand is a vital skill.

Other entries in "List of Books" represent some of Franklin's personal favorites, including Melchisédic Thévenot's swimming manual, *L'art de nager*. Franklin had read this book as a boy and used it to teach himself many different swimming strokes. The Passy copy is the 1780 Paris edition. Franklin's acquisition seems like another purchase inspired by nostalgia. When the new edition of this old favorite appeared, Franklin obtained a copy and shared it with his grandsons.[13]

Louis Lefebvre de La Roche recalled Franklin going down to the Seine "to teach one of his grandsons how to swim, [and] crossing the width of the river with him." This recollection presents another Temple-or-Benny mystery. The presence of Thévenot's manual in Temple's Passy library suggests that he was the grandson who learned to swim, but in his journal Benny recorded crossing the river and performing one of Thévenot's moves, swimming with a bundle of clothes balanced on his head.[14]

Benny and Alexander, a local friend, crossed the Seine one day to go fishing. Night fell with no luck. Benny suggested they swim back. Having trouble balancing his clothes on his head, Alexander got dressed and waited for the boat. Benny chose to swim. When he was three-quarters of the way across the river, a speedy galliot almost ran him down. Benny pirouetted, keeping his head above water and his bundle teetering atop his head. Turning back toward Passy, he once again reached the three-quarter mark, when gravity snatched the bundle, which slipped off his noggin into the water. Stroke by stroke, Benny nudged the sodden bundle forward. Once ashore, he undid the bundle, unwadded his clothes, threw on his wet coat, pulled on his wet breeches, put on his wet shoes, wrapped his wet undergarments in his wet handkerchief, and ran to Valentinois, squelching all the way.

Another entry in "List of Books" represents another Franklin favorite: Edward Young's *Love of Fame: The Universal Passion*. Having read *Love of Fame* in London when it first came out, Franklin cherished this poem. He had reread it numerous times while compiling *Poor Richard's Almanack* and knew parts by heart. It was an ideal book for Temple to read as a young man. Not only was it good poetry, it also supplied valuable life lessons. Since Temple had an eye toward establishing himself in French society, he could stand a lesson in humility. Franklin's literary tastes rubbed off. Three decades later, Temple would read a new edition of Young's *Poetical Works*.[15]

Whereas the presence of Thévenot and Young on the list suggests that Franklin was sharing favorites from his youth with his grandson, another entry shows Temple actively acquiring items his grandfather recommended. "List of Books" contains an entry for a six-volume English edition of Plutarch's *Lives*. From Paris, Temple corresponded with his old school chum William Caslon III. A dandy like Temple, Caslon asked him to buy some *mille fleur* pomatum. Temple, in turn, asked Caslon to buy some fancy monogrammed handkerchiefs. He also asked Caslon to buy some books. Caslon purchased the edition of Plutarch's *Lives* that Temple requested. The first volume of the Passy Plutarch survives with Temple's autograph and acquisition date: "W. T. Franklin 1780."[16]

Though "List of Books" is undated, the identifiable titles show that it was compiled in 1781. A letter written three years later provides the surest evidence about where the collection was shelved. While visiting Passy in 1784, Jonathan Williams browsed Temple's books for something to read. Voltaire's memoirs caught his eye. Williams pulled the book down, took it back to his room, and started reading. After Williams left Passy, Temple accused his kinsman of purloining the book. Williams replied, "I did not bring away the *Memoires de Voltaire*—they should be found either in your room or mine for I had them only in those two places."[17] This letter verifies that Temple shelved his books in his room, not in the office library.

Overall, "List of Books" represents a fairly standard set of books that any young man seeking to establish himself in French society might read. Benjamin Franklin told others that Temple planned to study law, but the list puts the lie to that idea. It does not mention any law books.

One unusual entry in "List of Books" stands out: "English cookery." This title represents Samuel Pegge's recent edition of the earliest known cookbook in the English language, *The Forme of Cury*. Caslon bought this cookbook for Temple at the same time he acquired Plutarch's *Lives*. The Passy copy does not survive, but a copy of Menon's *Cuisinière bourgeoise* autographed by Temple survives at the Boston Public Library. Another cookbook also appears in the list, Antoine Augustin Parmentier's treatise on breadmaking, *Le parfait boulanger*. Parmentier had presented the book to Franklin, who passed it along to his grandson.[18]

Temple, it seems, was developing a personal interest in the art of cooking. Menon's best-selling cookbook told readers how to prepare *cuisine bourgeoise*, thus making it possible for middle-class gourmands to approach *haut cuisine*. *The Forme of Cury*, Pegge's scholarly edition of a fourteenth-century manuscript, marks the start of English culinary antiquarianism. The word "cury" is an obsolete term for "cookery." Remember the gruesome scene in Thomas Malory's *Morte d'Arthur* when Arthur enters the giant's lair, finds cattle and Christians skewered on the same roasting spit, and exclaims, "Here es cury unclene!"[19]

The Middle English of *The Forme of Cury* is no more difficult than the language of *Morte d'Arthur*. The two works are almost exact contemporaries. Many recipes from *The Forme of Cury* have withstood the test of time. James

Beard thought "Perrey of Peson"—purée of peas—sounded delicious. Simmer the peas until they burst; strain them through a cloth; season with oil, salt, onion, sugar and saffron; and serve. *The Forme of Cury* introduced the word "salad" to the English language, advising readers to take fresh greens, vegetables, and herbs—garlic, leeks, onions, parsley, sage, watercress—and "waische hem clene" (wash them clean); mix well with oil, vinegar, and salt; and serve.[20] Temple's double interest in the history of cooking and its modern trends shows him developing a taste for luxury: a potentially dangerous impulse.

Another entry reflects another sensual impulse: Nikolai Detlef Falck's *Treatise on the Venereal Disease*. Though Franklin had an excellent medical library, Temple, now an adult, was growing curious about one particular malady: sexually transmitted diseases. Falck provided a detailed anatomy of male and female genitalia, a little too detailed, the fastidious William Bewley thought. Reviewing the book, Bewley observed, "Though the author every where professes the highest regard to decency and good manners, this description is, in many parts, unnecessarily loose, and even voluptuous."[21]

Unwilling to see his grandson get mixed up in any dangerous liaisons, Franklin tried to give him some stability. By 1781, he had decided that the Brillons' 17-year-old daughter Cunégonde would make the best of all possible granddaughters-in-law. The Brillons did not consider Temple a suitable match for their older daughter, however. They rejected the union, citing Temple's Protestantism as a convenient excuse. Instead, the Brillons arranged a match for Cunégonde that would benefit them socially and financially.

After Cunégonde was wed, Temple turned his attention to the Brillons' younger daughter Aldegonde, hoping little sister would not do what her big sister had done. Though she was barely 15 when Temple made his move, Aldegonde responded favorably. The Brillons were none too thrilled with Temple's attachment to her. By the time they warmed to the possibility of a match, Temple had begun an affair with Blanchette Caillot, a married Passy neighbor. Mme. Caillot soon discovered she was pregnant with Temple's child. They would name their son Théophile.

Calling the "List of Books" collection Temple's library is an arbitrary distinction. It was located within the villa where Benjamin Franklin lived, and Temple was financially beholden to his grandfather, whose household expenses provided the funds for Temple's book purchases. Franklin let Temple assemble a library of his own, but he would have expected him to share his books with other members of the household, especially his cousin Benny.

Jean L'Air de Lamotte, who compiled "Liste du livres," came to Franklin in a roundabout way. His uncle, Jacques Barbeu-Dubourg, had withdrawn his nephew from medical school and made him confidential secretary for his American affairs. When his uncle died in 1780, Jean found himself with neither money nor prospects. Franklin hired him as a personal secretary and moved him into Valentinois. Like so many other young men who entered Franklin's orbit, Jean became devoted to him. He would remain at Valentinois through the rest of Franklin's time in France.[22] Jean excelled as a library cataloguer and would help organize Franklin's vast collection of pamphlets, splitting them into volume-sized bunches, preparing manuscript title pages, and having them bound.

Though it represents a smaller collection than "List of Books," "Liste des livres" is more diverse. It contains books on numerous subjects: agriculture, industry and technology, including cider making, fruit culture, lumber, and machinery; biography; criminal law; demography; economics; history; medicine, including asphyxia, communicable diseases, electrotherapy, and smallpox inoculation; music and poetry; Native American culture and language; political theory; and the sciences: chemistry, geology, meteorology, oceanography, and, of course, electricity.

The demographic book named in "Liste des livres" is Jean-Baptiste Moheau's *Recherches et considérations sur la population de la france*. A landmark in the field of population studies, this work takes a statistical approach to the subject but also explains the causes and effects of population growth, examining economic, political, and social factors. Having written his own work on the subject, Franklin revealed his ongoing interest in the field when he acquired Moheau's book.

Moheau cited Franklin as an authority. Since Barbeu-Dubourg had included "Observations Concerning the Increase of Mankind" in his French edition of Franklin's writings, Moheau read the work and incorporated aspects of it. Citing Franklin's statistics about population growth in Pennsylvania, Moheau found excessive Franklin's projection that its population would double every twenty years. He did accept Franklin's argument that the limits of population are fixed solely by the number of humans the earth can sustain.[23]

Overall, the "List des livres" collection is quite recent. Many listed books appeared in 1781. Surviving bills from Parisian bookseller J. G. Cressonier show that Franklin had purchased several items within the previous two months. The list begins with the four-volume edition of *Don Quixote* Joaquin Ibarra published in Madrid, which Franklin had purchased on November 17th. That same day, he also acquired *The Oceana and Other Works,* John Toland's edition of James Harrington's collected writings. The following day,

Franklin bought an eight-volume quarto edition of Gaspard de Réal de Curban's *La science du gouvernement*. Looking forward to the United States forming a permanent government all its own, Franklin was filling some gaps in his knowledge of political theory.[24]

Gaspard de Réal de Curban, grand seneschal of Forcalquier, died before completing his massive treatise of political science, which was published posthumously in the 1760s. Voltaire did not care for it. Informing a correspondent of the publication, Voltaire called its author the "most boring seneschal you have ever seen." Boring perhaps, but Réal de Curban was nonetheless one of the era's most enlightened politicians. He believed that men were born free and equal. But Réal de Curban was also a realist. An egalitarian in theory, he considered changing the established class system impossible in practice. Instead of advocating republicanism, he accepted monarchy but argued that a monarch has the responsibility to understand political theory. Written as a guide for royalty, *La science du gouvernement* gives monarchs a historical survey of political systems from antiquity to modern times to facilitate their decision-making.[25]

Since the "Liste des livres" collection contains the books Franklin had been shelving in his private quarters but was moving to the office library and since it largely consisted of books he obtained in 1781, it reveals much about how Franklin treated recent acquisitions. He shelved his new books in his private quarters, so he could read and savor them alone. Franklin would read every morning. In "Dialogue between the Gout and Mr. Franklin," another bagatelle he wrote at Passy, Mme. Gout chastises him for his sedentary ways, asking, "Why, instead of gaining an appetite for breakfast by salutary exercise, [do] you amuse yourself with books, pamphlets, or newspapers, which commonly are not worth the reading?"[26] Once he had devoured a sufficient number of books in his private quarters, he would transfer them to the office library. Dated December 31, 1781, "Liste des livres" suggests that this transfer of books was a year-end rite.

Shelved in the office library, the books could be readily shared with visitors. Since the *Don Quixote* was a beautiful example of the art of printing, Franklin enjoyed showing it off. One Passy visitor found its typography and engraving practically unsurpassed. An American traveler reacted similarly to Franklin's Baskerville Bible. Describing the edition for his visitor, Franklin paid homage to Massachusetts printer Isaiah Thomas: "It was printed by Baskerville, the greatest printer in England; and our countryman, Mr. Thomas of Worcester, is the Baskerville of America."[27]

Not all the books Franklin bought from Cressonier that November reached the office library. One work listed in a surviving bookseller's bill does not appear in "Liste des livres": Nicolas Rétif's *Le pornographe*.[28] Perhaps Franklin had not finished reading it by the end of the year, or perhaps he decided that a book called *Le pornographe* should remain in his private quarters.

Like Bernard Mandeville a half-century earlier, Rétif identified prostitution as a nagging social problem, mainly because of its overt nature. Walking the streets of Paris, prostitutes were visible signs of debauchery, offending innocent passers-by and arousing less innocent ones. To solve this social problem Rétif proposed a system of public stews. Unlike Mandeville's, Rétif's proposal for establishing state-run brothels was serious, not satiric. His ideal house of prostitution would provide a discreet entrance for its clientele and mandate regular medical inspections to minimize the spread of sexually transmitted diseases.[29]

Beyond what it reveals about Franklin's reading and book-collecting habits, "Liste des livres" sheds light on his interaction with John Adams. Afflicted with jealousy-fueled paranoia, Adams thought Franklin was out to get him, but Franklin was not as opposed to him as Adams imagined. They clashed in terms of personal conduct, but Franklin was willing to consider his colleague's political theories. Though Adams was in the Netherlands when Franklin acquired Réal de Curban's *Science du gouvernement* and Harrington's *Oceana*, these two acquisitions reflect his influence. Adams took two of his most fundamental ideas from Harrington's *Oceana*: the concept of a natural aristocracy and the preference for a bicameral legislature. Purchasing a copy of Harrington's works, Franklin was rethinking the possibility of a bicameral legislature, which he had so far opposed.

It is not hard to see what attracted Franklin most about Harrington's literary style. To illustrate both the natural aristocracy and the theory underlying a bicameral legislature, Harrington created a fable about two little girls and a cake. One day, the girls receive a cake to share, but they must decide for themselves how to cut it. "Divide," says one girl to the other, "and I will choose; or let me divide, and you shall choose."[30]

According to Harrington, this process of dividing and choosing reveals the whole mystery of a commonwealth. The girl who cuts the cake represents the senate or upper house of a legislature, which contains the nation's natural aristocracy. The senators use their intellect to debate the issues and draft legislation. The other girl represents the assembly or lower house of a legislature. Her process of choosing is akin to passing resolutions. Upon drafting a piece of legislation, the senate presents it to the assembly, which must pass resolutions determining its fate. Harrington summarizes: "Dividing and choosing in the language of a commonwealth is debating and resolving."[31]

Franklin understood both the rhetorical power of fables and the allure of cake as a storytelling motif. Years earlier, he had written a religious parody featuring a greedy boy and his cake. The preacher says that our earthly lives do not matter because each of us will become a lump of clay; Franklin says that it hardly matters whether the boy cannot have his cake and eat it too because the cake itself will quickly become one big, stinky bolus of sir-reverence.[32] But Harrington's fable of the two girls and their cake failed to convince Franklin of the superiority of a bicameral legislature, which he found less democratic than a unicameral legislature and less efficient. To illustrate the drawbacks of a bicameral legislature, Franklin wrote a fable of his own, trading the cake for a snake.

One day, a two-headed snake is slithering toward a brook to have a drink. Before reaching the water, it must navigate a prickly hedge. A twig projecting from it impedes the snake's progress, stopping it from going straight to the brook. One head goes right, the other left. With the twig notched in its neck, the two heads debate which direction to go. Their debate lasts a long time. Bucking the proverb about two heads being better than one, the snake's two heads cannot reach a consensus, and it dies of thirst.[33]

"Liste des livres" has no discernible organizational scheme, but a few similar books are paired together. *La science du gouvernement* is next to Harrington's *Oceana*; Pierre Bertholon's treatise on electrophysiology, *De l'electricité du corps humain*, is next to Franz Anton Mesmer's *Précis historique des faits relatifs au magnétisme-animal.*[34] Shelving Bertholon and Mesmer together, Franklin expressed his openmindedness toward mesmerism and his consideration of its possible relationship to electrophysiology.

Mesmer theorized that animal magnetism, an imperceptible fluid supposedly pervading the cosmos, affected the movement of all bodies within it from planets to people. Furthermore, he contended that any illness could be cured using magnetic forces to restore the body's internal harmony. In the late 1770s, Mesmer had established his Paris practice. He added many evocative touches to enhance his magnetic therapy: mood lighting, strategically placed mirrors, and even a glass armonica—the musical instrument Franklin had invented—to contribute to the eerie atmosphere. Mesmer seems like a charlatan, but he genuinely believed in animal magnetism. Well-to-do clients visited his clinic seeking cures for all sorts of ailments. The business proved quite lucrative, but Mesmer wanted more than money. He longed for scientific recognition.

In the face of Mesmer's burgeoning popularity, Louis XVI created a commission to examine the practice of mesmerism in March 1784. Franklin was chosen president of the commission: another indication of the profound respect the French had for his scientific prowess. The commission would release its findings in August 1784. After observing numerous supposedly successful cures, they concluded that magnetism had little or no effect on the body. Animal magnetism was bogus.[35]

Taken together, "List of Books" and "Liste des livres" give rise to some nagging questions. If "List of Books" represents Temple's Passy library and not the contents of Franklin's office library, then where is the catalogue of the office library? If "Liste des livres" represents Franklin's Passy book list from 1781, where are the book lists from his other years at Passy? If Franklin catalogued his books when he moved them from his private quarters to his office library, then surely he would have catalogued the collection when he moved it from Passy to Philadelphia? If so, what happened to that list?

Franklin soon turned his attention from book lists to peace talks. In March 1782, he began informal negotiations with British envoy Richard Oswald. The following month, Franklin suggested that Britain should cede

FIGURE 23.1 *John Jay* (1888–1889), after a painting by Joseph Wright. Library of Congress, Prints and Photographs Division, Washington, DC, LC-USZ62-95399.

Canada to the United States. When John Jay, another American commissioner, arrived in June, he insisted on the recognition of American independence as a precondition before formal peace negotiations could begin. The
delay slowed the peace talks and let Britain get the upper hand in the war at
sea, thus weakening the American bargaining position.[36]

Jay and Franklin proposed their terms to Oswald, who secured a new commission in September that recognized the United States and satisfied Jay's
precondition, so they could finally start formal peace negotiations. In late
October, Adams finally returned to Paris from the Netherlands. Gazing into
the past, John Dos Passos could see him clearly, though his image of Adams is
hardly flattering: "He arrived all puffed up from the success of his negotiations with the Dutch bankers. Adams was a stubby rotund New Englander,
blue eyes, redfaced and shortnecked."[37]

Adams's face got even redder upon learning that Franklin had managed to
get Temple appointed secretary to the peace commission. Despite his absence
at the start of the peace negotiations, Adams thought he should be the one to

FIGURE 23.2 C. M. Bell, *John Adams*, c. 1900. Library of Congress, Prints and
Photographs Division, Washington, DC, LC-DIG-bellcm-25587.

choose the secretary, and he had a kinsman of his own picked out for the position. Toward the end of the next month, Henry Laurens arrived from England and, on November 30, 1782, Oswald and the four American commissioners signed the preliminary articles of peace.

The peace was still not definitive. Five months later, Laurens wrote George Washington that they were continuing to negotiate, but he remained skeptical: "So many things however have lately fallen out between the cup and the lip as tend to keep my expectations in a state of due moderation." Not until September 3, 1783, would Adams, Franklin, and Jay sign the Treaty of Paris on behalf of the United States officially ending the Revolutionary War. When Adams wrote his wife Abigail to tell her about the peace, she replied by quoting Addison's apostrophe to Liberty: "Hail! Goddess heavenly bright profuse of joy, and pregnant with delight."[38]

On May 12, 1784, the peace treaty with Great Britain was formally ratified. The next day, Franklin wrote Congress and asked to be relieved from his post. Though his French friends hoped he would end his days at Passy, Franklin, like W. C. Fields, would rather be living in Philadelphia, even though it would mean facing his petty, jealous, and mean-spirited political enemies. After reading one Connecticut newspaper article accusing him of extravagance at Valentinois, he told Adams, "If I could sit down to dinner on a piece of their excellent salt pork and pumpkin, I would not give a farthing for all the luxuries of Paris."[39] Franklin would be happy to eat pumpkin at morning and pumpkin at noon provided he could eat pumpkin at home. His pumpkin-spiced remark confirms Franklin's homesickness. He looked to the west, and his spirit was crying for leaving.

Instead of permission to return, Franklin received another assignment from Congress. When Jefferson reached Paris that August, he brought a new commission. Adams, Franklin, and Jefferson were to negotiate treaties of amity and commerce with other European nations and the Barbary states. Jefferson also informed Franklin that David Humphreys, one of Washington's aides during the war, had been appointed secretary of the new commission. Franklin was shocked and disappointed. He had pleaded with Congress to appoint Temple to some kind of diplomatic post. The appointment of Humphreys, who could not even speak French, was a slap in the face.[40]

In December, Polly Hewson, now widowed, and her three children came to Passy to spend the winter with the Franklins. She enjoyed the company of her old friend and mentor, but Polly was dismayed upon seeing Temple, whom she had known since he was little. The bouncing baby had become a dashing blade. She told a friend, "He has such a love of dress and is so absorbed in self-importance and so engaged in the pursuit of pleasure that he is not an amiable nor a respectable character."[41]

Franklin's political enemies continued to resent his maneuvers and machinations on behalf of his grandson. Temple never would obtain the diplomatic post for which his grandfather had groomed him. Instead, he would return to Philadelphia with his grandfather—but not with his son. As if to prove Polly correct, Temple left Théophile behind. A few years later, Blanchette wrote to inform him of Théophile's death from smallpox. Temple cruelly replied that she should have been more careful.[42]

Benny, who would soon turn 16, showed more promise. Polly was impressed: "He is sensible and manly in his manner without the slightest tincture of the coxcomb."[43] Given the difficulties Franklin had placing Temple in the diplomatic corps, he decided to give Benny more practical training. Having installed a small printing press at Passy to facilitate his diplomatic work—printing passports, promissory notes, and other official documents—Franklin taught Benny the printing trade. Once Benny had learned to operate the press, Franklin apprenticed him to a Parisian type-founder for further training. Franklin cut the apprenticeship short once he received permission from Congress to return home.

Before Franklin had arranged to transport himself to Le Havre, where he would board a vessel for the next leg of his journey home, he started packing up his household goods. The fourth week of May, a carpenter arrived to construct the shipping cases. Franklin wanted the cases to do double duty. They would transport his goods home to Philadelphia, where he would turn them into bookcases. The carpenter made 128 cases, initialing each with "B. F." and numbering every one. Besides the several hundred books that comprised the Passy library, the heavy baggage included the Passy printing press and Temple's fancy cabriolet. Nearly a month would pass before the heavy baggage was ready to transport.[44]

Happily, Franklin received a letter from Le Duc de Coigny, the royal equerry, who offered him the use of Queen Marie Antoinette's royal litter, a curtained couch in which the passenger would sit. It was suspended on long shafts harnessed to two large Spanish mules. A conductor rode a third mule to guide the litter. Temple and Benny would follow in a coach. They would take the road to Rouen, where they planned to meet up with the heavy baggage, which would travel down the Seine. At Rouen, according to their plan, the heavy baggage would be transferred to a larger vessel that would transport them the rest of the way to Le Havre.[45]

The water diligence, a horse-drawn barge, was scheduled to reach Passy on Wednesday, June 29th. Benny took it upon himself to supervise the shipment.

He rose before dawn Wednesday morning to watch the barge arrive, but there was no sign of it. The weather had been hot and dry that year, so the Seine was shallow in spots. The water diligence got stuck on a sandbar somewhere between the center of Paris and Passy. Franklin had the heavy baggage moved to the river's edge in anticipation of the barge's arrival.

Franklin had been in Paris for nine years, and he kept buying books that whole time, besides receiving numerous presentation copies from distinguished authors throughout Europe. Picture all those boxes stacked at the river's edge and consider the books they contained. Besides the "List of Books" collection and the "Liste des livres" collection, the boxes contained many other valuable books: Ariosto's *Satyres* in Robert Tofte's Renaissance English translation; Ignaz Born's *Travels*, which described the mines and mineral resources of Transylvania; Captain Cook's *Voyage to the Pacific Ocean*; and William Cowper's *Poems*, a collection that revitalized Franklin's love of poetry.[46]

The list goes on: a copy of Crèvecoeur's *Letters from an American Farmer* presented by the author; a French translation of *Robinson Crusoe* presented by the translator; *Constitutions des treize états-Unis de l'Amerique*, a copy of all the state constitutions, which the Duc de Rochefoucauld had translated into French at Franklin's behest; several Greek and Latin classics published at Zweibrücken by the Societas Bipointis, which contained new commentary and republished the commentaries of James Logan's old friend Johann Albert Fabricius; several pamphlets about the experimental balloon flights that had captivated Paris for the past few years; and many, many more books.[47]

By nightfall, the barge had yet to arrive, but storm clouds were fast approaching. Franklin scrounged up some sails to cover the boxes and protect them against the wet weather. He also hired a sentinel to guard them against thieves and vandals. The great French library that Franklin took nearly a decade to assemble spent its last night at Passy on the banks of the Seine in the rain.

24

Franklin Court

CARRYING ITS DISTINGUISHED American passenger, Marie Antoinette's royal litter clip-clopped into Rouen about 5 o'clock Thursday afternoon, July 14, 1785. Benjamin Franklin accepted an invitation to lodge with a Rouen banker. His reputation preceded him, and he began receiving visitors bearing gifts. On Saturday, he received a package from Dr. Louis Lépecq de La Clôture, a prominent epidemiologist who had devoted years researching the relationship between geography, meteorology, and disease, deriving his empirical data from the Normandy region. The package contained a three-volume quarto set presenting the results of his research, *Collection d'observations sur les maladies et constitutions épidemiques*. This bookish present enabled Lépecq to share his research with America's leading scientist, but it also had social value, letting him pay tribute to Franklin.[1]

Traveling by water, Jean-Antoine Houdon and his men reached Rouen two days after Franklin, but there was still no sign of their heavy baggage. The water diligence kept getting stuck, often for days at a stretch as it continued down the Seine. In its absence, Franklin would keep using the royal litter to Le Havre, hoping the heavy baggage would catch up with them there. It did not. They left France without it on Friday, July 22nd. Franklin's books and the other heavy baggage would not leave Le Havre until November, meaning that Houdon and his men would cross the Atlantic without their luggage. Given a lifetime of fundraising for good causes, Franklin knew how to help. During the ocean voyage, he would take up a "subscription of shirts and stockings" to allow better-equipped passengers to supply Houdon and his men with undergarments and other basic necessities.[2]

They had planned to sail from Le Havre to the Isle of Wight, where they were supposed to board the *London Packet*, skippered by Captain Thomas Truxtun. Since stormy weather made it impossible to land on the Isle of Wight, they went to Southampton instead, arriving there Sunday morning. They found comfortable lodgings at the Star Inn.

Franklin's library continued to grow as his journey progressed. Later that Sunday, some London friends arrived. One brought him two books, Samuel Gale's *Essay on the Nature and Principles of Public Credit* and John Coakley Lettson's edition of John Fothergill's *Works*. Gale, an American Loyalist who had worked as a paymaster for the British army, had been denied an annuity by its government. Explaining how Britain could extinguish its public debt, Gale wrote the tract to strengthen his claim for an annuity.[3]

Franklin, who knew about Lettsom's plan to collect and edit their friend's writings, retained a profound respect for Dr. Fothergill. Learning of his death four years earlier, Franklin had written a letter of condolence to a mutual friend, in which he offered his highest compliment: "He was a great doer of good."[4] Lettsom's edition includes a biography of Fothergill, which recounts his unsuccessful efforts to negotiate with Franklin a nonviolent agreement between Great Britain and its American colonies.

William Franklin, who had left America and settled in England, came to Southampton to see both his father and his son. Franklin convinced William to sell Temple his New Jersey estate—Franklin Park—and his other New Jersey holdings. The transaction required a huge document. Mr. Puzzle's prediction that it would take as much paper to convey a piece of land as to cover it almost came true: The deed for 577 acres filled thirteen folio pages.[5] All that paper still could not cover the raw emotions of the moment. As they came together at Southampton, father, son, and grandson knew the three would never come together again.

Franklin visited a local attraction in Southampton: Martin's Salt Water Hot Bath. Immersing himself in the salt water, he instantly relaxed. Floating on his back, Franklin soon fell asleep. Before he knew it, an hour had passed. He had slept that whole time without sinking or turning. Franklin had never done anything like that before; he could hardly believe it was possible. For an hour, his pain had subsided. Leaving the salt bath as if from the womb, Franklin felt like a new man.[6]

Bishop Shipley and his daughter Georgiana also came to Southampton to see their old friend. Shipley brought Franklin another book, William Paley's *Principles of Moral and Political Philosophy*. After finishing it, Franklin wrote Shipley a letter of thanks: "I am to thank you however, for the pleasure I had after our parting, in reading the new book you gave me, which I think generally well written, and likely to do good; tho' the reading time of most people is of late so taken up with news papers and little periodical pamphlets, that few now-a-days venture to attempt reading a quarto volume. I have admir'd to see, that in the last century, a folio, *Burton on Melancholy*, went through six editions in about twenty years. We have, I believe, more readers now, but not of such large books."[7]

Franklin's remarks offer an insightful comment on late-eighteenth-century reading habits. Few people read books any more, he complains, especially not 700-page ones. They much preferred reading newspapers or magazines. Curmudgeonly, yet familiar, his words are those of any true booklover. That people no longer read is a perennial complaint.

The irony is that Franklin's own writing had accelerated the preference for shorter works over larger ones. In his treatise, Paley critiques authors who treat the subject of moral philosophy with brevity. Instead of developing their ideas at length, they use a "sententious, apothegmatizing style," a style that prevented readers from concentrating on any one subject and stopped them from understanding. After writing *A Dissertation on Liberty and Necessity* as a young man, Franklin concluded that moral philosophy is best expressed in apothegms and sententiae, which could reach a much wider audience than a quarto volume, giving people moral philosophy they could remember and share. Phrased in the form of Poor Richard's saws and sayings, Franklin's moral philosophy would exert a greater and more democratic influence than weighty treatises like Paley's *Moral Philosophy*.

Decades had passed since Franklin wrote his last almanac, but Poor Richardisms continued being repeated and reprinted. A half dozen years earlier, Benjamin Vaughan had published his edition of Franklin's nonscientific writings: *Political, Miscellaneous, and Philosophical Pieces.* The work appeared in a 500-page quarto. Though it included *The Way to Wealth*, Joseph Johnson—Vaughan's publisher—also issued *The Way to Wealth* separately as a broadside suitable for framing. The format proved hugely popular. Publishers from Bath to Canterbury subsequently issued their own broadside editions of *The Way to Wealth*. Across Great Britain, people hung Franklin's apothegms on their parlor walls.[8]

Upon learning that Franklin was in Southampton, Vaughan came down to visit. Franklin enjoyed their reunion. Vaughan, 34 and married, was living in London and working in his father-in-law's mercantile business, but he was active in political, literary, and scientific circles. Like Franklin, Vaughan was curious about lead poisoning, a subject that dominated their conversation in Southampton. Franklin promised to write Vaughan a letter describing in more detail the topics they touched on in conversation.[9]

Jonathan Williams, who had been living in England, traveled to Southampton to join Franklin on the journey home. Williams was fascinated with his research on the Gulf Stream and agreed to help him measure the air and water temperature throughout the voyage. Williams would continue Franklin's research, eventually publishing his results as *Thermometrical Navigation*. His subsequent career further reflects Franklin's influence. The first superintendent of West Point, Williams would establish an innovative curriculum to make the military academy the first school of scientific engineering in the United States.[10]

Houdon befriended Benny during the voyage. On August 23rd, a ferocious storm beset them. The sailors took in all the sails but the one on the bowsprit, which the wind broke off with a terrible crash. The wind blew so hard, the mainyard dipped into the water three times. Neither Houdon nor Benny cowered in fear in the face of the storm. Together, they ignored Aeolus for Longinus, contemplating the sublimity of this spectacular storm. By 4 o'clock that afternoon, the storm abated, and Benny helped bail out the ship. Water was everywhere. The driest thing aboard the *London Packet* that day was Paley's *Moral Philosophy*.

The *London Packet* passed between Cape May and Cape Henlopen on Tuesday, September 13th, to enter Delaware Bay. Franklin recorded the moment in his diary: "water smooth, air cool, day fair and fine." On Wednesday morning, a light breeze brought the *London Packet* above Gloucester Point, putting its passengers, as Franklin exclaimed, "in full view of dear Philadelphia!" They had to weigh anchor and await the health officer to inspect the crew and passengers before they could land. Richard Bache came with a boat for Franklin and his grandsons, and they sailed to Market Street Wharf, where they disembarked to the sound of cannon salutes, pealing bells, and cheering crowds.

Franklin headed for Franklin Court, the home Samuel Rhoads had designed and built for him and Deborah to live out their golden years, but where they had never lived together. Richard and Sally Bache had been living there in her father's absence. The house had filled up with little Baches in Franklin's absence: Sarah and Richard now had six children, counting Benny, whom they had not seen in nine years.

Franklin had been looking forward to his retirement, but his state and his nation still needed him. On October 11th, he was elected to the Supreme Executive Council of Pennsylvania for a three-year term. The following week, the council and assembly together elected him president. They would unanimously reelect him to the presidency for the next two years: the maximum the state constitution allowed. As president of the Supreme Executive Council, Franklin effectively performed the role of governor of Pennsylvania. Soon afterward, he informed a correspondent of the "unanimous desire of my country folks": "They engrossed the prime of my life. They have eaten my flesh, and seem resolved now to pick my bones."[11] The dreams he had entertained of a relaxing retirement disappeared with this new responsibility, but he was proud to serve Pennsylvania.

Visitors kept him busy. Many travelers passing through Philadelphia in the mid-1780s hoped to meet Franklin. Andrew Ellicott, whose surveying career fostered his scientific interest in astronomy and mathematics, met Franklin the first week of December. He invited Ellicott to spend that Sunday at Franklin Court. After entering his home, Ellicott found Franklin in a little room containing a table and some stools and crowded with books, papers, and various "old philosophical instruments."[12] The cramped quarters reveal the problem Franklin faced on his return. With so many grandchildren running around all over the place, Franklin did not have enough room for his books and scientific equipment. When his Paris library arrived three months later, he took action. Finding room for all his books, which amounted to over 4,000 volumes, was a daunting task. He decided to build a large addition to his home. The first floor would be a dining room that could seat twenty-four. The library, 16 × 30 1/2 feet, occupied the entire second floor of the new wing.[13]

Franklin devised an innovative cataloguing scheme that would let him easily access his books. He converted the shipping crates into bookcases. Each case would hold one shelf of books. Since his Paris carpenter had numbered all the boxes, Franklin used the numbering system to catalogue his books. Into each volume, he would inscribe the case number and the shelf position. Into his copy of William Brownrigg's *Art of Making Common Salt*, for example, he wrote "C17 N18," meaning that the book was the eighteenth volume in case 17. Franklin would then record the book titles, case numbers, and shelf positions in his library catalogue, thus making it easy to locate any given volume.

After he created a scheme for coding his books and cataloguing his library, Franklin did some rearranging. Perhaps no work illustrates this better than his multivolume edition of François Rozier's *Cours complet d'agriculture*, which forms part of Franklin's excellent collection of agricultural books. Franklin had corresponded with Rozier and knew him as the editor of the *Journal de physique*, a scientific journal that Arthur Young, a contemporary agricultural writer, called the "best journal that is to be found in Europe." Young also had great respect for Rozier's encyclopedia, though it contained more theory than praxis.[14]

Initially, Franklin planned to shelve Rozier's encyclopedia in case 67. He inscribed its first volume with the shelfmark, "C67 N8." But case 67 was already bulging with scientific periodicals, so he relocated it and the next four volumes to the start of Case 72 and inscribed shelfmarks into all five. Dissatisfied with this location, Franklin canceled these shelfmarks, moved Rozier's volumes to Case 88, and reinscribed them with new shelfmarks. All this rearranging took place before 1789, when Franklin received Rozier's next two volumes. The fact that these two contain no shelfmarks indicates that Franklin's plan to inscribe his books was an ongoing process.[15]

His innovative organizational scheme is consistent with other clever devices Franklin created to enhance his reading. Most importantly, he invented bifocals, enabling him to see from far and near without switching glasses. Precisely when he invented the bifocal is unknown, but his fullest description occurs in a 1785 letter.[16] Franklin also invented a chair that transformed into a stepladder for accessing the topmost shelves of his library, which extended to the ceiling. In addition, he devised a mechanical hand that could gently remove individual volumes from the upper shelves.

Franklin would write the detailed letter about lead poisoning that he promised Vaughan, but it took him nearly a year to do so, mainly because he had a book in his library he wished to access but could not get to it until he had unpacked his books and organized his library. While living in Boston during his apprenticeship, Franklin learned of a complaint from North Carolina that New England rum was poison, causing both the dry gripes and the dangles. Boston physicians verified that the lead used in the distillation process caused these diseases, so the Massachusetts Assembly passed a law against using lead in distilling spirits, the first public health law enacted in British North America to protect consumers. Before writing Vaughan, Franklin wanted to consult his copy of *Acts and Laws of His Majesty's Province of Massachusetts-Bay in New-England*. He transcribed the act and enclosed it with his letter.[17]

Once his new library was finished, Franklin enjoyed giving visitors a tour. Winthrop Sargent stopped by in 1786. After a distinguished military career during the Revolutionary War, Sargent turned his attention to surveying, and Congress appointed him surveyor of the Northwest Territory. Sargent passed through Philadelphia the last week of June on his way to survey land north of the Ohio River. An excellent observer with a good sense of the material culture, Sargent recorded his dinner with Franklin, mentioning their simple fare: beer and russet potatoes. After dinner, Franklin gave Sargent a tour of his library. As he often did, Franklin selected a volume ideally suited to his guest's interests. Given Sargent's interests in the mathematics of surveying, Franklin showed him *Connoissance des temps*, a compendium of astronomical and meteorological calculations that Jérôme de La Lande compiled for the Académie Royale des Sciences.[18]

Franklin's home became the meeting place for a new organization he founded, a nonpartisan group named the Society for Political Inquiries. At its first meeting on February 9, 1787, Franklin was elected president. Family members Richard Bache, Temple Franklin, and Jonathan Williams joined, as did Henry Hill, Francis Hopkinson, John Jones, Thomas Paine, Samuel Powel, Benjamin Rush, and James Wilson.[19]

The organization was part Junto and part American Philosophical Society. It met twice a month, usually in Franklin's dining room or upstairs in his library. Like the Junto and the Club of Honest Whigs, the new society would assign questions for discussion beforehand but focusing on political science. Discussion topics included commercial policy, freedom of the press, prison reform, and the relevance of the study of Greek and Latin. The Society for Political Inquiries welcomed diverse opinions and showed that men from different ends of the political spectrum could come together for fruitful discussion.[20]

In May 1787, delegates from throughout the United States came to Philadelphia to attend the Constitutional Convention at Independence Hall. As they had during the Continental Congress, Samuel and Elizabeth Powel opened the doors of their home on Third Street and welcomed the delegates. Joining her guests' discussion, Elizabeth Powel would "animate and give a brilliancy to the whole conversation," as her sister Anne Willing boasted. Anne, who worried about Elizabeth's zeal for politics, shared her concerns with a third sister, Mary Willing Byrd: "Her patriotism causes too much anxiety. Female politicians are always ridiculed by the other sex." The Powels were excellent hosts. Their lavish hospitality included whipped syllabub and other delights.[21]

Franklin, who was elected a delegate to the Constitutional Convention to represent Pennsylvania, welcomed other delegates to his home. When George Washington entered Philadelphia the second week of May, he went to Franklin Court to renew their friendship. They had not seen one another since 1775, when Franklin had visited the headquarters of the Continental Army in Cambridge, Massachusetts, on behalf of Congress. They were happy to see each other after a lapse of a dozen years. Washington would often return to Franklin Court during his time in Philadelphia for the convention.

On one visit, Franklin showed off his library to Washington. He made a point to share the four-volume edition of *Don Quixote* published in Madrid by Joaquin Ibarra. Commissioned by the Real Academia de la Lengua, which oversaw its publication, the gorgeous edition was printed on elegant paper using a new, specially designed typeface and illustrated with handsome engravings. Paradoxically, England regarded *Don Quixote* as a classic before

Spain did. The Spanish formerly saw the work as little more than a burlesque of chivalric romance, but the Real Academia edition established *Don Quixote* as a Spanish classic. After seeing Franklin's *Don Quixote*, Washington would add a copy to his library at Mount Vernon.[22]

The convention was scheduled to begin on Monday, May 14th, but delegates from many states had yet to reach Philadelphia by then, preventing a quorum and delaying its start. Franklin accepted the delay with grace and hosted a party in the interim. On the 16th, those delegates already in town gathered at Franklin Court for dinner. Having recently received a cask of porter from London brewer Thomas Jordan, Franklin could think of no better time to share it. Writing Jordan a letter of thanks, Franklin described how his guests received the cask: "Its contents met with the most cordial reception and universal approbation." Jordan's porter was the best the delegates had ever tasted.[23]

Not until Friday, May 25th, did the states reach a quorum and begin the Constitutional Convention. Washington was elected president of the convention. A hard rain prevented Franklin from attending the first day, but he took his seat on Monday and diligently attended every day for the next four months. He did not speak on the convention floor very often, but he coaxed others toward his point of view, using his charm and storytelling ability to help them see things more clearly.

On June 4th, Franklin spoke against giving the national executive an absolute veto over the legislature, concerned that it would lead to an abuse of power akin to what colonial Pennsylvania had experienced under the proprietary governors. An absolute executive veto could lead to monarchy, he observed. The convention unanimously agreed.

Toward the end of June, the convention approached the contentious issue of legislative representation. Delegates from the smaller states argued that every state should be equally represented in the legislature. The larger states argued that representation should be directly proportionate to each state's population. On July 2nd, Franklin was elected to a committee to settle the issue. He initially advocated proportionate representation in both houses, but the smaller states refused.

The larger states were willing to accept equal representation in the Senate, provided that representatives in the House were proportionate and that the House of Representatives would control the spending bills. Debate over this scheme, which became known as the Great Compromise, lasted until July 11th. Franklin thought that giving the House of Representatives power over the spending bills made good sense and sought to persuade others. He ultimately persuaded enough to pass the measure. In short, Franklin helped keep the convention together at a crucial moment when the delegates were ready to return home without forming a federal government.[24]

Throughout that summer, convention delegates and travelers passing through Philadelphia visited Franklin Court. None left a fuller account than the Reverend Dr. Manasseh Cutler, who came to Franklin Court with a prominent convention delegate from Massachusetts, Elbridge Gerry. After dark, Franklin invited his guests into the library. In his account, Cutler does not say precisely how they entered, but the passage was tricky. In the new wing of Franklin's home, it was impossible to go directly from the first-floor dining room to the second-floor library because Franklin had excluded a staircase, which would have taken too much space away from his books. To access the library, they had to go through the main house. It was a little cumbersome, but Franklin liked going that way as he led guests to his library. The intricate passage added mystery and allure. They either went through his bedroom, or they entered through one of the closets in the old drawing room.

Recording the girlhood memories of Franklin's granddaughter Debby Bache, her daughter Elizabeth Duane Gillespie called the door between his bedroom and the library a "noiseless door."[25] Writing at the start of the twentieth century, Gillespie used a term that, in builders' circles, had remained an unachieved goal through the nineteenth. People longed for a door that would not slam, squeak, or screech. In American literature, noiseless doors are often found in utopian novels. Not until the ideal future would doors achieve noiselessness. No one outside Franklin's family circle knew that he had already perfected the noiseless door in the 1780s.

Franklin showed his guests many curiosities, natural and manmade. The night Cutler visited, the other guests continued to discuss politics. To his great delight, Cutler had their host to himself. Since Franklin typically shaped a tour of his library to suit his guest's interests, he showed him books about botany, which was Cutler's passion. That year, Franklin had received a copy of Linneaus's *Families of Plants*, a presentation copy from Erasmus Darwin. Cutler spent the most time looking at a related book, Johann Sebastien Mueller's *Illustration of the Sexual System of Linnaeus*. Dr. Fothergill had given Franklin this huge folio to present to the American Philosophical Society. It would eventually end up there, but Franklin held onto it for the time being and even inscribed it with his distinctive shelf mark.[26] Cutler enjoyed the book very much. It contained Linneaus's classification of plants, complete with engraved and hand-colored illustrations: "It was a feast to me, and the Doctor seemed to enjoy it as well as myself. We spent a couple of hours in examining this volume."[27]

On Friday, July 20th, debate in the convention turned toward the issue of impeachment. A resolution had been introduced that included a clause allowing the national executive to be impeached and removed from office for malpractice or neglect of duty. Two delegates moved to strike that part of the resolution, arguing that the national executive should not be impeachable while in office. Their motion met vehement resistance.[28]

"If he be not impeachable whilst in office," William Richardson Davie, a delegate from North Carolina, argued, "he will spare no efforts or means whatever to get himself re-elected."

"No point is of more importance than that the right of impeachment should be continued," said George Mason, concurring with Davie. "Shall the man who has practiced corruption and by that means procured his appointment in the first instance, be suffered to escape punishment, by repeating his guilt?"

Franklin agreed, arguing that impeachment would be the best way to punish the president when his misconduct should deserve it. Impeachment proceedings would also allow his acquittal should he be unjustly accused. Without an impeachment process built into the Constitution, Franklin argued, the only way to remove a corrupt president would be assassination.

James Madison concurred. He thought that an impeachment process should be built into the Constitution to defend against a corrupt, unprincipled, or incompetent national executive. Madison listed several possible outcomes resulting from a corrupt national leader. Read in retrospect, Madison's words are bone-chilling. Though often quoted, they deserve to be repeated. Considering what would happen in the case of a corrupt president, Madison observed, "He might pervert his administration into a scheme of peculation or oppression. He might betray his trust to foreign powers," Madison argued. "In the case of the executive magistracy which was to be administered by a single man, loss of capacity or corruption was more within the compass of probable events, and either of them might be fatal to the republic."

Monday, September 17th, was the last day of the Constitutional Convention. The Constitution was ready for the delegates to sign, though some remained unsure whether they should. After the Constitution was read, Franklin rose with a written speech, which he handed to fellow Pennsylvania delegate James Wilson to read. Franklin urged every member to "doubt a little of his own infallibility," put aside specific reservations, and vote to approve the Constitution.[29]

Franklin's speech in favor of the Constitution—his "blessing," John Updike called it—moved the delegates. Updike explained, "This blessing, which did much to quiet popular resistance to the centralized form the

FIGURE 24.1 H. B. Hall, *James Madison*, engraving. From Lyon Gardiner Tyler, *Encyclopedia of Virginia Biography* (New York: Lewis Historical Publishing, 1915), vol. 2, facing page 23. Kevin J. Hayes Collection, Toledo, OH.

Constitution had taken, was Franklin's last great gift to his nation."[30] Only three delegates refused to sign. When they had almost finished signing, Franklin made a clever and characteristic remark. He said that throughout the time the convention had been meeting, the sun that was painted on Washington's chair puzzled him. He could not tell whether it was a rising or a setting sun. But now that the Constitution was signed, he could tell that it was indeed a rising sun.

Once the Constitutional Convention adjourned, the delegates went to City Tavern to dine together. Some delegates ended up at the Powels' home Monday night. After enduring the secrecy of the convention proceedings all summer, the politically savvy Elizabeth Powel was eager to hear what the delegates had decided. No longer bound by secrecy, they could now talk freely about the convention proceedings.[31]

"Well, Doctor," she asked once Franklin entered their home, "We are happy to see you abroad again: pray what have we got?"

"A republic, madam, if you can keep it," Franklin told her.

"And why not keep a good thing," she asked, "when we have got it?"

"Because madam," Franklin replied, "there is in all republics a certain ingredient, of which the people having once tasted, think they can never get enough."

The month before the Constitutional Convention began Franklin had been elected president of the local anti-slavery organization. With the Constitution written and the convention adjourned, he could devote his energy to abolition. The organization had originally been founded in 1775, but it languished during the Revolutionary War. It was reorganized in 1784, and, in 1787, a new constitution was adopted and it was renamed the Pennsylvania Society for Promoting the Abolition of Slavery, for the Relief of Free Negroes Unlawfully Held in Bondage, and for Improving the Condition of the African Race.

In February 1790 on behalf of the Society, Franklin petitioned Congress against slavery and the slave trade, urging it "to countenance the restoration to liberty of those unhappy men, who, alone, in this land of freedom, are degraded into perpetual bondage."[32] When the petition came up for discussion on the floor of Congress, James Jackson, a congressman from Georgia, spoke at length in an elaborate defense of slavery. His ignorant remarks inspired Franklin to write "Sidi Mehemet Ibrahim on the Slave Trade," which satirized Jackson's defense of slavery. Written as a letter to the editor of *The Federal Gazette* and signed "Historicus," this work gave Franklin a new opportunity to indulge his passion for hoaxes. Historicus, having read a speech in a seventeenth-century history of the Barbary Coast, presents it to the readers of *The Federal Gazette*.[33]

Sidi Mehemet Ibrahim speaks in defense of the Muslim practice of enslaving Christians. His speech amounts to a paraphrase of the speech Jackson gave on the floor of Congress. It reveals Jackson's prejudice, hypocrisy, and narrow-mindedness. William Lloyd Garrison, who would reprint Franklin's hoax in *The Liberator*, a nineteenth-century abolitionist newspaper, remarked, "Not a slave owner, probably, not a single excuser of the slave system, on perusing the speech of Sidi Mehemet Ibrahim, can be so blind as not to perceive himself represented in *propria persona*, as in a mirror, or so obtuse as not to comprehend the folly of his own logic."[34]

"Sidi Mehemet Ibrahim on the Slave Trade," which appeared in *The Federal Gazette* on March 25, 1790, would be the last piece Franklin published, but he kept working on his autobiography, a project he had resumed in 1788. He had begun part 3 in August 1788 and wrote part 4 in late 1789 and early 1790. In addition, he tinkered with part 1. The surviving manuscript shows Franklin's hand trembling more and more as he revised, but he kept going.[35]

Some of his last revisions involved changing a word or two here and there. One day, he altered the story about the time he convinced Samuel Keimer to become a vegetarian. Franklin originally wrote the following sentence: "He was usually a great gormandizer, and I promis'd my self some diversion in half-starving him." He crossed out "gormandizer" and substituted "glutton."[36] The two words are synonymous, but glutton had greater resonance. It gives the episode the quality of a parable, channeling the rich glutton from the Bible who goes to Hell for his gluttony.

In his waning years, Franklin developed a reputation for his reading and writing among the neighborhood children. Robert Carr, then an adolescent, left a vivid picture of him: "When able to be out of bed, he passed nearly all his time in his office, reading and writing, and in conversation with his friends; and, when the boys were playing and very noisy, in the lot front of the office, he would open the window and call to them: 'Boys, Boys, can't you play without making so much noise. I am reading, and it disturbs me very much.'"[37]

Franklin continued expanding his collection of books, mainly by acquiring presentation copies from authors, friends, and well-wishers. During the last year of his life, he obtained books about a variety of subjects, including agriculture, astronomy, bee culture, botany, China, chemistry, commerce, drama, Greek antiquities, meteorology, philanthropy, physics, printing, prison reform, political science, and public finance. Illness confined him to bed in early 1790 and kept him from his library, but his grandchildren stayed busy running back and forth to fetch books for him. Even in his final illness, Franklin always had something to read nearby, as Polly Hewson's reminiscence confirms.

Having taken Franklin's advice, Polly had left England and emigrated to America, settling in Philadelphia with her three children. She stayed near her friend and mentor to comfort him at the end of his life. Sometimes Franklin's bladder stones hurt so much that Dr. John Jones, the leading surgeon in the nation and his personal physician, would occasionally administer laudanum to alleviate the pain. Complicating matters, pleurisy struck Franklin the first week of April. The pulmonary disease he had survived twice before now threatened his life again.

When Polly found him confined to bed in great agony one day, she lingered by his side until the worst had passed. As his pain abated, she asked if he would like her to read to him. Of course, he replied. Noticing the last volume of Samuel Johnson's *Lives of the Poets* by his bedside, she read to him from the life of Isaac Watts. She thought the book might lull him to sleep, but instead it triggered fond memories. He repeated several of Watts's lyrical poems and extolled their admirable qualities.[38]

Franklin's opinion of Watts's poetry closely resembles Johnson's. Watts's hymns and devotional poems for children are his best-known writings, but his other poetry appealed to more discriminating readers. In *Lives of the Poets*, Johnson observes, "He has provided instruction for all ages, from those who are lisping their first lessons, to the enlightening readers of Malebranche and Locke." As a printer, Franklin had published editions of Watts's *Hymns and Spiritual Songs* and *Divine Songs for Children*, but Johnson reminded him of poems from *Horae lyricae*. Johnson, too, preferred his lyrical verse. The narrow subject matter of Watts's devotional verse limited its possibilities, Johnson observed, but Watts's lyric poetry demonstrated his well-tuned ear, elegant diction, and *copia verborum*.[39]

Polly's reminiscence of Franklin's final days identifies a pattern: Reading Johnson's *Lives of the Poets* sparked Franklin's memory of poems from his past. Johnson's early chapters covered Abraham Cowley, John Milton, and Samuel Butler, three poets Franklin had known since encountering their collected works as an apprentice in his brother's printshop. Johnson had lengthy chapters on John Dryden and William Congreve, two authors whose dramatic works were performed on stage during Franklin's first visit to London, when he and James Ralph often attended the theater. Johnson also wrote a lengthy chapter about Joseph Addison, whose poetry Franklin read while working in London, where he may have helped set Addison's *Miscellaneous Works* in type. Edward Young, the subject of another long chapter in Johnson's *Lives*, was a Franklin favorite. Having first read Young's *Love of Fame* in London, he had since reread it so often, he practically knew the book by heart. Johnson's chapter on Alexander Pope could have reminded Franklin about his first trip to London, when Pope published his translation of *The Odyssey*, which Franklin read on the voyage home.

The list goes on. When Franklin returned to Philadelphia, he compiled an idiosyncratic religious creed that incorporated an excerpt from Richard Blackmore, a poet Johnson insisted his editors include. Once Franklin and his friends formed the Junto, Nicholas Scull nicknamed him "Denham," after the author of *Cooper's Hill*, the subject of Johnson's second chapter in *Lives of the Poets*. For decades, members of the Library Company of Philadelphia read the poets Johnson profiled.

Discussing Dryden's literary criticism, Johnson remarked, "With Dryden we are wandering in quest of Truth; whom we find, if we find her at all, drest in the graces of elegance; and if we miss her, the labour of the pursuit rewards itself."[40] What Johnson says about reading Dryden's prose applies to Franklin's reading process as a whole. Almost up to the moment of his death at 11 o'clock on the evening of April 17, 1790, Franklin still loved to read. Reading expanded his mind and broadened his world, putting him in touch with the great literature of the past and present and helping him make the world of the future a better place.

Sources

The Papers of Benjamin Franklin, the multivolume set of Franklin's writings sponsored by the American Philosophical Society and Yale University and published by Yale University Press, began appearing in 1959. It now fills over forty volumes but has yet to be completed. Bound in earthy brown buckram with gilt lettering and shelved together, *Papers* has such an authoritative appearance that it can be deceiving. It may look authoritative, but Franklin scholars have made many new discoveries during the six decades since the first volume appeared. In 1986, J. A. Leo Lemay published *The Canon of Benjamin Franklin, 1722–1776: New Attributions and Reconsiderations*, which adds numerous articles and essays to the canon of Franklin's writings. The following year, Lemay edited the Library of America edition of Franklin's *Writings*, which reprints his new attributions. Everyone who writes about Franklin's Boston years discusses Silence Dogood; few mention his other early personae: Dingo, Hugo Grimm, Jethro Standfast, Abigail Twitterfield, or Timothy Wagstaff.

Neither Dingo nor Jethro Standfast are mentioned in Lemay's *Canon* or included in his Library of America edition, but they are named in his *Life of Benjamin Franklin* because Lemay continued to make new attributions after completing his *Canon*. The appendices to Lemay's three-volume *Life of Benjamin Franklin* list more recent attributions. The editors of Franklin's papers at Yale have expanded its scope, including not just his writings and letters to him, but also letters of family and friends. These are included in their companion online project, The Digital Franklin Papers.

Papers forms the principal source for primary works quoted here. Lemay's edition of writings comes next. Writings not included in either are cited from previously published editions. Unpublished documents come from the digital edition. Texts have been slightly modernized. Franklin conventionally capitalized his nouns. His capitalizations, which add little meaning to his texts, have been standardized according to modern usage. Capitalized nouns have been retained when they do have meaning, that is, when they represent instances of personification. In his printed works, Franklin would use italics for emphasis, so his italics have been retained. Spelling eccentricities have been retained, except in a handful of instances when contemporary spellings create too much confusion. In those few cases, misspellings have been silently emended.

Some of the most useful secondary sources have been cited often enough to make it convenient to provide abbreviations and list them here.

ANB
Garraty, John A., and Mark C. Carnes, eds. *American National Biography*. 24 vols. New York: Oxford University Press, 1999.

Bell, *Patriot Improvers*
Bell, Whitfield J., Jr. *Patriot Improvers: Biographical Sketches of Members of the American Philosophical Society, Volume One: 1743–1768*. Philadelphia: American Philosophical Society, 1997.

CHAL
The Cambridge History of American Literature. Ed. William Peterfield Trent, John Erskine, Stuart P. Sherman, and Carl Van Doren. New York: Macmillan, 1917–1921.

Digital Edition
The Papers of Benjamin Franklin: Digital Edition. Packard Humanities Institute, 2022. franklinpapers.org.

Douglass, *British Settlements in North-America*
William Douglass, *A Summary, Historical and Political of the First Planting, Progressive Improvements, and Present State of the British Settlements in North-America*. 2 Vols. London: R. Baldwin, 1755.

ESTC
English Short Title Catalogue. British Library, 2022. estc.bl.uk.

Genetic Text
Franklin, Benjamin. *The Autobiography of Benjamin Franklin: A Genetic Text*. Ed. J. A. Leo Lemay and P. M. Zall. Knoxville: University of Tennessee Press, 1981.

Hamilton, *History of the Tuesday Club*
Hamilton, Dr. Alexander. *The History of the Ancient and Honorable Tuesday Club*, ed. Robert Micklus. 3 vols. Chapel Hill: University of North Carolina Press, 1990.

Hayes, *Colonial Woman's Bookshelf*
Hayes, Kevin J. *A Colonial Woman's Bookshelf*. 1996. Eugene, OR: Wipf and Stock, 2016.

Hayes, *Library of William Byrd*
Hayes, Kevin J. *The Library of William Byrd of Westover*. Madison, WI: Madison House, 1997.

Hayes, *Shakespeare*

Hayes, Kevin J. *Shakespeare and the Making of America*. Stroud, UK: Amberley, 2020.

Hayes and Bour

Hayes, Kevin J., and Isabelle Bour, eds. *Franklin in His Own Time: A Biographical Chronicle of His Life, Drawn from Recollections, Interviews, and Memoirs by Family, Friends, and Associates*. Iowa City: University of Iowa Press, 2011.

Lemay, *Calendar*

Lemay, J. A. Leo. *A Calendar of American Poetry in the Colonial Newspapers and Magazines and in the Major English Magazines through 1765*. Worcester, MA: American Antiquarian Society, 1972.

Lemay, *Life*

Lemay, J. A. Leo. *The Life of Benjamin Franklin*. 3 vols. Philadelphia: University of Pennsylvania Press, 2006–2009.

Miller

Miller, C. William. *Benjamin Franklin's Philadelphia Printing, 1728–1766*. Philadelphia: American Philosophical Society, 1974.

Newcomb, "Sources"

Newcomb, Robert. "The Sources of Benjamin Franklin's Sayings of Poor Richard." Ph.D. diss., University of Maryland, 1957.

Norton Critical Edition

Franklin, Benjamin. *Benjamin Franklin's Autobiography: A Norton Critical Edition*. Ed. J. A. Leo Lemay and P. M. Zall. New York: Norton, 1986.

ODNB

Matthew, H. C. G., and Brian Harrison, eds. *Oxford Dictionary of National Biography*. 60 vols. Oxford: Oxford University Press, 2004.

OHEAL

Hayes, Kevin J., ed. *Oxford Handbook of Early American Literature*. New York: Oxford University Press, 2008.

Papers

Franklin, Benjamin. *The Papers of Benjamin Franklin*. Ed. Leonard W. Labaree et al. 44 vols. to date. New Haven, CT: Yale University Press, 1959–.

PBSA

Papers of the Bibliographical Society of America

PG

The Pennsylvania Gazette

PMHB
The Pennsylvania Magazine of History and Biography

PPL
Library Company of Philadelphia

Russell, *Benjamin Franklin*
Russell, Phillips. *Benjamin Franklin: The First Civilized American.* New York: Brentano's, 1926.

Tilley
Tilley, Morris Palmer. *A Dictionary of the Proverbs in England in the Sixteenth and Seventeenth Centuries.* Ann Arbor: University of Michigan Press, 1950.

Whiting
Whiting, Bartlett Jere. *Early American Proverbs and Proverbial Sayings.* Cambridge, MA: Belknap Press, 1977.

Wolf, *Library of James Logan*
Wolf, Edwin, 2nd. *The Library of James Logan of Philadelphia, 1674–1751.* Philadelphia: Library Company of Philadelphia, 1974.

Wolf and Hayes
Wolf, Edwin, 2nd, and Kevin J. Hayes. *The Library of Benjamin Franklin.* Philadelphia: American Philosophical Society and Library Company of Philadelphia, 2006.

Writings (Lemay)
Franklin, Benjamin. *Writings.* Ed. J. A. Leo Lemay. New York: Library of America, 1987.

Notes

PROLOGUE: CIRCLES OF THE MIND

1. *Genetic Text*, 11.
2. *Genetic Text*, 37, 49.
3. *Genetic Text*, 53, 61.
4. Carl Van Doren, *Benjamin Franklin* (1938; repr., New York: Penguin, 1991), 41.
5. Edwin Wolf, 2nd, "A Key to the Identification of Franklin Books," *PMHB* 80, no. 4 (October 1956): 407–409; Edwin Wolf, 2nd, "The Reconstruction of Benjamin Franklin's Library: An Unorthodox Jigsaw Puzzle," *PBSA* 56, no. 1 (1962): 1–16.
6. Wolf and Hayes, 55–56.
7. Verner W. Crane, "The Club of Honest Whigs: Friends of Science and Liberty," *WMQ* 23, no. 2 (April 1966): 213–14.
8. Wolf and Hayes, nos. 2329, 2331.
9. Edwin Wolf, 2nd, "Great American Book Collectors to 1800," *Gazette of the Grolier Club*, no. 16 (June 1971): 47–52.
10. *Genetic Text*, 100.
11. J. A. Leo Lemay, "The Life of Benjamin Franklin," in *Franklin in Search of a Better World*, ed. Page Talbott (New Haven, CT: Yale University Press, 2005), 45.
12. Kevin J. Hayes, *Benjamin Franklin* (London: Reaktion, 2022), 151–52.
13. Jean-Luc Godard, *Godard on Godard*, ed. Jean Narboni and Tom Milne (New York: Da Capo, 1972), 238.

CHAPTER I

1. [Jonathan Smedley,] *Gulliveriana: or, A Fourth Volume of Miscellanies* (London: J. Roberts, 1728), 131; "Record of Birth" and "Record of Baptism," in *Papers*, 1:3; George P. Fisher, *Life of Benjamin Silliman, M.D., LL.D.* (New York: Scribner, 1866), 1:73. According to the old-style calendar, Franklin was born on January 6,

1705/6. The new style calendar would not be officially adopted in Britain and its colonies until 1752. Before then, dates from January 1 to March 25—the first day of the year according to the old-style calendar—were given as a dual date, as in Franklin's birth year, 1705/6. In the present work, dates will be supplied according to the new style.

2. Herman Melville, *Moby-Dick: or, The Whale* (New York: Harper, 1851), 122.

3. BF, *Poor Richard, 1746*, in *Papers*, 3:63; Tilley, no. S452; Whiting, no. S214.

4. Nian-Sheng Huang, *Franklin's Father Josiah: Life of a Colonial Boston Tallow Chandler, 1657–1745* (Philadelphia: American Philosophical Society, 2000), 12–14, 40–41.

5. Daniel Neal, *The History of New-England* (London: J. Clark, 1720), 2:590; Wolf and Hayes, no. 2404.

6. *Genetic Text*, 6; Nathaniel Hawthorne, *Biographical Stories for Children* (Boston: Tappan and Dennet, 1842), 111; Ezra Stiles, *The Literary Diary*, ed. Franklin Bowditch Dexter (New York: Scribners, 1901), 2:376.

7. Cotton Mather, *Corderius Americanus: An Essay upon the Good Education of Children* (Boston: John Allen, 1708), 29; J. A. Leo Lemay, *The Canon of Benjamin Franklin, 1722–1776: New Attributions and Reconsiderations* (Newark: University of Delaware Press, 1986), 113.

8. Benjamin Rush, "The Wisdom and Experience of Mellow Old Age, 1785–1789, 1805, 1806," in Hayes and Bour, 105.

9. *Genetic Text*, xxxiii; Thomas J. Haslam, "An Infidel's Progress: Benjamin Franklin's Twyford Manuscript Part One Reconsidered" (Ph.D. diss., University of Delaware, 1996), 11.

10. *Genetic Text*, 21.

11. *Norton Critical Edition*, 9.

12. Steven Gilbar, ed., *The Open Door: When Writers First Learned to Read* (Boston: David R. Godine, 1989), 3.

13. Haslam, "Infidel's Progress," 122–23; Lori Humphrey Newcomb, "What Is a Chapbook?" in *Literature and Popular Culture in Early Modern England*, ed. Matthew Dimmock and Andrew Hadfield (Burlington, VT: Ashgate, 2009), 68.

14. Kevin J. Hayes, *The Library of John Montgomerie, Colonial Governor of New York and New Jersey* (Newark: University of Delaware Press, 2000), 45.

15. *Genetic Text*, 10.

16. John Bunyan, *The Life and Death of Mr. Badman, Presented to the World in a Familiar Dialogue between Mr. Wiseman and Mr. Attentive* (London: Nath. Ponder, 1680), 100.

17. Leopold Damrosch, Jr., "John Bunyan," in *British Novelists, 1660–1800*, ed. Martin C. Battestin (Detroit: Gale, 1985), 82.

18. Clifford K. Shipton and James E. Mooney, *National Index of American Imprints through 1800: The Short-Title Evans* (Worcester, MA: American Antiquarian Society, 1969), 1:122–23; "Thomas Fleet's Inventory," in *Suffolk County*

(*Massachusetts*) *Probate Records, 1636–1899* (Salt Lake City: Genealogical Society of Utah, 1969–1971), 54:395.

19. *Genetic Text*, 11; *The Life and Errors of John Dunton* (London: J. Nichols, 1818), 1:206.

20. Worthington Chauncey Ford, *The Boston Book Market, 1679–1700* (Boston: Club of Odd Volumes, 1917), 118.

21. Ibid., 120; Roger Thompson, "Worthington Chauncey Ford's *Boston Book Market, 1679–1700*: Some Corrections and Additions," *Proceedings of the Massachusetts Historical Society*, 3d ser., 86 (1974): 75–76.

22. Edwin Wolf, 2nd, "Report of the Librarian," in *The Annual Report of the Library Company of Philadelphia for the Year 1966* (Philadelphia: Library Company of Philadelphia, 1967), 45; R. B. [Nathaniel Crouch], *The Surprizing Miracles of Nature and Art* (London: Nath. Crouch, 1683), 107.

23. Crouch, *Surprizing Miracles*, 161; BF, "The Grand Leap of the Whale," in *Writings* (Lemay), 561.

24. Hayes, *Colonial Woman's Bookshelf*, 96.

25. Herbert Schneider and Carol Schneider, eds., *Samuel Johnson, President of King's College: His Career and Writings* (New York: Columbia University Press, 1929), 1:498.

26. John Simons, introduction to *Guy of Warwick and Other Chapbook Romances: Six Tales from the Popular Literature of Pre-Industrial England*, ed. John Simons (Exeter: University of Exeter Press, 1998), 4.

27. John Hales, *A Modest Enquiry into the Nature of Witchcraft* (Boston: B. Green and J. Allen, 1702), 27–28, 40, 58; BF to Noah Webster, December 26, 1789, in *Writings* (Lemay), 1174; Increase Mather, *[Remarkable Providences:] An Essay for the Recording of Illustrious Providences* (Boston: Samuel Green, 1684), 2, 64, 110, 319; Increase Mather, *Cases of Conscience Concerning Evil Spirits Personating Men* (Boston: Benjamin Harris, 1693), 24, 47, 62; Cotton Mather, *Magnalia christi americana: or, The Ecclesiastical History of New-England* (London: T. Parkhurst, 1702), book 2, 60.

28. BF, "Account of the Devices on the Continental Bills of Credit," in *Writings* (Lemay), 734.

29. R. B. [Nathaniel Crouch,] *Delights for the Ingenious, In Above Fifty Select and Choice Emblems, Divine and Moral, Ancient and Modern* (London: Nath. Crouch, 1684), 207 (Yale University BEIN Jc30 23n); David D. Hall, *Worlds of Wonder, Days of Judgment: Popular Religious Belief in Early New England* (Cambridge, MA: Harvard University Press, 1990), 278.

30. Wolf and Hayes, no. 1313; Crouch, *Delights for the Ingenious*, 160; BF, *Poor Richard Improved, 1750*, in *Papers*, 3:449.

31. R. B., *Unparallel'd Varieties: or, The Matchless Actions and Passions of Mankind*, 2d ed. (London: Nath. Crouch, 1685), 18; BF, *Poor Richard Improved, 1748*, in *Papers*, 3:262.

32. Kevin J. Hayes, *Folklore and Book Culture* (1997; repr., Eugene, OR: Wipf and Stock, 2016), 5; Hamilton, *History of the Tuesday Club*, 1:22.

33. Ford, *Boston Book Market*, 118–19; James Parton, *Life and Times of Benjamin Franklin* (New York: Mason, 1865), 2:639.

34. *The Mad Conceits of Tom Tram of the West* (Edinburgh: John Reid, 1722); Tom Tram [Thomas Fleet,] "A Trip to the World on the Moon," *New-England Courant*, January 15, 1723; Kevin J. Hayes, "Fleet, Thomas," in *ANB*, 8:95.

35. Michael J. Eamon, "'Don't Speak to Me, But Write on This': The Childhood Almanacs of Mary and Katherine Byles," *New England Quarterly* 85, no. 2 (June 2012): 349–50.

36. BF to Deborah Franklin, September 6, 1758, in *Papers*, 8:145–46; James Brome, *Travels over England, Scotland and Wales* (London: Abel Roper, 1700), 72.

37. BF to Cadwalader Evans, May 9, 1766, in *Papers*, 13:269; BF to David Hartley, May 4, 1779, in *Papers*, 29:427.

38. *The Most Famous History of the Learned Fryer Bacon* (London, [1700]), sig. A3v–A4r; Whiting, no. E91.

39. *Most Famous History of the Learned Fryer Bacon*, sig. B1v–B3r.

40. Ibid., sig. C3v; Hayes, *Folklore and Book Culture*, 59–73.

41. Dixon Wecter, *The Hero in America: A Chronicle of Hero-Worship* (1941; repr., New York: Scribner, 1972), 61.

CHAPTER 2

1. *Genetic Text*, 11.

2. Plutarch, *The Lives of the Noble Grecians and Romans, Compared Together*, trans. Thomas North (London: William Lee, 1657); *Plutarch's Lives* (London: Jacob Tonson, 1683–1700); *Plutarch's Lives* (London: Tho. Bullock, 1710); *Plutarch's Lives* (London: Tho. Baker, 1713); Pierre Jean Georges Cabanis, "A Short Account of Benjamin Franklin," and Louis Lefebvre de La Roche, "On Franklin," in Hayes and Bour, 156, 124.

3. *Plutarch's Lives* (London: Jacob Tonson, 1711), 4:223–24.

4. Theodore Hornberger, *Benjamin Franklin* (Minneapolis: University of Minnesota Press, 1962), 10; Benjamin Vaughan to BF, January 31, 1783, in *Papers*, 39:115.

5. *Plutarch's Lives* (London: Jacob Tonson, 1703), 5:147; *Genetic Text*, 107; Edwin E. Slosson, "Voices in the Air," *Independent*, April 22, 1922, 385.

6. Jack P. Greene, *The Intellectual Heritage of the Constitutional Era: The Delegates' Library* (Philadelphia: Library Company of Philadelphia, 1986), 35; Frances B. Titchener, "Plutarch," in *Ancient Greek Authors*, ed. Ward W. Briggs (Detroit: Gale, 1997), 329.

7. *Genetic Text*, 11.

8. Russell, *Benjamin Franklin*, 13.

9. *Joe Miller's Jests: or, The Wits Vade-Mecum* (London: T. Read, 1742), 119; *Genetic Text*, 58.

10. Hayes, *Colonial Woman's Bookshelf*, 43; Lawrence C. Wroth and Marion W. Adams, *American Woodcuts and Engravings, 1670–1800* (Providence: Associates of the John Carter Brown Library, 1946), 7, 17; Lewis Bayly, *The Practice of Piety* (London: Edward Brewster, 1708), 156.

11. *Genetic Text*, 11; Edgar Allan Poe, "*Robinson Crusoe*," *Southern Literary Messenger* 2, no. 2 (January 1836): 127–28.

12. Maximillian E. Novak, "Daniel Defoe," in *British Novelists, 1660–1800*, ed. Martin C. Battestin (Detroit: Gale, 1985), 150.

13. H. M. Posnett, "Benjamin Franklin," *Westminster Review* 168, no. 6 (December 1907): 637–40.

14. [Daniel Defoe,] *An Essay Upon Projects* (London: Tho. Cockerill, 1697), 118; BF, "Silence Dogood, No. 5," in *Papers*, 1:20; Defoe, *Essay Upon Projects*, 283–84.

15. BF to Samuel Mather, May 12, 1784, in *Papers*, 42:236–37.

16. [Cotton Mather,] *Bonifacius: An Essay upon the Good* (Boston: Samuel Gerrish, 1710), 23, 37.

17. Ibid., 163; BF, *Poor Richard, 1737*, in *Papers*, 2:168; Whiting, no. L62.

18. Mather, *Bonifacius*, 50.

19. Thomas Prince, *A Funeral Sermon on the Reverend Mr. Nathaniel Williams, Who Deceased Tuesday January 10, 1737/8* (Boston: S. Kneeland, 1738), 26; *Genetic Text*, 6.

20. Ezra Stiles, *The Literary Diary of Ezra Stiles*, ed. Franklin Bowditch Dexter (New York: Scribners, 1901), 2:376; *Genetic Text*, 7.

21. "The Rev. Mr. Nathaniel Williams," *New England Weekly Journal*, January 17, 1738; Clifford K. Shipton, *Sibley's Harvard Graduates: Biographical Sketches of Those Who Attended Harvard College* (Cambridge, MA: Harvard University Press, 1933–1975), 4:111.

22. Cotton Mather, *Corderius Americanus: An Essay upon the Good Education of Children* (Boston: John Allen, 1708); Wesley T. Mott, "Ezekiel Cheever," in *American Colonial Writers, 1606–1734*, ed. Emory Elliot (Detroit: Gale, 1984), 62.

23. Herman Melville, *Moby-Dick: or, The Whale* (New York: Harper, 1851), viii; John Milton, *Paradise Lost: A Poem in Twelve Books* (London: Henry Bentley, 1691) (Harvard University, Hollis, no. *EC65.M6427P.1691).

24. Peter Heylyn, *Cosmographie in Four Books* (London: Henry Seile, 1652), 110 (Harvard University, Hollis, no. EC65.H5164652cb); BF, "A Large and Valuable Collection of Books," *New-England Courant*, July 2, 1722; Prince, *Funeral Sermon*, 26.

25. Kenneth B. Murdock, "The Teaching of Latin and Greek at the Boston Latin School in 1712," *Publications of the Colonial Society of Massachusetts* 27 (1932): 23; John F. Latimer and Kenneth B. Murdock, "The 'Author' of Cheever's Accidence," *Classical Journal* 46, no. 8 (May 1951): 391–97.

26. R. C., *Nomenclatura trilinguis anglos-latin-graeca: or, A Short Vocabulary, English, Latin, and Greek*, 6th ed. (London: for George Conyers, 1704), 73–78.

27. Leonhard Culmann, *Sententiae pueriles*, trans. Charles Hoole (Boston: Samuel Philips, 1702), 1.

28. Ibid., 2, 14.

29. Ibid., 12, 16, 27.

30. BF, "Preface to *Cato's Moral Distichs*," in *Papers*, 2:130; Miller, no. 99.

31. Charles Hoole, *Maturinus Corderius's School-Colloquies, English and Latin* (London: Company of Stationers, 1709), 6.

32. ESTC, no. N50037.

33. BF, "Apology for Printers [June 10, 1731]," in *Papers*, 1:199.

34. Thomas Dilworth, *A New Guide to the English Tongue* (Philadelphia: B. Franklin, 1747), 139; Miller, no. 415.

35. Dilworth, *New Guide*, 144, 145, 147; Whiting, nos. H264, T294.

36. *Materials for a Catalogue of the Masters and Scholars Who Have Belonged to the Public Latin School, Boston, Massachusetts, from 1635 to 1846* (Boston: Crosby and Nichols, 1847), 9–10; Lemay, *Life*, 1:49; Shipton, *Sibley's Harvard Graduates*, 7:111.

37. "Advertisements," *Boston News-Letter*, March 9, 1713; Lynne Zacek Bassett, "Rebecca Kingsbury Petticoat," in *Massachusetts Quilts: Our Common Wealth*, ed. Lynne Zacek Bassett (Hanover, NH: University Press of New England, 2009), 25.

38. Robert Francis Seybolt, *The Private Schools of Colonial Boston* (Cambridge, MA: Harvard University Press, 1935), 94; Barbara Lambert, "Social Music, Musicians, and Their Musical Instruments in and Around Colonial Boston," in *Music in Colonial Massachusetts, 1630–1820*, ed. Barbara Lambert (Boston: Colonial Society of Massachusetts, 1985), 2:487–90.

39. Cotton Mather, *A Cloud of Witnesses* [Boston, 1700?], 3.

40. Nancy Beadle, *Education and the Creation of Capital in the Early American Republic* (New York: Cambridge University Press, 2010), 110; Kate Van Winkle Keller and John Koegel, "Secular Music to 1800," in *The Cambridge History of American Music*, ed. David Nicholls (New York: Cambridge University Press, 1998), 52; Lambert, "Social Music," 448.

41. BF to Jane Mecom, September 16, 1758, in *Papers*, 8:154–55; Whiting, no. M54.

42. *Genetic Text*, 7.

43. *Genetic Text*, 7.

44. *Genetic Text*, 7.

45. BF, *Poor Richard, 1745*, in *Papers*, 3:5.

46. New Comer into America, *The Loyal American's Almanack for the Year 1715* (Boston, 1715).

47. Ibid.

48. "To Old Janus the Couranteer," *New-England Courant*, March 11, 1723.

49. William Congreve, *The Way of the World: A Comedy*, 2d ed. (London: Jacob Tonson, 1706), 50.

50. *Genetic Text*, 7; BF, *The Autobiography of Benjamin Franklin*, illustrated by Thomas Hart Benton (New York: Illustrated Modern Library, 1944), facing 28.

51. Benjamin Franklin, Sr., "On Ecton 1702," in *Papers*, 8:136.

52. BF to Jane Mecom, September 16, 1758, in *Papers*, 8:153; Appleton P. C. Griffin, ed., "Commonplace-Book of Benjamin Franklin (1650–1727)," *Publications of the Colonial Society of Massachusetts* 10 (1907), 224–25.

53. Wolf and Hayes, 940–42; Kevin J. Hayes, "Prospects for the Study of Benjamin Franklin," *Resources for American Literary Study* 33 (2008; issued 2010): 8–9.

54. Campbell, *London Tradesman*, 178; *Genetic Text*, 10.

CHAPTER 3

1. Mark Twain, "The Late Benjamin Franklin," *Galaxy*, July 1870, 138.

2. BF, "A Large and Valuable Collection of Books," *New-England Courant*, July 2, 1722; Anne Barbeau Gardiner, "John Oldham," in *Seventeenth-Century British Nondramatic Poets: Third Series*, ed. M. Thomas Hester (Detroit: Gale, 1993), 190; John Adams, *Diary and Autobiography*, ed. L. H. Butterfield, Leonard C. Faber, and Wendell D. Garrett (Cambridge, MA: Belknap Press of Harvard University Press, 1961), 1:72; John Dryden, "To the Memory of Mr. Oldham," in *The Works of Mr. John Oldham, Together with His Remains* (London: Jo. Hindmarsh, 1684), sig. A4r.

3. Oldham, *Works*, 92.

4. [BF,] *Hoop-Petticoats Arraigned and Condemned by the Light of Nature, and Law of God* (Boston: James Franklin, 1722), 2.

5. John Milton, *Areopagitica: A Speech of Mr. John Milton for the Liberty of Unlicenc'd Printing* (London, 1644), 13; Oldham, *Works*, 167.

6. BF, "Large and Valuable"; Oldham, *Works*, 178.

7. *Genetic Text*, 12.

8. *Genetic Text*, 12, 30.

9. *Genetic Text*, 13; BF, "Large and Valuable."

10. BF, "Silence Dogood, No. 14," in *Papers*, 1:45; Lemay, *Life*, 168–69.

11. BF, *Poor Richard, 1736*, in *Papers*, 2:138.

12. Thomas J. Haslam, " 'In Compliance with the Advice Contained in These Letters': Benjamin Franklin's Correspondence Networks and the Making of the *Autobiography*," *Rupkatha Journal on Interdisciplinary Studies in Humanities* 9, no. 3 (2017): 81.

13. *Genetic Text*, 17; Alexander Pope, *An Essay on Criticism*, 2d ed. (London: W. Lewis, 1713), 29.

14. *Genetic Text*, 14; *Guardian*, no. 155.

15. *Genetic Text*, 14.

16. *Genetic Text*, 14; Plutarch, *The Philosophie, Commonly Called, The Morals*, trans. Philemon Holland (London: Arnold Hatfield, 1603), 571–79; Louis Lefebvre de La Roche, "On Franklin," and Pierre Jean George Cabanis, "A Short Account of Benjamin Franklin," in Hayes and Bour, 125, 156.

17. Sylvester Graham, *Lectures of the Science of Human Life* (London: Horsell and Shirrefs, 1854), 528.

18. Tryon, *Way to Health*, 17, 379.

19. *Norton Critical Edition*, 12–13.

20. James Fox, "Numeracy and Popular Culture: *Cocker's Arithmetick* and the Market for Cheap Arithmetical Books, 1678–1787," *Cultural and Social History* 19, no. 5 (2022): 536; Paul C. Pasles, *Benjamin Franklin's Numbers: An Unsung Mathematical Odyssey* (Princeton, NJ: Princeton University Press, 2008), 37; *Genetic Text*, 15; Michael Richey, introduction to John Seller, *Practical Navigation* (Delmar, NY: Scholars' Facsimiles and Reprints, 1993), 19; Kevin J. Hayes, *George Washington: A Life in Books* (New York: Oxford University Press, 2017), 25–26.

21. Ian Higgins, "Explanatory Notes," in Jonathan Swift, *Gulliver's Travels*, ed. Claude Rawson (New York: Oxford University Press, 2005), 301.

22. BF, *The Charter, Laws, and Catalogue of Books, of the Library Company of Philadelphia* (Philadelphia: B. Franklin and D. Hall, 1757), 60.

23. John Locke, *An Essay Concerning Humane Understanding in Four Books* (London: Tho. Basset, 1690), 8, 37.

24. For the fullest discussion of Franklin and the cabinet of curiosities, see Kevin J. Hayes, *Benjamin Franklin* (London: Reaktion, 2022), 19–38.

25. Xenophon, *The Memorable Things of Socrates*, trans. Edward Bysshe (London: G. Sawbridge, 1712), iv; Wolf and Hayes, no. 3726; Cabanis, "Short Account," 158.

26. BF, "Large and Valuable,"; Antoine Arnauld and Pierre Nicole, *Logic: or, The Art of Thinking*, trans. John Ozell (London: William Taylor, 1717); Wolf and Hayes, no. 154.

27. John Ozell, "To the Right Honorable Sir Joseph Jekyll, Master of Rolls," in Arnauld and Nicole, *Logic*, sig. A3r; Jean Racine, *Britannicus*, trans. R. Bruce Boswell (London: George Bell, 1898), 308; BF, "Journal of a Voyage, 1726," in *Papers*, 1:78.

28. S. S. Nelles, *Chapters in Logic: Containing Sir William Hamilton's Lectures on Modified Logic, and Selections from the Port Royal Logic* (Toronto: Wesleyan Methodist Book-Room, 1870), vii–viii.

29. Arnauld and Nicole, *Logic*, 1; Kerry S. Walters, *Benjamin Franklin and His Gods* (Urbana: University of Illinois Press, 1999), 31; Thomas J. Haslam, "An Infidel's Progress: Benjamin Franklin's Twyford Manuscript Part One Reconsidered" (Ph.D. diss., University of Delaware, 1996), 180–81.

30. Arnauld and Nicole, *Logic*, 11; Newcomb, "Sources," 187; Andrew Amos, *Martial and the Moderns* (Cambridge, UK: Deighton, Bell, 1858), 29; BF to Peter Collinson, 1752, in *Papers*, 4:393–94.

31. Arnauld and Nicole, *Logic*, 70; BF, "Preface to Joseph Galloway's Speech, August 11, 1764," in *Papers*, 11:277; Lemay, *Life*, 1:168–69.

32. Blaise Pascal, *The Mystery of Jesuitism, Discovered in Certain Letters, Written upon Occasion of the Differences at Sorbonne, between the Jansenists and the Molinists* (London: John Vallange, 1695); Cabanis, "Short Account," 157; Blaise Pascal, *Les provinciales* (Cologne: Henry Schouten, 1738); Wolf and Hayes, no. 2555.

33. *Genetic Text*, 15; *Norton Critical Edition*, 13.

34. H. M. Posnett, "Benjamin Franklin," *Westminster Review* 168, no. 6 (December 1907): 640–41; Stuart P. Sherman, "Franklin," in *CHAL*, 1:109.

35. Alfred Owen Aldridge, "Shaftesbury and the Deist Manifesto," *Transactions of the American Philosophical Society*, new ser., 41, part 2 (1951): 297–98.

36. Cabanis, "Short Account," 157; Wolf and Hayes, nos. 674–75; J. Dybikowski, "Anthony Collins," in *British Philosophers, 1500–1799*, ed. Philip B. Dematteis and Peter S. Fosl (Detroit: Gale, 2002), 133–34.

37. Marquis de Condorcet, *Writings on the United States*, ed. and trans. Guillaume Ansart (University Park: Pennsylvania State University Press, 2012), 80.

38. J. Dybikowski, "Collins, Anthony," in *ODNB*, 12:692; Wolf and Hayes, no. 2081.

39. John Locke to Anthony Collins, October 29, 1703, in *A Collection of Several Pieces of Mr. John Locke, Never before Printed, or Not Extant in His Works*, ed. Pierre des Maizeaux (London: R. Francklin, 1720), 272; Wolf and Hayes, no. 2081.

40. John Locke, "Some Thoughts Concerning Reading and Study for a Gentleman," in *Collection of Several Pieces*, 231.

41. Ibid., 232.

42. Ibid., 239–40; BF, "Large and Valuable."

43. Locke, "Some Thoughts," 241–42; Wolf and Hayes, no. 2808; BF, "Large and Valuable."

44. BF, "A Letter from Father Abraham to His Beloved Son, August 1758," in *Papers*, 8:124; Kevin Slack, "On the Sources and Authorship of 'A Letter from Father Abraham to His Beloved Son,'" *New England Quarterly* 86, no. 3 (September 2013): 467–87; Wolf and Hayes, nos. 3554–3555; Obadiah Walker, *Of Education, Especially of Young Gentleman* (Oxford: At the Theatre, 1672), 113.

45. Walker, *Of Education*, 122.

CHAPTER 4

1. Charles E. Clark, *The Public Prints: The Newspaper in Anglo-American Culture, 1665–1740* (New York: Oxford University Press, 1994), 79; Walter Isaacson, *Benjamin Franklin: An American Life* (New York: Simon and Schuster, 2003), 21.

2. Clark, *Public Prints*, 87.

3. Ibid., 123–24, 132.

4. Cotton Mather, *The Angel of Bethesda*, ed. Gordon W. Jones (Barre, MA: American Antiquarian Society, 1972), 107.

5. Lemay, *Life*, 1:87–108.

6. BF's annotated file of *The New-England Courant*, the source for most attributions, is available online as part of the Seventeenth and Eighteenth Century Burney Newspapers Collection, which can be found on the Gale Primary Sources database.

7. William F. Dawson, "An Interview with Malcolm Cowley," in *Conversations with Malcolm Cowley*, ed. Thomas Daniel Young (Jackson: University Press of Mississippi, 1986), 37.

8. [Cotton Mather,] "To the Author of the *Boston News-Letter*," *Boston News-Letter*, August 28, 1721; Aubry La Mottraye, *Travels through Europe, Asia, and into Parts of Africa* (London, 1723), 2:391–92; *The Hell-Fire-Club Kept by a Society of Blasphemers: A Satire* (London: J. Roberts, 1721).

9. "Account of the Hell-Fire Club," *New-England Courant*, February 12, 1722.

10. George Francis Dow, *The Arts and Crafts in New England, 1705–1775* (Topsfield, MA: Wayside Press, 1927), 285–86; Alden Bradford, *Biographical Notices of Distinguished Men in New England: Statesmen, Patriots, Physicians, Lawyers, Clergymen, and Mechanics* (Boston: S. G. Simpkins, 1842), 19–20.

11. *Genetic Text*, 11–12.

12. H. W. Brands, *The First American: The Life and Times of Benjamin Franklin* (New York: Doubleday, 2000), 22, describes Adams's library as "an impressive if quirky collection." J. A. Leo Lemay, "Recent Franklin Scholarship with a Note on Franklin's Sedan Chair," *PMHB* 126, no. 2 (April 2002): 333, questions Brands's description, observing, "No one knows anything about Matthew Adams's library." Well, I know a little, and, like Lynyrd Skynyrd, maybe I can guess the rest. The generalization that closes this paragraph stems from Adams's subscription to the following books: Samuel Mather, *The Life of the Very Reverend and Learned Cotton Mather, D.D. and F.R.S.* (Boston: Samuel Gerrish, 1729); Thomas Prince, *A Chronological History of New-England in the Form of Annals* (Boston: Kneeland and Green, 1736); and Samuel Willard, *A Compleat Body of Divinity in Two Hundred and Fifty Expository Lectures on the Assembly's Shorter Catechism* (Boston: B. Green and S. Kneeland, 1726).

13. BF, *A Catalogue of Choice and Valuable Books* (Philadelphia: B. Franklin, 1744), 7.

14. [Matthew Adams,] "A Letter, etc.," *New-England Weekly Journal*, March 18, 1728; Lemay, *Calendar*, no. 87; Charles Leslie, *The Finishing Stroke: Being a Vindication of the Patriarchal Scheme of Government* (London, 1716); Henry Dodwell, *An Epistolary Discourse, Proving, from the Scriptures and the First Fathers, that the Soul Is a Principle Naturally Mortal* (London: R. Smith, 1706); J. Dybikowski, "Anthony Collins," in *British Philosophers, 1500–1799*, ed. Philip B. Dematteis and Peter S. Fosl (Detroit: Gale, 2002), 131.

15. [Matthew Adams,] "Unhappy Divisions," *New-England Courant*, January 1, 1722; John Shower, *Serious Reflections on Time, and Eternity* (London: Joseph Watts, 1689), 104–105.

16. Lemay, *Life*, 1:114; James Franklin, "In My Own Vindication," *New-England Courant*, December 4, 1721; Carla Mulford, "Pox and 'Hell-Fire': Boston's Smallpox Controversy, The New Science, and Early Modern Liberalism," in *Periodical Literature in Eighteenth-Century America*, ed. Mark L. Kamrath and Sharon M. Harris (Knoxville: University of Tennessee Press, 2005), 11; Kevin J. Hayes, "Fleet, Thomas," in *ANB*, 8:94–95.

17. Renuncles [Madam Staples,] "The Fool by His Wit," *New-England Courant*, October 9, 1721; Lemay, *Calendar*, no. 12.

18. See, for example, Charles Johnson, *The Generous Husband: or, The Coffeehouse Politician* (London: Bernard Lintott, [1711]), 2; Tilley, no. H623; BF, *Poor Richard, 1734*, in *Papers*, 1:352.

19. Lucilius [James Franklin,] "To Mr. P——p M——e, P——st-M——r of B——n," *New-England Courant*, January 8, 1722; BF, *Poor Richard Improved, 1749*, in *Papers*, 3:342; Whiting, nos. B31, H124.

20. Tom Tram [Thomas Fleet,] "A Trip to the World on the Moon," *New-England Courant*, January 15, 1723. BF, "A Letter from a Gentleman in Crusoe's Island," [April? 1764,] *Papers*, 11:184. Fleet's use of the term "gump," which means a foolish person, antedates by a century the earliest usage recorded in *Oxford English Dictionary*, s.v., "gump."

21. BF to John Whitehurst, June 27, 1763, in *Papers*, 10:303; Whiting, no. L185.

22. Desmond MacCarthy, "A Citizen of the World: Benjamin Franklin," *Sunday Times*, March 12, 1939, 6; D. W. Brogan, "Life of a Salesman," *Spectator*, September 9, 1949, 331; Vernon L. Parrington, *Main Currents in American Thought: An Interpretation of American Literature from the Beginnings to 1920* (New York: Harcourt, Brace, 1927–1930), 1:166.

23. [Nathaniel Gardner,] "Agreeable Society and Conversation," *New-England Courant*, April 23, 1722.

24. [Nathaniel Gardner,] "Clan of Honest Wags," *New-England Courant*, September 4, 1721; Whiting, no. M296.

25. Gardner, "Clan of Honest Wags."

26. *Genetic Text*, 17; BF to Joseph Priestley, October 3, 1775, in *Papers*, 22:218.

27. [Nathaniel Gardner,] "Sword, Famine and Pestilence," *New-England Courant*, November 6, 1721; [Nathaniel Gardner,] "In Favour of Inoculation," *New-England Courant*, November 20, 1721.

28. Corydon [Nathaniel Gardner,] "Of Beauty's Sacred, Conquering Powers I Sing," *New-England Courant*, January 29, 1722; Lemay, *Calendar*, no. 20.

29. Harry Meanwell [Matthew Adams], "Pernicious Principles," *New-England Courant*, April 30, 1722; Abigail Afterwit [James Franklin], *New-England Courant*, January 29, 1722; *Oxford English Dictionary*, s.v. "after-wit"; Tilley, no. A58.

30. Colin T. Ramsay, "From the *Boston News-Letter* to the 'Couranteers': Epistolarity, Reportage, and Entertaining Literature in Colonial American Newspapers," in *The Routledge Companion to American Literary Journalism*, ed. William E. Dow and Roberta S. Maguire (New York: Routledge, 2020), 23–24.

31. Henry David Thoreau, *Walden*, ed. J. Lyndon Shanley (Princeton, NJ: Princeton University Press, 1971), 74.

32. *Genetic Text*, 18.

33. Crowdero, "To Mrs. Silence Dogood, on the Letter in the Courant of the 14th Instant," *New-England Courant*, June 4, 1722; Lemay, *Calendar*, no. 24.

34. BF, *The Nature and Necessity of a Paper Currency*, in *Papers*, 1:140–41.

35. Lewis Bayly, *The Practice of Piety, Directing a Christian How to Walk, that He May Please God* (London: Edward Brewster, 1708), 156.

36. William Walker, *A Dictionary of English and Latin Idioms*, 6th ed. (London: W. Taylor, 1712), 238.

37. Ibid., 177.

38. Richard M. Gummere, *The American Colonial Mind and the Classical Tradition: Essays in Comparative Culture* (Cambridge, MA: Harvard University Press, 1963), 129; Lemay, *Life*, 2:20.

39. Isaac Watts, *Horae lyricae: Poems Chiefly of the Lyric Kind* (London: N. Cliff, 1709), 212.

40. BF, "Silence Dogood, No. 12," in *Papers*, 1:40.

41. BF, "Silence Dogood, No. 8," in *Papers*, 1:27; Kevin J. Hayes, *Benjamin Franklin* (London: Reaktion, 2022), 16; Suzy Platt, ed., *Respectfully Quoted: A Dictionary of Quotations Requested from the Congressional Research Service* (Washington, DC: Library of Congress, 1989), 132–33.

CHAPTER 5

1. BF, "A Large and Valuable Collection of Books," *New-England Courant*, July 2, 1722.

2. [Nathaniel Gardner,] "Another Dialogue between the Clergyman and Layman," *New-England Courant*, January 22, 1722; Gilbert Burnet, *The Bishop of Salisbury's New Preface to His Pastoral Care, Consider'd* (London: A. Baldwin, 1713), 17–18.

3. Carla J. Mulford, *Benjamin Franklin and the Ends of Empire* (New York: Oxford University Press, 2015), 62–63.

4. John Wise, *A Word of Comfort to a Melancholy Country; or, The Bank of Credit Erected in the Massachusetts-Bay* (Boston: [James Franklin,] 1721), 3, 18; BF, *Poor Richard, 1737*, in *Papers*, 2:165; Whiting, nos. S377, L177.

5. [Nathaniel Gardner,] *A Friendly Debate: or, A Dialogue between Rusticus and Academicus* (Boston: J. Franklin, 1722), 1, 19.

6. William Davis, *An Olio of Bibliographical and Literary Anecdotes and Memoranda Original and Selected* (London: J. Rodwell, 1814), 108.

7. Cotton Mather, *Magnalia christi americana: or, The Ecclesiastical History of New-England* (London: T. Parkhurst, 1702), book 3, 122; Charles Tanford, *Ben Franklin Stilled the Waves: An Informal History of Pouring Oil on Water with Reflections on the Ups and Downs of Scientific Life in General* (New York: Oxford University Press, 2004), 57.

8. Pliny, *The Historie of the World: Commonly Called, The Naturall Historie*, trans. Philemon Holland (London: Adam Islip, 1634), 2:192.

9. Charles Whibley, "Translations," in *The Cambridge History of English Literature*, ed. A. W. Ward and A. R. Waller (Cambridge, UK: Cambridge University Press, 1910), 4:14; BF to William Brownrigg, November 7, 1773, in *Papers*, 20:464.

10. Pliny, *Historie of the World*, 1:46.

11. Russell B. Goodman, *American Philosophy before Pragmatism* (New York: Oxford University Press, 2015), 92–93.

12. Samuel Sewall to Nathaniel Byfield, January 4, 1706, "Letter-Book of Samuel Sewall," *Collections of the Massachusetts Historical Society*, 6th ser., 1 (1886): 322–23.

13. *The Athenian Oracle* (London: Andrew Bell, 1704), 1:545–48; *The Athenian Oracle: The Second Edition, Printed at London, 1704* (Boston: Bartholomew Green, 1705).

14. "Pray, Gentlemen, Favour the Querist," *British Apollo*, April 23, 1708.

15. "On Monday Next," *British Apollo*, July 30, 1708; BF, "To the Royal Academy of [Brussels]," *Writings* (Lemay), 953.

16. "We Read in the New Testament," *British Apollo*, October 5, 1709.

17. "The Town Bull," *New England Chronicle*, November 23, 1775; Eric Partridge, *Shakespeare's Bawdy*, 3rd ed. (1968; repr., New York: Routledge, 2001), 264.

18. BF, "Jethro Standfast," *New-England Courant*, October 8, 1722; Kevin J. Hayes, "Benjamin Franklin, An American Satirist," in *Satire*, ed. Robert C. Evans (Amenia, NY: Grey House, 2020), 210.

19. [BF,] "Dingo," *New-England Courant*, July 15, 1723; Lemay, *Life*, 1:204.

20. Hayes, *Colonial Woman's Bookshelf*, 59–61; Richard Allestree, *The Ladies Calling in Two Parts* (Oxford: at the Theatre, 1705), 161, 245.

21. Virginia H. Aksan, "Is There a Turk in the *Turkish Spy?*" *Eighteenth-Century Fiction* 6, no. 3 (April 1994): 201–202.

22. *The Athenian Oracle: Being an Entire Collection of All the Valuable Questions and Answers in the Old Athenian Mercuries* (London: Andrew Bell, 1716), 3:5; Aksan, "Is There a Turk," 208; Wolf and Hayes, no. 2186.

23. Kevin J. Hayes, *Shakespeare and the Making of America* (Stroud, UK: Amberley, 2020), 29–30.

24. Ernest Hemingway to Maxwell Perkins, July 12, 1938, *The Only Thing That Counts: The Ernest Hemingway-Maxwell Perkins Correspondence, 1925–1947*, ed. Matthew J. Bruccoli (Columbia: University of South Carolina Press, 1996), 263.

25. [Nathaniel Gardner,] *A Friendly Debate: or, A Dialogue between Rusticus and Academicus* (Boston: J. Franklin, 1722), 5–6; Lemay, *Life*, 1:135; John Oldmixon, *The British Empire in America* (London: John Nicholson, 1708), 1:109; Douglass, *British Settlements in North-America*, 1:202.

26. John Oldmixon, *The British Empire in America* (London: John Nicholson, 1708), 1:ix (Thomas Prince's annotated copy at the Boston Public Library); Cotton Mather to Daniel Neal, July 5, 1720, *Diary of Cotton Mather* (New York: Frederick Ungar, 1957), 2:598.

27. *S. Augustine's Confessions: With the Continuation of His Life to the End Thereof, Extracted out of Possidius, and the Father's Own Unquestioned Works*, trans. Abraham Woodhead (N.p., 1679); Vernon Louis Parrington, *Main Currents in American Thought: An Interpretation of American Literature from the Beginnings to 1920* (New York: Harcourt, Brace, 1927–1930), 1:178.

28. William C. Spengemann, *The Forms of Autobiography: Episodes in the History of a Literary Genre* (New Haven, CT: Yale University Press, 1980), 53–54.

29. Mather, *Magnalia*, book 7, 86; James Franklin, "Bloody Fishing," *New-England Courant*, January 22, 1722.

30. Mather, *Magnalia*, book 3, 77.

31. Ibid., 20.

32. BF, "Silence Dogood, No. 1," in *Papers*, 1:10; Lemay, *Life*, 1:146.

33. "A Peculiar Blackness," *New-England Courant*, July 2, 1722.

34. BF, "Articles of Belief and Acts of Religion," in *Papers*, 1:106–107.

35. [Nathaniel Gardner,] "Agreeable Society and Conversation," *New-England Courant*, April 23, 1722; "Poems," *British Apollo*, April 21, 1708, 84.

36. [Matthew Adams,] "Female Impudence," *New-England Courant*, February 26, 1722.

37. Jonathan Swift, *A Tale of a Tub* (London: John Nutt, 1704), 138–39.

38. Samuel Butler, *Hudibras*, part 1, canto 1, lines 51–52 and 81–82.

39. Butler, *Hudibras*, part 1, canto 1, lines 281–83; William Douglass, *Inoculation of the Small Pox As Practised in Boston* (Boston: J. Franklin, 1722); Emily Cock, *Rhinoplasty and the Nose in Early Modern British Medicine and Culture* (Manchester, UK: Manchester University Press, 2019).

40. BF, "Silence Dogood, No. 7," in *Papers*, 1:26.

41. BF, "Rules for *The New-England Courant*," *Writings* (Lemay), 46.

42. Tilley, no. F400.

43. [Andrew Bradford,] "P.S.," *American Weekly Mercury*, February 26, 1723.

CHAPTER 6

1. *Genetic Text*, 20; Russell, *Benjamin Franklin*, 40; "New York, September 30," *American Weekly Mercury*, October 4, 1723; William C. Schermerhorn, "History of the Schermerhorn Family," *New York Genealogical and Biographical Record* 36, no. 4 (October 1905): 146–47.

2. Pierre Jean Georges Cabanis, "A Short Account of Benjamin Franklin," in Hayes and Bour, 156.

3. *Genetic Text*, 21, 26; Pattie Cowell, "Rose, Aquila," in *ANB*, 18:857–58.

4. *Genetic Text*, 22.

5. "A Short, a Safe, and a Sure Fever-Killer," *Boston News-Letter*, August 29, 1723; David Gentilcore, "From 'Vilest Bevereage' to 'Universal Medicine': Drinking Water in Printed Regimens and Health Guides, 1450–1750," *Social History of Medicine* 33, no. 3 (2018): 700; Wolf and Hayes, no. 1558.

6. *Norton Critical Edition*, 19.

7. Ibid.

8. [Charles Cotton,] *Scarronnides: or, Virgile Travestie* (London: Henry Brome, 1667), 1.

9. [Jacob Bailey,] *The Association, &c. of the Delegates of the Colonies at the Grand Congress, Held at Philadelphia, Sept. 1, 1774, Versified* ([Philadelphia,] 1774).

10. Jack Kerouac, *Lonesome Traveler* (1960; repr., New York: Grove Press, 1970), 174.

11. Hannah Benner Roach, "Benjamin Franklin Slept Here," *PMHB* 84, no. 2 (April 1960): 128–29.

12. *Genetic Text*, 26.

13. Samuel Marion Tucker, "The Beginnings of Verse, 1610–1808," in *CHAL*, 1:161.

14. Edmund S, Morgan, *Benjamin Franklin* (New Haven, CT: Yale University Press, 2002), 44, is typical; he calls Keimer "a born loser."

15. James N. Green, "English Books and Printing in the Age of Franklin," in *A History of the Book in America*, ed. Hugh Amory and David D. Hall (New York: Cambridge University Press, 2000), 1:251.

16. [Samuel Keimer,] headnote to *The Independent Whig: Number 1*. Philadelphia: Samuel Keimer, 1724, 1.

17. Alfred Owen Aldridge, *Benjamin Franklin, Philosopher and Man* (Philadelphia: Lippincott, 1965), 8, 17.

18. Kevin J. Hayes, "Prospects for the Study of Benjamin Franklin," *Resources for American Literary Study* 33 (2008; issued 2010): 8–9, identifies five of the nine pamphlets the volume contained. Since none are listed in Wolf and Hayes, let me delineate them here: Richard Bulkeley, *An Answer to Several Treatises Lately Published on the Subject of the Prophets* (London: B. Bragg, 1708); *Reflections on Sir Richard Bulkeley's Answer to Several Treatises* (London: J. Morphew, 1708); John Humphrey, *An Account of the French Prophets, and Their Pretended Inspirations* (London: Thomas Parkhurst, 1708); Richard Kingston, *Enthusiastick Impostors No Divinely Inspir'd Prophets* (London: J. Morphew, 1707); Joseph Keble, *A Essay of Humane Nature; or, The Creation of Mankind* (London: for S. Keble, 1707).

19. Samuel Keimer, *Brand Pluck'd from the Burning: Exemplified in the Unparallel'd Case of Samuel Keimer* (London: W. Boreham, 1718), 1, 6.

20. [William Keith,] *The Observator's Trip to America, in a Dialogue between the Observator and his Country-Man Roger* ([Philadelphia: Andrew Bradford,] 1726), 19–20.

21. Edwin Wolf, 2nd, "Great American Book Collectors to 1800," *Gazette of the Grolier Club*, new ser., no. 16 (June 1971): 7.

22. Cotton Mather, *Manuductio ad ministerium: Directions for a Candidate of the Ministry*, ed. Thomas J. Holmes and Kenneth B. Murdock (New York: Columbia University Press, 1938), 30.

23. Kevin J. Hayes, "Cotton Mather," in *American Book-Collectors and Bibliographers, First Series*, ed. Joseph Rosenblum (Detroit: Gale, 1994), 157.

24. William Powell Jones, *The Rhetoric of Science: A Study of Scientific Ideas and Imagery in Eighteenth-Century English Poetry* (Berkeley: University of California Press, 1966), 86–89.

25. BF, "Articles of Belief and Acts of Religion," in *Papers*, 1:105; Jones, *Rhetoric of Science*, 8.

26. BF to Samuel Mather, July 7, 1773, in *Papers*, 20:287.

27. *Genetic Text*, 32–33.

28. Douglass, *British Settlements in North-America*, 1:480; BF, "A Large and Valuable Collection of Books," *New-England Courant*, July 2, 1722.

29. *Genetic Text*, 37.

30. "Philadelphia, July 16," *American Weekly Mercury*, July 16, 1724; "Advertisements," *American Weekly Mercury*, July 30, 1724.

31. *Genetic Text*, 40.

32. Burton Alva Konkle, *The Life of Andrew Hamilton, 1676–1741: "The Day-Star of the American Revolution"* (Philadelphia: National, 1941), 36–37; *Genetic Text*, 40–41.

33. "Philadelphia, November 5," *American Weekly Mercury*, November 5, 1724.

34. William G. Whitely, "The Principio Company: A Historical Sketch of the First Iron-Works in Maryland," *PMHB* 11, no. 1 (April 1887): 63–68; James M. Swank, *History of the Manufacture of Iron in All Ages, and Particularly in the United States from Colonial Times to 1891*, 2d ed. (Philadelphia: American Iron and Steel Association, 1892), 241.

35. Stephen Onion was born February 10, 1694, and died August 26, 1754. See Helen W. Ridgely, *Historical Graves of Maryland and the District of Columbia* (New York: Grafton, 1908), 110.

36. Russell Mortimer, ed., *Minute Book of the Men's Meeting of the Society of Friends in Bristol, 1667–[1704]* (Bristol: Bristol Record Society, 1971–1977), 1:185, 198, 219; 2:168, 202, 252.

37. *Genetic Text*, 50.

38. George Johnston, *History of Cecil County, Maryland* (Elkton, MD, 1881), 233.

CHAPTER 7

1. Wolf, *Library of James Logan*, no. 859.

2. "Ships Enter'd Inwards, at the Custom House Since Our Last," *Weekly Journal*, January 2, 1725; *Genetic Text*, 41.

3. BF, "Appeal for the Hospital," in *Papers*, 4:151; Daniel Defoe, *The Tour through the Whole Island of Great Britain, Divided into Circuits or Journies* (London: G. Strahan, 1724–1727), 3:137; Daniel Defoe, *Life of Colonel Jack*, ed. Edward E. Hale (New York: Crowell, 1891), 15.

4. J. C. Platt, "The Custom House," in *London*, ed. Charles Knight (London: Charles Knight, 1842), 2:402.

5. *Genetic Text*, 41.

6. Bernard Christian Steiner, ed., *Archives of Maryland: Proceedings and Acts of the General Assembly of Maryland, July, 1727–August, 1729* (Baltimore: Maryland Historical Society, 1916), 569.

7. Abraham Cowley, *The Complete Works in Verse and Prose*, ed. Alexander B. Grosart (Edinburgh: Edinburgh University Press, 1881), 318.

8. Lemay, *Life*, 1:268.

9. Samuel Keimer, *Brand Pluck'd from the Burning: Exemplified in the Unparallel'd Case of Samuel Keimer* (London: W. Boreham, 1718), 52; Lemay, *Life*, 1:288.

10. [Thomas Gordon,] *The Humourist: Being Essays upon Several Subjects* (London: for T. Woodward, 1725), 12.

11. William West, *Fifty Years' Recollections of an Old Bookseller* (Cork: for the author, 1835), 53; Washington Irving, *History, Tales and Sketches*, ed. James W. Tuttleton (New York: Library of America, 1983), 969; [John Macky,] *A Journey through England* (London: for John Hooke, 1724), 1:290; Jonathan Swift to Alderman Barber, August 8, 1738, in *The Works of Dr. Jonathan Swift, Dean of St. Patrick's, Dublin* (Edinburgh: for John Donaldson, 1774), 13:156.

12. "Advertisement," London *Daily Journal*, November 28, 1724; Wolf, *Library of James Logan*, nos. 1107, 390.

13. *Genetic Text*, 42.

14. [Nathaniel Gardner,] "Advertisement," *New-England Courant*, September 25, 1721.

15. Jacob Bell, "Memoir of Anthony Purver," *British Friend*, December 1, 1882, 299; David Norton, "Purver, Anthony," in *ODNB*, 45:585; Wolf and Hayes, no. 319.

16. Anthony Purver, *A New and Literal Translation of All the Books of the Old and New Testament; with Notes, Critical and Explanatory* (London: W. Richardson, 1764), 1:656; *Hamlet*, 1.5.186.

17. James Boswell, *Boswell's Life of Johnson*, ed. George Birkbeck Hill (New York: Harper, 1904), 1:118–19.

18. Hazel Wilkinson, "Benjamin Franklin's London Printing, 1725–26," *PBSA* 110, no. 2 (June 2016): 147.

19. "Advertisements," *Grub Street Journal*, March 15, 1732.

20. George Baker, *Medical Tracts Read at the College of Physicians between the Years 1767 and 1785*, ed. Frederick Francis Baker (London: W. Bulmer, 1818), 396–97; BF to Benjamin Vaughan, July 31, 1786, in *Writings* (Lemay), 1164.

21. J. C. Ross, "A Progress Report upon a Study of Samuel Palmer: A London Printer as Icarus," in *An Index of Civilisation: Studies of Printing and Publishing History in Honour of Keith Maslen*, ed. R. Harvey, W. Kirsop, and B. J. McMullin (Melbourne: Monash University Centre for Bibliographical and Textual Studies, 1993), 113–28.

22. BF, *A Catalogue of Books Belonging to the Library Company of Philadelphia* (Philadelphia: Benjamin Franklin, 1741), 21.

23. *Genetic Text*, 37.

24. Alfred Owen Aldridge, *Benjamin Franklin, Philosopher and Man* (Philadelphia: Lippincott, 1965), 279.

25. *Genetic Text*, 203.

26. Emmett L. Avery, *The London Stage, 1660–1800 . . . Part 2: 1700–1729* (Carbondale: Southern Illinois University Press, 1960), 2: 806; Kevin J. Hayes, *Shakespeare and*

the Making of America (Stroud, UK: Amberley, 2020), 49–50, 58–59; William Shakespeare, *The Works of Mr William Shakespeare*, ed. Thomas Hanmer (London: J. and P. Knapton, 1750–1751), vols. 4 and 7 inscribed on the flyleaf, "W. T. Franklin" (University of Pennsylvania, Kislak Center for Special Collections, Furness Collection C90 1750H; not in Wolf and Hayes).

27. Avery, *London Stage*, 798, 802, 804, 808, 815, 817–819, 822; Wolf and Hayes, no. 907.

28. Avery, *London Stage*, 803, 805, 807; Samuel Johnson, *The Lives of the Most Eminent English Poets* (London: C. Bathurst, 1781), 3:50; Russell, *Benjamin Franklin*, 66; BF, "Extracts from the *Gazette*, 1738," in *Papers*, 2:211.

29. Avery, *London Stage*, 818, 804.

30. BF, *Reflections on Courtship and Marriage: In Two Letters to a Friend* (Philadelphia: B. Franklin, 1746), 35–36.

31. Ben Jonson, *The Works* (London: J. Walthoe, 1716), 5:194.

32. Avery, *London Stage*, 806, 809, 812, 816, 818, 826.

33. BF, "Articles of Belief and Acts of Religion," in *Papers*, 1:101.

34. BF, "The Busy-Body, No. 3," in *Papers*, 1:119–20; Avery, *London Stage*, 753.

35. Kevin J. Hayes, *Benjamin Franklin* (London: Reaktion, 2022), 26.

36. Robert Campbell, *The London Tradesman: Being a Compendious View of All the Trades, Professions, Arts, Both Liberal and Mechanic, Now Practised in the Cities of London and Westminster* (London: T. Gardner, 1747), 207; Hayes, *Benjamin Franklin*, 27; Amy Louise Erikson, "Eleanor Mosley and Other Milliners in the City of London Companies, 1700–1750," *History Workshop Journal*, no. 71 (Spring 2011): 156; Amy Louise Erikson, "Mistresses and Marriage: or, A Short History of the Mrs," *History Workshop Journal*, no. 88 (Autumn 2014): 39.

37. *Genetic Text*, 44.

38. *Genetic Text*, 45; Alan D. McKillop, "James Ralph in Berkshire," *Studies in English Literature, 1500–1900* 1, no. 3 (Summer 1961): 44.

39. John Dos Passos, "Two Eighteenth-Century Careers: I. Benjamin Franklin," *New Republic*, November 11, 1940, 654.

40. Edward G. Porter, "Diary of Ezra Stiles," *Proceedings of the Massachusetts Historical Society*, 2d ser., 7 (1892): 344.

41. [Edward Young,] *The Universal Passion: Satire I* (London: J. Roberts, 1725), 4; BF to Jared Eliot, September 12, 1751, in *Papers*, 4:194.

42. [Edward Young,] *The Universal Passion: Satire II* (London: J. Roberts, 1725), 16; Hayes, *Shakespeare*, 51–52.

43. *Genetic Text*, 45.

CHAPTER 8

1. Hazel Wilkinson, "Benjamin Franklin's London Printing, 1725–26," *PBSA* 110, no. 2 (June 2016): 139–80.

2. Anthony Blackwall, *An Introduction to the Classics* (London: for Charles Rivington, 1725), sig. A2r; William Mavor, "Advertisement," in *Blackwall's Introduction to the Classics* (London: Lackington, Allen, 1809), iii.

3. Blackwall, *Introduction*, 20–21; Wolf and Hayes, no. 1696.

4. Blackwall, *Introduction*, 70.

5. Ibid., sig. A3r–v; Susan Hunter, "Anthony Blackwall (1674–1730)," in *Eighteenth-Century British and American Rhetorics and Rhetoricians: Critical Studies and Sources*, ed. Michael G. Moran (Westport, CT: Greenwood Press, 1994), 17; Kevin J. Hayes, *Shakespeare and the Making of America* (Stroud, UK: Amberley, 2020), 238; Wolf and Hayes, no. 879.

6. George Saintsbury, "Lesser Verse Writers," in *The Cambridge History of English Literature*, ed. A. W. Ward and A. R. Waller (New York: Putnam, 1913), 9:211–12; Alexander Pope, *An Essay on Criticism*, 2d ed. (London: W. Lewis, 1713), 35; Samuel Johnson, *The Lives of the English Poets; and a Criticism on Their Works* (Dublin: Whitestone, 1781), 3:24.

7. Marco Girolamo Vida, *Vida's Art of Poetry*, trans. Christopher Pitt (London: Sam. Palmer, for A. Bettesworth, 1725), 5.

8. Johnson, *Lives of the English Poets*, 3:26; *Poor Richard Improved, 1756*, in *Papers*, 6:326. Though BF's editors do not identify it, this almanac includes a six-line passage from Pitt's translation of *The Aeneid*, which Franklin found in Henry Baker, *Medulla poetarum romanorum: or, The Most Beautiful and Instructive Passages of the Roman Poets* (London, 1737), 2:11.

9. Martin Murphy, "John Stevens (c. 1663–1726): Hispanist and Translator," *Dieciocho* 41, no. 1 (2018): 52; Wilkinson, "Benjamin Franklin's London Printing," 170.

10. William Robertson, *The History of America* (Dublin: Price, 1777), 2:369; *The Charter of the Library Company of Philadelphia* (Philadelphia: B. Franklin, 1746), 12.

11. William Carew Hazlitt, *The New London Jest Book* (London: Reeves and Turner, 1871), 298.

12. Wolf and Hayes, no. 1716; Richard H. Popkin, "The High Road to Pyrrhonism," *American Philosophical Quarterly* 2, no. 1 (January 1965): 23; Douglass, *British Settlements in North-America*, 1:165.

13. Pierre Daniel Huet, *A Philosophical Treatise Concerning the Weakness of Human Understanding* (London: [Samuel Palmer] for Gysbert Dommer, 1725), 168–69.

14. BF, "The Prodigious Growth of Infidelity," *PG*, March 30, 1732; Lemay, *Canon*, 58.

15. Richard Barcroft, ed., *The Rules of Conscience: or, Bishop Taylor's Ductor Dubitantium Abridg'd* (London: S. Billingsley, 1725), 2:289; Jeremy Taylor, *Ductor dubitantium: or, The Rule of Conscience in All Her General Measures* (London: Richard Royston, 1671) (Boston Public Library, Adams 112.6 Folio).

16. Bell, *Patriot-Improvers*, p. 66.

17. Wilkinson, "Benjamin Franklin's London Printing," 166–67.

18. *Genetic Text*, 43.

19. Lemay, *Life*, 1:272–77.

20. Mark Twain, "Three Statements of the Eighties," in *What Is Man? and Other Philosophical Writings*, ed. Paul Baender (Berkeley: University of California Press, 1973), 56–59; Gregg Earl Camfield, "The Influence of Sentimental Moral Philosophy on the Works of Mark Twain" (Ph.D. diss., University of California, Berkeley, 1989), 341.

21. William Powell Jones, *The Rhetoric of Science: A Study of Scientific Ideas and Imagery in Eighteenth-Century English Poetry* (Berkeley: University of California Press, 1966), 79, 84.

22. John Reynolds, *A View of Death; or, The Soul's Departure from the World: A Philosophical Sacred Poem* (London: John Clark, 1725), 12.

23. Lemay, *Life*, 1:277–83; BF, *Dissertation on Liberty and Necessity*, in *Papers*, 1:68.

24. Kevin J. Hayes, "Benjamin Franklin," in *OHEAL*, 436–37.

25. Wilkinson, "Benjamin Franklin's London Printing," 165–66; Michael Brian Schiffer, *Draw the Lightning Down: Benjamin Franklin and Electrical Technology in the Age of Enlightenment* (Berkeley: University of California Press, 2003), 20; Wolf and Hayes, no. 408; BF, *An Account of the New Invented Pennsylvanian Fire-Places*, in *Papers*, 2:440–41.

26. *Genetic Text*, 58.

27. Lemay, *Life*, 1:272; BF, *Dissertation*, 58; Wolf and Hayes, no. 909.

28. Edward Bysshe, *The Art of English Poetry* (London: Sam. Buckley, 1705), 142; *Thesaurus dramaticus: Containing All the Celebrated Passages, Soliloquies, Similes, Descriptions, and Other Poetical Beauties in the Body of English Plays* (London: Sam. Aris, 1724), 1:131.

29. BF, *Dissertation*, 59; Lemay, *Life*, 1:274.

30. BF, *Dissertation*, 71.

31. Hayes, "Benjamin Franklin," 432–33; A. Owen Aldridge, "Benjamin Franklin and Philosophical Necessity," *Modern Language Quarterly* 12, no. 3 (September 1951): 309.

32. [James Ralph,] *A Critical Review of the Publick Buildings, Statues and Ornaments in, and about London and Westminster* (London: C. Ackers, for J. Wilford, 1734), 25.

33. *Genetic Text*, 47.

34. *Genetic Text*, 48.

35. *Genetic Text*, 45–46. In addition to cataloguing the books Palmer issued when Franklin worked at his printing house, Wilkinson has catalogued the books Watts printed while Franklin worked for him.

36. Joseph Addison, *The Campaign*, in *Miscellaneous Works in Verse and Prose*, ed. Thomas Tickell (London: Jacob Tonson, 1726), 1:67–69.

37. Ibid., 71; BF, *Reflections on Courtship and Marriage: In Two Letters to a Friend* (Philadelphia: B. Franklin, 1746), 24.

38. Joseph Addison, "A Letter from Italy," in *Miscellaneous Works*, 1:53.

39. BF, "Books Added to the Library Since the Year 1741," in *Laws of the Library Company of Philadelphia* (Philadelphia: B. Franklin, 1746), 12.

40. David Lewis, ed., *Miscellaneous Poems, by Several Hands* (London: J. Watts, 1726), sig. A4r.

41. "[Winifreda]: Translation from the Ancient British," in Lewis, *Miscellaneous Poems*, 53–54.

42. [Samuel Wesley,] "The Monument," in Lewis, *Miscellaneous Poems*, 290.

43. *Cooper's Hill* calls to mind a personal experience. While studying for my doctoral examination in English Renaissance literature at the University of Delaware, I sought advice from my friend Patrick "Whitey" White, who had taken his the previous year. "Read *Cooper's Hill*," he recommended. "No matter what they ask, you can use it." After my examination, I went to the Crab Trap, the graduate student hangout near campus, and found Whitey there. I told him about my test; he was pleased to learn that I had indeed used *Cooper's Hill*. The Crab Trap has since burned down; *Cooper's Hill* endures.

44. Anne Janowitz, "'What a Rich Fund of Images Is Treasured up Here': Poetic Commonplaces of the Sublime Universe," *Studies in Romanticism* 44, no. 4 (Winter 2005): 474.

45. Iolo A. Williams, "Dyer's 'Grongar Hill,'" *Bookman*, July 1934, 203.

46. [John Dyer,] "Grongar Hill," in Lewis, *Miscellaneous Poems*, 228.

47. Wilfred P. Mustard, "Poor Richard's Poetry," *Nation*, March 22, 1906, 239; Wolf and Hayes, no. 2051.

48. Quoted in Anthony Kaufman, "Thomas Southerne," in *Restoration and Eighteenth-Century Dramatists: First Series*, ed. Paula R. Backscheider (Detroit: Gale, 1989), 209.

49. Newcomb, "Sources," 194.

50. Jonathan Swift, "On Reading Dr. Young's Satyrs, Called the Universal Passion," in *The Works* (Dublin: George Faulkner, 1735), 2:299–301; Edward Young, *The Universal Passion: Satire the Last* (London: J. Roberts, 1726), 8.

CHAPTER 9

1. "Extract of a Letter from Jamaica," *St. James's Evening Post*, December 17, 1726.

2. Percy G. Adams, "Benjamin Franklin and the Travel-Writing Tradition," in *The Oldest Revolutionary: Essays on Benjamin Franklin*, ed. J. A. Leo Lemay (Philadelphia: University of Pennsylvania Press, 1976), 42; Hazel Wilkinson, "Benjamin Franklin's London Printing, 1725–26," *PBSA* 110, no. 2 (June 2016): 156; John Dos Passos, "Two Eighteenth-Century Careers: I. Benjamin Franklin," *New Republic*, November 11, 1940, 657; BF, "Journal of a Voyage," in *The Oxford Book of the Sea*, ed. Jonathan Raban (New York: Oxford University Press, 1992), 92–108; James Hamilton-Paterson, "Marine Dreams," *New Republic*, October 25, 1993, 38.

3. BF, "Journal of a Voyage, 1726," in *Papers*, 1:86; *Genetic Text*, 51.

4. Thomas Kinsella and Willman Spawn, "Learning from Binders: Investigating the Bookbinding Trade in Colonial Philadelphia," in *Teaching Bibliography, Textual*

Criticism, and Book History, ed. Ann R. Hawkins (London: Pickering and Chatto, 2006), 136; "Lyons' *Infallibility of Human Judgment*," *Philobiblion*, April 1862, 106.

5. W. B. McDaniel, 2d, "John Jones' Introductory Lecture to His Course in Surgery (1769), King's College, Printed from the Author's Manuscript," *Transactions and Studies of the College of Physicians of Philadelphia*, 4th ser., 8, no. 3 (December 1940): 187.

6. "Lyons' Infallibility," 105.

7. *Genetic Text*, 44; David Runciman, *Political Hypocrisy: The Mask of Power, from Hobbes to Orwell and Beyond* (Princeton, NJ: Princeton University Press, 2008), 82–83.

8. [Bernard Mandeville,] *The Fable of the Bees: or, Private Vice, Publick Benefits* (London: Edmund Parker, 1723), 428.

9. James Steintrager, *The Autonomy of Pleasure: Libertines, License, and Sexual Revolution* (New York: Columbia University Press, 2016), 101–102; *Oxford English Dictionary*, s.v. "stew."

10. Kevin Slack, *Benjamin Franklin, Natural Right, and the Art of Virtue* (Rochester, NY: University of Rochester Press, 2017), 137.

11. *Connoisseur*, 3d ed. (London: R. Baldwin, 1757–1760), 1:3.

12. Benjamin Rush, "The Wisdom and Experience of Mellow Old Age, 1785–1789, 1805, 1806," in Hayes and Bour, 104.

13. Anita Guerrini, "Mead, Richard," in *ODNB*, 37:639.

14. John Lyons, *The Infallibility of Human Judgment*, 4th ed. (London: J. Brotherton, 1724), 248; Wolf and Hayes, no. 2125; Nick Bunker, *Young Benjamin Franklin: The Birth of Ingenuity* (New York: Knopf, 2018), 179.

15. "London, August 21," *Daily Journal*, August 21, 1723; "London, September 6," *Weekly Journal*, September 7, 1723.

16. Lyons, *Infallibility of Human Judgment*, 248–49.

17. Richard Mead, *Medical Precepts and Cautions*, trans. Thomas Stack (London: J. Brindley, 1751); Wolf and Hayes, no. 2280.

18. Edwin Wolf, 2nd, "Frustration and Benjamin Franklin's Medical Books," in *Science and Society in Early America: Essays in Honor of Whitfield J. Bell, Jr.*, ed. Randolph Shipley Klein (Philadelphia: American Philosophical Society, 1986), 57–91; Hayes, *Benjamin Franklin*, 32.

19. "Character of Dr. Franklin," *London Public Advertiser*, June 10, 1790; "Memoirs and Character of Dr. Franklin," *London Chronicle*, June 10, 1790; David Boyd Haycock, "Folkes, Martin," in *ODNB*, 20:222–24.

20. W. Johnson, "Pemberton, Henry," in *ODNB*, 43:505; *Genetic Text*, 44.

21. Wolf and Hayes, no. 2429; BF to Cadwallader Colden, September 14, 1752, in *Papers*, 4:354.

22. Isaac Newton, *Opticks: or, A Treatise of the Reflections, Refractions, Inflections and Colours of Light*, 3d ed. (London: William and John Innys, 1721), 1; A. Owen Aldridge, "Benjamin Franklin and Philosophical Necessity," *Modern Language Quarterly* 12, no. 3 (September 1951): 292–309.

23. Wolf and Hayes, no. 676; Sarah Dry, *The Newton Papers: The Strange and True Odyssey of Isaac Newton's Manuscripts* (New York: Oxford University Press, 2014), 205–206.

24. ESTC, no. T114069.

25. Quoted in Wolf, *Library of James Logan*, 349.

26. BF, *Poor Richard, 1748*, in *Papers*, 3:251; Wolf and Hayes, no. 676.

27. Rudi Verburg, "The Dutch Background of Bernard Mandeville's Thought: Escaping the Procrustean Bed of Neo-Augustinianism," *Erasmus Journal for Philosophy and Economics* 9, no. 1 (Spring 2016): 50.

28. Jaap Nieuwstraten, "Why the Wealthy Should Rule: Marcus Zuerius Boxhorn's Defence of Holland's Aristocratic Mercantile Regime," in *Public Offices, Personal Demands: Capability in Governance in the Seventeenth-Century Dutch Republic,* ed. Jan Hartman, Jaap Nieuwstraten, and Michel Reinders (Newcastle upon Tyne: Cambridge Scholars, 2009), 137–38; BF to "Charles de Weissenstein," July 1, 1778, in *Papers*, 27:7.

29. "*Arcana imperii detecta*," *History of the Works of the Learned* 2, no. 12 (December 1700): 753–54.

30. *A Catalogue of the Valuable and Extensive Library of the Late Rev. Jonathan Boucher* (London: Leigh and S. Sotheby, 1806), lot 195; Wolf, *Library of James Logan*, nos. 306–307; Prys Morgan, "Boxhorn, Leibniz, and the Welsh," *Studia Celtica* 8 (1973): 222.

31. Marie Elena Korey, *The Books of Isaac Norris (1701–1766) at Dickinson College* (Carlisle, PA: Dickinson College, 1976), no. 283.

32. BF to "Charles de Weissenstein," July 1, 1778, in *Papers*, 27:7.

33. Marcus Zuerius Boxhorn, *Arcana imperii detecta: or, Divers Select Cases on Government* (London: James Knapton, 1701), 318–23; Wolf and Hayes, no. 405.

34. BF to "Charles de Weissenstein," July 1, 1778, in *Papers*, 27:7.

35. BF, "Journal of a Voyage," 74.

36. Ibid.

37. Boxhorn, *Arcana imperii*, 35.

38. BF, "Journal of a Voyage," 92; Alexander Pope, trans., *The Odyssey of Homer* (London: Bernard Lintot, 1725–1726), 3:190.

39. Salem Pearse, *The Coelestial Diary: or, An Ephemeris for the Year of Our Blessed Saviour's Incarnation, 1726* (London: J. Dawks, 1726).

40. BF, "Journal of a Voyage," 95.

CHAPTER 10

1. Kevin J. Hayes, *Benjamin Franklin* (London: Reaktion, 2022), 42.

2. *Genetic Text*, 53.

3. *Genetic Text*, 53.

4. *Genetic Text*, 53; Whiting, no. 154; *William Byrd's Histories of the Dividing Line betwixt Virginia and North Carolina*, ed. William K. Boyd (1929; repr., New York:

Dover, 1967), 102. George Webb, "Goddess of Numbers, Who Art Wont to Rove," in Titan Leeds, *The American Almanack for . . . 1730* (Philadelphia: Nearegress and Arnot, 1729), signs himself, "Oxf. Schol."

5. Joseph Foster, *Alumni Oxonienses: The Members of the University of Oxford, 1715–1886* (London: Parker, 1888), 4:1516.

6. *Genetic Text*, 54.

7. Herman Melville, *White-Jacket: or, The World in a Man-of-War* (New York: Harper, 1850), 438–39.

8. BF, *Political, Miscellaneous, and Philosophical Pieces*, ed. Benjamin Vaughan (London: J. Johnson, 1779), 533.

9. John Locke, "Rules of a Society, which Met Once a Week, for Their Improvement in Useful Knowledge, and for the Promoting of Truth and Christian Charity," in *A Collection of Several Pieces of Mr. John Locke* (London: R. Francklin, 1720), 359; BF, "Standing Queries for the Junto," in *Papers*, 1:259.

10. Isabella James, *Memorial of Thomas Potts, Junior, Who Settled in Pennsylvania* (Cambridge, MA, 1874), 376–83; *Genetic Text*, 62.

11. Charles Biddle, *Autobiography of Charles Biddle: Vice-President of the Supreme Executive Council of Pennsylvania, 1745–1821* (Philadelphia: E. Clacton, 1883), 379–80; [Nicholas Scull,] *Kawanio che keeteru: A True Relation of a Bloody Battle Fought between George and Lewis, in the Year 1755* ([Philadelphia,] 1756), 2.

12. Biddle, *Autobiography*, 381.

13. Nicholas Scull, "The Junto," in *Colonial American Poetry*, ed. Kenneth Silverman (New York: Hafner, 1968), 372–73; Nicholas Scull, ["The Junto Room,"] in Nicholas B. Wainwright, "Nicholas Scull's 'Junto' Verses," *PMHB* 73, no. 1 (January 1949): 82–84.

14. BF, "Standing Queries for the Junto," in *Papers*, 1:257–58.

15. BF, *Political, Miscellaneous, and Philosophical Pieces*, 533; BF, "Rules for a Club Formerly Established in Philadelphia," *London Magazine* 48 (December 1779): 574–75; BF, "Rules for a Club Formerly Established in Philadelphia," *Annual Register* (London: J. Dodsley, 1780), 159–60; *Spectator* (London: Payne, 1788), 1:40.

16. BF, "Standing Queries," 257.

17. Francis Bacon, *The Essays, or Councils, Civil and Moral* (London: Timothy Childe, 1701), 135; BF, "Proposals and Queries to Be Asked the Junto," in *Papers*, 1:260.

18. Scull, "Junto Room," 82.

19. George W. Boudreau, "Solving the Mystery of the Junto's Missing Member: John Jones, Shoemaker," *PMHB* 131, no. 3 (July 2007): 314.

20. Scull, "Junto," 373.

21. BF, *Poor Richard's Almanack for 1750*, in *Papers*, 3:451.

22. John Dryden, *Essays of John Dryden*, ed. W. P. Ker (Oxford: Clarendon Press, 1900), 1:7.

23. [Joseph Breintnall,] "The Busy-Body, No. 9," *American Weekly Mercury*, April 10, 1729; Plutarch, *The Philosophie, Commonlie Called, The Morals*, trans. Philemon

Holland (London: Arnold Hatfield, 1603) (PPL, no. *STC 20063 89.F); Xenophon, *The Memorable Things of Socrates*, trans. Edward Bysshe, 2d ed. (London: J. Batley, 1722) (PPL, no. O Greek Xeno Mem 1722 204.O); BF, *A Catalogue of Books Belonging to the Library Company of Philadelphia* (Philadelphia: B. Franklin, 1741), 6, 19, 33, 47, 48, 51; *Genetic Text*, 61.

24. David S. Shields, ed., *American Poetry: The Seventeenth and Eighteenth Centuries* (New York: Library of America, 2007); David S. Shields, "The Wits and Poets of Pennsylvania: New Light on the Rise of Belles Lettres in Provincial Pennsylvania, 1720–1740," *PMHB* 109, no. 2 (April 1985): 102; James N. Green, "News from Our First Secretary and Notes on Other Acquisitions," in *The Annual Report of the Library Company of Philadelphia for the Year 1989* (Philadelphia: Library Company of Philadelphia, 1990), 8–11.

25. [Joseph Breintnall,] *The Death of King George Lamented in Pennsylvania; Being Part of a Letter to the Author's Country Friend* ([Philadelphia: Samuel Keimer, 1727]) (PPL, #Am 1727 Brei 9058.F).

26. Kenneth Silverman, "Notes on the Poems," in *Colonial American Poetry* (New York: Hafner, 1968), 449; Scull, "Junto Room," 82.

27. Wolf, *Library of James Logan*, no. 530.

28. [Joseph Breintnall,] "Salkeld, from Silent Sitting, Slow Would Rise," *American Weekly Mercury*, January 3, 1740; Lemay, *Calendar*, no. 544.

29. Scull, "Junto," 373; Lemay, *Life*, 1:343.

30. "The Rats and the Cheese," *Weekly-Journal: or, Saturday's Post*, December 7, 1717. Paul Bunyan Anderson, "Bernard Mandeville," *Times Literary Supplement*, November 28, 1936, 996, first attributed "The Rats and the Cheese" to Mandeville. Daniel Z. Gibson, "A Critical Edition of the Poems of Bernard Mandeville" (Ph.D. diss., University of Cincinnati, 1939), 205, accepts Anderson's attribution.

31. "The Rats and the Cheese," in *A Collection of Miscellany Letters, Selected out of Mist's Weekly Journal* (London: N. Mist, 1722), 1:21–22; Wolf and Hayes, no. 2343.

32. "The Rats and the Cheese: A Fable," *PG*, September 24, 1730; Lemay, *Calendar*, no. 161.

33. Scull, "Junto Room," 84; T. Z. [George Webb,] "No More a Willing Muse Her Aid Bestows," *PG*, April 8, 1731; Lemay, *Calendar*, no. 182; Shields, "Wits and Poets," 126–27.

34. Shields, "Wits and Poets," 123.

35. BF to Hugh Roberts, September 16, 1758, in *Papers*, 8:159.

36. Hannah Benner Roach, "Benjamin Franklin Slept Here," *PMHB* 84, no. 2 (April 1960): 140; Silvio A. Bedini, "Godfey, Thomas," in *ANB*, 7:616; Bell, *Patriot Improvers*, 63.

37. Miller, no. 1; *Genetic Text*, 62.

38. Miller, *passim*; J. A. Leo Lemay, "Recent Franklin Scholarship, with a Note on Franklin's Sedan Chair," *PMHB* 126, no. 2 (April 2002): 338.

39. H. W. Brands, *The First American: The Life and Times of Benjamin Franklin* (New York: Doubleday, 2000), 110.

40. Samuel Keimer, *Advertisement, October 1, 1728*. [Philadelphia: Keimer, 1728.]

41. Hayes, *Benjamin Franklin*, 46–48.

42. Kevin J. Hayes, "Benjamin Franklin," in *OHEAL*, 434–35.

43. BF, "The Busy-Body, No. 4," in *Papers*, 1:125–26; Henry Maundrell, *A Journey from Aleppo to Jerusalem at Easter A.D. 1697* (Oxford: at the Theater, 1703), 30.

44. Tim Nubibus [Samuel Keimer,] "Hue and Cry after the Busy-Body," *Universal Instructor*, March 13, 1729.

45. [Joseph Breintnall,] "The Busy-Body, No. 9," *American Weekly Mercury*, April 10, 1729.

46. [Joseph Breintnall,] "The Busy-Body, No. 16," *American Weekly Mercury*, June 5, 1729.

47. Hayes, *Benjamin Franklin*, 50; Ephraim Chambers, *Cyclopaedia: or, An Universal Dictionary of Arts and Sciences*, 2 vols. (London: J. and J. Knapton, 1728) (not in Wolf and Hayes).

48. Charles E. Clark, *The Public Prints: The Newspaper in Anglo-American Culture, 1665–1740* (New York: Oxford University Press, 1994), 175.

49. Hayes, *Benjamin Franklin*, 50–51.

50. *Genetic Text*, 65.

CHAPTER 11

1. Lemay, *Calendar*, no. 129.

2. Richard Lewis, "To Mr. Samuel Hastings (Shipwright of Philadelphia) on His Launching the *Maryland-Merchant*, a Large Ship Built by Him at Annapolis," in *American Poetry: The Seventeenth and Eighteenth Centuries*, ed. David S. Shields (New York: Library of America, 2007), 382; J. A. Leo Lemay, *Men of Letters in Colonial Maryland* (Knoxville: University of Tennessee Press, 1972), 133.

3. Lewis, "To Mr. Samuel Hastings," 382.

4. "To the Publisher of the *Weekly Rehearsal*," *Weekly Rehearsal*, January 27, 1735; Lemay, *Calendar*, no. 348.

5. B. L., "What Silly Wretch Would Prostitute His Name," *American Weekly Mercury*, August 4, 1737; Lemay, *Calendar*, no. 475; [BF,] "The Author of a Copy of Verses," *Pennsylvania Gazette*, August 11, 1737.

6. David S. Shields, "Henry Brooke and the Situation of the First Belletrists in British America," *Early American Literature* 23, no. 1 (1988): 4–27.

7. [Joseph Breintnall,] "An Encomium to Aquila Rose, on His Art in Praising," in *Poems on Several Occasions*, by Aquila Rose, ed. Joseph Rose (Philadelphia: New Printing Office, 1740), 3–12; Miller, no. 207; David S. Shields, "The Manuscript in the British American World of Print," *Proceedings of the American Antiquarian Society* 102 (1993): 415.

8. [Joseph Breintnall,] "To the Memory of Aquila Rose, Deceas'd," in Rose, *Poems*, 3–12; David S. Shields, "Eighteenth-Century Literary Culture," in *A History of the Book in America*, ed. Hugh Amory and David D. Hall (New York: Cambridge University Press, 2000), 439.

9. Breintnall, "To the Memory of Aquila Rose," 12; Michael C. Cohen, "Poetry of the United States," in *The Princeton Encyclopedia of Poetry and Poetics*, ed. Roland Greene et al., 4th ed. (Princeton, NJ: Princeton University Press, 2012), 1482.

10. Breintnall, "To the Memory of Aquila Rose," 11.

11. Lemay, *Calendar*, nos. 35, 53, 57.

12. Gerald D. McDonald, Stuart C. Sherman, and Mary T. Russo, *A Checklist of American Newspaper Carriers' Addresses, 1720–1820* (Worcester, MA: American Antiquarian Society, 2000), nos. 1–3; Keith Arbour, "The McDonald-Sherman-Russo *Checklist*," *PBSA* 95, no. 3 (September 2001): 370–73.

13. Joseph Rose to Jacob Taylor, November 11, 1741, in Gilbert Cope, "Jacob Taylor, Almanac Maker," *Bulletins of the Chester County Historical Society* (1908), 19.

14. [Joseph Breintnall,] *The Yearly Verses on the Printer's Lad Who Carrieth about the Pennsylvania Gazette to the Customers Thereof, Jan. 1, 1739: The Spreading News* ([Philadelphia: New Printing Office, 1738]); Miller, no. 154.

15. [Joseph Breintnall,] *The Yearly Verses on the Printer's Lad, Who Carrieth about the Pennsylvania Gazette to the Customers Thereof, January 1, 1740* ([Philadelphia: New Printing Office, 1740]); Miller, no. 172.

16. [Joseph Breintnall,] *The Yearly Verses on the Printer's Lad, Who Carrieth about the Pennsylvania Gazette to the Customers Thereof, Jan. 1, 1741* ([Philadelphia: New Printing Office, 1740]); Miller, no. 205; Kevin J. Hayes, preface to *The Cambridge Companion to Edgar Allan Poe*, ed. Kevin J. Hayes (New York: Cambridge University Press, 2002), 2.

17. David S. Shields, "The Wits and Poets of Pennsylvania: New Light on the Rise of Belles Lettres in Provincial Pennsylvania, 1720–1740," *PMHB* 109, no. 2 (April 1985): 110–11; James Logan to William Penn, March 7, 1702, *Correspondence between William Penn and James Logan, Secretary of the Province of Pennsylvania, and Others*, ed. Deborah Logan and Edward Armstrong (Philadelphia: J. B. Lippincott, 1870), 1:93. The only known copy of Taylor's first almanac, published in 1699 for 1700, consists of a single leaf that survives at PPL (*ESTC*, no. W5349).

18. Keith Arbour, "The First North American Mathematical Book and Its Metalcut Illustrations: Jacob Taylor's *Tenebrae*, 1697," *PMHB* 123, nos. 1–2 (January–April 1999): 87–98.

19. One poem in Jacob Taylor, *Pensilvania, 1737: An Almanac or Ephemeris, for the Year of Our Lord, 1737* (Philadelphia: Andrew Bradford, [1736]), mentions "Garth's *Enchiridion*," but Dr. Samuel Garth did not write any works by this title. "Garth" is a misprint for "Quarles."

20. Joseph Breintnall to Andrew Bradford, August 29, 1739, in Cope, "Jacob Taylor," 18.

21. Samuel Keimer, "The Printer's Preface," in *A Compleat Ephemeris for the Year of Christ 1726* (Philadelphia: Samuel Keimer, [1725]), n.p. Subsequent quotations from this almanac will not be separately cited.

22. Hayes, *Colonial Woman's Bookshelf*, 88–89.

23. This discussion of hudibrastics calls to mind the start of my teaching career. Once I began teaching early American literature at the University of Central Oklahoma, I rewrote the course description for the English department catalogue to reflect my syllabus. As it stood, the description emphasized the prominence of Puritan sermons. I cut the phrase "Puritan sermons" in favor of a different literary genre: "bawdy hudibrastics." The next edition of the catalogue appeared with my new course description. Without my knowledge or consent, another professor in the department altered my course description for a later edition of the catalogue. Bawdy hudibrastics were gone, and Puritan sermons were back.

24. Sylvia Plath, *The Collected Poems*, ed. Ted Hughes (New York: HarperPerennial, 2008), 222.

25. Jacob Taylor, "To S. K.," *American Weekly Mercury*, January 25, 1726; Lemay, *Calendar*, no. 59.

26. Joseph Breintnall, "A Plain Description of One Single Street in This City," *American Poetry*, 353; Lemay, *Calendar*, no. 117.

27. [George Webb,] "Let Philadelphia's Generous Sons Excuse," *American Weekly Mercury*, July 3, 1729; Lemay, *Calendar*, no. 122.

28. [George Webb,] "Goddess of Numbers, Who Art Wont to Rave," in Titan Leeds, *The American Almanack for . . . 1730* (Philadelphia: Nearegress and Arnot, 1729).

29. George Webb, *Batchelors-Hall: A Poem* (Philadelphia: New Printing Office, 1731), 6 (American Philosophical Society 811 W38); Miller, no. 46.

30. David S. Shields, "British-American Belles Lettres," in *The Cambridge History of American Literature*, ed. Sacvan Bercovitch and Cyrus R. K. Patell (New York: Cambridge University Press, 1994), 1:317.

31. Samuel Marion Tucker, "The Beginnings of Verse, 1610–1808," in *CHAL*, 1:162; Kevin J. Hayes, "Poetry in the Time of Revolution," in *The Cambridge History of American Poetry*, ed. Alfred Bendixen and Stephen Burt (New York: Cambridge University Press, 2015), 135–36.

32. [Richard Lewis,] "A Journey from Patapsco to Annapolis," *PG*, May 20, 1731; Lemay, *Calendar*, nos. 184, 198, 215, 252a, 253a, 268; Edward Kimber, *Itinerant Observations in America*, ed. Kevin J. Hayes (Newark: University of Delaware Press, 1998), 11–12.

33. William C. Spengemann, *A Mirror for Americanists: Reflections on the Idea of American Literature* (Hanover, NH: University Press of New England, 1989), 47; J. A. Leo Lemay, "A Newtonian Universe," in *An Early American Reader*, ed. J. A. Leo Lemay (Washington, DC: United States Information Agency, 1988), 559.

34. Clifford K. Shipton, and James E. Mooney, *National Index of American Imprints through 1800: The Short-Title Evans* (Worcester, MA: American Antiquarian Society and Barre Publishers, 1969), 1:424; Wolf and Hayes, no. 1278.

35. Richard Lewis, *Carmen Seculare, For the Year M,DC,XXXII*, in *Colonial American Poetry*, ed. Kenneth Silverman (New York: Harfner, 1968), 311.

36. Kenneth Silverman, introduction to *Colonial American Poetry*, 8; Allen Ginsberg, *Howl and Other Poems* (San Francisco: City Lights, 1956), 9.

37. Wolf and Hayes, no. 1278; Lemay, *Calendar*, nos. 408, 1081, 1135–37, 1144, 1178, 1179, 1204; Lemay, *Life*, 2:306.

38. Lemay, *Life*, 2:299–305.

39. "Teague's Orashion," *Gentleman's Magazine* 5 (January 1735): 44; Lemay, *Calendar*, nos. 349, 610; BF, "Teague's Advertisement," in *Papers*, 2:305; Cotton Mather, *Magnalia christi americana: or, The Ecclesiastical History of New-England* (London: T. Parkhurst, 1702), book 7, p. 74.

40. Hayes, "Poetry in the Time of Revolution," 141.

41. BF, "The Speech Versyfied," in *Papers*, 3:137–40; J. A. Leo Lemay, "Franklin and the Autobiography: An Essay on Recent Scholarship," *Eighteenth-Century Studies* 1, no. 2 (Winter 1967): 189; J. A. Leo Lemay, "Hamilton's Literary History of the *Maryland Gazette*," *William and Mary Quarterly* 23, no. 2 (April 1966): 279; John Updike, "Many Bens," *The New Yorker*, February 22, 1988, 113.

42. BF, "Teague's Advertisement," in *Papers*, 2:305.

43. Lemay, "Hamilton's Literary History," 280; Henry Lee Smith, "Dr. Adam Thomson, the Originator of the American Method of Inoculation for Small-Pox," *Johns Hopkins Hospital Bulletin*, no. 215 (February 1909): 49–52; Town Side [Adam Thomson], "Teague Turn'd Planter," *Maryland Gazette*, July 28, 1747.

44. Enroblos [Jacob Taylor,] "O Heavenly Muse My Darling Breast Inspire," *American Weekly Mercury*, February 19 and 26, 1740; Lemay, *Calendar*, no. 557; Shields, "Wits and Poets," 114.

CHAPTER 12

1. Joseph Breintnall to the Directors of the Library Company, November 8, 1731, in *Papers*, 1:208–10; Lemay, *Life*, 1:337; BF, *Experiments and Observations on Electricity, Made at Philadelphia in America*, 4th ed. (London: David Henry, 1769), 5; Bell, *Patriot-Improvers*, 11–15, 67.

2. Edwin Wolf, 2nd, *"At the Instance of Benjamin Franklin": A Brief History of the Library Company of Philadelphia*, rev. ed. (Philadelphia: Library Company of Philadelphia, 1995), 5.

3. R. B. [Nathaniel Crouch,] *Delights for the Ingenious, in Above Fifty Select and Choice Emblems, Divine and Moral, Ancient and Modern* (London: Nath. Crouch, 1684), 90.

4. Ibid., 138.

5. Lemay, *Life*, 2:97; Miller, no. 39; George W. Boudreau, "Solving the Mystery of the Junto's Missing Member: John Jones, Shoemaker," *PMHB* 131, no. 3 (July 2007): 307–17.

6. Kevin J. Hayes, "Logan, James," in *Encyclopedia of the American Enlightenment*, ed. Mark G. Spencer (New York: Bloomsbury Academic, 2015), 2:663–64.

7. BF, *Proposals Relating to the Education of Youth in Pennsylvania*, in *Papers*, 3:401.

8. Edwin Wolf, 2nd, "The First Books and Printed Catalogues of the Library Company of Philadelphia," *PMHB* 78, no. 1 (January 1954): 46; Wolf, *Library of James Logan*, no. 1060.

9. Wolf, *Library of James Logan*, no. 1480.

10. Wolf, "First Books," 62, 64, 69.

11. Ibid., 57; Jean Barbeyrac, "An Historical and Critical Account of the Science of Morality," trans. George Carew, in *Of the Law of Nature and Nations*, by Samuel Pufendorf, trans. Basil Kennett, 4th ed. (London: J. Walthoe, 1729), 15; Kevin J. Hayes, "Benjamin Franklin, An American Satirist," in *Satire*, ed. Robert C. Evans (Amenia, NY: Grey House, 2020), 208.

12. James N. Green, "Bound/Unbound," *Early American Studies* 16, no. 4 (Fall 2018): 616; Dorothy F. Grimm, "A History of the Library Company of Philadelphia, 1731–1835" (Ph.D. diss., University of Pennsylvania, 1955), 61.

13. James N. Green, "Peter Collinson, Benjamin Franklin, and The Library Company," in *The Annual Report of the Library Company of Philadelphia for the Year 2012* (Philadelphia: Library Company of Philadelphia, 2013), 16; Robert Southey, *The Doctor, &c* (London: Longman, 1837), 4:61–62.

14. Wolf, "First Books," passim; Herbert A. Johnson, *Imported Eighteenth-Century Law Treatises in American Libraries, 1700–1799* (Knoxville: University of Tennessee Press, 1978), no. 207.

15. Wolf, "First Books," 60–61; David Armitage, "Every Great Revolution Is a Civil War," in *Scripting Revolution: A Historical Approach to the Comparative Study of Revolutions*, ed. Keith Michael Baker and Dan Edelstein (Palo Alto, CA: Stanford University Press, 2015), 63; Kevin J. Hayes, *The Library of John Montgomerie, Colonial Governor of New York and New Jersey* (Newark: University of Delaware Press, 2000), nos. 669–671; Stan V. Henkels, *The Valuable Library of the Hon. Samuel W. Pennypacker: Part II* (Philadelphia: Davis and Harvey, 1906), lots 165, 415.

16. BF, *A Catalogue of Books Belonging to the Library Company of Philadelphia* (Philadelphia: B. Franklin, 1741), 48.

17. Douglass, *British Settlements in North-America*, 1:406–407.

18. Wolf, "First Books," 46; Blanche Henrey, *British Botanical and Horticultural Literature before 1800* (New York: Oxford University Press, 1999), 1:80; *Laws of the Library Company of Philadelphia* (Philadelphia: B. Franklin, 1746), 2–3, 7; Edwin Wolf, 2nd, "Report of the Librarian," in *The Annual Report of the Library Company of Philadelphia for the Year 1960* (Philadelphia: Library Company of Philadelphia, 1961), 34.

19. Wolf, "First Books," 46; Joseph Sabin, Wilberforce Eames and R. W. G. Vail, *Bibliotheca Americana* (New York: Bibliographical Society of America, 1898–1936), no. 18373.

20. Carl Thompson, "Dampier, William (1651–1715)," in *Literature of Travel and Exploration: An Encyclopedia*, ed. Jennifer Speake (New York: Fitzroy Dearborn, 2003), 1:312–13.

21. William Dampier, *A Collection of Voyages* (London: James and John Knapton, 1729), 1:255–56.

22. BF, "Notes on Colds [1773?]," in *Papers*, 20:535.

23. Dampier, *Collection of Voyages*, 1:330.

24. BF, "Maritime Observations," in *Writings* (Smyth), 9:381; Dampier, *Collection of Voyages*, 1:412; Kevin J. Hayes, *Benjamin Franklin* (London: Reaktion, 2022), 164.

25. Wolf, "First Books," 64–68.

26. Ibid., 59; Andrew Janiak, *Newton* (Malden, MA: Wiley, 2015), 30; Tina Skouen and Ryan Stark, ed., *Rhetoric and the Early Royal Society: A Sourcebook* (Leiden: Brill, 2014), 16; Wolf, "First Books," 58; *Laws of the Library Company*, 8; Peter Collinson to John Bartram, May 20, 1737, in *Memorials of John Bartram and Humphry Marshall*, ed. William Darlington (Philadelphia: Lindsay and Blakiston, 1849), 96.

27. John Noorthouck, *An Historical and Classical Dictionary*, vol. 1 (London: W. Strahan, 1776), s.v. "Collinson, Peter"; John Smith, *The Generall Historie of Virginia, New-England, and the Summer Isles* (London: Michael Sparkes, 1624) (PPL *Am 1624 Smith 245.F); Kevin J. Hayes, *Captain John Smith: A Reference Guide* (Boston: G. K. Hall, 1991), xvi.

28. "Home Ports," *Daily Journal* [London], August 12, 1732; Grimm, "History of the Library Company," 64–65.

29. Hannah Benner Roach, "Benjamin Franklin Slept Here," *PMHB* 84, no. 2 (April 1960): 141–42; Thomas Kinsella and Willman Spawn, "Learning from Binders: Investigating the Bookbinding Trade in Colonial Philadelphia," in *Teaching Bibliography, Textual Criticism, and Book History*, ed. Ann R. Hawkins (London: Pickering and Chatto, 2006), 136; Wolf, "Report of the Librarian," 34.

30. Hugh Roberts to BF, June 1, 1758, and BF to Hugh Roberts, September 16, 1758, in *Papers*, 8:84, 159.

31. Green, "Bound/Unbound," 616–19.

32. Joseph Breintnall to Peter Collinson, November 7, 1732, in *Papers*, 1:248–49; Green, "Peter Collinson," 16.

33. "Agreement between Louis Timothée and the Directors of the Library Company," in *Papers*, 1:250–52.

34. Wolf, "First Books," 46.

35. Ibid., 47; Miller, no. 71; Robert B. Winans, *A Descriptive Checklist of Book Catalogues Separately Printed in America, 1693–1800* (Worcester, MA: American Antiquarian Society, 1981), no. 11.

36. BF, *Catalogue* (1741), 51; BF, *A Catalogue of Choice and Valuable Books* (Philadelphia: B. Franklin, 1744), 3.

37. Jon Parkin, *Taming the Leviathan: The Reception of the Political and Religious Ideas of Thomas Hobbes in England, 1640–1700* (New York: Cambridge

University Press, 2007), 121, 123–24; Alexander Ross, *Leviathan Drawn out with a Hook: or, Animadversions upon Mr Hobbs His Leviathan* (London: Tho. Newcomb, 1653), 22.

38. Amédée François Frézier, *A Voyage to the South-Sea, and Along the Coasts of Chili and Peru, in the Years 1712, 1713, and 1714* (London: Jonah Bowyer, 1717), 1; BF, *Catalogue* (1741), 19.

39. BF, *Catalogue* (1741), 7; *The Charter, Laws, and Catalogue of Books of the Library Company of Philadelphia* (Philadelphia: B. Franklin and D. Hall, 1764), 26.

40. Lemay, *Life*, 2:103–104; BF to Hugh Roberts, September 16, 1758, in *Papers*, 8:159.

41. Lemay, *Life*, 2:101–109.

42. Edwin Wolf, 2nd, "Report of the Librarian," in *The Annual Report of the Library Company of Philadelphia for the Year 1964* (Philadelphia: Library Company of Philadelphia, 1965), 7–8.

43. BF, "Extracts from the *Gazette*, 1734," in *Papers*, 1:383.

44. BF, "On Amplification," in *Papers*, 2:146–47; Richard Steele, *The Dramatick Works* (London: J. T., 1723), 13; Wolf and Hayes, no. 3251.

45. Benjamin Rush, "The Wisdom and Experience of Mellow Old Age," in Hayes and Bour, 103–4; BF, "Extracts from the *Gazette*, 1734," in *Papers*, 1:383.

46. Miller, no. 108; Winans, *Descriptive Checklist*, no. 14.

47. BF, *Catalogue* (1741), 4.

48. Ibid., 5.

49. *Catalogue of the Library of Charles Carroll of Carrollton* (Baltimore: Gibson & Co., 1864), lot 1191; Gordon W. Jones, *The Library of James Monroe (1758–1831), 5th President (1816–1824) of the United States* (Charlottesville: Bibliographical Society of the University of Virginia, 1967), 21; Robert C. Bartlett, *The Idea of Enlightenment: A Postmortem Study* (Toronto: University of Toronto Press, 2001), 14; Herman Melville to Evert Duyckinck, April 5, 1849, in *Correspondence*, ed. Lynn Horth (Evanston, IL: Northwestern University Press, 1991), 128; Anthony Gottlieb, "The Tolerant Philosopher: Pierre Bayle, the Forgotten Hero of the Enlightenment," *New Statesman*, August 18, 2016, 38.

50. Pierre Bayle, *The Dictionary Historical and Critical*, trans. Pierre des Maizeaux, 2d ed. (London: J. J. and P. Knapton, 1736), 3:653.

51. Edward Gibbon, *Miscellaneous Works* (London: A. Strahan, 1796), 1:51.

52. BF, *Catalogue* (1741), 3.

53. BF, *Catalogue* (1741), 22; Hamilton, *History of the Tuesday Club*, 3:109.

54. M. G. Sullivan, "Rapin de Thoyras, Paul de," in *ODNB*, 46:70.

55. BF, *Catalogue*, 4; BF, *Poor Richard Improved, 1750*, in *Papers*, 3:455.

56. BF, *Catalogue* (1741), 5.

57. John Wilkins, *An Essay towards a Real Character, and a Philosophical Language* (London: Sa: Gellibrand, 1668), 415.

58. Umberto Eco, *From the Big Tree to the Labyrinth: Historical Studies on the Sign and Interpretation* (Cambridge, MA: Harvard University Press, 2014), 45.

59. Isabella James, *Memorial of Thomas Potts, Junior, Who Settled in Pennsylvania* (Cambridge, MA: 1874), 381; BF, *Catalogue* (1741), 6.

60. BF, *Catalogue* (1741), 48; Hazel Wilkinson, *Edmund Spenser and the Eighteenth-Century Book* (New York: Cambridge University Press, 2017), 58.

61. Hayes, *Library of John Montgomerie*, no. 620; Hamilton, *History of the Tuesday Club*, 1:119, 2:228.

62. Thomas Jefferson to Samuel Henley, March 3, 1785, *The Papers of Thomas Jefferson*, ed. Julian P. Boyd et al. (Princeton, NJ: Princeton University Press, 1953), 8:13; Wilkinson, *Edmund Spenser*, 140; Thomas Warton, *Observations on The Fairy Queen of Spenser*, 2d ed. (London: R. and J. Dodsley, 1762) (PPL, no. O Eng Wart Obs 1762 1471.D).

63. BF, *Catalogue* (1741), 6, 51.

64. Ibid., 22; Wolf, "First Books," 38.

65. The copy of the 1741 catalogue that Edwin Wolf reproduced in *A Catalogue of Books Belonging to the Library Company of Philadelphia: A Facsimile of the Edition of 1741 Printed by Benjamin Franklin* (Philadelphia: Library Company of Philadelphia, 1956), 33, lists Montaigne's *Essays*, trans. Charles Cotton (London: T. Basset, 1685), which ends with the donor's initials, which had been altered in manuscript to "B. R." Consequently, Wolf and Hayes do not list this title. The American Antiquarian Society copy of the 1741 catalogue clarifies that the donor's initials were indeed "B. F.," so this item should be considered as an addendum to Wolf and Hayes.

66. Montaigne, *Essays*, 1: 265.

67. Robert Newcomb, "Benjamin Franklin and Montaigne," *Modern Language Notes* 72, no. 7 (November 1957): 489–91; Stuart P. Sherman, "Franklin," in *CHAL*, 1:109–110.

68. BF, *Catalogue* (1741), 56.

69. *Norton Critical Edition*, 57; Grimm, "History of the Library Company," 34.

CHAPTER 13

1. Miller, no. 5.

2. Clifford K. Shipton, and James E. Mooney, *National Index of American Imprints through 1800: The Short-Title Evans* (Worcester, MA: American Antiquarian Society and Barre Publishers, 1969), 1:93, 312–13, 387, 414; 2:822.

3. *Genetic Text*, 68.

4. *Genetic Text*, 69; Wolf and Hayes, no. 1849.

5. Lemay, *Life*, 2:171.

6. Miller, nos. 52–54.

7. Miller, no. 54.

8. Sydney George Fisher, *The True Benjamin Franklin* (1898; repr., New York: Skyhorse, 2014), 145.

9. William A. Pencak, *Contested Commonwealths: Essays in American History* (Bethlehem, PA: Lehigh University Press, 2011), 170.

10. *Genetic Text*, 68.

11. Herbert Leibowitz, *Fabricating Lives: Explorations in American Autobiography* (New York: Knopf, 1989), 45; Blake Gopnik, *Warhol* (New York: Ecco, 2020), 120.

12. Tim Nubibus [Samuel Keimer,] "Hue and Cry after the Busy-Body," *Universal Instructor*, March 13, 1729; Lemay, *Life*, 1:388–89.

13. BF, *Poor Richard, 1733*, in *Papers*, 1:315.

14. Elizabeth Carroll Reilly, *A Dictionary of Colonial American Printers' Ornaments and Illustrations* (Worcester, MA: American Antiquarian Society, 1975), 443–46, reproduces the various Men of Signs from the colonial era, making it easy to compare Franklin's with earlier ones.

15. Jason P. Shurley, Jan Todd, and Terry Todd, *Strength Coaching in America: A History of the Innovation that Transformed Sports* (Austin: University of Texas Press, 2019), 15.

16. BF, *Poor Richard, 1734*, in *Papers*, 1:351; Henry David Thoreau, *Walden*, ed. J. Lyndon Shanley (Princeton, NJ: Princeton University Press, 1971), 37.

17. *The National Union Catalog Pre-1956 Imprints* (London: Mansell, 1971), 183:128.

18. Wilfred P. Mustard, "Poor Richard's Poetry," *Nation*, April 5, 1906, 279; Colin Gibson, introduction to *Witts Recreations: Selected from the Finest Fancies of Moderne Muses, 1640* (Aldershot, UK: Scolar Press, 1990), xii–xiii; James N. Green, "Poor Richard's Sources Revisited," in *The Annual Report of the Library Company of Philadelphia for the Year 2004* (Philadelphia: Library Company of Philadelphia, 2005), 17; Samuel Eliot Morison, "The Reverend Seaborn Cotton's Commonplace Book," *Publications of the Colonial Society of Massachusetts* 32 (1937): 323.

19. BF, *Poor Richard, 1733*, in *Papers*, 1:312.

20. *Witts Recreations Refined Augmented, with Ingenious Conceites for the Wittie, and Merrie Medicines for the Melancholie* (London: M. Simmons, 1654), no. 168; Morison, "The Reverend Seaborn Cotton's Commonplace Book," 343; BF, *Poor Richard, 1733*, in *Papers*, 1:313.

21. BF, *Poor Richard, 1733*, in *Papers*, 1:316.

22. Ibid., 317.

23. BF, "Extracts from the *Gazette*, 1733," in *Papers*, 1:347.

24. BF, *Poor Richard, 1734*, in *Papers*, 1:349–50.

25. Ibid., 358.

26. Ibid., 358, 352, 353; BF, *Poor Richard, 1733*, in *Papers*, 1:317.

27. Newcomb, "Sources," 181.

28. *A Collection of Epigrams*, 2d ed. (London: J. Walthoe, 1735), no. 295; BF, *Poor Richard, 1737*, in *Papers*, 2:171.

29. BF, *Poor Richard, 1738*, in *Papers*, 2:191.

30. Ibid., 192.

31. Ibid., 196; Newcomb, "Sources," 339; Francis Bacon, *The Essays, or Councils, Civil and Moral* (London: Timothy Childe, 1701), 135–36.

32. [Jonathan Swift,] "On His Own Deafness," in *A Collection of Epigrams*, no. 412.

33. BF, *Poor Richard, 1739*, in *Papers*, 2:221.

34. A. Franklin Parks, "The Establishment of the Printing Press," in *A History of Virginia Literature*, ed. Kevin J. Hayes (New York: Cambridge University Press, 2015), 78.

35. BF, "Extracts from the *Gazette*, 1745," in *Papers*, 3:58; BF, *Poor Richard, 1746*, in *Papers*, 3:6, 62.

36. BF, *Poor Richard, 1738*, in *Papers*, 2:192.

37. Thomas Fuller, *Directions, Counsels and Cautions, Tending to Prudent Management of Affairs in Common Life* (London: J. Wyat, 1725), 7; Newcomb, "Sources," 264.

38. Newcomb, "Sources," 50.

39. James Howell, *Lexicon tetraglotton: An English-French-Italian-Spanish Dictionary* (London: Thomas Leach, 1660), 4, 12.

40. Charles Augustin Sainte-Beuve, *Portraits of the Eighteenth Century, Historic and Literary*, trans. Katharine P. Wormeley (New York: Putnam, 1905), 333; Wolf and Hayes, no. 1522.

41. Lodovico Guicciardini, *Houres of Recreation, or Afterdinners, which May Aptly Be Called the Garden of Pleasure*, trans. James Sandford (London: Henry Binneman, 1576), 209; BF, *Poor Richard, 1733*, in *Papers*, 1:315.

42. Robert Newcomb, "Franklin and Richardson," *Journal of English and German Philology* 57, no. 1 (January 1958): 35; Miller, nos. 293, 338; Samuel Richardson, *Clarissa: or, The History of a Young Lady*, 3d ed. (London: S. Richardson, 1750–51), 8:364; BF, *Poor Richard Improved, 1752*, in *Papers*, 4:252.

43. Jacob Taylor, *Pennsylvania, 1745: An Almanack* (Philadelphia: Bradford, [1744]), n.p.

44. BF, *Poor Richard, 1747*, in *Papers*, 3:101.

45. Alan D. McKillop, "Some Newtonian Verses in Poor Richard," *New England Quarterly* 21, no. 3 (September 1948): 383–85.

46. BF, *Poor Richard Improved, 1748*, in *Papers*, 3:262.

47. BF, *Poor Richard Improved, 1753*, in *Papers*, 4:408.

48. Andrea Wulf, *Chasing Venus: The Race to Measure the Heavens* (New York: Vintage, 2013), 6; Lemay, *Life*, 3:141.

49. BF to James Bowdoin, February 28, 1753, in *Papers*, 4:446.

50. Miller, no. 574.

51. Jorge Luis Borges, *Other Inquisitions, 1937–1952*, trans. Ruth L. C. Simms (Austin: University of Texas Press, 1975), 11.

52. BF, *Poor Richard Improved, 1756*, in *Papers*, 6:326; Henry Baker, *Medulla poetarum romanorum: or, The Most Beautiful and Instructive Passages of the Roman Poets* (London, 1737), 2:11.

53. Baker, *Medulla*, 1:535; BF, *Poor Richard Improved, 1756*, in *Papers*, 6:326.

54. Baker, *Medulla*, 2:379.

55. BF, *Poor Richard Improved, 1758*, in *Papers*, 7:343.

56. Nathaniel Hawthorne, *Biographical Stories for Children* (Boston: Tappan and Dennet, 1842), 136.

57. Benjamin F. Palmer, *The Diary of Benjamin F. Palmer, Privateersman* (Hartford, CT: Acorn Club, 1914), 20.

58. Yvor Winters, "The Illusion of Reaction (II)," *Kenyon Review* 3, no. 2 (Spring 1941): 238.

59. Russell, *Benjamin Franklin*, 141.

CHAPTER 14

1. John Tennent, *Every Man His Own Doctor: or, The Poor Planter's Physician* (Williamsburg, VA: William Parks, 1734); Giles Jacob, *Every Man His Own Lawyer: or, A Summary of the Laws of England in a New and Instructive Method* (London: E. and R. Nutt, 1736); Thomas Mortimer, *Every Man His Own Broker: or, A Guide to Exchange-Alley* (London: S. Hooper, 1761); Francis Fuller, *Medicinia gymnastica: or, Everyman His Own Physician* (London: E. Curll, 1740); BF, "Books etc Sold by B. Franklin," *PG*, May 21, 1741.

2. BF, "Afterword to *Every Man His Own Doctor*," in *Papers*, 2:156.

3. Douglass, *British Settlements in North-America*, 2:352.

4. John Tennent, *Every Man His Own Doctor: or, The Poor Planter's Physician*, 3d ed. (Philadelphia: B. Franklin, 1734), 8–9.

5. BF, "Afterword," 156–58.

6. Hayes, *Colonial Woman's Bookshelf*, 91; Dr. Alexander Hamilton, *A Defence of Dr. Thomson's Discourse on the Preparation of the Body for the Smallpox* (Philadelphia: W. Bradford, 1751), 14; Philanthropos, "To the Author of the *Poor Planter's Physician*," *General Magazine* 1 (January 1741): 69; Lemay, *Calendar*, no. 599.

7. Raymond Phineas Stearns, *Science in the British Colonies of America* (Urbana: University of Illinois Press, 1970), 289–90.

8. Kevin J. Hayes, *Benjamin Franklin* (London: Reaktion, 2022), 60.

9. Joseph Rogers, *An Essay on Epidemic Diseases* (Dublin: S. Powell, 1734); Wolf and Hayes, no. 2910; Christopher Hamlin, *A Short History of Fever* (Baltimore: Johns Hopkins University Press, 2014), 109–10.

10. Rogers, *Essay on Epidemic Diseases*, 178.

11. BF, *Poor Richard, 1737*, in *Papers*, 2:166; Robert Newcomb, "The Sources of Benjamin Franklin's Sayings of Poor Richard" (Ph.D. diss., University of Maryland, 1957), 184.

12. Miller, nos. 518, 532.

13. Hamilton, *Defence*, 16.

14. Miller, no. 352; Ezra Pound, "L'Homme Moyen Sensuel," *Little Review* 4, no. 5 (September 1917): 16.

15. Stanley Finger, *Doctor Franklin's Medicine* (Philadelphia: University of Pennsylvania Press, 2006), 188.

16. Wolf and Hayes, no, 199; BF to Cadwalader Evans, February 20, 1768, in *Papers*, 15:51–52; George Baker, "An Examination of Several Means, by Which the Poison of Lead May be Supposed Frequently to Gain Admittance into the Human Body," in *Medical Transactions, Published by the College of Physicians in London* (London: S. Baker, 1772), 1:287–88.

17. BF, "Appeal for the Hospital," in *Papers*, 4:147; Kevin J. Hayes, "Benjamin Franklin and 'Good Old Mantuan,'" *Notes and Queries* 67, no. 3 (September 2020): 411–14.

18. Bell, *Patriot-Improvers*, 393.

19. BF to Peter Collinson, 1752, in *Papers*, 4:392–96. The ensuing dialogue comes from this letter and will not be documented separately.

20. Quoted in *Papers*, 3:458–59.

21. Peter Collinson to John Bartram, 1737, in *Memorials of John Bartram and Humphry Marshall, with Notices of Their Botanical Contemporaries*, ed. William Darlington (Philadelphia: Lindsay and Blakiston, 1849), 97; Isabella James, *Memorial of Thomas Potts, Junior, Who Settled in Pennsylvania* (Cambridge, MA, 1874), 54.

22. James, *Memorial of Thomas Potts*, 388.

23. Hannah Benner Roach, "Benjamin Franklin Slept Here," *PMHB* 84, no. 2 (April 1960): 146.

24. Theodore Hornberger, *Benjamin Franklin* (Minneapolis: University of Minnesota Press, 1962), 30.

25. BF, *An Account of the New Invented Pennsylvania Fire-Places*, in *Papers*, 2:424; BF, *A Catalogue of Books Belonging to the Library Company of Philadelphia* (Philadelphia: B. Franklin, 1741), 37.

26. BF, *Account of the New Invented Pennsylvania Fire-Places*, 425.

27. BF, *Catalogue*, 37.

28. BF, *Account of the New Invented Pennsylvania Fire-Places*, 427; *Tchang Seng: or, The Art of Procuring Health and Long Life*, in *The General History of China*, by Jean-Baptiste Du Halde (London: John Watts, 1736), 75.

29. "On the Device of the New Fire-Place," in *Papers*, 2:445–46.

30. J. F. Gronovius to John Bartram, June 2, 1746, in *The Correspondence of John Bartram, 1734–1777*, ed. Edmund Berkeley and Dorothy Smith Berkeley (Gainesville: University Press of Florida, 1992), 278; BF, *Beschreivinge van de Nieuwe Uitgevondene Pensilvanische Schoorsteenen* (Leyden: Cornelis Haak, 1746); BF to Cadwallader Colden, October 16, 1746, in *Papers*, 3:92; Joyce E. Chaplin, *The First Scientific American: Benjamin Franklin and the Pursuit of Genius* (New York: Basic Books, 2006), 96; Karel Davids, "The Scholarly Atlantic: Circuits of Knowledge between Britain, the Dutch Republic and the Americas in the Eighteenth Century," in *Dutch Atlantic Connections, 1680–1800: Linking Empires, Bridging Borders*, ed. Gert Oostindie, and Jesssica V. Roltman (Boston: Brill, 2014), 232.

31. Wolf and Hayes, no. 231; William J. Scheick, "John Bartram," in *American Colonial Writers, 1735–1781*, ed. Emory Elliott (Detroit: Gale, 1984), 25.

32. Wolf and Hayes, no. 1079; Jordan Kellman, "Mendicants, Minimalism, and Method: Franciscan Scientific Travel in the Early Modern French Atlantic," *Journal of Early Modern History* 26 (2022): 11.

33. Kellman, "Mendicants," 23–25.

34. Ibid., 32.

35. Wolf and Hayes, no. 957.

36. [William Bewley,] "Edward's *Gleanings, etc.*," *Monthly Review* 18 (March 1758): 237.

37. Thomas Short, *Medicina britannica: or, A Treatise on such Physical Plants as Are Generally to Be Found in the Fields or Gardens in Great-Britain*, ed. John Bartram, 3d ed. (Philadelphia: B. Franklin and D. Hall, 1751), 31, 287.

38. Short, *Medicina britannica*, 301, 261, 267.

39. John Bartram to Paul Dudley, c. 1738, in *Correspondence*, 106; "A Medical Society in Boston," *Boston Gazette*, October 2, 1738.

40. BF, A *Proposal for Promoting Useful Knowledge*, in *Papers*, 2:381.

41. J. A. Leo Lemay, "Spencer, Archibald," in *ANB*, 20:444–45; Hamilton, *History of the Tuesday Club*, 2:157, 192.

42. Wolf and Hayes, no. 662.

43. BF to William Vassell, June 19, 1746, and to Cadwallader Colden, July 10, 1746, in *Papers*, 3:79–81.

44. Kevin J. Hayes, "Cadwallader Colden," in *American Philosophers before 1950*, ed. Philip B. Dematteis and Leemon B. McHenry (Detroit: Gale, 2003), 52–53.

45. BF to Cadwallader Colden, April 5, 1744, in *Papers*, 2:406–407.

46. John Bartram to Cadwallader Colden, April 29, 1744, and October 4, 1745, *Correspondence*, 238, 261; Bell, *Patriot-Improvers*, 71.

47. Bell, *Patriot-Improvers*, 3; Hayes, *Benjamin Franklin*, 68.

48. BF, *Catalogue*, 19, 26; BF, *Account of the New Invented Pennsylvania Fire-places*, 424; Lemay, *Life*, 3:64.

49. Wolf and Hayes, nos. 3596–3597; Lemay, *Life*, 3:70.

50. Wolf and Hayes, no. 261.

51. Thomas S. Kuhn, *The Structure of Scientific Revolutions*, 4th ed. (Chicago: University of Chicago Press, 2012), 10–11.

52. Lemay, *Life*, 3:65, 67.

53. J. A. Leo Lemay, *Ebenezer Kinnersley, Franklin's Friend* (Philadelphia: University of Pennsylvania Press, 1964), 48–87.

54. Nicholas Scull to Jacob Taylor, July 19, 1743, in Gilbert Cope, "Jacob Taylor, Almanac Maker," *Bulletins of the Chester County Historical Society* (1908), 21.

55. Navin Sullivan, *Pioneer Germ Fighters* (New York: Scholastic, 1963), 1–13, does not meet the scholarly standards set for the present work, but I have a personal reason for citing it. When I was in second grade, our school held a book sale. After considerable browsing, I removed *Pioneer Germ Fighters* from the sale table and handed

it to the lady at the cashbox. Glaring at me through her cat's-eye glasses, Cashbox Lady refused to sell it to me. As I grew angry, she summoned our principal, Mr. Mallet, whose percussive name belies his kindly, soft-spoken nature. Mr. Mallet explained the problem. Written at the sixth-grade level, *Pioneer Germ Fighters* was inappropriate for second-graders. I can read it, I told him. He opened the book at random, pointed to a paragraph, and asked me to read it aloud. And so I did. After I finished reading, Mr. Mallet looked at me and smiled. Then he turned to Cashbox Lady and said, "Sell him the book." And so she did.

56. BF to William Strahan, February 12, 1745, in *Papers*, 3:13–14.

57. Christine Gerrard, "James Thomson, *The Seasons*," in *Companion to Eighteenth-Century Poetry*, ed. Christine Gerrard (Hoboken, NJ: John Wiley, 2006), 201–202.

58. James Thomson, *The Seasons* (London: A. Millar, 1744), lines 222–226.

59. Joseph Breintnall, "On the Lately Discover'd Wild Raspberries," in *Colonial American Poetry*, ed. Kenneth Silverman (New York: Hafner, 1968), 375–76.

60. Frederick B. Tolles, "A Note on Joseph Breintnall, Franklin's Collaborator," *Philological Quarterly* 21, no. 2 (April 1942): 247–49.

61. Erasmus Darwin, *The Botanic Garden* (London: J. Johnson, 1791), v.

62. Edgar Allan Poe, *Complete Poems*, ed. Thomas Ollive Mabbott (Cambridge, MA: Belknap Press, 1969), 91.

CHAPTER 15

1. BF, *Proposals Relating to the Education of Youth in Pensilvania* (Philadelphia, 1749), 4; [Elijah Fenton,] "The Life of Mr. John Milton," in John Milton, *Paradise Lost: A Poem in Twelve Books* (London: Jacob Tonson, 1730), xi.

2. BF, *Proposals*, 4; David Fordyce, *The Elements of Moral Philosophy*, ed. Thomas Kennedy (Indianapolis: Liberty Fund, 2003), ix; Isabel Rivers, *Reason, Grace, and Sentiment: A Study of the Language of Religion and Ethics in England, 1660–1780* (New York: Cambridge University Press, 2000), 2:154.

3. Obadiah Walker, *Of Education, Especially of Young Gentlemen* (Oxford: at the Theater, 1672), 41.

4. BF, *Proposals*, 4; John Adams, *The Earliest Diary of John Adams*, ed. L. H. Butterfield (Cambridge, MA: Belknap Press of Harvard University Press, 1966), 52; Rivers, *Reason, Grace, and Sentiment*, 2:176; George Turnbull, *Observations upon Liberal Education*, ed. Terrence O. Moore, Jr. (Indianapolis: Liberty Fund, 2003), xvii.

5. Theodore Hornberger, *Benjamin Franklin* (Minneapolis: University of Minnesota Press, 1962), 28; Wayne J. Urban and Jennings L. Wagoner, Jr., *American Education: A History* (London: Taylor and Francis, 2013), 48.

6. BF, *Proposals*, 5–6.

7. Ibid., 11.

8. BF, *The Ephemera*, in *Writings* (Lemay), 923; John Wise, *The Churches Quarrel Espoused* (New York: William Bradford, 1713), 88; Whiting, no. A122.

9. BF, *Proposals*, 13–14.

10. Abram Taylor's library list appears in *A Catalogue of Books, Sold by Rivington and Brown* (New York and Philadelphia, 1762), 83–88. The catalogue is anonymous, but Edwin Wolf II, *The Book Culture of a Colonial American City: Philadelphia Books, Bookmen, and Booksellers* (Oxford: Clarendon Press, 1988), 90, identifies it as Taylor's, based on a previous advertisement, "Rivington and Brown," *PG*, May 27, 1762.

11. [BF,] "A Large and Valuable Collection of Books," *New-England Courant*, July 2, 1722; Stuart P. Sherman, "Franklin," in *CHAL*, 1:109.

12. BF, *Proposals*, 20–21.

13. Ibid., 23; Renée Jeffrey, *Hugo Grotius in International Thought* (New York: Palgrave Macmillan, 2006), 77.

14. BF, *Proposals*, 26; Joyce Chapin, *The First Scientific American: Benjamin Franklin and the Pursuit of Genius* (New York: Basic Books, 2007), 70.

15. BF, *Proposals*, 26.

16. Hornberger, *Benjamin Franklin*, 27.

17. BF, "On the Need for an Academy," in *Papers*, 3:387.

18. BF, *Proposals*, 16.

19. Thomas Harrison Montgomery, *A History of the University of Pennsylvania from Its Founding to A.D. 1770* (Philadelphia: George W. Jacobs, 1900), 52.

20. *Genetic Text*, 103–104; Lemay, *Life*, 2:435–36.

21. *Genetic Text*, 118–19; Lemay, *Life*, 3:192–95.

22. Lemay, *Life*, 3:190, 195.

23. Quoted in Jared Sparks, ed., *The Works of Benjamin Franklin* (Philadelphia: Childs and Peterson, 1840), 1:570.

24. Lemay, *Life*, 3:196–97.

25. Quoted in Boyd Stanley Schlenther, *Charles Thomson: A Patriot's Pursuit* (Newark: University of Delaware Press, 1990), 24.

26. BF to Samuel Johnson, October 25, 1750, and "Idea of the English School," in *Papers*, 4:71–72, 102.

27. Samuel Croxall, *Fables of Aesop and Others*, 2d ed. (London: J. Tonson and J. Watts, 1724), sig. A3v.

28. *Catalogue of Books Sold by Rivington and Brown*, 86; BF, *A Catalogue of Books Belonging to the Library Company of Philadelphia* (Philadelphia: B. Franklin, 1741), 50.

29. Samuel Richardson, *Aesop's Fables: With Instructive Morals and Reflections* (London: J. Osborn, 1740), vii.

30. Croxall, *Aesop's Fables*, n.p.

31. BF, "Extracts from the *Gazette*, 1734," in *Papers*, 1:383; Wolf and Hayes, no. 66.

32. Croxall, *Aesop's Fables*, 238.

33. Ibid., 238–39.

34. Natalie M. Phillips, *Distraction: Problems of Attention in Eighteenth-Century Literature* (Baltimore: Johns Hopkins University Press, 2016), 29.

35. BF, *Proposals*, 19–20.

36. Stan V. Henkels, *The Valuable Library of the Hon. Samuel W. Pennypacker: Part II* (Philadelphia: Davis and Harvey, 1906), lot 343; Kevin J. Hayes, *Poe and the Printed Word* (New York: Cambridge University Press, 2000), 11.

37. BF to Mary Stevenson, May 17, 1769, in *Papers*, 9:117.

38. Cynthia J. Koepp, "Acknowledging Artisans and a New Social Order in Abbé Pluche's *Spectacle de la Nature*," *Princeton University Library Chronicle* 68, no. 3 (Spring 2007): 792–94.

39. Kevin J. Hayes, *The Mind of a Patriot: Patrick Henry and the World of Ideas* (Charlottesville: University of Virginia Press, 2008), 138; BF, "Idea of the English School," in *Papers*, 4:105.

40. William Temple to Lord Halifax, March 2, 1668, in *Letters Written by Sir W. Temple, Bart, and Other Ministers of State, Both at Home and Abroad*, ed. Jonathan Swift (London: J. Tonson, 1700), 300–301; A. A. Tilley, "The Essay and the Beginning of Modern English Prose," in *The Cambridge History of English Literature*, ed. A. W. Ward and A. R. Waller (Cambridge, UK: Cambridge University Press, 1920), 8:381.

41. William Temple, *Letters*, 116; Pliny, *The Letters of Pliny the Consul: with Occasional Remarks* (London: R. Dodsley, 1747), 326.

42. BF, *Poor Richard, 1738*, in *Papers*, 2:194.

43. BF, "Idea of the English School," in *Papers*, 4:106; Miller, no. 554.

44. Douglass, *British Settlements in North-America*, 1:165.

45. Mark Garrett Longaker, *Rhetoric and the Republic: Politics, Civic Discourse, and Education in Early America* (Tuscaloosa: University of Alabama Press, 2007), 143.

46. Wolf and Hayes, no. 293.

47. Samuel Johnson to BF, November 1750, in *Papers*, 4:75.

48. William Smith, *A General Idea of the College of Mirania* (New York: J. Parker and W. Weyman, 1753), 15; Robert Middlekauff, *Benjamin Franklin and His Enemies* (Berkeley: University of California Press, 1996), 43.

49. Smith, *General Idea*, 55; Wolf and Hayes, no. 3172.

50. William Smith, *A Poem on Visiting the Academy of Philadelphia, June 1753* (Philadelphia, 1753), 5–6; Miller, no. 582; Lemay, *Life*, 3:201.

51. Kevin J. Hayes, *Benjamin Franklin* (London: Reaktion, 2022), 59.

52. Peter Collinson to BF, August 12, 1753, in *Papers*, 5:20; Lemay, *Life*, 3:203.

53. Lemay, *Life*, 3:203.

54. Schlenther, *Charles Thomson*, 25.

CHAPTER 16

1. BF to William Strahan, July 10, 1743, in *Papers*, 2:383–84.

2. BF to William Strahan, July 4, 1744, in *Papers*, 2:410–11.

3. Glyn Williams, *Voyages of Delusion: The Quest for the Northwest Passage* (New Haven, CT: Yale University Press, 2002), 46–49.

4. Ibid., 54.

5. Ibid., 58.

6. Ibid., 59; Kevin J. Hayes, *George Washington, A Life in Books* (New York: Oxford University Press, 2017), 52–55.

7. Glyn Williams, "George Anson's *Voyage Round the World*," *Princeton University Library Chronicle* 64, no. 2 (Winter 2003): 303–304; Richard Walter, *A Voyage Round the World in the Years MDCCXL,I,II,III, IV by George Anson, Esq.*, 6th ed. (London: Knapton, 1749) (PPL [Log Rm] Am 1749 Ans 77894.O [Wolf]); "Books Just Imported in the Ship *Salisbury*," *PG*, March 14, 1749; John William Wallace, *An Old Philadelphian, Colonel William Bradford, The Patriot Printer of 1776: Sketches of His Life* (Philadelphia: Sherman, 1884), 448.

8. [Richard Walker,] *A Voyage Round the World* (London: Dent, 1942), 151; BF to Richard Jackson, June 1, 1764, in *Papers*, 11:216.

9. C. F. Beckingham, "Lancaster, Sir James," in *ODNB*, 25:379; Clements R. Markham, ed., *The Voyages of Sir James Lancaster, Kt., to the East Indies* (London: for the Hakluyt Society, 1877), 62; BF to Richard Jackson, June 1, 1764, in *Papers*, 11:216.

10. Samuel Purchas, *Hakluytus Posthumus: or, Purchas His Pilgrimes, Contayning a History of the World in Sea Voyages and Lande Travells by Englishmen and Others* (Glasgow: James MacLehose, 1907), 13:387.

11. Williams, *Voyages*, 66, 72.

12. BF, *Poor Richard Improved, 1748*, in *Papers*, 3:245.

13. Ibid., 246.

14. [James Sterling,] *An Epistle to the Hon. Arthur Dobbs, Esq; in Europe from a Clergyman in America* (Dublin: J. Smith, 1752), 13.

15. BF, *Poor Richard Improved, 1748*, in *Papers*, 3:247.

16. Ibid., 248.

17. Glyndwr Williams, "Middleton, Christopher," in *ODNB*, 38:51; Christopher Middleton, *A Vindication of the Conduct of Captain Christopher Middleton, in a Late Voyage on Board His Majesty's Ship the Furnace, for Discovering a North-West Passage to the Western American Ocean* (London: Jacob Robinson, 1743), 163.

18. Douglass, *British Settlements in North-America*, 1:274–75; Peter Collinson to Cadwallader Colden, September 4, 1743, *Forget Not Mee and My Garden: Selected Letters, 1725–1768 of Peter Collinson, F.R.S.*, ed. Alan Armstrong (Philadelphia: American Philosophical Society, 2002), 110.

19. Williams, *Voyages*, 113; Dobbs, *Remarks*, 148; Glyndwr Williams, "Wigate, John, Naval Clerk," in *Dictionary of Canadian Biography*, ed. George W. Brown et al. (Toronto: University of Toronto Press, 1966–), 3:663.

20. Henry Ellis, *A Voyage to Hudson's-Bay, by the Dobbs Galley and California, in the Years 1746 and 1747, for Discovering a North West Passage* (London: H. Whitridge, 1748), 137; *Oxford English Dictionary*, s.v. "snow-blindness."

21. Ellis, *Voyage to Hudson's-Bay*, 330–31; Wolf and Hayes, no. 974.

22. Percy G. Adams, "The Case of Swaine versus Drage: An Eighteenth-Century Publishing Mystery Solved," in *Essays in History and Literature Presented by the Fellows of the Newberry Library to Stanley Pargellis*, ed. Heinz Bluhm (Chicago: Newberry Library, 1965), 157–68; Percy Adams, "The Man Who Married Hannah Boyte, and Other Cases from the Files of a Scholar-Detective," *Soundings* 82, nos. 1–2 (Spring/Summer 1999): 191–202; [Charles Swaine,] *An Account of a Voyage for the Discovery of a North-West Passage by Hudson's Streights, to the Western and Southern Ocean of America* (London: Joliffe, 1748), 1:16; Wolf and Hayes, no. 3299.

23. Douglass, *British Settlements in North-America*, 1:275.

24. William Barr and Glyndwr Williams, eds., *Voyages to Hudson Bay in Search of a Northwest Passage, 1741–1747* (London: Hakluyt Society, 1995), 2:355.

25. BF to Jared Eliot, April 12, 1753, in *Papers*, 4:466; BF to John Pringle, May 22, 1762, in *Papers*, 10:95; Wolf and Hayes, no. 872.

26. BF to John Pringle, May 27, 1762, in *Papers*, 10:96–97.

27. Hamilton, *History of the Tuesday Club*, 3:193; Joachim Camerarius, *Symbolurum ac emblematum ethico-politicorum* (Mainz: Ludocvici Bourgeat, 1702), 176. A four-volume set with 100 emblems per volume, this Latin work has never been translated into English, but British educator and essayist Vicesimus Knox coined the English title, the "Centuries of Camerarius." See Vicesimus Knox, *Essays Moral and Literary*, 5th ed. (London: Charles Dilly, 1784), 2:266.

28. Sterling, *Epistle to the Hon. Arthur Dobbs*, 26.

29. A. Owen Aldridge, *The Dragon and the Eagle: The Presence of China in the American Enlightenment* (Detroit: Wayne State University Press, 1993), 83.

30. *A Catalogue of Books, Sold by Rivington and Brown* (New York and Philadelphia, 1762), 87.

31. J. A. Leo Lemay, *Men of Letters in Colonial Maryland* (Knoxville: University of Tennessee Press, 1972), 271–72; Peter Collinson to BF, January 27, 1753, in *Papers*, 4:414.

32. "Petition of the Merchants of Philadelphia to the King," November 18, 1752?, in *Papers*, 4:380–84.

33. Lemay, *Life*, 3:154–55.

34. [Charles Swaine,] *The Great Probability of a North West Passage: Deduced from Observations on the Letter of Admiral De Fonte* (London: Thomas Jeffrys, 1768), 137–38.

35. BF to Richard Jackson, December 6, 1753, in *Papers*, 5:148.

36. Lemay, *Life*, 3:156.

37. "Philadelphia, May 2," *PG*, May 2, 1754; "Philadelphia, October 24," *PG*, October 24, 1754.

38. "Philadelphia," *Pennsylvania Journal*, October 24, 1754; Robert Levers to William Parsons, October 1754, in Edwin Swift Balch, "Artic Expeditions Sent from the American Colonies," *PMHB* 31, no. 4 (1907), 425.

39. Swaine, *Great Probability*, xii.

40. Balch, "Artic Expeditions," 425; *Charter, Laws, and Catalogue of Books of the Library Company of Philadelphia* (Philadelphia: B. Franklin and D. Hall, 1757), 22; *The Charter, Laws, and Catalogue of Books, of the Library Company of Philadelphia* (Philadelphia: B. Franklin and D. Hall, 1764), 25.

41. Wolf and Hayes, no. 902.

42. Wolf and Hayes, no. 542; BF, "Franklin's List of Books Lent, November 1778," in *Papers*, 28:179.

43. BF to Samuel Cooper, April 27, 1769, in *Papers*, 16:117; Jonathan Carver, *Travels through the Interior Parts of North-America, in the Years 1766, 1767, and 1768* (London: for the author, 1778), 540–41.

44. Henry Russell, "Rogers, Robert," in *ANB*, 18:772; Wolf and Hayes, no. 2911; Robert Rogers to BF, May 4, 1770, in *Papers*, 17:135.

45. Robert Rogers to BF, February 20, 1772, in *Papers*, 19:80; Wolf and Hayes, no. 2912.

46. John Adams, *Diary and Autobiography of John Adams*, ed. L. H. Butterfield (Cambridge, MA: Belknap Press, 1961), 3:108–109, 139–40; Wolf and Hayes, no. 224.

CHAPTER 17

1. Wolf and Hayes, no. 2484, does not identify Franklin's copy of Onasander as Peter Whitehorne's translation, but the bibliographical information in Fred Schurink, "War, What Is It Good For?: Sixteenth-Century English Translation of Ancient Texts on Warfare," *Renaissance Cultural Crossroads: Translation, Print and Culture in Britain*, ed. Sara K. Barker and Brenda M. Hosington (Leiden: Brill, 2013), 130–31, lets me identify it more precisely now.

2. Kenneth F. A. Openchowski, "The Role and Location of the Commander," *Military Review* 57, no. 4 (April 1977): 13.

3. Onasander, *Onosandro Platonico: Of the Generall Captaine, and of His Office*, trans. Peter Whitehorne (London: William Seres, 1563), fol. 11, 6.

4. *The Art of War in Four Parts* (London: J. Morphew, 1707), sig. A3v.

5. Ibid., sig. A3v–A4r.

6. *Oxford English Dictionary*, s.v. "contravallation"; Louis de Gaya, *The Art of War and the Way that It is at Present Practised in France* (London: Robert Harford, 1678), 113; *The Athenian Oracle: being an Entire Collection of All the Valuable Questions and Answers in the Old Athenian Mercuries* (London: Andrew Bell, 1703), 2:277.

7. Charles Ffoulkes, Introduction to *Gaya's Traité des armes, 1678*, ed. Charles Ffoulkes (Oxford: Clarendon Press, 1911), xxii.

8. Archibald Lovell, "The Epistle Dedicatory," in Sieur de la Fontaine, *Military Duties of the Officers of Cavalry, Containing the Way of Exercising the Horse, According to the Practice of This Present Time*, trans. Archibald Lovell (London: Robert Harford, 1678), sig. A3v.

9. Douglass, *British Settlements in North-America*, 1:336; Lemay, *Life*, 2:352.

10. Wolf and Hayes, nos. 425, 1266.

11. Lemay, *Life*, 2:314; Sheila L. Skemp, *William Franklin: Son of a Patriot, Servant of a King* (New York: Oxford University Press, 1990), 10–11; BF to William Strahan, November 28, 1747, in *Papers*, 3:214.

12. BF to William Strahan, October 19, 1748, in *Papers*, 3:321; Wolf and Hayes, nos. 425, 1266.

13. BF to William Strahan, June 1, 1747, in *Papers*, 3:140; Wolf and Hayes, nos. 1080, 2547.

14. James Falkner, "Parker, Robert," in *ODNB*, 42:735.

15. Stephen Austen, "The Publisher's Preface," in Robert Parker, *Memoirs of the Most Remarkable Military Transactions from the Year 1683, to 1718* (London: S. Austen, 1747).

16. "The Translator's Preface," in Marquis de Feuquières, *Memoirs Historical and Military: Containing a Distinct View of All the Considerable States of Europe* (London: T. Woodward, 1736), xx–xxi.

17. William C. Lowe, "Lindsay, John, Twentieth Earl of Crawford and Fourth Earl of Lindsay," in *ODNB*, 33:881.

18. Wolf and Hayes, nos. 751–758.

19. *ESTC*, no. R217907; BF, *A Catalogue of Books Belonging to the Library Company of Philadelphia* (Philadelphia: B. Franklin, 1741), 48.

20. X., ["A Translation of the Sentences Prefix'd to the Pamphlet Call'd *Plain Truth*,"] *PG*, November 19, 1747.

21. Miller, nos. 416–417, 413; "To Be Sold by B. Franklin," *PG*, December 3, 1747.

22. H. M. Stephens and Richard Harding, "Blakeney, William, Baron Blakeney," in *ODNB*, 6:133; Stephen Saunders Webb, *Marlborough's America* (New Haven, CT: Yale University Press, 2013), 205; "The New Manual Exercise," *General Magazine* 1 (February–March 1741): 127–31, 153–58.

23. Lemay, *Life*, 3:33.

24. *Genetic Text*, 110; Lemay, *Life*, 3:33; Sally F. Griffith, " 'Order, Discipline, and a Few Cannon': Benjamin Franklin, the Association, and the Rhetoric and Practice of Boosterism," *PMHB* 116, no. 2 (April 1992): 152; *A Catalogue of Books, Sold by Rivington and Brown* (New York and Philadelphia, 1762), 86; BF, *A Catalogue of Choice and Valuable Books* (Philadelphia: B. Franklin, 1744), 8; Miller, no. 413.

25. "Philadelphia, May 26," *PG*, May 26, 1748.

26. Philomuseus [Adam Thomson,] "An Ode, Humbly Inscribed to the Associators of Pennsylvania," *PG*, September 1, 1748; Lemay, *Calendar*, no. 886.

27. Robert Harford, *English Military Discipline; or, The Way and Method of Exercising Horse and Foot* (London: Robert Harford, 1680), 112–13; BF, "Colors of the Associator Companies," in *Papers*, 3:268–69.

28. BF, "Colors," 268–69; Lemay, *Life*, 3:44.

29. Stan V. Henkels, *The Extraordinary Library of Hon. Samuel W. Pennypacker, Governor of Pennsylvania: Part I* (Philadelphia: Davis and Harvey, 1905), lot 61.

30. Miller, no. 456; Wolf and Hayes, nos. 3331–3332, 3165.

31. [Nicholas Scull,] *Kawanio che keeteru: A True Relation of a Bloody Battle Fought between George and Lewis, in the Year 1755* ([Philadelphia,] 1756), 10.

32. Quoted in *Papers*, 3:186.

33. Kevin J. Hayes, "The Board of Trade's '*cruel* Sarcasm': A Neglected Franklin Source," *Early American Literature* 28, no. 2 (1993): 171–76.

34. BF, "Rattlesnakes for Felons," in *Writings* (Lemay), 360.

35. BF to William Strahan, August 20, 1752, in *Papers*, 4:352.

36. J. S. G. Blair, "Pringle, Sir John, First Baronet," in *ODNB*, 45:399.

37. Eliga H. Gould, "To Strengthen the King's Hands: Dynastic Legitimacy, Militia Reform and Ideas on National Unity in England, 1745–1760," *Historical Journal* 34, no. 2 (June 1991): 339–40.

38. Lemay, *Life*, 3:315, 337.

39. Hutcheson Macaulay Posnett, "Benjamin Franklin," *Westminster Review* 168, no. 6 (December 1907): 637–38.

40. Lemay, *Life*, 3:389.

41. Posnett, "Benjamin Franklin," 638.

42. James Belich, "Grey, Sir George," in *ODNB*, 23:843–44.

43. Jack Kerouac, *On the Road* (1957; repr., New York; Penguin, 2016), 105–106.

44. BF, "Pennsylvania Assembly: Reply to the Governor," in *Papers* 6:242.

45. BF to James Read, November 2, 1755, in *Papers*, 6:235.

46. A. O. Exquemelin, *The History of the Bucaniers: Being an Impartial Relation of All the Battels, Sieges, and Other Most Eminent Assaults Committed for Several Years upon the Coasts of the West-Indies by the Pirates of Jamaica and Tortuga* (London: Tho. Malthus, 1684), 187–88.

47. Thomas Lloyd to ———, January 30 [31?], 1756, in *Papers*, 6:381.

48. Wolf and Hayes, no. 758; J. Bennett Nolan, *General Benjamin Franklin: The Military Career of a Philosopher* (1936; repr., Philadelphia: University of Pennsylvania Press, 1953), 68.

49. Lemay, *Life*, 3:554.

50. BF to William Strahan, January 31, 1757, in *Papers*, 7:115–16.

CHAPTER 18

1. Kevin J. Hayes, "New Light on Peter and King, the Two Slaves Benjamin Franklin Brought to England," *Notes and Queries* 60, no. 2 (June 2013): 205.

2. *Genetic Text*, 166; James Kennedy, *A Description of the Antiquities and Curiosities in Wilton-House* (Salisbury, UK: E. Easton, 1769), 13.

3. Sydney George Fisher, *The True Benjamin Franklin* (1898; repr., New York: Skyhorse, 2014), 211; BF to Mary Stevenson, May 17, 1760, in *Papers*, 9:117.

4. Hayes, *Colonial Woman's Bookshelf*, 128–29.

5. BF, *Experiments and Observations on Electricity* (London: David Henry, 1769), 444–63, 469.

6. BF to Mary Stevenson, [November 1760?], in *Papers*, 9:251; Walter Hopps, "Introduction: Rauschenberg's Art of Fusion," in *Robert Rauschenberg: A Retrospective*, ed. Walter Hopps and Susan Davidson (New York: Guggenheim Museum, 1997), 20.

7. George Simpson Eddy, "Account Book of Benjamin Franklin Kept by Him During His First Mission to England as Provincial Agent, 1757–1762," *PMHB* 55, no. 2 (1931): 102, 107, 112, 118; Wolf and Hayes, no. 3500.

8. *Genetic Text*, 166–67.

9. *Genetic Text*, 167.

10. *Genetic Text*, 168.

11. David T. Morgan, *The Devious Dr. Franklin, Colonial Agent: Benjamin Franklin's Years in London* (Macon, GA: Mercer University Press, 1996), 27.

12. BF to John Fothergill, October 1757?, in *Papers*, 7:271.

13. William Congreve, *Love for Love: A Comedy* (London: Jacob Tonson, 1704), 14; "The Royal Bagnio," *London Public Advertiser*, January 10, 1757.

14. BF to Mary Stevenson, June 11, 1760, in *Papers*, 9:120.

15. BF to the Earl of Buchan, March 17, 1783, in *Papers*, 39:346.

16. Eddy, "Account Book," 104; Wolf and Hayes, no. 1280; "Monthly Catalogue," *Monthly Review* 17 (October 1757): 377.

17. *A Genuine Account of the Late Grand Expedition to the Coast of France* (London: R. Griffiths, 1757), 41–42.

18. Wolf and Hayes, no. 1876; "Miscellaneous," *Monthly Review* 18 (June 1758): 623.

19. BF to Deborah Franklin, November 22, 1757, in *Papers*, 7:276; Eddy, "Account Book," 105.

20. "A List of Subscribers," in Susan Smythies, *The Brothers* (London: R. and J. Dodsley, 1758).

21. "Dr. Franklin's Life," *Saturday Review*, January 22, 1859, 102; Hutcheson Macaulay Posnett, "Benjamin Franklin," *Westminster Review* 168, no. 6 (December 1907): 640.

22. Eddy, "Account Book," 107; [Richard Twiss,] *Chess* (London: Robinson, 1787), 190; Wolf and Hayes, no. 2646.

23. Thomas Osborne, "Bill and Receipt," September 27, 1758, in *Papers*, 8:169; Isaac Norris to BF, April 7, 1757, in *Papers*, 7:176; BF to Hugh Roberts, September 16, 1758, in *Papers*, 8:160.

24. Edwin Wolf, 2nd, introduction to Marie Elena Korey, *The Books of Isaac Norris (1701–1766) at Dickinson College* (Carlisle, PA: Dickinson College, 1976), 6.

25. Alexander Pope, *The Dunciad, in Four Books* (London: M. Cooper, 1743), book 2, lines 155–158.

26. BF to David Hall, April 8, 1759, in *Papers*, 8:319–20.

27. Wolf and Hayes, no. 3500.

28. Verner W. Crane, "The Club of Honest Whigs: Friends of Science and Liberty," *William and Mary Quarterly* 23, no. 2 (April 1966): 214–15.

29. John Nichols, *Literary Anecdotes of the Eighteenth Century* (London: for the author, 1812), 5:313.

30. Abraham Rees, *Cyclopaedia*, s.v. "Furneaux, Philip."

31. James Boswell, *The Journal of James Boswell, 1769*, ed. Geoffrey Scott (Mount Vernon, NY: Rudge, 1930), 122; Josiah Quincy, Jr, "The London Journal, 1774–1775," in *Portrait of a Patriot: The Major Political and Legal Papers of Josiah Quincy, Junior*, ed. Daniel R. Coquillette and Neil Longley York (Boston: Colonial Society of Massachusetts, 2007), 1:244; BF to Benjamin Vaughan, March 14, 1785, in *Papers*, 43:492; Wolf and Hayes, no. 2155.

32. John Densham to John Canton, August 26, 1769, "The Canton Papers," *Athenaeum*, February 17, 1849, 163; Robert Aspland, "A Conversation with Franklin's London Friends, 1821," in Hayes and Bour, 146.

33. Abraham Rees, *A Sermon Preached at the Meeting House . . . upon Occasion of the Much Lamented Death of the Rev. Andrew Kippis* (London: G. G. and J. Robinson, 1795), 33–34; Andrew Kippis, *Biographia Britannica: or, The Lives of the Most Eminent Persons Who Have Flourished in Great Britain and Ireland* (London: A. and A. Strahan, 1778), 1:31. Not in Wolf and Hayes, this manuscript is known solely by Kippis's reference to it.

34. Benjamin Christian Nangle, *The Monthly Review, First Series, 1749–1789: Indexes of Contributors and Articles* (Oxford: Clarendon Press, 1934), 1:16–37. Subsequent attributions of *Monthly Review* articles come from Nangle and will not be documented separately.

35. Brian Hill, "The Philosopher of Massingham, William Bewley, 1726–1783," *Practitioner* 196 (April 1966): 580–84.

36. Wolf and Hayes, no. 2959; BF, *Political, Miscellaneous, and Philosophical Pieces*, ed. Benjamin Vaughan (London: J. Johnson, 1779), 63.

37. BF to Thomas Hubbard, April 28, 1758, in *Papers*, 8:53; Charles Thomson to BF, May 14, 1758, in *Papers*, 8:79.

38. Isaac Norris to BF, May 26, 1758, in *Papers*, 8:80.

39. Wolf and Hayes, nos. 2329, 2331.

40. Miller, no. 79.

41. BF to Isaac Norris, January 14, 1758, in *Papers*, 7:361–62.

42. Hayes, "New Light on Peter and King," 207.

43. Daniel Defoe, *A Tour thro' the Whole Island of Great Britain*, 4th ed. (London: S. Birt, 1748), 2:411–12; Ronald S. Crane, "The Vogue of Guy of Warwick from the Close of the Middle Ages to the Romantic Revival," *PMLA* 30, no. 2 (1915): 169.

44. Thomas J. Haslam, " 'In Compliance with the Advice Contained in These Letters': Benjamin Franklin's Correspondence Networks and the Making of the *Autobiography*," *Rupkatha Journal on Interdisciplinary Studies in Humanities* 9, no. 3 (2017): 83.

45. Wolf and Hayes, no. 2404.

46. Wolf and Hayes, no. 2246.

47. Wolf and Hayes, nos. 894–895.

48. Laurence Sterne, *The Life and Opinions of Tristram Shandy, Gentleman* (London: Oxford University Press, 1928), 66.

49. [William Rose,] "Douglass's Summary of the British Settlements in North-America," *Monthly Review* 13, no. 4 (October 1755): 268.

50. Douglass, *British Settlements in North-America*, 2:243; BF, *The Interest of Great Britain Considered* in *Papers*, 9:70.

51. BF, "A Defense of the Americans," in *Writings* (Lemay), 518–30.

52. Wolf and Hayes, no. 3471; BF to Deborah Franklin, [January 1758], in *Papers*, 7:368.

53. William Whitehead, *A Charge to the Poets* (London: R. and J. Dodsley, 1762), 14; Wolf and Hayes, no. 3471.

54. BF to Mary Stevenson, March 25, 1763, in *Papers*, 10:234.

55. Wolf and Hayes, nos. 888, 131, 1275, 2020, 2039, 473, 2961.

56. Wolf and Hayes, no. 473.

57. Kevin J. Hayes, "Benjamin Mecom," in *ANB*, 15:232–33.

58. "Meadley's *Life of Paley*," *British Critic* 37 (April 1811): 330; Thomas J. Haslam, "Benjamin Franklin, David Hume, Autobiography, and the Jealousy of Empire," in *Finding Colonial America: Essays Honoring J. A. Leo Lemay*, ed. Carla Mulford and David S. Shields (Newark: University of Delaware Press, 2001), 301.

59. BF, *The Interest of Great Britain Considered*, in *Papers*, 9:91.

60. BF, "Causes of the American Discontents before 1768," in *Papers*, 15:3.

CHAPTER 19

1. Kevin J. Hayes, "Libraries and Learned Societies," in *Encyclopedia of the North American Colonies*, ed. Jacob Ernest Cooke (New York: Scribners, 1993), 3:129.

2. Ibid.

3. John C. Van Horne, ed., *Religious Philanthropy and Colonial Slavery: The American Correspondence of the Associates of Dr. Bray, 1717–1777* (Urbana: University of Chicago Press, 1985), 509.

4. BF to John Waring, January 3, 1758, in Van Horne, *Religious Philanthropy*, 124.

5. William Sturgeon to John Waring, June 12, 1759, and Deborah Franklin to BF, August 9, 1759, in Van Horne, *Religious Philanthropy*, 136–37.

6. BF to Deborah Franklin, March 28, 1760?, in *Papers*, 9:38.

7. Van Horne, *Religious Philanthropy*, 20–23.

8. John Waring to Thomas Dawson, February 29, 1760, in Van Horne, *Religious Philanthropy*, 146.

9. Henry Dixon, *The English Instructor: or, The Art of Spelling Improved* (London: C. Hitch, 1760), 7, 10, 11, 13.

10. Miller, no. 11.

11. Brontë Short, " 'It Is a Terror . . . that Men Should Be Handeled So in Pennsylvania': Early Quaker Reasoning, Debate, and the Abolitionist Influence of *The*

Germantown Friends' Protest against Slavery," *Pennsylvania History* 90, no. 1 (2023): 112–13; BF to John Wright, November 4, 1789, in *Writings* (Lemay), 1172; [George Keith,] *An Exhortation and Caution to Friends Concerning Buying or Keeping of Negroes* [New York: William Bradford, 1693] (not in Wolf and Hayes).

12. Keith, *Exhortation and Caution*, 1–3.

13. Miller, no. 31.

14. Paul Rosier, "Lay, Benjamin," in *ANB*, 13:305.

15. Roberts Vaux, *Memoirs of the Lives of Benjamin Lay and Ralph Sandiford, Two of the Earliest Public Advocates for the Emancipation of the Enslaved Africans* (Philadelphia: Solomon W. Conrad, 1815), 25–27.

16. Benjamin Rush, "The Wisdom and Experience of Mellow Old Age," in Hayes and Bour, 106–107; Marcus Rediker, *The Fearless Benjamin Lay; The Quaker Dwarf Who Became the First Revolutionary Abolitionist* (Boston: Beacon Press, 2017), 73.

17. Michael E. Woods, "A Theory of Moral Outrage: Indignation and Eighteenth-Century British Abolitionism," *Slavery and Abolition* 36, no. 4 (2015): 662–83.

18. Benjamin Lay, *All Slave-Keepers that Keep the Innocent in Bondage Apostates* (Philadelphia: for the author, 1737), 110.

19. BF to Deborah Franklin, June 10, 1758, in *Papers*, 8:92; David Waldstreicher, *Runaway America: Benjamin Franklin, Slavery, and the American Revolution* (New York: Hill and Wang, 2004), 82.

20. Lemay, *Life*, 2:426; Miller, no. 224.

21. George Whitefield, "A Letter from the Rev. Mr. George Whitefield to the Inhabitants of Maryland, Virginia, North and South Carolina," *PG*, April 17, 1740.

22. Lemay, *Life*, 2:278; Kevin J. Hayes, "New Light on Peter and King, the Two Slaves Benjamin Franklin Brought to England," *Notes and Queries* 60, no. 2 (June 2013): 205.

23. BF, "Observations Concerning the Increase of Mankind," in *Papers*, 4:231.

24. Ibid., 229.

25. BF, *The Interest of Great Britain Considered, with Regard to Her Colonies, and the Acquisitions of Canada and Guadaloupe; to which Are Added, Observations Concerning the Increase of Mankind, Peopling of Countries, etc.* (London: T. Becket, 1760), 52; Maurice Jackson, *Let This Voice Be Heard: Anthony Benezet, Father of Atlantic Abolitionism* (Philadelphia: University of Pennsylvania Press, 2009), 111.

26. BF, "Observations Concerning the Increase of Mankind," in *Papers*, 4:234.

27. Hayes, "New Light," 208.

28. Ibid., 208–209.

29. Quoted in William S. Bartlett, *The Frontier Missionary: A Memoir of the Life of the Rev. Jacob Bailey, A.M.* (Boston: Ide and Dutton, 1853), 63.

30. Ronald W. Clark, *Benjamin Franklin: A Biography* (1983; repr. London: Phoenix, 2001), 170.

31. BF to John Waring, December 17, 1763, in Van Horne, *Religious Philanthropy*, 204.

32. *A Plan for Improving the Trade at Senegal* (London: R. and J. Dodsley, 1763), 2–3.

33. Ibid., 3.

34. Thomas Jefferson Hogg, *The Life of Percy Bysshe Shelley* (London: Edward Moxon, 1858), 2:292–93.

35. BF, *Poor Richard, 1747*, in *Papers*, 3:106; Kevin Kenny, *Peaceable Kingdom Lost: The Paxton Boys and the Destruction of William Penn's Holy Experiment* (New York: Oxford University Press, 2009), 7, 152.

36. John Updike, "Many Bens," *New Yorker*, February 22, 1988, 108.

37. BF, *A Narrative of the Late Massacres*, in *Papers*, 11:48; Alfred Owen Aldridge, *Benjamin Franklin, Philosopher and Man* (Philadelphia: Lippincott, 1965), 112–13.

38. BF, *Narrative of the Late Massacres*, in *Papers*, 11:55.

39. Kevin J. Hayes, "Benjamin Franklin," in *OHEAL*, 439.

40. BF, *Narrative of the Late Massacres*, in *Papers*, 11:62.

41. Alexander Pope, trans. *The Odyssey of Homer*, vol. 5 (London: Bernard Lintot, 1726), book 18, line 107.

42. Wolf and Hayes, no. 293.

43. BF, "A Conversation on Slavery," in *Papers*, 17:43–44.

44. Wolf and Hayes, no. 57; *Encyclopaedia Britannica*, 11th ed., s.v. "Adanson, Michel."

45. "The Translator's Preface," in Michel Adanson, *A Voyage to Senegal, the Isle of Goree, and the River Gambia* (London: J. Nourse, 1759), vii–viii.

46. Adanson, *Voyage to Senegal*, 54.

47. Ibid., 254.

48. Wolf and Hayes, no. 270; Jack P. Greene, *Evaluating Empire and Confronting Colonialism in Eighteenth-Century Britain* (New York: Cambridge University Press, 2013), 186; [William Bollan,] *Britannia libera: or, A Defence of the Free State of Man in England* (London: J. Almon, 1772), 43.

49. [Andrew Kippis,] "Britannia libera," *Monthly Review* 46 (May 1772): 535.

50. Anthony Benezet to BF, April 27, 1772, in *Papers*, 19:113, 115; Anthony Benezet, *Some Historical Account of Guinea* (Philadelphia: Joseph Crukshank, 1771), 87 (not in Wolf and Hayes).

51. Benezet, *Some Historical Account of Guinea*, 15–17.

CHAPTER 20

1. Stuart P. Sherman, "Franklin," in *CHAL*, 1:98.

2. Eric Nellis, *An Empire of Regions: A Brief History of Colonial British America* (Toronto: University of Toronto Press, 2010), 316.

3. BF to Cadwalader Evans, May 9, 1766, in *Papers*, 13:269.

4. Alfred Owen Aldridge, *Benjamin Franklin, Philosopher and Man* (Philadelphia: Lippincott, 1965), 138.

5. BF to Deborah Franklin, June 13, 1766, in *Papers*, 13:315–16.

6. [BF,] "Method of Making Salt-Petre at Hanover, 1766," in *Several Methods of Making Salt-Petre; Recommended to the Inhabitants of the United Colonies by Their Representatives in Congress* (Philadelphia: W. and T. Bradford, 1755), 7–8.

7. BF to Mary Stevenson, September 14, 1767, in *Papers*, 14:251.

8. Ibid., 255.

9. William Caslon to William Temple Franklin, June 20, 1780, in Digital Edition; Christopher Smart, *Poems on Several Occasions* (London: W. Strahan, 1752), 211–13.

10. BF to Benjamin Vaughan, July 31, 1786, in *Writings* (Lemay), 1165–66.

11. Wolf and Hayes, no. 740.

12. George Simpson Eddy, "Account Book of Benjamin Franklin Kept by Him during His First Mission to England as Provincial Agent, 1757–1762," *PMHB* 55, no. 2 (1931): 106.

13. Abraham Rees, *Cyclopaedia*, s.v. "Chappe d'Auteroche."

14. Thomas D. Cope, "Some Contacts of Benjamin Franklin with Mason and Dixon and Their Work," *Proceedings of the American Philosophical Society* 95, no. 3 (June 12, 1951): 232; Wolf and Hayes, no. 1062; [William Bewley,] "Ferguson's *Method of Determining the Parallax of Venus, &c.*," *Monthly Review* 24 (March 1761): 180.

15. Andrea Wulf, *Chasing Venus: The Race to Measure the Heavens* (New York: Vintage, 2012), 38, 62.

16. Ibid., 49, 60, 65, 92.

17. "List of Fossils Sent by George Croghan to the Earl of Shelburne and Benjamin Franklin," February 7, 1767, in *Papers*, 14:28–29; BF to Jean Chappe d'Auteroche, January 31, 1768, in *Papers*, 15:34; Jean Chappe d'Auteroche, *Voyage en Sibérie* (Paris: Debure, 1768), 1:684–85; [William Bewley,] "Philosophical Transactions, for the Year 1768," *Monthly Review* 42 (February 1770): 110.

18. Cope, "Some Contacts," 235–36.

19. Randolph Cock, "'The Finest Invention in the World': The Royal Navy's Early Trials of Copper Sheathing, 1708–1770," *Mariner's Mirror* 87, no. 4 (November 2001): 453; Douglass, *British Settlements in North-America*, 1:125.

20. John Hawkesworth, *An Account of the Voyages Undertaken by the Order of His Present Majesty, for Making Discoveries in the Southern Hemisphere, and Successively Performed by Commodore Byron, Captain Wallis, Captain Carteret, and Captain Cook* (London: W. Strahan and T. Cadell, 1773), 1:458 (American Philosophical Society, no. 910.4 C77.f.v.1–3).

21. Wolf and Hayes, nos. 2836, 3105, 1589, 1698.

22. [Ralph Griffiths,] "Hasselquist's *Voyages and Travels*," *Monthly Review* 34 (February 1766): 128–29.

23. BF to John Pringle, December 1, 1762, in *Papers*, 10:158–59.

24. [William Bewley,] "Franklin's *Experiments, &c. on Electricity*," *Monthly Review* 42 (March 1770): 199.

25. *Genetic Text*, xx; Herbert Leibowitz, *Fabricating Lives: Explorations in American Autobiography* (New York: Knopf, 1989), 54.

26. D. W. Brogan, "Life of a Salesman," *Spectator*, September 9, 1949, 331.

27. Wolf and Hayes, no. 442.

28. Charles Tanford, *Ben Franklin Stilled the Waves: An Informal History of Pouring Oil on Water with Reflections on the Ups and Downs of Scientific Life in General* (New York: Oxford University Press, 2004), 85–86.

29. BF to Jacques Barbeu-Dubourg, [November 12–16 1772,] in *Writings* (Smyth) 5:552–53; BF to Deborah Franklin, July 14, 1772, in *Papers*, 19:207.

30. [Mary Hewson,] "Extract from a Copy of Verses on William Hewson, Esquire," in *Forty Years' Correspondence between Geniusses ov Boath Sexes, and James Elphinston* (London: W. Ritchardson, 1791), 6:210. Elphinston edited the poem according to his idiosyncratic method of spelling, which is regularized here.

31. David Turnquist, "A Brief History of Benjamin Franklin's Residences on Craven Street, London: 1757–1775," *Journal of the American Revolution*, March 23, 2016, allthingsliberty.com.

32. BF to William Franklin, November 3–4, 1772, in *Papers*, 19:361.

33. [William Bewley,] "Hawkesworth's *Account of the Voyages for Making Discoveries in the Southern Hemisphere, &c.*," *Monthly Review* 49 (August 1773): 137.

34. Hawkesworth, *Account of the Voyages*, 1:4.

35. Ibid.; Wolf and Hayes, no. 1543.

36. Hawkesworth, *Account of the Voyages*, 5.

37. Jeremy Bentham, *The Works*, ed. John Bowring (Edinburgh: William Tait, 1843) 10:59.

38. BF, "Journal of Negotiations in London," in *Papers*, 21:581.

39. Ibid., 583.

40. William Franklin to BF, December 24, 1774, in *Papers*, 21:402–403.

41. Joseph Priestley, "Science, Religion, and Politics in London, 1769, 1795, 1802," in Hayes and Bour, 43.

CHAPTER 21

1. ["A Mighty Argument with Popularity,"] *Public Ledger*, March 12, 1774.

2. BF to Joseph Priestley, May 16, 1775, in *Papers*, 22:44; Whiting, no. O25.

3. Kevin J. Hayes, "Benjamin Franklin and 'Good Old Mantuan,'" *Notes and Queries* 67, no. 3 (September 2020): 412.

4. *Catalogus bibliothecae loganianae* (Philadelphia: Peter Miller, 1760), 80; Wolf, *Library of James Logan*, no. 1737.

5. BF, "Account of the Devices on the Continental Bills of Credit," in *Writings* (Lemay), 734.

6. Diego Saavedra, *The Royal Politician Represented in One Hundred Emblems*, trans. James Astrey (London: Matt. Gylliflower, 1700), 2:95–96.

7. Karl Enenkel, "Camerarius's Quadrupeds (1595): A Plinius Emblematicus as a Mirror of Princes," in *Emblems and the Natural World*, ed. Karl A. E. Enenkel and Paul J. Smith (Boston: Brill, 2017), 92.

8. Ibid., 97.

9. Joachim Camerarius, *Symbolorum ac emblematum ethico-politicorum centuriae quatuor* (Mainz: Ludovici Bourgeat, 1702), 1:22, 34; Marin Le Roy, sieur de Gomberville, *Moral Virtue Delineated*, ed. Penelope Aubin, trans. Thomas Manington Gibbs (London: J. Darby, 1726), 16–17.

10. Camerarius, *Symbolorum ac emblematum*, 1:82; BF, "Account of the Devices," 735; Eric P. Newman, "Continental Currency and the Fugio Cent: Sources of Emblems and Mottoes," *Numismatist*, December 1966, 1596; Hosea 2:6; BF, *Poor Richard Improved, 1754*, in *Papers*, 5:184.

11. Camerarius, *Symbolorum ac emblematum*, 1:100; Newman, "Continental Currency," 1596; BF, "Account of the Devices," 737.

12. Camerarius, *Symbolorum ac emblematum*, 1:116; Newman, "Continental Currency," 1596; BF, "Account of the Devices," 735–36.

13. Camerarius, *Symbolorum ac emblematum*, 1:168; Newman, "Continental Currency," 1596; BF, "Account of the Devices," 736; J. A. Leo Lemay, "The American Aesthetic of Franklin's Visual Creations," *PMHB* 111, no. 4 (October 1987): 484.

14. Camerarius, *Symbolorum ac emblematum*, 2:44; Newman, "Continental Currency," 1596; BF, "Account of the Devices," 736.

15. Camerarius, *Symbolorum ac emblematum*, 2:96; Newman, "Continental Currency," 1596; BF, "Account of the Devices," 734.

16. Camerarius, *Symbolorum ac emblematum*, 2:192; Newman, "Continental Currency," 1596; BF, "Account of the Devices," 735; Whiting, no. B94.

17. Camerarius, *Symbolorum ac emblematum*, 3:64; Newman, "Continental Currency," 1596; BF, "Account of the Devices," 735.

18. BF, "New Fables," in *Papers*, 17:3.

19. BF, "Account of the Devices," 735.

20. Newman, "Continental Currency," 1596; BF, "Account of the Devices," 737; Lemay, "American Aesthetic," 488.

21. *PG*, September 20, 1775; *Providence Gazette*, October 7, 1775; *Massachusetts Spy*, October 13, 1775; *Norwich Packet*, October 16, 1775; *Connecticut Journal*, November 1, 1775; *Essex Journal and New-Hampshire Packet*, December 8, 1775; *Wilmington Almanack, or Ephemeris for . . . 1777* (Wilmington, DE: James Adams, 1776).

22. Wheeler Case, "A Contest between the Eagle and the Crane," in *Historical Sketches of American Paper Currency: Second Series*, ed. Henry Phillips (Roxbury, MA: W. Eliot Woodward, 1866), 256–57.

23. Nicholas Cresswell, *The Journal of Nicholas Cresswell, 1774–1777* (New York: Dial Press, 1924), 130; "Revolutionary," *Salem Gazette*, July 19, 1825.

24. "Revolutionary," *Salem Gazette*, July 19, 1825.

25. Lemay, "American Aesthetic," 482–84.

26. BF to Jonathan Shipley, September 13, 1775, in *Papers*, 22:199.

27. BF, "The Rattlesnake as a Symbol of America," in *Writings* (Lemay), 744.

28. Dr. Alexander Hamilton, *Gentleman's Progress: The Itinerarium of Dr. Alexander Hamilton, 1744*, ed. Carl Bridenbaugh (Chapel Hill: University of North Carolina Press, 1948), 77; Whiting, no. C253.

29. BF, "Rattlesnake," 745.

30. Ibid., 745–46.

31. Quoted in Thomas Paine, *The Writings of Thomas Paine*, ed. Moncure Conway (New York: Putnam, 1896), 4:465.

32. Thomas Jefferson, *Jefferson's Memorandum Books: Accounts, with Legal Records and Miscellany, 1767–1826*, ed. James A. Bear, Jr., and Lucia C. Stanton (Princeton, NJ: Princeton University Press, 1997), 1:367; Whiting, no. B363.

33. John Adams to Abigail Adams, August 14, 1776, in *The Adams Family Correspondence*, ed. L. H. Butterfield, L. H., Wendell D. Garrett, and Marjorie E. Sprague, (Cambridge, MA: Belknap Press of Harvard University Press, 1963–), 2:96–97.

34. Ibid., 96.

35. Wolf and Hayes, no. 3614.

36. "Franklin's Proposal," in *The Papers of Thomas Jefferson*, ed. Julian P. Boyd (Princeton, NJ: Princeton University Press, 1950–), 1:494–95.

37. Kevin J. Hayes, *Benjamin Franklin* (London: Reaktion, 2022), 129.

38. "Du Simitière's Proposal" and "Report of the Committee," in *Papers of Thomas Jefferson*, 1:495–97.

39. BF to Lord Howe, August 20, 1776, in *Papers*, 27:575; Hayes, *Benjamin Franklin*, 137–39.

40. Richard S. Patterson and Richardson Dougall, *The Eagle and the Shield: A History of the Great Seal of the United States* (Washington: GPO, 1976), 95–99; Paul J. Smith, "Joachim Camerarius's Emblem Book on Birds (1596), with an Excursus of America's Great Seal," in *Emblems and the Natural World*, ed. Karl A. E. Enekel and Paul J. Smith (Boston: Brill, 2017), 178–81.

CHAPTER 22

1. Ernest Hemingway to Ezra Pound, March 17, 1924, in *The Letters of Ernest Hemingway*: Vol. 2, 1923–1925, ed. Sandra Spanier, Albert J DeFazio III, and Robert W. Trogdon (New York: Cambridge University Press, 2013), 103; BF to Mary Hewson, January 12, 1777, and to Emma Thompson, February 8, 1777, in *Papers*, 23:155, 298.

2. Richard Brilliant, *Portraiture* (London: Reaktion, 2004), 137.

3. *The Andy Warhol Collection: Sold for the Benefit of the Andy Warhol Foundation for the Visual Arts* (New York: Sotheby's, 1988), vol. 5, lot 3232.

4. BF, *La science du bonhomme Richard*, trans. A. F. Quétant (Paris: Ruault, 1777); Stacy Schiff, *A Great Improvisation: Franklin, France, and the Birth of America* (New York: Henry Holt, 2005), 85; Wolf and Hayes, no. 2511.

5. Jean-François de La Harpe, "Authentic Anecdotes of M. De Voltaire," *Monthly Mirror* 3, no. 2 (February 1808): 111.

6. Carl Van Doren, *Benjamin Franklin* (New York: Viking, 1938), 430.

7. C., "Epigram," *St. James's Chronicle, or The British Evening Post*, November 8, 1777.

8. "Epigram," in *An Asylum for Fugitive Pieces, in Prose and Verse, Not in Any Other Collection*, ed. John Almon (London: J. Debrett, 1785–1786), 1:61 (Wolf and Hayes, no. 88).

9. Achille-Guillaume Lebègue de Presle, October 1, 1777, and BF to Lebègue de Presle, October 4, 1777, in *Papers*, 25:5, 25–26.

10. Desmond MacCarthy, "A Citizen of the World: Benjamin Franklin," *Sunday Times*, March 12, 1939, 6.

11. John C. Fredriksen, "Williams, Jonathan," in *ANB*, 23:483.

12. Edwin Wolf, 2nd, "The First Books and Printed Catalogues of the Library Company of Philadelphia," *PMHB* 78, no. 1 (January 1954): 66; BF, *A Catalogue of Choice and Valuable Books* (Philadelphia: B. Franklin, 1744), 14.

13. A. Owen Aldridge, *Voltaire and the Century of Light* (Princeton, NJ: Princeton University Press, 1975), 83–84.

14. *The Charter, Laws, and Catalogue of Books, of the Library Company of Philadelphia* (Philadelphia: B. Franklin and D. Hall, 1757), 43; BF to Samuel Mather, July 7, 1773, in *Papers*, 20:286; Lemay, *Life*, 1:43–44; Aldridge, *Voltaire*, 193.

15. Peter Collinson to BF, August 15, 1752, in *Papers*, 4:342; [William Rose,] "The Age of Lewis XIV," *Monthly Review* 7 (August 1752): 116–17.

16. *Charter, Laws, and Catalogue*, 75, 86, 100, 111.

17. Aldridge, *Voltaire*, 75; Voltaire, *Letters Concerning the English Nation* (London: C. Davis, 1733), 45.

18. Voltaire, *Zadig: or, The Book of Fate, An Oriental History* (London: John Brindley, 1749), 53; BF to Benjamin Vaughan, March 14, 1785, in *Papers*, 43:493; Suzy Platt, *Respectfully Quoted: A Dictionary of Quotations Requested from the Congressional Research Service* (Washington, DC: Library of Congress, 1989), 183.

19. Voltaire, *Candidus: or, All for the Best* (London: J. Nourse, 1759), 94.

20. Pomponne Vincent to BF, after December 8, 1778, in *Papers*, 28:208; Wolf and Hayes, no. 3515.

21. André Maurois, *Franklin, The Life of an Optimist* (New York: Didier, 1945); Gordon S. Wood, *The Americanization of Benjamin Franklin* (New York: Penguin, 2004), 121; BF to Jane Mecom, March 1, 1766, in *Papers*, 13:188; J. A. Leo Lemay, *Benjamin Franklin: Optimist or Pessimist?* (Newark: University of Delaware, 1990), 23.

22. *Norton Critical Edition*, 102; Thomas J. Haslam, "An Infidel's Progress: Benjamin Franklin's Twyford Manuscript Part One Reconsidered" (Ph.D. diss., University of Delaware, 1996), 196–97.

23. BF to Henry Bouquet, September 30, 1764, in *Papers*, 11:367–68.

24. Voltaire, *A Treatise upon Toleration* (Glasgow: Robert Urie, 1765), 37.

25. BF to Henry Bouquet, September 30, 1764, in *Papers*, 11:367.

26. [William Rose,] "A Defence of My Uncle," *Monthly Review* 37 (December 1767): 498–99; Wolf and Hayes, no. 3533.

27. Aldridge, *Voltaire and the Century of Light*, 355.

28. BF to Mary Stevenson, June 27, 1769, in *Papers*, 16:161.

29. BF to Mary Hewson, late 1771?, in *Papers*, 18:272.

30. "Variétés," *Journal de Paris*, February 21, 1778.

31. Voltaire to Louis Larent Gaultier, February 20, 1778, in *Voltaire's Correspondence*, ed. Theodore Besterman (Geneva: Institut et Musée Voltaire, 1964), 97:110.

32. Wolf and Hayes, no. 3531.

33. BF to Charles Thompson, December 29, 1788, in Digital Edition.

34. Richard Henry Lee, *Life of Arthur Lee, LL.D.* (Boston: Wells and Lilly, 1829), 1:63.

35. Pierre Jean Georges Cabanis, "A Short Account of Benjamin Franklin, 1825," in Hayes and Bour, 166.

36. Cabanis, "Short Account," 159; John Adams, *Diary and Autobiography of John Adams*, ed. L. H. Butterfield, Leonard C. Faber, and Wendell D. Garrett (Cambridge, MA: Belknap Press of Harvard University Press, 1961), 4:119.

37. Claude-Anne Lopez, *My Life with Benjamin Franklin* (New Haven, CT: Yale University Press, 2000), 150–51.

38. William Weisberger, "Benjamin Franklin: A Masonic Enlightener in Paris," *Pennsylvania History* 53, no. 3 (July 1986): 168.

39. Maurois, *Franklin*, 71.

40. John Adams, "Franklin as a Congressman and a Diplomat, 1775–1778," in Hayes and Bour, 65.

41. Francisco de Quevedo, *The Visions of Dom Francisco de Quevedo Villegas*, trans. Roger L'Estrange, Knt. (London: Richard Sare, 1702), 208.

42. Adams, "Franklin," 65.

43. Ibid., 65.

44. Claude-Anne Lopez, *Mon Cher Papa: Franklin and the Ladies of Paris* (New Haven, CT: Yale University Press, 1966), vii; Kevin J. Hayes, *Benjamin Franklin* (London: Reaktion, 2022), 145.

45. BF, "The Ephemera," in *Papers*, 27:433.

46. Ibid., 435.

47. Theodore Hornberger, *Benjamin Franklin* (Minneapolis: University of Minnesota Press, 1962), 42; J. A. Leo Lemay, "Benjamin Franklin," in *Major Writers of Early American Literature*, ed. Everett Emerson (Madison: University of Wisconsin Press, 1972), 238; Stuart P. Sherman, "Franklin," in *CHAL*, 1:110.

48. Lopez, *My Life*, 152–53.

49. Wolf and Hayes, no. 3536; "The Maid of Orleans," *Monthly Review* 19 (September 1758): 309; "John Q. Adams on Voltaire," *Boston Recorder*, July 20, 1843, 114.

50. Aldridge, *Voltaire*, 26–31.

CHAPTER 23

1. BF to John Adams, November 26, 1781, in *Papers*, 36:115; Lester C. Olson, *Benjamin Franklin's Vision of American Community: A Study in Rhetorical Iconology* (Columbia: University of South Carolina Press, 2004), 141–94.

2. "List of Books" and "Liste des livres de Mr. Franklin apportés de sa chambre dans le bureau le 31. Xbre. 1781," in *Papers*, 36:330–43. Franklin's modern editors annotated both lists as part of his published papers, but they did make one assumption the evidence does not support. They assumed the "List of Books" recorded what volumes were shelved in the office library before the books from Franklin's private quarters were transferred there. Since the two lists are mutually exclusive, the assumption makes sense, but the "List of Books" collection was not necessarily shelved in the office library. It could have been shelved elsewhere in the sprawling villa.

3. "Franklin's List of Books Lent, November 1778," in *Papers*, 28:178–79; James N. Green, "A Newly Discovered Book from Benjamin Franklin's Library," in *The Annual Report of the Library Company of Philadelphia for the Year 2016* (Philadelphia: Library Company of Philadelphia, 2019), 55. Since this bound volume has surfaced since the completion of Wolf and Hayes, let me record its contents here in the order they are bound: *The Out-of-Door Parliament* (London: J. Almon, 1780); *Opposition Mornings* (London: J. Wilkie, 1779); William Jones, *A Speech on the Nomination of Candidates to Represent the County of Middlesex* (London, 1780); George Walker, *Substance of the Speech of the Rev. Mr. Walker* (London: Society for Constitutional Information, 1780); *The System Occasioned by the Speech of Leonard Smelt*, 2d ed. (London: J. Almon, 1780); James Ogden, *The Contest: A Poem in Two Parts* (Newcastle upon Tyne: T. Robson, 1776); William Johnston Temple, *On the Abuse of Unrestrained Power: An Historical Essay* (London: E. and C. Dilly, 1778) (PPL Am 1780 Gentl 113793.O.1–7).

4. Wolf and Hayes, no. 407; BF to Jacques Barbeau-Dubourg, December 26, 1772, in *Papers*, 19:437.

5. Thomas Nugent, *A New Pocket Dictionary of the French and English Languages* (London, 1767); Hayes, *Library of William Byrd*, no. 1995; Wolf and Hayes, no. 2459.

6. Wolf and Hayes, no. 1981.

7. Wolf and Hayes, nos. 517, 2937, 1896; Abraham Rees, *Cyclopaedia*, s.v. "Cahusac, Louis de"; Friedrich Melchior, Freiherr von Grimm, *Historical and Literary Memoirs and Anecdotes* (London: H. Colburn, 1814), 1:71.

8. "Foreign Articles," *Critical Review* 41 (February 1776): 150; Wolf and Hayes, no. 1731.

9. Wolf and Hayes, nos. 406, 2874.

10. Wolf and Hayes, nos. 76, 100, 3497, 1057, 361. A. Owen Aldridge, "Polly Baker and Boccaccio," *Annali institutio universitario orientale* 14, no. 1 (January 1972): 5–18, identifies a parallel between "The Speech of Miss Polly Baker" and an episode in the *Decameron*, but Aldridge could not say how Franklin got his hands on Boccaccio. I think he borrowed James Logan's copy. Wolf, *Library of James Logan*, no. 266, records that Logan gave away his copy of Boccaccio; perhaps he gave it to Franklin.

11. Wolf and Hayes, nos. 516, 639, 1697, 1838, 2074, 2999, 3502, 1953.

12. Wolf and Hayes, no. 508.

13. Wolf and Hayes, no. 3345.

14. Louis Lefebvre de La Roche, "On Franklin," in Hayes and Bour, 129; Sarah B. Pomeroy, *Benjamin Franklin, Swimmer: An Illustrated History* (Philadelphia: American Philosophical Society, 2021), 40–41.

15. Editing BF's autobiography, Temple quoted a long passage from Edward Young's *Two Epistles to Mr. Pope* to gloss the part about BF copying one of Young's satires in 1725 and sending it to James Ralph to dissuade him from pursuing a career as a poet. Temple was mistaken. *Two Epistles* did not appear until 1730. Franklin copied part of Young's *Love of Fame*. Temple's specific citation does show him reading Young's collected works. See *Memoirs of the Life and Writings of Benjamin Franklin*, ed. William Temple Franklin, 3d ed. (London: Henry Colburn, 1818–1819), 1:66–67.

16. William Caslon to William Temple Franklin, December 7, 1779, and March 10, 1780; William Temple Franklin to William Caslon, April 5, 1781, in Digital Edition; Wolf and Hayes, no. 2683.

17. Jonathan Williams to William Temple Franklin, July 16, 1784, in Digital Edition.

18. Wolf and Hayes, nos. 2571, 2293, 2550.

19. Leonard N. Beck, "Two 'Loaf-Givers': or, A Tour through the Gastronomic Libraries of Katherine Golden Bitting and Elizabeth Robins Pennell," *Quarterly Journal of the Library of Congress* 38, no. 2 (Spring 1981): 79; Thomas Malory, *Morte Arthure: or, The Death of Arthur*, ed. Edmund Brock (London: Early English Text Society, 1865), 32.

20. James Beard, "As Cozy as Two Pease in a Pod," *Boston Globe*, December 2, 1981, 1; Samuel Pegge, ed., *The Forme of Cury: A Roll of Ancient English Cookery* (London: J. Nichols, 1780), 39, 41–42.

21. Wolf and Hayes, no. 1046; [William Bewley,] "Monthly Catalogue, Medical," *Monthly Review* 48 (March 1773): 244.

22. Stacy Schiff, *A Great Improvisation: Franklin, France, and the Birth of America* (New York: Henry Holt, 2005), 227.

23. Jean-Baptiste Moheau, *Recherches et considérations sur la population de la france* (Paris: Moutard, 1778), 272–74.

24. Wolf and Hayes, nos. 576, 1569, 2838.

25. Voltaire, *Oeuvres completes de Voltaire* (n.p., 1785), 58:186; R. R. Palmer, *The Age of Democratic Revolution: A Political History of Europe and America* (Princeton, NJ: Princeton University Press, 2014), 47–48.

26. BF, "Dialogue between the Gout and Mr. Franklin," in *Writings* (Lemay), 944.

27. Wolf and Hayes, nos. 576, 318.

28. Wolf and Hayes, no. 2875.

29. James Steintrager, *The Autonomy of Pleasure: Libertines, License, and Sexual Revolution* (New York: Columbia University Press, 2016), 101–102, 112.

30. James Harrington, *The Commonwealth of Oceana*, ed. Henry Morley (London: Routledge, 1887), 29.

31. Ibid., 31.

32. BF, "Parody and Reply to a Religious Meditation," in *Writings* (Lemay), 232.

33. BF, "Queries and Remarks Respecting Alterations in the Constitution of Pennsylvania," in *Writings* (Smyth), 10:57–58.

34. Wolf and Hayes, nos. 305, 2303.

35. Stanley Finger, *Doctor Franklin's Medicine* (Philadelphia: University of Pennsylvania Press, 2006), 225.

36. J. A. Leo Lemay, "Franklin, Benjamin," in *ANB*, 8:391.

37. John Dos Passos, *The Men Who Made the Nation* (Garden City, NY: Doubleday, 1957), 45.

38. Henry Laurens to George Washington, April 30, 1783, in *Papers of Henry Laurens*, ed. David R. Chesnutt and C. James Taylor, vol. 16 (Columbia: University of South Carolina Press, 2003), 74; Abigail Adams to John Adams, April 28, 1783, in *Adams Family Correspondence*, vol. 5, *October 1782–November 1784*, ed. Richard Alan Ryerson (Cambridge, MA: Belknap Press, 1993), 141.

39. BF to John Adams, August 6, 1784, in *Papers*, 42:465–466.

40. Schiff, *Great Improvisation*, 377.

41. Quoted in Claude-Anne Lopez and Eugenia W. Herbert, *The Private Franklin: The Man and His Family* (New York: Norton, 1975), 265.

42. Ibid.

43. Ibid.

44. Charles F. Jenkins, "Franklin Returns from France—1785," *Proceedings of the American Philosophical Society* 92, no. 6 (December 1948): 421.

45. Ibid., 422.

46. Wolf and Hayes, nos. 149, 383, 713, 742.

47. Wolf and Hayes, nos. 761, 825, 3467.

CHAPTER 24

1. Wolf and Hayes, nos. 1976–1977.

2. Charles F. Jenkins, "Franklin Returns from France—1785," *Proceedings of the American Philosophical Society* 92, no. 6 (December 1848): 431.

3. J. I. Little, "Gale, Samuel (1747–1826)," in *Dictionary of Canadian Biography*, ed. George W. Brown et al. (Toronto: University of Toronto Press, 1966–), 6:269.

4. BF to David Barclay, February 12, 1781, in *Papers*, 34:366.

5. Jenkins, "Franklin Returns from France," 425.

6. Ibid.

7. BF to Jonathan Shipley, February 24, 1786, in *Writings* (Lemay), 1161.

8. *National Union Catalog* (London: Mansell, 1968–1981), 183:133.

9. BF to Benjamin Vaughan, July 31, 1786, in *Writings* (Lemay), 1163–64.

10. Jonathan Williams, *Thermometrical Navigation* (Philadelphia: R. Aitken, 1799); John C. Fredriksen, "Williams, Jonathan," in *ANB*, 23:484.

11. BF to Mr. and Mrs. John Bard, November 14, 1985, in *Writings* (Smyth), 9:476.

12. Andrew Ellicott, "The Venerable Nestor of America, 1785," in Hayes and Bour, 100.

13. Wolf and Hayes, 19.

14. Arthur Young, *Travels during the Years 1787, 1788, and 1789* (Bury St. Edmund's, UK: W. Richardson, 1792), 261.

15. Wolf and Hayes, 21.

16. BF to George Whatley, May 23, 1785, in *Writings* (Lemay), 1109.

17. BF to Benjamin Vaughan, July 31, 1786, in *Writings* (Lemay), 1164; Stanley Finger, *Doctor Franklin's Medicine* (Philadelphia: University of Pennsylvania Press, 2006), 187; *Acts and Laws, of His Majesty's Province of the Massachusetts-Bay in New-England*, (Boston: B. Green, 1726) 304–305 (not in Wolf and Hayes).

18. Winthrop Sargent, "My Dinner with Franklin, 1786," in Hayes and Bour, 108–109; Wolf and Hayes, no. 701.

19. Michael Vinson, "The Society for Political Inquiries: The Limits of Republican Discourse in Philadelphia on the Eve of the Constitutional Convention," *PMHB* 113 (1989): 188–89.

20. Ibid., 189.

21. Anne J. Willing to Mary Willing Byrd, March 19, 1808, "The Papers of Richard Evelyn Byrd I, of Frederick County, Virginia," *Virginia Magazine of History and Biography* 54 (1946): 117.

22. Kevin J. Hayes, "Discovering a Landmark of Literature: How George Washington Read Don Quixote," *Mount Vernon Magazine*, Winter 2018: 30.

23. BF to Thomas Jordan, May 18, 1787, in *Writings* (Smyth), 9:582.

24. Carl Van Doren, *Benjamin Franklin* (1938; New York: Penguin, 1991), 749–50.

25. E. D. Gillespie, *A Book of Remembrance* (Philadelphia: Lippincott, 1901), 23.

26. Wolf and Hayes, nos. 2067, 2386.

27. Manasseh Cutler, "A Visit to Franklin Court, 1787," in Hayes and Bour, 114.

28. Max Farrand, ed., *The Records of the Federal Convention of 1787* (New Haven, CT: Yale University Press, 1911), 2:64–66. The following speeches come from this source and will not be cited individually.

29. "Franklin's Speech," in *The Documentary History of the Ratification of the Constitution*, ed. John P. Kaminski and Gaspare J. Saladino (Madison: State Historical Society of Wisconsin, 1981), 13:214.

30. John Updike, "Many Bens," *New Yorker*, February 22, 1988, 106.

31. [James McHenry,] *The Three Patriots: Or, The Cause and Cure of Present Evils* (Baltimore: B. Edes, 1811), 6, the source of the following exchange.

32. Quoted in William Frederick Poole, *Anti-Slavery Opinions before the Year 1800* (Cincinnati: R. Clarke, 1873), 65.

33. BF, "Sidi Mehemet Ibrahim on the Slave Trade," in *Writings* (Lemay), 1157–60.

34. William Lloyd Garrison, "A Mirror for Apologists," *Liberator*, December 17, 1831.

35. *Genetic Text*, xxxi–xxxiii, 218.

36. *Genetic Text*, 36, 226.

37. Robert Carr, "Personal Recollections of Benjamin Franklin (1864)," in Hayes and Bour, 181.

38. Mary Stevenson Hewson, "Closing Scenes of Dr. Franklin's Life: In a Letter from an Eye-Witness," in Hayes and Bour, 120.

39. Miller, nos. 144, 266, 494, 519; Samuel Johnson, *The Lives of the Most Eminent English Poets; with Critical Observations on Their Works* (London: C. Bathurst, 1783), 4:283.

40. Johnson, *Lives*, 2:107.

Acknowledgments

In Bibliography and Research Methods, the introductory graduate course I used to teach every year, I helped my students understand literary historiography by introducing them to the concept of academic genealogy. In other words, it is important to understand who studied under whom. I had the fortune to study at the University of Delaware with J. A. Leo Lemay, the greatest Franklin scholar of his generation, who studied at the University of Maryland with A. Owen Aldridge, the greatest Franklin scholar of his generation. The present work reflects the profound influence of both men, who deserve my deepest thanks.

Occasionally, I have visited historical societies and universities to talk about my research concerning the history of books and reading in early America. One such trip brought me to Washington College in Chestertown, Maryland. Adam Goodheart, director of the Starr Center for the Study of the American Experience at Washington College, had invited me to present a lecture about my award-winning biography, *George Washington, A Life in Books*. While I was there, we discussed what project I might tackle next. Adam suggested I do a book about Benjamin Franklin. I already did, I told him, meaning *The Library of Benjamin Franklin*. But that was not what he had in mind. He suggested I write a book about Franklin akin to *George Washington, A Life in Books*. Adam Goodheart is my Mr. Great-heart. His suggestion triggered the present work.

Related research projects have also helped me develop this work. While researching *Jefferson in His Own Time*, I happily received a fellowship from the Robert H. Smith International Center for Jefferson Studies. This fellowship is the gift that keeps on giving. As one benefit, the Smith Center gave me off-site access to its online databases and thus facilitated my research. In addition, the present work has let me use much material I had left unused from previous Franklin research at the Library Company of Philadelphia and the American Philosophical Society, two other institutions that deserve my thanks. I would also like to thank the librarians at the Sanger Branch of the Toledo Lucas County Public Library. During the composition of this book, I made numerous requests from OhioLink, the statewide consortium of public and academic libraries, which the Sanger Branch filled kindly and expeditiously.

Many other individuals deserve recognition. At Oxford University Press, I thank Susan Ferber for thoroughly reading my manuscript and encouraging me to rethink and reshape parts of it. Her detailed suggestions have helped improve this work immensely. As always, my wife Sooki has provided unceasing love and support throughout the composition of this work. Finally, I would like to thank my parents, whose love of reading set a pattern to emulate.

Index

For the benefit of digital users, indexed terms that span two pages (e.g., 52–53) may, on occasion, appear on only one of those pages.